The Problem of Freedom

Johns Hopkins Studies in Atlantic History and Culture

Thomas C. Holt

The Problem of Freedom

Race, Labor, and Politics in Jamaica and Britain, 1832–1938

THE JOHNS HOPKINS UNIVERSITY PRESS
Baltimore and London

The Johns Hopkins University Press
2715 North Charles Street
Baltimore, Maryland 21218-4363
www.press.jhu.edu

Library of Congress Cataloging-in-Publication Data

Holt, Thomas C. (Thomas Cleveland), 1942–
  The problem of freedom : race, labor, and politics in Jamaica and Britain,
1832–1938 / Thomas C. Holt.
     p.   cm. — (Johns Hopkins studies in Atlantic history and culture)
  Includes bibliographical references and index.
  ISBN 0-8018-4216-6 (alk. paper)   ISBN 0-8018-4291-3 (pbk.)
  1. Plantations—Jamaica—History. 2. Peasantry—Jamaica—History
3. Indigenous peoples—Jamaica—History. 4. Capitalism—Jamaica—
History. 5. Slavery—Jamaica—History. 6. Jamaica—Race relations—
History. 7. Jamaica—Politics and government—To 1962. 8. Great Britain—
Colonies—History. I. Title. II. Series.
HD1471.J3H65   1992
326´.097292—dc20   91-17694

A catalog record for this book is available from the British Library.

Frontispiece: Paul Bogle, leader of the Morant Bay Rebellion, 1865.

For my children,
Karis Scott, Katherine Michelle, and Michael Kenyatta

Contents

Tables, Figures, and Plates

Tables

Figures

Plates

Preface

It has been said that prefaces enjoy a strange and deceptive status: they present themselves to a reader as the first words introducing a text, when in fact they are almost always the last words written. This one is no exception to that rule. The themes of this study evolved in the process of writing. It began as a comparative analysis of the politics of the postemancipation eras in the United States and the British West Indies, but in the course of research and writing it became both more and less ambitious. This preface is my effort to reformulate in intellectual and political terms both what that process wrought and the relation of process to final product.

This is a study of emancipation and the postemancipation society of Jamaica, beginning with the slave revolt of 1831–32 and ending with the labor rebellion of 1938 and its immediate aftermath. The first event precipitated the abolition of slavery throughout the British colonial empire, the second marked the beginning of the end of that empire. The symmetry of these two events embraces two forms of emancipation: at issue in the first instance was the freedom of the individual slave; in the second the question involved the nation as a whole. The century that separated these watersheds in Britain's colonial history was one of extraordinary transformations in British ideology, in its economic and social policy, and in the fate of Jamaican freed people and their descendants. All of these—ideology, politics, labor, and racism—are the interrelated subjects of this study.

Over the course of that century Afro-Jamaicans at first maintained a tenuous balance between peasant farming and labor on the failing sugar estates, then created a vital economy based on the fruit trade, but eventually were reduced to a quasi-proletarian status by the corporate monopoly that developed within that trade. During this period, and in close step with these transformations, British elite ideology and official policy moved from nonracist to racist premises, at the same time that the destruction of slavery cleared the way for that elite's more robust embrace of imperialist ambitions. The racism that made it possible to think of people as slave labor gave way to a racism that freed individual slaves while justifying the domination of entire nations. Eventually, like the sovereignty of the slave master, imperial dominion also had to be relinquished. But here, again, the policy change was framed in ways that masked a new coercion even as it yielded new opportunities for self-determination.

These propositions, the subject matter of this study, are historical matters, concerned with developments in a somewhat distant time and place. But histories are not generally written merely about historical matters, and only the most narrowly conceived are motivated solely by historical debates. This study grew out of, is connected with, and was partly formed by the concerns of my historical present—the decade of the 1980s. That amazing decade began with the election of Ronald Reagan to the American presidency; it ended with the collapse of communism in Eastern Europe and the threat of its collapse in the Soviet Union itself. Reagan's simple and forceful message was that the best policy was to let the market govern social relations and that those who did not make it in modern America had only themselves to blame. Thus, while in contemporary usage Democrats claimed the liberal label, Reagan and his modern conservative allies took up many of the essential elements of the original nineteenth-century liberalism, which differs from the so-called advanced liberalism of the late nineteenth century.[1]

Reagan's seemingly new and fresh approach had a powerful appeal, especially to people looking for respectable ways to evade the failure of American society to satisfy the basic needs of large sectors of its population. It is not irrelevant to the composition of this book that the 1980s were a period when the gap between rich and poor grew wider and racial tensions and despair grew worse. At the same time, self-determination and free enterprise were conflated in public discourse, and democracy and capitalism became synonyms.

Reagan's 1980 campaign formed the backdrop against which I began wrestling with the problem of British emancipation and wrote early drafts of the first three chapters. At first, I moved almost unreflectively between my reading of the daily newspapers and the Colonial Office memoranda of Henry Taylor, Earl Grey, and others you will meet in this study. Only slowly did I realize that what was going on around me in the contemporary political world and in the distant historical world of my documents was beginning to supply the outline of the problematic that slavery emancipation in the Western world had posed for me. Measured against the goal of bringing self-determination, justice, and dignity to former slaves, emancipation had failed. What successes it did enjoy must be credited to the unrelenting struggles of freed people themselves rather than to the determined policies of governments. But that failure was not so simple a matter as a wish by the powerful not to see it succeed, or errors of judgment or policy. Something was amiss in the very project of emancipation, in the very premises on which it was founded. And those premises appeared to be linked to its outcomes and to the extreme racism that followed in its wake in the late nineteenth century.

As I worked on Jamaica and observed America embracing the new conservatism—which was but the old liberalism—I saw that emancipation was a moment of truth in which the internal contradictions of classical liberalism stood exposed. The development of racist thought was not a natural outgrowth or legacy of slavery; it arose in part from the seemingly nonracist (or racially neutral) premises of liberal ideology. Indeed, what is striking about the force of that ideology is how, almost by sleight of hand, it makes market-governed social relations into *natural* phenomena, ignoring even as it does so the fact that historically such relations initially were nearly always coerced and that the places and peoples who have been slow to conform have been harshly dealt with. Such is the dogma posited, for example, in a recent article celebrating the imminent victory of capitalism over communism, which declares "the end of history" and the "universalization of Western liberal democracy." First, Francis Fukuyama dismisses whole peoples and nations as irrelevant to history. He then goes on to declare that in contemporary America "the root causes of economic inequality do not have to do with the underlying legal and social structure of our society, which remains fundamentally egalitarian and moderately redistributionist, so much as with the cultural and social characteristics of the groups that make it up, which are in turn the historical legacy of premodern conditions. Thus black poverty in the United States is not the inherent product of liberalism, but is rather the 'legacy of slavery and racism' which persisted long after the formal abolition of slavery." African Americans and Third World peoples may be fit subjects for charity, Fukuyama argues, but they are irrelevant to the unfolding of the larger human destiny. The world will be safer and richer if governed by individual self-interest mediated by the market.[2]

This "blame the victim" approach so popular with contemporary conservatives parallels the reactions of many classical liberal apologists to emancipation. The internal contradictions of their ideology and of the economic and political system founded on it are displaced onto the people who are its victims. Just as members of the black urban "underclass" who have failed to become integrated into the social system of the late twentieth century are deemed culturally and socially deficient, the refuse of a premodern era, former slaves in the nineteenth century who failed to respond to the market as they were supposed to were relegated to the status of wards of a superior civilization. Moreover, the fact that historically some of these same attitudes were also adopted toward white laborers who failed liberalism's cultural tests suggests that "racism" was embedded in the very premises of a presumably nonracist liberalism; that the virulently racist ideology of the late nineteenth century was not merely some aberrant anachronism, or throwback to slavery, but in large part a creature of the ostensibly nonracist ideology that had undermined and destroyed slavery. It also suggests that the same ideology continues to pose a major obstacle to resolving the legacies of slavery emancipation in the late twentieth century.

By thus framing this study by the political environment in which it was written, I do not intend to suggest that my investigations were entirely limited by presentist concerns; I merely want to reveal one of the standpoints from which I looked out on the world as the book took shape. For reasons of personal history I care deeply about the fate of emancipation and the emancipated peoples; in large measure the unfolding of contemporary events during the 1980s fueled those concerns with energy and passion and shaped my perspectives and insights. It is this context too that explains why I ventured onto such wide-ranging disciplinary terrain, attempted to cover such an un-wieldy time span, and dared to broach such broadly conceived questions. For me this was no mere academic exercise.

What this study attempts, therefore, is a multifaceted exploration of "freedom" as idea and reality—multifaceted in the sense that I try to explore the notion as represented in both economic and political life, as well as the tensions and connections between these two spheres. Examining those multiple facets of this century of emancipation requires multiple approaches and perspectives. It is at once a problem in the social and economic reconstruction of the lives of freed people, a problem in British intellectual and political history, and a problem in race relations, colonialism, and imperialism. Yet, this study is not solely an intellectual history nor even a social history but an attempt to integrate both. It must be both because the struggle to define the content of freedom was at bottom a contest for social power, a struggle at once intellectual and political, social and economic.

Defining the contested terrain of that struggle requires nearly equal attention—to the extent that sources permit—to the perspectives of both those who made colonial policy and those who were its objects. Exploring that terrain requires recognizing that ultimately and philosophically freedom is a problem of social relations, at its core a problem of how human beings sustain and reproduce themselves. Clearly, this means that it is susceptible to determination by material forces and must be understood in its material context. But there is also a tension throughout between how we see the world and the realities of our experience in the world. As a practical consequence, this involves the exploration of a complex epistemological phenomenon: we observe, on the one hand, how ideas, beliefs, and values shaped perceptions and actions and, on the other, how the results of actions and events shaped ideas and beliefs.

The first problem I engage, therefore, is to understand just what freedom for ex-slaves meant, both as an idea and as a reality. And by that I mean not only the conditions of life following slavery but what the various principals involved—British policymakers, Jamaican planters, and freed people themselves—expected freedom for ex-slaves to entail and how those expectations and understandings, or rather conflicts in what was understood or believed, shaped the actual outcome of emancipation. In brief, the freedom of ex-slaves, I argue, was determined first by the array of material realities they confronted, but those material realities were shaped in turn by men whose minds were prepared to accept one reality but not another. This book is on one level a study of ideas, but the ideas arise out of, and interact with, material conditions and objective social relations.

The reality that abolitionists and the men who fashioned and implemented emancipation policies were prepared to accept was determined by their adherence to a liberal democratic ideology in which humans' behavior was believed to reflect primarily their acquisitive, materialist appetites. The sources of social action and the criteria for political and economic justice were to be understood in terms of these basic innate drives for gain and self-improvement. This liberal democratic thought was part and parcel of the rise of capitalism, and it helped to explain and justify the emerging bourgeois social relations of the seventeenth and eighteenth centuries that produced the English working class. These developments form the ideological background for slave emancipation in the mid-nineteenth century, because in many ways the task of compelling the "voluntary" transformation of slaves into wage laborers bore striking similarities to the problem of creating a white working class.

Thus the freedom that emancipation proffered was neither natural nor indigenous, but a historically particular and socially constructed phenomenon. Slavery, as a system and an ideology, was supplanted by free labor, which ushered in its own embedded coercive forms, ideological and systemic. Consequently, the "problem of freedom"—understood as the task of socializing ex-slaves to respond to the work incentives of freemen—could be addressed only by thoroughly reforming the ex-slaves' culture so as to make them receptive to the discipline of free labor. Specifically, a social environment needed to be created that would make them discontented with a mere subsistence-level existence; their material aspirations needed to be gradually expanded. This process would instill the internal discipline required to make them a reliable working class.

But by the 1840s a second facet of the problem of freedom had emerged. Bourgeois freedom was both an aspect of the social relations of labor and a feature of political relations, in part because the men who urged the former tended to be political insurgents challenging aristocratic privilege. Thus was a new moral basis for political relations linked with the new order in the marketplace. But if the linkage between economic and political liberty was advantageous to bourgeois insurgents, it could also prove risky for an established bourgeois elite. Given that the economic system was (quite literally) man-made and not a "natural" phenomenon, it could be changed by men through the exercise of state power. It followed, then, that those ruling men committed to the system as given must either make its "givenness" ideologically transparent and self-evident to the ruled or deny them access to that state power with which they might alter the putatively natural order of things.

Thus arose the contradiction between the "self-possession" or autonomy implied by economic liberalism and selective dispossession within the political sphere. This contradiction could be negotiated, and the problematic nature of liberal democratic premises evaded, only by prescribing rules for inclusion or exclusion, by redrawing the boundaries of membership in the body politic. Ultimately, then, the defense of the "natural" social order depended on how one understood or conceptualized human nature. Critical to sustaining social structures founded on blatant inequalities, within the terms of such an ideology, was the notion that some people—because of their fundamental natures—should be restrained, should not be free. In the West Indies racialist ideologies came to be essential to sustaining the overarching ideology of freedom. At home, in Ireland, and elsewhere, the language invoked to exclude "residual" humanity was hauntingly familiar and served strikingly similar functions.

But ruling elites are not all-powerful, nor are ideologies—racial or otherwise—thoroughly hegemonic. The evolution of policy came not merely from the working out of the logic of freedom in an unfolding capitalist system but from the necessity on the part of policymakers and planters to confront and interpret intractable realities on the one hand, while defending against determined challenges on the other. Some of these realities and challenges involved dramatic collective actions of the dispossessed within the West Indies—including the slave revolt of 1831, the Morant Bay Rebellion of 1865, and the labor rebellion of 1938. Also relevant were the unrest in Canada during the 1830s and 1840s, in India in the 1850s, and in Ireland in the 1880s. But most of all there was the quiet reality of the ex-slaves' refusal to follow the scripts envisioned by either planters or policymakers. While planters preferred coercion, and policymakers voluntary wage labor, neither accepted the right of the freed people to choose an alternate path. Meanwhile, in large numbers freed people moved away from the major sugar parishes and established new villages and market centers, devoting most of their time to raising foodstuffs and working on the estates only intermittently. Consequently, by mid-century there had been a precipitous decline of the Jamaican plantation economy and the rise of a black peasantry. By this quiet initiative and the more violent one at Morant Bay, Afro-Jamaicans laid claim to an alternative vision of freedom that challenged bourgeois assumptions. At the same time, those challenges opened them to a virulent racist counterattack that justified their exclusion from political processes for three-quarters of a century. As if to underscore some ironic, fated symmetry, they would reclaim political self-determination—again through violent initiatives—at precisely the moment when their transformation into plantation proletarians was nearly completed and their economic enthrallment to a neocolonial world order was about to begin.

This book, then, is not precisely a monograph on Jamaica or even a case study intended to illuminate larger processes. Rather, using Jamaica as its terrain, it proposes to trace the definition and the quality of freedom in the modern world by drawing together and illuminating the links among crucial social, economic, and intellectual developments on both sides of the Atlantic over the course of a century. There are two structural consequences that follow from this: first, the vast and diverse historiographies relevant to this study can be addressed only selectively; and second, there are occasional digressions from the main plot of the story, the struggle in Jamaica, into subplots of British colonial and domestic politics as they were shaped by events in other parts of the empire. It may be useful, therefore, to sketch the general organization of the parts prior to beginning the narrative.

Part 1 examines the meaning of freedom and the structured transition from slavery to free labor as these related to earlier and parallel developments in Britain. Part 2 discusses the establishing of a new plantation economy, the emergence of the peasant economy, the planters' uneven reorientation to being employers rather than slave masters, and the ex-slaves' response to becoming free agents. Part 3 explores the implications for state power and the Jamaican political system particularly of the potential threat of a politically empowered and mobilized peasantry. Despite their prior ideological commitments to political enfranchisement for ex-slaves, British policymakers found ways to back off from pure ideals of liberal democracy, much as they were beginning to do with economic idealism. This culminated in a new crisis, the essentially peasant war at Morant Bay. Part 4 examines the new departure in British policy toward its former slave colonies: benevolent guardianship and trusteeship in political life coupled with support for peasant proprietorship, a coupling that attempted to seal off state power from the now economically empowered masses. Eventually it became clear that political impotence undermines economic self-determination. In the aftermath of Morant Bay and the rise of the fruit trade, monopoly capitalists turned peasants into de facto proletarians, the sugar industry was reorganized with a proletarian core, and a casual labor pool developed in the cities. These transformations provided the tinder ignited by the social crisis of the Depression years, leading to the conflagration of 1938. That conflagration forced another departure in British policy—this time toward eventual decolonization—and the beginnings of yet another recasting of liberal democratic and racial ideologies. But again, as in 1838, the policy and its ideological analogue sought to embed dependence within independence, to confine self-determination within vaguely defined, nonthreatening limits. As in 1838, what was envisioned was a "freedom" drained of the power of genuine self-determination: materially, a freedom stripped of control over basic material resources; ideologically, a freedom that internalized its own antithesis. After a century-long struggle for freedom, Afro-Jamaicans confronted new forces on new terrain, yet the fundamental structure of the contest—the combatants, the ideological content and discourse—remained much the same.

This philosophical and historical excursion will, I hope, illuminate the meanings and contradictions of Western concepts of freedom. In one sense it is a philosophical flight, but its foundation is an analysis at ground level of the material life as well as the *mentalité* of a people for whom freedom was something to be brought into being, created, and struggled for rather than merely accepted or taken for granted; for whom defining freedom was part of the politics of everyday life rather than philosophical speculation; for whom freedom had to be wrenched, as it were, out of its antithesis and in the midst of social revolution. The raison d'être of this book is that we have much to learn from such a people, from their struggle, and even from their ultimate failure.

Acknowledgments

Having been at this project for some time, I have accumulated a ton of debts along the way. It is likely that those most recently acquired will come most readily to mind; I apologize in advance to any I might inadvertently slight in this public acknowledgment. It seems needless to add that acknowledging the sources from which I have drawn my intellectual capital in no way makes them accountable for the results.

My earliest intellectual debts for this project are owed to C. Vann Woodward and Eugene D. Genovese, the former for a series of lectures at the Yale Law School in 1969 on comparative perspectives on emancipation and the latter for a course on comparative slavery. Both of those events, occurring within a few months of each other, not only stimulated my interest in studying slavery and emancipation outside the American South but offered challenging models of how to go about it. I will be eternally grateful to Professor Woodward as well for strongly advising me *not* to undertake anything like this book as a dissertation. Given that this project has proved formidable for a relatively experienced scholar, it might well have been impossible for a beginning graduate student to complete. Had it not been for Woodward's counsel, therefore, I probably would be in some other line of work today.

My most recent and profound debts are to Frederick Cooper, Barbara Fields, and Rebecca Scott, all former colleagues at the University of Michigan, who have influenced this work in somewhat different but complementary ways. Each of them has written splendidly and provocatively on the subject of slavery and emancipation, and their work has become so integrated with my own thinking that I fear I will have failed to properly acknowledge them in this text. For example, the introductory chapter of Fred's book on slavery emancipation in East Africa provided the clues for my earliest formulation of "freedom" as an ideological problematic in capitalist societies. In the conclusion of her book on slavery and emancipation in Maryland, Barbara broaches the idea that "freedom is a constantly moving target," which resonates with the themes I pursue in the final chapters of this book regarding the fate of Jamaican workers in the twentieth century. To Rebecca's constant admonition to find the stories of ordinary people, which her own study of Cuba exemplifies so well, I owe whatever measure of balance I have managed to achieve between space devoted to British policymakers and that to Jamaican workers. Not only has the example of her own work been important to this project, but undoubtedly Rebecca has run up bigger phone bills talking about and has read more versions of this manuscript than anyone else. The only repayment I can offer for her advice, unselfish commitment, and encouragement over the years is a public acknowledgment that the debt is greater than I can ever possibly repay.

Although I never met him, the late Walter Rodney's work on the making of the working class in postemancipation Guyana has influenced my conceptualization of themes in this book. Other scholars and friends have also been generous with their time. Sidney W. Mintz and Gad Heuman read the entire manuscript and gave me very helpful suggestions for improvements. Ira Berlin, David Brion Davis, and Seymour Drescher were helpful with some of the early chapters in various stages of their development. I hope my footnotes reflect my intellectual debts to their published work as well. Charles and Louise Tilly not only made helpful comments on early versions of chapters 1 and 5, but their Sunday evening seminars provided an opportunity to "battle test" some of my original thoughts about the problems addressed here. Peter Railton offered some helpful suggestions about my reading of John Stuart Mill's *On Liberty*. My thanks to Barry W. Higman for reading the first full draft and providing excellent suggestions for changes and additional reading. I thank Richard Wentworth, of the University of Illinois Press, for arranging to secure Barry's comments. August Meier read a penultimate draft of this book and generously bestowed his customarily detailed commentary. Although Auggie and I did not always agree and this is probably not the book he would have wished, I am certain that it is better in many ways because of his intervention.

Among my more recent debts are those to Jacqueline Wehmueller, the acquisitions editor at Johns Hopkins University Press, and to Joanne Allen, my copyeditor. Both have been patient, generous, and supportive in the difficult and laborious process of transforming a manuscript into a book.

I have accumulated other, but not dissimilar, debts to my research assistants, Anne McKernan and Melinda Collins Campbell, who have given me extraordinarily diligent and careful help on this project. Qualitatively and quantitatively, each gave me far more aid than I expected or could pay for. Anne's expertise in computer analysis and in Irish history were crucial to completing the data analysis in chapter 7 and to the research and writing of chapter 9. Melinda's tenacious pursuit of fugitive footnotes and keen editorial eye were essential in preparing the final draft of the manuscript. I am grateful to the Center for Afroamerican and African Studies and to the Rackham Graduate School at the University of Michigan for funding Anne's services and to the Postemancipation Studies Project at Michigan and to the Department of History and the Social Sciences Division at the University of Chicago, which funded Melinda's.

My research has benefited, too, from the very generous assistance of archival staffs at the Jamaica Archives, the National Library of Jamaica, and the Public Records Office at Kew and at Chancery Lane before that. Except for the photograph of Henry Taylor on page 44, which is from *Autobiography of Henry Taylor, 1800–1875*, 2 vols. (London: Longmans, Green, 1885), all the plates for this book were reproduced through the courtesy of the National Library of Jamaica. I would especially like to thank Val Carnegie and June Vernon, of the National Library of Jamaica, for helping me locate illustrations and my friend Nesha Haniff for facilitating that search. I also appreciate the excellent graphics prepared by David L. Oliver and Eugene G. Leppanen, of the University of Michigan Division of Research and Development. My travel to these archives and time for research and writing were made possible by timely fellowships in 1975–76 from the National Endowment for the Humanities, in 1979–80 from Stanford's Center for Behavioral Studies in the Social Sciences, and a travel grant in the summer of 1979 from the Social Science Research Council. In 1987, during a crucial stage in the completion of this project, I was supported by the Woodrow Wilson Center in Washington, D.C. Down the home stretch I enjoyed a year's leave with colleagues and friends in the Postemancipation Studies Project and the Center for Afroamerican and African Studies at the University of Michigan through the generosity of the Office of the Provost and Vice President for Academic Affairs. Help with indexing, proofreading, and managing the final steps was cheerfully provided, respectively, by Lisa Lindsay at Michigan, Jill Dupont and Hannah Rosen at Chicago, and Therese Boyd at the Johns Hopkins University Press.

I have been blessed with the spiritual and intellectual support of several good friends, many of whom have read little, if any, of this manuscript. Opal Burt guided me and my family through our first days in Jamaica. I fear that we have never adequately expressed to her how much her generous and gracious welcome meant to each of us. Christopher ("Kit") Davis-Roberts never read a line of this book, but many long conversations with her about her own work in African anthropology, about intellectual issues, or just about life in general profoundly shaped how I thought about the larger meaning of what I was doing. Leora Auslander did read and comment on parts of the manuscript, but her influence, too, has been felt largely through the example of her own writing and thinking about French social history, feminism, and "doing history." Nancy Lungé Holt accompanied me on my first trip to Jamaica, talked me through some of the early plans to do a statistical survey of some plantation accounts, helped me collect and code some of those as well as the wills and inventories in the Island Record Office. She has not yet seen the results of all that effort; I hope she will be pleased.

Finally, this work is dedicated to my children, Karis Scott, Katherine Michelle, and Michael Kenyatta. More than anyone, they know its true cost. With this I acknowledge that I know as well.

Abbreviations

Add.Ms.	Additional Manuscripts, British Library, London
AHR	*American Historical Review*
CO	Colonial Office, Public Records Office, Great Britain, Kew, England
DNB	*Dictionary of National Biography*
Hansard	*Hansard's Parliamentary Debates*, 3d series
IUP	Irish University Press
PP	Great Britain, Parliament, House of Commons, *Parliamentary Papers*
SES	*Social and Economic Studies*
Votes	*Votes of the Honourable House of Assembly of Jamaica*

The Problem of Freedom

[The capitalist transformation] can itself only take place under particular circumstances, which meet together at this point: the confrontation of, and the contact between, two very different kinds of commodity owners; on the one hand, the owners of money, means of production, means of subsistence, who are eager to valorize the sum of values they have appropriated by buying the labour-power of others; on the other hand, free workers, the sellers of their own labour-power, and therefore the sellers of labour. Free workers, in the double sense that they neither form part of the means of production themselves, as would be the case with slaves, serfs, etc., nor do they own the means of production, as would be the case with self-employed peasant proprietors.

KARL MARX, *CAPITAL* (1867)

The only part of the conduct of any one, for which he is amenable to society, is that which concerns others. In the part which merely concerns himself, his independence is, of right, absolute. Over himself, over his own body and mind, the individual is sovereign. It is, perhaps, hardly necessary to say that this doctrine is meant to apply only to human beings in the maturity of their faculties. We are not speaking of children. . . . For the same reason, we may leave out of consideration those backward states of society in which the race itself may be considered as in its nonage. The early difficulties in the way of spontaneous progress are so great, that there is seldom any choice of means for overcoming them; and a ruler full of the spirit of improvement is warranted in the use of any expedients that will attain an end, perhaps otherwise unattainable. Despotism is a legitimate mode of government in dealing with barbarians, provided the end be their improvement, and the means justified by actually effecting that end.

JOHN STUART MILL, *ON LIBERTY* (1859)

Prologue

The Problem of Freedom
in an Age of Revolution

The nineteenth century has been called "the long century." Like a premature infant, it was ripped from the womb of the preceding century by determined revolutionaries; like a senile patriarch, it died an agonizing, lingering death in the trenches of the Great War of 1914. Thought of in this way, its measure is taken not so much by the calendar as by transformations in the lives of human beings and human societies. By these measures it was one of the great watersheds of human history, encompassing fundamental changes in how human beings relate to nature and to each other, sheltering the beginnings of modernity. Born in world revolution, ending in world war, it has left us a legacy, yet to be fully calculated or clearly determined. It bequeathed us not only the main contours of contemporary thought but the language with which to express it. Like child with parent, we are—even in this nuclear age—still too close perhaps fully to take its measure, to see clearly which parts of that legacy to keep and which to discard.[1]

The first half of that century was an "age of revolution," inaugurated by simultaneous, radical breaks with the past in Great Britain and in France. The first was economic, the second political, but both sought to maximize the unfettered realization of individual capacities. In the 1780s, Englishmen perfected in Lancashire cotton mills a division of labor and wealth that fundamentally transformed the social relations of production. Ostensibly in the interest of humans' insatiable appetite for material consumption, they created a radically different economic order, with exponentially accelerating production, self-sustained growth, and infinitely greater disparities between the social power of those who labored and that of those who owned. In that same decade French men and women stormed the Bastille demanding greater political participation, equal justice before the law, and increased satisfaction as citizens. Subsequently, to fulfill an impassioned desire for self-determination and self-respect, they waged almost twenty years' continuous warfare to spread their revolution, redrawing the political maps of Europe and America in the process.[2]

One of the nineteenth century's more important legacies to the twentieth, therefore, was the concept of individual freedom. The word *freedom* was not among that century's many new additions to our vocabulary, but the struggles of that era invested it with new meanings. The dual revolutions ushered in new relationships between the individual and society, relationships articulated as ones involving greater freedom of action, self-possession, and autonomy of self in relation to others. These relationships were themselves the culmination of classical bourgeois liberal thought fashioned in the seventeenth and eighteenth centuries. Beginning with Hobbes in the seventeenth century, philosophers had deduced political rights and obligations, not from Christian natural law, but from the interests and will of dissociated individuals. The basic building block of society was no longer the family, the clan, the tribe, but the individual self. Society consisted of an aggregation of individuals, all of whom were the proprietors of their own person and capacities, for which they owed nothing to society. Given this premise, all forms of social interaction could be conceptualized as exchange relations between individual proprietors. The mainspring of the economic system was the proclivity of people to "calculate their most profitable courses and to employ their labour, skill, and resources as that calculation dictates," while the political order existed merely as "a calculated device for the protection of this property and for the maintenance of an orderly relation of exchange."[3]

In such a society human freedom can be defined as autonomy from the will of others, and social relations are fundamentally contractual, entered into voluntarily with a view to one's own self-interest. Consequently, one finds the commercial terminology of the contract invoked to express all manner of human relations. For example, the society itself was said to be founded on a social contract between independent primitive beings living in a state of nature. The moral legitimacy of the contract depended, theoretically, on the freedom and equality of the contracting parties. Their freedom consisted of their capacity to dispose of their possessions and powers and to receive an equivalent value in return. Their equality was embodied in the formal reciprocity of the relationship, that is, their like capacity or legal standing to make the contract and to receive equivalent values in the exchange. Both political and economic liberalism, in short, were grounded in exchange relations between self-possessed individuals. The notion of contract presupposed individual autonomy and rights; its reciprocity presupposed formal equality.[4]

This was a radical change in the way people were accustomed to thinking of themselves—indeed, in the way most people in the rest of the world continued to think of themselves. Life's goals for most humans who have walked this earth are better described in terms of the relative absence of scarcity and peril than in the full achievement of satisfaction and security. Given those circumstances, the modern ideal of individual autonomy might well be a dysfunctional, if not alien, notion. For most of humankind throughout most of human history the highest value or good has been to achieve a sense, not of autonomy, but of belonging, that psychic and physical security of incorporation into the group. In fact, under some circumstances, among some groups, individual detachment or independence could be a synonym for slavery; individual self-aggrandizement could be an antisocial act. In some African societies it brought on suspicions of sorcery.[5] The transformations Europeans endured, therefore, were novel in human experience and far-reaching in their effects.

Though increasingly obscured for their descendants, the novelty was well understood by those who inaugurated the change. Freedom, both economic and political, was problematic. The debut of the new economic liberty required a process Karl Marx describes as "primitive accumulation," the forcible separation of the laborers from the physical means of applying their labor. They were now free in a bitterly ironical "double sense," free of customary obligations to a lord and free of means to evade the obligation to work for another. Thus detached and deprived, the "free" worker discovered that new forms of coercion lay at the heart of the new freedom.[6]

John Stuart Mill encountered a parallel contradiction in the political domain. Heir to Jeremy Bentham's political economy and the key mid-century spokesman for the evolving liberal democratic doctrine, Mill agonized over the tension between the autonomy of the individual and the needs of society. An important though muted purpose behind his great treatise, *On Liberty*, was to justify protection of the intellectual elite from the presumably illiberal masses. Defining their conflict as one of enlightenment versus ignorance rather than wealth versus poverty, he argued that the well-being of the whole society, rather than the special interests of the elite, was at stake. But Mill also recognized that the education of humans for the obligations of the new political liberty might encounter "early difficulties" requiring an expedient, benevolent despotism, especially for primitive races. Again, the way to freedom lay through coercion.[7]

But perhaps the most profound difficulty at the practical level was reconciling economic and political liberties within the evolving system of social relations. A capitalist society required for its justification a postulate of equal natural rights and rationality, yet inherently it generated class differentiation in the effective rights, powers, and possessions of its members. That is, freedom as defined by capitalist market relations inevitably produces unequal class relations, which undermine the substantive freedom of most members of society. On the other hand, the freedom defined by civil and political institutions—to the extent that society actually is democratic and egalitarian—must threaten an economic system based on inequality.[8]

Consequently, though theoretically conjoined, the dual revolutions rushed down two separate, mutually incompatible courses: the economic demanded greater scope for individual expression; the political required greater constraint. The anxious British reaction to the French Revolution reflects the fear that the one might undermine or contaminate the other. After all, a genuine democracy would enable men and women at the bottom of the social order to change that order, and this threatened the property of those who ruled. Put another way, transactions in the political domain could imperil the rules of the game for the economic domain. In the seventeenth century this incompatibility had surfaced as anxiety about sustaining stability and social order once the basis for traditional moral authority was removed. In the nineteenth century it resurfaced as concern for balancing the commitment to liberal economy and political democracy. For a good part of the nineteenth century, therefore, men in power wrestled with various formulas for political legitimacy and authority that would rein in the more radical implications of the French Revolution.

In the end, they did it with mirrors. By the end of the century, intellectuals had succeeded in severing in theory the political and the economic domains, even as political control of economic life became in practice more blatant and thorough. Thus the early nineteenth-century intellectual's political economy eventually became our separate, less substantial disciplines of economics, politics, and sociology.[9] Meanwhile, premises about economic relations were reified into liberal dogma, sealed off from political challenge from below. One consequence of these trends was that many of the fundamental contradictions in the new order that had been openly debated at the outset of the dual revolution now became shrouded from view, a development that complicates our current task of historical retrieval. The nineteenth-century conception of freedom is so much a part of our intellectual baggage that it requires effort to see it merely as an artifact of history rather than one of the givens of human nature and desire.

The dual revolution, then, is both the intellectual and historical prologue to the age of slavery emancipation—the other front of liberty's advance. This is true not simply because this revolution provided the context for emancipation and its aftermath but also because the liberation of slaves was both a partial consequence of the new political and economic freedom and its most profound challenge. The political upheavals inspired by the French Revolution set the destruction of slavery in motion; the ideology thrown up by Britain's free labor economy provided the model for what should replace slavery. At the turn of the century Haitian slaves rose in revolt and eventually succeeded in establishing an independent state; the French Revolution inspired their revolt. The European wars that followed that revolution helped loosen the bonds of Spain's American colonies and opened the way for abolition on the South American mainland. Over the course of the century, slave militancy, wars of national liberation, and the internal conflicts between social classes eroded and finally swept away the last vestiges of human bondage in the Americas.

During the age of revolution Great Britain took its first steps toward dismantling its American slave empire, which, amounting to three-quarters of a million slaves, was the third largest slave population in the hemisphere and the second largest to be emancipated at one time.[10] Britain abolished the slave trade in 1807, required British slaveowners to ameliorate the living and working conditions of slaves in 1823, abolished slavery as a legal institution in 1833, and proclaimed complete emancipation in 1838. Jamaica, the jewel in the British colonial crown, had the largest slave population and the most demographically and politically complex society; as such it provided the model for British policy and thought before, during, and long after emancipation. This despite the fact that it was being overtaken in production and general economic importance by other colonies, especially Guiana, and that its experience was clearly atypical in many respects. Nonetheless, that experience and what was thought about it served as a test of evolving British policy and its problematic ideology of freedom.

Slavery abolition forced British policymakers to be explicit about the meaning of freedom. Their notions of economic and political liberty had evolved over the previous century and were grounded in novel premises about human nature, which were in turn the distillate of specifically European—indeed, English—historical experience. But in time, the very historicity of that experience was lost. So when British policymakers looked to the abolition of West Indian slavery, focusing explicitly on Jamaica as their model, they saw the problem through an ideological lens fashioned according to their own culturally and historically defined notions of what freedom was and blind to all its inherent contradictions and flaws. For British emancipators, the nature of bourgeois man *was* human nature; all else was at worse deviant and savage, at best primitive and undeveloped human potential. Both the original development and subsequent shifts in British policy oscillated about this central premise. Of course, to recognize this fact is not to claim that emancipation would have proceeded differently or more successfully had the British been more self-reflective, but such recognition may provide us clues as to why freedom unfolded as it did and help us to see that to which *we* might otherwise be blind.

Thus the age of revolution was a thematic as well as a temporal prologue to British slavery emancipation. As Napoleon marched through Europe, for example, Georg Wilhelm Friedrich Hegel was composing *Phenomenology of the Spirit* (1807), a treatise addressing some of the philosophical problems raised by the dual revolution. The men and women of this new age would confront the problem of determining the boundaries of individual autonomy, the self, and balancing these against the claims of dependence and community. Significantly, Hegel turned to slavery, to the struggle between lord and servant, for a model of human self-realization. With that struggle he attempted to illustrate how freedom emerges out of absolute domination; how autonomy can require interdependence; how the realization of the individual self can depend on the recognition of an other and, more specifically perhaps, of a community. Hegel's initial premise was that "it is only through staking one's life that freedom is won." But in the completion of his parable, freedom emerges not as just a state of being or even a relationship but as a process of becoming, something to be achieved only through struggle and work.[11]

That Hegel chose to place the image of the slave's struggle for self-determination at the center of his analysis suggests something of its continuing power as metaphor and experience. The complexity of that analysis helps underscore two themes that have guided this work. First, to understand the emancipation experience, we must track simultaneously the struggle for mastery and the resistance to being mastered through their diverse forms and domains. Though much of what follows focuses on deconstructing the ideology of elites and policymakers, I hope to make clear that these elite ideologies and policies always developed in dialectical relation to the thought and action of the Afro-Jamaican masses. Second, the struggle of master and slave, of freed people and their erstwhile emancipators, poses issues of continuing relevance to freedom struggles whatever their forms or venues. The emancipation of slaves helps to frame freedom as a problematic for us all. Paradoxically, it is from ex-slaves that we may well learn much of what it means to be free.

Part One

The Mighty Experiment

The question will not be left to the arbitrament of a long angry discussion between the Government and the planter. The slave himself has been taught that there is a third party, and that party himself. He knows his strength, and will assert his claim to freedom. Even at this moment, unawed by the late failure, he discusses the question with a fixed determination.

F. B. ZINCKE TO GOVERNOR BELMORE, 23 MAY 1832

Emancipation, properly understood, does not imply the right to be indolent when profitable labour is to be had, but only the right to labour moderately in obedience to a general law for a fair compensation, subject to such penalties for disobedience as the law may have prescribed, and as the Magistrate alone shall inflict.

HENRY GEORGE GREY TO LORD JOHN RUSSELL, 11 JANUARY 1833

1

The Meaning of Freedom

The first flames appeared shortly after seven in the evening. It was Kensington, a small estate belonging to John Henry Morris, located in the high country of St. James Parish. From that height, as planned, the blaze was a beacon visible throughout the surrounding countryside. Within hours torches were set to the flammable dried sugar cane trash at Blue Hole, Leogan, Leyden, Palmyra, Windsor, Hazelymph, Belvedere, and Content. Later that night observers at Montego Bay reported a pattern of flame stretching across the dark horizon like a red arc. The slaves of Jamaica's western parishes were in revolt.[1]

The rebellion began shortly after Christmas, on 27 December 1831. For several days small parties of rebels moved methodically among the plantations of St. James, Trelawny, Hanover, St. Elizabeth, and Westmoreland, leaving in their wake a wide swath of burnt sugar factories and devastated cane fields. The resistance continued into January and eventually implicated several thousand slaves. Fighting was limited mostly to guerrilla attacks on the estates, but there was a skirmish at Old Montpelier in St. James between 150 slaves, organized as the Black Regiment, and the Western Interior Regiment, a militia made up mainly of local estate personnel. With a mere fifty guns among them, the rebels forced the militia to retreat to the safety of Montego Bay, where, humiliated, they awaited reinforcements.[2]

Although the rebels established hidden caches of arms and organized themselves into military units on some estates, there is considerable evidence that they actually intended to mount an armed general strike rather than an all-out war. In fact, there were "sit down" strikes both before and after the violent phase of the uprising. In both rhetoric and tactics theirs was a defensive war, intended to maintain rights, privileges, and territory they thought they had already won. Rumors circulated widely that the king had freed them but that their masters were conspiring to withhold the "free papers." From the outset, the rebel leaders urged their followers to inflict property damage selectively in order to halt the harvest, but to shed no blood. In several instances, white constables and overseers were disarmed and held prisoner but not physically injured. Only when the militia and army marched against them did the leaders release their followers from this curious nonviolent discipline.[3]

By the end of January the rebels had been subdued, but not before spreading their rebellion over 750 square miles of Jamaica's most prosperous region and embroiling almost a fifth of its entire slave population. Two hundred twenty-six estates sustained damages totaling more than £1 million sterling, and 540 slaves lost their lives, almost 200 in combat and another 344 before a firing squad or on the gallows.[4]

The rebels failed in their announced objective of driving whites and free coloreds from the island and working the plantations for their own benefit, but their revolt was a harbinger of events that would eventually destroy Jamaican slavery. On 20 August 1833, little more than a year and a half after the revolt had been crushed, the British Parliament abolished slavery throughout its West Indian colonies. The authors of the abolition law cited the Christmas revolt of 1831 as a major factor compelling their action.[5]

That this particular revolt should have proved so decisive in the antislavery cause is ironic. Although conspiracies and rumors of conspiracy were common, this was actually the first and only major rebellion of plantation slaves in nineteenth-century Jamaica. Compared with the slave risings of the eighteenth century, it was a relatively bloodless affair—at least for whites. Only fourteen whites were killed in 1831, as compared, for example, with sixty in Tacky's Revolt in

Attack on Montpelier Old Works Estate during the "Baptist War"

1760. In the 1831 revolt, much of the damage intentionally inflicted upon property was confined to residences and the outbuildings used to store dried sugar cane trash. The rebels made an effort not to torch the growing canes because they intended to harvest them later for their own benefit. The destruction of cane fields that did occur was caused primarily by cattle left unattended during the fighting, or fires that got out of control. Moreover, government loans and grants rescued the planters from financial losses suffered in the course of the rebellion.[6]

Jamaican planters and British policymakers were most disturbed by the unique character of this revolt. Investigations in Jamaica had uncovered a deep involvement of the plantation elite—the black drivers and artisans—which unnerved Jamaican whites. The rebel leaders were men who had enjoyed their masters' trust. "Daddy" Sam Sharp, reputed to be the chief leader of the resistance, belonged to Croydon Estate but worked at Montego Bay and traveled freely throughout St. James. An eloquent and passionate speaker, he had become a class leader in the Baptist church and a "ruler" among the independent

Baptist congregations. George Taylor was a saddler in Montego Bay and a Baptist deacon; his business permitted him to move freely among the estates smuggling arms and information. John Tharp was a driver and "doctor-man" at Hazelymph, Charles Campbell was a carpenter at York, and Thomas Dove, a literate headman at Belvedere. These men were among the most privileged slaves, enjoying significant material advantages and considerable autonomy in their personal lives and generally protected from the harsher features of slave life. Robert Gardner, one of the condemned rebel leaders, acknowledged that he had always been treated well. "If Dove and I were to be stripped, our skins would be found to be as smooth as any white man's, for we have never been flogged. I was quite happy."[7]

The eighteenth-century revolts had been instigated by African field slaves; indeed, such rebellions were often confined to a single African ethnic group, such as the Coromantes in 1760. By 1831 the Jamaica slave population was largely creole, so it was not surprising that the rebels were predominantly Jamaican-born. But the rebel leaders were also exceptionally acculturated. Many of them were literate and had been inspired to rebel by newspaper accounts of the abolitionist movement in England, of the British government's highly publicized effort to ameliorate and abolish slavery, and of the planters' strident calls for resistance. During the summer and fall preceding the outbreak, planters had held a series of angry meetings, which were filled with inflammatory speeches threatening armed revolt against the Crown. Affiliation with the United States, then the major slave power in the hemisphere, was debated.[8]

Moreover, the principal rebel organizers were all class leaders or deacons in the Baptist Church, a circumstance that reinforced their natural authority as plantation foremen by lending religious legitimacy to their habit of command. They drew on that authority to build up an "invisible church" outside the control of the English Baptist missionaries, including separate services and an independent organizational network. They drew on the Bible to justify their actions, proclaiming as the slogan of the rebellion "No man can serve two masters." At least a quarter of those court-martialed at Montego Bay were affiliated with a Baptist congregation. Indeed, so thorough was its identification with the Baptists that the slaves soon labeled this revolt the Baptist War.[9]

The striking religious, indeed Baptist, character of the uprising provided the planters with a convenient scapegoat. The white Jamaican elite were quite convinced that "the unceasing and unconstitutional interference" of the British government, "the false and wicked reports of the Anti-Slavery Society," and "the machinations of crafty and evil-disposed persons," namely, the Baptist missionaries, had caused the rebellion. Generally, planters were convinced that the missionaries and abolitionists constituted a "bigotted faction" whose incessant agitation of the slavery issue had put "the knife at [their] throats" and "cheer[ed] on the blacks to [their] destruction." As soon as the rebels were brought under control and martial law had been canceled, therefore, whites began a sustained assault on the Baptist and Methodist missionaries, destroying their chapels and threatening their lives.[10]

These actions dissipated the initial sympathy the planters had gained in England and helped mobilize support for the abolitionist cause. Baptist missionary leaders survived the pogrom and beat a hasty retreat to England, where they related their tribulations and oppression to a parliamentary committee and to their fellow Dissenters, who just recently had been mobilized by the campaign for parliamentary reform. Over previous decades, the large Dissenter sects had maintained a kind of uneasy compromise with British slaveholders, even though they decried the sinfulness of slavery. They now became uncompromisingly vocal foes of slavery and joined with evangelical Anglicans and secular abolitionists to demand immediate abolition. They flooded Parliament with petitions and organized the provincial electorate to demand that every candidate for Commons pledge himself to the abolitionist cause. In the fall of 1832, abolitionists won a stunning victory in the parliamentary elections. By December 1832, one year after the "Baptist War," a majority of the House of Commons was sympathetic to abolition, and the government was studying ways to effect it.[11]

The role of the 1831 revolt as a precursor to abolition lay not only in its political impact in mobilizing antislavery opposition but also in its discursive reverberations, which transformed the very terms of the debate over abolition at Whitehall. The rebellion had a marked effect on the attitudes of government officials; they, too, had come to accept the necessity of *immediate* abolition. This shift in sentiment was evident well before the great abolitionist mobilization in the summer and fall of 1832. As soon as his staff had finished digesting the accounts of the rebellion, but before he could have learned about the religious repression that followed, Viscount Goderich, the Whig colonial secretary, wrote to Jamaica's Governor Belmore, relaying the home government's interpretation of recent events in the colony. Goderich portrayed the planters as fighting a rearguard action against inexorable progress. The 1831 revolt demonstrated that it was a struggle they must inevitably lose.[12]

By 1832 the argument for abolition's inevitability was pervasive in both private discussions and public debates on emancipation. It had two separate but mutually reinforcing thrusts: first, that the 1807 abolition of the slave trade was a kind of promissory note for emancipation for which the 1823 amelioration laws were a first remittance; and second, that amelioration of the slave regime and acculturation of the slave population, both necessary precursors to free labor, made the slaves dangerously discontented with slavery. Given these views, the unique character of the 1831 revolt seemed to prove that the cultural advancement of slaves, their access to information, and the continued agitation of the slavery issue in Britain and the colonies guaranteed that another, possibly more successful revolt would occur, and soon.

With this argument the Whig government gave a decidedly abolitionist twist to the history of recent legislation on slavery. Parliament's vote to abolish the slave trade, the ministers now claimed, was actually a pledge to terminate slavery as well. It had been expedient for opponents of the trade to declare at the time that they had no intention of disturbing slavery itself, they conceded, but the steady unfolding of policy since 1807 made it clear that the ultimate result of this first breach in the walls was total destruction of the entire edifice. The slave trade abolitionists had expected that planters, deprived of African replacements, would be moved to reform and ameliorate the conditions of slavery so as to preserve, if not reproduce, their existing labor force. When the planters failed to respond to such clear market incentives to reform, the government, under pressure from the abolitionists, had taken more direct steps to encourage amelioration and reform. This was the intent of the Amelioration Acts, presented to Parliament nearly a decade earlier by George Canning, the Tory leader in the Commons. The planters were encouraged to move with all deliberate speed to prepare their slaves to join a free labor force. Slaves should be given religious instruction; marriages and families should be protected; physical coercion, especially whipping, should be controlled if not abolished; and manumission should be encouraged. Consciously copying the Spanish system of *coartación*, the Colonial Office sought to achieve a gradual emancipation by enabling individual slaves to buy their freedom. Parliament had approved these resolutions as an alternative to Thomas Fowell Buxton's motion for the immediate emancipation of all slave children after a certain date. It was, therefore, only the mode and pace of emancipation, not the fact, that had been disputed. Yet the response of West Indian governments had been obstinate delay and obstruction of Parliament's clear intent. In Jamaica, especially, the planters' intemperate and excessive protests, widely publicized in the colonial press, were misconstrued by the slaves, exciting unrest among them. The recent slave revolt was its fruit, and it now made direct and more forceful intervention by the home government imperative. Since the West Indian planters had proved they would not act, Parliament must do the job for them.

But if government intervention was now required to fulfill the original goals of amelioration, successful reform actually seemed to imperil the gradualism of the amelioration-acculturation process. By Goderich's reckoning the decision a quarter-century earlier to abolish the slave trade had unleashed impersonal social forces that, irrespective of government action now, would inevitably destroy slavery:

> It is also well worth while to reflect upon the inevitable tendencies of the laws for the abolition of the slave trade. So long as the islands were peopled by the importation of native Africans, who lived and died in heathenism, the relation of master and slave might be expected to be permanent. But now that an indigenous race of men has grown up, speaking our own language and instructed in our religion, all the more harsh rights of the owner, and the blind submission of the slave, will inevitably at some period, more or less remote, come to an end.[13]

According to this policy, therefore, education and religious conversion were necessary prerequisites to the creation of a free labor force, but the 1831 revolt made clear that such reforms also harbored the seeds of slavery's violent destruction. Given this paradox of reform, the planters' frustration and anger are understandable. The colonial secretary's bland assertion, in passing, that Christianity brought new knowledge and habits of reflection that necessarily undermined habits of servility must have unnerved them. His nonchalant conclusion that looking toward eventual emancipation, a policy of religious proselytizing among the slaves had to be pursued regardless of the dangers it posed to the master's authority and to the institution's survival must have confused and infuriated them.

Surprisingly, the planters made no effective response to this argument, possibly because a variant of it had long been so prominent a part of their resistance to reform. They had protested that continued government interference and public agitation on the slavery issue invited unrest and endangered their lives. Of course, their conclusion was that the agitation should be squelched and the government should leave them to their own devices. Unlike the slaveholders of the American South, West Indian planters did not defend slavery as a positive good that should be expanded and continued indefinitely, but protesting the "hasty and ill-digested measures of wrong-headed enthusiasts," they insisted that it was inexpedient to make changes too rapidly or at that moment.[14]

The government's argument was circular in many respects, but one that the planters were never able to dismantle: abolition of the slave trade necessitated amelioration and acculturation in order to reproduce the slave population; amelioration and acculturation necessitated gradual emancipation. Abolition of the slave trade and amelioration had made the slaves restive, however, and likely to seize their freedom by force at any moment. The most striking evidence for this view was the chilling warning of Linton, one of the condemned rebels, on the eve of his execution: "In about three or four years the negroes will break out again, for they cannot help believing that the King has given them freedom, especially as they hear so much about it from newspapers."[15]

The calm resolve with which Linton and his fellow rebels went to their death boded ill for the future, mused one of the authors of the emancipation policy: it would foster a legacy of martyrdom and instill a revolutionary ethos among other slaves. Moreover, in the aftermath of the revolt, the planters' wanton destruction of the Baptist chapels—which had been built largely with money supplied by the slaves themselves—was expected to engender fresh animosity. Nor were matters helped much by the general attack on Dissenter religious groups, actions that had alienated the predominantly Methodist free brown class. The largely colored western militia had been instrumental in putting down the slave revolt of 1831, but they would be less likely to perform the same service in future.[16] All of this crystallized, in debates and memoranda, into an official discourse of abolition's inevitability.

Edward Stanley, the new colonial secretary, in presenting the government's plan for emancipation to the House of Commons in the spring of 1833, put the situation succinctly: The status quo was untenable; "the only course left to you is to advance. The only dangerous course is happily impracticable—you cannot recede—you cannot stand still." Arguing for the same proposals before the House of Lords some months later, Goderich, recently created the earl of Ripon, declared that the issue was no longer whether the slaves were fit for freedom but the dangerous fact that they were "now unfit for slavery." He was seconded by Lord Suffield, an abolitionist spokesman, who observed curtly that since "the slave was prepared to take [his freedom], if their Lordships were not prepared to give it," it would be wise to give "that which they could no longer withhold."[17]

The only acceptable solution to the paradox of reform, therefore, was "immediate" emancipation. The idea that the amelioration policy itself should be reversed and the slave trade reopened was never entertained. Change must be quickened, not reversed. Since the slaveholders appeared loath to cut this Gordian knot, the government must do it for them; but cut it must surely be. Within a year after the Jamaican rebellion, therefore, Colonial Office staff were sifting through various proposals for the "immediate" and complete abolition of British slavery.

The Matrix of Reform: Providence's Immanent Design, Adam Smith's Invisible Hand

What made the government's abolitionist argument tenable, perhaps, was the larger context of progressive reform whence it sprang. Thirteen months before the slavery abolition measure passed its third reading, Parliament had enacted the Great Reform Act of 1832, a major change of its system of electoral representation and suffrage. Though not nearly as sweeping as was claimed at the time, it did bring important new groups into the political process and laid the basis for the Whig and Liberal parties' ascendancy over the next three decades. Just prior to parliamentary reform, Protestant religious dissenters and Jews had gained full civil rights. A year after the Abolition Bill passed, the same Parliament enacted major changes in the laws governing poor relief. Over the decade that followed, factory regulation, education, prisons, policing, and other social issues would be addressed by new legislation and institutions. Contemporaries were acutely conscious of living in the "Age of Reform."

Undoubtedly, it was this context that Colonial Secretary Edward Stanley was referring to when he told Parliament that the Abolition Bill reflected "the liberal and humane spirit of the age." Given this spirit, he insisted, the pecuniary interest of West Indian planters and merchants was overawed by the great popular abhorrence of slavery, "which no one can deny or wisely despise." Thus, he concluded, expediency, consistency, and morality all demanded an end to slavery. Invoking the memory and legacy of Wilberforce and the abolition of the slave trade, Stanley urged that Parliament "for a second time set the world a glorious example of a commercial nation, weighing commercial advantages light in the balance against justice and religion."[18]

Indeed, the idea that the British were moved to abolish slavery by a groundswell of humanitarian sentiment that overrode their own economic interests soon became the orthodox interpretation of these events and of this era. It was an interpretation not seriously challenged until the mid-twentieth century, when West Indian historian Eric Williams argued that economic, not humanitarian, concerns motivated the destruction of colonial slavery. Williams saw a causal relation between the rise and fall of mercantilism and the rise and fall of slavery. Stated simply, the rising British bourgeoisie, embracing a laissez-faire ideology and rejecting monopoly on general principle, soon came to reject West Indian slavery and the monopoly that slaveholders enjoyed in British markets. Having been isolated ideologically, the West Indian planters were rendered even more vulnerable because of their declining economic power both as a trading partner with Britain and from the internal weaknesses of the slave economy, which was caused by a host of maladies, especially absenteeism, soil exhaustion, and overproduction. The decisions to abolish the slave trade in 1807, to free the slaves in 1833, and to adopt free trade in 1846 were all rooted in the expansion of capitalism and the triumph of laissez-faire ideology. That proponents of emancipation in 1833 saw their efforts as an extension of the movement to abolish the slave trade and that many of the leading emancipationists were active in the free trade movement lent credibility to Williams's thesis.[19]

That credibility has been undermined by recent studies, however, especially those of Roger Anstey and Seymour Drescher. Anstey contended that the abolitionists used economic arguments to cloak their genuine humanitarian objections to the slave trade rather than the other way round. Both Anstey and Drescher criticized Williams for failing to link laissez-faire ideology to any *specific* groups, in or out of Parliament, who might have been mobilized to support the abolition of the slave trade. In fact, it appears to them much easier to establish the opposite linkage, that is, that the new British industrialists, much like those in the United States, were more likely to oppose the abolitionists than to support them. Moreover, rather than declining, the slave empire was booming at the turn of the nineteenth century, according to Drescher, whether viewed from the perspective either of its share of British trade or of the productive capacity of the plantations themselves. All this seems to suggest that the British abolished the slave trade despite their economic interests, not because of them.[20]

Williams made an easy target. His punchy, bold rhetoric did not concede much to the nuances and complexities of human motivations. But his fundamental insight was correct: the advent of slavery abolition was a function of the rise of capitalism. This point even his most severe critics now willingly concede.[21] Where modern scholars differ with Williams (and with each other) is in determining the crucial nexus of these simultaneous developments. Capitalism prompted new social relations, new institutions, and a new psychology, they all agree. But which aspect of that transformation was most salient to the advent of abolition? Was it the mere fact that market relations gave rise to new ways of understanding human relations generally, to new conceptions of moral responsibility? Was it that capitalism stimulated countervailing reactions among workers and evangelical religious groups, one form of which was an intense empathy for slaves? Or is the connection to be found in the anxieties of the new bourgeoisie, which led them to use antislavery as an illustration of how the old morality and the new economic order could be reconciled?

Williams's second most important insight—admittedly more implicit than explicit—was that abolition as a process of policy formulation must be considered separately from abolition as a social movement. Contrary to the impression conveyed by most contemporary summaries of his thesis, Williams never denied the sincerity of the so-called Saints, whom he praised, nor the genuineness and importance that humanitarian sensibility played in destroying slavery, which he readily conceded. He simply claimed that sentiment played a subordinate, auxiliary role in the process. Public pressure was necessary but not sufficient to make abolition an accomplished fact of public policy. Politics, on the other hand, was essential, and politics was shaped by the economic interests of the dominant classes. "The humanitarians," he wrote, "in attacking the system in its weakest and most indefensible spot, spoke a language that the masses could understand. They could never have succeeded a hundred years before when every important capitalist interest was on the side of the colonial system."[22]

It was to explain that political process, the action of the governing classes, that Williams devoted his efforts. His argument does not rest on proving that abolitionists in general were moved by self-interest (although he clearly thought some were), nor even that the capitalists as a group actively promoted abolition. Rather, his argument seems to be that British capitalists were an essential prop to the status quo, holding abolition at bay; and when they turned against slavery, the West Indian slaveholders and merchants were left vulnerable to the moral outrage of the abolitionists. Of course, even in this form the argument still has its weaknesses (the capitalists' hostility to slavery is still motivated by economic interests narrowly defined), but the point here is not so much to defend Williams as to recognize and build on his contributions. Once abolitionism is seen not as a transcendent moral crusade but as a product of the social relations of its time, we can better probe both its successes and its failures. And the exploration of both the successes and the failures is framed by two questions: What influences did the rise of capitalism exert on the destruction of slavery? and What factors shaped the government's decision to abolish slavery?[23]

David Brion Davis has done the most to build on Williams's insight that abolition was linked to the rise of capitalist social relations. In contrast with Williams, however, Davis argues that it was not the specific economic interests of particular capitalists but their bourgeois ideology that conflicted with slavery. By the late eighteenth and early nineteenth centuries, "enlightened" people had come to view slavery as anachronistic and "unprogressive" on both religious and economic grounds. Simultaneous with "the dual revolutions" of the late eighteenth century, traditional justifications of slavery—as biblically sanctioned and economically progressive—came under increasingly critical scrutiny. The rise of secular philosophies and evangelical religions stripped away slavery's ideological "screening mechanisms," exposing it as merely a blatant power relationship sustained by the material greed of the master. Those attuned to the new liberal political economy pioneered by Adam Smith could condemn slavery as less efficient and more expensive than a free labor system. It was also more costly for society as a whole because it inhibited the growth of population, industry, and national wealth. On the other hand, for evangelical Protestants, slavery inhibited the master's moral progress at the same time that it brutalized the slave. The master's godlike power over another human being and the denial of moral agency to slaves enthralled to another's will were inevitable sources of sin and corruption. The system stymied the progressive transformation of human feeling and was contrary to God's immanent historical design. Thus stripped of both its economic and its religious defenses, slavery became just another pecuniary interest vulnerable to competing interests. These competing interests generally arose among the bourgeois class that emerged from the ongoing capitalist revolution. But equally important, this class, not coincidentally, also made up a core constituency of the dissenting religious sects and commanded an increasing share of political power after the electoral reforms of 1832.[24]

In fact, Davis argues, the majority of the early abolitionist leaders—from the 1780s to the 1820s—came from a narrow, affluent cross section of commercial and professional elites. In their minds, antislavery was linked to a broad reform agenda featuring a commitment to replace the older, external, overt mechanisms of physical constraints with internalized restraint. In their hands, slavery was a useful antonym for the emerging "free" wage labor system because it allowed "issues of freedom and discipline to be faced in a relatively simplified model. And by defining slavery as a unique *moral* aberration, the ideology tended to give sanction to the prevailing economic order," by reshaping "attitudes toward work, liberty, exploitation, and proper discipline."[25]

Although Davis's argument has been subjected to attacks much like those made against Williams's, actually his core thesis is not vulnerable to the same objections. His argument is less about specific economic interests and political maneuver than about the ideology that informed both. Its chief virtue is that by recovering the ideology of the class primarily responsible for formulating the abolitionist argument, it points us a way out of the historian's cul-de-sac formed by the simplistic choice between economic interests and humanitarian ideals as competing motivations for abolition. If we define ideology or world-view as a particular systematic conjuncture of ideas, assumptions, and sentiments that mediates between our objective experience and our subjective interpretation of that experience, then it acts like a lens through which the light of experience passes. It is the mental framework that lends order to and vests meaning in experience. On the other hand, experience—as shaped by religion, race, gender, and class—can in turn be a key generative force determining ideology.[26]

A fundamental part of the experience of those elites who led the abolitionist movement was the ongoing capitalist revolution and its problematic implications for human relations. How was one to conceptualize freedom in a society where social relations of labor were rapidly changing? Freedom was an abstract concept, difficult to define in substance; consequently, it was feared, liable to misuse. Slavery, on the other hand, being clear-cut and concrete, could be used to symbolize "all the forces that threatened the true destiny of man."[27] In this way slavery helped locate the outer boundaries of freedom; it was the antithesis of freedom. If slavery meant subordination to the physical coercion and personal dominion of an arbitrary master, then freedom meant submission only to the impersonal forces of the marketplace and to the rational and uniform constraints of the law. If slavery meant involuntary labor for the master's benefit, freedom meant voluntary contracts determined by mutual consent, which theoretically should guarantee the enjoyment of the fruits of one's labor. Slavery meant little, if any, legal protection of property, person, or family; freedom meant equal protection of the law. Historians might empirically determine that slavery and capitalism were compatible, but to contemporaries of the Reform Era, slavery was logically synonymous with irrational monopoly power in both labor markets and commodity markets. The power of the antislavery movement in this era derived in large part, then, from the fact that slavery was such a convenient foil for free markets, free labor, and free men.[28]

But new ways of thinking—an ideology, a new language—simply provided the *materials* for creating social movements and government policies. Ideas in themselves do not create either movements or policies. To account for the political decision to emancipate we must close the gap between an enabling discourse and social action. Moreover, ideas can be fickle guides to social action. When widely shared by people who are antagonists, they can be applied very differently.

Such was the case, Seymour Drescher argues, with the ideology of British abolition. It was not the bourgeois class, but the working class, in particular the artisans, who provided the troops and the energy of the abolitionist movement. They made abolition a reality. Their antislavery commitments sprang from sources very different than those of the abolitionist elite. Their genuine empathy for West Indian slaves was rooted in their own experience as workers, and they shaped antislavery ideas and language to their own ends—to resist capitalist expansion, not endorse it. Their movement was caused neither by factory expansion nor by evangelicalism. Indeed both evangelicalism and abolitionism were spawned independently by the social conditions of England's industrial regions. The antislavery message played well among the boom towns of the north and west, where recently displaced workers responded with empathy for the slave's plight. The movement sprang up in these areas because they enjoyed the unique combination of psychological and political insulation from slavery as a social system, yet experienced close involvement with slave societies through commercial relations. Similarly, early industrialization patterns created a class of workers outside the factory, a class recently freed of traditional paternal labor relations yet close enough to that past to appreciate in human terms what freedom and slavery meant.[29]

Quakers and other elites may have founded the antislavery movement, Drescher argues, but they soon lost the initiative to this segment of the new working class, most of whom were members of the fast-growing Methodist and Baptist sects. These were the people who perfected the petition as a mechanism for simultaneously creating "a climate of opinion" and exerting political pressure in a premodern electoral system. Religious enthusiasm, therefore, was not a determinant of antislavery motivation, but the well-traveled, overlapping maps of evangelicalism and commerce forged communications networks and made increasingly massive political mobilizations possible. In 1788 about a hundred petitions bearing over sixty thousand names demanded abolition of the slave trade; by 1833 the abolitionists had flooded Parliament with five thousand petitions endorsed by almost 1.5 million people demanding the abolition of slavery.[30]

But should we characterize a movement by the people attracted to it, or by how its leadership defined its objectives? The answer depends very much on the question one wants to address. If one wants to examine abolitionism as a social movement, the appeal of its message is important. The supporters that it attracted reveal a great deal about the *mentalité* of that movement. If one is concerned with abolitionist outcomes, however, then the content of ideology as framed by its leaders may be its most salient feature. Abolitionism existed on several levels. It was an aspect of humanitarian sentiment, which raises questions about the sources of this new empathy. Why, as Davis has asked, did men suddenly define as immoral an institution that had been an accepted part of Western culture and morality for centuries? It was a social and political mass movement, which raises questions of who joined and why, and what the mechanism was for their mobilization. Why and how did people collectively attack slavery and force their moral perceptions onto the larger public and the government? But ultimately we must deal with the issue of abolitionism as public policy, which, in turn, raises questions of statecraft, of the mediation among contentious forces, of political judgments, of the principles of legislation and implementation. In short, it is a question of governance and of how those who governed, given their own internal dynamics of ideology and mobilization, were moved to particular actions. The question why men of one class would lead an antislavery campaign is likely to be separable from why others would follow and participate. Similarly, the question why the governing class—the Ministry and

Parliament—would accept and promulgate a policy of emancipation is related to, but quite different from, those addressed in trying to account for a social movement.

For our purposes, then, the original question—Why did men suddenly define as immoral an institution that had been an accepted part of Western culture and morality for centuries?—needs to be focused much more sharply: Why did British government policymakers define slavery as a social and moral evil after it had served the nation's interests so well for so long? And even more to the point, what forces—intellectual or other—shaped their perceptions of the alternatives to slavery and of how to achieve those alternatives?

The circumstances surrounding the decision to abolish slavery were not analogous to the situation in 1807.[31] In contrast with the case in the earlier period, West Indian planters *were* experiencing some distress in the 1830s because of overstocked markets and low prices. The Versailles peace ending the Napoleonic Wars brought an end to the war years' dramatic expansion and lower profits for British agriculturalists at home and in the colonies. During the postwar adjustment, therefore, British West Indian sugar and coffee prices were puffed up by protective tariffs just as English grain prices were. But West Indians faced the added problem of becoming increasingly less important as a trading partner with the mother country during the postwar decades. This must have made emancipation easier for government officials to contemplate. If free black labor turned out to be a disaster, the nation risked less in 1833 than it would have in earlier decades. Certainly British capital was already beginning to turn to other outlets, and it would do so even more aggressively during the following decade.[32]

In any case, by 1833, government policymakers were treating the economic effects of emancipation in a surprisingly cavalier fashion, at least to the extent one may judge from the correspondence and speeches of the responsible officials. West Indian cries of imminent ruin had been heard in the halls of Parliament too often to be credible any longer. Sugar production might well continue its decline after emancipation, observed Edward Stanley in his presentation to the Commons, but this might actually benefit the colonial economies by bringing supply into a more profitable relationship with current demand. Thus spoke a future Tory prime minister. His future Liberal antagonist, Henry George Grey (Viscount Howick at the time), wrote much the same thing in a confidential memorandum. And as if that were not enough to chill the planters, Stanley went on to advise them that given the "inevitability" of slavery's destruction, they would be wise to minimize their losses. Small comfort that.[33]

Behind this cavalier attitude toward West Indian prosperity a growing condescension toward the West Indian planters was evident. Indeed, for the West Indian interests a major difference between 1807 and 1833 was their declining political power as well as their diminished economic importance. The West Indian members of Parliament tended to find their allies among the Tory landlords and sugar merchants, the former sharing their concern with preserving monopoly markets for agricultural products, the latter, their interest in the sugar trade. The political power of this coalition of sugar and corn had been based on the malapportioned House of Commons, which gave rural areas and "rotten boroughs" a disproportionate number of seats. That power base was a major casualty of the 1832 Parliamentary Reform Act, which had created a broader electoral base in general and increased in particular the power of urban constituencies, the industrial bourgeoisie, and dissenting religious groups.[34]

But perhaps even more important than the growing number of parliamentary enemies, sugar and corn M.P.'s found fewer sympathizers within the Whig ministry elected under the new system of representation. For example, Henry George Grey, son of Prime Minister Earl Grey, suggested that the slaves deserved financial compensation as much as the planters did. Meanwhile, one of his Colonial Office colleagues, assessing potential opposition to emancipation from the West India interests, contemptuously dismissed colonial residents as politically insignificant. They were, after all, mostly attorneys and overseers who feared the loss of employment if plantations were abandoned after emancipation. The actual owners of the land and slaves and the merchant mortgage-holders were residents of England and would probably welcome any plan that offered to minimize their losses. Plantations were less an investment than a gamble. Gamblers should be prepared to take losses.[35]

The Whig ministry's hostility to the slaveholders was based more on ideology and partisan allegiances than on any specific economic interest it sought to foster or destroy. Thus its ministers demonstrate the impact of the new ideology quite apart from economic interests. For the most part, these officials were neither new industrialists nor members of the rising bourgeoisie nor evangelicals or Dissenters. The Whig party was still controlled by wealthy landed magnates, and this was reflected in the composition of the Grey ministry. But they were receptive to the prevailing liberal ideology of the new bourgeoisie and sought to reform society in its interest. Ideological and political needs neatly coincided in the 1830s. Assessing the political environment in 1832, Henry Taylor, one of the architects of British emancipation policy, urged his superiors at the Colonial Office to draft an emancipation measure that would satisfy the middle class, because its concerns were more "durable" than the "evanescent" prejudices of the larger populace.[36]

Who might Taylor have had in mind when he invoked "the middle class"? Certainly, he would have included the Quakers, the cutting edge of the antislavery movement and also the vanguard of the Industrial Revolution in Britain. No other group better illustrates the connections between liberal ideology and religion, on the one hand, and the problematic linkage of abolitionism and free labor ideology, on the other. Heavily peopled by bankers, merchants, and industrial entrepreneurs, the largely urban Quaker community was likely not only to be concerned as a group with problems of social order and labor discipline but also to be disturbed by the ethical basis for capital accumulation and economic success. Men who were the veritable linchpins of the Atlantic world market professed a religion that renounced worldly values. Perhaps this critical contradiction produced the guilt and self-flagellation historians have uncovered in the diaries and personal papers of the various reform leaders. Among the antislavery men in particular, one discovers a pattern wherein young men earned their fortune, retired, and devoted the rest of their life to a variety of humanitarian causes, including reform of prisons, hospitals, education, and poor relief, as well as antislavery. All these social causes betrayed a single principle and objective: to free individuals from arbitrary, personal, and physical dominion, on the one hand, and to promote self-discipline, individual responsibility, and human "betterment," on the other. All this was to be achieved by appealing to man's innate desire for self-improvement. Thus the Quakers were perhaps the most striking embodiment of the intimate connections between the ideals of social reform and self-reform.[37] Perhaps also they provide us some glimpse into the melding of religious sentiment and bourgeois acquisitiveness within society at large. By the middle of Victoria's reign, one would be hard pressed to separate the one from the other, or to tell when one ended and the other began: both piety and material wealth defined middle-class respectability.

Despite their small number, Quaker abolitionists were also important partly because their endogamy reinforced the connectedness and interlocking memberships of a host of nineteenth-century reform movements. A seamless web of business, religious, and family connections magnified this small community's impact on a wide range of social reform movements. Samuel Gurney the elder was a wealthy Quaker banker who financed the antislavery campaign. His son, who became president of one of the abolitionist societies in 1864, sat on eleven different philanthropic committees. His brother J. J. Gurney was a leader in the radical Joseph Sturge wing of the abolitionist movement during the 1830s. His sister Elizabeth Fry organized the reform of the women's section of Newgate Prison. Sister-in-law of abolitionist Thomas Fowell Buxton, Fry was a friend of Joseph Lancaster and a supporter of his model school system. Abolitionist William Allen, manager of a London chemical works, organized the Prison Discipline Society, which advocated new methods of penal management aimed at rehabilitating inmates.[38]

Many non-Quaker abolitionists displayed a similarly eclectic range of activism. William Wilberforce supported Sir Thomas Bernard's Society for Bettering the Condition and Increasing the Comforts of the Poor (S.B.C.P.), which sought to ameliorate conditions among the lower classes by appealing to man's innate desire for self-improvement. Wilberforce was also interested in reforming the poor laws and defended on the floor of Parliament Jeremy Bentham's prison reform scheme and John Howard's reformed management of Gloucester Prison. Abolitionist Henry Brougham served as president of the Working Men's Club and Institute Union, a middle-class-led organization designed to teach workers self-control and the pleasures of more temperate and "rational" use of their leisure time.[39]

The dissemination of such ideas was not simply through written texts. The autobiographies and diaries of this period unfold an extensive intermingling of elites—in salons, debating societies, and intellectual friendships. Gatherings at Lord Shelburne's Bowood Estate, a meeting place for policymakers, philosophical radicals, and philanthropists, illustrate the many concentric and intersecting circles that imparted social force to personal ideas and sentiments. Abolitionist William Allen, intimate of utilitarian philosophers Jeremy Bentham and James Mill, enlisted their support for James Lancaster's model schools. James Stephen, who later drafted the Abolition Act, identified Nassau Senior, a Benthamite who authored the poor law reforms in 1832, as "one of my intimate and habitual associates."[40]

Henry Taylor, who wrote so many of the key policy decisions at the Colonial Office during the emancipation era, also enjoyed close social ties to a number of reformers, especially Bentham converts.

During the early 1830s Taylor shared a house and developed a close friendship with Thomas Hyde Villiers, initially his superior at the Colonial Office and subsequently a member of Parliament. Villiers was the second son in a wealthy and influential family; two of his brothers also served in government, one in Parliament, the other in the Cabinet. The Villiers brothers gathered around them a number of bright young men. Most were recently graduated from Cambridge; many were committed to and active in movements for free trade, abolition, and poor law reform; most were Benthamites. They formed a club, calling themselves the Academics, and held regular debates. Though clearly awed by the brilliance of his friends, decades later Taylor insisted that he was not converted to Benthamism, but remained "an ardent conservative." Indeed, he recalled defending the virtues of the upper class in a club debate with John Stuart Mill. Nevertheless, Taylor's approach to problems of social action betrays the influence of the "philosophical radicals" of his day. As we shall see, when he sat down to develop a plan for emancipation, Taylor drew, consciously or not, on Malthusian demographic principles and Benthamite notions of human motivation.[41]

The pervasiveness of reform ideas, the interactivity of reform schemes and organizations, and their intellectual circulation among the elites expose their common philosophical roots. All was sketched over a common template. Adam Smith's great principle that "the desire of bettering our condition . . . comes with us from the womb, and never leaves us until we go into the grave" was not merely a principle of political economy: it was a fundamental maxim for understanding human nature and the human condition. By the nineteenth century such ideas had become merely the givens of ordinary intellectual discourse. Thomas Malthus's "scientific" political economy and Jeremy Bentham's utilitarian philosophy commanded the attention if not the total allegiance of policymakers as well as intellectuals. "Nature," declared Bentham, "has placed mankind under the governance of two sovereign masters, *pain* and *pleasure*. It is for them alone to point out what we ought to do, as well as to determine what we shall do."[42] Thus the values of Adam Smith's self-seeking economic man became the norms for moral and social behavior generally.

In sum, fundamental tenets of capitalist ideology were pervasive among intellectuals, bureaucrats, and the politicized elites. Perhaps it was as an ideological and political force rather than an injured economic interest that Williams's rising bourgeoisie made their most important contribution to the destruction of slavery. In this expanded context one might better interpret David Brion Davis's observation that the "new hostility to human bondage cannot be reduced simply to the needs and interests of particular classes. Yet the needs and interests of particular classes have much to do with a given society's receptivity to new ideas and thus to the ideas' historical impact."[43] Davis's thesis may not provide a complete explanation for the rise of antislavery sentiment (i.e., the empathy for ex-slaves, the expanded boundaries of moral responsibility) or of abolitionism as a social movement (its broad reach and political clout), but it does provide an indispensable clue to the frame of reference for the governing authorities who fashioned emancipation policy. It is also true that those authorities could not have remained indifferent to the burgeoning social movement Drescher describes, especially when it threatened to spill over into larger issues of political and economic order in British society.

Bourgeois ideology provided the essential language for abolitionist legislation, and the abolitionists helped to create the political climate that made emancipation legislation possible, but it was government officials who became the emancipators. They wrote and administered the law. Embedded in their motives for abolition is a rationale for the specific schemes adopted and the policies subsequently pursued. In ascertaining why, or how, they were moved to destroy slavery, perhaps one can gain a better understanding of the nature and the meaning of the freedom they hoped to bestow on the former slaves. Such an analysis might also provide some insight into the evolution of emancipation policy thereafter and the problems encountered by both ex-slaves and their former masters. The immediate choices—whether to abolish slavery and what form that abolition would take—were dictated by the political and class relations of the early 1830s. But the formulation of those choices, that is, what options were seen and not seen, was determined by the received liberal ideology. The forces that produced the political climate making abolition possible were multifaceted, overlapping, sometimes even contradictory.[44] But the nature of the emancipation law they framed—the meaning they gave to freedom—was a clear expression of the ideology that Eric Williams's rising bourgeoisie had created. It also reflected the internal contradictions and political difficulties of that ideology.

The Problem of Free Labor

For British policymakers the problem of abolition was, at its root, a labor problem: how safely to transform a dependent laborer into a self-motivated free worker. Or as one Colonial Office staffer framed it, their primary objective in fashioning an emancipation scheme was "to pass from bondage to freedom without overthrowing the existing apparatus of social order in the passage." For solutions to that problem they could draw on the historic transformation of their own agricultural workforce into a proletariat, but that history was not unproblematic, as events on the eve of emancipation would remind them.

Emancipation schemes would be founded on the fundamental maxim that all humans shared an innate desire for material self-betterment. It was a maxim about human nature that Adam Smith's *Wealth of Nations* had made famous, but it predated Smith's work by at least a century. Indeed, Nicholas Barbon articulated in 1690 a view of human nature identical with the policy a colonial secretary would urge on Jamaican governors in the 1840s. "The Wants of the Mind are infinite, Man naturally Aspires, and as his Mind is elevated, his Senses grow more refined, and more capable of Delight; his Desires are inlarged, and his Wants increase with his Wishes, which is for everything that is rare, can gratifie his Senses, adorn his Body, and promote the Ease, Pleasure, and Pomp of Life." Furthermore, it was not necessities but luxuries that spurred consumption, added Barbon's contemporary Dudley North, those "exorbitant Appetites of Men, which they will take pains to gratifie, and so be disposed to work, when nothing else will incline them to it; for did Men content themselves with bare Necessaries, we should have a poor World."[45] Given this view of human nature, the role of government in the economy could be greatly reduced.

But this materialist psychology and laissez-faire ideology was rejected by other seventeenth-century thinkers, and their rejection is instructive for gaining perspective on the sources of ambiguity, ambivalence, and contradiction in postemancipation policy of the nineteenth century. As historian Joyce Appleby points out, many seventeenth-century Englishmen saw danger in embracing "the idea that society was an aggregation of self-interested individuals tied to one another by the tenuous bonds of envy, exploitation, and competition." The commercial sector of the economy, anxious to expand trade, touted the new laissez-faire doctrine, but industrialists and landowners, as employers of labor, rejected it in favor of mercantilism, with its reassuring corporate view of society wherein economic individualism was subordinated to the ideal of the national interest.[46]

There was from the outset, then, tension between those who made theory or counted money and those who had to command labor and maintain social order. Seventeenth-century employers, witnessing a vast and unnerving redistribution of the agricultural workforce because of enclosures and the growth of an urban wage labor force, were acutely sensitive to the issue of social order and stability. "The new economic ideas undermined the rationale for lower-class discipline and upper-class direction," writes Appleby.[47] Just how was one to establish social order in a society of self-interested individuals seeking to maximize their personal gains? If one accepts the individual's right to autonomy and self-sovereignty, where does one draw what a student of a later period has called "the moral boundaries of social authority"?[48] Would not the same envy and desire that urged men to work also lead them to social and political pretensions that would undermine the existing social hierarchy? Was it possible to believe that the working class they knew actually shared the character traits laissez-faire advocates attributed to all human beings? Many among the privileged classes had their doubts; it seemed to them that the British lower class was an innately lazy and unambitious lot. They would never work three days "if two days' pay would keep them a week."[49] Thus seventeenth-century political economists never fully accepted the liberal premises, because they were unable to resolve the seemingly inherent contradiction between the ethic of liberalism and the labor needs of a capitalist economy, between individual freedom and social order and utility.

The men of the Reform Era thought they had learned the answers. Their objective, as David Brion Davis summarizes it, was "to inculcate the lower classes with various moral and economic virtues, so that workers would want to do what the emerging economy required."[50] Or, as William Wordsworth, the representative poet of the Reform Era, put it, they sought to replace the discipline of slavery with "the discipline of virtue." But since the poor, all agreed, were not yet virtuous and certainly not disciplined, their education in market values could not be left to chance. Given the lower class's economic irrationality, the problem was "to train them up to habits of work." They had to be taught to calculate advantage and to allocate time and resources by the unitary principle of the likelihood of gain. What was required was a thorough cultural reconstruction of the working class. "To train a rising society in the right way, is a process of comparatively little difficulty," declared a government official in 1850, "but to change a great uneducated mass requires a well directed effort of many years." This reference was not to West Indian ex-slaves but to English mineworkers.[51]

Of course, the specific policies pursued in Jamaica owed more to concrete experience than to philosophical speculation. The problems British entrepreneurs confronted in their attempt to turn white agricultural laborers into an industrial workforce prefigured the problems and possible solutions for turning black slaves into free agricultural workers. The fact that the great seal of the Anti-Slavery Society, which showed a kneeling slave and the motto "Am I Not a Man and Brother," was designed by Josiah Wedgwood is emblematic of this connection. Wedgwood was best known to his contemporaries as owner of a pottery factory at Etruria and as a major innovator of techniques for inculcating industrial discipline. Workers were summoned to Etruria by a bell, and their work day was strictly regulated by the clock. They were assigned to a single, specific task on a production line, and differential pay rates were set according to the skills required. Quality control was maintained by frequent inspection. Wedgwood prepared written rules and regulations, providing for punctuality, constant attendance, fixed hours, scrupulous standards of care and cleanliness, avoidance of waste, and a ban on drinking and sex during working hours. His objective was to render his employees "steady, remorseless and efficient," to assimilate men to machines, or as he put it, to "make such *machines* of the *Men* as cannot err."[52]

Wedgwood did not enjoy complete success in reeducating his workers and crushing their preindustrial culture. They continued to take Monday as a holiday, to abandon their tasks for days on end to attend wakes and fairs, to drink on the job, and even to commit occasional sexual indiscretions. Obviously, the cultural reform of the working class would require the attentions not only of the rulers of industry but also of the rulers of state. Among other things, the state must establish a comprehensive and universal system of education. Dr. James Phillips Kay, who became the government's chief architect of educational policy in the 1840s, observed in his 1832 pamphlet on the condition of Manchester cotton workers that the primary goal of state-sponsored education was not simply to impart skills but to teach the worker "the nature of his domestic and social relations . . . his political position in society, and the moral and religious duties appropriate to it."[53]

James Roebuck, a Benthamite and prominent radical member of Parliament, put the matter even more bluntly than Kay when he introduced a resolution to establish a national education system. In a speech that followed immediately upon the emancipation debate in

1833, Roebuck described specific political gains that he expected to flow from public education:

> Of all the knowledge that can be conferred on a people, this is the most essential; let them once understand thoroughly their social condition, and we shall have no more unmeaning discontents—no wild and futile schemes of Reform; we shall not have a stack-burning peasantry—a sturdy pauper population—a monopoly-seeking manufacturing class; we shall not have a middle class directing all their efforts to the repeal of a single tax, or to the wild plan of universal robbery; neither will there be immoral landlords wishing to maintain a dangerous corn monopoly; or foolish consumers, who will suffer it to remain. We shall have right efforts directed to right ends. We shall have a people industrious, honest, tolerant and happy.[54]

But what of those who persisted in stack-burning, begging, and idleness? Obviously, different modes of social control and cultural reform were required for the deviants and incorrigibles. Thus the same Parliament that debated and approved the abolition of slavery and entertained proposals for universal education enacted legislation to reform prisons, poor relief, and the police. There were striking similarities in the governance and discipline that they established in penitentiaries, mental hospitals, workhouses, schools, and reformatories. Like the factories on which they were modeled, these institutions enforced regularity, punctuality, uniformity, and routine. By assimilating men to machines, they sought to instill behavioral norms of rationality and self-control. The managers of these institutions were also to be rational, uniformed, and self-controlled. Discipline was to be cadenced and impersonal. Therefore, personnel were recruited from among half-pay officers and retired military men to serve as policemen, prison guards, and even teachers.[55]

As we shall see, the same types of recruits were sent to the West Indies as stipendiary or special magistrates to supervise the resocialization of the newly emancipated slaves. In fact a rural constabulary was organized in Jamaica even before one was dispatched to Lancaster to instruct misbehaving English workers. Schools and prisons, organized on reform principles, were promoted in the colonies almost simultaneously with their development in England. And though both white and black Jamaicans resisted many of these innovations, colonial officials adopted others enthusiastically. For example, in his search for a thoroughly impersonal and thus humane system of corporal punishment for his model prison system, Jeremy Bentham designed a whipping machine that made punishment "self-evidently rational."[56] The treadmills erected in Jamaica to punish refractory freedmen bore a haunting similarity to Bentham's design.

The great irony, of course, is that so much of the paraphernalia of the new institutional discipline bore such a striking resemblance to that of the slave plantation. Centralized surveillance, regimentation, division of labor, strictly controlled work pace, written rules and regulations, were all standards pursued by every planter, though not always attained. It was as if part of society would have to be enslaved to preserve the liberties of the rest.

This anomaly provides a crucial clue to the internal contradictions of the liberal idea of freedom. Assuming a universal human nature, it rejected as culturally deficient those who did not respond according to its theory. Bentham defended the infringement of liberty he prescribed for his poorhouses by pointing out how unfit for liberty the paupers were. They were "a sort of forward children—a set of persons not altogether sound in mind—not altogether possessed of that moral sanity without which a man can not in justice to himself any more than to the community be intrusted with the uncontrolled management of his own conduct and affairs."[57] The idea that those who did not take readily to the new cultural values should be forced to submit to the tyranny of publicly sanctioned slavery also figures in some of the proposals for emancipation.

There was, then, an ever-present tension between the ideals of free labor and social realities which made consistency of theory and practice difficult to achieve, thus requiring a variety of transitional institutions and expedient compromises. Describing the compromises resorted to by the poor law reformers in 1834, for example, historian J. R. Poynter wryly observed that in their conscious remaking of the English working class, they "looked to the carrot rather than the goad to stimulate labour, but it is not surprising that goads were fashionable while carrots remained in short supply."[58]

Prefigured in Britain's experience, too, was the difficulty of maintaining a distinction between political equality and the equality implied in the freedom to contract one's labor. The recognition of the universality of certain traits in human nature was not intended to invite social pretensions from the lower orders. The sameness of human striving did not imply equality of conditions among all people. As one student of Reform politics has observed, "in the scale of Whig values, liberty was conditioned by and subordinated to the maintenance of a traditional hierarchical order in society."[59] Thus the few would rule and the many would serve; some would employ, most would labor. Ultimately, the liberal state was founded on Marx's "double freedom": the free worker was expected to offer social and political deference without claiming economic dependence.

Yet, despite the new penitentiaries, workhouses, police forces, and schools, the superior classes remained anxious and uncertain of their ability to control or remake the lower orders. In an 1845 report on the public schools, an English school inspector fretted about the inscrutability of these lower orders. "The fact is that the inner life of the classes below us in society is never penetrated by us. We are profoundly ignorant of the springs of public opinion, the elements of thought and the principles of action among them—those things which we recognize at once as constituting our own social life, in all the moral features which give to it form and substance." William Taylor, manager of a Jamaican plantation, anticipated those thoughts in confessing his utter surprise at the slave revolt of 1831: "There may be living hundreds at your very door, and you do not know what they feel or what they are going to do."[60]

Those who attended the parliamentary hearing on slavery abolition heard much the same message about blacks, in much the same words, that they might have heard elsewhere in its halls about white labor. In a sense, the British experience with its own working class was a rehearsal for the formulation of policy for West Indian freed people. If government officials had been inclined to miss that resemblance, the prevailing unrest in the English countryside was likely to remind them. The Whig government that plotted the course of abolition had first to confront the threat of agrarian rebellion at home.

The Swing Rebellion of 1830 made clear that the process of creating an agricultural proletariat in the English countryside, begun centuries earlier, was still incomplete. By the early nineteenth century British agricultural laborers were wage earners who had no claims to the land, but labor relations in the countryside had not yet been reduced entirely to an antipaternal cash nexus. This was true especially of the farm servants hired for the year and receiving in-kind payments for their work in addition to cash. Demobilization after the Napoleonic Wars, however, brought falling prices, a labor surplus, and accelerated changes in the social relations among landlords, their tenant managers, and the rural labor force. The situation was exacerbated by a system of poor relief, put in place ostensibly on a temporary basis during the booming war years, that in effect used the poor rates to subsidize low wages by institutionalizing a system of family allowances. Under postwar conditions this welfare system was overburdened, and in many areas the combination of poor rates and low wages fell below the level a worker and his family required to subsist. Meanwhile, labor became increasingly seasonal, cash replaced in-kind payments, and farmers adopted labor-saving machinery, particularly threshing machines.[61]

In 1830, after experiencing two seasons of disastrous harvests, farm laborers in the cereal-growing parishes were pessimistic about the coming harvest and fearful of another hard winter. Rumors of the July Revolution in France and agitation over parliamentary reform fed a "vaguely stirred expectation" of imminent violence. The chief targets of anger were the threshing machines that stole their jobs, Irish migrant laborers who undercut their wages, and the increasingly impersonal, hierarchical nature of rural social relations, especially as they were manifested in the callous administration of poor relief. Much like Jamaican slaves the following year, these English laborers spread word that the king was on their side, had outlawed the hated machines, and was sending his emissaries to restore justice.

By late summer the rumors gave way to action, beginning in eastern Kent and spreading westward across twenty counties in southern England. Farm laborers, often led or assisted by local town artisans, organized marches through their parishes and sent threatening letters to landlords demanding the destruction of their machines. In other instances more direct action was taken: in broad daylight riotous crowds visited the farmer and dismantled his threshers; at night incendiaries fired the barns and storehouses. Historians have estimated that the damage from arson and wrecked farm machinery alone exceeded a hundred thousand pounds.[62]

Although the major thrust of the uprising had spent itself by early December, incendiary incidents continued sporadically for more than a year. Earl Grey's Whigs, who had taken office in November, outdid their Tory predecessors in their stern repression of the unrest. Because local communities could not be trusted to return guilty verdicts, almost 2,000 people were tried by a Special Commission. The death sentence was ordered for 252, of whom 19 were executed; those whose sentences were commuted were among 481 rioters transported to Australia. These penalties were far more severe than any imposed for similar incidents of unrest and reflect the inordinate fear among Britain's ruling class. But repression was not enough, however harsh. The Whig government's overriding concern was to stem the possible spread of this rural revolt to the industrial workers in the north and west. For the governing class, the connections between various "clamors for reform" were palpable and threatening.[63]

Working class spokesmen articulated a range of views on the slavery issue. Certainly those rural workers and artisans who gathered in the village beerhouses listening to the village shoemaker read from *Cobbett's Weekly Political Register* were treated to racist diatribes and attacks on abolitionists that West Indian planters would have heartily approved. But in the politically charged environment of the Reform Era, even Cobbett eventually gave a wavering endorsement to abolition. And the fact that counties swept by the Swing Rebellion showed a propensity to Methodism is suggestive evidence of new political connections being forged.[64]

Slavery was a powerful metaphor, for workmen no less than for middle-class reformers. It provided a language that intensified their sense of dispossession and oppression. Of course, it could be (and had been) invoked to claim priority for their own situation by denigrating the abolitionist campaign. But it could also be invoked to support both their own and the slaves' cause, as it was increasingly in the 1830s. By 1833, therefore, this chief metaphor for oppression had spilled headlong into the broader political discourse. With it, spokesmen for workingmen as well as for the middle classes implied a connection, verbal and political, between the fate of West Indian slaves and their own.[65]

For a government increasingly sensitive to the need to keep middle-class and popular grievances separate, this development raised a problem of "containment" that was not just military but ideological, political, and social. It is not coincidental that the same Whig administration that promoted parliamentary reform, new poor laws, education, and slavery abolition also carried out a brutal repression of its own "stack-burning peasantry." When they faced the tasks of defining what freedom would mean for West Indian blacks and designing new social and political infrastructures for plantation societies, therefore, British policymakers drew on perspectives and precedents learned from the centuries-old process of "liberating" their own rural workforce. But they could hardly have been oblivious to the fact that such transitions were fraught with peril to established hierarchies of social status and power. On 6 May 1833, a little over a week before Edward Stanley presented the Abolition Bill to Parliament, the last shipload of Swing rebels were landed in Australia.[66]

Planning the Transition to Free Labor

The various emancipation proposals discussed in 1833 were themselves not fully consistent with laissez-faire principles, therefore, because policymakers knew that the real world required more than ideological consistency. Like any effort at statecraft, their proposals were fashioned according to what was perceived to be politically viable. Nevertheless, they were all rooted in the liberal democratic ideology that had evolved over the preceding century. One must judge them by the options that the authors of emancipation ruled out as well as the ones they chose. They did not attempt to replace slavery with any new form of *permanently* bound labor or seigneurial relationship. They dismissed any racist grounds for limiting the freedom of action of the former slaves. All the proposals were designed to transform slaves into free laborers, and slaveholders into employers, equal before the law, their social relations mediated by the market.

Several plans were considered, but two—Henry Taylor's and Henry George Grey's—are especially useful in exposing the fundamental concepts shaping emancipation and the difficulties that would be encountered in its implementation. Their plans were unusually detailed, clearly specifying their assumptions and reasoning. Although neither plan was adopted in total, together they clarified the principles of legislation and framed the problems all other schemes had to address. Equally important for our purposes, the men who drafted them would play predominant roles in shaping the outcome of emancipation in later years.

At thirty-three, Henry Taylor was still a relatively young man in 1833, but he had already been a clerk at the Colonial Office for eight years. He would remain there for almost forty more, retiring in 1872. During that period he would play a key role in decisions on almost every issue related to emancipation, and he provided an unparalleled institutional memory for a succession of colonial secretaries. Taylor also reflects the diverse influences of the postwar reform age on a "disinterested" mind. His family's roots were in the Northumberland gentry, but his father, being the youngest son, had had to make his own way, managing a farm during the Napoleonic Wars and engaging in various other occupations afterwards, including secretary to the Poor Law Commission of 1834. Henry Taylor was largely self-educated but developed some talent for poetry. In 1824, he went down to London seeking to establish himself as a writer. It was a profession that brought him some modest contemporary fame, but he had to take on a government clerkship to secure his "fortune." For much of the rest of his life he would pursue a dual career, poet and bureaucrat.

A close friend of Southey's and Wordsworth's, and strongly influenced by them, in his poetic work Taylor combined the influences of the Lake School romantics with the worldly-wise caution one might expect of a civil servant. The dispatches and minutes he prepared for the Colonial Office reflect these qualities as well. During the thirties he circulated among the Whig salons, and his circle of acquaintances included politicians, intellectuals, and the London literati, most notably John Stuart Mill and Thomas Carlyle. During his long service in the Colonial Office, Taylor had ample opportunities for promotion—an offer of the governorship of Upper Canada in 1835 and of permanent undersecretary in 1847—but declined all of them, preferring to continue his part-time literary career.[67]

Taylor presented his plan to the Cabinet in January 1833. The central problem of freedom, he noted, was how to create a free working class out of former slaves. The problem was particularly acute in colonies such as Jamaica, where population density was low and large areas of the interior had not been engrossed by plantation staples. Jamaican planters had encouraged their slaves to grow foodstuffs on such land to supplement their weekly rations of salt fish and corn. They allocated garden plots either on the plantation itself or on land leased from others. By custom, slaves had come to treat these so-called provision grounds as their private property. They sold their surplus produce in the weekend markets of nearby villages and towns and retained the profits for themselves. Taylor noted that testimony before the House of Commons had shown conclusively that freed people would be able to earn their accustomed subsistence needs by working their own provision grounds for little better than one day a week. The key question, therefore, was "What, except compulsion, shall make them work for six?"

Taylor brushed aside abolitionist testimony that the slaves' industry on their provision grounds showed that they would continue to work on plantations after emancipation. The slaves who worked one or two days to purchase necessities would not necessarily work five or six more days for superfluous luxuries. They could be expected to expand their work week sixfold only if their needs and wants were likewise expanded, which was an "extremely improbable" occurrence in the foreseeable future. "It is true that the wants and desires of mankind are indefinitely expansive," wrote Taylor, echoing a basic premise of Adam Smith's *Wealth of Nations*, "but when the habits of a

Henry Taylor

whole population are concerned, the expansion must be necessarily gradual. Their habits cannot be suddenly changed." For the moment, one must expect that the freedmen would strive for those possessions they were accustomed to, those enjoyed by persons of slightly higher status, that is, the black headmen and estate artisans. It would be reasonable to assume that "it will only be in a long course of years and progress of society that their wants will creep up the scale of luxury, and be characterized by that exigency in the higher degrees of [those desires] which might suffice to animate and prolong their labours."[68]

Obviously, the dangers of the present moment and the needs of society would not permit such delay. It was necessary that industrious habits be inculcated in some manner; work discipline must be internalized by the freedmen without the normal spur of necessity or desire. The problem was to overcome the legacy of slavery. "The state of slavery, if it implies much injustice, implies also much ignorance and want of moral cultivation," Taylor concluded. Being "ignorant, destitute of moral cultivation, and . . . habituated to dependence," slaves required "both a sense of subordination in themselves, and the exercise by others over them of a strict and daily discipline." But there was reason to believe that under "disinterested instructors" they would advance in civilization. Once it had been thought that blacks were intellectually inferior, but preponderant evidence presented to Parliament revealed striking cultural progress. Under the tutelage of missionaries, the slaves showed a strong desire to learn and were "a quick and intelligent race of people." Of course, some racial differences remained. Taylor rejected one witness's testimony that the slaves possessed a "shrewd"—he might have said "calculating"—intellect. He thought their mental character might better be described as rash, volatile, and somewhat shallow, "the intelligence, in short, of minds which had neither discipline nor cultivation, and nothing but natural vivacity to enlighten them."[69]

Given their character and the absence of material incentives to work, freedmen were likely to relapse "into a barbarous indolence" if suddenly or completely emancipated. Experience showed that where population density is low, people have "a strong propensity to scatter themselves" and live in the wild as hunter-gatherers. A society must be "condensed" to be civilized; otherwise a situation develops wherein "capitalists [will be] shorn of their profits by the want of labour, and . . . those who *should be* labourers, turning squatters and idlers, and living like beasts in the woods." In lavish detail Taylor described future Jamaican villages, which would become "scenes of savage sloth, unstimulated by the motives of human nature in a cultivated state, unactuated by *opinion,* the great regulator of civilized societies, and perhaps interrupted only by such broils and acts of violence as idleness and the ardour the Negro temperament might give birth to."[70]

The government's objective, then, should be "to devise a system of civil government" that would redeem West Indian communities from barbarism. An emancipation measure must be drafted "which shall preserve the frame-work of the present system of society in the West Indies, whilst it calls into immediate operation a power calculated to place that system substantially in a state of rapid transition." Taylor's plan, consciously modeled after the Spanish system of slave self-purchase, *coartación,* was designed to achieve this end. "On this plan," he recalled years later, "I conceived that before [the slave's] bondage ceased, he would have acquired habits of self-command and voluntary industry to take with him into freedom, by which habits *he* would be saved from a life of savage sloth and the planter from ruin."[71]

Taylor's plan provided that the value of all slaves between six and seventy years of age would be calculated and the British government would purchase one-sixth of their work week, that is, one day. Thereafter the slave could use the earnings of that "free" day to purchase another day, and so forth, until he or she would be entirely free. The key feature of the system was that the slaves would earn their freedom by their own industry. Thus "the operation of the measure would be in accordance with the great moral principle of the government of men, which would call their own powers and virtues into action for their own profit and advantage; and bring home to them the consciousness of a moral agency and responsibility, by making the good and evil of their lives the result of their own conduct."[72]

Surely there could have been no clearer statement of liberal ethics and market-oriented values. It was the laboring portion of one's day, week, or life that defined one's status as free or slave; freedom was parceled out into six equal parts congruent with a six-day work week. After the first day had been purchased, the slave's access to freedom would be determined solely by a desire for self-improvement and capacity for hard work. Taylor recognized that inequalities in the circumstances as well as the character of slaves would enable some to achieve freedom sooner than others, but such inequities—of industriousness, physical power, and local environment—exist naturally and justly "amongst men at all times and under every system of society." The able and worthy slaves would quickly gain their freedom, "leaving only an idle and spendthrift residue, whose liberation from arbitrary control would be duly retarded." Like Bentham, therefore, Taylor believed that those who refused or were unable to embrace the values of a capitalist economy ought to remain slaves.[73]

Henry Taylor's detailed analysis never got beyond the Colonial Office. Henry Grey rejected this mode of freeing the slaves and threatened to resign should it ever be adopted. The heir of one of the chief Whig magnates, Grey was a fierce advocate of laissez-faire economic theory and free trade. Two years Taylor's junior, he was undersecretary of state for the Colonial Office in 1833. Over the next two decades he would hold a variety of government positions, the most important being colonial secretary during the crisis years of 1846 to 1852. Like Taylor, Grey would exert a major influence on the implementation of emancipation policy.[74]

In a letter to John Russell, Grey critiqued Taylor's plan. In his view, Taylor had violated the central tenets of political economy. "The essential difference between the slave & the free labourer is that the latter is induced to work by motives which act upon his reason, the former by the fear of bodily pain, & it appears to me that upon your plan neither stimulus wd act with effect." Setting wages by law removed the first incentive; taking the whip from the master and handing it to a magistrate removed the second.[75]

Despite the planters' insistence that blacks would only work under the lash, however, Grey saw no reason to suppose that as free people they would not respond to rational incentives. If they acted differently, "it was not because they differ from others in character, but because their circumstances are different; and just in proportion as they are brought within the reach of those motives by which Europeans are governed, will their conduct resemble that of the natives of Europe."[76]

The "rational" stimulus to labor was institutionalized in the wage contract, which summed up the vital difference between freedom and bondage.

> Wages correctly speaking must be matter of agreement between the labourer & his employer, & must be regulated by the demand for labour & the real value of that which is performed, if they are determined in any other manner, & if the labourer is required to accept of such remuneratn as either the employer or some third party may consider sufficient, the whole nature of the bargain is altered, & altho another name may be given to such a mode of obtaining labour, it is practically slavery: in what indeed does it differ from the existg system except in the fact that the remuneratn assigned to the labourer is to be given to him in money instead of in supplies, a change which no more does away with the real existence of slavery than the truck system in England converts those who are so pd into slaves.[77]

Both plans, however, were grounded in the same basic premises about market relations and human nature. Unlike Grey, the pragmatic Taylor was not an ideologue of political economy, but the language and concepts of liberal ideology came to him naturally and unselfconsciously. Indeed, he was a bit put off by Grey's strong condemnation of his attempt to square political economy with the practical difficulties involved in an orderly transition from slavery. Taylor was especially resentful when Grey asked to make selective use of the arguments presented in *Taylor's* memorandum in support of his own scheme.[78]

The distinguishing feature of Grey's emancipation scheme (some of which he would urge again during his tenure as colonial secretary in the 1840s) was a system of taxation on nonplantation land designed either to discourage settlements off the plantations or at least to encourage such settlers to work for wages in order to pay the tax. Taylor sharply criticized the scheme as one designed to "starve the Negro out of his idleness." Grey's plan was rejected by the Cabinet primarily because of Lord Brougham's strong objections and the observations received from the Jamaican governor, Lord Mulgrave, that such a tax would be impossible to collect. Grey resigned as undersecretary in April 1833, after a Cabinet shakeup that brought Edward Stanley to head the Colonial Office.[79]

After a false start of his own that was roundly condemned by abolitionists and coolly received by West Indian planters and merchants, Stanley asked James Stephen, son of the prominent abolitionist family, to draft appropriate legislation. Since 1813, Stephen had been legal counselor to the Colonial Department, digesting and evaluating colonial laws. Though an admirer of John Stuart Mill's work and a friend of Nassau Senior, Stephen was attuned to the law more than to political economy. His father, the elder James Stephen, had been one of the chief leaders of the evangelical abolitionists, and his brother organized the Agency Committee in 1830. Stephen was sympathetic to abolition and religiously devout, but he kept his distance from both the evangelicals and Exeter Hall. Nevertheless, he brought to his official work a sense of moral duty. "This task devolved upon me by inheritance," he wrote a cousin in 1829, "and although I believe that nothing further remains for me to do, and that therefore my conscience is acquitted from all further solicitude on the subject, I should carry away from England a very heavy heart if I left that question under any degree of doubt." Four years later, he wrote his intimate friend and coworker Henry Taylor: "If I cannot do some good to the children of Ham, I shall never do any in my day."[80]

Stanley had promised to submit the legislation by a given date in order to forestall a competing abolitionist initiative. Consequently he gave Stephen his assignment on a Saturday morning with orders to report back by Monday noon. According to Stephen's daughter, the formidable task of drafting sixty-six sections of legislation within forty-eight hours subsequently broke his health. Given this short notice, Stephen's proposal must have been basically a collation from earlier plans and discussions—largely, it appears, Taylor's.[81]

On the evening of 14 May 1833, Stanley rose in the House of Commons to present the emancipation scheme that Stephen had drafted and Earl Grey's ministry had adopted. With some significant modifications in details but not in principles, it was passed four months later. This plan provided for the immediate abolition of legal slavery, to be followed by a period of apprenticeship during which ex-slaves would be required to work for their former masters in return for their customary allowances of food, clothing, housing, and medical care. Part of the laborers' week, however, would be reserved for their own use. During this "free time" they were expected to work for their former masters or other planters for wages. Special magistrates from England (Taylor's "disinterested instructors") and a plantation police force of free blacks would be appointed to enforce discipline, through whipping or incarceration in a public workhouse. It was originally proposed that the planters be compensated by a loan of £15 million sterling, but eventually this was made an outright grant of £20 million. During debate, the proposed twelve-year apprenticeship was shortened to six, commencing on 1 August 1834 and ending in 1840.

Reportedly against the urging of his father, the prime minister, and to the distress of his mother, Grey launched a strong attack on the ministerial plan for emancipation. Stanley had taken three hours to present the plan; Grey followed him with a two-hour rebuttal. In it he reiterated the objections he had raised to Taylor's plan four months earlier. The real difference between freedom and slavery, he lectured the members, was that free men work "because they are convinced that it is in their interest to do so"; theirs was a rational calculation of the relative advantages to be gained from industry over the privations to be expected if they "indulge in their natural inclination for repose." Slaves worked from fear of punishment and for the benefit of others. Thus the government's emancipation scheme retained the central features of slavery. Although under a so-called contract, the apprentice laborer would be free neither to choose his master nor to negotiate his wages. He would be compelled to give three-fourths of his work week for subsistence, but that amounted to only a fifteenth part of the actual value of his labor when compared with prices paid for slaves hired out by their owners. It is axiomatic, Grey continued, that "men can only be taught industry" if their labor is voluntarily given from motives of gain. The proposed apprenticeship system violated both these principles in that labor would be coerced by fear of punishment and compensated below its market value. Thus the apprentice would still work at "a task unjustly imposed upon him by superior power." Echoing Taylor's memorandum, Grey pointed out that the major portion of the apprentice's "wages," that is, the subsistence given in kind, would not increase if he worked harder or better, nor decrease if he shirked his duty. The government therefore had attempted to build a halfway house between freedom and slavery which must fall, because "competition [is] the essence of free labour; . . . there is no intermediate state." One cannot mix coercion and the incentives of free labor. If there is to be any coercion at all, "it is better for all parties that the master should be a completely irresponsible despot."[82]

Nevertheless, despite Grey's insistence that major philosophical differences compelled his break with his father's government, the broad areas of agreement in the schemes and discussions of Taylor, Grey, Stephen, and Stanley are far more important than any points of disagreement. No doubt they and their contemporaries took their political and philosophical differences seriously, but in retrospect the most interesting features of their debate are the basic principles they agreed on. All four rejected racist interpretations of slave behavior and insisted that blacks shared the basic, innate traits of other human beings, that is, that all human beings could be motivated by self-interest and the desire for self-improvement. This was the mainspring of social action in a rationally ordered society. They were committed to laissez faire, though to differing degrees. Artificial and arbitrary constraints on the free exercise of self-interested behavior must be removed to ensure an efficient and productive economy. While historians might conclude retrospectively that slavery was logically compatible with capitalism, the men who fashioned the emancipation law completely rejected such a notion. For them, as for their mentor Adam Smith, there was no question that free laborers, having the greater incentive for efficient and productive work, were more profitable to employ than slaves.

This was, as Howard Temperley has noted, a conclusion arrived at by deduction rather than the type of cost accounting historians have applied to New World plantations. In truth it was a "faith" just as powerful, perhaps, as the belief in Providence's immanent design. It was an article of faith demanded by the assumptions about human nature and psychology that undergirded the liberal world-view. Like its religious counterpart, it was grounded in the conception of humans as autonomous beings who must find their way to God and to the market as individuals.

By the 1830s these economic ideas were more than a century old and were generally accepted by men of diverse political persuasions. For example, in 1824 the Tory-controlled Select Committee on Labourers' Wages had anticipated Grey's lecture to Parliament: "There are but two motives by which men are induced to work: the one, the hope of improving the condition of themselves and their families; the other, the fear of punishment. The one is the principle of free labour, the other the principle of slave labour."[83] By 1833 such notions had become simply the givens of the intellectual and political discourse of those looking to "reform" society.

In sum, the great political and social reforms of the 1830s were undertaken by essentially the same groups of people, were aimed at similar goals, were based on similar premises about human nature and social order, and were inspired by similar fears and hopes. During the months immediately preceding the reform of Parliament and poor relief, Lord Russell recalled, the Swing Rebellion riveted the attention of him and his colleagues. There were nights when "the whole atmosphere was lighted up by fires . . . and the whole framework of society seemed about to yield to force and anarchy." The king was advised not to visit London "lest his presence should excite tumult and disorder. . . . A certain vague desire, and a fear equally undefined, seemed to possess all classes of men." He related a vignette in which a Westminster tradesman, when asked why he carried a musket, replied: "In the first place to get Reform of Parliament, and in the next place to defend my house against a mob." Like that tradesman, Whigs saw themselves standing in the middle, between a brave new liberal social order and the chaos of the unleashed mob. Something like their perspective may be inferred from the reminiscences of Charles Kingsley, an aging Tory, describing the disorders of the 1830s to his Cambridge undergraduates in 1862. He recalled that his generation had believed "that the 'masses' were their natural enemies and that they might have to fight any year, or any day, for the safety of their property and the honour of their sisters." Such a state of mind West Indian slaveholders would have readily understood.[84]

Burned haystacks in England's southern counties mirrored the burned-out sugar works of Jamaica's western parishes. The relevance of the one to the other was not lost on British policymakers. Popular unrest at home made it necessary to approach the slavery question cautiously, wrote Taylor. To grant immediate emancipation to West Indian slaves without compensating the planters would offend the Whig party's middle-class constituency and might excite further unrest among the masses. Such a decision

> would affect the course of other political opinions and events, add force to popular influences, and by inspiring in the public mind an

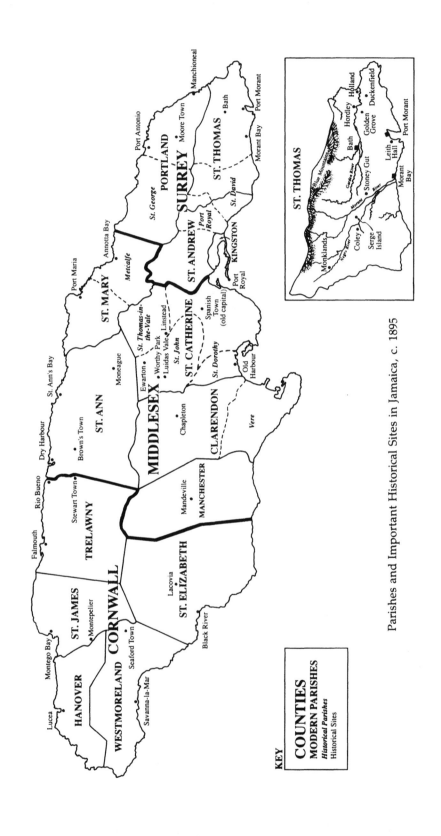

Parishes and Important Historical Sites in Jamaica, c. 1895

KEY

COUNTIES
MODERN PARISHES
Historical Parishes
Historical Sites

CORNWALL

HANOVER

ST. JAMES

Lucea
Montego Bay
Montepelier

WESTMORELAND

Savanna-la-Mar
Seaford Town

ST. ELIZABETH

Black River
Lacovia

TRELAWNY

Falmouth
Rio Bueno
Stewart Town

MANCHESTER

Mandeville

MIDDLESEX

ST. ANN

Dry Harbour
Brown's Town
St. Ann's Bay
Moneague

CLARENDON

Chapleton
Vere
Old Harbour

ST. MARY

Port Maria
Metcalfe
Annotta Bay

ST. CATHERINE

St. Thomas-in-the-Vale
Ewarton• •Worthy Park
•Luidas Vale Linstead
St. John
St. Dorothy
Spanish Town (old capital)

SURREY

PORTLAND

Port Antonio
Moore Town
Manchioneal
St. George

ST. ANDREW

Port Royal
St. David

KINGSTON
Port Royal

ST. THOMAS

•Bath
Morant Bay
Port Morant

ST. THOMAS

Monklands
Yere River
Coley
Serge Island
Morant River
Stoney Gut
Garden River
Blue Mountains
Bath
Hordley
Holland
Duckenfield
Golden Grove
Leith Hall
Morant Bay
Port Morant

increased consciousness of instability and change, with a redoubled disregard of the right of property, accelerate the progress of the [reform] party, and probably tend to precipitate the policy of the Government upon the vital questions of popular interest, which may be considered as the necessary *sequelae* of the Reform Bill. In the present political state of the country no one of these great questions can be wholly yielded up to the people, without giving an impulse to others, and to some extent carrying them along with it.[85]

It was this social and political context, then, that both motivated and constrained freedom for West Indian slaves. They would be free, but only after being resocialized to accept the internal discipline that ensured the survival of the existing social order. They would be free to bargain in the marketplace but not free to ignore the market. They would be free to pursue their own self-interest but not free to reject the cultural conditioning that defined what that self-interest should be. They would have opportunities for social mobility, but only after they learned their proper place. This at least was the intent of the British policymakers who framed and implemented emancipation. The planters had already expressed their doubt and confusion about the viability of such a social reconstruction. The reaction of the freed people remained to be seen.

To make them labour, and give them a taste for luxuries and comforts, they must be gradually taught to desire those objects which could be attained by human labour. There was a regular progress from the possession of necessaries to the desire of luxuries; and what once were luxuries, gradually came, among all classes and conditions of men, to be necessaries. This was the sort of progress the negroes had to go through, and this was the sort of education to which they ought to be subject in their period of probation.

RIGBY WATSON, MEMBER OF PARLIAMENT, 10 JUNE 1833

If the desires of the Negroes were limited to what Labourers in other Countries are forced to be content with; If they were not fond of Luxuries, smart Clothes, and good Furniture, and riding Horses, or had not the better motives of educating their children or supporting their church, they would hardly have any inducement to labour.

GOVERNOR CHARLES METCALFE TO COLONIAL SECRETARY, 30 MARCH 1840

2

An Apprenticeship for Ex-Slaves

The day abolition took effect, 1 August 1834, passed peacefully in Jamaica. Richard Robert Madden, a special magistrate recently come from England, observed acidly that "not a single riot occurred throughout the island, and not a single man, woman, or child, was butchered to make a negro holiday." Madden charged that proslavery advocates, having predicted a general conflagration, were disappointed by the freed people's calm response. Abolitionists, uncertain that their opponents' predictions of violence would prove incorrect, were greatly relieved. James Spedding reported that his Colonial Office colleagues were equally relieved. Since Parliament's approval of emancipation twelve months earlier, all had waited nervously to see "whether the driver's whip could indeed be laid down without blood." They were pleased to see that it could be, and that "sudden destruction had not come to man or beast."[1]

According to the recently appointed governor, the marquis of Sligo, the only exception to this quiet transition from bondage to apprenticeship occurred on the Shaw Park Estate in St. Ann, where, claiming an immediate and concrete rather than a prospective liberty, the freed people refused to work. But the expeditious arrival of companies of the Thirty-seventh Regiment and a sound flogging of the strike leaders quickly restored the peace. Freed people on the rest of the island, apparently content and patient with their probationary status, obediently returned to work after spending most of their first day of freedom in various Baptist and Methodist churches. The freed people attending secular celebrations were also decorous and restrained. The Honourable House of Assembly of Jamaica had declared 1 August a holiday, and on many estates the now ex-slaves were given special rations of rum and beef.[2]

In some ways these initial signs of peace and contentment were deceptive. Former slaves could hardly be expected to understand fully their ambiguous, ill-defined status as apprentices, given that it had confused the supporters of emancipation in the British government itself. One elderly African, highly skeptical of the new law as it was explained to him, reportedly observed that *apprenticeship* was a term used for children put out to learn a trade. "What," he asked, "was he to learn? He was too old to become a cooper, carpenter or mason; he knew how to plant the cane, to weed, to hoe—what was he to learn? Such was not the law the King had made."[3]

Of course, the analogy was more apt than he realized: drafters of the apprenticeship system did regard the slaves as children needing to be reeducated as wage laborers and resocialized as citizens. The problem posed by the transition from a slave to a free society, as James Spedding succinctly put it, was "to change a slavish multitude into an orderly and happy peasantry [and] a slave driving oligarchy, deformed and made fierce by their false attitude, into a natural upper class." Indeed, it is significant that the latter part of Spedding's statement recognized that it was equally important to reeducate and resocialize the planters and the "childlike" slaves. In this connection Governor Sligo's exasperated outburst shortly after his arrival in Jamaica is ironic. Commenting on the planter-dominated Jamaica Assembly, he declared: "I never saw such a set of children. I really think my children would make up nearly as wise a community."[4]

Apprenticeship was a half-way covenant in which the relationship between the planter and the worker was much the same as that between master and slave for forty and one-half hours of the work week, but during the balance of the week they were to assume the respective statuses of employer and employee freely negotiating conditions of work and wages. During the forty and one-half hours, the apprentices

Emancipation Day Celebration at Dawkin's Caymanas, 1838

were to receive all the customary rations and indulgences they had received as slaves. For any labor agreed to above this base period, they were to receive wages. During their "free" time, apprentices were at liberty either to hire themselves to their former master or to another employer or not to work at all.

Combining the roles of judge, teacher, and taskmaster, the special magistrates were the key to the proper functioning of the system. Initially, thirty-three special magistrates were allotted to Jamaica, but the demands of the work eventually required their number to be increased to sixty-three before the end of the apprenticeship period. Drivers and free colored men were recruited as constables and assigned to the plantations to assist in maintaining order. The specials traveled from plantation to plantation, hearing complaints from both planters and workers. Their duties beyond this had been left vague by the emancipation law, but in Jamaica they made periodic reports on conditions in their district, held weekly court sessions, and inspected the jails and workhouses in their area. Not only were their circumstances complicated by onerous travel conditions but they were harassed by the Jamaica Assembly and subjected to discriminatory taxes.[5]

The special magistrates assumed the role of the former masters in enforcing work discipline. Punishments they could invoke included fines in the form of extra labor, imprisonment in plantation dungeons or parish workhouses, and flogging. No offense was punishable by more than fifty lashes (twenty lashes for work-related offenses), and females could not be flogged at all. The Colonial Office preferred to hire half-pay officers from the army and navy to fill the special magistrate positions; such men reputedly knew how to enforce discipline. Indeed, the evidence from Jamaica suggests that such magistrates were more likely to use flogging as a means of punishment than were those recruited from civilian occupations.[6]

In general, the framers of the emancipation law preferred to bring special magistrates from England, thereby ostensibly ensuring their objectivity and disinterest. But problems of recruitment soon led many West Indian governors to grant special commissions to the regular local magistrates, even though many of them were former slaveholders. Although the Jamaican governors resisted pressure to follow that course, many of the Jamaican special magistrates were recruited locally, though not from among former slaveholders. Of the 119 specials who served in Jamaica, the origins of 105 have been identified. Sixty of these were recruited from England, including former military or naval officers, seven were colored Jamaicans, and twenty-four were white creoles.[7]

Although blacks did not raise an insurrection on 1 August 1834, it was not at all clear that they would work as diligently under the special magistrates' authority as they had under their masters'. The typical Jamaican slave had been employed on a sugar plantation, and its rhythms and social organization dictated the planning and implementation of emancipation policy. It was this system that the special magistrates would have to master in order to oversee the supplanting of slavery's coercion by wage labor discipline. The dominant feature of sugar cultivation was that it was both an agricultural and an industrial regime. Consequently, the workforce of the typical estate was divided into four field gangs, constituted according to age and physical ability, and a mill crew of skilled workers. During the final decades of slavery the first, or "great," gang of field laborers tended to be predominantly female and black, while the industrial workers were exclusively male and often mulatto.[8] As we shall see, the fact that labor regimentation

Depiction of Cane Hole Digging

A Sugar Mill at Work

and control were enmeshed with gender and kinship greatly complicated the magistrate's task.

Certain botanical aspects of cane cultivation also shaped the labor regime. The growth of the canes required about fifteen months, including a labor-intensive period for preparing the ground (digging cane holes) and planting and a less intensive period of three or four months for weeding and fertilizing, usually with fresh cow dung, which workers carried to the fields in baskets African-style—on their heads. Of these tasks, digging cane holes with crude hoes in often hard and rocky soil was the most difficult and debilitating. For this reason many estates contracted this task to professional contractors who organized "jobbing gangs" of slaves specially constituted for that purpose. During the "out-of-crop" period field slaves worked from daybreak to sundown, from about 5:00 A.M. to 7:00 P.M., or eleven and one-half hours, excluding meal breaks. There was a half-hour midmorning break for breakfast in the field and a two-hour break at noon for dinner, during which time slaves might rest or attend to personal chores and gardens. In addition, there were always personal chores waiting at the end of the day as well as "before day jobs," that is, miscellaneous maintenance tasks around the estate.[9]

This already strenuous pace increased dramatically during the in-crop season. Since cane juice ferments and sours within a day or two after it is cut, the processing into raw sugar, molasses, and other by-products must be accomplished quickly. At the mills the cane juice was extracted by crushing the freshly cut stalks between mechanical rollers, boiled, and finally allowed to crystallize in large wooden, one-ton barrels called "hogsheads." The combined labor demands of mills operating around the clock, six days a week, an accelerated demand for field workers to keep pace supplying the machines, and a simultaneous need to replant for future crops while keeping up routine maintenance meant that the labor adequate for the normal out-of-crop period had to be supplemented by jobbing gangs or greatly prolonged, or both. Even estates with adequate manpower required their field laborers to work one of the three shifts that divided the ten-hour night, in addition to their day's labor. Those on short-handed estates had to work one of two five-hour evening shifts. Thus the work day ranged from seventeen to twenty hours during the four- to five-month harvest season, or a minimum of eighty hours a week, excluding meal breaks. Since the emancipation law mandated a mere forty and one-half hours per week, with the balance to be coaxed by the offer of wages, its first crucial test was likely to come at the first harvest.[10]

A Sugar Boiling Room

It was clear after 1 August that freedom would not trigger violence, but it was not at all clear whether a wage labor system would command labor discipline comparable to slavery. Since the special magistrates were charged with ensuring that the apprentices worked, freed people soon grew to resent their authority as much as they had that of the head drivers, seeing little difference between the two. By late fall Governor Sligo's pleasure at the peaceful initiation of apprenticeship gave way to growing concern about frequent reports of insolence and insubordination. There was no immediate threat of general violence, he reassured the Colonial Office, but "a general appearance of sullenness & bad disposition" was worrying. Increasing numbers of apprentices were refusing to work any more than necessary during the obligatory forty and one-half hours, were refusing generally to work for wages during their free time, and were increasingly litigious over working conditions and hours.[11]

More ominous were those instances when the apprentices' sullenness broke out into open violence. At Belvedere, an estate belonging to President Cuthbert, of the Jamaica Privy Council, the workers staged a slowdown to protest a cutback in their customary allowances and indulgences. Cuthbert sent for a special magistrate, who after a brief investigation sentenced some of the men to the workhouse. As the prisoners were being led away, a seventy-year-old woman, the es-

Carting Sugar for Shipment

tate's midwife, with "the most violent language & impassioned ges-
tures," called upon the other apprentices to prevent the police from
taking her three children, who were among the prisoners, to the workhouse, because this would be the third time they had been jailed
since Christmas. A group of workers surrounded the police as they
prepared to lead their captives away. A trash house was set afire, and
none of the field hands, drivers, or principal tradesmen would assist
in putting it out. Eventually, two men were convicted of arson at
Belvedere and given a sentence of death, which was later commuted
to banishment by the island's chief justice.[12]

Most of the violence that did occur was directed, as at Belvedere,
at property rather than at persons and involved groups acting on
collective grievances rather than individuals exacting revenge for slavery. One exception was James Ellis's murder of a bookkeeper at St.
Helen's Pen, Augustus Jones, who was strangled and beaten while
bathing in a river on a Sunday morning. Ellis's action was atypical,
however. Not only was the crime rate among apprentices lower than
that among free persons (1 in 3,802 as compared with 1 in 357) but
most apprentices' offenses were against property, while those of free
persons were personal assaults. Furthermore, the apparent increase
in criminal behavior among apprentices was deceptive because public

authorities were now adjudicating disputes formerly settled on the private authority of plantation managers.[13]

In fact, much of the violence and most of the disputes in the apprenticeship period involved mainly questions of working hours and conditions during the harvest season. The apprentices wanted to divide the required forty-and-one-half-hour work week into four nine-hour days plus four and one-half hours on Fridays, which would allow them a long weekend for travel to and work on their provision grounds. The planters, on the other hand, wanted to divide the week relatively evenly into four eight-hour days plus eight and one-half hours on Fridays in order to maximize the operation of the mill. During the spring of 1834, Governor Sligo, under the mistaken impression that Parliament had legally required a nine-hour system, issued a proclamation explaining that the apprentices were legally required to work the four-and-one-half-day system. The governor's confusion exacerbated the conflict between the apprentices and their masters over which system to adopt.[14]

On Gibraltar Estate, in St. George, the overseer attempted to implement a system of overlapping shifts similar to slavery practices. When the workers refused to turn out, he sent for a special magistrate to discipline them. During the ensuing controversy, the estate's trash house was set on fire and the workers refused to extinguish the blaze. At Golden Grove Estate, in St. Thomas-in-the-East, the workers were said to have rioted when a special magistrate insisted that although they were legally required to work only forty and one-half hours per week, those hours could be arranged any way the plantation managers saw fit. In an attempt to quell the disturbance, the special magistrate ordered that one of the leaders (a woman) be confined in the plantation dungeon, whereupon "the people declared they would all go into the dark room, and followed her towards the place of confinement; when near it, they rescued her, and took her away; when they came to the gate near the house they gave three cheers in triumph." Order was restored only after a detachment of police and troops were called out, eight men were flogged, and nine people were confined in the house of correction. However, the Reverend Richard Panton, the local chaplain, reported that this punishment, "instead of intimidating people, put them in a state of frenzy." Although the apprentices at Golden Grove returned to work that afternoon, in the evening they sent the overseer an "extraordinary" message declaring their intention to leave the plantation immediately. Only mediation by the chaplain allowed for a peaceful resolution of this crisis.[15]

Events like those at Belvedere, Gibraltar, and Golden Grove continued into 1836. Among the more striking features of all these disturbances was the solidarity of the workers and the prominence of women among the activists and leaders. The latter phenomenon was especially ironic, given that the emancipation law was conceived and written in an unreflectively masculine gender. It was explicable, however, since women made up a disproportionate share of the field labor force on sugar estates. The most militant resistance to the apprenticeship regime came from women workers; and eventually the methods used to tame them—the treadmills at the houses of correction—created a scandal discrediting the whole apprentice system and paving the way for its abolition.[16]

During the first months of the new era, an unnamed female apprentice at Pusey Hall refused to go out to the fields because she wanted to stay with her child, who had had a fever the night before. John Melmoth, the planting attorney, examined the child's pulse and concluded that the mother's concern was unwarranted. After all, there were two female nurses and a male attendant at the estate's hospital, he later offered as justification, so the child would have received the care usually given to weaned slave children. But the woman adamantly refused to go to work, so Melmoth sent for the special magistrate. The woman, however, did not await events. With hoe in hand as if going to the fields, she took a shortcut to the magistrate's office to personally give him her side of the story first. Although the record is silent on the magistrate's specific response to this situation, Melmoth testified that the officer never came out to Pusey Estate and never gave this stubborn apprentice the punishment Melmoth thought she deserved.[17]

During the harvest season of 1836, special magistrate Thomas J. Baines was called to Leith Hall because two women, Catherine Stanford and Diane Clarke, refused to work "on so poor an estate." When Baines ordered Stanford and Clarke to return to the fields, nine other women came forward, declaring that "they would not cut another cane; that they would die on the treadmill first." Baines threatened to select five of them and send them to jail for ten days if they did not turn out to work the next morning. If he was intending to cow them, he was sadly disappointed. The following morning, "they all insisted upon going to the treadmill." Baines sent five to the Morant Bay House of Corrections, confined seven in the plantation dungeon, and requisitioned a detachment of police. The next day, after the police arrived, the seven were brought before him but showed "the same obstinate determination" not to work. "I ordered the police to take them to the cane-piece to work, but the sergeant came back, and reported that they all sat down, and did so in defiance of any entreaty or remonstrance of his." Baines thereupon sent these seven to join their five confederates at the Morant Bay House of Corrections. In jail the women continued their defiance of authority. Eventually one of them, Louisa Beveridge, died from injuries received on the treadmill. The others were then placed in solitary confinement.[18]

These instances of resistance and disruption suggest a more general reservoir of hostility to the probationary "freedom" Jamaican slaves had been granted. Their determined protests also suggest that the apprentices understood and were prepared to defend what little freedom of choice the emancipation law did allow them. James Spedding's image of "a slavish multitude" awaiting instruction misperceived the reality special magistrates actually confronted.

Both planters and magistrates often condemned the apprentices for being suspicious and overfond of litigation. However, in many of the cases in which they refused to work, reported the Reverend Mr. Panton, their agitation reflected the fact that "they do not expect to be honestly dealt with." R. S. Cooper, special magistrate for St. James Parish, confirmed that most disputes could be traced to the idea among the workers that they were being cheated, which he sadly conceded: "I am sorry to add, that with one exception I have found that idea correct."[19]

The authors of the emancipation law conceived of ex-slaves as an aggregation of individuals—and male individuals at that—seeking individual gains. While this may have been true in part, it is also clear that the freed people saw themselves as a community, if not a class, with community interests to protect and defend not only against their former masters but against the special magistrates as well. Some apprentices ran away, just as slaves had run away before abolition. Indeed, free black settlers in St. John Parish became infamous for harboring and encouraging runaway apprentices. Most apprentices, however, simply refused to work under conditions they found objectionable. In attempting to explain what appeared to be an inconsistent pattern of apprentices' working for wages on some estates while refusing to work on others, the special magistrates discerned that the way an estate was managed and its general working conditions could be as important as wage rates in attracting workers. Apprentices refused to work for people who abused them or cheated them. There were several reports of apprentices turning down the wages offered by their former masters only to accept the same or even lower wages from another planter. They preferred to work in plantation factories manufacturing sugar rather than in the fields harvesting or planting cane. They preferred to work at individual, self-paced tasks rather than in gangs, suggesting a desire to escape the regimentation of the overseer and the driver. Although children under six were completely freed in 1834, it was expected that they would be apprenticed voluntarily to the estates, but parents generally refused to apprentice children to their former masters. Indeed, many parents removed their children from the plantations altogether and settled them in towns with friends or relatives.[20]

As both the planters and Colonial Office policymakers had expected, the most important factor determining the apprentices' inclination to refuse work on the estates was the availability and productivity of their provision grounds. This provisioning system developed out of necessity, since many planters had been unable or unwilling to provide all the subsistence needs of their slaves. The American Revolution and the cutoff of the slave trade appear to have been crucial historical determinants in the development of the system. The first event prompted a rationing crisis by cutting off sources of cheap imported foodstuffs; the latter necessitated urgent measures to reproduce the slave labor force by supplementing the meager traditional ration of salt fish and corn with increased home production. A minority of planters, like those in Vere Parish, responded by growing food crops with supervised slave labor, but most set aside land and time for slaves to raise their own food on their own account. Each slave hut had a small plot of land attached to it that could support vegetable gardens, fruit trees, chickens, and pigs. In addition, each household was assigned a more substantial lot, generally located at some distance away on estate backlands, on which to raise plantains, yams, other root crops, and sometimes goats. In good seasons these "grounds" produced a surplus above a family's subsistence needs which could be sold at market for a profit to the laborer. Indeed, plantation personnel often bought a portion, and the rest was bartered at weekly Sunday markets to small tradesmen in exchange for imported goods, to other slaves in exchange for handicrafts, or to townspeople and higglers for cash.[21]

Control of one's own subsistence involved risks, for example, bad seasons when crops failed or were destroyed; but it also involved a measure of autonomy that was paradoxical, given the legal and social status of the slave. Although slaves could hold no legal title to these gardens or provision grounds, from a very early date the grounds were treated as their private, inheritable property. Slaves willed them to their children; and planters reimbursed their slaves when properties were sold. Furthermore, the system of self-provisioning required planters' concessions on working hours. The kitchen gardens, or "shell-blow grounds," could be worked during the slaves' dinner break or after working hours. But the more distant provision grounds required sufficient time for travel to and from, as well as for cultivating, harvesting, and gathering the surplus for consumption and marketing. Although the slave code of 1792 and the amelioration act of 1816 prescribed the minimum number of days slaves should receive to work their grounds (one day every fortnight), customary practices and the planters' self-interest were sufficient to ensure that the system functioned. Without it, not only slaves but most of the rest of Jamaica would starve.[22]

Because the provision grounds returned so much more income for apparently so much less labor, planters and officials feared that after emancipation, freed people would convert these or other grounds into small truck farms and abandon plantation labor altogether. Thomas McCornock, the attorney for Golden Grove Estate, reported that his apprentices often sold as much as £50 to £60 worth of produce in one day, carrying it to the wharf at Morant Bay in the estate's wagons and selling it to boats from Kingston. Arthur Welch, the special magistrate in Manchester, estimated that provision grounds could earn a worker 2s. sterling a day, or £30 sterling per year. Another magistrate reported that wages in his area were 1s. 8d. per day but that one could earn six times that amount by raising provisions.[23]

Of course, the rosy picture painted by these observers ignores the perennial uncertainties of agriculture. First, not all slaves were willing or able to participate in the provisioning and marketing systems, nor did all benefit equally from them. Indeed, some worked as the hired labor of other slaves, a development that almost caricatures the classic process of capitalist class differentiation.[24] Droughts, excessive rainfall, and other natural disasters, moreover, could wipe out even a successful apprentice's livelihood in any given year. Successful marketing of provisions required proximity to cities and towns and either land or water transport. Indeed, G. D. Gregg, special magistrate for St. David Parish, disputed the idea that growing provisions offered an attractive alternative at all, provided reasonable wages were offered by the planters:

> The apprentice makes this calculation: he goes to his own grounds, plants his ground provisions, for which he has to wait, watch and attend to, for at least three months; then he is obliged to carry them on his head to market a very long distance, part of which he can sell well, but as his hours are numbered, he is usually obliged to sacrifice the remainder to the "higgler", (as they are usually termed,) who, knowing that the apprentice has to return by a stated period, waits like a hungry shark for the moment to "oblige" the apprentice, (as I once heard one of those "higglers" say); so that in reality "higglers" are the persons who make the most money.[25]

The apprentice would do better, Gregg argued, "not [to] lay himself open to the disappointment of not being able to sell his provisions," but to work for wages on an estate, where "in one week or two, he can obtain what formerly took him as many months." The trouble with Gregg's analysis, however, was that the planters were far from agreed on what would be a "reasonable" wage for the apprentices' free time. In the fall of 1834, planters testifying before the Jamaica Assembly reported a wide range of wages and hours on their estates. The work day might be defined as eight, nine, or ten hours. For this, a worker might receive 1s. 8d. or 1s. 6d. or as little as 1s. One attorney, while insisting that the apprenticeship system was a failure, maintained that a wage of only 1 penny per hour was a sufficient wage. By his calculation, working ten hours per day and 250 days a year, an able-bodied person could earn a little over £10 per annum (about U.S. $42).[26]

Obviously, then, the workers' disposition and behavior were determined to a large extent by the disposition and behavior of their employers. As James Spedding observed, "If any planter be a loser under the new system, it is only because he has not used his capital judiciously." As an example of judicious use of capital Spedding offered Henry Shirley, a former absentee proprietor who came to Jamaica during the apprenticeship to manage his properties. In determining an appropriate wage, Shirley used as a standard the amount paid jobbers during slavery, which was also the standard used by the Colonial Office in drafting the Abolition Act. Although Shirley's wages were considerably above those offered elsewhere in the colony, they were covered almost completely by the interest on the slave compensation money he had received. Testifying before the Jamaica Assembly in the fall of 1834, Shirley reported that his apprentices were performing fair and reasonable labor "and in a cheerful and ready way."[27]

Although Spedding reported that Shirley's testimony was received contemptuously by the legislators, there were a number of other planters and attorneys who reported success at inducing the apprentices to work for wages. George Gordon, an attorney for more than a score of properties with a total of eight thousand apprentices, declared the system an unqualified success. Matthew Farquharson, a resident proprietor and attorney, testified that he saw "no alteration in their labor from what it was before." S. B. M. Barrett, son of the Speaker of the House of Assembly, wrote Sligo in December 1834: "I never was half so confident as I am now of the peaceable disposition of the negroes. I never knew them so greedy for money—so industriously anxious to earn it." In 1835 the attorney for the numerous Tharp properties wrote his employer that the apprentices were working well and that he was optimistic about the coming crop. A survey of the island in July and September 1835 revealed that 68 percent of the estates had been able to hire workers during their free time, 24 percent had not offered employment, and on just 8 percent of the estates had the apprentices refused to work beyond the statutory forty and one-half hours.[28]

Nevertheless, apprenticeship must be judged a failure if success is measured by the production of sugar. Sugar output for the island as a whole declined by more than 10 percent from what it had been during the last four years of slavery. It is still difficult, however, to determine the precise nature and causes of the decline. The *Falmouth Post*, in a survey of twenty estates in Trelawny Parish comparing their 1834 crop with that of 1835, found an overall increase of 9.7 percent; furthermore, thirteen estates had an increase in production, while only five showed a decline. Although Trelawny was one of the more prosperous sugar parishes, this survey does suggest the extent of variation on the island as a whole and among individual properties particularly.[29]

Some observers argued that the estates with declining production were primarily those that had been short-handed during slavery. Georgia Estate, the property of absentee Rowland Alston, is a case in point. Almost two years before emancipation was voted by Parliament, Alston was considering selling Georgia if the expenses could not be cut back and if he could get a reasonable price. Upon hiring a new attorney in the fall of 1832, Alston complained that his former manager had extended production beyond the capacity of the plantation labor force. For many years he had depended upon job laborers, a practice Alston found unprofitable in the long run. Indeed, in the 1830s the price of West Indian produce fell to such an extent that his only alternative was to cut back production. One of the problems faced by properties such as Georgia was that many of the jobbing gangs, on which they depended to supplement their resident labor force during the harvest season, were disbanded during the apprenticeship period.[30]

The uncertainty created by the vast change in social relations after emancipation also contributed to the decline in production. Since Jamaican sugar cane was cultivated over a fifteen-month growing season, it was planted more than a year in advance of its expected harvest. Apprehensive about the system of free labor, many planters simply did not put in new canes for future years. Even George Gordon, though asserting his confidence in the new system before the Jamaica Assembly in 1834, added that in anticipation of labor difficulties he did not plan to plant as much sugar cane for the following year. Other planters who were expecting the new system to fail had concentrated their labor force during the winter of 1833 on harvesting the current crop rather than on planting future crops. The situation was further complicated by unstable weather—droughts followed by severe flooding—a problem that would continue to plague Jamaica over the next several decades.[31]

Although they were not clear on the extent to which the decline in sugar production could be attributed to labor problems, the special magistrates and the governor did agree on the character of the black workers. Writing to the colonial secretary in 1836, Sligo labeled the popular idea of an inscrutable Negro character "nonsense."

> I have watched these people now for more than two years with the closest attention; I find their "proverbial indolence" to be nothing more than could be discovered in the English man, if compelled to labour without any personal payment or advantage, except what the negroes have here, and be liable, besides, to corporeal punishment if the quantum of labour done does not please the proprietor. How much work does your Lordship think that you would get on such terms from the majority of the white people in England? In my opinion not half as much as is now given by the negro.[32]

"Upon the whole, I have no hesitation in saying that the negro obeys the same impulses as other men," reported R. S. Cooper from St. James, "is actuated by the same hopes (of gain especially), and if, placed on the same footing, will discharge as well the obligations (social and moral) of his condition." Edward D. Baynes was not at all optimistic about the moral progress of the ex-slaves; indeed, he found their habits "gross and licentious." Nonetheless, he found "no natural inferiority on the part of the negro" and felt that blacks would be as responsive to opportunity as Europeans. In order to elicit such responsiveness, John Daughtrey recommended that "the interest [in working for wages] must be shown to be obvious and sufficient." Blacks would respond to material incentives, Daughtrey thought, because they were "capital reckoners" and "characteristically fond of money." "There can be no intrinsic fascination in cane-hole digging," another special magistrate pointed out, so clearly the consumer impulse of the blacks must be developed. Daughtrey thought he saw evidence of this impulse in St. Elizabeth Parish, where apprentices were spending conspicuously to equip themselves with horses and new clothes. "Every step they take in this direction is a real improvement; artificial wants become in time real wants. The formation of such habits affords the best security for negro labour at the end of the apprenticeship."[33]

The cultivation of "artificial wants"—socially stimulated desire—as a means of reconciling black freedom with the continued prosperity of the sugar economy was, of course, precisely the theory upon which the emancipation law had been founded. The drafters of the law believed that social order could be preserved in a society of autonomous individuals only by raising those individuals to a higher level of civilization and aspiration. But the problem of applying the principles of a liberal political economy to the former slave colonies continued to engross the attention of British policymakers during the apprenticeship period. Having succeeded in their initial goal of putting those societies "in a state of rapid transition," they now turned their efforts to formulating a more precise definition of the freedom that would follow apprenticeship and how it might be rendered compatible with social order and utility.

Defining Freedom for a Malthusian World

During the last full year of apprenticeship, Lord Glenelg, the colonial secretary, urged the governors of the West Indian colonies to amend laws left over from the slavery period, taking special note of those that made "innumerable distinctions of the most invidious nature in favor of Europeans and their descendants, and to the prejudice of persons of African birth or origin." Not only should all these be abolished, Glenelg insisted, but all "disguised references" should be struck from colonial laws. Writing in late 1837, Glenelg, a former liberal Tory who had converted to Whiggery, offered a definition of the meaning of freedom that was much more detailed and far-reaching than had been suggested in 1833 during discussions of the emancipation law. "The great cardinal principle of the law for the abolition of slavery is, that the apprenticeship of the emancipated slaves is to be immediately succeeded by personal freedom, in that full and unlimited sense of the term in which it is used in reference to the other subjects of the British Crown."[34]

He ordered that the governors and their attorneys general should survey colonial laws and report on them to his office with regard to access to the elective franchise, schools, churches, the militia, and other publicly supported institutions. They should note any restraints on such occupations as peddler, porter, and boatman. They should study the administration of poor relief, vagrancy laws, the tax system, road maintenance, Crown land sales, and prison discipline. All these should be reviewed to ensure that they did not involve any racial discrimination. This, he pointed out, was "the essence of the contract between Great Britain and the colonies."

Among the resolutions passed by Parliament in abolishing slavery was one that called for a general plan to educate apprentices. Late in 1835, Lord Glenelg informed the West Indian governors of the government's intention to ask Parliament for twenty thousand pounds sterling, which would be used for matching grants in the colonies to erect school buildings and support education. Rather than establishing government-run schools, the grants would support and expand those run by existing religious societies. The government would, however, set up normal schools in each of the colonies in order to train competent teachers. An inspector of schools would be appointed in each colony to report on school conditions and efficiency.[35]

A number of observers thought these plans did not go far enough. Lord Glenelg urged Governor Sligo to encourage the Jamaica Assembly to enact compulsory education. He thought the objections raised to compulsion in "more advanced societies" were irrelevant in a colony where "the great mass of the people have just emerged from slavery." However, Patrick Dunne, special magistrate for St. David Parish, warned Sligo to expect the freed people, naturally associating coercion with slavery, to resist compulsory education. Other observers, however, felt that the freed children should be removed entirely from the influence, if not control, of their parents. Even John Daughtrey, who was usually supportive of the apprentices and optimistic about their moral progress, was convinced that freed children had to be "trained in entirely new principles and new habits" and that this could be achieved only by separating them from their parents, who were a source of "inevitable contamination."[36]

The decision to renounce coercion and affirm laissez-faire principles with a people recently emerged from slavery and in a society not yet fully developed posed a number of difficulties. Early in 1836, Lord Glenelg forwarded to all the West Indian governors a dispatch addressing one of these policy problems. He began by noting that during slavery, labor could be compelled to be applied wherever the owner desired. Now, with the end of apprenticeship, the laborer would apply himself only to those tasks that promised personal benefit. Therefore, if the cultivation of sugar and coffee were to continue, "we must make it the immediate and apparent interest of the negro population to employ their labour in raising them." He was apprehensive about their ability to do this, repeating the now familiar maxim that given the demographic patterns of former slave colonies such as Jamaica—"where there is land enough to yield an abundant subsistence to the whole population in return for slight labour"—blacks would not work. Eventually, a proper equilibrium between land and labor would be established by the inexorable flywheel of natural forces that govern the social order, but the colonies could not afford the luxury of waiting.[37]

> Should things be left to their natural course, labour would not be attracted to the cultivation of exportable produce, until population began to press upon the means of subsistence, and the land failed (without a more assiduous and economical culture) to supply all its occupants with the necessaries of life. As soon as the natural labouring population should thus arise and the growing necessity of making the most of the land should ensure the proper application of their labour, it might be expected that the present staples would again be brought into cultivation. But the depreciation which would take place in property, and the rude state into which society would fall back in the mean time, make it desirable to adopt measures to check this apparently natural course.[38]

Having conceded that the freed people's behavior, by Malthusian and Wakefieldian dicta, was natural, Glenelg went on to prescribe the means by which the government would interdict these natural proclivities. It was essential that the ex-slaves be prevented from obtaining land. While he was uncertain how to proceed with the land that was already in private hands, he recommended that persons without land titles be excluded from occupying Crown lands and that the price be raised so as to keep those lands "out of the reach of persons without capital." Following a policy successfully employed in Canada and Australia during this period, Glenelg recommended that a minimum price be set for all Crown land, that it be sold only to the highest bidder, and that a 10 percent down payment be required for purchase. Furthermore, he recommended that an investigation be launched immediately into the means by which squatters could be prevented from occupying public land.

Lord Glenelg offered the following arguments justifying these extraordinary steps to constrain the free enterprise of the apprentices. First, the prosperity of any society depended upon maintaining an appropriate balance between labor supply and demand. If that definition of social utility were accepted, then it followed that government intervention was justified to establish conditions for its realization. "In new countries, where the whole unoccupied territory belongs to the Crown, and settlers are continually flowing in, it is possible, by fixing the price of fresh land so high as to place it above the reach of the poorest class of settlers, to keep the labour market in its most prosperous state from the beginning." With this policy the government not only assured an adequate supply of landless laborers to the estates but boosted the value of land, which in turn would make "it more profitable to cultivate old land well than to purchase new."[39] But the ultimate goal of these economic maneuvers was moral: to domesticate "natural" desires and behavior, to hold safe the boundary between civilized life and a Hobbesian jungle.

> The natural tendency of the population to spread over the surface of the country, each man settling where he may, or roving from place to place in pursuit of virgin soil, is thus impeded. The territory, expanding only with the pressure of population, is commensurate with the actual wants of the entire community. Society, being thus kept together, is more open to civilizing influences, more directly under the control of Government, more full of the activity which is inspired by common wants, and the strength which is derived from the division of labour; and altogether is in a sound state, morally, politically and economically, than if left to pursue its natural course.[40]

Glenelg's policy was intended to prevent situations such as those Henry Taylor had conjured up in his 1833 memorandum—scattered villages descending steadily into "savage sloth." Glenelg hastened to add, however, that the government's policy was not intended to favor one class over another. The object of the government was not to force the freed people to stay on the plantations by depriving them of alternative employment "but merely to condense and keep together the

population in such a manner that it may always contain a due proportion of labourers." Since "the most profitable produce will always
afford the highest wages, and the highest wages will always draw the
largest supply of labour," the government should not discourage the
cultivation of nonplantation crops. "But some security should if possible be taken, that all the territory which is cultivated at all shall be
cultivated well. The minimum price of land, therefore, should be high
enough to leave a considerable portion of the population unable to
buy it until they have saved some capital out of the wages of their
industry, and at the same time low enough to encourage such savings
by making the possession of land a reasonable object of ambition to
all."[41]

Observers in Jamaica shared Glenelg's fears that the freed people
would abandon the plantations after the apprenticeship period and
become petty settlers on Crown lands, but they did not necessarily
share his putative concern for ensuring justice to all classes. Early in
1835, planters in Trelawny requested government aid to finance white
immigration to Jamaica. Their plan was to settle white families in the
interior, where the climate was temperate and where these immigrant
Europeans might grow coffee, ginger, provisions, and other minor
products. Some of the immigrants could be recruited into the police,
and some could be employed on the estates, where "by their industry,
they would set a good example to the apprentices." But the most
important benefit to be derived from such settlements was that they
would preempt Jamaica's vast open spaces and "prevent the idle and
dissolute negroes from making them places of resort when the period
of absolute freedom arrives."[42]

Governor Mulgrave and his successor, the marquis of Sligo, whom
the planters thought hostile to their interests, both urged similar policies. Early in 1834, Governor Mulgrave sent the Colonial Office his
plans for establishing a temporary police force. The plan called for
twenty-six police stations to be distributed throughout the colony,
manned by a total of 770 men. Each police station would provide the
core settlers for the eventual colonization of the interior of each parish.
Later that same year Governor Sligo embellished the plan further,
urging that the Colonial Office recruit Chelsea pensioners (that is,
old ex-soldiers) as policemen for Jamaica. Sligo proposed that these
recruits be offered Crown lands in lieu of part of their pension. Not
only would this enable him to fill the 300 vacancies in his police force
but, "what is most desirable, a nucleus for a white establishment could
be formed." The Colonial Office was unenthusiastic about Sligo's pro-

posal, however, noting that the pensioners were generally addicted to the use of strong spirits, "an indulgence for which that island would offer to their existing predispositions . . . considerable and dangerous facilities." They urged that the recently arrived German immigrants might offer a better source of recruits.[43]

The concerns of Richard Hill, a freeborn colored special magistrate, were similar to, though slightly different in perspective from, those of the governor and the planters. Having traveled frequently to Haiti, Hill was very impressed by the African American immigrants in that country. He felt that they would offer the best example to the Jamaican freed people of the virtues of hard labor. Certainly he was more impressed with the African Americans than with Afro-Jamaicans.[44] During the early 1840s, the United States and Canada would provide the first substantial numbers of immigrant settlers.

At this very early stage, therefore, two fundamentally incompatible ideas were urged to justify immigration: first, to create a more favorable balance of land and labor so as to discourage agriculture outside the plantation economy; second, to recruit workers—black as well as white—who would offer role models for Jamaican freed people. The major flow of immigrants who actually arrived during the following decades, coming from "benighted" Africa and "backward" Asia, satisfied neither of these criteria. They were far too few to fill up Jamaica's vast interior, and rather than being models for others, they themselves required indoctrination into Western culture and the work ethic. Thus, they simply provided planters with another dependent, unfree labor force, albeit one restrained by legal contracts rather than whips.

Nevertheless, these early discussions provide a key to contemporary ideas about disciplining a free labor force, and immigration provides a testing point for differences between British government authorities and Jamaican planters on the nature of a free society. The government seems to have been concerned at this time less with preserving the plantation economy per se than with fostering its particular ideal of a civilized political economy. Glenelg's land policies were ostensibly designed to keep the freed people on the estates primarily because this was the best means of bringing them under civilizing influences. Of course, these British authorities defined civilization in their own terms and according to their own value system, a system honed over the past century as Britons shaped and were shaped by a capitalist political economy. Civilized men and women aspired to material goods; their aspirations were unlimited and indefinite, thus spurring unlimited economic growth. This consumption ethic was balanced, somewhat uneasily, by one of ascetic frugality, which was necessary to generate savings. But the ultimate motive for frugality was investment to increase one's capital and thereby one's potential social and economic power and status, which eventually required an even higher level of consumption.

As the special magistrates' reports show, not only were these ideas pervasive among British intellectuals and policymakers but they were imbibed and articulated by their agents in Jamaica. The ideals of classical political economy shaped what many of the special magistrates observed, what they reported, and how they "instructed" the freed people. This was just as true of the specials recruited among Jamaican natives, such as Richard Hill and Alexander J. Fyfe, as it was of those sent out from Britain, such as John Daughtrey and Thomas Baines.

When the freed people from the Manchoineal district of St. Thomas-in-the-East gathered to celebrate the ending of apprenticeship and the beginning of their real emancipation, special magistrate Richard Chamberlaine, a colored Jamaican native, instructed them carefully on the "duties and responsibilities of a rational and unfettered freedom." They were the objects of international scrutiny, he said, and the fate of black slaves in foreign nations would be determined by their conduct. They must prove "that black men are as susceptible of the value and responsibility of freedom as any other race of human beings." They would meet this responsibility by remaining on the plantations and working diligently. Chamberlaine was confident that they would continue working because their tastes were becoming more refined and their material desires more numerous and expensive.[45]

> You are not going to be satisfied with the oxnaburgh and rontoon clothing, which you have heretofore been accustomed to receive; you are not now, much less will you be hereafter, contented with a pot of coco soup and a herring tail for your dinners. Your wives and your daughters will require their fine clothes for their chapels, churches, and holidays. You will visit your friends with your coat and your shoes, and you will require your dinners prepared for you with some respect to comfort and cleanliness; your soup will be seasoned with beef and pork; and in order to obtain these, the comforts and necessaries of civilized life, you will have to labour industriously—for the more work you do, the more money you must obtain, and the better will you be enabled to increase and extend your comforts.[46]

That Chamberlaine's message was uttered in a masculine register was not accidental; one boon of freedom would be the newfound prospect of establishing gendered spheres of activity and authority. Growing more and more expansive as he spoke of the "comforts" the freedmen's labor would bring, the magistrate painted veritable word pictures of an ideal bourgeois domestic scene:

> Your wives, hitherto accustomed to be partakers in your daily toils, running to the fields with you in the morning, and returning with you down-spirited and dejected at sun set day by day, bringing no alleviations, will be enabled to remain at home, to look after your clothes, and your children's clothes—your household affairs—your stock—your comfortable dinner, so that whilst you are at work at the field, as the day advances, instead of lagging in your work, you are more cheerful, more industrious, because moving in the certainty of finding every thing comfortable when you get home.[47]

Comfortable with this domestic hierarchy, the freedmen should willingly acquiesce to the principles of social order: personal accumulation and deference to authority. Thus, even if they could satisfy their desires for civilized comfort by working only two days each week, freedmen should work the other four days as well, in order to accumulate savings "for the winter of your days, when you will have no master's bounty or humanity to appeal to." And even as they foreswore paternal dependence on the propertied classes, they should affirm that men without masters must still defer to their betters. All were now "as free as the Queen," and no man was more "free than another," but still it was necessary "for the purposes of civilized society, that there should be gradations of rank in all communities." They must be civil, respectful, and obedient, not only to their masters but to all in authority over them. Thus did the claims of deference and authority extend from the fireside to the public sphere.

Chamberlaine urged the freed people not just to obey their former masters but "to forgive, and if possible to forget," their grievances from slavery. They must remember that slavery—"the monster," "the thing," "the curse"—corrupted the masters as well as the slaves, because "civilization and slavery are incompatible." Chamberlaine did not choose to press this line of reasoning, but his colleague Richard Hill did. Both white and black freemen in Jamaica offered very poor examples to the apprentices, Hill lamented. "Liberty . . . has its own corruptions, and, unfortunately for the example of the negro, West Indian freedom has too much been associated with licentiousness. . . . The cock pit and the gambling table, which have their numerous votaries in the upper classes of society, work with a pernicious force on such a community, and the law finds in these examples one of the sources of public vice."[48]

Richard Hill's indictment of the Jamaican white ruling class exposed a problem that would be crucial to the success of emancipation. Yet not only did the emancipation law provide no solution for the problem, it compounded it. Parliament had provided the framework and the broad principles of abolition but had left the details of implementation to the colonists themselves. The larger question whether the planters were themselves culturally equipped to reorganize Jamaican society along the lines envisioned by British policymakers—to reform themselves—had not been seriously addressed. Although the planters were full participants in a capitalist economy producing for the world market, their accustomed methods of commanding labor were not congruent with the evolving liberal democratic ideology; their social system was not amenable to liberal ethics; their mores and values were in many ways as alien from the British as were those of the blacks. They might parrot British policymakers in speaking of immigration as a means to right the balance between the land and labor supply, but it soon became evident that their real objective was direct, personal control of their labor force rather than the indirect, impersonal controls advocated in the metropolis. Thus it soon became clear that—like their ex-slaves—the planters needed to be reeducated, needed to be apprenticed to a new system of labor management and political governance. Ultimately, the failure to accomplish this task proved the most serious threat to the free system.

As the question now stands a race has been freed but a society has not been formed.

GOVERNOR HARRIS OF TRINIDAD, 1848

Men used all their lives to coercion, cannot be well acquainted with persuasion deprived of power.

SLIGO TO SPRING RICE, 25 DECEMBER 1834

3

An Apprenticeship for Former Masters

Six months before emancipation became law, Lord Mulgrave wrote to Lord Goderich warning him that the government's emancipation plans had been founded on an erroneous assumption about the nature of the Jamaica Assembly. The planners appeared to assume that "the House of Assembly is composed of rational creatures likely upon consideration to sacrifice their past prejudices to their permanent interest," Mulgrave observed, "but you are none of you sufficiently aware that they have hardly any of them any permanent interest in the Country. They are part and parcel of the present system of Slavery. They are mostly persons in the enjoyment of a large percentage for the management of a troublesome and precarious species of property for absentees. The moment emancipation on any terms takes place their occupation's gone."[1]

Mulgrave of course was wrong when he stated that the government policymakers were not aware of this distinction between proprietors, the most important of whom were residents of Britain, and the plantation managers and staff who were residents of Jamaica. Henry

Taylor had taken note of this in 1833 in assessing the possible political consequences of emancipation. "The Colonists, generally speaking, are not the proprietors. No principle of compensation for loss of property would reach their case or mitigate their opposition; for their ruin would not come by the loss of property, but the loss of employment. Attorneys, Managers, Overseers, and Bookkeepers, would receive no part of the indemnity, and their occupation would be gone. Their destruction would be complete." But what Taylor concluded from this analysis was that the absentee proprietors could be convinced that they should make the best of the situation to protect their investment, while the resident colonists could be safely ignored.[2]

It is easy to see why Taylor would draw such sharp political distinctions between the absentee proprietors and the Jamaican plantation managers. One of the most influential men in Whig circles was an absentee owner of vast Jamaican properties. Henry Richard Vassall Fox, the third Lord Holland, had become a Jamaican proprietor through his marriage to Elizabeth Vassall, daughter and heir of a wealthy Jamaican planter, Richard Vassall. Lord Holland, who had held a seat in the House of Lords since 1796 and had served in several Cabinet posts, was a strong supporter of many reforms and a consistent advocate of emancipation and the abolition of the slave trade. Lord Holland was not simply a Whig: as the grandson of Henry Fox, the first Lord Holland, he was heir to a family name synonymous with the Whig party in the early nineteenth century. His grandfather had been something of a political wheeler-dealer who earned his private fortune through the deft, if not entirely honorable, use of public influence. The third Lord Holland's political principles, as one student has pointed out, were "strongly conditioned by his personal and intellectual inheritance." He conceived of "politics as an arena for display of virtue." Liberty became the overarching theme and core of his political philosophy. "His politics in opposition acquired consistency in his vigorous dissent from governmental measures which he deemed detrimental to liberty." He spoke out in favor of the rights of Jews, Catholics, and evangelical Dissenters. He condemned the slave trade as "repugnant to the principles of natural justice."[3]

The third Lord Holland never held a major cabinet post; nonetheless, he enjoyed a disproportionate influence on Whig policies and politicians. Holland House, in the Kensington section of London, was a focal point of English social life and reputedly one of the last continental-style salons. The Hollands played host to "that brilliant circle of statesmen, wits, men of letters, and other people of distinction which gave the house a European celebrity." Furthermore, during that long period in which the Whigs were out of power, their leadership reputedly held council at Holland House every Sunday.

Presiding over this sparkling court was Elizabeth Vassall Fox, who had inherited her estates in 1800 from her grandfather Florentius Vassall. Yet Lady Holland was as staunch a Whig as her husband and shared many of his libertarian sentiments. She was invariably described as beautiful, vivacious, highly opinionated, and blunt. Always something of a controversial figure, Elizabeth's relationship with Lord Holland began in adultery and resulted in the birth of an illegitimate son. She was an admirer of Napoleon, sending him messages of sympathy while he was imprisoned at Elba and St. Helena, as well as some books and Neapolitan sweetmeats. Upon his death she inherited his gold snuffbox, and she procured other relics, including a sock he had worn at the time of his death.[4]

Despite his wife's eccentricities, Lord Holland maintained considerable influence in the Whig government until his death in 1840. It is not surprising that he was consulted by the colonial secretary during the apprenticeship period on the appropriate person to appoint as governor of Jamaica. While there is no evidence that he ever visited Jamaica, he did keep in close contact with the attorney for his properties, Friendship and Greenwich estates and Sweet River Pen. Even before the abolition of slavery he had issued very strict rules governing the use of corporal punishment on these estates. After Parliament approved the Abolition Act, but before it went into effect, Holland instructed his attorney to cease referring to his workers as slaves; thereafter he was to refer to them as his "people." During the apprenticeship Holland advised his attorney to offer premiums and bonuses as an incentive for more diligent labor.[5]

If Holland's eccentricities and decidedly liberal views preclude generalizing from his attitude to that of other absentees, the views of Charles Rose Ellis, the first Lord Seaford, can be put forth as clearly authoritative if not representative of the West Indian planters resident in London. Indeed, Lord Seaford was the acknowledged leader of the West Indian interests. He came into his Jamaican properties in a more traditional, if not more typical, fashion than did Holland. Seaford was a grandson of George Ellis, a former chief justice of Jamaica, and a descendant of Colonel John Ellis, who had settled in Jamaica in 1665 and founded the family fortune. Unlike Lord Holland, Seaford was a Tory, albeit a supporter of the liberal Canning wing of that party. He was elected to the House of Commons in 1793 and entered the House of Lords after being elevated to a peerage in 1826. Although he himself held no government post, his son Charles Augustus Ellis had served as the undersecretary of state for foreign affairs during the Canning administration.[6]

Lord Seaford owned Old Montpelier and New Montpelier estates in St. James in the valley of the Great River twelve miles from Montego Bay; the first was established in 1745, the second in 1775. He also owned Shettlewood Pen in Hanover Parish, at the border of St. James. The two Montpeliers covered ten thousand acres, of which one thousand were planted in cane in the 1820s. In 1825 there were 864 slaves on the three properties. It is probable that Lord Seaford was a supporter of Canning's amelioration policies in the 1820s. In 1831 he asked Moravian missionaries to convert and instruct his slaves.[7]

Lord Seaford, the liberal Tory, and Lord Holland, the moderate Whig, maintained an active correspondence, consulting each other not only about their respective Jamaican properties but also about government policy on slavery generally. Late in 1831, Seaford informed Holland that he was ready to concede that slave labor was in principle more expensive than free labor but felt that there were practical limitations to the implementation of that principle. Seaford and Holland held several private meetings with Goderich after the slave insurrection of 1831, advising him on the best strategy to pursue in getting Parliament to look into the condition of the slaves. They both urged a moderate course on the part of the government, which should seek a rapprochement with the planters. Lord Seaford did not identify with the resident Jamaican planters, however, and was very upset about the violent and alarming resolutions that they passed in 1831 condemning the government.[8]

In August 1833, shortly before final passage of the Abolition Act, Lord Seaford visited Old Montpelier, which had been heavily damaged during a major pitched battle between slave rebels and the militia during the revolt in 1832. From Jamaica, Seaford expressed his concurrence with Governor Mulgrave's opinion of the character of the Jamaica Assembly. They were men of "ruined fortunes," he wrote Lord Holland, and the government should not trust them to implement the emancipation law fairly. He advised the government to seek the support of the absentee planters in England, who could be expected in turn to influence their attorneys in Jamaica. Furthermore, he felt that if the absentee proprietors took a leadership role in encouraging cooperation with the government, then the resident proprietors were likely to follow suit.[9]

Seaford distrusted the local magistrates in Jamaica and urged ample funding for the specials sent from England. And though he regretted that the emancipation law contained no provision enabling employers to compel apprentices to work for wages on their own time, he himself sought nonphysical means of encouraging work. He felt that the home government should provide ample funding for ministers and teachers in the postslavery period, because the cultural improvement of the freedmen was just as important as legal coercion, if not more so. Jamaica needed "as many schoolmasters as magistrates."[10]

Yet aside from the question how representative men such as Holland and Seaford were of the absentee owners, it is also an open question how much influence they could exert on local affairs. The historian W. L. Burn makes much of the fact that after Holland's order to his attorney, Thomas McNeil, to support the government in the 1833 elections in Westmoreland, the antigovernment candidates—Beaumont and Whitelocke—were defeated. Even if we concede the dubious assertion that Holland's influence turned the tide on that occasion, it is obvious that the occasion was exceptional: in 1833 and for much of the following decade the Jamaica Assembly was notoriously antigovernment.[11]

Even the degree to which McNeil's opinions were shaped by his employer is uncertain. The attorney's letters to his employer show a deferential tone but not a subservient one. A small, self-made proprietor and estate manager such as McNeil would be expected to yield some general deference to a peer of the realm; aside from immediate employment, such a powerful friend could offer assistance on the island as well as at home. It would not be unreasonable, I think, to infer that Governor Sligo appointed McNeil custos of St. Dorothy with the blessing of Lord Holland, if not his instigation. Nevertheless, McNeil's behavior was probably less a response to his employer's influence than a reflection of his own convictions. Lord Seaford wrote Holland in the spring of 1834 that he was not impressed with McNeil's abilities as a planter but felt that he was willing to make the new system work.[12]

Actually, McNeil was not at first very sanguine about being able to get blacks to work after their complete emancipation, and he was very much concerned that Jamaica's high land-labor ratio would make wages exorbitant. In order to compensate for the expected loss of field labor, he sought to introduce new technology, especially the plow and harrow. He also favored immigration, and in 1837 he imported five Scottish plowmen on three-year indentures. He felt, however, that the best way to secure the continued, faithful labor of the ex-slaves was to gain their affection. Good labor relations were essential. The rights of the worker must be respected. In 1836 he reprimanded the overseer at Greenwich for entering the workers' cabins without their permission. The following fall he reported approvingly to Lord Holland that policemen who had conducted unauthorized searches of the apprentices' houses had been convicted and fined. He was also pleased that the Colonial Office had disallowed an act of the Jamaica Assembly that would have disenfranchised many black voters.[13]

Not only were McNeil's attitudes and opinions exceptional; he was very aware that his fellow attorneys were behaving quite differently. Jamaica's leading men were not helping to make the transition from slavery to freedom a smooth one. "There are," McNeil wrote Holland, "some men amongst us (and of my profession) that this country would in my opinion benefit by the absence of. The conduct pursued towards the apprentices on many properties will to a certainty be the ruin of the properties on the very first day of August 1840, by the labourers being then free to engage themselves to labour and settle on the properties of those now acting most friendly towards their people."[14]

If McNeil's assessment of his fellow attorneys was correct, then the absentee proprietors must not have exercised any significant influence to encourage the attorneys' cooperation with the new system. The most influential attorneys managed between twenty and thirty properties, thus representing a number of absentees. Such dispersion of interests probably encouraged independent opinions and behavior, just as it ensured independent income. Furthermore, it must be remembered that many absentees never visited their properties or did so infrequently; the only information they received came from the attorney. Consequently, the employee was apt to shape the opinion of the owner, rather than the other way around. What impact the attorneys' reports had on absentees we cannot know, but we do know that most were unfavorable to the altered circumstances of production. Clearly, then, the strategy Henry Taylor recommended in 1833—which divided the planter group into absentee proprietors and resident managers and urged that the latter be ignored in the resolution of the political problem of freedom—was a colossal blunder. The resident whites in Jamaica proved to be a far more troublesome factor in the transition from slavery to freedom than did the slaves, and a far more powerful adversary than the absentee proprietors. Colonial

Office policymakers were soon to discover that they should have devoted as much attention to the origins, evolution, and character of white Jamaican residents as they had to those of the black slaves.

A World "Beyond the Line": The Jamaican Planter Class

By the time the Abolition Act was implemented the white Jamaican population, having reached a peak of 34,152 in 1824, was experiencing a precipitous decline. A population that had grown by almost 90 percent over the thirty-eight years before 1824 declined by 56 percent over the next decade. This vast demographic change, however, did not seem to alter the fundamental character of Jamaican residents, at least as they were described and perceived by travelers. Unlike the North American mainland colonies, Jamaica had no tradition of founding fathers; "it started off with major generals and pirates." Unlike the pilgrims of New England, the Europeans who came to Jamaica sought, not to establish a New Eden, but to exploit an El Dorado. John Stewart, a twenty-year resident of the island and one of the more perceptive observers of its society, described its founders in this way: "The Europeans who are settled in Jamaica come to it with one invariable view—that of making or mending their fortunes." According to Stewart, even the clergy of the island were more interested in making money than in saving souls. The materialistic impulse was pervasive and all-consuming, "a passion naturally hostile to literary pursuits and intellectual enjoyments . . . alive only to the voice of interest, and . . . success. The pride of wealth, not of virtue, . . . is in this country the great desideratum." Although Stewart's observations were made at the beginning of the nineteenth century, they were reiterated by a young Frenchman, the son of the abolitionist Brissot, in 1831. Brissot described the Jamaicans as "entirely a commercial people."[15]

Of course, the materialistic emphasis of Jamaican culture is what one would expect of a frontier society. Although British Jamaica was seized from the Spaniards in the mid-seventeenth century, the fabled prosperity of her sugar economy was sustained for only a very brief period in the late eighteenth century. The island's spectacular growth came between 1740 and 1775, when the aggregate value of the colony's economy increased more than 300 percent and the number of slaves and sugar plantations more than doubled. By 1775 Jamaica was exporting ten times the sugar products, and had three times as many slaves, as Barbados, the former leader of British West Indian production.

During the first half of the eighteenth century Jamaica's sugar cultivation was still restricted primarily to the southeastern part of the island, but with the conclusion of peace with the Maroons in the 1790s the west was opened to production as well.[16]

The 775 sugar plantations in 1774 represented not only a four-teenfold increase in the number of estates over the past century but a greater efficiency of production and concentration of wealth as well. The average output per plantation rose from 11.8 tons of sugar in 1670 to 56.6 tons in 1774. Production and slave population grew in tandem, and both were concentrated on larger and larger units. The pattern continued to some extent during the last two decades of slavery. On the eve of emancipation almost half of Jamaica's slaves were held on estates having more than 150 slaves, with a quarter of them living on estates with over 250 slaves.[17]

The overall social impact of this vast expansion and concentration of Jamaica's sugar economy is paradoxical and uncertain. It is clear that during the late eighteenth century many of the beneficiaries of Jamaica's unparalleled prosperity abandoned the island for a life of ease in London, where they lived on the proceeds of their investment. Many, such as Elizabeth Vassall, married into the nobility. Others, such as Lord Seaford, gained political influence and, with the patronage of their grateful allies, were recreated as noblemen. On the other hand, it would appear that there were proprietors who abandoned the island in failure rather than in triumph, who moved to England to repair their fortunes rather than enjoy them. For example, William Beckford and his wife, heirs of Richard Beckford's vast holdings in Westmoreland, immigrated to Jamaica in 1774. After thirteen years, however, the Beckfords returned to England broke. It is probable that the experience of the Beckfords was more typical during the second and third decades of the nineteenth century than earlier. The precipitous decline of the sugar industry during those decades made it less feasible for a proprietor to retire to a life of luxury at home. It also probably encouraged the out-migration of the less prosperous white settlers, evident in the population decline of the 1820s.[18]

It is not possible to say which of these patterns was most typical of Jamaican absentees. It is clear that contemporaries began to recognize absenteeism as a significant phenomenon and a problem even during the height of the island's prosperity. By 1740 it was significant enough to lead the Jamaica Assembly to pass a law designed to prevent fraud by requiring attorneys to submit annual reports certifying the production of the properties they managed. By 1775, historian Richard Sheridan estimates, absentees owned 30 percent of all Jamaican properties and produced 40 percent of the island's sugar and rum. Therefore, one might conclude that in their career pattern the wealthiest absentees were representative of the more influential proprietors resident in Great Britain, although not necessarily representing a majority of that group.[19]

Many of the great planters enjoyed similar careers. They were the heirs of early settlers who had received some of the original Jamaican land grants; their children, benefiting from the eighteenth-century growth of the sugar monoculture, had expanded and consolidated their holdings through advantageous marriages as well as purchases. The third and fourth generations of the family were educated in England, where many of them stayed. Some of these emigrés purchased landed estates in England and married into noble families. Some might return to their Jamaican estates for brief periods, but during most of the nineteenth century ownership was divorced from management.[20]

"Almost all the great proprietors reside in Great Britain," observed John Stewart in 1823, "leaving their estates to the care and management of agents, or attorneys, as they are here called." The attorneys usually received a 6 percent commission on all sales of an estate, although after 1809 a few estate managers were put on fixed salaries. Attorneys usually represented more than one property, and the so-called "great attorneys," often representing twenty or more, could earn between eight thousand and ten thousand pounds sterling a year.[21]

Like most observers, Stewart felt that management by attorneys was ultimately bad for the sugar economy. The deleterious effect of absenteeism was assumed to derive from the lack of permanent interest on the part of the would-be absentee owner, who was concerned with getting rich quick and returning home, as well as on the part of the resident manager, who desired to raise the largest crop possible so as to maximize his commission, even if that meant inadequate maintenance of the property and slaves. It was also assumed, given the class biases of the day, that the migration of the absentees, who tended to be the wealthiest proprietors on the island, robbed Jamaica of its natural leadership and lowered the moral and cultural tone of society generally.

As Douglas Hall has observed, however, there is a tendency in these arguments to confound the absenteeism of white people generally with the absenteeism of the white elite. It is also an open question whether the absentee proprietors would have provided more expert management or raised the cultural and moral tone of island society. Hall notes that many proprietors fled to Britain in the late eighteenth century because their plantations were failing, and they sought a political rather than a strictly economic solution to their problems. Indeed, among the major proprietors there are examples to sustain Hall's arguments. William Beckford and Sir Charles Price embarked for England leaving not flourishing estates but nearly bankrupt ones. And as for the superior morality of the wealthy elite, Sir Rose Price left behind two illegitimate colored children after a stay of only three years. Not many Jamaican creoles would match the sexual license or libidinous energies of this future English baron.[22]

The assumption that the attorneys themselves had no permanent interest in the development of the island economy is also open to question. It has been pointed out that many of the resident proprietors were also attorneys and indeed earned the greater proportion of their income from their fees or salaries. But it could just as easily be said that many of the attorneys were also resident proprietors, albeit small ones, who had more than a transient interest in the island's economic welfare. And while Governor Mulgrave correctly noted that such people earned most of their income from their commissions for managing other people's property, that fact does not vitiate their genuine proprietary interest in the island.

Historians as well as contemporaries have indicted the exploitative and materialistic culture of the West Indies, depicting it, in one analyst's words, "as a monstrous distortion of human society." The source of the problem, it is argued, was that white Jamaicans were not interested in building permanent social infrastructures in the islands, but only wanted to return to England, which they considered their real home. In a sense, then, all white Jamaicans were psychological absentees. Yet, where "home" was for most of the planter class is a real question. As Richard Sheridan points out, the planter class was increasingly a multinational group; by the 1770s about half the largest proprietors were of non-English origins. Irish immigrants were a majority in the militia in 1729, and Scotsmen were estimated to constitute about one-third of the entire white population in the 1760s. Scotsmen came to the island in large numbers after 1710 and enjoyed considerable success in acquiring plantation properties. During the eighteenth century the classical route to proprietorship was to begin as an overseer or as the owner of a gang of jobbing slaves, but it appears that when the sugar industry began to decline, local merchants were more likely to succeed in taking over estates. Not only the Scots but also the Portuguese Jews of Jamaica successfully pursued this route to colonial wealth.[23]

Objecting to the thesis that white Jamaicans were culturally deprived, Edward Brathwaite protests that they did indeed have a "real and living culture of their own, with its own sense of rewards, dignity and destiny." It had "a practical, not an aesthetic focus," but this is what one would expect in a frontier society concerned with power and profit. During the 1770s and 1790s, apparently the very period when the flight of the white elite was growing apace, Brathwaite describes a building boom in which an impressive array of great houses, bridges, public buildings, and monuments were created.[24] Much like the more settled planter classes of Brazil and the American South, the Jamaicans developed distinctive architectural styles, cuisine, modes of hospitality, and codes of personal honor that were rooted in the physical and social climate of the island.

Even Brathwaite must confess, however, that white Jamaica failed to evolve an alternative, integrated colonial culture and instead created "a dichotomy of thought, action, and attitude which finally weakened the possibility of action." The "creatively 'creole' elements" of society were, it seems, always at war with the "reactionary 'colonial'" elements. The American Revolution severed Jamaica's cultural ties with her northern neighbor, reinforcing her dependence on Britain materially and culturally at a time when escalating attacks on slavery undermined her self-confidence and challenged the fundamental values of creole culture.[25]

However one chooses to evaluate the efforts of Jamaican elites to foster an indigenous culture, theirs was nonetheless a culture founded on and inextricably tied to slavery. That overriding fact gave rise to an increasingly unbridgeable difference between creole and British culture, which posed major obstacles to the implementation of British emancipation policy. It was recognized that men born or even long-resident in a slave society developed not just different economic interests but different mores and values from those of even the absentee planters. This is perhaps in part what Spedding had reference to in defining the other half of the problem of freedom from the British perspective, that is, to transform "a slave driving oligarchy, deformed and made fierce by their false attitude, into a natural upper class." After the first five months of the apprenticeship, Governor Sligo was more confident of the transformation and moral progress of the blacks than he was of a similar change in planters habituated to command rather than persuasion.[26]

Sligo's judgment was confirmed a few months later by St. David's special magistrate Patrick Dunne, who judged the behavior of the apprentices "good and forebearing" but could not say the same for that of their managers and overseers. Indeed, their hostility to emancipation was so great "that one would be led to think the non-working of it, however inexplicable it may appear, would give them delight." Dunne was perplexed to discover that such men appeared "in their intercourse with society in general to act with apparent kindness and good nature." At work, however, "their manner of speaking to and of the negroes is haughty, intemperate and disgusting in the extreme; their disposition to have corporal punishment inflicted is manifested on almost every occasion of preferring complaints."[27]

The essence of slavery was the unlimited and arbitrary power that one man exercised over another. Such power, critics argued, broke down self-restraint; the daily brutality in a slave society soon sapped finer human sentiments. "Doubtless, too, there is in the very nature of slavery, in its mildest form, something unfavourable to the cultivation of moral feeling," John Stewart wrote in 1823. Observers of Jamaican society shared Thomas Jefferson's view that slavery corrupted the planter just as it debased the slave. The *Falmouth Post* in 1835 described in detail the process by which a young man sent out from England to the tropics, released from restraint and cut off from his family, was soon "initiated to vices which his previous habits had taught him to regard as the crime of human profligacy." First, his conscience was destroyed, "trampled in the dust."

> Then, this youth was made a king—a little king—a petty despot. Into the hands of this boy was committed the happiness of hundreds of his fellow creatures, from whom he had to compel by all means, or any means, a given amount of labour, for which he had no money given to him to pay. Could he, thus situated, retain the vestiges, the last shreds of his moral being? He could not—he must have seen that to bend or break was inevitable.[28]

In some ways, therefore, Jamaicans never outgrew their seventeenth-century image as "England's most lawless colonists," highlighted by the buccaneers at Port Royal, that "Sodom of the Indies." Indeed, for many travelers the physical landscape itself seemed to foster passions and discourage restraint. Stewart warned any potential sightseer looking for well-laid gardens or public monuments, mansions or churches, that he would be disappointed. "But if he be an admirer of the wild magnificence of nature, he will here have ample . . . gratification." Little wonder, then, that such a wild and romantic society gave birth to a people who were "too lively, too volatile, too indolent, and too fond of pleasure." Although by 1823 Stewart believed that the primitive creole customs and manners were giving way to the polished manners of European life, he found this to be true primarily among the more genteel families.[29]

Certainly the feature that horrified most travelers in Jamaica, including Stewart, did not give way to European convention. The unlimited power of men over other men implies the unlimited power of men over women. "Every unmarried white man, and of every class, has his black or brown mistress, with whom he lives openly," wrote Stewart in 1823. No doubt the extreme imbalance in the ratio of white males to white females contributed to this situation, but even married white men were known to keep colored concubines. Indeed, what offended most visitors was not simply that interracial sexual liaisons were tolerated but that they were countenanced at the highest levels of society. Some sense of the pervasiveness and openness of the practice of keeping concubines can be grasped by looking at the personal lives of the Jamaican political elite. Sixty-four men elected to the Jamaica Assembly before 1833 also served during the apprenticeship and may be considered to some degree representative of the white slaveholding class. The wills of forty-two of these legislators include information on their family status, at least to the extent that they named heirs and family relationships. Thirty-eight percent of these men acknowledged and left property to colored mistresses, illegitimate children, or both.[30]

By mid-Victorian standards such confirmation of the planters' sexual immorality merely reinforced the idea of the *general* immorality of West Indian societies and their utter heedlessness of European moral conventions. In the seventeenth century, sailing to the West Indies was to go "beyond the line," which originally meant outside the territorial limits of European treaties but soon came to mean outside the moral boundaries of European society and culture. In the nineteenth century, West Indian societies were still socially and culturally "beyond the line." Their sexual licentiousness seemed to contemporary Britons merely emblematic of their general social and political character, which featured abuse of power, lack of self-restraint, and personal intemperance.

On the other hand, eighteenth-century Jamaican historian Bryan

Edwards described the wild West Indies much as one would have described the Wild West of the nineteenth-century United States; the colonies were characterized by a spirit of independence and equality, "an impatience of subordination." Certainly in their own eyes West Indians were not so peculiar or unreasonable. They laid claim to the same cultural and political heritage as Britons resident in England. However, they also claimed sovereignty in internal affairs, which had developed not through legal prescription but rather through default of the British government. Unlike those of their northern neighbors, these claims never raised any serious prospect for separation and nationhood, but they did complicate the problem of creating a free society in Jamaica. Problems of labor discipline and social control were conflated inextricably with issues of governance and power.[31]

Creating a Free Society

The Jamaica Assembly's initial reception of the news that the Abolition Act had been passed seemed to bode well for its implementation—under the circumstances. James Spedding described it as "a kind of sullen tranquility." On 8 October 1833, in reply to Governor Mulgrave's opening speech requesting the passage of local legislation to implement the imperial Abolition Act (an act-in-aid), the Assembly declared: "The people of Jamaica have never advocated slavery in the abstract, but as connected with their rights of property, upon the principle of compensation, they are ready to relinquish the system, and will be proud to show that they have feelings as favorable to the improvement of the labouring population as their fellow subjects in the mother country. All they desire is to be fairly dealt with." In a satirical paraphrase of the planters' position, James Spedding wrote some years later: "They were willing that it should be so; they had never advocated slavery as a good thing in itself, but only as a thing profitable to them[selves]; no Englishman could desire the improvement of the negro population more sincerely than they,—let but the proof of this cost them nothing, and they would be proud to prove it."[32]

The Jamaica Assembly did pass the Act-in-Aid of the Abolition Act in December 1833, which Lord Mulgrave approved and forwarded to the Colonial Office. Unfortunately, it was found to be "extremely deficient" because of the omission of obligatory clauses as well as the inclusion of a number of objectionable ones. Far from providing specific details on how the apprenticeship system would operate, the

Jamaican law tended to leave many matters vague. Offenses for which apprentices would be culpable and penalties to which they would be subject were not defined. The masters' specific obligations to the apprentices were also left vague. For example, the supplies of food, clothing, and medicine were merely required to be "customary" or "sufficient." The decision on the adequacy of such provisions was left to the parish vestries, which were, in fact, composed of the masters themselves. There was no protection against improper punishment, and masters were still allowed on their own authority to confine apprentices to plantation dungeons for up to twenty-four hours if a special magistrate was not immediately available. Despite these deficiencies, Edward Stanley, the colonial secretary, was disposed to be liberal, and much to the chagrin of his subordinates, "most liberally did he redeem his pledge." Stanley chose to regard the law's defects as "oversights" and asked the governor to point them out to the Assembly. He then proceeded to declare the act "adequate and satisfactory," thus entitling Jamaica to her share of the compensation money; "the deed was done—the money was paid."[33]

The Assembly did respond to the government's request for amendments to the act-in-aid. On 4 July 1834 it passed a law to repeal and amend the earlier legislation. However, in that perverse spirit which would characterize the Assembly's relations with the Colonial Office for the next thirty years, it provided that these amendments would expire on 31 December 1835, while the act to which they applied would continue until 1840. Since emancipation was scheduled to take effect the very next month, the Colonial Office again reluctantly approved the Assembly's actions.

On 22 December 1834 the Assembly passed yet a second Act-in-Aid of the Abolition Act. But now, having experienced five months of the apprenticeship, it was determined to regain as much local control as the British government could be forced to concede. The second act-in-aid allowed the owners of sugar estates to so arrange the hours of labor as to secure eighteen continuous hours out of twenty-four, provided only that individual laborers not work more than nine hours a day; required apprentices to remain in agriculture unless they could demonstrate their ability to support themselves otherwise; barred them leaving the estate without the permission of their employer, except to attend church, work on their provision grounds, or sell produce at weekend markets; prohibited them from proceeding in a body of five or more to seek a special magistrate, or to attend "any public meeting." Workers were forbidden to have meetings or revels or to

Peter Howe Browne, the Marquis of Sligo

have drummings on any estate after 9:00 P.M. Special justices were required to set up penal gangs on plantations. Proprietors were allowed to destroy the hogs, goats, and other animals belonging to apprentices which depredated property or provision grounds. Plantation constables were given the power to arrest and confine apprentices and loiterers. With the altercations at Belvedere and Gibraltar fresh in their minds, the legislators made it a legal requirement that apprentices assist in putting out fires on plantations.[34]

This time the Assembly had gone too far. On 13 June 1835, Lord Aberdeen informed the governor that the second act-in-aid had been disallowed. In Aberdeen's view the intent of this law was not to implement the imperial act but rather to supersede it by placing too much authority into local hands. He objected particularly strongly to a provision giving the Jamaica Court of Quarter Sessions jurisdiction over the apprentices, because the employer regained through the courts "the exercise of much of that invidious authority of which he was deprived by the slavery Abolition Act." He felt that the ambiguity of some of the provisions for confinement on the plantation raised the specter of a return to slave law practices, and he objected to the clause that barred five or more apprentices from leaving the estates to go to the special magistrates, on the ground that a person might need witnesses. Worse yet, the new act actually repealed many beneficial clauses in the earlier legislation. For example, the right to go to market and to church and to use nonworking hours freely were dropped from the new law. So was the requirement that apprentices confined by their master be released after twenty-four hours if no special magistrate could be secured and that subsequently an official complaint had to be made relative to that confinement. The Assembly had also neglected to reenact the prohibition against flogging women, as well as the provision that penal labor be limited to fifteen hours a week.[35]

The British government's belated efforts to assert its authority and to define the substance as well as the framework of black freedom exacerbated rather than resolved the difficulty. The government's relations with the Jamaica Assembly were alternately hostile and conciliatory, and its substantive policy was never entirely certain, the whole of which resulted, as Henry Taylor described it, in "a slow, never-ending, rankling quarrel."[36]

At the center of this controversy was the governor, who represented British authority but had no real power. Five months before the emancipation law went into effect, Lord Mulgrave resigned as governor of Jamaica, ostensibly for health reasons, to be replaced by Peter Howe Browne, the second marquis of Sligo. Lord Seaford, who was in Jamaica at the time and who had been very favorably impressed with Lord Mulgrave, was extremely disappointed with the choice of his successor. "Could you find no one better qualified to succeed him than Sligo!" he wrote to Holland. It is not clear exactly why Lord Seaford objected, but Sligo's proud, volatile, impulsive temper did not bode well for executing so sensitive an assignment as governing Jamaica in this critical transition period. Like his good friend Lord Byron, Sligo had a reputation as something of an adventurer. Having spent four months in prison in 1811–12 for harboring seventeen British deserters on his private ship in the Mediterranean, he was not known as a man of caution or tact.[37]

It may be that Sligo's appointment owed something to his close friendship with Spring Rice, then the colonial secretary, but he also possessed qualities that might have fitted him ideally to deal with the vituperative Jamaica Assembly. Lord Holland was disturbed by Sligo's lack of judgment but found him "zealous and honest in his views and full of attention to business." James Spedding described him as "really a noble lord; humane and earnest in his purposes—clear and frank in his dealings; teeming with unwearied activities; plunging boldly into the middle of all businesses in the confidence of a just intention, and writing like a man."[38]

There were other factors that made Sligo's appointment appear, at first blush, to be politically astute. He was himself the owner of two plantations in Jamaica's St. Dorothy Parish with a total of 286 apprentices. Indeed, one of his first acts upon arrival in the spring of 1834 was to inspect his own properties. He also took it upon himself to inform his absentee planter friends of the condition of their estates. Furthermore, unlike Lord Holland, Sligo was only a recent convert to the necessity of emancipation. Indeed, he had become convinced of that necessity only while attending the 1832 hearings in the House of Lords on the condition of the slave populations. Undoubtedly these factors in his background contributed to his warm reception by the planters in the spring and summer of 1834. The editor of the *Jamaica Dispatch* praised him as "a nobleman of conservative principles, and whose interest is so closely identified with our own," while he dismissed Mulgrave as "just a Whig."[39]

But as Sligo was to discover, this era of good feelings was to last only as long as he behaved like a planter willing to concede extraordinary powers to the local assembly rather than as a governor intent on executing British policy. And as governors coming after him realized, the Jamaican chief executive had little power other than his personal influence. Assessing the situation at the end of the decade, James Spedding wrote: "The prerogatives of the Crown are vested in a governor, who has no natural influence or authority in the colony—whose name commands no reverence, whose powers are sufficient to make him obnoxious, without procuring for him either fear or respect; who represents nothing but the policy of the British Government, which, for the last fifty years, the dominant classes in Jamaica have always hated." Indicative of the governor's political weakness was the fact that the mayor of Kingston could and did decline Governor Sligo's invitation to dinner.[40]

One of Sligo's first actions in Jamaica was to test the formal powers of the governor and find them wanting. Following the model of the British parliamentary system, the governor was empowered to dissolve the Assembly and thereby force new elections. But the Jamaican electorate was small, election campaigns were inexpensive, and the constituency to which one had to appeal was extremely narrow; thus members had little to fear from the threat of a dissolution. Sligo found in 1834 that most Jamaican politicians were opposed to the government and that there were no consistent partisan divisions he might profitably exploit. Worst of all, the governor had no patronage to bestow upon individuals to secure their loyalty. The custodeship (the custos was head magistrate of a parish) had once been a patronage plum that the governor could bestow upon his friends, but ironically the appointment of special magistrates under the emancipation law undercut not only the authority but also the prestige of local justices. Sligo found it difficult to attract men of substance to this position; the governor, rather than the prospective officeholder, became the supplicant. Worse yet, even some of the men who held government appointments were among its most vehement opponents. For example, in the summer and fall of 1835 Sligo was forced to remove Edward T. Guy, the adjutant general of the militia, and John Edward Panton, the King's Advocate, because of their refusal to support emancipation policies.[41]

With a degree of prescience, Sligo recognized that the Crown needed some official representative in the Assembly to put forth its measures and to defend them. He toyed with the idea of appointing the attorney general from among the resident lawyers; such patronage might give him leverage with lawyers in the Assembly. But since many lawyers were either planters themselves, the scions of planter families, or dependent upon estates for their private income, they obviously would not make consistent opponents of the planter class. Thus no such policy was implemented, and twenty years elapsed before the more general proposition of government representation in the Assembly was adopted. Even that reform required, as Sligo soon recognized, a party loyal to the government that would serve as a counterweight to the planter interest.[42]

With that realization it also became clear to Sligo, as it had to Lord Mulgrave earlier, that the Jamaicans most loyal to the British government were the freeborn colored people. For two decades prior to the abolition of slavery the Jamaica Assembly had gradually liberalized laws restricting the economic and political rights of brown men, culminating in complete civil and political equality in 1830. When Sligo arrived in Jamaica, at least two mulattoes—John Manderson and John Campbell—had served in the Jamaica Assembly. Sligo's predecessor Lord Mulgrave, recognizing the potential of a politically mobilized colored sector, had begun to appoint free brown men to public office.

Sligo, however, was hesitant to pursue such a policy at first. During his first tour of the island in the spring of 1834, he was appalled to learn that a black tailor named Johnson had defeated a respectable white property holder in a local vestry election. "This may be a just return for the inequities they had previously suffered from the whites, but it is an unpleasant proof of what is in their minds. There are certainly few of the men of colour at all refined, or educated, for which reason it will be necessary to [hurry] forward on every occasion any so qualified, & thereby enable opposition to be given to such as are unfit." By summer of 1835, however, he informed the Colonial Office of his eagerness to appoint free colored men whenever possible.[43]

During the next several years it appeared that the brown class would in fact become a major factor in Jamaican politics. There were two islandwide elections during the apprenticeship period—in 1835 and 1837—and in each of them brown Jamaicans were an active force. In 1835 there were colored challengers in St. Catherine, St. Andrew, St. James, Westmoreland, Port Royal, and St. Ann, the last running against the Speaker of the Assembly, Richard Barrett. In Hanover the colored electorate supported a liberal white candidate, Alexander Grant. Colored candidates were successful in four of these parishes and in the city of Kingston, electing six of their number to the Assembly in all, of whom four were new members. The breadth and vigor of the challenge itself was enough to excite anxiety among white Jamaicans. The *Kingston Chronicle* labeled the challengers that "vagabond revolutionary faction." During the campaign in St. Ann Parish, Speaker Barrett presented himself as a liberal and claimed credit for the political rights now enjoyed by the free colored population. When Richard Hill rose to dispute Barrett's claims, the Speaker, visibly shaken, retorted that in years past, men such as he would not have been allowed to speak at all.[44]

If the brown men's political challenge of 1835 appeared to undermine white hegemony, their successes in the election of 1837 seemed to threaten its total destruction. Eleven of the forty-three members returned in the 1837 election were new members; three of them were brown men, raising their total membership to eight. Furthermore, their strength was no longer confined to cities such as Kingston and Spanish Town, but emerged impressively in the very heartland of the planter oligarchy. J. S. Brown and Charles Lake were elected to represent Westmoreland; Richard Hill amassed the highest vote total of any candidate in the Trelawny election. The almost totally rural sugar parish of St. John was said to belong to "the radicals," leading the *Kingston Chronicle* to lament that "the mob" controlled the parish now. In contrast, "the gentlemen" seemed apathetic and unresponsive. Baptist missionaries were seen electioneering for colored candidates, a new development that excited fear of an eventual political revolution. "Believe me, gentlemen," declared a planter who had just been elected with a total of sixty-three votes, "this is the last popular and independent election for Manchester, at which the voters will be so confined in numbers. . . . Next time . . . there will be at least a thousand."[45]

As one would expect in a society where an embattled political minority controlled the economic wealth, the planter-controlled Assembly reacted by raising the property qualifications for voting and holding office. In December 1834, prior to the colored political challenge, the Assembly had passed a relatively liberalized franchise act extending the vote to anyone paying £5 per annum in taxes or £50 in rent, and a 2s. 6d. registration fee, renewable every eight years. Members of the Assembly, however, had to have an annual income of £300 or unencumbered property worth £3,000.[46]

Governor Sligo felt that this legislation was as good as he was likely to get out of the Assembly, so he approved it despite strict instructions from the Colonial Office not to approve franchise legislation without a clause suspending its effective date pending review by the home government. Several colored leaders did not agree with Sligo. Edward Jordon sent the Colonial Office a strong protest against the new act, claiming that it would disfranchise colored voters and that it would prejudice the interests of urban groups as opposed to those living on plantations. Jordon's principal objection was to the provision allowing renters who paid no taxes to vote, because it was felt that persons in "middling circumstances" would not be encouraged to acquire property. Furthermore, he charged that attorneys on estates would be able to control the votes of their tenants. Jordon's objections also included an anti-Semitic tirade against potential political competitors in Kingston who, entitled to vote as rent payers, would "sell their Votes to the highest and best bidder."[47]

Following the 1835 elections, the Assembly changed the franchise again. In an amendment apparently aimed at disfranchising small farmers in rural areas, the 1836 law raised the property qualifications from £10 to £30 clear annual value, while keeping the alternative qualifications of £5 in annual taxes or £50 in annual rent. The fact that persons who had registered under the previous, more liberal qualifications would be allowed to continue to vote represented a kind of Jamaican "grandfather clause." Members of the Assembly still had to have either £300 in income per year or £3,000 in real property but now could also qualify with a combined £5,000 in real and personal property. The intent of this law was so obvious that the Colonial Office disallowed it in April 1837.[48]

The political mobilization of colored voters and the Assembly's efforts to suppress it seem to have resulted in a standoff. Afro-Jamaican political activity was dramatic when compared with that of the preemancipation period, but it was never sufficient to overthrow planter control of the Assembly or to assure the government success in its efforts to protect the freed people. That success would still be dependent upon the outcome of the test of wills between the planters on the one hand and Governor Sligo and the Colonial Office on the other.

After receiving the Colonial Office's objections to the second act-in-aid, Sligo convened a special session of the Assembly in August 1835 and demanded that the law be amended. Not only did the Assembly refuse to amend the act but it passed new legislation placing the police under the control of the custodes rather than the governor. Sligo reacted by dissolving the Assembly and calling for new elections.[49]

The Colonial Office was not pleased with Sligo's drastic action. Glenelg thought Sligo had been "too sensitive" to the personal abuse he had received from the opposition press. Although the governor felt that his action was congruent with his general instructions from the Colonial Office, Glenelg disclaimed authorization for so drastic a step as dissolution. Glenelg's official dispatch of 13 October 1835 amounted to a public reprimand. Writing in his diary during this period, Lord Holland probably expressed the feeling of many members of the government in concluding that the reprimand was necessary but hoping that it would not force the governor to resign. Such a resignation would be "a triumph for the faction of the Old Slavedrivers [and] would be very unfortunate." Thus he hoped Sligo would uncharacteristically swallow his pride and stay.[50]

Sligo did not resign in the fall of 1835, very probably because he felt the elections following the dissolution had vindicated his actions. In his earlier dispatch announcing the dissolution, he confessed that he did not expect it to bring about any material change in the membership of the Assembly. This concession had contributed to the feeling at the Colonial Office that it was poor judgment to take so drastic a step when it offered so little hope of success. By mid-November, however, Sligo was ecstatic at the changes that had occurred in the

Assembly. Eleven new members had been elected, including three new colored members, Richard Hill, Charles Lake, and Robert Russell. The liberal, pro-government faction in the Assembly had been very much strengthened. One visible indicator of what Sligo took to be a change of temper among the island elite, and by no means a small thing, was the large attendance at the governor's dinner and ball in late November.[51]

The calm was broken again, however, when Jamaica's official lobbyist in Britain, William Burge, forwarded to the Assembly copies of Sligo's dispatches to the Colonial Office. Sligo's letters gave a very frank assessment of the island elite that offended the Assembly. In this highly charged atmosphere, resolution of the differences between the governor and the Assembly on the Police Bill and amendments to the Act-in-Aid of the Abolition Act proved impossible.

Exasperated and impatient, Sligo sent a message directly to the Assembly, proposing certain minor amendments to resolve the differences. The Assembly seized upon the message as a breach of its privileges and demanded that the governor apologize. After several weeks of agitation Sligo informed the Colonial Office that the only course remaining was to ask Parliament to override the local assembly by enacting the Police Bill and the act-in-aid itself. Glenelg's ambiguous reply seemed to leave the governor no recourse but to apologize to the Assembly or offer his resignation. Hearing of the governor's intent to resign, colored voters in the Spanish Town area mobilized a demonstration pledging their support and requesting that he reconsider. Sligo changed his mind about resigning. The disposition of the Assembly also improved, and it appeared ready to resolve its differences with the governor and to reenact the Police Bill and the act-in-aid measure. Ironically, when Sligo finally did resign shortly thereafter, it was over an issue unrelated to his struggle with the planters: his dismissal of a special magistrate had been overruled by the Colonial Office, and the governor took this as a vote of no confidence in his administration. In August 1836 the marquis of Sligo left Jamaica for good.[52]

It soon became evident that Sligo's departure would not resolve the problem of governance despite the appointment of a successor, Sir Lionel Smith, who had enjoyed the warm approval of Barbadian planters for his administration of that colony's apprenticeship as well as a strong recommendation from the Tory leader, the duke of Wellington. Smith openly expressed his disdain for Sligo and reversed many of his policies. In general he deemphasized the special magistrates, even taking away the uniforms that Sligo had insisted they wear. To the planters' delight, Smith opposed appointing colored special magistrates and was disdainful of Sligo's attempt to build a government party.[53]

Smith was determined to pursue a conciliatory policy with the planters, and he did so for more than a year and a half. From mid-1836 to the end of 1837 there was a surface calm on the affairs of Jamaica. James Spedding, however, reflecting on the Colonial Office's experience in encouraging the colonies to ameliorate conditions of slaves before emancipation, was less than sanguine about the outcome of Smith's policies. "But all was worse than fruitless. Everything turned into bitterness. The whole conciliatory process served only to fill them with false ideas of their own importance; to render them more obstinate in their prejudices, more tenacious of their rights, more reckless in their actions;—to aggravate the original difference into an abiding system of hostility."[54]

It soon became evident how fruitless Governor Smith's policy had been. A celebrated exposé of the conditions in the workhouses and prisons of Jamaica, together with the belated realization that the Assembly still had not remedied any of the defects in the legislation governing apprenticeship, led Governor Smith to a sudden, devastating acknowledgment of the abject failure of his policies. "I am almost broken-hearted," he wrote to Glenelg, " . . . in reality I am the only slave in the whole island." Like Sligo before him and others to come, he recognized the almost total impotence of the governor under the present system. He was amazed at the recklessness of the white creole elite. He had heard of plots to call out the militia without his authorization and rumors that he would be assassinated. "It is impossible for any one to answer for the conduct of the House of Assembly. Many are there in the island who would be delighted to get up an insurrection for the pleasure of destroying the negroes and missionaries. They are, in fact, mad."[55]

Actually, it was not all the Assembly's fault. It was difficult enough to govern a society in the midst of the momentous transition from slavery to freedom, but the division of authority between Britain and the colonial assemblies exacerbated that difficulty. The Jamaica Assembly was alternately recalcitrant and temporarily compliant; the Colonial Office, conciliatory and briefly forceful and determined. At times it seemed that they were the proverbial two ships passing in the night. Thus, on 19 March 1838, Glenelg asked Parliament to amend the Jamaican Abolition Act directly. Meanwhile, the Assembly, having grown more compliant, passed an amended act-in-aid on 24 March 1838, which met some of the complaints that had been lodged against earlier laws. Their action was mooted, however, by a parliamentary act, which became law on 11 April 1838, that gave the governor discretionary power to legislate by proclamation and directly prohibited certain abuses, such as putting women on the workhouse treadmills or in penal gangs, whipping them, or cropping their hair. Furthermore, no male apprentices were to be whipped after 15 August 1838, except in cases where free persons would be also.[56]

By the spring of 1838 both the planters and their abolitionist opponents had become dissatisfied with the apprenticeship—the latter because of the abuses suffered by the apprentices, the former because of the continued interference of England in their internal affairs. In the summer of 1835 Speaker Barrett had spoken publicly in favor of ending apprenticeship just to get rid of the special magistrates. Toward the end of 1837 Edward Jordon, leader of the Afro-Jamaican legislators, introduced a bill in the Assembly designed to end Jamaica's apprenticeship system; but no action was taken on it. Pressures began to build, however, after Montserrat abolished apprenticeship in 1837. Several other colonies—Nevis, St. Kitts, the Virgin Islands, and Barbados—followed suit during the winter and spring of 1838. By the spring of 1838 a bipartisan consensus had formed in Jamaica favorable to immediate abolition. In June 1838 the Assembly passed legislation abolishing the system effective 1 August 1838.[57]

If the planters thought that abolition of apprenticeship would free them from British government interference, however, they were wrong. It had become all too obvious that the former slaveholders were not apt pupils of a free labor ideology and liberal democratic statecraft. As in most societies, the testing point was the system of justice. It is ironic and suggestive of the interaction of political and economic domains that the prison system (the state's methods for controlling deviance) rather than the labor system (the planter's methods for extracting profits) was the terrain on which the issue was joined.

The Jamaican Panopticon

The most visible and compelling symbol of the difference between a free society and a slave society was the latter's reliance upon the whip to control human behavior. In the view of English liberals, free men exercising their rational choice did not require direct external coercion.

Persons who deviated from that norm, because of a lack of education or improper socialization, could be confined to special institutions designed to reform them—prisons, workhouses, asylums. Here they would be disciplined and taught self-restraint. But that discipline would be deliberative, impersonal, and rational as opposed to the arbitrary, impassioned lashes of a driver's whip. Under the apprenticeship system recalcitrant workers were sent to the parish house of correction. Although it was expected that the apprentices would sometimes be flogged there, it was also expected that they would normally be subjected to a more rational system of discipline. Their primary mode of punishment was intended to be subjection to hard labor. To achieve this, Governor Sligo, shortly after his arrival in Jamaica, recommended the general adoption of the treadmill.

Invented by Samuel Cubitt in 1818, the treadmill had come into widespread use in England as a result of the efforts of the Prison Discipline Society, a group intent on reforming the English prison system. The device consisted of a hollow cylinder of wood on an iron frame with a series of steps around its circumference. With wrists strapped to a bar above the machine, the prisoner was forced to turn the wheel continuously by walking the steps, or "dancing the treadmill." The treadmill was considered a rational and humane way to impose discipline. In fact, it combined the two senses of "discipline"—punishment and routinized labor. As implemented in Jamaica, its design bears a striking similarity to the whipping machine recommended by Jeremy Bentham in his great prison reform tract, the *Panopticon*.[58]

Throughout the apprenticeship period disturbing reports were being received in England that the workhouses and jails of Jamaica were not conforming to the rational, reform ideal. Instead, treadmills—so poorly constructed that they whipped and lacerated the prisoners rather than simply "worked" them—had become instruments of torture. In response to these reports, Captain J. W. Pringle was appointed by the Colonial Office in September 1837 to investigate the system of prisons in the West Indies. What Pringle found was systematic "licentiousness" and cruelty, violating all the norms and reform ideals then accepted in England. Male and female inmates were separated only at night in most cases. Male warders forced sexual relations on their female prisoners. There was no orderly system for feeding the prisoners; they simply were given an allowance and purchased their own food from hucksters. Cleanliness was not enforced; there was no soap allowance. Recidivism was high. The sys-

A Treadmill Scene in Jamaica, c. 1837

tem of justice seemed altogether arbitrary and harsh. Pringle found one person who had been sentenced to death for sheep stealing but had had his sentence commuted to twelve months imprisonment; meanwhile another prisoner was hanged for horse stealing. At the end of this report Pringle could only conclude that "it must be evident that [the prisons] hardly hold out a chance of bringing about reform in the character of the inmates."[59]

The treadmill became emblematic of the abuses of the Jamaican prison system, which in turn symbolized that colony's general failure to make the transition from a slave to a free society. In the British government's view both failures could be traced primarily to the former slaveholders' hostility to the philosophy and modes of control of the employers of free labor. "The West Indian legislatures have neither the will nor the skill to make such laws as you want made," Henry Taylor declared to James Stephen, "and they cannot be converted on the point of willingness, and they will not be instructed." Taylor went on to indict the entire political infrastructure of Jamaican society. "The superior courts were partisans of slavery; the legislatures were worse than the judicatures; all were embittered and enraged against the negroes and their friends, and the police were fit agents for giving effect to the passions of their employers."[60]

The Colonial Office moved to remedy the abuses of the Jamaican prison system in much the same way as it had handled the act-in-aid of abolition. They requested Parliament to pass imperial legislation overriding the local laws. In July, Parliament passed the Act for the Better Government of Prisons of the West Indies, which empowered the Privy Council or the governor-in-council to make all regulations necessary for the governance of such institutions. The law was published in Jamaica on 25 September 1838. Thinking that they had rid themselves of direct parliamentary interference by abolishing the apprenticeship system, the assemblymen were incensed. When they met on 30 October, they voted a resolution declaring the parliamentary action a violation of their "inherent rights as British subjects" and refused to do any business. Despite successive prorogations and dissolutions, the deadlock continued. On 24 December Governor Smith informed the Colonial Office that there was no prospect of breaking the impasse. Seventeen annual acts expired, taxes could not be levied, the police were discharged.[61]

This crisis exposed the dangers of the confused, piecemeal policy the British government had pursued. As Henry Taylor later confessed, the policy of conciliation was actually misnamed, because it involved an insistence that the local legislatures make only such laws as the Colonial Office designed and approved; consequently, it amounted to a "constant setting up and knocking down of their authority." Such a policy was clearly ineffective. It was also inadequate to respond to abuses that had occurred on an ad hoc basis by superseding the authority of the Assembly on particular issues. In a private letter to Stephen in October 1838, Taylor declared:

> I cannot help expressing to you privately my persuasion that the Government is in danger of falling into a system of erroneous policy on this question and creating great and continual discontent to no purpose. What they are doing and about to do is, in fact, a repetition of the policy pursued from 1823 to 1834, on Slave melioration, . . . the experience of . . . which . . . should teach us a different lesson. . . . That assuming the objects of the Government to be necessary to the establishment of the liberty and promotion of the industry of the negroes, and that the habits and prejudices, if not the interests of the planters, are strongly opposed to them, then the only method of accomplishing them effectually and completely, and the best method as regards irritation and discontent, will be by exerting at once and conclusively, a power which shall overrule all opposition and set the question at rest.[62]

Three months later, on 14 January 1839, the Colonial Office decided to seek broad changes in the mode of colonial governance. Taylor was ordered to draw up a minute for submission to the Cabinet by Lord Glenelg. Taylor's minute began by listing five classes of laws that were required for the smooth transition from a slave to a free society, all of which the Jamaican legislature had failed to enact. These included the reform of the court system, the establishment of a police force, the reform of the poor laws, new laws for the regulation of contracts, and the repeal of all slave laws together with the imposition of some limits on the jurisdiction of the planter-dominated local magistrates. Moving quickly from the details, arguments, and counterarguments of the existing crisis over the prisons, Taylor raised what he saw as the critical question: "whether the West Indian Assemblies be or be not, by their constitution and the nature of the societies for which they legislate, absolutely incompetent and unfit to deal with the new state of things." The Jamaican social structure was composed of 320,000 ex-slaves "still in the depths of ignorance and by their African temperament highly excitable," 28,000 poorly educated colored people of free origins, who were alienated socially from the black majority, and 9,000 whites "possessed by all the passions and the inveterate prejudices growing out of the slave system." Such a society offered no real basis for representative democracy and must inevitably tend toward oligarchy. In short, the black majority should have power but could not, the large colored group could have power but should not, the white minority should not have power but will.[63]

Taylor went on to describe how the Assembly had been able over a course of years to usurp many of the functions normally exercised by the executive and to reduce the power of the governor and thereby the home government on the island. The Jamaica Assembly was totally prejudiced against the blacks and not disposed to undertake the steps necessary to encourage their civilization and development. By abolishing slavery the British government had forced a fundamental change in Jamaican society, but "to force this social change, and yet to leave the political frame-work of the totally different society the same as it was, would seem even in a mere theoretical view to be in the nature of a political solecism." Given their character, the West Indian planters were "eminently disqualified for the great task of educating and improving a people newly born into freedom as it were."

All efforts to "temperately and courteously" reason with the assemblies, to conciliate them, to show them "how essentially the interest of the planters are bound up with the good treatment and the civil and moral advancement of the negroes," had failed. This failure resulted, not from temporary mistakes in policy or personality conflicts, but from "the inherent and permanent incongruity of the system with the state of society." Clearly influenced by the derogatory image of the creole elite that had built up over the years, Taylor declared emphatically that appeals to the assemblymen's property interests would not convince them to act rationally. "They are composed of agents and attorneys, seldom of proprietors. The motives which affect them are connected with authority, station, and certain rooted feelings concerning class and colour. Men cannot be delivered out of these feelings by an appeal even to pecuniary interest,—not even when the interest are [sic] their own, much less when their employers are the parties solely or chiefly concerned; nor can they be reasoned out of them."

The recent reforms in the government of lower Canada, which Taylor interpreted as essentially a Crown colony system, would serve as his model for changes in the West Indian assemblies. The assemblies would be abolished, and appointive legislative councils similar to the existing privy councils would be instituted. Judges would be sent from home to reform and administer the system of justice.

It was expedient, Taylor warned, that decisive action be taken at once. The Jamaica Assembly's intemperate and vicious attack on Parliament vitiated any possible political support they might have enjoyed at home. Thus, the prospect for changing the mode of government and abolishing the Assembly was good. If the government waited, however, changes in the political situation of Jamaica might make future action more problematic. There was ample evidence of growing political mobilization among the black freedmen. Very soon the situation might be reversed, therefore, and a black oligarchy would be oppressing the white minority. The home government's latitude for action in such a situation would be much more restricted. The government's support for the black majority over and against the white minority had resulted only in the temporary paralysis of colonial government. A future situation in which the government should be called upon to support the white minority against a black majority enjoying control of state power "would be totally different in its features from those we have been accustomed to, and of a far more dangerous character." Taylor predicted political difficulties in Britain if the government ever tried to mobilize support for suppression of a black majority, especially when that suppression would almost inevitably be of a military character. "It is at the present moment therefore, if ever, that the Assembly can be got rid of."[64]

For the second time in six years, Henry Taylor had drafted a bold and far-reaching policy statement only to see it receive a lukewarm reception by his superiors. "Lord Glenelg's support of his adopted child," Taylor remembered some years later, "was but faint-hearted." As a result, opponents in the Cabinet were able to gut the measure by limiting it to Jamaica alone and for five years' duration. For Taylor, the ministry's acceptance of such a watered-down bill was tantamount to surrendering the whole raison d'être for action. His entire justification for the measure was that the former slave colonies were intrinsically unfit for self-government by virtue of the character of creole society.[65]

The discussion of Taylor's plan and the substitute proposal precipitated a minor crisis in the Cabinet. Secretary of War Henry George Grey, offended by Glenelg's timidity on this issue as well as his colonial policy in general, threatened to resign if the colonial secretary were not replaced. And while Grey, known for his rashness, might not have been such a great loss, the threat by John Russell to follow him out of office made for a difficult situation. According to Lord Holland, Prime Minister Melbourne offered Glenelg the sinecure of the privy seal in return for his resignation from the Colonial Office. But while Glenelg was by no means anxious to remain in office, he was loath to resign during Parliament's hostile review of his Canadian policy. The crisis was resolved when Grey agreed to remain at his post on the condition that Melbourne arrange to get rid of Glenelg "ere long."[66]

But the weakness of the Whig government can by no means be charged solely to the timid personalities of Glenelg and Lord Melbourne. Although the Whigs had held a majority in Commons since the elections following passage of the Reform Bill, it was a fractious and uneasy majority. As Lord Russell described it, it was a "majority [that] consisted of every shade, from the most moderate of the Whigs to the most resolute of the Radicals." In fact, it was only the Whigs' ad hoc coalition with liberal Tories between 1830 and 1866 that made their reforms, indeed their government, possible. Politicians in Jamaica were not unaware of the weakness of the Whig ministry. "We have now a government of expediency—nothing more," Richard Barrett declared in 1836. "The government is kept in office by a small majority in the House of Commons. They cannot bring forward a measure in that House that they can with certainty carry."[67]

Unfortunately for the resolution of the Jamaica crisis, the Tories decided to make the bill suppressing the Jamaica Assembly an issue of confidence in the Whig ministry. On 6 May the measure passed the

House of Lords by a mere five-vote margin. Lord Melbourne decided that such a small victory necessitated the resignation of his government. Because the Tories were unable to form a government, however, Melbourne was returned to office within a week. A second Jamaica bill was introduced on 30 May and eventually passed. That bill, however, did not suspend the Jamaica Assembly for any definite period; it merely required the Assembly to submit certain remedial legislation before its functions would be restored.

Sir Lionel Smith was recalled and appointed governor of Mauritius, where he served until his death in 1842. Sir Charles Metcalfe, the former governor of India, was appointed to succeed him. Metcalfe inaugurated an ostentatiously conciliatory policy toward the planters and the Assembly that was in a general sense continued by his successor, the earl of Elgin. Years later Jamaican planters would see the six years of Metcalfe-Elgin administration as a golden age in the postemancipation era. There was relative economic prosperity and peace as planters and freed people were left to adjust to a new system of social relations.

It was, however, a deceptive economic progress and a false peace. The apprenticeship system had failed to remold the ex-slaves, their former masters, or Jamaican society as a whole. The authors of that system had decided by 1839 that a society composed of ex-slaveholders and ex-slaves was incapable of self-government. Their drastic solution, direct rule from Britain, was not politically feasible in 1839; it would become so a quarter-century later as a result of radical change in the racial and political climate of Great Britain and a long history of political and economic failure in Jamaica.

Part Two

The Free Labor Economy

But there is on both sides a tenacity to the old connexion, which keeps them together. The Landlord does not like to eject those whom he still regards as his proper Labourers, although he cannot obtain Labour from them, and the Labourer clings to his House and Ground on the Estate where he has long held them, although he is harassed by vexatious demands on account of Rent.

**GOVERNOR CHARLES METCALFE TO LORD JOHN RUSSELL,
30 MARCH 1840**

4

The Planters: Managing a Free Labor Economy

Twenty years after passage of the slavery abolition bill, Governor Henry Barkly, following a tour of Jamaica to assess conditions, reported to the Colonial Office that "as a sugar growing country she is never likely again to hold a very high rank." In St. Thomas-in-the-Vale, previously one of the most prosperous of the interior parishes, he found that over half the estates had been abandoned; of those remaining only fifteen deserved to be called genuine "estates." On the northwestern coast he found similar, if less severe, adversity. In Trelawny, eighty-six estates had produced 8,000 tons of sugar in 1834; now sixty-two produced 4,800 tons. St. James's eighty-two sugar estates were now just fifty, producing less than half the parish's former crop. Of the fifty-eight estates that had received imperial loans following the 1831 slave rebellion, eleven, barely 20 percent, remained under cultivation in 1854; indeed, only three were fully cultivated, the rest being at some stage along the road to ruin.[1]

Enclosed with Barkly's report were those of his special magistrates—the first since such reports were discontinued in 1846—describing similar stories of distress and blight from almost every parish. Indeed, conditions in the eastern parishes were even worse than those seen by Barkly during his western tour. Perhaps the most devastated was the northeastern parish of Portland, where only four sugar estates remained, and those just partially cultivated. There had been eleven in 1846 and twenty-eight the decade before that. From the southeastern parish of St. David, Alexander J. Fyfe reported that the eleven sugar estates he had found there in 1838 had shrunk to four by 1854, and one of these was near abandonment. In the earlier period, a thousand hands had worked five and one-half days to produce 800 hogsheads; now 300 workers averaged slightly more than four days to produce 350 hogsheads. In other words, there had been declines of 64 percent and 70 percent in the numbers of estates and workers, respectively; yet this 75 percent reduction in man-days worked per week was resulting in just 56 percent less sugar produced.[2] In recounting these statistics, special magistrate Fyfe noted that only estates blessed with the richest soil had survived; but given the discrepancy between the decline in labor and the smaller drop in output, he might also have added that only those estates able to exploit their workforce to the maximum survived.

Barkly was wrong, of course; Jamaica would become a major sugar producer again, but not until the Great War of 1914 brought a renewed prosperity through increased demand and better prices. For the balance of the nineteenth century these images of blight would be commonplace in contemporary references to the Jamaican sugar industry. Ten years after Barkly, another governor touring the island painted a graphic portrait of a lost paradise: "In every direction were to be met with the remains of handsome entrances to Estates now decayed and overgrown with bush; houses dilapidated and untenanted, expensive works in ruins, and dense jungles occupying fields that formerly were waving in sugar canes."[3]

Attempts to determine the causes of this decline and to remedy them occupied many of the best political minds in Britain and Jamaica. Numerous government commissions studied the problem. Every government administration formulated policies intended to reverse the precipitous skid into bankruptcy. To the island's economic fortunes were linked the competence of Jamaica's planters, the credibility of British policymakers, and the reputation of Jamaican blacks. As we have seen, the policies that guided emancipation and its aftermath were formulated on the basis of liberal democratic conceptions of human behavior and aspirations. Involved, therefore, in the apparent failure of those policies were transformations of thought as well as life. The answer to the question what went wrong in Jamaica's new economy had consequences beyond its particular boundaries and in domains other than the economic.

King Sugar's Fall

Richard Hill, an Afro-Jamaican who had served as a special magistrate since 1835, contributed one of the reports attached to Governor Barkly's 1854 dispatch to the Colonial Office. In a sweeping overview of Jamaica's economic history, Hill argued that the introduction of free trade in colonial produce, not the emancipation of the slaves, was the real cause of Jamaican distress. Indeed, there had always been a roulettelike aspect to the island's sugar business; decline and distress were evident even in the earliest records of the island. His conclusion that "insolvency was not a casual occurrence but a constant calamity" was illustrated by the facts that 177 estates had been sold for debt between 1772 and 1792 and 92 others were in the hands of their creditors; that there was a loss of confidence in the industry again in 1804, and consequently another credit crunch; that in 1807 one-quarter of the sugar estates in the colony had been up for sale. In contrast, emancipation, by relieving the industry of the "dead weight" of slavery, which was "perishable capital," freed its energies and resources for innovation. Certainly paying day labor was less expensive than maintaining a large body of slaves. If the supply of labor had been sufficiently flexible—"that is to say, little when little was enough and abundant when such was required"—the sugar estates would have been profitable after emancipation and able to replace hand labor with machinery "without raising wages beyond a subsistence rate." But even so, "there was really an excellent spirit in the planter when the magistrates made their last report in 1846; the staple industry was upon the increase; agricultural societies were promoted; science was resorted to to augment the productiveness of the surface; the maxim was to cultivate well; a hopeful feeling predominated, and the hazards of the present were cheerfully encountered for the promises of the future."[4]

Rudely intruding onto this hopeful scene of innovation and enterprise came the Sugar Duties Act of 1846. By gradually equalizing the duties on foreign and British colonial produce, this law threw West Indian staples into direct competition with the slave-grown produce of Cuba and Brazil. The increased availability of the product in the

British market and the fact that slaveholders could undersell their free labor competitors meant a lower price. By 1854 the price in Britain, exclusive of duty, was twenty shillings per hundredweight. Jamaican planters insisted that they could not earn a profit at this price and that in most instances it amounted to less than their production costs.[5]

From Hill's discussion one can discern the major propositions offered to explain the decline of Jamaica's postemancipation economy, which elicited conflicting contemporary interpretations (or were given different emphasis) and which have continued to dominate the debate among twentieth-century historians as well: that the postemancipation abandonments were part of a longer secular decline already in progress; that free labor was cheaper and more flexible than slave labor; that slave compensation money should have provided the capital necessary for readjustment to free labor; that the surviving planters were optimistic, progressive, and willing innovators; that free trade policy was the *coup de grâce* to their hopes of recovery; that ultimately the planters' ability to recruit and control labor was the key to their survival. On one point, at least, all could agree: contrary to Hill's hope, the labor supply was not pliant; little was *not* offered when little was enough, nor was it abundant when such was required.

There is evidence to support Hill's contention that some of the contraction in Jamaica's sugar production was evident well before abolition and for causes unrelated to emancipation as such. The apogee of the island's sugar output came in 1805, when 99,600 tons were shipped to Britain. This peak was framed by a fifteen-year "golden age," 1801–15, during which the Haitian slave revolt and independence together with the Napoleonic Wars induced supply problems that inflated prices and encouraged expansion throughout the West Indies. In 1820 British West Indian colonies were still supplying about 40 percent of the sugar cane reaching the world market, and Jamaica was producing about half of that (see fig. 4.1). By the eve of slavery abolition, sugar and coffee production had been pushed deep into the interior parishes and onto marginal lands everywhere.[6]

The fifteen years following Napoleon's defeat, 1816–30, brought new problems, however. The abolition of the slave trade in 1807 had left Jamaica dependent on the biological reproduction of its labor force, yet during that fourteen-year period the slave population declined by 9.4 percent. Average annual production fell off proportionately, more than 7,000 tons, or just under 9 percent. Like pincers, the labor shortage and falling prices forced short-handed estates on marginal soils into an ever-tightening compass. As one special magistrate observed,

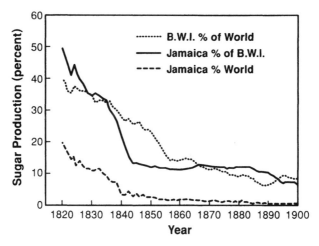

Figure 4.1. Shares of Cane Sugar Production, 1820–1900. Data from Deerr, *History of Sugar*, 2:35–40.

these estates extracted their meager profits "out of the very hearts' gore" of the slaves. With the advent of emancipation, their days were numbered.[7]

Jamaica's average annual sugar crop during the apprenticeship (1834–38) was almost 23 percent less than that produced during the decade preceding abolition (see table 4.1). The first ten years of freedom, 1839–48, saw a further slide to less than half (49 percent) of the preabolition production level. Although the decline was less rapid during the second decade and even rebounded slightly during the 1860s, by the eve of the Morant Bay Rebellion in 1865 the annual product stood at just 38 percent of the preabolition level. Therefore, though it is true that a secular decline in Jamaican production from the dizzying heights of the Napoleonic era was under way even before the abolition of slavery, it is also clear that bigger plunges came with apprenticeship in 1834 and after complete emancipation in 1838. The island produced roughly 20 percent of the world's cane sugar in 1820, 11 percent in 1830, 3 percent in 1840, and less than 2 percent after 1851 (see table 4.1 and fig. 4.1).

Furthermore, though the free labor period saw a 35 percent decline in sugar production throughout the British West Indies, Jamaica's 51 percent fall placed it among the severest cases. Its decline was greater not only in absolute terms but relative to its sister colonies. Moreover,

Jamaican production continued to fall even as the others rebounded or held their own. In 1825–34, Jamaica produced more than a third of British West Indian sugar annually, compared, for example, with Barbados's 7.5 percent. By the 1850s, Barbados had surpassed Jamaica in share of annual output. By the end of the century their preabolition positions had almost exactly reversed: Barbados's share was about 20 percent, while Jamaica's was 16 percent (see table 4.1).[8]

Therefore, while adverse movements of prices and capital in international markets may explain some of Jamaica's distress, its sluggish performance in comparison with its neighbors facing similar problems leaves the issue of causation unresolved. Indeed, there is considerable evidence that much of the initial decline in sugar production, that occurring during the apprenticeship years, might well be charged to management decisions by the planters rather than solely to difficulties with the labor force. Special magistrates reported from all regions of the island that planters, apprehensive about the new system and anticipating labor shortages later, deliberately reduced the number of canes planted and harvested other plants prematurely. The effects of such decisions in the 1830s would reach well into the future, affecting later planting as well as harvests. Thus at least some of the loss of product was the result of the planters' self-inflicted wounds.[9]

The bulk of the decline in production came after apprenticeship, however, and appears to have been caused by difficulties peculiar to Jamaica, in particular to the struggle between its planter class and its black labor force. All indicators suggest that the critical period of that struggle and of planters' adjustment to the new regime fell during the

Table 4.1. Changes in Sugar Production in Key Periods, 1825–1868

Years	World		British West Indies	
	Metric Tons (avg.)	Change (%)	Metric Tons (avg.)	Change (%)
1825–34	533,365		181,997	
1835–38	599,695	12.4	159,928	−12.1
1839–48	894,781	49.2	119,155	−25.5
1849–58	1,209,531	35.2	140,193	17.1
1859–68	1,459,947	20.7	177,350	26.5

Sources: Moreno Fraginals, *El ingenio: complejo económico social cubano del azúcar*, 35–40; Deerr, *History of Sugar*, 2:193–203.

first decade following complete emancipation, before the full impact of free trade. By the time Barkly toured the island in 1854—the same year the equalization of sugar duties was completed—the pattern of the transformation had been set and the basic outlines of Jamaican economic history for the next half century could be discerned.

Distinctions in crops and geography are also important to comprehending Jamaica's economic transformation. Although Kingston was the main port for the island's commerce, high transport costs and convenience dictated that planters use regional ports to embark their staple exports. Kingston, Old Harbour, Port Morant, and Morant Bay served the southern and eastern end of the island; Annotto Bay, Port Maria, and Port Antonio the northeast; St. Ann's Bay and Falmouth the north-central parishes. Montego Bay, Lucea, and Savannah-la-Mar served the northwestern and southwestern end of the island. Together with other information, trade data from these ports suggest trends in production for different regions and crops.

Sugar estates, which employed about 50 percent of the slave labor force in 1832, were concentrated on the most fertile soils of the northwestern coasts, the interior river valleys, the Vere district on the southern coast, and along the southeastern corner of St. Thomas-in-the-East. Another forty-five thousand slaves (14 percent) worked the coffee plantations, and forty thousand more, the cattle pens. Coffee properties (with the exception of those in Manchester), cattle pens, and many smaller sugar estates tended to locate in the island's interior or on the less fertile, hilly areas of the coastal lowlands. Many of these less well endowed areas were being abandoned even before abolition,

Jamaica		Barbados		Cuba	
Metric Tons (avg.)	Change (%)	Metric Tons (avg.)	Change (%)	Metric Tons (avg.)	Change (%)
61,244		13,616		86,761	
47,190	−22.9	18,562	36.3	120,358	38.7
29,881	−36.7	15,320	−17.5	186,868	55.3
23,021	−23.0	27,904	82.1	376,020	101.2
23,367	1.5	34,960	25.3	524,663	39.5

as indicated by the movement of slaves from the interior parishes to the west.[10]

After producing their largest crop ever in 1814, Jamaican coffee planters witnessed an inexorable decline for most of the rest of the century. During the interval between abolition and free trade legislation, 465 coffee plantations, which had engrossed 188,000 acres and employed 26,830 slaves, were abandoned.[11] Trade figures from the island's regional ports indicate that coffee exports fell by 76 percent between 1834 and 1850. Indeed, the major coffee parishes on the western end of the island appear to have been hardest hit by abolition, and by mid-century almost 70 percent of coffee exports came out of Kingston and other southeastern ports.[12] This had the effect of reinforcing sugar as the island's main export earner and employer, even though it too was in decline.

Sugar estates differently situated, regionally and economically, were affected differently by the loss of slave labor. Emancipation appears to have left the western parishes indisputably the predominant sugar sector in Jamaica, and the larger, absentee-owned estates, the predominant producers. Most Jamaican sugar continued to be shipped from its northwestern and north-central ports, suggesting that estates in or contiguous to the parishes in which those ports were located weathered the storms of abolition and free trade much better than others. Indeed, almost half the island's total sugar crop in 1850 was collected from the area between Falmouth and Montego Bay. At a time when production for the island as a whole was less than half what it had been before abolition, these estates were shipping cargoes almost 60 percent the size of preabolition cargoes.[13]

The regional pattern of declining exports is consistent with, but not precisely proportionate to, the pattern of abandonment of estates. Between 1836 and 1858, 35 percent of the sugar estates in the island's central parishes (Middlesex), 40 percent in the west (Cornwall), and 63 percent in the east (Surrey) stopped production.[14] Yet, the decline in output does not appear to have been proportionate to the attrition in numbers of estates, suggesting that larger, better-situated estates took up the slack. For example, the ports at Morant Bay and Port Morant shipped a slightly larger proportion of the island's sugar in 1850 (11.9 percent) than in 1834 (11 percent) despite the drastic decline in the number of contiguous estates.

It appears likely, then, that changes in the world market for sugar—that is, falling prices and the loss of protection—combined with the loss of control over labor to push marginal and smaller estates offstage during the first decade after emancipation. But the demise of some estates may have actually strengthened the survivors by making more land and labor available at cheaper prices. Barkly, for example, describes such a process at work in St. Thomas-in-the-Vale, and the history of Worthy Park and other estates reveals that they did indeed profit from their neighbors' misfortunes.[15] Nevertheless, it is also clear that the consolidation of the estate labor forces did not go very far, nor did it return Jamaica to a competitive position in the world market, even in comparison with other British colonies. In any event, external market forces merely set the stage for an internal struggle between former slaveholders and former slaves to determine the nature as well as the success of production in a free labor economy.

Costing Out Slavery and Freedom

To most contemporary analysts, control of labor was the dominant internal factor determining the profitability and thus survivability of an estate.[16] Of course, the nature and means of controlling labor was the fundamental and controversial difference between slavery and freedom. Theoretically, slave labor could be applied when, where, and under whatever conditions the planter chose, at a cost determined primarily by the need to sustain the life of the slave and reproduce the labor force. Under slavery some estates were able to achieve a labor yield of two hogsheads of sugar for each worker, but one finds no examples of estates in the postemancipation period able to match that productivity. For example, thirty-two estates (managed by nineteen owners and thirteen lessors) reported to the Colonial Office in 1847 an average yield of one hogshead per laborer.[17]

The advantage of free labor was supposed to lie in the fact that the planter would not have to sustain the subsistence cost of a worker who was only needed seasonally. This had been one of the basic assumptions of emancipation policy, which Henry Taylor reiterated in 1840 when he pointed out that the wages of free laborers (then 1s. 6d.) were still much lower than payments formerly made to slave jobbers (about 2s. 6d.). The advantages of slave labor to the planter, he observed, appeared to be only "in the continuity and the certainty of his supply of labor."[18] But that was precisely the difficulty. The theoretical advantages of free labor were not immediately evident to planters, who considered *continuity* and *certainty* the essential attributes of labor recruitment and control.

Planters' expenditures for slave maintenance were usually covered by receipts from rum sales (a by-product of sugar manufacture) and cattle sales within the island, were handled through a British agent, and thus were relatively invisible. The payment of wages, however, was highly visible, frequent, and pressing. A cursory survey of the register of the reports of accounts current from several Jamaican estates reveals that pitifully small sums were expended to purchase food and clothing for slaves. Indeed, sugar planters provided so small a portion of the total food, clothing, and household furnishings slaves consumed that it provoked their comment when adverse conditions necessitated such allocations. Medical care was the most consistent item in these accounts, and many of the foodstuffs, for example, beef, were obviously for the white staff and possibly the black headmen rather than field hands. For example, Tilston Estate had 477 slaves in 1830, on whom it expended £355 for maintenance, while receiving £2,416 for its exports; thus maintenance was 15 percent of receipts. By contrast, in 1841 Aboukir Plantation expended £1,211 for wages and received £1,489 for its exports; thus its wages were 82 percent of receipts.[19]

Unfortunately, the accounts current reports are so fragmentary that it is difficult to determine any consistent pattern of wages in relation to income. Nevertheless, the preponderance of evidence suggests that wages bore down much more heavily on estate budgets than had slave maintenance. Michael Craton finds that slave maintenance costs for Worthy Park, for example, rarely exceeded one-third of the total expenditures, which were in turn only one-half or less of the revenues received. In the early 1840s wages consumed about 50 percent of the estate's revenue. Craton's examination of wage records for 117 weeks out of 214 between 1 January 1842 and 14 February 1846 shows that free wage labor was "almost twice as expensive as the cost of labor in the last days of slavery." Labor costs rose from 30 percent of total cost of production to over 60 percent. Of course, this reflected not only higher labor costs but reduced expenses in other areas, for example, insurance, freight, management, commissions paid on sales, and in the case of Worthy Park the fact that no attorney's commissions had to be paid because the owner was resident during these years.[20]

These last items suggest further difficulties with broad comparisons between systems of slave and free labor. Strictly speaking, it may have been cheaper to run a slave than to hire a free worker, if one only considered the direct cost of slave maintenance versus wages. But aside from the charges against the investment in slave property, it is clear that the institution required, or was encumbered by other expenses necessitated by, a social system founded on coercion. Supervisory costs were high because physical coercion was the only means of commanding labor or securing the labor force. Taxes were higher because the slave estates monopolized taxable real and personal property values. Freed people paid taxes; slaves were the basis on which taxes were charged to an estate.

Special magistrate Hall Pringle's analysis of the accounts of a sugar estate in Clarendon, formerly comprising four hundred slaves and three thousand acres of land, illustrates both the problems and the nuances of comparative analysis. Pringle found, consistent with the figures of Craton and others, that the cost of slave maintenance was equal to just one-third of the wages later paid the free worker. Although his figures did show that the cost of production under freedom was, in fact, higher (by 2.4 percent) than the cost under slavery, Pringle argued that recalculating these figures to reflect the £528 in compensation and interest that the planter received for his four hundred slaves during their four years of apprenticeship would reveal free labor to be cheaper than slave labor. But there are items of interest in Pringle's analysis other than the aggregate totals. For example, the estate paid 88 percent less in taxes after emancipation than before. This deduction reflected the fact that only land tax, quitrent, and a small poll tax on stock were levied during the 1840s, as compared with the additional levies during slavery of poll taxes on slaves and stock, and road taxes. Another major reduction (45 percent) was from the salaries and maintenance of supervisory personnel during the slavery period, which sustained one overseer, a clerk, and seven bookkeepers. After emancipation, only an overseer, a clerk, and two bookkeepers were required.[21]

It is clear, too, that some of the increased labor costs were offset by the deletion of jobbing gangs. The rationale for using jobbers had been to save the estate's labor force and to assist short-handed estates, but these were no longer an imperative with free laborers. Not only were supervisory costs less after emancipation because of the reduced need for slavery-style coercion and control, but it was now unnecessary to maintain large numbers of white personnel. Slave-era deficiency laws required estates to employ one white male for a given number of slaves for security against revolts; in a free labor system the responsibility for security shifted to the state. Indeed, Governor Sligo reported that many discharged white estate employees enlisted in the police after 1834.[22]

Naturally, since the wage bill constituted the major remaining item in their expense accounts, planters directed their attention to reducing its impact. Bargaining between planters and their workers over the wage rate had begun in the apprenticeship period and continued well into the postemancipation years. In 1840 the Colonial Office reported prematurely that this bargaining had subsided, although wages were by no means uniform or consistent at that point. Estimates from the special magistrates' reports showed wages to be higher than in 1838, when 1s. 8d. per diem was the highest reported. Now this figure was the lowest, and wages as high as 2s. 6d. had been found.[23]

During the early years of the postemancipation era planters had been unable to dictate wage rates. Planters in St. Dorothy Parish, for example, had met in 1838 and agreed to set wages at 1s. per diem. The planters' solidarity broke down rapidly, however, as Alexandre Bravo gave his workers 1s. 3d. at Kelly's and was quickly matched by the attorney at Lodge. Bravo then upped his offer to 1s. 6d., which became the established rate. In St. Mary, meanwhile, William F. Marlton reported that workers struck when the planters tried to reduce their wages from 1s. 6d. to 1s. sterling. At a subsequent meeting in Port Maria the planters were unable to unite on a rate and so eventually gave in to the strikers, who stayed out until the old rates were restored.[24]

Some planters, however, tried to reduce the rates indirectly by switching from day rates to job and task work.[25] Job work was a certain amount of work for a specified sum: for example, seventy-two shillings to clear six acres of cane. Task work was a fixed amount of work to be performed *within a given day* for wages; for example, seventy or eighty cane holes for two shillings. The main difference was that job work could be undertaken by a squad of workers over several days, while a task was assigned to an individual and amounted to a standardization of work pace. Often laborers hired others to work for them in the job work system (something like subcontracting). Under the task system, daily wage rates could be reduced de facto by increasing the size of the tasks. Nonetheless, the task system appears to have been attractive to both the laborer and the planter because it involved less direct supervision.[26]

By the mid-1840s, however, day wages had been reduced throughout the island, with the apparent approval of the Colonial Office. Successive failures of the workers' provision crops because of drought and the lack of alternative sources of employment were cited as the most likely causes. But over the long term, it is likely that the drastic reduction in the number of estates bidding for workers, together with increasing numbers of African and East Indian indentured laborers, affected the supply side of the wages-labor equation. Although planters in sparsely populated interior parishes were unable at first to reduce their wages to the levels prevailing on the seacoast, eventually the modal wage for an adult sugar worker fell to one shilling per diem. In Manchester, meanwhile, wages for coffee pickers dropped 25 percent, from one shilling at peak season to nine pence. In some cases, however, the nominal wage rate was reported to be misleading, because "the day" actually worked was shorter than the traditional nine hours; but for that longer day workers demanded a higher rate.[27]

Nevertheless, a reduction from 1s. 6d. per diem to 1s. represented a 33 percent reduction in the wage rate. A reduction to 9d. represented a decline of 50 percent. A wage rate of 1s. 6d. sterling would mean £17 8s. received by the laborer annually, assuming the 232 workdays that had been standard during apprenticeship. But a wage rate of 1s. meant an annual income of £11 12s., and 9d. meant only £8 14s. for the year.

When one compares these rates with the cost of living during this period, it becomes clear that workers were forced to supplement their earnings from other sources. Captain J. W. Pringle's report on West Indian prisons, for example, showed that the cost for a prisoner feeding himself in 1837 was approximately 3s. 6d. per week (or 6d. per diem). Given this subsistence standard, a wage of 1s., and the typical four-day work week, a worker could barely feed himself from his estate earnings. Even with a maximum work week of five and one-half days and top wages of 1s. 6d., the prisoner's boarding standard amounted to 42 percent of a worker's income. Obviously, without supplementary income, the average black Jamaican worker did not and could not eat that well.[28]

Even so, 3s. 6d. per week does not appear to have been an excessive standard, considering that *white* prisoners spent 10s. 6d. on food. Using other reference groups gives an even higher estimate. For example, the weekly ration for the troops of the West India Regiment required expenditures of 6s. 11d. in 1840, 5s. 5d. in 1860, and 5s. 6d. in 1863 (all of these figures excluding their rum allowance). Of course, troops used mostly fresh beef in their diet, while black Jamaicans favored pork; but according to the *Blue Book* figures, salt pork was equal in cost to beef during most of this period and sometimes even more expensive.[29]

Even at reduced wages, planters were often either unwilling or unable to meet their wage bills. There were numerous reports from the late forties through the fifties and sixties of nonpayment of wages owed. For example, the Baptist missionary Walter Dendy reported during 1848 that many workers had not been paid for weeks. In 1854, special magistrate Charles Lake wrote that nonpayment of wages had become a major problem on the estates. Indeed, in many instances laborers took their case to court in order to secure the wages due them. Many observers concluded, therefore, that the difficulty estates experienced in getting labor was due primarily to the inability of the proprietors to pay for work done. A *New York Daily Tribune* correspondent wrote in 1854 that estates that paid wages regularly and on time had no difficulty obtaining labor.[30]

In contrast to some planters in the American South, however, there is no evidence that Jamaican planters resisted the wage labor system as such. Of course, they wanted to pay the lowest possible price for their labor, and often they did not meet their payrolls, but there are no examples of Jamaican planters reacting with a genuine psychological revulsion at paying wages.[31] This suggests that slavery as a social system—as opposed to a system for commanding labor—was less critical to the Jamaican planter's world-view than for former slaveowners elsewhere. The high degree of absenteeism, the fact that many estates were managed by attorneys responsible for several properties, the relatively low incidence of family life among those most directly responsible for plantation management (the overseers and bookkeepers), the fact that even resident white families often thought of Britain as home—all these factors may have contributed to the relative lack of commitment to the social values of a slave regime and thus promoted flexibility toward change. Of course, this is not to say that the planters' responses to emancipation did not involve reactionary attempts to retain features of the former system as well as a receptiveness to innovation. But their reactionary tendencies appear to have been confined more narrowly to labor management issues rather than social relations in general. To a greater extent than one finds in the American South, for example, Jamaican planters looked to the bottom line.

Thus planters responded to the depressed prices in the sugar market during the decades following emancipation with a variety of managerial, technical, and entrepreneurial innovations. One such change involved experiments with the ratio of rum to sugar, which was susceptible to considerable manipulation. When prices for the former were high and those for the latter low, many planters responded by increasing their rum production. Indeed, this strategy for responding to world market conditions continued to be used well into the twentieth century, with some properties soon becoming known as "rum estates."[32]

A similar strategy can be discerned with cattle pens. In the early 1840s many estates began to emphasize meat production, a part of their operation that previously had been only secondary. During slavery, most pens were owned by and/or closely associated with sugar estates. They supplied the working stock for the sugar factories and draft animals for the cane fields; old, worn-out stock was fattened, butchered, and sold to the estates for meat. Even when under common ownership and management, however, the pen accounts were usually maintained separately from those of the estates. Since pens required far fewer workers than the estates and their labor regime was much less onerous, they experienced far fewer labor problems in the postemancipation period.[33]

Thus, in 1842 John Blagrove reported that Orange Valley Estate was clearing land to plant guinea grass rather than cane, and the new pastures would be hired out to fatten cattle. Indeed, according to Blagrove, what little profit Orange Valley Estate had earned the previous year could be credited to income from the attached Belle Air and Pear Tree Bottom Pen.[34]

Similarly, by 1846 the butchery attached to Harding Hall was reported to be carrying the entire estate.[35] Between September 1840 and July 1841 Fort George Pen increased its meat sales by 147 percent (from £7,499 to £18,493) and the proportion of its income from meat sales by 58 percent; by 1853 it had opened its own butchery. As a result of such shifts, apparently, a new occupation was created as transient butchers appeared in the countryside buying animals from the pens and slaughtering them for sale. But the expansion of the meat industry was so rapid that by the mid-1850s prices were falling and profits were shrinking.[36] Nevertheless, as with the rum-sugar ratio, increased emphasis on meat production became a common part of the planters' repertoire of responses to the difficulties of the postemancipation era.

Sugar still remained the main source of profits, however, and it exacted the greatest demand for labor. Any innovations having significant impact on the general economy would have to occur in its production or manufacture. Innovations were aimed at reducing labor requirements in the fields by substituting plowing for the more arduous, labor-intensive cane hole digging and at increasing cane yields per acre. In the factory, the objective was to increase the yield of sugar per ton of canes. Steam power was recommended for faster and finer grinding of the canes, and the vacuum pan and other devices were recommended for more efficient evaporation of cane juice. During his tenure in the early 1840s, Governor Elgin was especially active in encouraging an "active spirit of invention."[37] He and other observers affirmed Richard Hill's contention that Jamaican planters were receptive to innovation and willing to adopt new methods and machinery.[38]

But there were numerous obstacles to the introduction of new machinery in Jamaica. The diversity of the Jamaican landscape made general adoption of the plow problematic, for example. The heavy soils and hilly terrain of the wet parishes (those that received heavy annual rainfall) made plowing difficult and often impossible. And although the lighter soils of the dry parishes were suitable for plowing, estates there tended to make more extensive use of ratooning (i.e., taking successive crops from the same roots rather than replanting annually) and thus had less need for the plow. There is also evidence that workers resisted the adoption of the plow because such tools reduced the need for their labor and thus for wages. Consequently both Barkly and Elgin identified the control of or cooperation of labor as an essential prerequisite to the successful adoption of machinery.[39]

Several waterwheels were in use in Jamaica. Hanover, for example, was too wet for growing guinea grass for cattle, so waterwheels were common there. But few steam engines were introduced, because for many planters it made little sense to invest in expensive machinery that no one on the island would be able to fix. For that reason, those who did buy steam engines chose models of very simple design.[40] Others calculated that given the market for sugar, their expected return would not justify the investments; either prices were too low or, as one planter observed, the fact that only the coarse muscovado sugar could be sold in the United Kingdom nullified the advantages of more efficient factory processes.[41]

The most important obstacle to technological innovation, however, was the shortage of capital. One purpose of the slave compensation money—of which Jamaica received 30 percent (£6,161,927)—besides assuaging the planters' resistance to emancipation, was to fund the transition to new labor-saving, capital-intensive systems of production. But the impression of most contemporaries was that British merchants, who held mortgages and other debts on Jamaican properties, received the bulk of the compensation money. British merchants had been the indispensable middlemen and creditors of the slave system throughout the West Indies. They accepted sugar on consignment from the planter, handled its sale to British refiners and grocers, and—after deducting commissions and fees (about 3 percent) and the principal of and interest on outstanding debts—credited or debited the balance to the planter's standing account. Debits consisted of loans extended during the year toward slave purchases, plantation supplies, personal expenditures, and annuity payments due family or heirs in Britain. In addition to these short-term debts, large numbers of plantations were mortgaged. By 1832 almost a fifth of all Jamaican estates were in receivership or had been repossessed by their mortgagee.[42]

Kathleen Butler's examination of the largest slave compensation claimants reveals that 15 percent of Jamaican slave compensation was paid directly to twenty-three major merchant firms. Having cleared their books, many were loath to reinvest in the sugar islands; like John Gladstone, they found more attractive lures in American and British rails, the East Indian trade, and South America. Consequently, as one Colonial Office analyst concluded, in such cases compensation payments actually amounted to the withdrawal of capital from the islands.[43]

There was also increased capital investment and money circulation within the island, but it was not enough, apparently, to realize the major restructuring of the industry that some policymakers envisioned. The compensation money that found its way to island residents was often reinvested, but more often in buying new estates or expanding existing ones than for technological improvements. Those planters who signed their compensation checks over to their merchant-factors might have gained renewed liquidity and thus creditworthiness, but they too were likely to seize the opportunity for renewed speculation rather than modernization of production.[44] In any event, most planters, far from buying new labor-saving equipment, were unable even to meet their payrolls regularly. By the late 1840s the brief bubble of optimism generated by the flow of compensation cash was broken by the deepening distress of the Jamaican economy. The problem, however, was not the lack of cash, as some believed, but the lack of credit. Thus Henry Taylor's acid comment in a marginal note to a proposal for establishing a Jamaican government bank to serve the planters' needs is quite apt: the planters, he observed, were in need "rather of the *subject* in matter of credit than of channels for conveying it."[45]

One source of new capital investment and more energetic management was the attorneys, merchants, and proprietors resident on the island. Absentee ownership had been the traditional whipping boy for the evils of the plantation system. It was contended that not only would an owner's management be more careful, efficient, and conducive to the long-term prospects of the properties but the large fees presently paid to attorneys could be diverted by resident owners into improvements. During the 1840s the *Falmouth Post,* edited by colored assemblyman John Castello, sponsored a sharp campaign to drive absentee owners out of Jamaica. "The great body of our proprietors are non-resident, and whatever the land yields in clear revenue, is carried out of the island and spent elsewhere. Under this system Jamaica must ever be poor." The attorney system that absenteeism required was condemned as wasteful and inefficient, "a hireling, irresponsible agency," "a semi-feudalism." The great attorneys, scorned as arrogant and parasitic, were tagged with the moniker "golden feet." Castello urged absentee owners to lease their properties to their overseers or other Jamaica residents.[46]

Reports suggest that there were indeed numerous sales to resident proprietors during the late 1830s, 1840s, and early 1850s. A number of resident slaveowners—mainly small proprietors and attorneys—used their compensation awards to buy land, much of it smaller sugar properties, coffee plantations, pens, or even portions of estates. Scanning the 1840s rosters of the Jamaica Assembly, one finds a number of new men emerging into prominence among the planter class; some, such as Henry Westmorland, were newly arrived investors, while others, such as John Blagrove, were newly resident absentees. But although they were politically significant, the economic impact of their purchases on the sugar industry was slight; the overall rate of absentee ownership did not change appreciably.[47]

In any event, the experience of resident owners does not suggest that this could ever have been an adequate source of new capital for the Jamaican economy or of model management for the estates. By the mid-1840s, Alexandre Bravo was proclaiming himself one of the largest and wealthiest of the island's resident proprietors. Owner of Marley Mount, Knight's, and Mount Moses in St. Dorothy, Vere, and Clarendon, respectively, he received £12,588 compensation for 593 slaves. The son of a wealthy Kingston merchant-planter, Bravo also inherited a share of his father's slave compensation money. He immediately used his legacy to purchase a number of estates: Deeside and Cabbage Hall in Vere and Clarendon, respectively, in 1837 and Kelly's and Cocoa Walk in St. Dorothy Parish from Governor Sligo sometime later. After spending £30,000 on improvements, Bravo found his working capital insufficient to withstand the total crop failures caused by devastating droughts in the early 1840s. By the late 1840s he was heavily in debt. Even his attempt to turn Kelly's into a cattle pen failed. By the 1850s he was being sustained by government patronage alone and still seeking ways to extricate himself from massive debts. Ironically, he was eventually appointed assignee of the Insolvent Debtors Court, an appointment he begged to relieve his own perilous financial condition.[48]

Hugh A. Whitelocke was somewhat more fortunate than Bravo, but he too fell on hard times. In 1846 Whitelocke purchased Glasgow Estate for £5,500 cash. Anticipating that the asking price would be inflated if it were known that the prospective purchaser was a resident of the island, he sought to make his purchase through a third party in England. Whitelocke also purchased Morelands for £2,050 and leased other estates. The passage of free trade legislation gave him cause to hesitate about these investments, but he proceeded with the purchases, nonetheless. He moved his residence to Glasgow, obtained thirty-nine indentured East Indian laborers, ostensibly through his political connections, and got married. But by the late forties, Whitelocke reported that he was struggling to meet the high expenses of his new properties and expressed some regret about his investments. "I have overdone the thing by being too greedy in speculations."[49] In later years Whitelocke became a major conservative political figure in Jamaica, and although the evidence is less clear than with Bravo, it is probable that patronage helped ease his financial difficulties as well.

Although Whitelocke may have represented the new blood infusing the sugar economy during its brief period of optimism in the 1840s, he also reflected some of the more reactionary attitudes of the old planter class. He wrote enthusiastically about the East Indian indentured laborers, or "coolies," who constituted the core workforce on both his own estates and those for which he was attorney. The quality of his new workers that he appreciated most and most frequently contrasted with the character of the blacks was what he called their "docility."[50] Undoubtedly, the value Whitelocke put on maintaining control of his "docile" workers, having them responsive to his every command, was representative of planters generally. New money was not in itself sufficient to change old ways.

According to free labor theory, the wage payment was the entire and sufficient mechanism for exercising control over the worker. But planters feared—and not without reason it turned out—that wages would be an insufficient instrument of control under Jamaican conditions. Edmund B. Lyon, one of the Afro-Jamaican special magistrates, reported from St. Thomas-in-the-East in 1836 that he saw little hope that sugar production could be maintained at the end of the apprenticeship because of the workers' opportunities for independent farming, as well as the attractions of other less onerous, less debilitating, and less seasonal labor, such as that on coffee plantations and pens. "In my opinion, the only probability the sugar planter has of continuing cultivation of any extent after the termination of the apprenticeship consists in his seizing the golden opportunity afforded him in the remaining term of compulsory labor, of creating in his laborers a strong local attachment to their present homes and lands and by identifying their interests with his own success."[51]

The planters, however, chose to do just the opposite. They seized upon the houses and provision grounds that apprentices had occupied gratis during slavery as an additional control over their workers as well as a way to reduce their operating expenses. Generally slave housing in Jamaica had been built and maintained by the slaves themselves, with little if any supervision or financial and technical assistance from the planters. Constructed according to African-inspired designs, typically the huts' walls were made of wattle and daub (wood sticks, mud, and plantain leaves) and their roofs of palm thatch. Encompassing an area no more than fifteen feet square, they generally consisted of two rooms, sometimes separated by a hall, with an outdoor lean-to kitchen, a dirt floor, shuttered windows, and an unvented fire. Their flimsy construction made them especially vulnerable to destruction by high winds and fires—both of which were frequent—and their occupants susceptible to exposure during cold and damp weather. Furnishings were sparse: assorted calabashes, pots, and gourds; a table and chairs; beds, made up of boards covered with homemade matting. But they were home; their surrounding yards provided both kitchen gardens and burial plots for family and kin. On many plantations they clustered in African-style compounds with a common yard shared by kinspeople. It was not uncommon for slaves to secure their houses with homemade locks or bolts—visible, if incongruous, symbols of possession and autonomy.[52]

Rather than exploit the freed people's attachment to these homes, planters chose to risk alienating them by collecting rents. Moreover, resentment at this usurpation was deepened by the fact that the rents charged were so variable and collected so arbitrarily. In some cases rent was charged to the family, in others, to each member of the

A Peasant's Hut

family. Both houses and grounds were rented in some cases, while in others grounds were rented separately. A report in 1842 from Port Royal indicated that rent charges throughout that small parish varied from situations in which just the husband and wife paid rent (1s. per week) to cases where working children were charged as well. In 1844 another report from Port Royal described charges for cottages and grounds of 2s. per week for married men and 1s. per week for all other adults. An 1842 report from St. James indicated that the rent varied between 2s. and 2s. 6d. on most estates and that in cases where no rent was charged, wages were reduced to 1s.[53]

Lord Seaford instructed his attorney McNeil to distinguish between rent for cottages and their surrounding gardens and charges for the distant provision grounds, with low rents being asked for the former and higher for the latter. Seaford's objective apparently was to encourage laborers to stay on the estates by exacting a higher money rent for the provision grounds than for the cottages. In fact, at Lord Holland's suggestion McNeil had attempted to begin the system of renting houses and gardens even during apprenticeship, but these efforts had been premature and unsuccessful; the apprentices had simply refused to rent the cottages.[54]

After emancipation, rent charges could be backed up by the threat of eviction; and the rents sugar estates collected were substantial, sufficient in many cases to defray a significant portion of their operating expenses. In an 1842 sample of thirty-two properties, rent averaged 5 percent of estimated sugar receipts. Rent in most cases fell between 3 percent and 7 percent of receipts but on one estate amounted to 17 percent. Ten years later, fewer than half of the sampled sugar estates (fifteen of thirty-three) reported rent collections. Rent as a percentage of sugar receipts ranged from less than 0.1 percent to 6.9 percent and averaged just under 2 percent. For most estates rent amounted to between 1 percent and 3 percent of total receipts. Rent collections were reported by none of the coffee plantations and by only three of the pens, with all but one of these showing negligible amounts (0.4 percent and 0.6 percent of receipts).[55]

Clearly, during the first ten years of the postemancipation period, rent charges contributed substantially to paying the operating expenses of sugar estates, but not thereafter. Worthy Park, for example, began charging rents in 1838; they amounted to £342, or 15 percent of its wage bill in 1839. In 1840 Worthy Park collected £2,570 for rent, or more than its total wage payment. By 1842, however, it was able to collect only £50 in rent.[56]

Similarly, Fort George Pen employed eighty-seven laborers, of whom fifty-five rented houses and grounds at 6s. per month, twenty-seven rented just the grounds at 4s. per month, and five rented houses alone for 4s. The total rents at Fort George amounted to £353, which was 12 percent of its receipts that year. In 1842 Fort George expended 25 percent of its total gross receipts on labor (£490 out of £1,962). And although only eight people paid rent, their payments constituted 11.4 percent of its total receipts and recouped 45.7 percent of its wage costs. In 1843, sixty-four laborers paid rent, which amounted to 6.8 percent of total receipts. As late as 1848, seventy-seven people were reported as paying rent totaling £122, thirty-four were listed as paying nothing, and fifty-seven others were listed in arrears.[57]

It was clear that these rent charges were designed not simply to reduce the expenses of the estate but also to manipulate the worker. A Colonial Office analyst concluded as early as 1840 that these charges were not a true rent but really a "fine" for not working, because those who worked on the estate usually were charged less rent than were nonemployees.[58] Even Governor Metcalfe, generally considered friendly to the planters' interests, agreed with this assessment: "The chief cause of the misunderstanding respecting rent is that the landlord cares little for rent and solely regards labour. Were the rent taken for its own sake distinctly it would soon be settled on a proper footing."[59] According to Metcalfe, in their attempt to tie rent to labor, the planters altered the charges on "every failure of labour," thus creating constant disputes between workers and management.

Generally, the weekly rent was deducted from the weekly wages "and [was] often diminished or increased according to the continuance and punctuality of labor or the reverse." A few planters had referees set rent on houses and gardens that were charged irrespective of family size. But generally rents were levied to exact labor and sometimes were not charged at all, or only a moderate charge was made to "faithful" laborers resident on the property. Double rents were sometimes demanded of those who did not work on the property, and rents for grounds were demanded of wives and children as well. In other cases, rent was charged only to residents who were not also employees on the estate. For example, Fort George Pen, which employed 107 persons in February 1843, charged rents amounting to £17 5s. for the month of April, but 60 percent of this was paid by nonemployees. Between April 1843 and January 1844 the pen's rents ranged from £11 14s. to £17 10s., but 54–75 percent was paid by nonemployees.[60] Howard de Walden instructed his staff even as late as 1852 that all workers who were located near the sugar factory were expected to labor on the estate. The staff was instructed to deny any indulgence, grazing of animals, use of grounds, and so on, to those who did not work when they were requested. "In all instances, preference to be given to the poor, well conducted, [and] industrious, over the wealthy idler."[61]

Governor Metcalfe expressed surprise that given the mutual hostility over the rent situation, planters nevertheless refrained from evicting their tenants, and the tenants from leaving. Both planter and tenant were bound, he thought, by "the old connexion," the landlord not wanting to lose *his* laborers, the laborer holding on to *his* house and grounds. The freedmen were disappointed with the operation of the new system, however, having "cherished the idea that the change to freedom was to be in all respects, an improvement. The payment of rent is a disappointment."[62] The effect of the planters' effort in this instance, therefore, was to increase not the docility of their labor force but rather its litigiousness.

The situation of the early forties contrasts sharply with Metcalfe's observations about the planters' reticence to evict their laborers. Indeed, Metcalfe himself urged in March 1840 that changes be made in the judicial system, including the addition of circuit-riding judges, because he anticipated a large increase in landlord-tenant disputes.[63] By 1842 Blagrove found the courts in Falmouth crowded with cases for nonpayment of rent.[64] Extant court records from other parishes confirm that both planters and workers had recourse to the courts. As late as September 1852, Fort George Pen won forty-five judgments and had distress warrants issued against several workers for failure to pay rent.[65]

The planters experienced some difficulties, however, when they took their cases to court. In some instances they did not receive the total amount from the jurors that they claimed from the laborer. In one case, Charles Smith, the attorney for Richmond Estate in St. Ann, the property of Ralph Bernal, Esq., an M.P. in Great Britain, had five men imprisoned for nonpayment of rent. The men were freed after an appeal to the Supreme Court in *Bernal v. Green* on 22 June 1839. They later sued in the Surrey Assizes and received £50 6s. 11d. for illegal commitment to jail. *Bernal v. Green* was decided on a technicality, but in their decision the judges ruled that a wife could not be charged extra rent in a place rented by her husband, thus effectively severing labor from residence.[66]

The planters soon turned to other legal means for exercising their authority. Included in the act abolishing the apprenticeship was a provision that tenants, excepting the aged and the infirm, could be evicted with three months' notice to quit, unless they had an unexpired contract for house and grounds.[67] In 1840 the Assembly passed a Petty Debts Act, aimed at recovering rents or wages that were in arrears, and a Summary Ejectment Law. The latter drew objections from Baptist missionaries Knibb and Clark because it placed the tenants in danger of losing their crop. To Metcalfe's argument that the tenant could reap the crop before leaving, they countered that it was useless to harvest a crop that was not yet ripe. Lord John Russell agreed with these objections, and the Colonial Office instructed the governor to ask for amendments.[68] The governor reported in January 1842, however, that the Assembly had refused to amend the Ejectment Law to satisfy Colonial Office objections, but he claimed that in any event only one case had been prosecuted under it. In the ensuing discussion of whether to disallow the law, the Colonial Office decided that the laborers now had the upper hand in Jamaica and would force the disassociation of rent from labor contracts without additional assistance from Whitehall. It decided, therefore, to leave the law to its operation.[69]

It is true that by the mid-1840s reports from many parishes suggested that the rents controversy was beginning to subside. A special magistrate from St. James Parish declared in 1840 that rents were no longer the subject of dispute for court action in his parish.[70] Part of the reason for the decline in litigation apparently was that even where rents were still charged, they were applied to the heads of families rather than to each member.[71] In November 1844, C. H. Darling informed Governor Elgin that the rental of houses for residence on estates was 1s. per week charged to the head of family only, or about £2 6s. per year.[72] And after a tour of the western districts of the island in 1843, Governor Elgin confirmed these reports, finding that disputes over rents were rarely occurring. Rents were still charged, but they were kept separate from the labor issue.

Many proprietors had ceased to demand rents at all, but their properties were in most cases fairly distant from good provision grounds; they were also unwilling or unable to sell land to their laborers.[73] Others perhaps shared the situation of George Price at Worthy Park, who abandoned rent charges because of the weekly collisions with his workers over its payment.[74]

In any case, rents clearly came to represent a declining proportion of the receipts of the various estates. In August 1850, for example, Content Estate in St. James (consisting of 235 acres) paid £76 in wages and received £10 18s. 6d. (14 percent) of this back in rent payments. But the wage bill for the year ending July 1851 was £1,500 and rent was £80; that is, 5 percent of the total wages were returned in rent. For the year ending in July 1852, £1,377 was paid in wages and £49 was received in rents, or 3.6 percent. By the following year only 1.2 percent of the wages paid out came back in the form of rents (£16 out of £1,380).[75]

Of course, some planters persisted in their attempts to use rent collections as a lever for labor control throughout the first two decades of the postemancipation era. In 1852, James Prestridge, the overseer for Fort George Pen, reported that he was demanding six months' rent in advance. The measure was designed primarily to "prevent an accumulation of arrears," he claimed. Demanding and collecting were entirely different matters, however: some of the tenants paid Prestridge; others refused. Apparently those who did not pay cash rent were encouraged to work it out on the property, but very few were willing to do this either. Indeed, only the people still working on the pen paid regularly, and almost no one paid on time, but waited until the last moment in December, just before the notices to quit became due.[76]

Even as early as 1840, Governor Metcalfe had reported that many planters were beginning to see the mistake of initiating the rent controversy in the first place and were now thinking of selling land to workers in order to keep them close to their estates.[77] Others, such as a group of proprietors in St. Ann, offered to delete rent charges in exchange for wage reductions.[78] It would appear, however, that by the mid-forties, when rents were generally being discontinued or at least made less vexatious, the damage had already been done. If there ever had been emotional ties that might have kept the workers on the estates, they had now been irreversibly damaged.

It will be perceived I do not argue against the negro, I may admit him equal to the English labourer, but that only strengthens my argument, for human nature is always the same, and no man of common sense will work for a single day's hire when he can become the original proprietor of a farm, however small, provided that farm (as I have shown the negroes' will) give him a comfortable livelihood.

SPECIAL MAGISTRATE THOMAS DAVIES, 29 MARCH 1836

Though many work on the same property and no other, still not continuously, as they all take a certain time, a week or two at a time, to replant or otherwise attend to an acre or half of an acre of land usually at some distance from the property on which they work, and unfortunately, this happens in rainy seasons, the time when they are most wanted for the cultivation of the staples or other produce supplied by the planter.

SPECIAL MAGISTRATE W. A. BELL, 1 JANUARY 1854

5

Peasants and Workers: Building a Free Society

The planters' bungled efforts to gain greater control of their labor force only heightened the freed people's desire to leave the plantations. It is equally clear, however, that the desire to establish independent freeholds predated the rents controversy. Writing in the *Royal Gazette* during the first year of the apprenticeship, one planter urged a massive white immigration from England and Ireland, whole villages if possible. "We must not be deluded—our present apprentices will answer our necessities only in proportion to the facilities of their becoming petty settlers being withheld from them."[1]

In the years that followed, other observers confirmed the planters' fears and the freed people's hopes. A special magistrate reported from St. Thomas-in-the-East that although the apprentices were generally inclined to work for wages, they were also "hoarding up their money for the purpose of purchasing land after the apprenticeship."[2] In St. Ann Parish during 1837, a magistrate described properties changing hands rapidly, some rented and others purchased for between fifty shillings and five pounds per acre for uncleared mountain land.[3] In most cases, "mountain land" referred to the sections of a plantation's holdings set aside for growing provisions for slaves. This is probably what John Daughtrey, a special magistrate in St. Elizabeth Parish, had in mind when he reported two years after abolition that some apprentices were already purchasing small plots of such land to work at the end of their apprenticeship either in their spare time or exclusively. The buyers, paying as much as four to five pounds per acre, were anxious for "mountain land" fit for growing ginger but preferred also a socially developed neighborhood and proximity to a church.[4] At about the same time, in St. Thomas-in-the-East, Edmund B. Lyon observed that land and a house were the first priority of freed people who had purchased their freedom before the expiration of the apprenticeship. In the easternmost district of the parish an aggregate of 150 acres had been sold at prices ranging from five to ten pounds per acre. Noting how these apprentices made careful arrangements for titles to pass on to their children in the event of their death, he concluded that such activities "must remove all apprehension of the unrestricted Negro sinking into listless apathy, content to live upon the spontaneous productions of the soil."[5]

Some indication of the freed people's demand for land can be gleaned from the skyrocketing land prices and brisk real estate market. John Clark, of the Baptist Missionary Society, claimed that prices in the interior settlements of Jamaica rose by 66 percent between 1833 and 1838.[6] By the fall of 1839, newspapers carried extensive advertisements of lots offered for sale to "the labouring peasantry."[7] The ensuing registration of freeholds following emancipation in 1838 was dramatic. Between 1 August 1838 and June 1840 alone, 2,074 freeholds of less than twenty acres were registered.[8] By 1845 the number of properties of less than ten acres settled and legally registered reached 20,724, which might have embraced a population of more than 66,000 people (given a conservative estimate of 3.2 persons per family). That would mean that just seven years after full emancipation more than 21 percent of the apprentice population of 1838 had become residents on peasant freeholds.[9]

As early as 1840, just two years after the end of apprenticeship, it was clear to all that a significant change in the demography and economy of Jamaica was in process. It was noted in the Colonial Office that freed people were buying land, although the extent, rate, and consequences were not yet clear. Associated with the growth of these small freeholds was a dramatic expansion in the number of towns and villages, which served as marketing centers for the settlers. The island's internal retail commerce increased dramatically, as reflected in the large number of new shops, the circulation of small silver coin, and the rising volume of imports coming into the island. Contemporary analysts also noticed, however, that the land purchases were generally quite small, 1.5 to 3 acres, and the soil was often unproductive.[10]

By the mid-1840s the pattern was clearer. Often entire plantations were purchased and subdivided among the tenants. For example, 106 acres known as Turner's Land, located near Retirement Estate in St. Ann Parish, were purchased by twelve parties in March 1846. The largest purchase was of 20 acres, eight others bought 3 acres or fewer, and only two people could afford more than 10 acres. The modal purchase was 3 acres at about £3 per acre. John Clark, the attorney negotiating the sales, collected a total of £130. Apparently the freed people were not a docile crowd; Clark complained about their sharp bargaining over prices, calling them "most tantalizing [i.e., aggravating] to deal with."[11]

The growth of smallholdings continued into the next decade and beyond, as the sugar industry fell into deeper and deeper distress following equalization of sugar duties. In 1855 a special magistrate described how one Port Royal estate was cut up into lots and sold for £4–£6 per acre. The new owners grew coffee, which they sold in Kingston for £5 and £6 per hundred-pound lots.[12] In 1857 another magistrate reported from St. David that there were a large number of peasant proprietors in that parish. Coffee was now produced on a very few settlements, and only one of eleven sugar estates remained in cultivation. One "peasant" proprietor had purchased Belle Clair, a two-hundred-acre coffee property that once belonged to an assemblyman. Another had bought Middleton, also a coffee property.[13]

Over the course of the century following emancipation, freeholds of fifty acres and less grew rapidly, suffering only a minor decline in the 1890s (see fig. 5.1). The available statistics make it clear that while the small farmer or settler class (holding fewer than fifty acres) increased significantly over this period, most of these new landowners held fewer than ten acres, in fact, usually just three to five. Many of the new settlers then rented two or more additional acres, often several miles from their homestead, on which they grew provisions. By one estimate, during the thirty years between emancipation and the Morant Bay Rebellion of 1865, black freeholders amassed property valued at £2.5 million and were able to deposit almost £50,000 in banks.[14] By the 1890s, peasant proprietors and their families may well

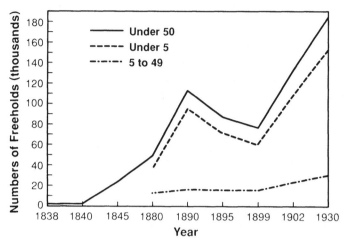

Figure 5.1. Growth of Small Freeholds, 1838–1930. Data from Hall, *Free Jamaica*, table 19; and Eisner, *Jamaica, 1830–1930*, table 30.

have embraced as much as half the population of Jamaica. By the 1930s, peasant families conceivably constituted somewhere between 60 percent and 80 percent of the population.[15]

Explaining the Growth of the Peasantry

This phenomenal shift from a society in which most of the working population was employed by sugar or coffee estates to one in which most were freehold proprietors seemed to represent the realization of the worst fears of the men who had fashioned British policy. Released from the restraints of the plantation before new social values and aspirations took hold, the freed people had apparently moved into the Jamaican hills, beyond the reach of civilizing forces, and reverted to an African barbarism. This, of course, was the outcome Henry Taylor had feared when he argued for apprenticeship as a way of forestalling such a development.

Thus many of Taylor's contemporaries formulated the problem as one of "cultural regression," or what one might call (invoking the contemporary stereotype) the "Quashee" syndrome. Stripped of its racist assumptions, this interpretation echoes a phenomenon modern economists call "a backward bending supply curve of labor": ex-slaves were culturally endowed with relatively simple aspirations that could easily be satisfied in a tropical environment and worked just enough to gratify immediate desires. Even in this sanitized form the "Quashee" thesis has not been argued consistently by any modern historian, but the suspicion that freed people were somehow less responsive to material incentives than whites does make its way into contemporary analyses. Thus William A. Green writes that "the needs of former slaves could be easily satisfied: land was plentiful and productive; fuel was unnecessary; and clothing was relished for style, not warmth." And despite his explicit *rejection* of the notion of a backward-bending labor supply curve, Philip Curtin concludes an analysis of the Jamaican peasantry with the observation that "the Negro settler was not principally interested in economic success." "Economic gain meant less to the black, than to the white, Jamaican, and the Negro was drawn away from estate work by many factors having nothing to do with the wages offered." The result of this withdrawal, he concluded, was the development of two competing cultures in Jamaica, a European-oriented plantation sector and an African-oriented peasant sector.[16]

Other analysts, both contemporaries and historians, have dissented from such views and emphasized the economic rationality and self-aggrandizing behavior of ex-slaves. According to their view, freed people were, in the language of modern economists, "marginal utility maximizers." Of course, during apprenticeship, many special magistrates and other observers had taken note of rapidly expanding consumption among blacks, as well as their disposition to work for wages to pay for that consumption. There were reports that they were purchasing new clothing, riding horses, and other luxuries, all of which suggested that they would not be content with a subsistence-level existence and therefore would continue to work on the estates.[17]

Later adherents of this view would insist that the withdrawal of freed people from estate labor and the consequent failure of the plantation economy was caused, not by the cultural deviance of peasants with subsistence-level wants, but by the inability of the plantations to provide adequate and reliable wages. For example, William Sewell, an American correspondent, expressed most tersely this thesis of economic rationality. "While proprietors say that the Negroes are too independent to work," he observed in 1861, "the Negroes say that proprietors are too poor to pay or that they will not pay regularly, which is a great grievance to people who live from hand to mouth." Of course, Sewell did note the powerful pull of the desire for economic independence and recognized that it might be a force different from and more complex than the material benefits of higher wages. "By a law of nature that cannot be gainsaid," he wrote, "they prefer independence to labor for hire. Why should they be blamed?" Nevertheless, Sewell's emphasis was on the purely economic differential between wages and the profits of provision growing.[18]

Many later students of the Jamaican peasantry have given much less credence than Sewell to the desire for autonomy as a significant concurrent motivation. Thus Gisela Eisner offers a blunt restatement of the economic rationality principle: "Slaves had acquired standards of taste in food and clothing that presupposed an exchange economy and which complete self-sufficiency in the mountains rendered impossible. . . . Had they been assured of attractive wages and conditions of employment there is no reason to suppose that they would not have remained on the estates." Peasants did work for wages on the plantation; the problem was that they worked only six hours a day, four days a week, and an unreliable number of weeks a year. Eisner reasons that this resistance to giving full time to the estates must have reflected their calculation that the "marginal return" for maximizing their output was less than they could realize from their provision grounds.[19]

Lord Sydney Haldane Olivier, who had a long association with Jamaica as governor and in other roles between 1897 and the 1930s, articulated yet a third view of the ex-slaves' motivation and behavior. Olivier, a Fabian, writing at a time when the British government had tilted toward the peasant sector in its colonial policy, recognized the economic rationality of the ex-slaves' action, but he did not accept it as a full explanation of their behavior. Clearly, working provision grounds often proved materially more rewarding than estate labor, and generally it was more secure. But Olivier emphasized what was to Sewell and many other observers only a minor theme—the desire for a measure of autonomy from the plantation and for control of one's labor. Olivier rejected the economic premises Henry Taylor's generation had taken as truisms; it was clear that "because in the vocabulary of academical [classical] economics in which all Englishmen are brought up, the words 'labour' and 'work' always mean occupation for an employer at wages, the fact that many freed Negroes refused or are unwilling to occupy themselves in that manner gave rise both in this country and the colonies to an inveterate habit of representing that they did no work at all."[20]

Because of this peculiar, culturally determined definition of legitimate work, Olivier argued, observers had misrepresented the real significance of the freed people's preferences. By combining estate labor and provision gardening, which necessitated travel to distant grounds and head porterage to market, freed people actually expended more physical effort than in either of these activities alone. Those who accused black Jamaicans of indolence had left such "work" out of their accounting because "it was not apparent to economic results or has even been censured as an unthrifty waste of time."[21]

Olivier's interpretation, which we will label "social autonomy," implies that the freed people's choice of working their provision grounds was not simply the result of their calculating the highest marginal return for their labor. Although Olivier did not reject the economic rationality of ex-slaves, neither did he abstract those economic calculations from their other social concerns. On the other hand, while he accepted the notion that freed people's cultural experience and resultant world-view was different from Europeans', he did not consider that world-view necessarily deviant or regressive to African roots.

Among contemporary analysts, Sidney Mintz most emphatically emphasizes this perspective on freed people's behavior. Mintz rejects the view that the peasant adaptations of West Indian ex-slaves were the result of a low level of economic aspirations, reflected deficient skills, or were evidence of regression to an African past. Rather, the repository of agricultural and marketing skills learned during slavery were adapted to the conditions of postemancipation society. The reconstitution of the peasantry after slavery was "simultaneously an act of westernization and an act of resistance." The freedmen exploited demographic and ecological conditions and, what is more important, political conflicts within the metropolitan and colonial ruling classes to reconstruct themselves "economically as men." Thus they were neither economically irrational nor marginal utility maximizers; they simply refused to refract their economic selves from their larger social beings. What they sought was a fuller measure of autonomy from the estates and from their former masters. What was at stake was "access to a life style that would allow them to retain both a sense of patrimony and a sense of self-respect."[22] Theirs was not, then, a choice between economic success and self-determination but an effort to realize both.

By emphasizing contrasting motivations and values, these three interpretations of the freed people's behavior imply different policy response to, and suggest different explanations for, the failure of the plantation economy after emancipation. If the freed people were culturally regressive, then only a thorough and forceful reformation of their culture would resolve the difficulty. Given this premise of cultural deficit, the black Jamaicans' character becomes the subject of study. If, however, they were highly responsive to economic incentives, then the estate system must either be made to work better, and therefore pay better, or be abandoned altogether. Given this premise of cultural sameness, or at least indifference to culture as a category of analysis, the economic system becomes the subject of study. But if freed people sought autonomy from estate wage labor, then a just policy required that those sectors of the economy outside of estate agriculture should be encouraged. Here cultural difference but not deficiency is presumed; the freed people's choices are structured by both the historical experience of slavery and the unfolding struggle with their former masters to determine the conditions and nature of their work.

Unfortunately, in the absence of surviving testimony from the freed people themselves, their motivation, intent, and values cannot be examined directly. We can only approach the question how *they* defined the problem of freedom, or guess the meaning of the freedom they sought, through an interpretation of their behavior. By determining when the peasantry developed, where it first appeared, and how it developed, we may be able to at least infer something about the freed people's view of the world they confronted.

The postemancipation scenario most consistent with the view that freed people were culturally regressive and subsistence-oriented would be one in which they responded to emancipation by immediately ceasing work on the estates and moving into the hills to establish provision grounds. Those who see freed people as marginal utilitarians generally describe a more gradual transition from estate labor to peasant cultivation in response to the decline of the plantation sector. The two key events during this transition period are the controversy between planters and their workers over rents, which sparked the first exodus from the estates in 1841–42 and the sugar duties crisis of 1846, which undermined the planters' ability to pay competitive wages by denying them a monopoly price for their sugar. Neither of these scenarios is necessarily inconsistent with the social autonomy interpretation, which emphasizes the evolving peasantry as an arena for resistance to the demands of the plantation; its primary concern is with the unfolding struggle between the former masters and the ex-slaves to define the terrain and nature of work. In other words, the freed people's choices were not predetermined by some essentialist character trait, cultural or racial, but evolved out of their struggle with the planter class, during slavery as well as after.

In fact, the withdrawal of labor from the plantations was both immediate and gradual. Immediate in the sense that shortly after 1 August 1838 the first response of many of the freed women and children was to cease or substantially reduce their commitment to field labor. By the terms of the Abolition Act, children six years old and under and persons over seventy were freed immediately on 1 August 1834. In 1834 there were 39,013 Jamaican slave children under six years old, or 12.5 percent of the slave population; the 15,692 elderly people constituted another 5 percent.[23] At the stroke of a pen, therefore, there were at least 17 percent fewer workers available to Jamaican estates.

British emancipators had anticipated that the children would continue to give labor to the estates through voluntary apprenticeship by their parents. But not only did black parents refuse to apprentice their children but in many cases they physically separated them from the estates by sending them to live with relatives and friends in urban areas.[24] One example of the result of such parental initiatives was an estate that had had fifty children (not counting babes in arms) reporting that by March 1836 only fifteen or sixteen were left; the rest, it was claimed, were "wandering in rags about Morant Bay." This meant, of course, that 70 percent had been taken away. Indeed, responding to such situations, S. H. Cooke, one of the governor's correspondents from Morant Bay, called for legislative interference to force the apprenticing of children to the estates.[25]

Some planters established schools on their estates in an attempt to encourage children to remain, but the success of that tactic varied. On Blue Mountain and Greenwall estates, parents did allow children under six to be formed into a separate gang in exchange for the proprietor's providing one and one-half hours of education per day.[26] Similarly, 14 of 21 students attending Mrs. O'Mealy's school on Lucky Valley Estate in St. Thomas-in-the-Vale were resident on the property. The Lucky Valley students also raised provisions in back of the school. But a school on Kellitt's Estate conducted by the bookkeeper apparently did not win the confidence of the black parents: only 2 of its 90 to 100 freed children actually attended.[27] In 1835, apprentices in St. Mary and St. David also refused to allow their freed children to work in the fields, even when free education and allowances were offered in exchange.[28]

Nevertheless, offering education appears to have been the only way that planters could encourage the apprenticing of children. Apparently the desire for education was a major motivation for their exodus from the estates in the first place. After visiting Jamaica in March and April of 1837 to report on Negro education, Charles Joseph Latrobe estimated that three-fourths of the students in day schools were the freed children of apprentices or of those who had purchased their freedom since 1834. The other one-quarter were the children of poor, free coloreds and Maroons. Latrobe's figures show that 8,321 children of apprentices were attending day school, which means—given that approximately 20,000 of the 38,754 freed children of apprentices were of school age by 1837—that just three years after abolition over 40 percent were in school. That figure is truly remarkable, considering that schools were not available in all parishes or districts.[29]

The withdrawal of women from estate labor at the end of the apprenticeship period was a much heavier blow to the workforce, because almost without exception they had constituted the bulk of the field labor force during the latter years of slavery. For example, women made up 61 percent of the apprentice population of Worthy Park and two-thirds of its field labor force.[30] On Friendship and Greenwich estates 86 percent of the ninety-five healthy female workers were assigned to the fields; they made up 71 percent of the field labor force. Exactly half of the apprentices on Sweet River Pen were women, and 53 percent of its field laborers.[31]

The differential was greater on sugar estates than on pens in part because the skilled jobs at sugar factories were reserved for men. Barry Higman's detailed demographic study shows a predominance of females in sugar parishes in 1832, while areas associated with coffee production and cattle rearing had considerably more males.[32] Despite their already disproportionate share of the heavy labor on sugar estates, moreover, at least some female apprentices were relegated to jobs previously performed by mules and light carts, such as carrying cane and cane trash, suggesting increased exploitation of female labor after slavery.[33]

Thus when women suddenly disappeared from estate labor forces in disproportionate numbers after the end of apprenticeship in 1838, they left a critical shortage of labor understated by their numbers alone. In Trelawny, for example, Baptist missionaries reported that of their 698 members working on sixteen estates, only 81 percent were still employed by March 1838. Eight percent of those leaving had been disabled by age or sickness, but 7 percent—mostly females—had simply ceased to work on the estates. The situation grew much worse after the termination of apprenticeship. Baptist missionaries Thomas Birchall and Walter Dendy, anxious to disprove charges that freed people would not work, surveyed fifty-six estates in the western parishes in the spring of 1839. They found 2,031 people at work, one-third of them females. But these same estates formerly had employed 4,341 people, 60 percent of them female. There had been, therefore, a 53 percent decline in the total workforce, but 84 percent of that decline was attributable to the withdrawal of female workers.[34]

The experience of many other estates was the same. Women dominated field labor forces before emancipation but not after. On Worthy Park Estate in 1842, for example, less than 40 percent of the workforce was made up of women; four years later there were fewer than one in four.[35] On Green Park Estate in 1848–49, there were twenty-five women out of ninety-five laborers (26 percent) working for one shilling a day or five shillings per week fertilizing cane plants with cow dung. By the following year only nine of these women remained, making up less than 10 percent of the workforce and mostly engaged in miscellaneous light tasks.[36] It seems clear that although women continued to give some work to the estates, a declining number gave their full time to wage labor. By the end of the first decade of freedom, the wage labor force was mostly male.

Another complication in the timing and patterning of the changes in the postemancipation labor force is the fact that the withdrawal from estate labor did not, in the early years, necessarily entail withdrawal from residence on some estate. Indeed, some estates experienced a dramatic growth in their resident population; for example, the resident population of Montpelier in St. James almost doubled by 1847 (from 800 to 1,500), even though its labor force did not increase. Similarly, Worthy Park, which had 500–600 apprentices, was home to 1,400–1,500 residents during the 1840s; but fewer than 20 percent of them worked on the estate.[37] Indeed, by 1842, Worthy Park had begun recruiting laborers from other parishes, who it formed into a "strangers' gang" and kept separate from its resident workers. By July 1845 the new workers, numbering nearly 100, were divided into two gangs; they now outnumbered the resident field hands and were no longer designated "strangers."[38]

Despite the earlier controversy over rents, the tenants on the various estates apparently continued to consider these former slave residences home and to lay claim to them.[39] For example, the tenants on Fort George Pen built fences around their rented plots and killed or injured livestock that trespassed onto them. In an interestingly back-handed concession to the tenants' proprietary claims, the overseer blamed them for the animals' depredations because they neglected to maintain *their* fences.[40]

Thus the initial withdrawal from estate labor, comprising mainly women and children, did not necessarily entail physical withdrawal from the estate. Withdrawal from estate residency came more gradually, and in the context of the freed people's struggle to define the proper limits of their former masters' authority not just over their work but over their lives as well. During the first three years of freedom, when planters tried to force the payment of rent for houses and provision grounds that slaves had occupied as de facto proprietors, thousands responded by moving off the estates, purchasing freeholds, and establishing free villages. Most villagers continued to work on some estate, however; and all indications are that their small freeholds were intended only to give them a homestead and with it a measure of independence from the planters. This is why observers at the Colonial Office initially found evidence that the growth of settlements could have a favorable effect on the labor supply of estates located in the vicinity of the new settlements.[41] In any event, free villagers remained a minority of the total freed population for some time, and substantial numbers of estate residents and village settlers continued giving intermittent labor for almost a decade after emancipation.

The motivation for the more general movement away from the estates, which began during the early 1840s and increased rapidly over the next four decades, can be understood best perhaps by examining *where* the peasantry developed. Over 20,000 new freeholds of under ten acres were registered in the island's record office within

Table 5.1. Changes in Land Tenure, 1840–1845

County	Under 10 Acres		10–49 Acres		50–249 Acres		250–499 Acres		Over 500 Acres	
	No.	%	No.	%	No.	%	No.	%	No.	%
Surrey	2,671	1,214	86	19.5	−38	−11.2	−16	−10.7	−20	−10
Middlesex	12,447	3,419	796	107.1	−111	−15.6	−8	−2.8	−76	−12
Cornwall	4,723	1,574	710	117.2	−9	−1.9	−18	−11.8	−55	−11
Total	19,841	2,249	1,592	91.2	−158	−10.8	−42	−7.3	−151	−11

Source: Hall, *Free Jamaica*, 160–62 (table 19).

just six years after emancipation. Most of these were established between 1840 and 1845, during which time more than 20 new peasant-sized freeholds were registered for every one already in existence. About 1,600 additional freeholds were established that ranged from ten to fifty acres in size, an increase of 91.2 percent (see table 5.1). Undoubtedly, there were many others that were not officially recorded; nevertheless, there is reason to believe that these official claims might give a fair indication of where the peasantry was developing. First, the numerous special magistrates' reports filed during this period did not mention squatters. And second, the number of new freeholds closely approximates the probable reduction in labor on sugar and coffee estates between 1840 and 1845. If the decline in produce is taken as proxy for the decline in full-time labor, then by 1845 there were approximately 31 percent and 63 percent fewer sugar and coffee workers, respectively, than in 1838. Since the 1838 labor force for these crops numbered about 155,000 and 45,000, the decline in production suggests that about 15,000 families probably departed from sugar estates, and another 9,000 from coffee plantations. This total displacement of 24,000 families is proportionate with the new freeholds registered during these years. Those apprentices who purchased their freedom before 1838, along with displaced managerial and skilled laborers, might well account for the modest growth in holdings of ten to fifty acres.[42]

The new peasant settlements were not randomly distributed across the island. Six parishes clustered at the island's center accounted for well over half of them—St. Ann, Manchester, St. Mary, St. Thomas-in-the-Vale, Clarendon, and St. Elizabeth (see fig. 5.2). Of course, these parishes also occupied almost 45 percent of the island's surface and probably held a comparable share of its vacant lands. Indeed, as one might expect, the size and growth (in absolute terms) of the peasant population correlates strongly with parish size.[43]

When we examine the *rate* of growth rather than the absolute numbers of freeholds, however, parish size has little or no effect, but other interesting patterns emerge. In table 5.2, the parishes are arranged in order of the rate of growth of their peasant proprietorships between 1840 and 1845. Among those parishes where peasant freeholds increased most rapidly just six can account for more than half the total increase. Their average growth rate was more than two and one-half times that of the island as a whole, and yet they encompassed less than half the island's surface (43.6 percent) and had a far greater median density of freeholds per ten square miles (60.5) than the island

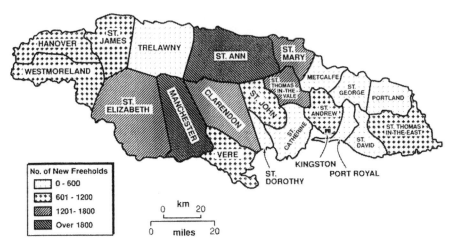

Figure 5.2. Geographical Distribution of New Peasant Freeholds, 1840–1845

as a whole (53). These six parishes were also home to more than a third of the major sugar estates on the island in 1844 and accounted for 43.3 percent of its capital assets (an index of economic activity).[44] Historically, two of these six parishes had been committed primarily to sugar production (St. Mary and St. James), two to coffee (Manchester and St. Elizabeth), and the two others (St. Thomas-in-the-Vale and St. Ann), respectively, to sugar and cattle and to cattle, coffee, and minor export crops. In many ways, the economic character of the parishes that freed people chose as the modal location for their freeholds was mixed. Their choices did not focus on the poorer parishes (Portland and St. George) nor, for the most part, on the wealthier ones (Hanover and Trelawny); they restricted themselves neither to sugar nor to non-sugar areas.

The mixed economic character of the parishes where peasant freeholders settled reinforces two contemporary interpretations of the freed people's choices: first, that they sought out areas for settlement where they could combine market gardening with wage labor; and second, that peasant proprietors moved quickly into the production of export as well as subsistence crops. Given these inclinations, parishes such as St. Mary and St. James were probably chosen because they combined opportunities for working on functioning estates with access, through their major shipping ports (Montego Bay, Port Maria, and Annotta Bay), to outlets into local and interregional trade. On the other hand, the large numbers of new peasant holdings registered in parishes devoted primarily to coffee (Manchester and St. Elizabeth) and/or mixed cultivation (St. Ann) probably reflected the greater availability of land for purchase in those districts and possibly the better prospects for undertaking the production of minor staples.

The geographical concentration of the fast-growing "peasant" parishes in the center of the island, mainly in the county of Middlesex, may be significant in elaborating this scenario of settlement choices. During the late eighteenth and early nineteenth centuries, sugar cultivation had been pushed into the upper reaches of the interior regions in response to the inflated prices of the Napoleonic era. With the abolition of the slave trade, many of these properties must have begun a long slide into bankruptcy. Unable to compete on the world market, they were also unable to compete for slave labor with better-situated western and eastern coastal estates. Even before emancipation, many such marginal estates had been converted from sugar and coffee monocultures to producing diverse minor crops and to supplying jobbing gangs to more successful estates. About one-fourth of the island's slaves worked on properties of this mixed character, many of which were almost immediate casualties of the Abolition Act of 1833.[45]

Their fate may be reflected in the overall changes in tenure patterns on the island between 1840 and 1845 (see table 5.1). Although the growth of holdings of under 50 acres was spectacular, there was simultaneously a noticeable decline of properties among the 50- to 250-acre tenure class. Such freeholds were most likely to be small and medium-sized coffee estates or other properties of mixed cultivation. In Middlesex there were more than 15 percent fewer in 1845 than there had been five years earlier, and that one county accounts for 70 percent of the islandwide decline in this class of properties. It is likely that this statistic partly reflects the dismemberment and sale of such properties to peasants and small farmers as well as to small, resident estate proprietors.

Other evidence is also suggestive about the redirection of labor during this first decade. The rate and size of the decline in coffee exports were much greater than for sugar, especially in the northern and central parishes, where the peasant population grew most rapidly. Sugar planters resisted selling lands to freed people at least initially, but presumably hard-pressed coffee planters would have been much less resistant. This, as well as its size, may explain why Manchester had the largest number of peasant proprietors in 1845: it was

Table 5.2. Economic Character of Peasant Parishes, 1840–1845

Parish[a]	Peasant Growth			Parish Size	
	%	No.	Cum. %	Sq. Mi.	Cum. %
St. Mary	7916	1,979	10.0	205.2	4.7
Manchester	6653	2,129	20.7	339.8	12.4
St. Elizabeth	5664	1,393	27.7	474.4	23.1
St. Thomas-in-the-Vale	4761	1,571	35.6	181.2	27.3
St. James	3836	1,013	40.7	240.6	32.7
St. Ann	3789	2,652	54.1	481.0	43.6
Port Royal	3700	185	55.0	47.7	44.7
Clarendon	3298	1,550	62.9	289.0	51.3
St. Catherine	2547	433	65.0	137.1	54.4
St. John	2238	895	69.6	117.4	57.1
St. Thomas-in-the-East	2109	717	73.2	247.8	62.7
Vere	1896	910	77.8	178.9	66.7
Trelawny	1633	441	80.0	352.6	74.7
Westmoreland	1153	1,076	85.4	320.4	82.0
St. David	952	457	87.7	92.1	84.1
St. George	950	380	89.6	179.3	88.2
St. Andrew	763	702	93.2	137.7	91.3
St. Dorothy	630	328	94.8	47.6	92.4
Hanover	621	800	98.8	177.1	96.4
Portland	—[d]	230	100.0	158.3	100.0
Total		19,841		4,405.2	

Sources: Figures for peasant growth and numbers of sugar estates are based on Hall, *Free Jamaica*, 82, 160–62 (tables 10 and 19). Figures for parish size are based on Higman, *Slave Population and Economy*, 53 (table 6).

[a] In 1842, there were boundary changes between St. Mary and St. George to create Metcalfe (mainly from the former). I have combined the 1845 figures for Metcalfe with St. Mary's.

producing half as much coffee as it had in 1838, which very likely made its planters more willing to sell excess land to freed people.[46]

The fact that many of these settlers raised coffee lends further support to the supposition that they purchased land largely from the holdings of existing coffee plantations, since they would have had to rely initially on an existing stock of plants. By 1859, for example, only Albion and Morris plantations were still producing coffee full-scale in St. David, which left a major share of the parish's production in the

Peasant Density, 1845		Property Value[b]		Number of Sugar Estates		
No. per 10 Sq. Mi.	Rank	£1,000	Cum. %	1834	1844	1854
98	1	1,158.2	9.7	86	79	39
64	5	735.5	15.9	0	0	0
30	16	689.8	21.7	17	20	12
89	2	347.4	24.6	23	24	12
43	12	1,098.3	33.8	80	74	41
57	7	1,129.9	43.3	30	32	18
40	13	211.0	45.0	3	3	0
55	8	497.0	49.2	40	41	17
33	15	436.6	52.9	5	5	3
80	3	269.4	55.1	11	10	6
30	16	769.2	61.6	67	61	21
54	10	405.1	65.0	29	29	22
13	20	1,196.6	75.0	76	86	55
36	14	852.0	82.1	48	48	34
55	8	250.8	84.2	10	10	3
23	18	281.2	86.6	—[c]	—	—
58	6	548.8	91.2	14	18	5
80	3	204.5	92.9	11	10	5
52	11	644.0	98.3	71	70	34
15	19	202.2	100.0	25	24	3
		11,927.0		646	644	330

[b] This figure is the parochial assessment of the value of capital assets. Since in practice it was not collected from smallholders, it gives a fair index of estate and plantation activity.

[c] St. George's estate figures were totaled with St. Mary's in the original source.

[d] There were no data for Portland in 1840; therefore no growth figure can be calculated.

hands of small settlers. One observer judged their crop "equal in quantity although deficient in quality to that heretofore produced on the old established plantations." By 1864, on the eve of the Morant Bay Rebellion, Governor Eyre conceded that Jamaica's minor exports—ginger, arrowroot, honey, beeswax, and coffee—were raised by small settlers exclusively. Even in the formerly premier coffee parishes, Manchester and St. Elizabeth, Eyre found most estates abandoned and peasants and small farmers producing most of the coffee.[47]

Small freeholders also grew small quantities of sugar, which challenges the notion that they were somehow prejudiced against estate
crops per se, that is, that they identified them with slavery. In 1855
Richard Hill reported that small settlers were producing sugar, using
two or three sugar boilers to produce five to twenty barrels annually
of "exceedingly good quality." At about the same time, magistrate
Henry Crewe reported that no coffee estates were left in Clarendon
but that the small settlers grew "inferior" coffee for the American
market. Three years later, although only two sugar estates remained
in production, the coffee and sugar output of small settlers in that
parish was estimated to be worth twenty thousand pounds.[48]

Contrary to the Quashee stereotype, then, this first torrent of peasant settlements does not appear to have flooded into the remotest
regions of the Jamaican hills. Black freed people did not simply rush
into the vacant hinterland, like air into a vacuum. We know, of course,
that Jamaican authorities overestimated the island's size by one-third
and consequently misjudged the amount of vacant land available for
squatting. Given the assumption that ex-slaves would be content with
a subsistence-level existence, officials also underestimated the quality
of locations potential squatters would find attractive. Freed people did
not want undeveloped land, distant from markets, schools, churches,
communal institutions, and civilized amenities. It was for this reason
primarily that initial settlements following emancipation were made,
not by squatters on vacant Crown lands, but by *purchasers* of developed land on former sugar and coffee properties.[49]

It is important to recognize, however, that the peasant holdings
established during the early 1840s represent only the initial phase of
settlement. And indeed, when one overlays that pattern onto the
overall movement of the working population, other configurations
emerge. Like freed people in other former slave societies, Jamaicans
tested their freedom with physical movement. But figure 5.3 shows
that only nine parishes appear to have gained population during the
first six years of freedom; and only three of the parishes that experienced relatively large increases in their peasant population (St. Mary,
St. Elizabeth, and St. Thomas-in-the-Vale) appear to have attracted
settlers from outside their boundaries.[50] It is likely, then, that most
of the earliest peasant settlers established their freeholds within the
parishes where they had lived as slaves. Significantly, perhaps, it
was two sugar parishes—St. Thomas-in-the-Vale and St. Mary—that
experienced the largest in-migrations between 1838 and 1844. These

parishes may well have offered the best opportunity for combining estate work with independent proprietorship.

During the next intercensal period, however, the pattern was just the opposite. Between 1844 and 1861 there was a dramatic shift of population from the western and eastern parishes toward five parishes that formed a wide belt across the island's center. During this sixteen-year interval, blacks of working age resettled in Clarendon, Manchester, St. Elizabeth, St. Ann, and St. Thomas-in-the-Vale. Large numbers were also attracted to Westmoreland and St. Andrew (see fig. 5.4). Of these seven, only Westmoreland and St. Thomas-in-the-Vale continued to be important sugar producers, and St. Andrew was the hinterland and suburb of Kingston. Given the condition of the staple export economy during these years, this movement must have been aimed at establishing peasant farms. More than two-thirds of the island's coffee and half its sugar plantations had been abandoned. Consequently, hitherto prosperous sugar parishes, such as Hanover and St. James, were losing workers; but, then, so were the poorer parishes, such as Portland, St. David, and St. Catherine. The parishes that gained working-age people had been devoted primarily to coffee, cattle, and diversified production during slavery (again excepting Westmoreland). Most of these were also parishes that had experienced large absolute increases in peasant holdings between 1840 and 1845.[51]

Peasant proprietors apparently sought out a particular kind of area to settle. The parishes where the growth of freeholds was most explosive were also areas where some marginal sugar and coffee estates were abandoned and sold to freedmen, yet other coffee and sugar estates remained profitable and capable of offering occasional employment to the settlers. Freed people did not settle in the poorest, economically less active parishes or, by and large, in those dominated by sugar estates. It is likely also that they settled, not in undeveloped areas within these parishes, but on abandoned properties near other, more prosperous estates. Many of them purchased just enough land to establish freeholds and then rented grounds upon which they grew provisions for the market. All the contemporaneous descriptions we have indicate that they divided their labor between their own properties and the estates. The substance of the planters' complaints was that this division favored the freed people's own grounds rather than theirs.

A large part of the labor shortage planters complained about, however, was caused by the immediate redirection of a critical portion of

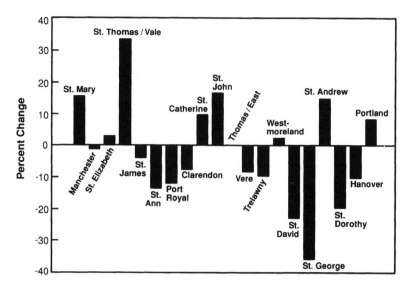

Figure 5.3. Black Migration, 1838–1844. Data from Higman, *Slave Population and Economy*, 140, 256, tables 26 and A3.7; and idem, "Jamaica Censuses of 1844 and 1861," 2–3, table 2.

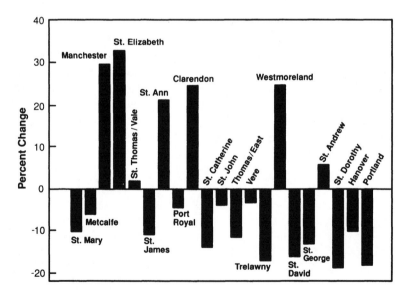

Figure 5.4. Black Worker Migration, 1844–1861. Data from Higman, "Jamaica Censuses of 1844 and 1861," table 6.

the freed family's labor.[52] The refusal of black parents to allow their young children to work on the estates during the apprenticeship period and the subsequent reduction in the labor women gave suggests that a family division of labor was taking place before and immediately after emancipation.[53] The entire family worked to cultivate provisions as they had during slavery, but women took primary responsibility for marketing the crop and possibly for the chickens, fruit, and other produce raised on their house plot rather than at the distant provision grounds. A magistrate in St. Dorothy, for example, observed in 1854 that the women usually did the marketing, while the young men in the family got work with neighboring planters.[54] The older women and younger children might give some labor to the estates, but at their own convenience, when it did not interfere with their other primary activities, when it was most profitable, or when droughts and other natural disasters destroyed their own crops. This would explain why planters found labor more plentiful at harvest time—a period of the most grueling and arduous labor but when pay was higher—than at other seasons.[55]

Authorities were not unaware of this interpretation of the freed people's behavior. As early as 1840 it had become apparent that the acquisition of freeholds did not mean complete abandonment of labor on an estate. "It appears to me that the land which they purchase is chiefly for the purpose of obtaining a secure home," Governor Metcalfe informed Colonial Secretary Russell, "that it is generally too little in extent to be looked to as a permanent source of subsistence, and that they must calculate either on obtaining additional means of comfort by going out to labor, or on taking more land on lease for their own cultivation. I do not therefore anticipate the unfavorable result which some predict." Thus he favored settlements because they apparently made blacks content.[56]

Similar observations were made by John Blagrove, who arrived in Jamaica in 1842 to take over management of his estates, which were located near some of the earliest and most successful settlements in the western parishes. Touring the area around Brown's Town, he commented favorably on the industrious, well-kept appearance of the cottages and gardens. "The land is sold out to them by [an] acre or two—and this enables them to raise provision enough for themselves and to sell at market—but still they are obliged to work in many parts of the Island."[57] Several special magistrates confirmed Blagrove's observations. For example, Peter Brown, reporting from Portland, insisted that the increased number of freeholders did not reduce the labor supply, "but on the contrary, I find that the persons who undertake, and execute the most Task work on the Estates are persons possessed of small freeholds."[58]

Other magistrates nonetheless continued reporting complete withdrawal from the estates. William Hewitt wrote that in St. George the settlers continued working the estates during their first year as landowners but ceased entirely thereafter. Still others reported a return to the estates in 1842 and again in 1844, attributing it to the effects of falling prices for provisions in some areas and drought in others.[59]

Attempting to make some sense from these conflicting reports regarding the disposition of freeholders toward estate labor, Henry Taylor was prepared to concede by late 1842 that on balance the settlements were a favorable development. He surmised that the conflicting reports reflected observations of freeholds in very different stages of development. Naturally, a freeholder in the initial stages of settlement would devote his whole time to building a house and preparing his grounds; only after these tasks were completed would he have time or be inclined to work for an estate. Furthermore, as his grounds and his neighbors came into full production, there was likely to be a glut that would reduce his earnings and make estate work more attractive. "One magistrate says that the negro, notwithstanding the glut still stupidly persists in raising provisions at a loss; another says that he finds his mistake and betakes himself to working for wages. Probably the one magistrate was speaking of new settlements where only one year's glut had been experienced, and the other of those where the glut had lasted two or three years." He added pointedly that "the Negroes are not the only producers with whom the earliest [appearance] of a glut is insufficient to check overproduction." Taylor concluded that the best policy was to encourage settlement in fully cultivated districts, a policy freed people already had embraced.[60]

Apparently, many planters had arrived at similar conclusions. Having failed to hold their workers close with various rental schemes, many began to sell land to prospective laborers. In some cases, as a magistrate reported from Manchester in 1842, portions of the plantation backlands, or "mountains," were sold to create nearby village settlements with the hope that these would be sources of labor.[61] In other cases, entire properties were cut up and sold in small lots to settlers. Mavis Bank, Dallas Castle, Halberstadt, and Tower Hall in Port Royal had all met this fate by 1844. These worn-out coffee properties sold readily for five to six pounds per acre.[62] Again, the willingness of such owners to sell is probably the reason that freeholds devel-

Falmouth Market

oped most readily in areas of marginal or abandoned properties and not in virgin wilderness.

On the other hand, the willingness of the freed people to buy, and at such inflated prices, suggests that they were in no danger of "relapsing into barbarous indolence" in the Jamaican hills. Indeed, when observers were honest, as John Blagrove was during his initial tour of Jamaica, they conceded that the freed people were hard workers when they chose to work, or better still, when they worked for their own benefit rather than the planters'.[63] The peasants prepared for market on Friday, went to market on Saturday, and attended church on Sunday. This left four days at most for estate work. Throughout the late nineteenth century observers commented on the energy and activity of the Jamaican markets. By Friday evening the roads were clogged with people on their way to town. They walked fifteen to twenty miles with a very small parcel of produce—bananas, coffee, chickens—in a basket on their heads.[64] These were not a lazy people.

Nor were they unresponsive to market incentives. Rather, as Governor Metcalfe had recognized begrudgingly, what they sought was to combine the occupations of market gardener and estate laborer.[65] The problem was that peasant production did not mesh well with plantation requirements. The strategy of encouraging settlements con-

Brown's Town Baptist Chapel and School

tiguous to estates had its natural limits. Over time the search for available land took settlers further and further into the interiors of parishes. As their distance from the estates increased, the settlers were less likely to work on them.[66] In later years it was not only the movement of the freed people but also the disappearance of more and more estates that created greater distance between settlement and estate zones. Thus by 1854 Thomas Witter Jackson, a magistrate in St. Thomas-in-the-Vale, noted that while cottages had formerly been close enough to estates to permit settlers working them to return home in the evening, the accelerated abandonment of estates left the settlements "more scattered and inaccessible to the few [estates] remaining in cultivation."[67]

Nevertheless, the conviction about black people's cultural regression persisted, despite all evidence to the contrary. Even while acknowledging that low wages offered "no inducement to the more independent class of people to work on estates," many still insisted that blacks were somehow at fault: "The people betake themselves to the mountains, buy an acre of land, and squat on it. Indolence begets its certain inheritances. We know the rest."[68] The "rest," according to Governor Barkly, writing in 1856 in language reminiscent of Henry Taylor's nightmarish prognosis of 1833, was a dangerously isolated peasantry. They did not even see whites from one year to the next,

Barkly wrote, and obeah practices and other African superstitions and religious beliefs were encouraged by the isolation. Indeed, during that very year, colored assemblyman John Castello introduced legislation outlawing obeah, which soon became law.[69]

Thus, despite the evidence, arose the legend of "Quashee"—lazy, morally degenerate, licentious, and heedless of the future. By the mid-1850s it laced the special magistrates' reports: the peasantry was unaffected by the moral sanctions of the larger society and adhered to an alternative moral system; for them no shame, but a kind of celebrity, attached to criminal convicts, who returned to their communities without stigma. "I regret to state," special magistrate Fyfe reported from St. David in 1854, "that I see little improvement in the laboring classes. They work for no prospective or moral object, the incentive is entirely present and physical. They are improvident, reckless of life, and almost indifferent to the ties of kindred. They are scarce grateful for charity in sickness, and whilst they will lavish pounds on a funeral, they grudge a shilling for the medicine which might avert it. Disease entails trouble, death is followed by merriment and feasting." And from Trelawny, magistrate Robert Emery added: "Their march back to barbarism has been rapid and successful."[70]

The magistrates' frustration is evident in the extreme remedies that even those most sympathetic to the freed people recommended. Richard Hill, for example, thought he saw progress in their "regularity in the observance of set hours and set forms, and decency in conduct and appearance," but insisted nonetheless that they required moral education to awaken their conscience as well as their intellect. He thought tuition charges for education would have a salutary effect and that infants should be separated from their parents: "In infant schools we at once get over the obstacles to regulated thought and action in the negro's cottage."[71]

These draconian measures, urged by the most liberal elements of the magistracy, suggest what the freed people were up against. Of course, the idea of educating blacks for free labor, of reforming their debased slave culture, of inculcating new values and desires—"regulated thought"—was at the heart of the original emancipation policy and was the primary goal of the aborted apprenticeship system. But now, twenty years after abolition, the idea of cultural reformation had a harder edge. After all, Taylor's original plan had presumed to build on the positive values associated with the slave provisioning and independent marketing system. Such indigenous values were hardly credited by the mid-1850s. Not only was there thought to be little to build on in a culture formed in slavery but the bearers of that culture were denounced as a baneful influence on their posterity. The power of the state must be interposed to raise a new generation with values appropriate to a free market society. It was a thoroughly totalitarian view.

The Moral Economy of Jamaican Workers

Events also proved it a mistaken view. What observers such as Richard Hill and Henry Taylor failed to appreciate—and what contemporary historians have only recently come to recognize—was that blacks could not have defended themselves against the cruelties of slavery without creating viable social structures and positive, life-affirming values. In all slave societies survival required blacks to learn a harsh discipline and adopt social values that would enable them somehow to make sense of their crippled lives.[72] It is not surprising that some of those values could be adapted to the harsh realities of freedom as well.

Thus the self-provisioning and marketing experience of slavery, which Taylor expected to provide raw material for the apprentices' education in wage labor discipline, laid the basis instead for the emergence of a peasant economy. The formation of this peasant class, however, was no more a matter of freed people automatically mobilizing a repertoire of skills and patterns learned as slaves than it was a simple, unmediated, reflex response to the availability of uncultivated land. Just as ex-slaves moved into the interstitial areas among the surviving estates rather than into the vacant Jamaican "outback," they also sought to combine provision gardening with estate work rather than depend exclusively on either. Both choices evolved out of a particular world-view that first emerged during slavery but took its distinctive form in the struggles following emancipation. The slave provisioning and marketing system was embedded in a network of communal, family, and gender relations that constituted a semiautonomous moral and social order. The choice to maximize their autonomy rather than their income provoked a struggle with the planters. Out of that struggle the Jamaican peasantry emerged; because of that struggle it assumed particular forms of practice and consciousness.

Colonial officials, missionaries, and planters correctly discerned an alternative world-view and morality among freed people, even though they distorted and misinterpreted them. For example, special magistrate W. A. Bell, of St. Dorothy, was surprised and perplexed by

The Ordinance of Baptism, 1842

the readiness with which the Afro-Jamaican villagers acknowledged a debt in absence of written proofs or receipts, given the agrarian dishonesty that he thought generally prevailed. "They are exact in their accounts, though slow, seldom make many mistakes, and understand their rights perfectly." He was impressed too with the fact that black villagers would not inform on one another, unless there was a private grudge or a dispute amongst themselves. Blagrove observed a similar community solidarity among his workers at Orange Valley Estate, although he interpreted it as mere conformity and lack of that independence ostensibly found among English workers. "To such an extent do they carry it that upon Estates where one man refuses to take a job at a certain price his neighbour will take it under no other terms. The Negroes so intermarry one with the other that a breach of the above conduct wd. perhaps cause an everlasting dispute between the families—& is not in one single case scarcely ever infringed."[73]

Blagrove's observation of intermarriage and kinship ties within the plantation community suggests the social basis for the moral order he observed. First, contrary to the image of slaves living in social chaos, recent studies describe diverse household structures, among which nuclear and extended patterns were the most dominant. In the decades immediately preceding abolition, the relatively small external and internal slave trades, together with the low incidence of manumission among field slaves, promoted a demographic and geographic stability that should have provided at least material support for the formation of strong family and communal ties.[74] Second, patterns of residence are suggestive of the social organization, values, and mores of slave communities. Slave huts appear to have been allocated primarily to family units and according to the size, nativity, and status of their households. In Jamaican slave households, couples and their children lived together; unattached individuals lived with their families, alone, or with other single persons of the same sex, depending upon their age, status, or nativity. Creole households differed in composition from those of recently imported Africans; older workers', from those of both the young and the superannuated; and artisans' and drivers', from those of field hands. Furthermore, residence patterns, such as those on Hope Estate, in St. Andrew, where houses belonging to kinfolk were enclosed within a common fence and shared a single gateway, suggest the importance of extended kin networks in the slave quarters.[75]

But household composition, anthropologist Raymond Smith warns, is not a reliable guide to the *meanings* of family and gender relationships. Anthropological fieldwork among West Indians in the twentieth century can help fill this lacuna in the historical record if we avoid the mistake of too readily conflating past and present. Social values and practices are not static but are grounded in historical and material relations that evolve over time. Some historically oriented contemporary ethnographies are helpful, however, because they describe values and practices that are ubiquitous, intergenerational, and sometimes directly traceable to the nineteenth century.[76]

Working-class West Indian families, these studies show, have tended to be matrifocal and matrilocal and to involve complex structures and highly nuanced relationships. The diversity of household structures and family formations reflects options exercised at different stages of the life cycle rather than deviant choices. Gender relations are not simply the result of economic conditions; they both reflect and shape life expectations and material relations. Erna Brodber's work, which studies women born as early as 1861, identifies a pattern of serial monogamy, in which the adult male in a household was both a meaningful presence and a temporary one. Solidary, multigenerational groups of women formed households through which men passed, their presence in their mates' subsequent interviews striking for its anonymity (for example, "the young man," or "the person"). Although such men were not necessary to a woman's day-to-day survival—a role fulfilled by kinswomen, young and old—they were valued for their emotional support, for their occasional interventions with public authority, for economic assistance, and for sexual pleasure and procreation. There is evidence, consistent with the postemancipation reaction against certain forms of heavy labor that had been imposed on women during slavery, of an ideology of female spheres evolving among later generations; that is, some crops and certain agricultural tasks had become gender-defined. For example, informants, many of them second-generation freedwomen, described deep-digging (required for planting both yams and sugar cane) as a male task that was taboo for women. They also articulated a strong convention that women should avoid wage employment, if possible, and focus their labor on "female crops" such as oil nuts and beans. Assistance with male tasks could be obtained by hiring or exchanging labor. Nonetheless, these women aspired to an "ideal" family structure wherein an adult male would be head of the household; at the same time they valued and insisted upon their own and their daughters' economic autonomy. The resolution of these apparently conflicting practices and values lay in the timing of roles and activities. The ideal or conventional marital relationship would be established only when a man was capable of providing a house and sustaining a household—usually in the middle of his life cycle. Both preceding and following that stage, households tended to be multigenerational, their young men and women working for wages outside the home.[77]

Whether nuclear or extended, all households were embedded within larger networks of kinspeople and communities. Contemporary field studies describe informants capable of recounting complex and extensive genealogies of kinfolk, more than twice as large, for example, as that of the typical urban white American informant. Thus despite their unconventional family and mating relations, individuals were "enmeshed in complex and ramifying networks of kinsmen, friends and neighbours" and enjoyed "dense and supportive social relationships."[78] Other studies suggest that these networks, among kinswomen especially, were singularly strong and crucial to sustaining economic life among rural populations and that labor sharing and exchange were common among agricultural villagers.[79]

These twentieth-century observations provide clues for interpreting nineteenth-century evidence; they suggest a link between the ex-slaves' economic choices and their social arrangements and values. Anthropological fieldwork has revealed the subtle and symbolic meanings of the rural Jamaicans' house and yard and their different understandings about various modes of land tenure.[80] The plots of land on which the peasants built their cottages were important to the establishment and maintenance of family life. According to oral tradition, this "family land" had been inherited or purchased by the first generation of freed people, its ownership must pass to all the children of a family, illegitimate as well as legitimate, and it could not be sold. Clear distinctions were made between this land and the distant tracts one rented or purchased to gain a livelihood. In the Jamaican economy, Edith Clarke has observed, "ownership of land is believed to be the only real and permanent source of security and of the means of satisfying the normal expectations which operate between men and women as prospective parents and between them and their children. And this has no connection, be it stated, with the income which the land can provide."[81] The role of these small, uneconomic house plots in larger social relationships is perhaps best illustrated by the Jamaican proverb, A man should not marry and live in a rented house. Likewise, a sense of the autonomy such plots symbolized is revealed by the fact that the statement "Get out of my yard!" means not simply the physical yard but the speaker's social affairs as well.[82] In contrast with the multitude of forces that pulled them apart, therefore, the house and yard both symbolized and were a potential means of realizing and sustaining the integrity of their family and kin networks.

Family land was functional to the extent that it provided refuge and support in time of need or a minimum subsistence that permitted resistance to exactions of the outside world, especially the sugar estates. At the same time, its significance was in large measure symbolic, because it could not provide actual material security for the entire group of claimants. It must be understood, then, as primarily supporting and affirming the corporate existence of the group. It was, as Jean Besson describes, an "inalienable corporate estate," representing "the spatial dimension of the family line, reflecting its continuity and identity."[83]

Thus family land was a kind of spatial metaphor for the family itself. Ostensibly, all family land claims could be traced to the immediate postemancipation era, but actually even recently purchased plots were often transformed by fiat into "family land." By this "invention of tradition" the claimant appropriated a whole history of collective struggle and bestowed upon that claim a mythic quality. In effect, freed people sought to reconstitute not simply the slaves' provisioning and marketing systems after emancipation but a broad spectrum of social relations that inhered in those economic activities.

The importance of family land to a larger set of social relationships was evident in the decades following emancipation. In 1842, Hall Pringle found that one-fifth of Clarendon's laborers had purchased freeholds, but their average holding was a mere two acres, and they appeared to make no effort to increase it, despite the fact that land was cheaper than at any time since emancipation. In Pringle's opinion, the cottages they erected were no better than their slave huts, yet the settlers bestowed names on them, for example, "Content."[84] A St. Ann magistrate noted similar increases in freeholds but insisted that "the chief object of the people is, apparently to secure to themselves a home without much regard to the quality or fertility of the soil." Obviously, such freeholders must continue working on the sugar estates "to enable them to realize the means of furnishing them with their increased wants." The issue, therefore, was not one of working for wages per se; freed people had done that during the apprenticeship and, by and large, continued to do so during the decade following their complete emancipation. Estate work continued to be an important part of their repertoire of strategies for making ends meet. What they resisted was the loss of autonomy, the coercion, inherent in the wage system. They resisted becoming proletarians.

It is also true that those difficult early years—years of drought, of shortages of capital and credit, of falling prices—taught them bitter lessons about the dependability of the plantations for earning a livelihood. Many planters could not meet their payrolls on time, others cheated, most sought every opportunity—through rents, the courts, changing work requirements—to squeeze their workers and make them absorb the shortfall in profits. Whatever attraction for market gardening the slavery experience had left them with was certainly reinforced by the realities and uncertainties of the postemancipation economy. Theirs was not, however, merely a calculation of the marginal utility of peasant farming over estate work.[85] A more relevant explanation of their responses to postemancipation conditions is their collective struggle with the planter class.

Freed people sought to create and define their freedom in the only terms they knew. They valued most the very things persistently denied them as slaves—a home and control of their family's labor. The planters, on the other hand, wanted to direct their labor when, where, and under conditions they dictated. As Richard Hill had phrased it, they wanted labor to be "little when little was enough and abundant when such was required." The freed people were equally anxious to apply their labor to the tasks, in the manner and at the times of their own choosing. This was exactly the opposite of what slavery had been; this was the only sensible and tangible meaning freedom could have for them.

But it was not possible to combine the occupation of market gardener with estate laborer, warned Governor Metcalfe. He acknowledged that the problem was not that blacks would not work but that they refused to give "continuous labour" to the estates. They worked "only just as much as they like." The success of the gardener deprived the planter of that control over his labor force essential to plantation discipline and survival, because "all labor must be at the option of the peasant to give or withhold." Access to land that could be turned to market gardening and/or minor export crops provided "the facility with which the Population [could] support themselves without labouring in the service of others."[86]

The "inevitable" conflict, then, came when the planters' insistence upon control confronted the laborers' insistence upon independence. The nuances of this conflict British policymakers did not always appreciate. At the height of the withdrawal from the estates, Tory Colonial Secretary Edward Stanley remained confident of an amicable solution. After all, the labor supply problem was less a matter of blacks' indisposition to work than it was a matter of local conditions enabling them to raise their demands, "which is not an evil of so hopeless a nature."[87] In the vocabulary of contemporary economists, Stanley might have said: the planter needed simply to meet the freed people's "high reserve price" for estate work. It was a problem of "marginal returns." But planters made clear that what they required was, not simply labor, but *laborers* under their complete control to work when, where, at the price, and under the conditions they determined. When one of the more liberal planters, Thomas Price, of Worthy Park, testified before a parliamentary committee in 1847, he was asked to clarify just what he meant by "a labor shortage." "What you want is this," the inquirer suggested, helpfully, "that at any moment when it suits your convenience you may be able to put your hand upon the labourer?" To which Price replied: "Undoubtedly; you could not have better expressed my meaning."[88]

If other interested observers were reluctant to label Price's condition of labor by its proper name, the ex-slaves were not. As one was reported to have declared: "What kind of free this? This the free them gee we. This Free worse than slave, a man cant put up with it."[89]

Slavery had been a mode of social as well as labor coercion. Market gardening had been the one area in which slaves had enjoyed a considerable measure of autonomy, socially as well as economically. Post-emancipation labor requirements that looked like slavery or that infringed upon socially relevant economic activities would be resented and resisted most fiercely of all.

Sometimes the freed people's resistance appeared irrational to those unappreciative of their determination to gain in freedom what slavery had denied. Dr. G. M. Lawson, the proprietor of Porto Bello, reported offering top wages in 1839, but workers still refused to work for him. In some cases workers struck their estates, won the strike, but refused to return, notwithstanding their victory. They preferred to forgo the higher wages of the estate and to buy or rent lands elsewhere. There was evidence of preference, too, for lower-paying work on pens and estates of mixed cultivation because the discipline was not as rigid, or the work as regimented, as on sugar estates.[90]

Thus the noneconomic motivations of the freed people were, not separate from, but interactive with the economic. One may choose to think of this interaction as one in which there was a "high reserve price" for estate labor, but that does not tell us much about why this would be so. And given the sugar estates' need for cheap, docile workers, matching that high reserve price under the constraints of the world sugar market of the postemancipation era was a moot issue in any case. Similarly, efforts to explain the freed people's motivations by simply labeling them are equally pointless. One doubts that they would have been impressed by efforts to fit them, according to some formula, into categories such as "peasant" or "proletarian."[91] In many ways they were both: an unfinished proletariat, a semi-peasantry.

As in other agricultural societies, members of the family might devote themselves alternately to estate labor or market gardening.[92] Sometimes they appeared as peasant cultivators completely divorced from the estates, providing their own subsistence and selling their surpluses in export as well as local markets. At other times they appeared as a militant agricultural proletariat, utilizing all the tools of labor agitation, including strikes, slowdowns, and sabotage to extract concessions of better pay and working conditions from the estates.[93] Different family members probably took on different roles, as they did later in the nineteenth and early twentieth centuries, when young men and women worked estates in roving migrant labor gangs, while their elders tended to gardens and marketing.[94] Over a given life cycle, an individual probably filled many different roles, roles to which definitions and labels cannot be unambiguously affixed and to which values and behavior cannot be simply ascribed. Ultimately, for the Jamaican freed people, as for us all, social identities are created out of oppositions and struggles. Thus the thread uniting their diverse roles into one fabric was the freed people's struggle to control the nature, meaning, and rewards not only of their work but of their lives. They sought to build not just a free labor economy but a free society. They sought to be not just free laborers but a free people.

Part Three

The Political Economy of Freedom

In truth, there is no justice in the general local institutions of Jamaica; because there is no public opinion to which an appeal can be made. Slavery has divided society into two classes; to one it has given power, but to the other it has not extended protection. One of these classes is above public opinion, and the other is below it; neither are, therefore, under its influence; and it is much to be feared, that owing to the want of sympathy between them, to the want of dependence and mutual confidence, to the poorer class being able to provide for the necessities of life without any application to the higher, there never will be in Jamaica, or in any other slave colony, a community of feeling on which public opinion can operate beneficially.

**[SLIGO], "JAMAICA UNDER THE APPRENTICESHIP SYSTEM"
(1838)**

The West Indian colonies are not things of natural growth which may be safely left to the care of nature, but artificial fabrications, formed and sustained for a long time by peculiar political contrivances, which being now discountenanced and prohibited have left a disjointed and discordant framework that has peculiar need of care and assistance.

CHARLES GREY TO EARL GREY, 21 APRIL 1849

6

Liberal Democratic Society in Theory and Practice

L ess than a year before the end of the apprenticeship system, Lord Glenelg, the colonial secretary, enunciated what he considered the essence of Britain's future policy toward West Indian freed people: "that the apprenticeship of the emancipated slaves is to be immediately succeeded by personal freedom, in that full and unlimited sense of the term in which it is used in reference to the other subjects of the British Crown."[1] According to the Glenelg doctrine, the ex-slaves' freedom was to have political and social as well as economic content; all Jamaicans would now enjoy the equal protection of the law. Henceforth all references, "disguised" or overt, to their race or former condition were to be expunged from colonial laws. Blacks would now have access to all public institutions and be able to vote on the same basis as whites, and even inadvertent social distinctions were to be eliminated from the legal codes.

Glenelg's tenure as colonial secretary ended less than fifteen months later, but his doctrine continued for several years more to inform the policies of his successors, despite waning official sympathy for West Indian blacks. The doctrine retained its force because it articulated the regnant ideology of liberal democracy; it expressed the ethos of the nineteenth century's dual revolution that had prepared the seedbed for emancipation. A well-ordered, self-regulating society depended on the unbiased mediation of the competing personal interests expressed by autonomous individuals. The ancient subject now became the modern citizen, upon whose participation in the political marketplace and exercise of individual choice was founded the perception of justice and consent.

Emancipation policies were developed, moreover, in an era of increasing agitation for a broader franchise in Britain itself. The expansion of the body politic was not uncontested, of course. Its middle-class beneficiaries were constantly glancing over their shoulders at proletarian hordes, who might exploit bourgeois democracy to make socialism. But they had not yet developed credible ideological defenses against the presumption of a gradual and inexorable democratization of political processes.[2] For all these reasons, the debates over the political and economic policies appropriate to the newly emancipated societies lay bare issues relevant to other human societies that otherwise would have remained unarticulated.

Classical liberalism posited an approximate symmetry between men's economic and political relations with society. That free laborers must be invested with civil rights—equality before the law—reflected, in principle, an integrated perception of man as economic animal and political actor. Without political equality, equality in the market was merely "nominal," wrote John Stuart Mill.[3] Freedom meant little if what was gained in the marketplace could be taken away in the legislature. Precisely this anxiety undergirded the Smithian principle of laissez faire, for which the mid-nineteenth century provided "a special kind of interlude" of unprecedented and unequaled hegemony.[4] It was a principle, however, that would soon become more a convenient fiction than an actual basis of political and economic practice. And if the reality of activist government was an unspoken truth in mature societies, it was explicit for those in the process of formation or transformation. As Mill himself would later concede, in such "backward states" even "despotism" might be "a legitimate mode of government."[5] Indeed, in the former slave colonies it became clear that government intervened as decisively by its inaction as by its action. Since state action—in one form or another—would likely determine the fate of critical economic and social processes, the outcome of the struggle to control state power would be decisive.

Colonial Office policymakers had anticipated that obstacles to the creation of free societies in former slave colonies would be posed less by the ex-slaves than by their former masters, and the apprenticeship years gave ample demonstration of the difficulties one might expect in coaxing enlightened public policies from the planters' political representatives. The objectives of the home government could be easily frustrated in the details of lawmaking and execution. Theoretically, Parliament was supreme, but there were practical limits to working its will in the distant colonies. The Colonial Office, or the governor it appointed, exercised a veto over colonial legislation, but this proved a blunt tool with which to achieve positive rather than negative goals. The home government could reject laws it did not like, but it experienced great difficulties in assuring the passage of laws it did want.

In Jamaica, legislative initiative lay almost entirely with the local assembly. Any governor so bold as to meddle in the business of lawmaking prior to final passage faced certain censure for breach of assembly privilege. More than once in recent years government had come to a grinding halt pending a governor's public apology for thus abusing the independence of the legislature. Indeed, the Jamaica Assembly had even arrogated many executive functions, such as spending the money it appropriated and letting public contracts. Against this formidable array the governor's small island bureaucracy and limited patronage lent him little weight with which to shape events. In a crisis, of course, Parliament could take matters into its own hands and pass the requisite legislation directly. But such a proceeding was by definition extraordinary. It remained a reserved power to be exercised only after extreme provocation, as it had been in 1833 and in 1839. Having failed to end Jamaican self-government in 1839, the Colonial Office had to rely on the colonists themselves to implement the Glenelg doctrine of racial equality. If a free society was to be created, it must be done by ex-slaves and their descendants, together with former slaveholders and their retainers.

Developments during the first decade of freedom greatly complicated the theory and practice of indirect rule in the West Indies. The adoption of free trade policies precipitated renewed and bitter conflict between planter representatives in the Jamaica Assembly and the British government. But this conflict, unlike those of the 1830s, occurred as brown and black men were achieving a formidable and, to whites, threatening presence in Jamaican politics. That presence was precursor to the intermittent struggles of the second decade of freedom, during which—in an ominous reversal of previous alignments—Afro-Jamaicans came increasingly into conflict with the governor.

As a consequence, Glenelg's doctrine was all but abandoned by the end of the 1850s. The political process was viewed almost wholly in racial terms, and the talent and skill of colonial officials were directed not toward protecting the rights of freed people but toward blunting black political power. Taylor's harsh judgment that democratic governance was impossible in a racially mixed society had now become the conventional wisdom. To most analysts, Jamaica was what twentieth-century social scientists would call "a plural society": fragmented into antagonistic racial groups, without mediating public institutions, without norm-creating public opinion, without community. It was, Governor Grey insisted, an unnatural growth, an artificial fabrication, a political contrivance.[6] By the early 1860s, colonial officials anxiously awaited the next major crisis that might be seized upon as a pretext to end what had once been called "the mighty experiment."

Liberal Democracy beyond the Line

For much of the British Empire the 1840s were economically expansive and politically turbulent. The economic doctrines of the so-called philosophical radicals were ascendant, the promulgation of free trade by successive Tory and Whig governments signaling their clear triumph. Meanwhile, the political radicals of the day, the Chartists, waxed and waned before finally being routed in 1848. Parliamentary politics were characterized by shifting factional alignments and weak control by the governing alliance. But the dominating presence of Sir Robert Peel and Lord John Russell lent a discipline to these alliances not founded on ideology or in the electoral constituencies. Approaching the era's problems from radically different perspectives, Peel and Russell met on the common ground of continued Whig-style reforms in the nation's economic and social life, that is, moderate reforms that appealed to the middle classes. Thus, above the partisan wrangling appeared an emerging liberal consensus; party conflict took place within the neat boundaries of liberal democratic ideals.[7]

Although this liberal consensus often broke down over specific policies, the ideals, or at least the language in which they were expressed, were consistent; almost all parties claimed as their own "progress" and "progressive" principles. The themes of the age were decidedly bourgeois: innovation, enterprise, practical education, self-reliance, the mutuality and interdependence of social classes. All was built on calculated appeals to the basic, innate human desire for material self-improvement. Such desire could be cultivated, nurtured, and made the moral linchpin of social action.

At the Colonial Office both Conservative and Whig administrations spoke this language and reflected this bourgeois view of the world. In part this was because of the continuity of the permanent staffers who drafted their dispatches. But it is significant that the Tory minister Edward Stanley could endorse "an active spirit of invention," labor-saving technological innovations, and the enterprising spirit as readily as the radical free trader Earl Grey.[8] Moreover, by the 1840s these premises about the sources of human motivation and the mainsprings of social action were pervasive among all colors and ranks of Jamaican society as well.[9]

Thus in 1846 Richard Hill, a former colored legislator and then head of the special magistrates' corps, bemoaned the drought-inflicted decline in Jamaican prosperity as much for its moral as for its economic consequences. "Active prosperity gives the means of supplying what is necessary, and sends out its stirring thousands to look abroad and find new and varied wants. We had opened up the moral excitements in the place of the physical inducements to labour . . . by varying the wants of their animal nature, and extending their rational desires." Here, he proclaimed, was "a lesson of timely wisdom." As Hill contemplated the efficiency of the railroad link between Kingston and St. Thomas-in-the-Vale, his language became almost panegyric. He was fascinated by the railway's "rapid communication," "untiring velocity," "ceaseless energy," "exactness and dispatch," "stirring punctuality." The moral impact of this new technology was pervasive and wondrous to behold. "Already the listless habit of the creole whatever be his lineage or complexion is exchanged for methodical energy in conducting intercourse with the business world." It was a propitious moment for all to learn "a lesson of vigilance and self dependent activity." More specifically, all this was an object lesson on the benefits to be expected from the proposed industrial schools, "for it is only through the instrumentality of education rendered practically useful by being applied to the purposes of life, that we can hope to change habits, the growth of a vicious freedom of over two hundred years."[10] Bourgeois freedom, then, would not have an immaculate conception; the state must plant and nurture its seed. Crucial tests of the colonial state's nurturing role emerged as it

Sir Charles Metcalfe

debated and implemented policies for the administration of civil and criminal justice, education, immigration, and taxation.

The impartial administration of the laws was fundamental to fostering liberal democratic values. Glenelg's policy required that new laws be crafted appropriate to the new social relations of freedom. The Colonial Office's early vigilance in detecting oppressive features in these proposed statutes owed mainly to the head of its West Indies division, James Stephen, who had gained valuable experience at this during the 1820s, when he pored over the amelioration acts. In addition, Glenelg invited representatives of abolitionist societies to the Colonial Office to scan West Indian laws, an invitation readily taken up by many of them.[11]

But despite this vigilance, colonial systems of justice became increasingly biased in favor of planter interests and against the freed people. Most students of postemancipation Jamaica date changes in attitude toward the freed people and vigilance in defending their rights from the crisis of 1839.[12] In Jamaica the changes were set in motion by the policy commitments of the governor, Charles Metcalfe, and shaped by the complexities of his relationship with the Colonial Office. Metcalfe's instructions had reflected the colonial secretary's desire for reduced tensions in his office's relations with the Jamaica Assembly following the aborted attempt to supersede it in 1839. But the governor's own background and predilections led him to stretch his instructions to the limit. Thus in one of the earliest efforts by the planters to regain control of their former slaves through the legal system, Metcalfe was their willing ally. Metcalfe's conciliatory policy seemed "fatuous" to veteran staffers such as James Stephen. The governor appeared "determined to think the Assembly virtuous till he finds it otherwise," Stephen sighed, whereas the Colonial Office staff, having known it longer, must "distrust it."[13]

Among the new laws that worried Stephen most was the Vagrancy Act, which, for reasons Metcalfe failed to explain, deviated from the provisions recommended by the British orders in council issued 7 September 1838, being generally "more severe." Particularly troubling was a provision giving summary jurisdiction to local magistrates, who, being planters in most cases, could be expected to harbor biases against allegedly "vagrant" laborers. Metcalfe had offered the disingenuous argument that he could hardly appoint men to positions implying public trust in their very title and terms and then decline to trust them. Finding it difficult to refute Metcalfe's logic, Russell demurred. He assented to the act provided the governor would revise the list of magistrates to weed out bad ones and not allow any new legislation to render these powers "vague, arbitrary & uncertain." Should the government find these powers used oppressively in the future, the law would be disallowed. Russell urged amendments immediately to those parts of the law that had aroused objection, but he cautioned the governor that his reticence to disallow the act was solely in deference to Metcalfe's opinion. "But you must be aware that no considerations of courtesy & no fear of reproach ought to deter me from affording the best protection in my power to those classes of the Queen's subjects who, as Labourers or Artisans, constitute the great majority of the Population of Jamaica."[14]

Metcalfe's reply was less than reassuring. He was apprehensive about suggesting amendments in a way that the Assembly might take as a breach of privilege. He assured Russell that he would urge the Assembly to accept the suggested amendments to the Vagrancy Act and to take other steps to satisfy the secretary's wishes, as long as they did "not involve an invasion of established rights and privileges." Not only was Metcalfe very solicitous of the Assembly's honor, he resisted

Russell's suggestion that he weed out bad justices. Declaring his absolute confidence in the local magistrates, he insisted: "I am ready to answer for the whole Body." This drew a marginal notation from one Colonial Office staffer: "This is strong." Perhaps Metcalfe thought better of it too, since he then reversed his field, arguing that it would be fruitless to try to prune away the bad magistrates anyway. The governor protested that he was very much aware of his duty to protect the laboring class, who were the great majority of Jamaicans. He would use his own methods, however. He would not be found "riding roughshod over the Island Institutions, and knocking down right and left every thing that stands in ones way." Rather he would achieve the government's objectives "by cordially cooperating with the Island Authorities, Legislative and Executive, profiting by their good feelings, taking them by the hand and leading them gently to every desired improvement, respecting their just rights as well as those of others; and above all by not suspecting and distrusting them." Warming to his subject, the governor went on to chide the Colonial Office for language in its dispatches that could be misconstrued to suggest its distrust and suspicion and that might lead to disgust and disaffection among both the assemblymen and their constituents. He was confident that by his gentler methods he could get them to adopt "the most perfect code of Laws in the World, securing in the utmost degree the Liberty and Protection of the Subject." Apparently this extraordinary declaration left at least one Colonial Office staffer at a loss for words. Beside it he wrote simply: "!!!"[15]

James Stephen, who long had been under violent attack for being an overly vigilant protector of black West Indian interests, was not content to leave matters there. Arguing that the entire issue of allowing former slaveholders to enjoy summary jurisdiction over their former slaves and current labor force remained dangerously "undecided & inconclusive," he urged Russell to pursue the matter further. "When a Govn. so urgently demands confidence for the local Institutions, Legislature and Magisterial, and so strongly deprecates, or rather censures (for the word is not too strong) the language and spirit of the Instructions conveyed to him, I confess myself to doubt whether some more full & direct encounter with such remarks is not necessary." But Russell waved off this suggestion, thinking it "unseemly to argue [his] instructions with the Governor." In a longer minute, he expanded upon his policy with Metcalfe. "I have been anxious to leave as much as possible to Sir C. Metcalfe, but to let him see that the objections to the Jamaica Acts were not over [trivial matters]." He felt that in the end "Sir C. Metcalfe will take more pains with the Acts, & will consult his own excellent understanding rather more than in his wish to conciliate he appears to have done." Consistent with that policy, the Colonial Office disallowed only five of the sixty-five Jamaican acts passed in the 1839–40 sessions, notwithstanding the serious questions raised by Stephen and his staff.[16] In this first test of Glenelg's policy the government failed.

Metcalfe's successor, Lord Elgin, arriving in Jamaica in March 1842, was also determined to follow a conciliatory policy, but his was of a different brand from his predecessor's. When the Assembly passed "an Act to prevent trespasses," the governor vetoed it. In doing so he ignored the favorable endorsement of his attorney general and accepted instead the negative evaluation of the Jamaican chief justice. He felt the need to act rather than leave the decision to the Colonial Office, because he feared a violent reaction to the legislation among black freeholders. The key objection to the bill was that it gave summary jurisdiction in land tenure and trespass cases to any two magistrates, one of whom even could be the complainant. These magistrates would have been given power, practically, to determine disputed land titles. Appeal of the magistrates' decision would be limited in time and would have required substantial appeal bonds.[17]

Elgin also reversed Metcalfe's policy of reducing the special magistrates' corps through attrition.[18] Only twenty-eight special magistrates remained in the colony, and Elgin did not favor reducing that number further. On the other hand, he also declined to increase their number, explaining that relations between the special and local magistrates were less tense now and that a new law allowing appeals of all local magistrates' decisions to the court of quarter sessions removed some of the need for the specials. Elgin's optimism about the improved administration of justice was not justified, however. By his own evidence, the costs of appeals to quarter sessions would be prohibitive for the peasantry, totaling five pounds in direct costs and requiring appellants to post a ten-pound security deposit besides. The record of recent appeals showed that of 685 convictions over the previous twelve months, only 5 had been appealed. Here was cause to question the attrition policy.[19]

Elgin won firmer home government backing on other law and order issues. The crisis of 1839 had been precipitated by Captain Pringle's devastating critique of Jamaica's prison system. As late as 1842, Elgin still found reason to worry about crime and punishment. His predecessor, Governor Metcalfe, had found the prisons not much im-

James Bruce, the Earl of Elgin

proved during his tenure; after a year in office, Elgin was convinced that the crime rate was still increasing and that more effective methods of punishment were required to control it. At the Colonial Office, Taylor agreed that the changing character of crimes committed was cause for concern. Violent crimes against persons were more frequent, and the outbreak of myalism during the early 1840s presaged the much-feared cultural regression among freed people to African barbarism.[20]

Myalism was a set of beliefs and practices that Jamaican slaves had fashioned specifically to defend themselves against witchcraft (obeah), but more generally it was a response to their experiences in America. It represented their way of understanding and exerting a measure of control over the harsh life they endured. Although coming from diverse ethnic origins, Afro-Jamaican slaves shared certain concepts about the relations binding the individual, the society, and the spirit world. Human misfortune was caused by malicious forces embodied in the spirits of the dead, which were activated by antisocial acts, such as sorcery and witchcraft. Spells could be cast by burying the Obi, a malevolent charm. In order to protect itself from these antisocial individualists (practitioners of obeah), the community enlisted the ritual services and powers of specialists who could identify the spirit causing the problem and exorcise it. Therefore, the myal tradition, as one scholar describes it, "formed the core of a strong, self-confident counter-culture."[21]

In 1840–41 there was a dramatic resurgence of these practices. In the St. James Court of Quarter Sessions, for example, more than sixty persons were tried for myalism, and forty of them were convicted and sentenced to hard labor. There were also convictions in petty sessions where criminal charges had been preferred against a number of people, mostly for trespass on property to dig for the Obi in places where he was supposedly buried and for assaults on people supposedly evil. Meanwhile, churches tried to suppress obeah by expelling members accused of the practice. Planters, however, were less concerned about religious deviance than they were about the loss of labor. Periodically, some estates had been completely deserted, "the laborers in a body abandoning their work and devoting themselves entirely to the celebration of the myalism rites."[22]

In his reports to the Colonial Office, Elgin appeared to link the resurgence of myalism, which was confined to the north side of the island, in Trelawny and St. James, to the influx of African indentured workers there. Obeah was usually present among Africans, he thought, and this sparked its antidote, myalism. But the fact that the myalism outbreak occurred before any significant African immigration and that the few African indentures then in Jamaica were often mere children suggests that they probably were not the primary cause of these developments. Furthermore, according to Elgin, the victims of these assaults were almost invariably old men and women long resident on the island, never Europeans or newly imported Africans.

On the other hand, the African content of myalism was unmistakable. The black population was overwhelmingly creole by 1840, but it included elderly Africans, and African traditions remained strong in Jamaican culture. "It would appear, moreover, that terms and expressions borrowed from Christianity were in the present case engrafted upon the original African superstition," Elgin wrote his superiors. "The leaders professed to be acting under the authority and in obedience to the command of Jesus Christ. The alliance with pseudo-Christianity, or rather this adoption of a Christian phraseology did not in any degree mitigate the barbarism of their rites." Those rites consisted chiefly of singing, digging for the Obi, and violently exorcising "the evil Spirit" out of the possessed. "I am moreover informed that some of their orgies were not altogether consistent with Morality and decorum," lamented the governor. Similar circumstances in 1802 had aroused fears of rebellion, but he thought that nothing had transpired in 1841 "to warrant the belief that the superstitious practices in question were connected with feelings of disaffection."[23]

Nevertheless, Elgin thought stern measures would be necessary to get on top of the situation. He recommended "the stocks or other degrading & humiliating punishments."[24] By the end of the decade, the Assembly had decided to go even further: they legalized corporal punishment for such "crimes." This return to slave-style discipline was swiftly implemented.[25]

On most other issues Lord Elgin's administration was in a much more liberal tradition than Metcalfe's. Perhaps the fact that he was a young man (thirty-one years old) with less administrative experience than most Jamaican governors gave Elgin a freshness of outlook, idealism, even a naive optimism. Certainly, more than any other governor's, his dispatches reflect the liberal idealism of that era. He found in Jamaica a duty to which he must respond. The manner in which Britain shepherded the transformation of the West Indies from slave to free societies would set an example for the world, he declared shortly after his arrival on the island. Now more than ever a close connection existed "between the course of Policy which ought to be pursued here and the interests of Christian civilization both within the Island and beyond it." British colonies could be examples of good government and successful policy in a plural community. Unhesitatingly, Elgin took up Glenelg's doctrine that it was Britain's obligation to raise the emancipated slave morally, intellectually, and socially, as well as to obliterate racial animosities. This emphasis on the social progress of the freed people was a return to first principles and contrasted sharply with the overbearing concern of his predecessor for the material prosperity of the planter class. But one must also understand that for Elgin material prosperity and moral progress were mutually interactive and inseparable.[26]

For Lord Elgin, the fundamental division of Jamaican society was defined by class: on the one side were the planters and those connected with or dependent on their welfare; on the other, the freed people and their supporters. The source of Jamaica's problem, then, was the incomplete deprivation of the means of production from that potential working class; or as Sligo had put it, "the poorer class [was] able to provide for the necessities of life without any application to the higher."[27] But in the fashion of a classic nineteenth-century liberal, Elgin contended that the interests of both classes were actually compatible and mutual. Describing the conflict as one arising between the moral and intellectual claims of the blacks, on the one hand, and the material interests of the planters, on the other, Elgin asserted that it gave a "false and party coloring" to practical questions of mutual interest. There was a need to find "common ground" and on this common ground to found "a scheme of policy sufficiently progressive to contribute towards the development of that new order of social relations into which the materials supplied by Emancipation were about to arrange themselves." He was convinced that "the interests of both classes, rightly understood, lie in the same direction." The role of government was to get the conflicting parties to recognize that mutuality of interest. That accomplished, the island's prosperity was assured.[28]

Repeating the standard formula of the day, Elgin insisted that "civilization" would stimulate tastes and habits in the black worker that could only be satisfied with a money income. Indeed, his very first tour of the island had convinced him that "civilization, the spread of knowledge, habits of greater expense in respect of living, dress and dwellings, will conspire to render a relapse to a former and lower condition distasteful and I trust improbable."[29] From this it followed that "the improvement of the negro is the first interest of the Planter." All other measures were subordinate to that principal objective.[30]

Planters would have to reform, too. They must be "weaned" away from the coercive management and wasteful cultivation techniques characteristic of slavery. Given an abundance of cheap land, it would be impossible to coerce labor by means of immigration or similar measures. "One scheme of policy" was to teach them the connection between education and industry. Elgin was also convinced that the planters would be much less reliant on immigration as a panacea once they recognized the virtues of scientific agriculture and the inefficiencies of slavery. Innovation and scientific agricultural practices would call, in turn, for higher skills and intelligence from the laborer and "redeem the pursuits of the husbandman from the discredit into which they had fallen as the avocation of slaves, and thus enlist the hearty co-operation" of the blacks' friends.[31]

For their part, laborers resisted innovation because "they are in some quarters keenly alive to the effect which the proposed change of system may have in reducing the value of their labor."[32] Industrial schools should be established to educate blacks in new methods and skills. In these schools they would be taught principles of scientific agriculture and gain practical experience by working the gardens and fields maintained by the schools. The Baptists objected to industrial education because they thought it was just a device to keep blacks on the estates. Elgin hoped to overcome their opposition by offering model, voluntary classes and inviting them to attend with their students. Such programs would "create . . . a feeling favorable to the subject by presenting it to the Public in its most attractive guise as connected with questions of scientific and practical interest."[33] Thus industrial schools would "harmonize well with the prevailing spirit of improvement" and provide a practical "illustration of that coincidence between the material interests of one class and the moral interests of another, the recognition of which is an indispensable condition to social progress in these communities."[34]

All this would require time and systematic rather than isolated, ad hoc measures. Required, too, were "conciliatory principles and sound economical views." Thus Elgin abjured "hasty condemnation of received opinions and the overzealous advocacy of new practices." Like his predecessors, he was sensitive to the governor's limited powers, the Assembly's monopoly of legislative initiative, and the scant patronage available to oil the machinery of government. Since the governor's influence was entirely moral and intellectual, he must conciliate and cajole, staying always above the fray of partisanship.[35] The governor's speech to the Assembly upon the opening of a new session was his best chance to address the issues, set priorities, and recommend legislative initiatives. Elgin resolved to make the most of it. Deciding early in his tenure that a lack of confidence was the critical problem, he sought to revive it by pointing out the strengths of the island and the brighter prospects before it. This speech was also intended to turn "the attention of English capitalists towards the Colony."[36]

Elgin reported some success in gaining the local press's approval of his policies. Private initiatives were also evident in the formation of agricultural societies and in the nineteen submissions he received in response to a prize offered for the best essay describing a system of industrial education suited to the colony. His efforts were not uniformly successful, however; for example, the plowing contests designed to encourage black workers to accept new techniques drew little support.[37] Nevertheless, by the summer of 1845 the governor could point to a revival of confidence evident in the good prices fetched by estates that previously had been unsalable. Indeed, by that date Elgin was himself confident about the island's future. Notwithstanding that crops were still far below slave-era standards, violent crimes were rising, and school attendance was falling, he concluded that "on the whole" the colony's prospects were favorable and "steadily advancing towards that condition of prosperity and social happiness in which the reasonable expectations of the friends of emancipation will be fulfilled."[38]

Many planters also were more confident by the mid-1840s, although their bets were hedged with reservations about good sugar prices, a steady labor supply, and falling wages. Nevertheless, the main lines of theoretical agreement one finds between the political economists and some of the practical planters illustrate the pervasiveness of liberal ideas. Recently arrived from England to superintend his Jamaican properties, John Blagrove jotted into his diary an analysis not entirely dissimilar from those of Taylor and Elgin. He began, predictably, with the declaration that immigration was essential to create labor competition and thereby bring costs down. But he also recognized that the impact of immigration would not be evident for generations hence, after natural increase of the population and acculturation had done their work. "Upon this score—combined with religious & temporal instruction, the promotion of marriage, and increased desire of industrious habits—Jamaica I conceive will yet hold up its head. The present prospects are far from flattering however. Still I see no reason to dispair—by the [ ] assistance & desire of both black & white to conduce to the welfare of one & the other—to lay aside all recollection of Olden Times—& each & all to remember that as Human-beings we are dependent one on the other." Meanwhile, staple production would increase "in proportion [to] the ideas & wants of Jamaica's indigenous 'habitants." Like Elgin, Blagrove was convinced that the moral and religious education of the blacks was the planters' essential ally.[39]

Almost at the same time as Blagrove's diary entry, Richard Lewis, attorney for Ballard's Valley, wrote his London suppliers describing a similar scenario for Jamaica's road to recovery. Lewis was not a recent arrival but a long-term resident planting attorney, yet his analysis shared with Blagrove's certain conceptions of economic and moral process. He agreed with Blagrove that immigration and natural population increase were essential to reduce labor costs. But his first condition for improvement was that blacks would become "more industrious" in the process of "acquiring more wants," a process he thought clearly evident already.[40]

Blagrove later sat in the planter-dominated legislature to which

Elgin addressed many of his lectures on political economy and sound public policy. For a time the assemblymen appeared to be apt pupils. In a private letter to Stanley, Elgin fairly bubbled with enthusiasm for "the hearty tone" of their response to his suggestions.[41] The Assembly echoed the governor's enthusiasm for industrial education. "A system of education for that large portion of the community who depend on daily toil for support can only be rendered effective by combining habits of manual labour with elementary instruction." Moreover, they appeared ready to take the long and indirect route to rebuilding their fortunes by investing in institutions that would mold future generations of workers. The state must rectify the failures of the parents.

> Schools which unite these two requisites at once meet the wants and circumstances of an agricultural population; what has hitherto been defective in the parent ought to be supplied in the tuition of the child; There can be little doubt that these deficiencies in a large and important class of our population are produced in a great degree by an injurious absence of parental guidance and control. At a maturer age these must infallibly result in the want of due appreciation of the restraints of social order; of the advantages of a steady pursuit of domestic happiness and comfort through a course of usefulness; and of a proper understanding of those relative interests in the fair rewards of labour which identify individual with general prosperity.[42]

Agreement on first principles did not lead to an agreement on an effective educational system, however. Although all conceded the importance of education, the state actually played a very limited role in funding and maintaining schools. Except for the few plantation classes set up during the apprenticeship period, most schools had been established by sectarian groups, primarily the Baptists and the Methodists. Even these had been built with money and labor contributed by ex-slaves and sustained by the substantial school fees paid by black parents.[43] In 1835 and 1836, Parliament appropriated almost fifty thousand pounds to subsidize these ecclesiastical schools; but the grants were discontinued in 1841, a step justified in part by the existence of such an extensive private system.[44] Possibly the home government also thought that such action would encourage greater public expenditure on education by the colonies themselves. But in Jamaica their cuts only led the Assembly to propose, with Metcalfe's endorsement, abolition of the special magistrate corps on the pretext of applying the savings to education. Seeing through this ingenuous ruse, Stephen convinced Stanley to reject the proposal.[45]

It was six years after emancipation before any significant colonial effort was made to organize and fund a public education system for the black majority. In 1844 Elgin secured passage of "An Act to Promote Education of the Industrial Classes in This Island," a law that established a board of education consisting of the governor, the bishop, the president of the Executive Council, the Speaker of the Assembly, and five other commissioners to examine the state of education and industrial instruction. Among its provisions was £1,000 to fund existing sectarian schools, including £300 to establish "a normal school of industry." But despite this hopeful beginning, the education system—if it can be called that—remained underfunded and served only a minority of the island's eligible youth. An 1847 report counted 178 schools with a total enrollment of 14,532, which amounted to about 20 percent of the eligible children in a school-age population estimated to be 75,558.[46]

By the mid-1840s the school fund had risen to £2,000, including £700 for the normal school, but the system's development was still inhibited by the controversy over sectarian versus state control of curriculum. Reflecting these controversies, the 1847 report included strong criticisms of what it considered to be the excessively religious orientation in the schools: reading was taught from the Bible, and instructors relied on a catechistic, rote learning regime in which children repeated lessons that were not explained. The report also recommended that "at an early age a portion of labor as agricultural apprentices" be combined with academic education.[47] Such comments exacerbated the Dissenter religious groups' distrust of state involvement that was already so prevalent. Indeed, the Baptists were already engaged in a broad-based political attack on the state-supported church establishment, and they remained the principal opponents of industrial education.[48] Consequently, the Baptists declined public financial assistance, as did the Church Missionary Society, the Roman Catholics, and the Jewish congregations. Only the Methodists, Presbyterians, Moravians, and the American Congregationalists accepted state funding.[49]

More than ten years after the Elgin initiative, therefore, the Jamaican educational system remained underfunded and inadequate. In 1856 Governor Barkly reported that educational accomplishments since emancipation were meager. Financing still came mainly from private sources through churches, missionaries, and the parents themselves, the parliamentary grants having declined each year. The colony's £2,000 appropriation was supplemented later by an additional £2,000 to £3,000 collected from the poll tax, but that total, too, was inadequate. And even these funding levels were not sustained during quarrels over retrenchment in the late 1840s and early 1850s. By the end of 1854, "education was at its lowest grasp." Teachers who received their salaries from government funds had not been paid for two years, and their schools had been closed as a result. A few schools had been kept open by Anglican clergymen but then closed when their salaries also stopped. In 1856 the governor reported that "scarcely half as many children were receiving instruction as had done so the year before."[50]

The obstacles to greater progress in education were not difficult to identify. Although planters may have agreed with educational reform in principle, they were loath to make this a priority when it came to appropriations. In 1850 the *Colonial Standard* insisted that education was the only solution to the indolence, crime, and immorality rampant on the island, but it still excused the limited appropriation because of the distress created by the free trade crisis.[51] There may be some merit to the *Standard's* excuse, but the fact is that planters showed little practical enthusiasm for education even before 1846. The main advocates of educational reform between 1838 and 1844 were the small cadre of colored assemblymen. In 1844 Edward Jordon tried to double education expenditures, and in 1850 Robert Osborn urged the establishment of more schools throughout the island and larger budgets. With Alexander Heslop, Osborn also sought to create local professional schools for doctors and lawyers. Other colored legislators advocated technical training schools, believing this could encourage crafts and cottage industries using local materials.[52]

By contrast, planters generally opposed all measures to expand education. Very likely the idea of spending money primarily for the benefit of the black majority did not appeal to most planters. Most of the white estate managers had no family or children, at least none they chose to recognize officially. The wealthier resident planters sent their children to a few select private academies on the island and to England. It is undoubtedly true that some feared the uncertain effects of education on their labor supply, the theory of increased wants be damned. So despite Barkly's long catalog of distress in the mid-1850s, in 1856 an education bill that colored and liberal whites managed to maneuver through the Assembly was vetoed by the planter-dominated Legislative Council.[53]

Even the most liberally disposed planters insisted that they required the more direct relief offered by immigration. Two theories were operative in thinking about immigration: the demographic rationale, that population would be increased so as to create a more favorable balance between land and labor; and the coercive rationale, that the "unreliable" creoles would be replaced by workers whose labor planters could command. Indentured workers, under contracts that restrained their movements, defined working conditions, and specified their pay, were not free to bargain for higher wages or to leave the plantation without legal penalties. In truth, they were a dependent and unfree labor force.

Although the Colonial Office staff was wary of the coercive intent of recruiting contract laborers, it shared the planters' conviction that an imbalance between land and labor was a bad thing and could have deleterious consequences. State intervention to correct that imbalance was accepted practice, for which Australian settlements were a good precedent. By 1840 the home government had formed the Colonial Land and Emigration Commission to sell colonial land and supervise emigration from Britain. Beginning with Sligo's efforts during the 1830s to recruit Germans and other Europeans to fill up the interior parishes, every Jamaican governor had given at least qualified approval to state-supported immigration. In April 1840 Governor Metcalfe signed a law initiating state-supported immigration to Jamaica. Under this act immigration agents were appointed to recruit and arrange transportation for immigrants in North America, Britain, and "elsewhere."[54]

Without awaiting Colonial Office approval, Metcalfe dispatched the new commissioner of immigration, Alexander Barclay, to seek out potential immigrants in the United States, Canada, and Great Britain. During the summer of 1840 Barclay traveled to Savannah, Charleston, Norfolk, and Philadelphia, meeting with black leaders in those cities and distributing a pamphlet on Jamaica. His reports were not encouraging, however. He encountered opposition from slaveholders as well as black and white abolitionists. The American Colonization Society and its slaveowning supporters wanted to send emigrants to Africa, not to other parts of the Americas. American abolitionists were opposed to emigration to any destination. Barclay also learned that Jamaica's prevailing wage offered little inducement for American workers. In fact, they could get higher wages in Trinidad, from which a contingent of black emigrants had just returned with a negative report on conditions that discouraged further interest in the West Indies generally. The only attractions Jamaica offered American blacks were the political and civil rights they stood to gain, not economic improvement.[55]

The 1840s and 1850s were years of steadily worsening political and social conditions for blacks in America, and their attitudes toward immigration changed dramatically during that period. Jamaica was one of many destinations black emigrationists considered, but as one of them, the Reverend James Pennington, pointed out to Governor Elgin in 1846, black Americans were unlikely to come as field laborers. They wanted land, not wages. Although Elgin thought immigration even under these conditions might be a useful cultural leaven for the Afro-Jamaican population, the Colonial Office was skittish about possible complications in its diplomatic relations with America should fugitive slaves find their way to the island as well. The American government had already rebuffed official overtures in 1843 to recruit among its free black population. This problem of American slavery continued to restrain British recruitment efforts among American blacks well into the 1860s.[56]

Fugitives from American slavery who had settled in Canada seemed to be another attractive source for Jamaican laborers. But for much the same reason as their fellows in the United States, Canadian blacks were not interested in Jamaica. Only 169 came between 1841 and 1845, all of them skilled laborers. They demanded higher wages and more food, especially meat, than native Jamaicans. The extra expense did not endear them to their Jamaican employers, nor did plantation work endear Jamaica to them. Many of them soon returned to Canada.[57]

Consequently, only a handful of American and Canadian blacks came to Jamaica in the 1840s. Indeed, most of Jamaica's 1,417 immigrants during the first year's operation of the new law were white. But this source proved inadequate to the island's labor needs and held little promise of shifting the demographic balance of the island's population. Europeans were more vulnerable to tropical diseases and even more likely to shun field work than blacks. Instead of establishing settlements in the interior, where they might have blocked access to native blacks, the whites were more likely to settle in the coastal towns, where they were alleged to have fallen into drunkenness and disorder. If one were seeking a political "counterpoise" to the freed people in the interior, advised Metcalfe, granting freeholds and voting rights to the native Maroons offered a better possibility than did European immigration. Moreover, such a policy would take advantage of the longstanding hostility between slaves and Maroons. Meanwhile, Barclay's recruiting tour of Britain and Ireland incited violent demonstrations in opposition. By the end of 1841 the idea of a European trek to the Jamaican outback was all but given up.[58]

Despite their hostile denunciation of native Jamaicans, planters strongly preferred new workers drawn from the same source—Africa. Having little to show for his trips to North America and Great Britain, Commissioner Barclay turned toward Sierra Leone, hoping to coax to Jamaica some of the Africans settled there, who had been liberated from the slave trade by the British navy. Eventually, Barclay managed to bring 267 indentured Africans from Sierra Leone, landing them in Port Royal in May 1841. But he had encountered a number of obstacles to his efforts that did not bode well for the future. Among them was the gingerliness with which John Russell's Colonial Office approached the subject, fearing that recruiting laborers in Africa might be interpreted as a surreptitious reopening of the slave trade that would embarrass the government.

The replacement of Melbourne's Whig government by Robert Peel's Tories in September 1841 removed one obstacle to African immigration by bringing Edward Stanley, a more sympathetic ear to planter complaints, to the Colonial Office. The endorsement of state-supported African and Asian immigration by a parliamentary select committee the following year was also helpful. During the twelve-month period ending in the fall of 1842 more than half (53 percent) of the 1,798 immigrants landed in Jamaica were Africans.

The planters did not have it all their own way, however. Seven months after Stanley arrived at the Colonial Office, Elgin was appointed governor. Much more skeptical than Metcalfe had been of what he called the immigration "panacea," Elgin gave it a very qualified endorsement. He insisted that immigration policy be pursued in the context of general improvement in agricultural techniques and management practices; be fiscally responsible; and be consistent with government efforts to protect the moral interests of the freed people. The planters' view of immigration, he rued, was premised on the continuation of slave-style management and coercion of the native workforce. They sought immigrant laborers in order to continue "the system of husbandry pursued during slavery." Immigration pursued from this motive threatened his policy of reconciling the interests of planters and creole laborers.[59]

What planters might well have countered to Elgin was that the demographic rationale offered little prospect of relief in their lifetime. As Herman Merivale, the Colonial Office's resident expert on emigration, pointed out in 1847, once their indentures expired, new immigrants could be expected to respond to Jamaican conditions just as the creoles had done: they would become settlers themselves. Thus the labor problem would not be solved by the trickle of immigrants Jamaica had received thus far. The requests for immigrant labor totaled 8,000 in 1845 alone; from all sources, just 25,094 indentured laborers were brought to Jamaica between 1834 and 1865.[60] The numbers required to preempt the interior would be several times that number.

Despite their lip service to political economy, therefore, most planters appreciated indentured immigrants as laborers on demand. They provided the steady, reliable core labor force and the "continuous" labor that planters insisted was necessary to operate the estates profitably. For example, his 39 coolies at Morelands allowed Hugh Whitelocke to dispense with the services of 100 creole laborers for most of the year, hiring the latter only at crop time. Despite the extra costs and taxes associated with procuring them, he was certain that indentured workers were no more expensive than creoles.[61] By the early 1850s, other estates also reported that indentured laborers constituted the core of their workforce, performing off-season jobs such as repairing fences and general maintenance that it was difficult to get creoles to take.[62] Similar to the situation in the American South after emancipation, planters had difficulty getting freed people to undertake routine maintenance tasks out of season. For American workers these tasks were not reflected in their crop shares; for Jamaicans they were remunerated at a lower rate of pay than crop work.[63] Indentured workers had no choice in the matter. They also worked on Saturdays and holidays.

Being able to lay their hands on their laborers when and where they wanted them bore strong resemblance to "the system of husbandry pursued during slavery" that Elgin sought to wean the planters away from. Apparently, a few planters found the resemblance irresistible. Mr. Lowndes, owner of Treadways Estate, flogged his African indentures regularly. After he and his overseer were convicted in 1849, Lowndes was fined twenty pounds, and his overseer, ten pounds plus one month's imprisonment.[64] But even those planters who did not succumb to old habits were likely to confound the obligations of a contract with the obligations of a slave. Some planters conveyed to Governor Charles Grey the impression "that the outlay of public money in effecting Immigration gives either to the Planter or to the Government a sort of property in the labourer which might justify such coercive exaction of labour in repayment of their purchase money as it would be difficult in any way to reconcile with substantial or even nominal freedom."[65]

The potential threat that a successful immigration program posed to their interests was clear to native Jamaican workers and their supporters. Under Jamaican conditions a genuinely free market in labor favored the worker, but by creating a class of quasi-free, contract laborers, the planters undercut the native workers' bargaining position. The prospect of state support for such recruitment programs drew quick responses from those dependent on a black working-class constituency. Baptist congregations fired petitions to the Jamaica Assembly and the queen. The petitioners denied the existence of a labor shortage requiring immigration; rather there was considerable unemployment and underemployment among native laborers. Furthermore, the introduction of "uncivilized" Indian and African laborers threatened the fragile cultural progress native blacks had achieved since emancipation. African indentured laborers were accused of "idolatry," "superstition, and vices the most debasing and demoralizing." Their presence threatened all the progress native blacks had made to escape "the darkness of Heathenism." But their main objection, as a second petition made clear, was to the unjustifiable expenditure of public funds to foster private interests. Taxes collected from the Afro-Jamaican majority would go directly to subsidize the planter minority, thereby enabling them to cut the wages and jobs of native workers.[66]

Such protests, attracting support mainly by the colored minority in the planter-controlled Assembly, made little impact during the first emancipation decade.[67] But after Parliament adopted the free trade policy, immigration funding fell prey to drastic cuts from its erstwhile friends. Anticipating dire effects from the Sugar Duties Act, planters scaled back their orders for contract laborers from eight thousand to twelve hundred during the first months following its final passage. And in the fall of 1846 the Assembly resolved to halt all further Asiatic immigration because of free trade.[68] Stung by what they saw as Britain's callous disregard for their welfare, planters insisted that the assumption of immigration costs by the imperial government was an appropriate quid pro quo for the imposition of free trade. At the very least a loan guarantee to cover public expenditures on immigration seemed fitting. Although Secretary Grey had offered such a loan himself in 1848, the colonies had declined such support at the time, feeling that political changes in England offered a better chance for relief. By 1850, Guiana and Trinidad had received immigration loans, but the

Colonial Office was now less than sympathetic to the idea of including Jamaica in such arrangements without governmental reform as a precondition.[69] Indeed, even the Afro-Jamaican politicians, perhaps foreseeing potential political advantages, began to offer qualified support for immigration by the late 1850s. By 1858, Jamaica had spent £231,488 to import immigrant workers and £21,404 for return passages—about ten times the educational expenditures over the same period. The net increase in its workforce could not have exceeded 10 percent.[70] Planters still complained of "a labor shortage."

Progressive Theory, Regressive Taxation, and Political Crisis

Whatever intellectual attractions liberal political economy held for Jamaican planters, therefore, the bottom line came before first principles. They were prepared to spend public money on immigration but not education. And in that same spirit they sought to shift the tax burden generally onto the black majority. Here again their basic instincts led them into policies that conflicted with the models and theories urged by the home government. As long as the conflict remained theoretical, there was room for maneuver and compromise, especially while the conciliatory policies of Metcalfe and Elgin benefited from the general optimism and relative prosperity of the early 1840s. By contrast, the decade following the Sugar Duties Act was one of pessimism and gloom, as well as real hardship. It was also a period when liberal political economy increasingly held sway at the highest levels of the Colonial Office bureaucracy.

The abolition of property in slaves posed major fiscal problems for raising colonial revenue. During slavery a poll tax of five to six shillings levied on slaves and other forms of personal property, such as livestock, dogs, and carriages, had raised the bulk of colonial revenues. But once blacks ceased to be taxable chattels, other sources of revenue had to be found.[71] For the planter-controlled Assembly, the tax substitutes of choice usually involved various regressive levies on persons or on consumption, such as head taxes for road repairs, duties on sugar and coffee sold domestically, and duties on imported consumer goods. These fiscal innovations drew immediate opposition from freed people and their supporters in Jamaica and Britain. But despite their protests and continued opposition from the Colonial Office, the shift in the tax burden proceeded apace, exposing in the process the difficulties that the home government confronted in exercising a positive, as opposed to a negative, influence on colonial governance.[72] Once again, it could block laws it opposed, but it could not mandate the laws it wanted.

In 1843 the Colonial Office, following James Stephen's lead, had objected to regressive taxes in general and to the principle of recruiting wage labor via the tax system specifically. Colonial Office staff objected to the four-shilling road tax imposed on every male fifteen to sixty years old and chided Governor Elgin for assenting to it. Aside from their general objection to the regressive nature of the tax, they cited "the present state of affairs in the West Indies." Stephen conceded that there might be "plausible arguments" for creating "an artificial poverty" through taxation so as to induce labor for wages, "but the imposition of direct Taxes with any such view, could not be vindicated, nor can I therefore regard without distrust and jealousy the introduction of a precedent directly tending towards that result." He worried, too, that sanctioning such a precedent in Jamaica would lead to its being imitated throughout the British West Indies.[73]

In his defense, Elgin protested that (1) the tax was merely an addition to an existing impost and not a new tax; (2) the peasant class also derived benefits as road users; and (3) they evaded the tax in any case. Stephen, for one, was not impressed with the governor's rejoinder, thinking it altogether evasive of the main issue: "a Capitation Tax is essentially unjust; and . . . in the West Indies at present it is peculiarly impolitic on account of its tendency to grow into a contrivance for coercing labour by creating an artificial pressure for money on the labouring classes, and so compelling them to work for wages." Stephen thought Elgin's insistence that this was not the law's intent to be irrelevant. "The principle of Capitation Taxes may teem with injurious consequences though the first example of such an Act may have no direct tendency to produce them. It [is] indeed always in this way that bad principles of legislation establish themselves, namely by appearing at first with their fairest aspects and most plausible apology." Colonial Secretary Stanley was apparently won over to his chief aide's view of the case and incorporated much of Stephen's language into his dispatch to Elgin. Subsequently, the tax was repealed.[74]

The major change in tax policy, however, was the emergence of customs duties and other indirect, regressive taxes on consumables as the major sources of island revenue. The first tentative steps in this direction, occurring just one year after passage of the Abolition Act, drew protests from British merchants anxious to maintain Kingston as an entrepôt for American trade and objecting to the expense and inconvenience of warehousing goods in transit. Glenelg instructed

Sligo not to assent to this bill, but the governor interpreted his earlier instructions from Stanley as allowing import duties for the purpose of replacing losses from abolition of poll taxes on slaves. He suggested, therefore, that differential, protective duties be imposed on foreign goods. But the Colonial Office and the Board of Trade objected to the imposition of differential duties on foreign as well as British colonial products because of the inevitable confusion and injury to foreign relations in allowing each colony to regulate its own rates.[75]

A measure enacted in December 1842 raised more serious policy issues, however. The duties were clearly much higher than required for revenue alone, and they were levied not on manufactured articles but on goods consumed primarily by the laboring classes; for example, the cost of salt beef and pork would be raised 40 percent. "On behalf of those classes," Stanley felt constrained to object. He neglected to disallow the act only because by the time his message would have been received in Jamaica, the fiscal year would be half over and commerce and fiscal affairs would be seriously disrupted by the change of schedules. Consequently, Elgin was simply inveigled to use his utmost influence to prevent future laws of this sort and commanded to veto such legislation if persuasion failed.[76]

Elgin professed his uncertainty about the effect of higher duties on consumption but sent a survey of imports over the past five years, which appeared to indicate that duties had not discouraged consumption of salt beef and pork.[77] For its part, the planter majority in the Jamaica Assembly was convinced by experience that import duties offered all "the advantages of indirect, over direct, taxation," and it promptly proceeded to impose new import duties during its next session.[78] Forwarding the new act to his superiors, Elgin argued that the Assembly had tried to accommodate the concerns raised by the Colonial Office the previous spring and urged approval. Most discriminating duties on foreign goods (except wines) had been eliminated, and duties on salt beef and pork had been reduced from twenty shillings per barrel to fifteen per barrel. He was now certain that the higher duty had had no effect on consumption; indeed, prices did not rise, because the higher duties were offset by extraordinarily low prices in New Orleans. Moreover, the governor argued, increased taxation was necessitated by the new programs appropriate to governing a free society, programs the home government itself had urged on the colony. The proprietary class could no longer "bare exclusively as heretofore the Public Burdens."[79] In the final analysis the planters got their way. By 1845, 65 percent of Jamaica's revenue came from import duties, £186,085 of £286,850. By contrast, the land tax garnered only £7,440, and taxes on stock, wheels, and trade, another £6,121.[80]

Having succeeded in shifting island taxes from direct to indirect sources, the planters moved to "reform" the tax system of the parishes as well. Parochial taxes were still mostly direct levies on various species of real and personal property. Since it proved extremely difficult to collect such taxes from estate workers and peasant farmers, these levies were also effectively progressive in nature. Perhaps it is also relevant that small settlers and peasants enjoyed their greatest political success at the local level. In any event, planters chose to attack the problem indirectly through the Assembly, which they still controlled, rather than through the vestries themselves, some of which they did not control.[81] Therefore, in 1847 the Assembly attempted to shift some of the parochial expenses onto the general island revenue, which was now thoroughly regressive because most island revenues came mainly from import duties, while parochial taxes tended to fall on the planters. By reducing the powers and responsibilities—and hence expenditures—of the parishes, planters hoped to shift the tax burden as well. By 1849 Governor Charles Edward Grey reported that indeed the planters had largely succeeded in relieving themselves of the bulk of the tax burden.[82]

The planters' success was not without costs, however. In 1849 there was a severe riot in St. Mary Parish that in Governor Grey's opinion was in truth "a tax revolt" by sugar workers and small settlers vexed at "the indiscret and irregular" procedures of the parish tax collector. Evidently this overly zealous taxman had attempted to collect hereditaments taxes from small tenants. Although legally liable to the tax, smallholders had traditionally evaded it, and collectors confined themselves in practice to the estates. So when Richard Rigg attempted to collect from workers at Goshen Estate and settlers at Guy's Hill, he was beaten. When police approached Goshen to arrest the perpetrators, they heard shells blowing from four directions and soon found themselves facing a mob of five hundred men and women armed with cutlasses and sticks. The extensive planning entailed in this "riot" is suggested by the fact that the mob was made up of participants from several parishes and included a few Maroons.[83]

The planters also encountered opposition from a Colonial Office bureaucracy that had otherwise grown relatively sympathetic to their plight. Just as they were succeeding in their efforts to shift the tax burden onto their workers, radical economic ideas began to dominate the Colonial Secretariat. In June 1846 Sir Henry George Grey, formerly

Viscount Howick and the future third Earl Grey, took the seals of the Colonial Office in John Russell's first administration. Well before the 1840s, Grey had been committed to "radical political economy" (in the mid-nineteenth-century sense of that appellation) in general and free trade in particular. In fact, he is credited with bringing Russell—and with him the Whigs generally—over to a free trade policy. He would now head the Colonial Office during the crucial six years when free trade policy was gradually imposed on colonial staples. At the time Grey directed the Colonial Office, his cousin, Sir Charles, was governor of Jamaica. Having reputedly left England just ahead of his creditors, Sir Charles had enjoyed an extensive colonial service in Canada, India, and Barbados.[84]

The planters' argument that they had been thrown into unfair competition with Cuban and Brazilian slaveowners by the free trade policy won them no sympathy from Henry Grey. They must entertain no hope of reviving "the old & vicious system of protection." If the planters would look to themselves, he insisted, "they would find no difficulty in competing with the slave owner."[85] Grey was convinced that protection merely encouraged planters to pay higher wages than a free market would have justified and that higher wages enabled freed people to work less. He argued that protection—by artificially raising the price of sugar—led the planters to bid up the price of labor to an equally artificially high level. These high wages actually brought less labor into the market because workers needed fewer hours of work "to buy all they want." There was evidence in the recent Antiguan experience, he argued, that a reduction in wages would in turn stimulate greater labor.[86]

Similarly, Grey was convinced that the tax system provided the planters their best opportunity for "real relief" from labor problems. The planters' determination to shift the tax burden to the working population was misguided, because it merely gave "artificial encouragement to the negroes to work rather in their own provisn grounds than for hire, by raising the price both of the articles they have to sell from their own grounds, & of those which if they worked for hire they wd. buy with their wages as a substitute for part at least of the provisns they produce for themselves." The taxes on stock and wheels discouraged improvements, and the high customs duties restrained trade. In place of these the Assembly should levy a tax on land, calculated so that it fell heaviest on unimproved acreage.[87]

In marked contrast to the position taken by the Colonial Office under Stanley, therefore, Earl Grey urged reliance on direct taxes on the means of production, especially on land, rather than indirect levies on consumption. This, of course, was a position he had held since the critical discussions over emancipation policy in 1833, when he had urged a land tax and high prices for Crown lands as measures necessary to coerce labor from freed slaves. When he returned to the Colonial Office in 1846, he felt that developments had vindicated his earlier position. "The experience we have had since 1833 & the contrast between Jamaica & Barbadoes in this respect clearly proves that the whole difficulty in commanding labour in the former arises (as in the former year I urged that it would) from the over abundance of land as compared to populatn."[88]

Tax policies could be manipulated so as to simulate a denser population, however. If revenue were raised from real estate taxes rather than import duties, land would be made more expensive and less accessible to would-be settlers. This would have the same effect on the supply of wage laborers as an increase in population. Meanwhile, lower import duties would tend to lower the cost of the planters' supplies and "at the same time to encourage the labourer to form tastes for the gratificatn of which he must earn money by working for hire." Land tax could be arranged to fall primarily on the small settlers by granting planters a rebate in the form of a bounty on his sugar exports, "so regulated that the amount of bounty on the ordinary produce of an acre wd. equal (perhaps somewhat more than equal) the tax upon that extent of land." The colonial secretary was proposing an income transfer from the workers and peasants to the planters, and he was distressed that the planters could be "so blind to their true interest in the matter" that they were pursuing exactly the opposite policy. He informed Charles privately that he was determined to resist such folly. "I have thought one measure of this sort, that for throwing on the general revenue a number of parochial charges so objectionable that I shall advise the disallowance of the act."[89]

The financial policies of the planters were just as bad, in Grey's opinion. By insisting upon retrenchment of government spending on essential public services, they merely relieved the blacks, who paid most of these taxes, of the necessity to work for wages to pay them, enabling them to do "as well as they wish to do upon less wages thus diminishing the motive to industry." Clearly, a more rational political economy dictated more government spending, not less, and direct taxes on the means of production, not indirect taxes on consumption. Thus tax and expenditure policies could instill labor discipline by means of cultural reformation.

> My convictn is that instead of reducing taxatn the wise policy for the Assembly wd. be to provide liberally for police, educatn, the administratn of justice, improvement of roads etc. & to raise the revenue required for these purposes by a direct tax upon land allowing a drawback upon sugar, coffee, etc. This wd. compel the negroes if they wish to continue to enjoy the same amount of comforts & luxuries as heretofore to do more work to earn the means of purchasing them & maintaining themselves.

Having tried unsuccessfully to get a similar message through to legislators in a dispatch the year before, he urged Charles to talk to legislators privately to get them to recognize the wisdom of this policy.[90]

Unfortunately for Secretary Grey and his cousin the governor, by the late 1840s taxation and spending were no longer matters for dispassionate, theoretical discussion. The economic interests of colonial planters deviated sharply from those of Britons at home. British industrialists wanted new markets abroad, which free trade promised to open up. Hard-pressed British consumers wanted lower food prices at home, which free trade promised to make possible. By 1846, British West Indian sugar cost British consumers 40 percent more per hundredweight than that of Cuba, its next nearest competitor, and about 72 percent more than sugar from Brazil. This at a time when falling West Indian production and declining British demand made the colonies' potential monopoly effective. Indeed, one scholar calculates that in 1841 British consumers would have saved £4 million had they been allowed to buy Cuban or Brazilian rather than colonial sugar. It is also probable that increased consumption would have more than made up the losses from lower customs revenues.[91]

On 25 June 1846, Sir Robert Peel maneuvered through Commons a bill eliminating the English Corn Laws, which had sustained the grain monopoly in the United Kingdom. His apostasy split his party and brought the Whigs back to power under Lord John Russell. Seizing the moment, the Whigs pressed the free trade principle to its logical conclusion, passing the Sugar Duties Act that August by a comfortable majority. All duties on foreign sugar were cut immediately to twenty-one shillings, setting in motion a program of gradual reductions designed to equalize colonial and foreign duties by 1851.[92]

The loss of their protected British markets sent shock waves through the colonial planter class. Partly in genuine anticipation of reduced income and general economic distress, and partly as a calculated policy to win relief from the home government, the Jamaica Assembly adopted austerity measures to slash spending and the public payroll. Refusing to vote a budget was the traditional weapon of the Jamaica Assembly in its struggles to maintain its prerogatives against imperial intrusions. Cutting the budget was a relatively new strategy, its precedents all appearing to date from the emancipation era.

In 1834, even before abolition had taken effect, the Assembly urged a cut in the salaries of the receiver general, a royal appointee paid from the island treasury, as an economy measure necessitated by the uncertainties of a free society. Anticipating the pattern of debate in later years, the Colonial Office ruled that the salaries of public officials could not be reduced during the tenure of an incumbent without appropriate compensation. Offices were a form of property; therefore, reducing a public official's salary was a form of expropriation, violating the faith and credit of the Crown.[93] By the mid-1840s the vast increase in public expenditure required to maintain the postemancipation state had become all too evident, and to many planters objectionable. Of course, the greater part of the island's debt—£155,042—was the result of immigration expenses, but this fact received little notice from the Assembly's planter faction. In December 1844 a large Assembly majority recommended cuts in the salaries of public employees ranging from 5 percent to 20 percent, as well as deep cuts in the allocations for police and military establishments. A hostile amendment to this report attracted only four votes.[94]

With passage of free trade legislation in 1846, retrenchment efforts took on a much more confrontational edge. In November 1846 the Assembly determined that it was impossible to maintain the colony's institutions following imposition of free trade. In the retrenchment bills that followed, the planter faction in the Assembly sought to shift the salaries of the governor and his secretary onto the British treasury and cut all other public salaries. The planters also sought to lower taxes, limit spending, and transfer costs of immigration to Britain. Furthermore, the planter faction sought to hold all revenue bills hostage until its retrenchment program was adopted by the Legislative Council, a body appointed by the governor that had veto power. Grey succeeded in beating back this first assault, when the bills came to the floor in February 1847, with the crucial votes of the Afro-Jamaican assemblymen, who made up half the eighteen members voting with the Crown.[95]

Grey's victory was short-lived, however, because 1847 saw the onset of a severe economic recession that increased pressures for economies in government service. The conjunction of a bumper sugar harvest in the West Indies (23 percent above the average for the preceding eight years), depressed demand in Europe, and vast increases in supplies from foreign producers (38 percent) responding to the lower duties forced sugar from 37s. per hundredweight in February to 22s. 7d. in November. Prices would remain below 26s. for almost a decade, forcing forty-eight West Indian merchant firms into bankruptcy. Planters were unable to redeem bills drawn on these insolvent creditors for consignments of sugar already shipped, and those lucky merchants who survived refused further credits to West Indian clients. Planters, in turn, defaulted on wages and short-term loans to local banks. Throughout the West Indies, banks closed their doors. In Jamaica, the Planters Bank suspended payments on its notes. Those planters who might have chosen to cut and run found their properties almost worthless, in many cases fetching no more than 20 percent of their previous value. Many planters lost their fortunes. Others lost more. Thomas McCornock, a Jamaican resident for forty years, manager of Golden Grove Estate, owner of Shenton, and custos of St. Thomas-in-the-East, was one of those stretched too thin by these events. The crisis cast McCornock into a deep depression. After an arsonist burned his trash house in December 1848, he cut his throat.[96]

The planters' protectionist allies in Parliament responded to this crisis with hearings before a Select Committee on Sugar and Coffee Planting, chaired by Lord George Bentinck. Most of Bentinck's committee colleagues were free traders, however, and their final report in May 1848 disappointed planter hopes that free trade would be reversed. The committee suggested only that a 10s. differential between foreign and domestic sugars be maintained for six years more. Russell disappointed them further when he rejected even that modest relief, offering instead a 7s. differential (as compared with the 4s. 6d. differential that was still in effect at that time) and postponement of final equalization from 1851 to 1854. Further, consistent with the liberal analysis of West Indian problems, he offered to guarantee the interest on colonial loans for immigration and development (that is, transportation networks, irrigation, and drainage).[97]

This crisis atmosphere and Russell's rebuff fueled renewed demands for retrenchment and lower taxes. But there was a well-founded suspicion at the Colonial Office that the planters were looking for more than tax relief. Evidently, the close vote on Grey's proposals in Commons and the apparent weakness of the government in Parliament generally encouraged the West India Interest to think that they could get more.[98] After trying unsuccessfully to humor the Assembly out of its "ill temper," Governor Grey became convinced that there was collusion between the Planter party in the Assembly and West Indian interests in England "determined to throw the Government of these Colonies both here and at home into a state of financial difficulty."[99] Certainly, there appears to have been a coordinated effort among West Indian colonies to force the home government's hand by slashing public payrolls in response to the free trade crisis.[100]

On the other hand, the crisis in government finance was real enough. Jamaica had run large deficits in 1847–48, and by June 1848 its treasury was empty. Governor Grey decided to call the Assembly into an extraordinarily early August session, ostensibly to allow time for tempers to cool before they had to vote a budget in October. It did not work: the Assembly adamantly refused to vote out revenue bills without concessions on retrenchment. The following January a legislative committee reported a bill that chopped 17 percent out of the budget, including salary cuts ranging from 10 percent to 33 percent. Predictably, the Legislative Council, some of whose members were public employees who would have been affected by the cuts, rejected the bill, and the governor prorogued the Assembly. The legislators reconvened in only slightly better humor. Backing away from shutting down the government completely, they passed a series of tax measures to pay for essential services, except the salaries of most public officials and the Anglican clergy.[101]

Ultimately, the Jamaican retrenchment crisis involved more than the short-term economic distress over taxes and spending. At stake, too, was the power of the Assembly, as well as who would rule that Assembly. In April 1847 the Assembly approved a measure offered by Alexander Barclay that shifted a significant portion of government revenues from permanent tax sources to sources requiring annual renewals.[102] This measure appears to have been the opening move in a sustained effort not simply to cut the civil service but to make it more dependent on annual appropriations by the Assembly. Clearly, such an arrangement would weaken the governor and the Crown further. Eventually, the home government insisted that statutory provision of a permanent revenue would be the price for any additional British financial assistance to the colony.[103]

Earl Grey's immediate response to Barclay's measure was to try to convince the planters that once again they were acting against their own long-term interests. He asked his staff to draft a confidential memo that Charles could circulate among the leading members of the Assembly. Should they fail to provide a permanent revenue for government operations, he warned, "the probability [was] that at the next general election the negro populatn may virtually return a majority of the Assby, [and] there is much danger that the European inhabitants & merchantile classes may stand greatly in need of protectn from the Executive Govt which it will not have the means of affording."[104] It is unclear whether this memorandum was actually circulated, but it is clear that the Assembly rejected Grey's advice. Two years later the situation had reached a dangerous stalemate. As the crisis deepened, the desperate governor asked that Parliament overrule the Assembly as it had in 1839 and continue the disputed revenue laws by its own authority.

But aside from race baiting the white assemblymen, Henry had little help or advice to offer cousin Charles. Asking his most experienced staff member to review the materials and recommend something for the Cabinet's consideration, Grey conceded that the options were limited, and "it wd be impossible however great may be the difficulties to be encountered to ask Parlt for any increase of power in order to meet them." He had written privately to Charles already that he could not help him. There were more important government measures before Commons and no time to devote to the Jamaican crisis.[105]

In a personal note to his cousin, the secretary explained further why on this particular trial of strength he must pass. He assured him that he had couched the official dispatch in terms intended to place Charles in the best light and cast the blame for the situation on the Assembly. He counseled a waiting game. "I conceive that our right policy is to use the power of the Crown with great firmness to check the caprices of the Assembly, at the same time making the inconvenience arising from their conduct as manifest as possible, trusting that by degrees the evil will raise up public opin. against them & compel them to give way." In preparation for that future test of strength, the secretary asked for a history of the Assembly's Committee of Accounts and how its powers had increased unconstitutionally. "If Parlt. ever shd. interfere I think it must be in a much more effective manner, & for the purpose of making a much more complete reform, for which matters are obviously not yet ripe, & which I hope will never be necessary."[106]

The "ripeness" Earl Grey awaited with dread was the maturing of black political power. That day was not nearly as far in the future as many people thought. When it arrived, the home government would confront a situation very much like that Henry Taylor had so feared in 1839; that is, it would have to support Jamaica's white minority against its black and brown majority. Thereafter the problem of governance, from a British perspective, would not be to cajole the planter class into adopting liberal democratic principles but to contain the aspirations of a politically insurgent black citizenry. No future governor would speak, as Elgin had, of Britain's liberal duty to the newly enfranchised freed people. None would think of Jamaica's problems in terms of the basic class conflict between the capitalist owners of the means of production and the laboring masses. Hereafter the racial dimensions of the political conflict would shape their approach to the island's problems. In this regard they had numerous affirmations among many sectors of Jamaican society. To achieve their economic ends planters found the racial analysis of the crisis convenient. Colored politicians, conscious of their minority status, were equally anxious to divert attention from issues of class privilege. Racial premises made more sense than ever to a British public increasingly self-conscious about the burdens of empire in the Southern Hemisphere. To Charles Grey's successor, Henry Barkly—lately the governor and still a planter in Guiana—racial divisions in Jamaica were the primary obstacle to its economic recovery. Indeed, at times they appeared the only obstacle.[107]

In describing these various elections I have noticed the colours of the candidates, but I ought to add that in no instance has the contest appeared to be between colours. . . . Party contests are now between those who advocate the supremacy of the upper classes and those who strive for their own advancement on the basis of popular representation; [that is, between] those who desire the rule of the few or the upper classes, and those who advocate the influence of the many or the lower classes.

**CHARLES M. METCALFE TO EDWARD G. STANLEY,
9 FEBRUARY 1842**

Looking to the comparative numbers of the black & white inhabitants of Jamaica, & to the absence of any real impediment to the acquisit'n of the elective franchise by the former, it seems impossible to doubt that at no very distant period they must acquire a paramount influence in the legislature [and] the power of the Assembly when it comes into their hands will be used with little regard to the interests of the planters or even to justice, & that therefore if the planters were wise they wd. use the authority they now possess, not to break down the power of the Crown but on the contrary to strengthen it, by restoring to the executive govt some of those functions which properly belong to it but which in Jamaica have been usurped.

EARL GREY TO CHARLES GREY, 16 MARCH 1849

The spontaneous reforms [of the Better Government Act of 1854] left the composition of the Assembly untouched and with the defects within it which had so completely incapacitated it before. Constituted of three great parties, or rather races, the only way I could form a Cabinet was by selecting representatives from two of them.

HENRY BARKLY TO SIR SIDNEY HERBERT, 10 APRIL 1855

7

Politics and Power in a "Plural Society"

The 1844 census, the first official count of Jamaica's entire population in its 189-year history, revealed a population of 15,776 whites, 68,529 browns, and 293,128 blacks.[1] Many contemporaries—like Earl Grey above—anticipated that these figures confirmed the political arithmetic of the Jamaican future: given Glenelg's doctrine of political equality, black power was imminent. All things being equal, black men should soon rule the island. But, of course, all things were not equal. Political power in Jamaica—as in all putatively democratic societies—was mediated by institutional arrangements that made realization of majority rule very difficult. Indeed, much of the political history of Jamaica in the second and third decades following abolition involved efforts to defy the political calculus of its demography. For fifteen years Colonial Office officials endeavored to maintain the forms of democratic practice while denying its substance.

In the process, racism became an essential solvent for dissolving the otherwise blatant contradictions between liberal democratic ideology and colonial practice. The stark reality of the Jamaican census abetted a discursive and ideological process wherein descriptive census categories became reified into analytic-explanatory variables.[2] By mid-century the recognition reflected in Governor Metcalfe's statement above that the Afro-Jamaican majority was also a *working class* majority with interests necessarily at odds with those of the largely white, planter-merchant elite was obscured. For Colonial Secretary Grey it was their *blackness* that was most relevant politically and most to be feared. Indeed, for Governor Barkly race and class had become so confounded as to be interchangeable categories; or rather, class was subsumed within race. With these transformations in thought, Glenelg's simple doctrine of equality under law—at least for men—gave way to imperialist justifications of white power. Potential black empowerment was to be thwarted through novel political arrangements. If, all things being equal, black men should rule the island, then all things could not be equal.

On the other hand, such efforts to thwart a rising black leviathan seemed superfluous to many other contemporary observers and to subsequent historians as well, because the black electorate never even remotely approached its potential nor even posed a viable threat. Moreover, in their view, no consistent partisan alignments emerged to represent the real needs and interests of the majority population or to sustain a liberal, much less radical, alternative to the planters. Indeed, the "black" party was not really black, but "coloured." Given this view, the threat of black political empowerment was imaginary and the practice of Jamaican politics incomprehensible. Blacks did not vote, and Jamaican legislative politics was entirely personalistic, opportunistic, and anarchic.[3]

On the surface there is much to sustain such views. Upon their emancipation, black men could exercise electoral rights if they owned real property worth six pounds or paid thirty pounds in rent or three pounds in direct taxes. Even under this restrictive formula roughly 20,000 of them—mostly black small freeholders—might have qualified under the property qualification alone. But the actual registration in 1839 was only 2,199, and over the next two decades it did not exceed 3,000. The number actually going to the polls never exceeded 1 percent of the population; indeed, elections in some parishes attracted little more than a score of voters.[4]

There is evidence, nonetheless, that black and colored voters did exert significant influence within this small electorate, enough to stimulate the fears of Grey and others. Indeed, a close study of suffrage by historian Gad Heuman has demonstrated that by the late 1840s small freeholders and estate workers predominated among Jamaican voters in four important parishes. His analysis of voting and landholding in St. Thomas-in-the-East, Vere, St. John, and St. Thomas-in-the-Vale shows that owners of 25 or fewer acres outnumbered owners of 100 or more acres in the electorate and that these small freeholders "generally supported either colored candidates or men who were allied to the Town party."[5]

The politics of the Jamaica Assembly, on the other hand, probably did represent a significant barrier to the expression of the majority's political will. Though restrictive, suffrage qualifications were low enough to permit a significant sector of the black population to vote; however, qualifications for the Assembly were high enough to exclude most voters from membership. Throughout this period assemblymen were required to prove receipt of a net annual income from an estate of £180, real property worth £1,800, or combined real and personal property worth £3,000. By these criteria few among the brown population need apply, and among blacks fewer still. Consequently, the black and brown electoral majority had to chose its representatives largely from among the white elite minority.[6]

Nevertheless, one could not dismiss the possibility that such relatively affluent assemblymen, owing their election to a working-class constituency, might, as Metcalfe put it, "strive for their own advancement on the basis of popular representation." And should that happen, predicted Earl Grey, blacks might yet "acquire a paramount influence in the legislature" and use that power to make laws in their own interests. Whatever our contemporary evaluation of its validity, therefore, this great fear shaped discussions of colonial political affairs during the second decade following the abolition of slavery. These years, 1844–54, constitute a transitional era in British politics, colonial policy, and racial ideology; changes in all these areas stimulated new approaches to the problem of freedom. The political dimensions of that problem for British policymakers paralleled the economic: how to reconcile freedom with coercion, or more specifically, how to structure a political system in the colonies nominally consistent with liberal democratic principles, while maintaining ultimate control over black political expression.[7]

The Great Fear: Black Power in Jamaican Politics

During the first two decades of the postabolition era, every governor predicted that brown and black power was imminent. During the first decade a few colonial officers even anticipated such a development with pleasure. When he dissolved the Assembly in 1832, Governor Mulgrave was hopeful that the newly enfranchised colored voters would have a significant impact on the coming elections. The results were disappointing, however; only one additional colored representative—John Campbell—was returned. Shortly after his arrival on the island, Sligo predicted that the brown class would soon dominate the government and control the Assembly. Six colored men were elected to the Assembly during Sligo's tenure, but resignations, deaths, and illnesses diminished their effective membership to three in a House of forty-seven members. Nevertheless, Colonial Secretary Glenelg approved Sligo's patronage of colored Jamaicans; he, too, felt that they would and should soon dominate the island and that therefore they should be allowed to gain experience for their future roles. Consequently, during Sligo's battles with the planters in the spring and summer of 1836, a distinct government faction emerged in the Assembly.[8]

Lionel Smith, Sligo's successor, feared rather than welcomed colored political activism. In fact, Smith came to Jamaica determined to dismantle Sligo's efforts to cultivate a government party among Afro-Jamaicans. Invoking the Haitian nightmare, he warned that under brown and black rule the island would "fall into a Waste, under all the Evils of Anarchy, Confusion, and Bloodshed." But when confronted by an intransigent, planter-dominated Assembly, he, too, looked for help from the colored representatives. During the continuing crises of the late 1830s, Afro-Jamaican legislators remained staunch supporters of the Crown and were solidly united on the various pieces of legislation affecting the recently freed slaves. They supported, for example, the early abolition of apprenticeship and opposed planter efforts to control the freed people through vagrancy laws, police regulations, and evictions. Occasionally they were joined by four to five white members, with whom they sustained a credible opposition to the planter majority. Despite their very different attitudes and styles, therefore, Sligo and Smith succeeded in nurturing the emerging political consciousness of the brown population.[9]

Over the next three decades Afro-Jamaican representation in the Assembly grew from this small minority of government loyalists to a large, vocal, and fractious plurality (see fig. 7.1). Collectively, with a small group of white allies, they constituted a political force that would be known by various labels over the years: "the King's House Men," "the Coloured party," "the Liberals," "the Town party." Of

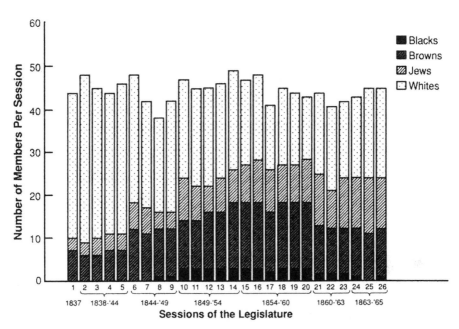

Figure 7.1. Racial and Ethnic Composition of the Jamaica Assembly, 1837–1865

course, *party* was something of a misnomer, because these legislators possessed none of the organizational apparatus associated with a modern political party. There were neither sanctions nor incentives with which to encourage "members" to act in concert—neither in the election canvasses nor in the legislature afterwards. Indeed, one student of Jamaican politics suggests that the Town party might be more accurately classified as "a floating faction" rather than a political party. But then modern parties had not yet fully taken shape in Britain either; political parties there were fairly volatile parliamentary coalitions, and "a stubborn tradition of personal political independence" persisted.[10] In this regard, then, Jamaica was not so far out of step with the mother country.

Notwithstanding the indistinctness of Jamaican political alignments, there was nascent party formation that is measurable; one of its obvious quantifiable indicators is the tendency of legislators to vote together. Calculating the percentage of times members voted alike and aggregating these "agreement scores" for the group provides a

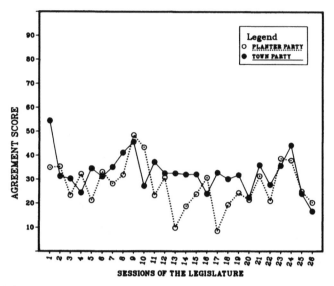

Figure 7.2. Mean Agreement Score by Political Party for Members of the Jamaica Assembly, 1837–1865.

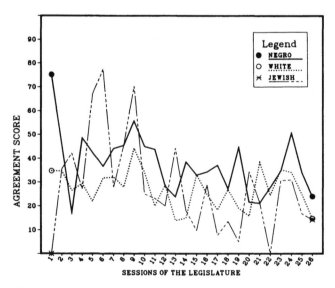

Figure 7.3. Mean Agreement Score by Ethnic Group for Members of the Jamaica Assembly, 1837–1865.

measure of party cohesion. With this measure, we can discern that Jamaican legislators did cluster into fairly consistent voting blocs.[11] Figure 7.2 plots the average agreement score for members of the two major political groups in the years 1837–65. It shows that a larger percentage of the so-called Town party members voted the same way more frequently than did members of the so-called Planter party. In fact, in fifteen of twenty-six legislative sessions convened during this twenty-eight-year period the Town party was more cohesive than the Planter party. The differential appears especially striking during the "crisis" decade of the 1850s. As we shall see, during the debate on governmental reform in 1852 and 1853, the Planter party appears to have begun coming apart. In only four of the seventeen legislative sessions after November 1852 (session 10) did the Planter party achieve greater cohesion than the Town party.

It is likely that the ties that bound members of the Town party together had much to do with its composition and the class interests that its makeup implied. First of all, the Town party was truly—as it was sometimes called—the "Coloured party." Between 1847 and 1860 brown and black members constituted more than half of its membership; and given their better attendance, their growing presence on the Assembly floor was probably even more dramatic visually. Moreover, since the colored legislators were generally more cohesive in their voting patterns than non-Jewish whites (see fig. 7.3), their political impact was greater than even their numbers would suggest. The seed of partisan differentiation was rooted in policy differences between these colored members and the planters. Although the party nomenclature implies that race, allegiance to the Crown, or the fate of the emancipated slave formed the core of their differences with the planters, such frictions tended to resonate with more fundamental conflicts over broader economic interests. More than a third of the brown representatives who served between 1831 and 1866 were lawyers, and before 1849 the predominance of legal professionals was even greater—six of ten. Several others were small merchants, editors, or public employees, nearly all of them "townsmen," pursuing urban professions and not dependent on agriculture to any significant degree. Unlike the planters or Whitehall, they did not identify the interests of the island exclusively with the success of its plantations.[12]

Gad Heuman's study of the colored assemblymen demonstrates that there was one dominant, unifying political theme for them: their "creoleness." Jamaican-born, they claimed commitment to the country and its future to a degree most planters did not. The distinction between those with "a merely temporary interest in the country" and "the men who are the bones and sinews of the country, [with] a permanent stake in its fortunes" became a staple of their political rhetoric.[13] Colored newspapers condemned absentee ownership of the estates and argued for a more diversified economy.[14] To Jamaica-born coloreds, the sojourning planters were parasites. "The history of the country shows," Robert Osborn told the Assembly, "the indelible fact that it has been the system of the planters, for three-quarters of a century past to take everything away from the country and to return nothing to it, except what is necessary to keep up their estates. . . . What have they done for the country? Nothing."[15]

Creole loyalties also found political expression during those times when the Assembly's power and prerogatives were perceived to be under attack. In February 1836, despite their steadfast support of Sligo, the brown assemblymen agreed with their planter colleagues that he had violated the Assembly's privileges by his attempts to influence the legislative process. On that occasion they did not go so far as to agree to suspend business until Sligo apologized—as the Planters demanded—but on a similar occasion in 1838 a majority of them (four members) did vote to suspend business to protest Parliament's imposition of prison reform on the island. The home government's only defenders were three public employees, Richard Hill, Charles Lake, and James Taylor.[16]

The colored faction did not fare as well under Charles Metcalfe as it had under Sligo and Smith. In pursuing his conciliatory policy with the planters, Metcalfe discouraged what he considered the political "pretensions" of the colored people. Indeed, the governor disparaged the colored members' capacity to form the basis of a government party, because in his view they lacked cohesion.[17] And, in fact, the colored legislators were much less unified during Metcalfe's tenure, because the assertion of Assembly prerogatives and independence against the British Parliament continued to divide them.[18]

Nonetheless, the number of members nominally associated with the Town party increased during Metcalfe's term with the addition of several more whites to their ranks. Unfortunately, there is very limited information on the occupational or personal backgrounds of the white legislators who associated themselves with the Town party, but the little that survives suggests that the party drew its white membership, as it did its brown, from people not primarily dependent on plantation agriculture. For example, there were fourteen Jews connected with the party between 1837 and 1865, and of the eleven for whom we have biographical information, eight were small merchants or shopkeepers.[19] Unlike Jews in the Planter party, these men were more likely to depend on customers among the black working population than on business from the planters. For example, George Lyons, a fish and provisions merchant, drew his main support from the Baptist villages in his district, appealing for the settler vote by advertising himself as the "friend of the people." By contrast, the Jewish merchants connected with the Planter party—such as the Bravo family—operated substantial import-export businesses, held mortgages on estate property, or were often planters themselves.[20]

The occupations of about half of the thirty-nine non-Jewish whites associated with the Town party have been identified. They included five lawyers, five planters, and a variety of other urban professionals (a doctor, a newspaper editor, a railroad executive, a blacksmith, a surveyor, two Kingston merchants, a bank manager, a director of the public hospital, and the governor's secretary).[21] The liberal sympathies of some of these men were longstanding. Dr. Archibald L. Palmer, a Scotsman, had been a stipendiary magistrate under Sligo and had published a weekly newspaper supporting the freed people. He was among that minority of Jamaican white men who had married their colored mistress.[22]

In general, labor rather than racial issues per se seems to have determined Planter party affiliation; practically all of its members who can be identified were directly dependent financially on the plantation economy—as owners, attorneys, or merchants.[23] But whatever their racial sympathies, many assemblymen felt the need to adjust their speech to the political realities of the new order. White conservatives sometimes felt constrained even to deny any allegiance to the old regime and to avoid racist comments. Thus planters John Vincent Purrier and Richard Barrett denied ever having opposed civil rights for colored men in the 1820s. When accused of having owned slaves in Cuba, merchant William Titley vigorously disputed it. According to the *Falmouth Post*, Titley assured his Kingston constituents that "no one in this island felt greater satisfaction at the abolition of slavery in the British possessions than he did." Meanwhile, planter Hugh Whitelocke's "indecorous remarks" against people of color were said to have cost his party the Westmoreland elections.[24]

If the image of "parliamentary anarchy" in the Jamaica Assembly is overstated, the common impression of planter domination and black powerlessness is totally erroneous. Contrary to the impressions given by the unsystematic observations of some contemporaries, planter interests managed to dominate the Assembly for only six years after emancipation was completed. Indeed, the opening session of the 1844–49 legislature was the last in which the Planter party enjoyed a clear numerical majority in the Assembly (about 56 percent). Over the next decade (1845–54) the parties would be fairly evenly balanced, at least in nominal membership (see table 7.1). During the late 1850s, in fact, the white, non-Jewish core of the Planter party would decline to as few as seven members, thus becoming a minority within their own party. Ironically, the Planter party's thinning ranks would be filled out thereafter by Afro-Jamaican and Jewish representatives. In terms of Assembly membership certainly, the great fear appeared to have a substantial basis in fact.

The earliest efforts to mobilize the dormant black electorate is-landwide came from the Baptist missionaries, who recognized the political potential of the dramatic growth of peasant freeholds during the early 1840s. Baptist ministers actively encouraged their members to purchase freeholds and to register to vote, fueling the white elite's fears of a radical political revolution. In 1844 Governor Elgin dissolved the legislature and called for early elections, admittedly in an effort to blunt the Baptists' registration drive.[25] It may be that Elgin's tactics did check the momentum of that voter mobilization, but the 1844 election still proved a crucial turning point in Jamaica's political history. When the new assemblymen convened, there were five more colored faces among them, three of whom were allied with the Town party. Joined with the eleven white Jamaican members, these legislators swelled the Town party's ranks to more than 43 percent of the Assembly's seats (see table 7.1, sess. 6).

Even before these additions to its numbers, however, the Town party had emerged as a force to be reckoned with in the Assembly, because of its members' better attendance and greater cohesion on roll call votes. Calculating the number of times each member voted with the winning side on roll call votes gives us a measure of legislative "success" for that member. Aggregating these "success scores" for each party's members provides, in turn, an index of the collective legislative effectiveness of one party relative to another.[26] The results for Jamaica, plotted in figure 7.4, show that 1844 marked a turning point in the fortunes of the Town party. Before 1844 the Planters had been practically unchallenged, but thereafter—beginning, fittingly, during the final session of the first new legislature elected during the postemancipation era (session 5)—the parties competed on surprisingly equal terms. Given the increased legislative strength of the Town party, Afro-Jamaican legislators also gained a stronger voice in political affairs (see fig. 7.5).

The exceptions to this pattern came in the sessions held between 1847 and early 1849, when their opposition to free trade and support of retrenchment produced an unprecedented level of cohesion among Jamaican planters (see fig. 7.2, sess. 9 and 10). The troubled Jamaican economy of the early 1840s had stimulated increasing sentiments for retrenchment of government spending. Following passage of free trade legislation in 1846, that debate took on a heightened political significance, becoming for planters a stratagem designed to extract major concessions from the home government, including possible rescission of the Sugar Duties Act. They were able to attract to their cause five putative Town party members. Some Afro-Jamaicans were also attracted to retrenchment by the seductive argument that lower salaries would benefit Jamaican creoles by discouraging European competition for government positions.[27] Most Afro-Jamaican legislators, however, continued to support the government. Of course, they may have expected to inherit these local posts anyway, and thus reducing the salaries would have been a self-inflicted wound. In any event, roll calls on the retrenchment issue confirm the crucial support black and brown members gave the government. Four roll calls attracted twenty-four to twenty-seven supporters for retrenchment and ten to thirteen opponents; 61 percent of the opponents were Afro-Jamaican.[28]

During this period, however, the Afro-Jamaican minority could not override the determined antigovernment majority coalition. As the impasse with the Assembly worsened, Governor Charles Grey feared that it would be necessary to dissolve the legislature and hold new elections. Dissolution was the governor's traditional riposte to a refractory legislature, but unlike Sligo under similar circumstances in 1835, Charles Grey dreaded that he might succeed in getting more of a new Assembly than he wanted. "But I am very far from wishing that the representatives of the English and planting interests should be at once made entirely subordinate to a colored or indigenous party and no endeavor shall be wanting on my part to prevail on all parties to join in such proceedings as may enable me to avoid the necessity of another general election." Before printing this dispatch for Parliament, Henry Taylor hastened to delete this statement, because he thought it might "deprive the Gov. of the support of the Coloured

Table 7.1. Partisian and Ethnic Composition of the Jamaica Assembly, 1837–1865

| Legislative Session | Planter Party | | | Total |
	Whites	Jews	Afro-Jamaicans	
1837–38				
1	32	3	0	35
1838–44				
2	31	1	0	32
3	30	2	0	32
4	26	2	0	28
5	30	2	0	32
1844–49				
6	22	3	2	27
7	17	3	1	21
8	18	2	1	21
9	20	2	1	23
1849–54				
10	19	2	0	21
11	19	2	0	21
12	19	2	2	23
13	16	2	2	20
14	16	2	2	20
1854–60				
15	11	5	3	19
16	11	6	3	20
17	9	6	2	17
18	10	5	3	18
19	9	5	3	17
20	7	5	3	15
1860–63				
21	11	5	2	18
22	12	4	2	18
23	13	6	2	21
1863–65				
24	11	6	1	18
25	13	6	2	21
26	11	5	2	18

Sources: See appendix 2.

[a] Because of their high absenteeism, the partisan affiliation of five members—Duncan Hamilton (sess. 2), Robert G. Bruce (sess. 8 and 9), Alexander James Brymer (sess. 10), John Andrew Pillon, and Frederick Levy Castle (both in sess. 21)—could not be determined. Pillon was an Afro-Jamaican whose election may have been challenged;

Town Party					
Whites	Jews	Afro-Jamaicans	Total	Unknown[a]	Total[b]
2	0	7	9		44
8	2	6	16	1	49
5	2	6	13		45
7	2	7	16		44
5	2	7	14		46
8	3	10	21		48
8	3	10	21		42
6	2	11	19	1	41
6	2	11	19	1	43
4	8	13	25	1	47
4	6	14	24		45
4	4	14	22		45
6	6	14	26		46
7	6	14	27		47
9	4	15	28		47
9	4	15	28		48
6	4	14	24		41
8	4	15	27		45
8	4	15	27		44
8	5	15	28		43
8	7	10	25	2	45
8	5	10	23		41
5	6	10	21		42
8	6	11	25		43
8	7	9	24		45
10	7	10	27		45

Castle was a Jewish merchant from Trelawny who became insolvent shortly after his election. All but Hamilton were probably affiliated with the Town party.

[b] Total varies because of extended leaves of absence and by-elections to fill vacancies.

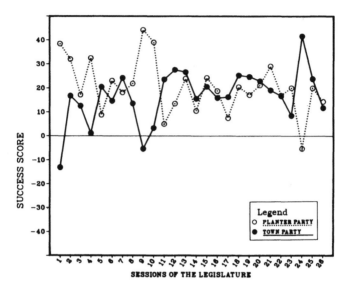

Figure 7.4. Mean Success Score by Political Party for Members of the Jamaica Assembly, 1837–1865.

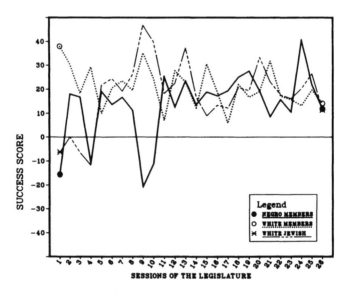

Figure 7.5. Mean Success Score by Ethnic Group for Members of the Jamaica Assembly, 1837–1865.

Party." Taylor's concern reflects the irony of a situation in which the principal architects of colonial policy were seeking to retard the growth of political representation among the very Jamaicans who provided their government its most consistent support.[29]

Despite his misgivings, however, Grey eventually had no choice but to dissolve the Assembly and call for new elections. Afro-Jamaican support of the government against the planters carried over from the Assembly into the electoral campaign that followed, which proved to be the most crucial of the postemancipation period. In this campaign Afro-Jamaican politicians brought out the black settler vote in unprecedented numbers, especially in St. John and St. Thomas-in-the-Vale (which had its highest turnout of the entire 1837–65 period). In those parishes, Gad Heuman has traced 62 percent and 63 percent of the votes, respectively, to small landowners; meanwhile, in St. Thomas-in-the-East and Vere they made up 49 percent and 46 percent. Six of eight members elected from these parishes (including four browns, one black, and one Jew) became staunch government supporters.[30]

Altogether, the 1849 elections produced startling changes in the ethnic makeup of the Assembly. The number of Jewish members in the Town party rose from two to eight; black and brown representation increased to thirteen.[31] Over the next two years, by-elections consolidated and expanded these changes, so that by the fall of 1852, black and brown assemblymen alone made up about 36 percent of the Assembly's membership.[32] Compared with their numbers in the year before emancipation, there were by 1860 more than twice as many Afro-Jamaican members in the Assembly, more than three times as many Jews, and fewer than half as many non-Jewish whites. Well over six of every ten members were at least nominally identified with the Town party, in contrast with just one in five at the end of 1837.

With these elections the Town party emerged as the dominant force in the Assembly, so much so, in fact, that the Planters could win consistently thereafter only by forging temporary alliances with various factions of that party. Their success scores demonstrate that in eight of the last thirteen sessions of the 1838–65 period, members nominally identified with the Town party were consistent winners in the legislature. The Planter party would never again exercise its accustomed control.

The Town party's success can be attributed more to its better attendance and cohesion than to greater numbers. Although it enjoyed a numerical advantage over the Planters after 1849, this was not true of the period 1844–49, when it held only 30 percent of the Assembly's seats. The party's success during this period is attributable largely to the fact that absenteeism among the Planters was extraordinarily high; during a typical session an average of almost 40 percent of the Planter party's membership failed to answer roll calls. By contrast, absenteeism among Town party members averaged about one-third over the entire period, reaching 40 percent or more in just two sessions.[33] It is also probable that over time, the greater longevity in office and thus legislative experience of a significant number of the Afro-Jamaican legislators gave them some advantages in parliamentary maneuvering.[34]

The 1849 election returns brought Governor Grey mixed feelings, however. He sighed relief that the canvass had gone peacefully but regretted that it apparently had confirmed a proretrenchment majority in the new Assembly.[35] Although Afro-Jamaican legislators continued providing stalwart support for Grey's administration, a cohesive group of fifteen Planter party members, aided by two defectors from the Town party, still managed to contain an equally cohesive opposition of eight colored members, supported by two defectors from the Planter party.[36] Occasionally, the high absentee rate of the planters provided an opening for the colored group to emerge with a critical victory, however, so that by the end of this second session of the new Assembly the government succeeded in getting its budget approved.[37]

After a brief period of political calm, induced perhaps by the cholera epidemic in 1850–52 and mistaken planter hopes that the Derby-Disraeli government would restore protective duties, conflict returned in the 1853 legislative session when the Assembly passed new retrenchment measures.[38] This rekindled conflict with the governor and Legislative Council took on a more ominous aspect than the last, however, because this time a much larger faction from the Town party, including several Afro-Jamaican leaders, joined the Planter party in voting for more limited spending, fracturing all previous coalitions and temporarily realigning the parties.[39] This unprecedented Afro-Jamaican–white planter coalition, though fragile, was very troubling to the Colonial Office. It was clear that many in the Planter party, alarmed at their shrinking majorities, sought to either restructure the government or abolish it in favor of direct rule from Britain. "The leaders of the party indeed do not scruple to say openly that they want to bring about a crisis," Grey warned the new colonial secretary, the duke of Newcastle, "and to have both Council and Assembly done away and some new form of Government established." By contrast, the colored advocates of retrenchment sought to strengthen the role of an Assembly they expected eventually to control. It was their goal, charged Grey, to keep "nine tenths of the revenue dependent upon annual grants and [to assert and exercise] the privilege of having money bills introduced by any member of the Assembly who may please to do it." He also thought that they wanted to reduce all public salaries to levels unappealing to Europeans. The Jewish merchants, meanwhile, were alleged to dislike duties and taxes of any kind, to care little for the judiciary or ecclesiastical establishment, and to profit by disruptions of imports and rum duties, because cessation of customs collections gave them an opportunity to stockpile duty-free merchandise. Whatever the merits of Grey's implicitly racist and anti-Semitic analysis, he clearly confronted a formidable coalition that allowed him less room for maneuver than in previous years.[40]

The governor held out little hope that another dissolution and new elections would change the composition of the legislature. On the contrary, he feared that the violent, black power surge he had expected in 1849 would become a reality. Premonitions of such a result were already evident in a recent series of local election riots with racial overtones. In Vere four years earlier, supporters of Afro-Jamaican assemblyman Charles Jackson had come to the polls armed with sticks. They attacked a prospective voter for their opponent and then the police who attempted to rescue him. According to Alexandre Bravo, the custos, the people "exhibited a spirit of insubordination and contempt for the constituted authorities." As police marched back to the barracks, they were stoned and their inspectors severely beaten, one sustaining a broken right hand.[41]

More recently, John Henderson, a white Baptist missionary in Falmouth, had been accused by an anonymous correspondent of inciting his "ragged regiment" against the educated and respectable merchant-planter James Dunstone in a recent election. Following the election several "followers" of Henderson, joined by a number of "loose" women, "rushed into the Court House, with sticks and other weapons." They were turned away by the police, but "a band of ruffians" threw rocks at "gentlemen who were returning to their homes."[42]

And, indeed, the worst was yet to come. St. David had long been a parish in which blacks were highly mobilized politically, the size of its registered electorate second only to Kingston's. In 1851 a very serious riot broke out when the candidate supported by blacks, John

Nunes, a mulatto owner of a livery stable, was defeated by James Porteous, a white planter-merchant. Police, the custos, magistrates, and "principle [sic] persons" of the parish were put to flight by a black mob brandishing cudgels and stones, and the courthouse was destroyed. The coroner, Mr. MacLean, was killed in the melee, and several others were hurt. Troops of the West India Regiment were sent in, and Porteous had to be guarded on his own estate. After investigations, stipendiary magistrates Fyfe, Hill, and Willis concluded that the riot was premeditated; fifty-five people were ordered to stand trial for rioting, and eight were indicted for the murder of MacLean.[43]

By mid-century, Afro-Jamaican assemblymen were speaking openly of their imminent assumption of power. Edward Vickars's slogan in the 1844 election had been "Vote for Vickars, the Black Man." In February 1849 Charles Jackson warned that the planters had better treat blacks justly and educate them to "fit them morally to occupy positions to which in the nature of things, they must arrive." They were destined to become "the permanent masters of the island."[44] Even some of the white Town party members seemed to welcome the militancy of their constituents. During a debate in March 1851, for example, William Smith, a railroad executive, declared that the Town party could command half the votes of the Assembly when "party considerations" required it and that within a few years it would command an "outright majority." All these events confirmed Grey's worst fears. Once again he insisted that parliamentary intervention like that in 1839 was the only viable option.[45]

But the new colonial secretary, the duke of Newcastle, was no more responsive to this suggestion than Earl Grey had been four years earlier. Thus the Jamaican situation drifted further into crisis. In April 1853, after the Assembly had reconvened and renewed its demands for retrenchment, which the Legislative Council once more rejected, it refused to do business. By midsummer, Jamaica was without either its senior naval officer, who had died of yellow fever, or its senior military commander, who had returned to England on sick leave. The police had not been paid since the end of May. Faced with an empty treasury, Governor Grey had begun releasing prisoners from the penitentiary, albeit most of them on work release programs.[46] In July the governor received notice that he was to be relieved at last. The same mail brought word of Newcastle's announcement to Parliament of a new initiative to reform the Jamaican system of government.[47]

Making a Better Government: Mid-Century Analyses
of Race, Power, and Governance

Resolution of the governmental crisis in Jamaica had had to await settlement of political difficulties in England. British politics in the late 1840s and early 1850s has been characterized as one of shifting coalitions, usually involving assorted Whigs and supporters of Robert Peel.[48] John Russell's six-year administration was the last formed on "a designedly Whig basis," according to that party's historian, Donald Southgate. Still, Russell depended on Peelite support in Commons, a kind of informal entente that was severely weakened by Peel's death in July 1850.[49] The temporary lull in the Jamaican crisis in 1851, then, coincided with a rapid series of governmental changes in Britain. Russell resigned in February 1851 only to resume office a few months later. But in February 1852 Palmerston's resignation over foreign policy issues brought the government down again. However, the administration of his successor, Edward G. Stanley (now created Lord Derby), could not withstand William Gladstone's withering attack on the budget prepared by Chancellor of the Exchequer Benjamin Disraeli.

In August 1852 George Hamilton-Gordon, the fourth earl of Aberdeen, now "the recognised leader of the Peelites," called for a fusion of Whigs and Peelites, which he dubbed "Liberal Conservatives." Aberdeen, "an aging and rather gloomy man," had been Peel's foreign secretary in 1834, and as a member of Peel's Cabinet again in the 1840s he had heartily endorsed his free trade policies. Late in 1852 he formed a "ministry of All the Talents" that included Russell, Gladstone, and Palmerston but excluded Earl Grey. The thirteen members of Aberdeen's first "Liberal" Cabinet included five fellow Peelites, seven Whigs, and one radical.[50] The new colonial secretary was Henry Clinton, the fifth duke of Newcastle, who also had been a member of Peel's first administration and endorsed free trade. The later action had so offended his father—"a rigid conservative" who had fought parliamentary reform to the bitter end in 1832—that he urged his son's constituents to defeat him in an 1846 by-election, thus forcing Henry to seek the suffrages of a new borough.[51]

While the new administration at Whitehall organized itself and consolidated its hold on office, the Jamaican troubles grew worse. Finally, on Thursday, 30 June 1853, Newcastle rose in the House of Lords to announce a plan for resolving the crisis. He made clear at the outset that the government was not prepared to call for either parliamentary intervention or crown colony rule "at present." Rather, he thought, "the quarrel was more likely to be adjusted by good management on the part of the Governor, and those who advised him, and by care and vigilance on the part of the Government at home, than by the intervention of the Imperial Parliament." Yet, it was clear from his remarks that should the Assembly refuse the carrots that the home government was now prepared to offer, the stick of direct intervention would be brought out in future.[52]

The root of the present crisis, according to Newcastle's analysis, lay in "the peculiar position of the constitution of the island." In his view, Jamaica had developed an anomalous and insupportable system of governance. Its finances were in shambles because its system of raising and expending public money was irresponsible. There being no annual estimates of revenues and expenditures, any individual member of the Assembly could propose a money bill, which also named the specific tax source to support its authorized allocation. A standing committee of the Assembly supervised the collection of taxes, administered expenditures, and audited the accounts, leaving the governor not only without control of finances but deprived of official channels even to communicate his views on these matters to the Assembly. The rise of debts, taxes, and inconvertible paper currency had been the inexorable result of such a system. During the current crisis, Newcastle estimated that the colony was losing a thousand pounds each day in uncollected revenues, an indicator of its inefficient system for collecting taxes. Meanwhile, essential social and government services were neglected, and the entire government was one of "extravagant and wasteful expenditure."[53]

A more proper system of financial management—including annual estimates, executive control, and clear separation of legislative, executive, and auditing functions—was essential to rectifying these defects of island governance. The civil service must be supported by a permanent fund based on permanent taxes, making a crisis such as the current one impossible thereafter. Essential government functions should never again be held hostage by a hostile Assembly. In exchange for these reforms, the home government was prepared to make generous arrangements to resolve the colony's current financial embarrassment and to put it on the road to fiscal and moral recovery by providing a total of £550,000 in loans at 3 percent interest. Newcastle's peroration underscored the urgency of reform by reminding white Jamaicans in a veiled way of the black leviathan rising in their midst: it was, he said, "the eleventh hour."

The clarity and confidence with which Newcastle presented his financial proposals contrasted sharply with his muddled and diffident discussion of possible political reforms. The irresponsibility of Jamaica's financial system required a more responsible government, it was agreed, but by 1853 the term "responsible government" had taken on meanings much broader than merely the efficient management of governmental affairs. It now referred to a set of political arrangements by which increased authority devolved upon the colonial electorate rather than the Crown. More specifically, it referred to the system of government that had recently evolved in Canada. In his speech to Parliament, Newcastle had compared Jamaica unfavorably with Canada; still, he was very hesitant about offering Canada's good example as a model for Jamaica.[54] To appreciate Newcastle's diffidence—the fears and hopes the phrase "responsible government" aroused, the reasons for the studied ambiguity with which those words were used, and how an evolving racial ideology hopelessly confounded all political analysis—one must examine the development of imperial thinking about the full range of British colonies.

By 1850 key British policymakers had begun to make distinctions between the future of their white colonies, such as Canada, and the black ones, such as Jamaica. The former were to be groomed for greater independence in their local affairs, while the latter were judged to be better suited for a "benevolent guardianship." Even so good a friend of freed people's interests as James Stephen was convinced by mid-century that England should never give up its tropical colonies. Colonies were "wretched burdens" the nation had assumed "in an evil hour . . . but which we have no right to lay down again." The white settlement colonies—the Canadian provinces, New South Wales in Australia, and the South African Cape—might decide to break the ties of empire, but the black West Indies were "unfit" for independence. "We emancipate our grown-up sons, but keep our unmarried daughters, and our children who may chance to be ricketty [sic], in domestic bonds," he wrote a friend. Here, then, the iconography of dependency formerly applicable to individual slaves came to characterize whole societies. Here, long before Rudyard Kipling popularized the phrase, was Britain's ostensibly altruistic imperial mission—"the white man's burden."[55]

Although Earl Grey rejected the notion that the colonies were a burden, he too believed that imperial power carried with it "a responsibility of the highest kind which we are not at liberty to throw off." Britain must spread "the blessings of Christianity and civilization."

But for Grey the materialistic and the idealistic justifications were always closely intertwined. Britain's power and influence depended "upon its having large colonial possessions in different parts of the world." On the West African coast, for example, British power was necessary to stop the slave trade and civilize the natives, but it also protected British property and ensured markets for British goods. Although the West Indies were no longer an economic asset, loosening the colonial bonds would unleash "a fearful war of colour . . . , and too probably all the germs of improvement which now exist there would be destroyed and civilization would be thrown back for centuries."[56] Thus the conflict Metcalfe had characterized in 1842 as one of class, workers versus planters, became for Grey mainly one of race, black versus white.

For an administration committed to free trade, Grey sketched out a nonmercantilist justification for empire. But his argument emphasized political rather than economic advantages, narrowly conceived: control of colonies enhanced the overall position of Britain as a world power. The economic wealth of a colony might contribute directly to the mother country or indirectly, in the sense that British possession kept that wealth out of rival hands. Canada, with its vast mineral resources and growing population, was an apt illustration of this principle. It was just as important to deny Canada's resources to Britain's rival power in the Western Hemisphere, the United States, as it was to acquire them for herself. And as for a colony's relationship to the mother country, or more precisely its fitness for self-government, this would be determined by the numbers and purposes of its white settlers. In the temperate-zone colonies whites were numerous and permanent settlers, while in the tropics they were a minority of "temporary sojourners."[57] Thus, by 1850 two very different men, beginning from different premises, had arrived at the same conclusion: Canadians could rule themselves; Jamaicans could not.

Ironically, neither Grey nor Stephen would have been comfortable with such an analysis ten years earlier. Much of Canada's history during the 1830s and 1840s had paralleled, even intersected with, Jamaica's. (Both Metcalfe and Elgin left Jamaica to become governor of Canada.) Although in later usage Canada would be classified with the "white" colonies, in the 1830s and 1840s it was discussed in much the same terms as the mixed societies to the south. Thus, attention to that earlier discussion and its subsequent changes might help strip away the racial mystifications and confusions attendant on similar developments in Jamaica a decade later.

Since 1791, Canada had been divided into two provinces with distinct populations under separate governments: Francophone Lower Canada and Anglophone Upper Canada. The French Canadians of Lower Canada, called *Canadiens,* occupied a position much like that of Jamaica's black and brown population in that they made up a majority of Canada's population. They also constituted a majority in the assembly of Lower Canada, but they did not enjoy commensurate political power. In the 1830s they rebelled. First, the Assembly precipitated a crisis in 1834, Jamaica-style, by stopping supplies. In 1837 the situation deteriorated into a series of bloody confrontations led in Lower Canada by prominent French political families demanding independence from Britain. British analysts interpreted this crisis as one of, in the words of the official investigation, "two nations warring in the bosom of a single state." Canada was on the verge of a "race war." The *Canadiens* were the other "race."[58]

In mid-nineteenth-century usage the term "race" had not yet acquired a strictly biological connotation but was a handy way of embracing what in the twentieth century might be called nationality, ethnicity, or culture. Nevertheless, the term strikes with some of the same resonance and communicates much the same social significance as in later years; it conveys the same sense of extreme "otherness." But in Canada, as in the West Indies, race was impossibly entangled with class and political factors. The "racial" struggle observers described in Lower Canada was between French agriculturalists and British commercial interests.[59] Meanwhile, French demands for reform were seconded by British allies in Upper Canada, who had also rioted in 1837. The latter were aggrieved by their province's corrupt oligarchic administration (called the Family Compact), inequitable distribution of public land, and state support of the established church. Indeed, it was the potential political alliance of these two disparate groups that, in Whitehall's view, made Canada especially dangerous.

Nonetheless, it was the "racial" rather than political and class dimensions that aroused anxiety in Britain; or, at least, it was in racial terms that class and political conflicts were discussed. In the minds of British officials, "racial" divisions, however calculated, rent the social fabric, threatened social order, and retarded progress. Of course, unlike biological differences, differences of culture (language, religion, and values) were mutable. Indeed, assimilation was not merely a possibility but a strategy for allaying political tensions. In fact, Charles Buller, a former tutee of Thomas Carlyle, saw assimilated French Canadians serving to check the democratic, "American" tendencies of

British reformers in Upper Canada.[60] There was no hint in his analysis that assimilation would mean amalgamation, however, at least not in the sense of eventual sameness or equality. The task was to design political structures that would preserve both peace and the empire; that would make "other" peoples British enough, yet keep the *real* British in control.

Along with Edward Gibbon Wakefield, Buller assisted Lord Durham—a radical Whig who had helped write the Reform Act of 1832—who was sent out in 1838 as high commissioner and governor general of British North America. Durham's assignment was to quell Canadian unrest and develop a scheme for a better system for governing British North America, a mission deemed crucial to "the preservation of the integrity of the British Empire."[61] Durham managed to exceed his rather extensive powers by deporting some rebels to Bermuda, which created political embarrassment for his superiors and forced him to resign his commission before the year was out. His six-month tenure had provided enough material, however, to fill a multivolume report that is generally credited with transforming British colonial administration. Durham recommended the reunification of the two provinces, British Upper and French Lower Canada, under a single governor armed with expanded powers over public affairs and finances but acting through a cabinet of ministers. The ministers would be selected from the Assembly and would be politically responsible to that body, in that—as in the British Parliament—a vote of "no confidence" could force them to resign. This popular control of the executive branch would be checked and balanced by a strong, independent judiciary and a nonelective legislative council.[62]

When Durham submitted these recommendations in January 1839, they provoked considerable discussion, some serious reservations, and a major Cabinet crisis that resulted in the dismissal of Glenelg—who had procrastinated on taking any action on the issue—from the Colonial Office. Glenelg's main antagonists, Lord John Russell and Durham's brother-in-law Earl Grey, were concerned that the plan ultimately would threaten British rule. Could a colonial executive serve two masters, the Assembly and the Crown? The essence of the colonial relationship was that the governor was appointed by and must respond to directives from the Crown. Could he do this if his main instrument for implementing those policies served at the pleasure of a popularly elected Assembly? And how much more complicated must this be in Canada, where the population majority was of an alien culture, of a different race?

For his part, Durham was far from intending to turn power over to the French Canadian majority. On the contrary, his intent was to ensure that the British minority in Lower Canada would never again be placed under the authority of a legislature dominated by *Canadiens*.[63] It is likely that Durham's analysis was strongly influenced by Wakefield, the authority on colonial demography, because the proposed concession of democratic government was made on the assumption that future immigration must inevitably give Canada a British majority. While this final solution unfolded, *Canadiens* would be gerrymandered to reduce their political strength and assimilated to British language, religion, and values. Thus the Act of Union of 1840, which grew out of Durham's report, made assimilation an official policy. The capital was moved to Kingston, and French was forbidden as a language of official discourse. Durham's scheme was in the venerable Whig tradition of ostensibly radical changes designed to achieve conservative ends. Ironically, subsequent generations would hail his responsible government plan as a liberal landmark in colonial governance.

Interestingly, Durham himself did not introduce—and in fact rejected—the phrase "responsible government," which soon came to describe his plan. The phrase had been used during the thirties as a slogan by British reformers in Upper Canada to express their demands for a greater role in colonial governance and dissolution of the Family Compact. The phrase made its way into the marginalia of Durham's report, placed there apparently by a clerk in an effort to summarize succinctly the author's lengthy paragraph on the weaknesses of the colonial executive. Thereafter colonial reformers seized upon it as a succinct expression of the expanded role they sought in colonial governance, thus bringing it into general usage; but it came in like the discursive analogue of the proverbial bull in a china shop. British authorities deprecated the phrase but could not free themselves of it. Over the next decade, they could neither define it nor confine its implications for colonial relationships.[64]

In fact, responsible government as such was not approved by Whitehall, nor was it officially implemented by the Act of Union. Indeed, Durham's notion of responsibility was positively rejected by the Cabinet. Russell was convinced that the colonial executive could not serve two masters and that the proposed constitution was incompatible with imperial authority or colonial status. A key point in Durham's argument was the possibility of making a distinction between colonial or local issues and imperial interests, but others in the government did not accept this distinction. Therefore, self-government eventually came to Canada, not by positive enactment, but through a series of concessions and practical politics, responsive to political insurgencies in the 1840s. By 1850 the doctrine was established, having evolved through a combination of determined pressure from below and "muddling through" at the top of colonial government, with the British government reacting to developments rather than shaping or dictating them.[65]

Traditionally, colonies—revealingly referred to initially as "plantations"—had been mere outposts for extracting surplus values for the mother country. As they grew into more complex societies requiring larger undertakings by government, they also required greater executive authority, and this, in turn, necessitated a party administration with a reliable majority in the assembly. The necessity of commanding the support of the majority of the assembly evolved inexorably into responsibility to that majority. It was an irresistible trend that Canadian political insurgents immediately recognized.[66] In the summer of 1840, for example, British reformer Francis Hincks wrote his French counterpart Louis-Hippolyte LaFontaine: *"We will make them give [responsible government] whether they like it or not."*[67]

Although Whitehall was anxious to evade recognition of the inevitable, it found it increasingly difficult to do so. Thus the British government found itself drawn inexorably into a situation like the one it would confront in Jamaica a decade later. Russell denounced responsible government for Upper Canada in principle but had to concede it in practice, forced by circumstances reluctantly to take a public position.[68] At the same time, however, the British succeeded in forestalling the full implementation of responsibility by refusing to recognize parties; that is, they avoided forming a government from any single partisan coalition.[69] This fear of parties was bound up with an inordinate fear of racial conflict; only the diminution of the latter would allow full acceptance of the former.

Somehow British policymakers never accepted that parties would be the necessary sequelae of Cabinet responsibility. Perhaps the fact that party organization was still in its infancy in Britain itself and partisanship was not yet fully accepted as appropriate for statesmen helps explain their naiveté. Durham's reforms were presented as measures by which the governor would gain initiative rather than lose power to a majority party in the Assembly. Indeed, Durham himself did not appreciate the significance of parties nor anticipate the development of party systems in British North America. His view of Canadian politics reflected much of the concurrent image of partisan chaos in Jamaica. Colonial political groups were merely ad hoc alliances of interest groups formed around specific issues, rather than more or less permanent alignments. Other governors shared this view. Elgin—who, following Metcalfe, served in Canada after his Jamaican tour—believed that fair dealings would break down racial or class cohesions and promote mutuality of interests across class or race lines. Thus, wise policies could be a solvent of racial and class divisions.[70]

The Colonial Office staff's distrust of partisanship was entangled with their fears of racial conflict. "Racial" differences seemed to give a permanence to partisan alignments not evident in more homogeneous polities. Not only did national or racial sentiment provide the basis for incipient parties but, once formed, such parties posed a danger because they made a mockery of that "mutuality of interests" between various classes and strata upon which good government and social order depended. The possibility of compromise for the common good was reduced. Given these premises, it followed that party formation in a racially mixed society must be discouraged; or more accurately, the non-British "race" must not be allowed to form a party. As a consequence, the home government was trapped in an awkward double-speak, its policies articulated in an obscurantist discourse. The consent of the governed was to be secured through an elected assembly, but their representatives must be denied the most obvious means of political expression and mobilization.

The policy was as difficult to implement as it was to articulate. As with any political system, patronage was necessary to govern, because it mediated real political differences among constituent groups in a legislature. An initial attempt by Secretary Stanley to maintain imperial control through the deft manipulation of patronage to individuals proved impossible to sustain. Their electoral successes made formal recognition of, and thus patronage for, French Canadians *as a political faction* irresistible. "Whether the doctrine of responsible government is openly acknowledged or is only tacitly acquiesced in," one governor declared after appointing French partisans to the Cabinet, "virtually it exists."[71] For many knowledgeable observers the Frenchmen's growing power in the Assembly required more formal recognition than the British had anticipated giving. It was clear to Wakefield, for example, that "the French could not *be* the majority but they could *give* the majority to any other considerable party."[72] British governors tried, counterproductively, both to oil the wheels of government with patronage and to deny control of its dispensation by the governing coalitions it was forced to recognize in the Assembly. Thus Whitehall set up a second line of defense with a formulation that proved ultimately indefensible: its parliamentary ministers were to have control over measures but not men.

Earl Grey entered the Colonial Office in 1846 still opposed to responsible government in Canada for many of the same reasons that he would invoke later in Jamaica. But like his successors Russell and Stanley, Grey was forced by a series of Canadian crises to recognize responsible government de facto. As then Canadian Governor Elgin wrote him in 1847, they must acknowledge the impossibility of denying the principle of self-government once the practice had been conceded.[73] Shortly thereafter, Elgin was forced to form a government exclusively of the *Canadien*-controlled reform party and to confirm its authority over patronage. Armed now with power over men as well as measures, the government was vested with executive responsibility in its fullest sense and could be fully responsive to the popular will as expressed through the majority party in the Assembly.[74]

It was against this background that the British mulled over what political reforms to recommend or accept in Jamaica. In their attempts to resolve the Jamaican crisis they confronted some of the same issues, made many of the same mistakes, and were plagued by exactly the same confusions about race and class as in Canada. Indeed, there had been earlier confidential discussions, concurrent with the unfolding of the Canadian experiment, of how it might serve as a model for Jamaica. As early as 1840 James Stephen had suggested adopting some specific aspects of the Canadian arrangement as a way for the governor to gain greater influence over the legislative process. But after an extended discussion, it was decided that the situation was not yet ripe for the application of the Canadian solution in Jamaica. "Ripeness" in this instance Metcalfe defined as that crucial transition period during which "the Democracy" would greatly increase their numbers in the Assembly yet remain a minority, while the "Aristocracy," though still in control, would recognize the inevitability of black domination. At that precise moment the government could expect maximum influence, because both sides would find their interests served by curtailing "the power of the popular branch."[75]

By the end of the decade the situation seemed "ripe." In the midst of the 1849 crisis, Charles Grey suggested to the Assembly the notion of revising the Jamaican constitution to a Canadian model. The governor's recklessness baffled the Colonial Office, however, because the Canadian "model" had evolved by 1849 into a system deemed inappropriate to Jamaican conditions. Canada, they declared, was "in a totally different state from Jamaica as to political elements." They no longer thought of Canada as a racially mixed society; it was "white." Officially, Earl Grey simply acknowledged that the governor's dispatch had been received, but in a private letter he argued strongly against his cousin's reckless notion of instituting responsible government in Jamaica. Afro-Jamaican assemblymen applauded the governor's suggestion, however, because responsible government offered them a means of institutionalizing the Assembly's power, and through it their own.[76]

Newcastle had reason, then, to be cautious with this subject when he urged constitutional reform in Jamaica. He wanted a system of government that was responsible in the generic sense, certainly, but he declined to "pledge himself to all the details of the Canadian system." The idea would require considerable modification before it could be applied to Jamaica. That island might choose simply to give the governor representation in the Assembly in order to facilitate the administration of public business rather than adopt fully responsible government, he suggested hopefully. Under such an arrangement, the executive officers could be removed from office by the governor but not by an adverse vote of the Assembly as in Canada. Evidently, Newcastle hoped that reforms would be adopted that would make the Assembly more "responsible" in its behavior but not in its power. In sum, for Jamaica, Newcastle used *responsible* as an adjective, not a noun.[77]

Jamaica's "peculiar circumstance," then, was that it had a black majority. Moreover, it was a culturally alien, potentially hostile majority. The same had been true of Canada in the early 1840s, when French Canadians stood in the place comparable to the one blacks occupied in the West Indies. The situations were parallel in the political sense as well, in that the ultimate objective in each instance was to secure British predominance and to quell disorder. Colonial acquiescence was to be achieved by democratic reforms that would win the consent of the popular majority, while ensuring continued imperial control. By 1854 the crucial difference between these two colonies, as British authorities perceived it, was in their demographic trends. Canada would grow inevitably more British and assimilated, that is, white; Jamaica would grow inevitably blacker and more alien.

Henry Barkly, the eldest son of a wealthy Scottish sugar merchant and legatee to several West Indian estates, was handed the task of shepherding Newcastle's ostensibly radical but actually conservative reforms through the fractious Jamaica Assembly. No stranger to West Indian troubles, his appointment was one both Stanley and Grey applauded.[78] Governor of British Guiana at the time of his appointment, Barkly had been a significant figure among West Indian lobbyists during the 1840s. In testimony to a select committee in 1842 he took the position of an enlightened planter, arguing against physical coercion and for programs that stimulated the "artificial" consumption desires of his laborers as a way to get a more disciplined workforce. But he also endorsed the importation of Asian indentured laborers as crucial to immediate recovery and survival. He had been a familiar figure at the Colonial Office, where he lobbied persistently for more indentured workers for his own estates. Elected to Parliament in 1845 as a "Liberal-Conservative," he had been a devoted follower of Robert Peel and had endorsed and voted for free trade; but he had also earned the sobriquet "Sugar Plum," because of his insistent advocacy of sugar interests.[79] Subsequently, as governor of Guiana he had achieved modest success in reforming its political system, at least to the extent of securing a long-term (though not permanent) revenue to forestall future crises, earning such popularity in the process that upon his departure the planters raised a subscription of five hundred pounds to purchase him a silver service. Thus began a career in the colonial service that would take him eventually to Australia (1856–63), Mauritius (1863–70), and the Cape Colony in South Africa (1870–77).[80]

Initially, Barkly's reactions to the state of the island and the task before him were very pessimistic. His first tour of the island and the reactivated reports of the stipendiary magistrates revealed growing economic distress and argued a deterioration of the moral fabric of Jamaican black society. And although the black majority seemed not to be fully mobilized politically—there were only 2,235 registered voters—the governor thought that political power still fell to "the least competent part of the community," an assertion substantiated, he thought, by the recent electoral violence in St. David and St. Mary. While one might agree, therefore, that an expanded franchise was desirable in principle, "it is evident that it must be set about with the greatest deliberation and care, owing to the very peculiar state of society which exists in this island."[81]

A flawed electorate had produced a flawed legislature, in Barkly's view. Political conflict in Jamaica was engendered solely by "differences of Race and its concomitant distinctions of both creed and complexion," all politely "concealed under the ordinary terms of party nomenclature." This made the Assembly a difficult body to work with, he found, "being so evenly balanced, or rather subdivided into so many variously influenced and slightly cohering sections, as almost to baffle conjecture as to the side on which a majority would be found in respect to any question that arose." The various factions waged "a sort of guerilla warfare on their own account." Barkly's assessment of the Assembly has been seconded by more disinterested analysts. An American correspondent in Jamaica to cover the constitutional crisis thought it absurd even to speak of a "coloured party": "Never was there a people, perhaps, more disunited than the colored people of Jamaica." Gad Heuman's authoritative discussion of Jamaican politics during this period also dates the disintegration of the colored faction from the retrenchment crisis of 1853.[82]

It is true that the constitutional reform crisis created new coalitions and alignments in the Assembly, but Barkly's description of a political "Tower of Babel" is surely overstated, and the New York correspondent's characterization of the colored members is misleading. Even Heuman's description of increased factionalism must be qualified. If one examines the overall voting pattern over the entire period rather than focusing on alignments on single roll calls, some interesting patterns emerge. The most striking of these, perhaps, is that by mid-century the Planter party appears practically to have collapsed as a consistent, identifiable voting bloc. Certainly, their extraordinarily high absenteeism during this period—averaging 51 percent between November 1852 and April 1853, compared with an average of 34 percent for Town party members—greatly reduced any possible influence the twenty-two Planter party men might have exercised. But even those Planters in attendance were not very cohesive during the crisis years: fewer than one out of four voted with another party colleague at least 70 percent of the time, a feat managed by well over half the Town party members. Contrary to many contemporary views, then, the Planters were the least united political faction in the Assembly.[83]

By the time the constitutional crisis came to a head, the Planter party had suffered some critical losses among its most veteran leaders, and those who remained seemed confused as to how best to deal with this crisis.[84] Apparently, some favored a stronger executive government and Legislative Council, while others—as Charles Grey had suspected—hoped the crisis would result in the abolition of the Assembly altogether and direct rule from Britain. Most of them appear to have cooperated with the new opposition faction led by Charles Jackson, colored member from Vere.

Charles Hamilton Jackson

Most of Jackson's group had voted in support of retrenchment, splitting the Town party and its colored core in the process.[85] Indeed, because of the high absenteeism of the Planters, legislative battles during these years sometimes had the appearance of an internal struggle within the erstwhile Town party coalition. In 1853 all but two effective members of Jackson's opposition coalition were identified with the Town party, including four other colored legislators (Alexander Heslop, Foster March, John Nunes, and Henry Franklin). They were joined by three planters, Henry Westmorland, George Barrett, and John R. Hollingsworth. The government was supported most consistently by a seven-member coalition comprising four colored members (James Taylor, Robert Russell, William March, and Robert Osborn), a planter (William Wright), and two white members of the Town party (Francis Lynch and John Bristowe).[86]

By 1854, however, the government coalition had gained strength because of the high absenteeism among Planters and defections by several colored members who had voted with Jackson's group. Thus, despite Jackson's prominence among the antigovernment faction, an overwhelming majority of colored members were now supporters of the proposed reforms. Ironically, then, Afro-Jamaican votes were critical in determining the success of a government measure spon-

Alexander Heslop

sored in part to constrain the future employment of black political power.[87]

Of course, the government's advantage did not guarantee success on every vote. Part of the problem, perhaps, was the lack of leadership from the governor, who was sometimes accused of being too aloof from the political process. But then Barkly's instructions from home were vague on the most critical points before the Assembly. Newcastle had emphasized the governor's need for a spokesman in the Assembly, control of finances by officers responsible to the Crown, and an annual budget framed by government ministers. He sidestepped, however, the question whether responsible government should mean that executive officers should serve at the pleasure of the Crown or of the legislature and just who would control patronage. He had hinted broadly at the difficulties popular control might entail: "That responsible Government should be established is the first thing necessary, but what form that responsibility should in the first instance assume, depends chiefly upon the composition of the Assembly, and the materials which it affords for what has been termed party Government; as also upon the control which public opinion may be likely to exercise over such a Government, and over the majority of the Assembly."[88] Given the Colonial staffers' current assessments of Jamaican public opinion, the Assembly majority, and the wisdom of party government in racially mixed societies, Newcastle obviously intended Barkly to oppose responsible government.

In the Jamaica Assembly, meanwhile, both proponents and opponents of reform also disavowed any desire for party government. Still, it was not clear how otherwise to constitute a strong executive authority armed with exclusive control of the budget and yet preserve a meaningful check on that power in the Assembly. The bill that finally emerged from their prolonged debate vested legislative powers in a popularly elected Assembly, which retained the initiative on money bills, and in an appointive Legislative Council, armed with veto power. No more than four government officials could serve on the council, and the qualifications for its nonofficial members were set to ensure that only resident planters would be selected. Administration of government, including drafting the budget, was vested in the Executive Committee, made up of two to three assemblymen and one of the council members. The Executive Committee was appointed by and served at the pleasure of the governor, who retained ultimate responsibility for government administration and patronage.[89]

The bill was a compromise, Barkly wrote, "the result of the struggles of parties having widely different objects in view."[90] By a one-vote margin it was approved in council, where the four planter representatives were its only supporters. Its opponents—including Jordon—expressed concern that the governor's choices for executive officers would be unduly limited by the provision excluding public officials from the Assembly. Barkly, too, regretted that he would not be allowed to select any of his ministers from among the heads of government departments, contending that the system placed them in an "anomalous position" with respect to the new ministers and implied a degree of responsibility to the Assembly that was undesirable. Overriding these objections, however, was the prospect that this act would lay "the foundations of a reform" that might be perfected in future. "When the new system has been fairly tested, and the character of the legislature, as a necessary consequence, raised, I do not despair of seeing those jealousies of class and colour which prevented the adoption of better arrangements now, assuaged, if not obliterated; and I am confident that then changes such as I have described will be the object of future legislation." Newcastle concurred with this judgment and, despite his own reservations, consented to the law.[91]

Just how, in Barkly's view, "jealousies of class and colour" were to be obliterated is not clear. Nor is it clear what he understood the relationship between race and class in Jamaica to be, but his earliest reports from Jamaica reflected his pessimism about the prospects of governing a racially mixed society. He spent his first Christmas trying to quell a riot at Montego Bay that had erupted when police attempted to suppress a "John Canoe" procession, a popular, African-influenced revel dating from slavery. After the police arrested five or six of the revelers, a mob stormed their station house to rescue them, and the military had to be called upon to restore order. Barkly thought that the procession itself cast doubt on claims made for the blacks' "progress in civilization." But he was especially offended that Town party politicians had condemned the actions of the police rather than those of the mob. This event was evidence for him of "the real spirit of the population" and underscored the dangers "of almost democratic institutions upon a people little fitted by previous training for self-government." Such propensity for disorder could be kept in check only through "a better organized system of police, and a more defined and vigorous central Executive Authority." The trouble was, he would soon discover, that the Better Government Act deliberately obscured the actual relationship between the people's will and the new "central Executive Authority."[92]

Taming Black Power

In order to inaugurate the new system, it was necessary to dissolve the Assembly and call new elections. The continuing financial emergency required immediate legislative action. But like Grey and Elgin before him, Barkly was fearful of what kind of Assembly the elections would produce. What those elections did produce was the largest number of black and brown legislators in the Assembly's history; fifteen colored men and three blacks would sit in the Assembly over the next six years. Three of the colored members were identified with the Planter party, but this still left a formidable nonwhite presence. There were now only eleven white, non-Jewish members in the Planter party. It seemed that the situation successive governors had dreaded had finally arrived.[93]

These election results required the governor's utmost tact in forming the new government. Barkly appointed Edward Jordon, Henry Westmorland, and Bryan Edwards as his Executive Committee, his choices dictated by a conscious attempt to represent major racial divisions in the Assembly. "Constituted of three great parties, or rather

250 | The Political Economy of Freedom

races, the only way I could form a Cabinet was by selecting representatives from two of them."[94]

Thus at least four facts were fully evident at the outset of the new government. First, the governor's policies would proceed from the assumption that party, class, and color were interchangeable, if not synonymous, categories; and having denied party as the basis for political organization and class as legitimate grounds for political desire, race became their substitute. Thus willy-nilly the feared politicization of race crept back into the system of governance. Second, although by statute the ministers would be hired and fired by the governor alone, they needed to maintain de facto a credible political base in the Assembly because their usefulness depended ultimately on that political influence. Thus, as in Canada, the system of "responsibility" stood poised at the back door ready to enter at the first major political crisis. Third, again much as in Canada during the 1840s, the government attempted to maintain the Assembly's support by representing its major conflicting sections within one "unity" ministry rather than allowing any one party to control the government. Therefore, having inadvertently conceded a partisan basis of political organization with one hand, the government sought to forestall it with the other, thus sowing the seeds of confusion about the actual basis of political reform. Even if successful, such a ministry would confound and possibly dilute partisan leadership but at the same time actually encourage divisive factional alignments. Clearly, the partisan leadership the home government most wanted to dilute was that offered by Afro-Jamaican assemblymen, what Barkly called "the popular party." The obfuscation of responsibility under the Better Government Act achieved that dilution temporarily but in the process sowed the seed of an even greater crisis.

In the short run, of course, it was a brilliant stratagem. Legislative initiative now lay with an Executive Committee that represented not one party but two. Therefore, any policy initiative would necessarily be a compromise, at best, regardless of the relative voting strengths of the two parties in the Assembly. The political will of a future black electoral majority could be thwarted through the intricacies of this political arrangement. By appointing Jordon to the Executive Committee, the government further constrained the most prominent member of the so-called popular party (meaning the former Town party coalition) to support its policies. As Henry Taylor would declare in another context some years later, given Jordon's influence, it was important that the government "have a permanent hold" upon him.[95] And more

Edward Jordon

often than not during the following decade, Jordon's colored colleagues did follow him in supporting the government.

In each of the first two sessions there were "no confidence" motions that Afro-Jamaican members helped turn back. On 24 October 1855, for example, the government's opposition, constituted now of splinter factions from the former Town party, introduced a resolution condemning the inadequacy of the proposed appropriation for education, health, and welfare. Recognizing this as a motion of "no confidence" in Jordon, colored legislators voted against it overwhelmingly, defeating it, 21–7. Of course, it is likely that motives other than sentiment prompted such loyalty. Although the governor had final authority, Jordon's position should have given him some influence over decisions on patronage and government contracts, and it is likely that his associates benefited from those decisions. It must be remembered, too, that the colored men had always been the group most consistently loyal to the Crown.[96]

Nevertheless, the new regime, of which Jordon was a part, pursued policies that were anathema to these members' constituents. It is probably for this reason that although they supported the ministry on some crucial challenges to its survival, their overall support was relatively soft. One can discern three clusters of legislators during the first session under the new constitution. First, there was the "ministerial" coalition, formed around Jordon and Westmorland. Its ten members were evenly divided between the Planter party and the Town party, but besides Jordon there was only one other colored member, Peter Espeut, an owner of two sugar estates. Afro-Jamaican legislators Foster March, Christopher Walters, and James Taylor joined two white Town party members to form an opposition, though apparently not a very consistent one. The six remaining colored members constituted a "swing" group, which voted with the government's ministers more often than against them but was not consistent. This softness in the government's coalition continued into the second session.[97]

Increasingly, however, Jordon found himself isolated politically from his colored colleagues because, as a minister, he was identified with policies offensive to the Afro-Jamaican majority. The priorities of the new administration included financial measures to increase taxes on imports, especially clothing, and to reduce export duties on estate produce. Christopher Walters became a vocal opponent of the import duties on clothing, arguing that they were intended to force laborers to work for lower wages. Although most of the colored legislators continued to support Jordon and the government, several others, including Taylor, March, and Vickars (known as the "Kingston Agitators"), held public meetings to condemn the government's policies.[98] More colored legislators joined the opposition on 6 February 1856 to defeat soundly a government proposal to revise the election laws. On the short end of this 13–10 vote, Jordon found himself in the company of six Planter and only three other Town party members. Among Afro-Jamaican Town party members, only Osborn supported him. By contrast, twelve of the measure's thirteen opponents were Town party members, nine of them Afro-Jamaican.[99]

But as the Colonial Office well knew, it was easier to oppose legislation than to enact it. By law, legislative initiative now lay with the governor and the Executive Committee rather than the Assembly. And even if the governor and his ministers could be prevailed on to sponsor a measure favorable to Jamaica's black majority, the measure still could be derailed by the planter-controlled Legislative Council. During the 1854–55 session, for example, Afro-Jamaican assemblymen had doubled the education appropriation that Jordon submitted by taking advantage of the planters' absences from the legislature in December to attend to their estates. The Executive Committee offered to resign because of these defeats, but Barkly dissuaded them. Having been thus put on notice, the following year the government finally took a modest step toward improving the educational and sanitary systems by providing better funding through a new house tax. Having used such a tax previously to pay off parochial debts contracted fighting the cholera epidemic, the government now sought to apply it to expanded education and sanitary services. The bill passed the Assembly with solid support from colored members and surprisingly strong backing from Planter party members but was "ambushed" in the Legislative Council. Despite George Price's strong advocacy of the bill in the council, the planters and their press insisted that the education system was good enough as it was and that peasants would not pay the tax anyway. Through the council, therefore, the planter minority was able to thwart one of the most cherished objectives of the black majority.[100]

In a dispatch describing this litany of defeat, Barkly realized that perhaps he should have disbanded the Executive Committee. He decided against such a step because he was certain that the Assembly would never return a "no confidence" vote and that he would not find a better cabinet anyway. The new government worked well enough in its administrative capacity, he thought, but "indifferently in a legislative point of view." Its executive officers "may be said in short to be strong enough to defy any combination which could by possibility be formed against them, but weak to an excess whenever they attempt to act." Although members would support the government on final passage of a bill, they felt no compunction against opposing it on crucial amendments. In the Assembly "personal or class interests [still] usurp the place of fixed political principles." What the governor was saying—apparently without realizing it—was that "a vigorous central executive authority" required a disciplined cadre of assemblymen. But how could one have a disciplined cadre, without a party?[101]

The month following this confused and disappointed assessment of what reform had wrought, Barkly left Jamaica. His successor, Charles Henry Darling, was even more experienced in West Indian affairs than Barkly had been and was equally anxious about his status as a commoner in a job traditionally reserved to the nobility. For much of his career he had served as private secretary to several colonial governors, beginning with his uncle, Sir Ralph Darling, in New South Wales, then Lionel Smith in Barbados and Jamaica, and Charles Grey. He had also been Elgin's agent-general of immigration. He left Jamaica in 1847 to become lieutenant governor of St. Lucia and subsequently went to the Cape of Good Hope and Newfoundland. He had the distinction of being the only Jamaican governor who had been a member of the Jamaica Assembly. Although identified with the Town party during his brief tenure, often he had voted with the planters. It was an allegiance he continued as governor.[102]

During Darling's administration, government policy tilted decisively and overtly against the black majority. Although he admitted the need for educational and health measures, he delayed them in favor of immigration and law and order issues. Jordon's presence in the administration no longer deflected Afro-Jamaican opposition to such policies, although it may have blunted that opposition at critical junctures. Indeed, on one occasion Jordon himself voted against the government, when in November 1858 it tried to expand the jurisdiction of local magistrates to cases involving property worth twenty shillings without consent of the accused and to cases involving ten pounds with consent. Christopher Walters objected that peasants already distrusted magistrates and that this would deepen their distrust. With the Executive Committee split, the Assembly divided evenly on the final vote. Jordon joined nine other black and brown members and five Jewish members to oppose the bill. William Hosack, also an Executive Committee member, lined up a solid Planter party behind the bill, including its three colored members. He was also supported by two colored assemblymen from the Town party. Speaker Morales's vote broke the tie in favor of the measure. This law would be a significant irritant in the events leading up to the Morant Bay Rebellion five years hence.[103]

But Afro-Jamaican legislators themselves contributed the deadliest blow to their political fortunes—the 1859 revision of the election law. Since the middle of the 1830s, planters had recognized the need to restrict the franchise if they were to have any chance of maintaining political power, but their previous efforts had been mostly rebuffed. In the early forties, all such attempts had come under the intense scrutiny of James Stephen and his colleagues committed to Glenelg's policy of "true equality," as well as of abolitionists and Afro-Jamaicans themselves. Consequently, the only measures planters were able to win consent for involved indirect approaches to discouraging the exercise of the franchise by black workers.

In 1840, for example, Metcalfe had recommended a law that purported not to change voter qualifications but merely to "streamline registration." The Colonial Office was properly dubious about this

Sir Charles H. Darling

characterization, since it turned out that the law did in fact disfranchise farm tenants by adding a taxpaying requirement on top of the existing property requirement; it was amended to permit £6 freeholders to vote without paying the tax.[104] A few years later, through his cousin, Earl Grey privately urged the Assembly to adopt a literacy qualification for voting. The measure would have to originate in the Assembly and be disguised as an effort to encourage education: "The political object ought to be kept entirely out of sight & the promot'n of educat'n by making it the means of obtaining the franchise, alone insisted upon."[105] Four years later, in December 1851, an effort was made along the lines Grey had recommended, but fooling no one, the proposal was defeated 13–11, with Afro-Jamaicans supplying eight of the negative votes.[106]

One of the first initiatives of the government inaugurated in the fall of 1854, therefore, was to instruct Edward Jordon to draft a new election law. The supposed inadequacies of the franchise had been one of the reasons Newcastle had adduced against responsible government. The home government and a succession of Jamaican governors all professed a desire to expand the franchise, without explaining how this squared with their deep fear of increased democracy. Shortly after his arrival, for example, Barkly complained about the smallness of the electorate but was also appalled that what he considered "the most ignorant and consequently least competent part of the community" controlled many elections. He was particularly disturbed that voters in St. David had elected to the parish vestry men just released from prison who had been participants in the 1851 election riot.[107]

Like many previous measures, Jordon's purported to simplify voter qualifications by substituting a single test of eligibility: an annual tax of £1. Barkly argued that the present multiple qualifications almost required "a man to keep a lawyer to look after his vote" and that this change would increase the electorate from two thousand to six thousand. But the government's proposal came under sharp attack from Afro-Jamaican assemblymen. John Castello, who had called for lower property and tax requirements just months earlier, charged that far from expanding the pool of eligibles as the government contended, the measure actually would disfranchise many of the peasantry. Robert Russell pointed out that since the £6 freehold voters presently paid only eight to twelve shillings in annual taxes, they would be disqualified. The measure was defeated by a two-vote margin, with nine of twelve brown and black representatives voting against it. Interpreting this defeat to the Colonial Office, however, Governor Barkly ignored the bill's disfranchising effects and blamed the opposition to it on "*soi-disant* liberals" who feared that an expanded electorate would endanger their safe seats.[108]

Ironically, a more successful effort to restrict the franchise was passed five years later with crucial support from Afro-Jamaican assemblymen. The Franchise Act of 1859 imposed a ten-shilling poll tax on all voters, which had the effect of slashing the voter rolls and drastically curtailing black and brown representation in the Assembly. The probable explanation for this act of political suicide is the confusion during the debate over the actual intent and effect of the law. The act became necessary, according to Darling, because of the discontinuance after 1858 of the tax on hereditaments. This tax on fixed capital assets and personal property was assessed on freeholds of £6 and over for which a claim to vote was made. It had come to the government's attention that discontinuance of the tax had the inadvertent effect of disfranchising voters who qualified under the property provision. The original government proposal was simply to waive any further obligation to pay the tax, but this was strenuously opposed by the planter faction in the legislature on very close votes, and it certainly would have been rejected by the planter-dominated Legislative Council. Consequently, a compromise was reached whereby a ten-shilling stamp duty would be required of all voter registrants. The reasoning here was that the minimum due from the previous tax would have been about eleven shillings for most peasant-sized freeholds. Therefore, the governor insisted that despite the appearance of adding an additional obstacle to the exercise of the franchise, the law actually changed nothing in a practical sense and was in fact "almost tantamount to universal suffrage." Having said this much, he then had to concede that the change would be in practice "a great discouragement of the exercise of the Franchise, by the more numerous and humbler Class of Freeholders, and that it was advocated in Assembly for no other reason."

Still, Darling protested, the government did not intend to restrict the franchise but simply felt that this compromise was "only the expedient and most liberal measure that could be gotten." It might even have the latent benefit of discouraging corruption. Previously, electors would sell their votes in exchange for having their taxes paid, "a substantial benefit." But now, since the stamp duty was voluntary, they gained nothing from having it paid.

Darling's explanation is not entirely credible, however. The memoranda accompanying his dispatch reveal sharp disagreement within the Executive Committee on the issue. One faction proposed to lower the stamp duty to about one shilling by estimating the indirect taxes a freeholder contributed to the import duties and crediting this amount (about ten shillings) toward the poll tax. Another faction objected that calculation of such a tax credit was impracticable. The main opposition argument, however, was that the present system was unfair to the planters, because they received only one vote despite paying more taxes. "The owner of three Estates in a parish has only one vote, and the owner of three acres has a vote of equal value: being put on a footing in this respect, they should, it seems to us, be put on the same footing in regard to the amount of stamp on their claims to vote." In contrast with earlier years, the colonial officers had very little to say about all this—except one, who commented dryly that he was not surprised that the people would object to paying a poll tax but saw no cause in that to disallow the act.[109]

There can be little doubt that this law favored planter interests. In addition to the stamp duty, it introduced a new voter qualification for salaried workers. This provision was expected to strengthen the estate owners' influence by adding clerks, bookkeepers, and other estate employees to the voter rolls. After passage of this law, freehold voters declined from almost 60 percent of the registered voters in 1858 to barely 30 percent in 1860. The impact on the £6 freeholders—the peasant voters—was especially devastating. Previously they had made up one-third of the voters, by 1860 they were one-sixth, and by 1863, one-eighth. Taxpayers and salaried employees now dominated the electorate.[110]

The Election Bill split the Town party and its colored membership in twain. John Nunes, Christopher Walters, and James Taylor were active opponents of the bill. Taylor led a public campaign to block it, and William T. March and George W. Gordon chaired mass protest meetings against it. An initial attempt to kill the proposal outright was defeated 25–8; all but one of the bill's opponents were Town party members, six of them colored. Ten Town party members joined Jordon and fourteen Planter party members to support the government, however; seven of this group were colored members. An attempt to strike the offending ten-shilling stamp duty was defeated, 21–11, by a similar racial and partisan alignment.[111]

Some black and brown assemblymen obviously voted against their own interests, as well as those of their constituents. Possibly some of them were ambivalent about the growth of a black electorate. Color and class differences were sharply drawn among Afro-Jamaicans and sometimes found political expression. Jordon and Osborn were, perhaps, acutely sensitive to such intraracial tensions because they had been frequently manifested in Kingston elections. Consequently, many brown assemblymen might have anticipated the imminent flowering of majority rule, with the uneasy realization that they might themselves not be part of that majority. Since three of the seven Afro-Jamaican supporters of disfranchisement were allied with the Planter party, however, it is possible that they identified their real interests as ones of class rather than color.

Of course, the measure probably would have passed despite a united colored opposition, because the critical votes came from the white members of the Town party. These men also owed their election to the black majority, however, and earlier they had resisted blatant efforts at curtailing the black vote. Why not this time? Part of the answer may lie in the confused objectives articulated and the government's insistent disclaimers that it was not a disfranchisement measure. Clearly, Jordon had had something else in mind originally. The government measure, it must be remembered, emerged from a debate among the executive officers that probably replicated much of the public debate later. From his dispatches it is evident that the governor cast his weight behind a "compromise" that favored planter objectives. For whatever reason, philosophical or self-interested, Jordon did not oppose that collective decision. Indeed, it was he who placed the bill before his colleagues, and years hence it would be referred to as "Mr. Jordon's bill." Here then was the new governmental system at its conservative best. Having ensnared the putative leader of the most populous party in the Assembly, the government succeeded in splitting its vote. This opened the way for a planter victory that might not otherwise have been possible, given the formidable Afro-Jamaican presence in the government.

Despite its success in hamstringing what Metcalfe was fond of calling the "Democracy" in the Assembly, the new system was still terribly flawed. Shortly after his arrival in Jamaica, Darling complained of the obvious defects in Jamaica's version of responsible government. Echoing Barkly's observations a few years earlier, Darling noted that Jamaica had a system "of imperfect ministerial responsibility without the concomitant of party organization"; consequently, one could not judge beforehand the success of government measures. Herman Merivale agreed: "It is the old story of constitutional government without party, & without patronage whereby to consolidate a party." In the hands of a circumspect governor, those flaws might have remained hidden. Neither Darling nor his successor, Edward John Eyre—both socially anxious men—was circumspect.[112]

Early in 1860, shortly after the new franchise act was passed, Darling found himself embroiled in a new controversy when he was threatened with censure for improprieties in the disbursement of road construction funds. In his defense, the governor insisted that the Executive Committee share "responsibility" for the policy. Possibly he reasoned that a censure vote against the ministers, which would require their resignation and force new elections, was much less likely to carry in the Assembly than one against himself alone. But the interpretation of the constitution he offered to support this demand was tantamount to an open embrace of the doctrine of responsible government. The Executive Committee—Jordon, George Price, and William Hosack—would not cooperate, however. They argued that under the Jamaican system the governor was solely responsible for policy. Responsible government, they warned, would lead to party governance.

To the Colonial Office Darling "emphatically" protested his innocence of any desire to establish party government. Reiterating the conventional wisdom that under party government political differences would become racial differences, he insisted that his intent had been that the Executive Committee "should be so composed, as adequately to represent from time to time, the sentiments and views which *prevail* in the legislature" and should retain office "only so long as they possess the confidence of the Legislature." The ministers should be responsible to the legislature and not to the governor. The governor should be responsible only to the queen.

The Colonial Office was not impressed by the governor's defense. In fact, they were more than a little perturbed that he had opened up this particular Pandora's box, especially when "the point at issue is so fine that at times the eye can hardly follow it." Henry Taylor thought the elegant argumentation on both sides was "superfluous," all intended to obscure the particular issue of the main roads appropriation by a larger debate over principle. Both sides were wrong, he argued: the governor in denying substantive responsibility for the implementation of policy and patronage, the Executive Committee in avoiding the inevitable fact that they could not serve without the "confidence" of the Assembly majority. The problem in the dispute was that the two sides confounded these two different senses of the term "responsibility," that is, the substantive and the political. But one doubts that either side found Taylor's own tortured explanation very helpful. The Executive Committee was responsible, he argued, "in the sense of a liability to consequences with reference not to merits but to the question whether the Acts done whether right or wrong & with or without the power of preventing them, have left the Committee capable of executing with advantage to the public service the particular functions for which their offices were created."[113]

After studying the papers very carefully, Newcastle could not do much better. He was simply amazed to find so much "ingenuity wasted on both sides," the dispute seeming to turn on "either a quibbling or a misunderstanding of words." But he recognized that the issue was not trivial and that once raised, it could not be ignored. No one ever pretended that the Better Government Act established a perfect system, he protested, "but it was intended to remedy great existing evils and to prevent the advent of still greater, in the shape of Government by Party of mixed Races." This overarching fact had necessitated a compromise of principles. Newcastle was disappointed in Darling, who, in contravention of carefully laid plans, seemed "anxious to tighten the power of the Democracy over himself and loosen that of the Imperial Government." He thought a lecture was in order.[114]

But the governor was isolated in his position. The "Democracy" did not rally to his support, and the "Aristocracy" railed against him. In London, the West India Committee lobbied the Colonial Office in support of the Executive Committee's position. Benjamin Vickers, a member of the Legislative Council, also supported them. Eventually, the dispute resulted in the resignation of the Executive Committee, which promptly formed a government opposition. The Assembly was dissolved, and elections were scheduled for the fall. The election quieted the debate over responsibility, allowing the home government to avoid any public intervention to clarify the issue. What is more important, being the first under the new election law, it also greatly diminished the number of Afro-Jamaican assemblymen. Darling was able to form a new Executive Committee composed—for the first time—wholly of Planter party members and including no Afro-Jamaican leader. No one commented on the fact that in the process he had formed a "party" government, after all. This was not the "party" that had been feared.[115]

The genie was back in the bottle, but there was cause to worry about how long it would stay. Benjamin Vickers divulged his fears to his London factors. The new constitution had brought order and prosperity back to Jamaica, he wrote, and its framers had studiously avoided instituting party government. Now the skeleton of partisan organization so carefully camouflaged by the Better Government Act had been dragged out of the closet. Should party government be inaugurated in place of the present system, he would, at "the earliest opportunity," abandon his estates, "so deeply impressed am I of the consequences which must inevetably [sic] result from 'party' Government in this Colony." Vickers was convinced that party government would bring "strife and bitter hatred . . . between the various creeds and Races." It would be the "apple of discord." Its inevitable result must be "a war of the Races."[116]

Isn't time for the negro to throw off the yoke and seek your liberty. See the heavy tax they put upon your donkey going to market, while the proprietors cows are taxed . . . at 3d. The taxes were only made for the black man and not for the white, there was one law for the black man and one for the white man, and they never received any benefits from the Government.

SAMUEL CLARKE AT KINGSTON RALLY, AUGUST 1865

It is now time for us to help ourselves—skin for skin. The iron bar is now broken in this parish. The white people send a proclamation to the Governor to make war, against which we all must put our shoulders to the wheels and pull together. The Maroons sent their proclamation to us to meet them at Hayfield at once without delay; that they will put us in the way how to act. Every one of you must leave your house. Take your guns; who don't have guns take your cutlasses down at once. Come over to Stony Gut, that we might march over to meet the Maroons at once without delay. Blow your shells, roal [sic] your drums house to house to house. Take out every man, march them to Stony Gut, and [them] that you find in the way takes them up, takes them down with their arms. War is at us, my black skin. War is at hand.

PAUL BOGLE ET AL. TO [THOMAS GRAHAM], 17 OCTOBER 1865

War down a Monk-land,
War down Morant Bay,
War down a Chigger Foot,
The Queen never know!

JAMAICAN SONG, N.D.

8

"A War of the Races"

Eighteen sixty-five was a grim year for Jamaicans. It marked the end of a decade in which the island had been beset by an almost biblical onslaught of plagues: cholera, smallpox, drought and floods. The political reforms of 1854 had not stanched the tide of bankruptcies in the sugar industry. The developing small farm sector was not yet able to fill the economic void. For four long years the American Civil War had curtailed the major source of supplements to homegrown provisions, driving the prices of imported food to unprecedented heights at a time when Jamaican workers were least able to pay. The Union blockade of Southern ports also raised the price of cotton goods and clothing. As the Jamaican economy fell into ever-deepening distress, both estate workers and peasants were hard-pressed in a grim struggle for survival. Not only did the British and local governments seem unsympathetic to their plight but they were pursuing policies designed to take away the one alternative many Afro-Jamaicans had for survival—squatting on vacant Crown lands or abandoned plantations and raising their own food.

Eighteen sixty-five was a violent year in Jamaica. Here, too, it climaxed a decade of steadily escalating social pressures and political tensions, visible to all who cared to see. During the 1850s and early 1860s, Afro-Jamaicans had petitioned, rallied, demonstrated, and sometimes taken direct, violent action to express religious, political, and economic grievances. But the newly reformed political system was even less responsive than in previous years, the political elite more insensitive. The white elite saw in these events not defective policies but a degraded people, not warnings of the coming storm but proofs of racial deficits.

In October 1865 the storm finally broke at Morant Bay in St. Thomas-in-the-East. There peasant occupiers of abandoned properties, caught in a protracted struggle to eke out a life in the interstices among the estates, raised an aborted rebellion. Yet even in failure they dramatized the major economic, political, and social issues of the postemancipation era. Laying bare the contradictions of British policy and ideology, their revolt summed up the whole unfortunate history of Jamaican emancipation. In its aftermath, problems of labor and politics, ideas about freedom and race, were unraveled and rewoven into new patterns, patterns that would have consequences for colonial peoples beyond Jamaica's borders.

"The Coming Storm"

The Baptist missionaries, the whites in closest contact with and having greatest sympathy for black workers, were among the first to see the gathering storm and to sound alarms. In the summer of 1859 a Baptist congregation in St. James had complained of high taxes, wasteful state expenditures on the established church and immigration, and the racially biased new election law. Moreover, there was actual hunger and nakedness, dilapidated housing and deteriorating morals. But their appeals to the home government had to be routed through Governor Darling, who dismissed them as inaccurate and unrepresentative.[1] Darling's refusal to acknowledge worsening Jamaican conditions contradicted the concurrent reports from his own stipendiary magistrates, who confirmed many of the Baptists' claims: provisions were scarce and expensive, wages were low. The next year these scarcities were exacerbated by a "disastrous drought" followed by heavy rains, a calamity often to be repeated over the next five years.[2]

The American Civil War compounded and intensified these problems by reducing the main alternative source for supplies, setting off an unprecedented inflationary spiral. By 1865 not only had the cost of cotton trebled but osnaburgh, the hempen substitute that had clothed workers since slavery, had more than doubled in price. The price of fish doubled. Cornmeal went up as much as 75 percent. Flour was up 83 percent. Moreover, floods in 1864, followed by droughts in 1865, ruined provision crops that might have alleviated the dearth. Only the northwestern side of the island reported normal prices for ground provisions. According to one recent calculation, the overall cost of living on the island rose 60 percent between 1859–61 and 1865.[3]

The causes of these sharp pangs of distress were less the temporary dislocations caused by war or the vicissitudes of weather, however, than the basic flaws in the Jamaican economy and in British colonial policy. For officials in Spanish Town and Whitehall, sugar *was* the Jamaican economy. Yet, the Jamaican sugar industry had not revived, despite the hopes aroused by governmental reform and the encumbered estates acts of the previous decade that had been intended to facilitate the sale of abandoned properties. Both were intended to make the island safe for capital investment, the first by rationalizing the public debt and taxes, the second by cutting through the web of private debt that made plantations unsalable.

Planters insisted, nonetheless, that there was plenty of work on their estates and that workers could earn high wages if they chose to work full-time. Their laborers insisted that there was not enough work. In any event, it seems unlikely that very many workers could have survived solely on the wages actually paid. Plantation payroll ledgers show payments to the average field hand totaling no more than 4s. to 6s. during most weeks, and even these wages were extremely seasonal. For example, the maximum earned by a field hand on St. Jago Estate in Clarendon during the ten-week crop time was 8s. 9d.; for ten weeks out of crop it was 7s. 1.5d. But the *average* pay for 138 workers on that estate was just 5s. a week in crop; 117 of these managed just 3s. 4.5d. out of crop. At best, then, a field hand could expect to be employed just twenty weeks, during which he or she would earn less than £8 for the year. But clearly most field workers—for whatever reason—earned just half that amount.[4]

Those fortunate enough to get work still faced the problem of getting paid. "Sometimes we labour for nothing," declared an African worker from Clarendon, "for when Friday comes, which is our pay day, there will sure be some fault or the other found with the work, and then our pay is stopped, and we are obliged to go starving until the next Friday." In fact this practice of "stopping" wages, that is, making deductions for alleged infractions or inadequacies in the work, was a rankling and widespread grievance. If any of these deductions were not reflected in the estates' ledgers, the pay actually received would be less than the records appeared to show.[5]

It is difficult to credit the planters' contention that such low wages were simply a matter of workers' being too lazy to work full-time. The planters' definition of "continuous labor" had not changed much over the years. Indeed, Peter Espeut, a brown assemblyman and owner of two estates employing up to 250 workers, responded to a parliamentary enquiry on the subject in 1866 much as Thomas Price had twenty years earlier. Continuous labor, he explained, was "persons that will work on estates whenever their services are required, but it so happens they do not do it. They have their own patches to cultivate, and you very often find that they are doing that when you require them." "By continuous labour," he was pressed for clarification, "do you mean that you hire men when you want them and discharge them when you do not?" "Certainly," Espeut replied.[6]

By the 1860s the decline of Jamaica's sugar industry reinforced Afro-Jamaicans' longstanding resistance to the complete proletarianization Espeut and his fellow planters desired, but at the same time economic distress intensified their need for some estate work to make ends meet. Even in good times, the so-called peasantry had gone to the estates for occasional work to supplement the earnings from their smallholdings. In bad times, when their provision crops had failed from droughts, flooding, or other causes, they had relied even more heavily on estate labor to survive. But now there were many fewer estates producing much less sugar; and since the lucky survivors had founded their prosperity on indentured labor, the few native workers they hired would necessarily be *under*employed. Consequently, from all over the island came reports of people wandering for miles in search of work, from Falmouth and lower Trelawny, from Bethel Town and Carey, from Portland. Burlington was the only estate in Portland, so people walked thirty-five miles to Amity Hall in St. Thomas-in-the-East for a single day's work. By the hundreds they came into Clarksonville and Mount Zion, in upper Clarendon and St. Ann, looking for work. So many Manchester peasants poured into Thompson Town in Clarendon that resident laborers complained that they were depressing wages. The "labor shortage" planters had long complained of was no more.[7]

The fact that the labor supply situation more nearly favored the planters now was reflected in the diminished bargaining power and independence of the minority of native workers who still lived on estates. "No labourer likes to live on the estates," one observer declared, "nor will he do so unless necessity constrains it, for fear of being turned off when any dispute arises, and the whole of his ground provisions be forfeited."[8] This statement echoes similar observations in the early 1840s, during the exodus from the estates; but now the depressed economy made it more difficult for those renting house and grounds from the estates not to hire on as occasional laborers for their landlords. And since landlords generally would not allow them to grow export crops on their rented grounds, their alternatives to estate labor were further reduced.

Apparently, it was common practice for estates to move these plantation villages frequently, which limited the varieties of provision crops that resident workers might raise for either export or subsistence. The planters' purpose, according to one minister, was "to prevent the labourers from profiting by the bread-fruits, coco-nuts and other trees of slow growth which they plant around their dwellings."[9] Thus, he observed, over the past decade every estate village in his district had been moved. Consequently, resident estate workers were being pushed toward producing solely for subsistence and squeezed out of the cash economy altogether; in other words, they were becoming a more thoroughly dependent proletariat.

For most Afro-Jamaicans, land seemed the obvious solution to their problems. Those who had none wanted a plot independent of the estate's control. Those who already had land wanted more. Consequently, by the 1860s, land disputes had become common throughout the island, usually erupting where settlers had taken possession of abandoned estates that subsequent purchasers or lessees tried to reclaim. The people had developed the idea, one official complained, that they had rights to the land. Such convictions were rooted deep in the moral economy of Afro-Jamaican peasants. They were convictions they were willing to fight for, sometimes in violent and angry confrontations.

In the summer of 1859, for example, settlers on Florence Hall, an estate in Westmoreland, were charged with trespass, and police were sent out to eject them. When the settlers resisted, they were arrested and confined to the jail in Falmouth. Before they could be tried, however, a crowd of several hundred supporters broke them out of jail. In the ensuing melee, ten or twelve other prisoners were rescued from police custody as well, and the station house was stoned. During this confrontation police fired into the crowd, killing two women instantly and wounding four or five others. Enraged, the crowd, led by Florence Hall settlers Emily Jackson and Samuel Sutherland, set fire to the police station and refused to allow anyone to help extinguish it. Instead, the mob marched around the burning building, singing: "In two hours time we will have down the station and if that won't do we will have down the Court House too." One of the rioters threatened to bring down the whole Maroon garrison "to make the buckra fly." Another declared that "it is now our time."[10]

Although this incident was recorded officially as a "riot," others insisted that there was "an organized conspiracy" and that Falmouth was "in a state of rebellion."[11] Whatever the credibility of such claims, they reflect a general uneasiness about the island's stability even during the earliest phases of its economic distress. That disquiet must have been increased by the larger black public's reaction to the violence. Almost one hundred people were indicted for the Falmouth riot, but it proved almost impossible to secure a conviction, apparently because of the strong community sentiment favoring the settlers' rights. So pervasive was that support that Governor Darling considered seeking legislation to have them tried by a special tribunal.[12]

The level of violence at Falmouth was exceptional, but the situation at Florence Hall was not. All over the island, once-abandoned sugar properties had fallen into the hands of workers. Sometimes these so-called squatters' claims were complicated, such as those at Hartlands, a pen in St. Catherine that had belonged to assemblyman Daniel Hart. In the early 1840s Hart had subdivided his property into five hundred to six hundred lots. After 1844 a number of other small settlers also established claims there, apparently without Hart's permission. Some professed that they had purchased their tracts; others said they had received them as gifts. Unfortunately, the records of all such transactions had been lost in a great Kingston fire in the fall of 1843. Hart's heirs later disputed all these claims, insisting that the settlers were actually squatters. Settled on the property now were an estimated eight hundred people, described by an apprehensive policeman as "a very rough and ignorant class of men," armed and determined to resist forcibly any attempt at eviction. In 1865 the situation remained a standoff.[13]

A similar predicament developed in St. Thomas-in-the-East, not far from Morant Bay. Augustus Hire, attorney for Amity Hall, complained that people had seized a run of land called Rowland's Field, located on Hector's River, an estate belonging to English investors, for whom he was agent. But apparently some of these people had paid quitrents on their land and thus considered themselves in rightful possession. All of them refused to pay rent to Hire. During the summer of 1865, when Hire attempted to have the land surveyed, his party was surrounded by "100 able-bodied negroes, amongst whom were a few women, all armed either with cutlasses, knives, or sticks." The crowd seized the surveyor's chain and threatened him bodily harm if he continued. When Hire asked William Doyley, one of the ringleaders, by what rights he claimed the land, he replied: "What God Almighty make land for? You have plenty; we have none." Others in the crowd declared: "If you want war, you shall have it."[14]

Cases such as these illustrate both the explosive tensions involved in the land issue and the difficulties in securing undisputed titles when transferring property through private sales. Even in the absence of complex searches of titles and liens, such purchases could be expensive, requiring charges for stamp duty, tithes, surveying, and recording. For these reasons, possibly, many Jamaicans turned their attention increasingly to the lands belonging to the Crown. The Crown controlled two types of property: (1) those lands forfeited to the government for failure to pay quitrents; and (2) the unsettled lands in the island's interior, the so-called backlands. In 1866 Richard Hill estimated that there were 815,303 acres in the first category, patented land on which quitrent had remained unpaid for twenty years. These acres alone would have made a significant dent in the land hunger of Jamaican workers, leaving aside the unpatented "backlands" of the interior, which were largely waste.[15]

The idea that abandoned estates had reverted back to the queen was evident in many of the confrontations described above and was a basic assumption of many of the petitions for relief. Afro-Jamaican petitioners are often accused of being pathetically naive in their reliance on Queen Victoria's justice. But what these petitions also suggest is a direct connection between popular notions of Crown land, public land, and the people's land. The peasants grounded their right to the land in the logically consistent belief that abandoned properties should revert to the queen, thereby returning it to the public domain. They were the public.[16]

This was not an argument the government was prepared to countenance, but it was not so far-fetched as it is often portrayed. No one in authority, however, in either Britain or Jamaica was prepared to concede either the justice or the wisdom of rebuilding the colony's economic fortune on the basis of peasant proprietorship and a more diversified agriculture. As far as the colonial authorities were concerned, Jamaica's future still lay with the large sugar estates, the survival of which depended on developing a disciplined wage labor force. This classically capitalist ideology had particularly pernicious effects when fused with the evolving racial ideology of the mid-Victorian era. Bourgeois and racist convictions acted in tandem to blind many of the British and Jamaican political elites to policy alternatives. Consequently, those most charged with the responsibility and authority to redress the island's decline were fundamentally hostile to Afro-Jamaican aspirations.

Their blindness cannot be excused on the grounds that clear policy alternatives were not laid before them. Not only were there petitions and protests from Afro-Jamaican workers and peasants but Jamaica's Baptist missionaries were persistent in their efforts to secure relief from the home government. Having been rebuffed by Governor Darling in 1859, they wrote their English colleagues, providing grim descriptions of Jamaican depression and its social consequences. One recipient of this correspondence in 1864 was Dr. Edward B. Underhill, an English Baptist minister who had visited Jamaica during a tour of the West Indies in 1859 and 1860 and published a book about it in 1862. Since his family had rendered Colonial Secretary Edward Cardwell some "valued assistance" in a recent general election, Underhill communicated with him directly, and his report received special attention.[17]

Underhill reiterated the grim portrait of Jamaican conditions that he had received from his colleagues. He went further than merely pleading for relief, however; he forcefully linked the evident social deterioration, not to impersonal economic forces, but to failed and misguided policies of the Jamaican and home governments. Foreshadowing colonial policy of the late nineteenth century, Underhill's remedy combined commitment to capitalist development and peasant proprietorship. Sugar estates now employed only a minority of the island's workforce, he wrote, yet they continued to monopolize the government's attention, while nothing was done to assist the majority of workers, the small-scale producers, whose enterprise might have absorbed some of the redundant estate labor. Indeed there was much to hinder them, including heavy, regressive tax levies and a land policy designed to keep large tracts of unsettled land out of the hands of those who might make it productive. Jamaica was not attractive to capital under present conditions, Underhill warned, and the government had not taken any action, such as developing the island's infrastructure, to make it so. The present situation, he concluded, required government assistance, lower taxes, and technical aid to encourage diversified development.[18]

The Colonial Office forwarded Underhill's letter to the new Jamaican governor, Edward John Eyre, for a reply. His personal temperament, political circumstances, economic convictions, and virulent racism made a constructive response from Eyre unlikely. The son of a Yorkshire vicar, Eyre had emigrated when he was just seventeen years old to Australia, where he had prospered as a sheep farmer. There—ironically, in light of the infamy he would earn in Jamaica later—he also gained a reputation as a great explorer and protector of the aborigine population. From 1846 to 1853 he served as lieutenant governor of New Zealand, followed by a succession of similar appointments in secondary roles in St. Vincent and the Leeward Islands, none of which satisfied his vaunting ambition or assuaged his feelings of social inferiority. He had come to Jamaica in March 1862 to fill in temporarily for Governor Darling, who was on a leave of absence. Darling's leave was unexpectedly prolonged, however, creating awkward political and financial problems for Eyre. He had to make sensitive political appointments but was anxious not to embarrass Darling, whose return was expected momentarily. He had to entertain in a manner befitting a chief executive, but on a lieutenant governor's salary, which was half as much. When Darling accepted the governorship of Victoria, Eyre expected promotion, but the Colonial Office delayed, thereby increasing his anxiety and sensitivity to perceived slights in the rough-and-tumble world of Jamaican politics. Indeed, by the time Darling made his decision not to return to Jamaica, Eyre had stirred up a political hornet's nest, having been charged with misappropriation of road funds and some ill-advised patronage decisions, which prompted letters to the Colonial Office demanding his removal. His good friend Frederic Rogers, the permanent undersecretary, prevailed on the incoming colonial secretary, Edward Cardwell, to promote Eyre to the governorship despite his unpopularity on the island. When Underhill's letter arrived on his desk, therefore, Eyre's promotion had been confirmed just eleven months earlier, under circumstances that did not increase his popularity or authority.[19]

The controversial circumstances surrounding his appointment and tenure possibly contributed to Eyre's determination to see no distress on the island. But it is also clear that despite his reputation for racial liberalism, Eyre's racist and bourgeois convictions profoundly shaped his response to the growing crisis. As was the case with many in Jamaica's officialdom, and indeed with many in the Colonial Office

Governor Edward John Eyre

itself, that ideological conjuncture made for a willful ignorance of Jamaican conditions. In fact, in a tour of the eastern parishes in the summer of 1864 Eyre had received an address from three hundred peasants in St. David spelling out many of the problems Underhill would describe six months later. There was not enough "continuous and remunerating labour," and the costs of food and clothing were "intolerable." They found it very difficult "to obtain land to cultivate extensively," and the government had provided them little protection or assistance. Cattle overran their provision fields, because the owners were not obliged to maintain fences. The roads serving their properties were in "the most deplorable condition—some resemble goat tracks, and not ways for human beings." On top of all this, their crops were stolen by people "too lazy to work for themselves."

Eyre's reply to their distress was laced with classic mid-Victorian platitudes and irrelevancies. The solutions to their problems were moral reformation, piety, and propriety. They must improve in "social habits and in domestic comfort, as well as in material prosperity." They required larger houses so that they could "distribute their families in separate sleeping rooms at night." They must attend more "to their ordinary daily dress, rather than sacrifice that to grand displays on Sundays." The remedy for the larceny of their crops depended upon their own moral choices: they must "improve in civilization;" they must educate their children in religion, industry, and respectability, "both by example and precept."[20]

His subsequent response to Underhill's letter continued in much the same vein, elaborating an official discourse of denial and distortion. Although he passed it along to the parish custodes for investigation, he did not wait to receive their reports before dismissing Underhill's claims as inaccurate and "exaggerated." The distress was not general, and its causes were not those Underhill asserted. Poverty did not beget demoralization, the governor insisted; rather, the low moral character of blacks caused poverty. In support of this proposition Eyre enclosed a letter from William Hosack, a member of his Executive Committee, stating that such poverty as existed resulted from "sheer idleness, and a growing dislike to steady industry, and a consequent preference to a dishonest mode of living, with the risks of occasional imprisonment, to one of honest labour, with the remote certainty of independence."[21]

That Hosack spoke for a large number of the Jamaican political elite was confirmed when the custodes finally did reply to Underhill's charges. Like Eyre, they first denied that a problem existed and then blamed the victims for whatever distress might be found. If Jamaicans were naked, it was because of the warm climate: they did not need much clothing. If they wore rags, it was because they chose to: they insisted on saving their "finery" for Sunday. If they were unemployed, it was because they refused to work.[22]

The greatest dangers to social order, Eyre informed his superiors, lay in the moral deficiencies of the blacks, not in their economic circumstances. Jamaican peasants were materially prosperous but in their social habits and relations "little better than absolute savages." The solution he recommended for the larceny problem, therefore, was a good whipping.[23] Indeed, the real problem with Jamaica, the governor advised, was that there were not enough white people. Whites were leaving the island and not being replaced "by any fresh influx of European energy, intelligence, experience, enlightened views and moral principles, qualities which are so essential as examples to stimulate and influence races, only just emerging from and without such influences likely to fall rapidly back into a state of barbarism."[24] Such was the sober analysis of the colony's distress that the Colonial Office received from Jamaica's political elite.

There were other political voices, prophetic voices, raised to challenge Eyre's and the custodes' view of Jamaican conditions. During legislative debates in February 1861, Andrew H. Lewis, a Jewish assemblyman, chastised his colleagues about imposing high taxation on the poor: "They were taxed on their bread, their salt, their lucifers, their clothes, and everything else they used." Referring to the great religious revivals of 1860–61, which had been deplored as disruptive of labor and the peace, Lewis warned that government policies raised the danger "of creating not revivals, but something worse, which would be regretted." Later that same year, George Henderson, a white Town party member, warned that the needs of the black majority could not be safely ignored any longer and that they must be given a greater voice in government. "I maintain, that those who look forward and see the coming storm, and do not provide against it, by wisely legislating for the people of this country are not performing their duty to the people." Four years later assemblyman George William Gordon wrote a friend: "I do not think we were ever in more dismal times than at present in Jamaica. The Governor succours wrong and oppression to the fullest extent in every quarter."[25]

Despite these exceptions, however, Afro-Jamaicans confronted a government that was, at all levels, mostly unsympathetic and unhelpful. Eyre was the appointee of a Colonial Office that itself had grown increasingly insensitive to and impatient with Jamaica's nonwhite majority. The custodes were the collective product of a reformed political system that had reduced Afro-Jamaican representation in the Assembly and deprived the Assembly majority of political responsibility for the fate of their constituents. And, of course, this crisis developed at a time when the political power of the black majority had been thwarted by a high poll tax, which reduced the number of registered voters to 1,903, just under 2 percent of the adult male population. Although more than three-quarters of these had actually turned out in the last election, in 1863, over a quarter of that vote was cast in Kingston alone.[26]

Consequently, Afro-Jamaican representation in the Assembly declined after 1860, and the Executive Committee and the Legislative Council continued to be effective institutional obstacles to any legislation planters opposed. Like his predecessors, Eyre continued to resist official recognition of parties, meaning in practice that the Executive Committee would never be constituted solely of Town party representatives. Clearly, this prohibition did not apply to the Planter party, because in 1861 Darling had appointed as his Executive Committee, Raynes W. Smith, Hugh Whitelocke, and Baron von Ketelhodt—all planters. Following the 1863 elections, an augmented and revived Town party had forced their resignations, but despite the obvious weakness of Planters in the Assembly, Eyre went to great lengths to ensure that the new committee was politically mixed.[27] His first ministry comprised George L. Phillips, a St. James merchant from the Planter party; Henry Westmorland, a substantial planter and attorney politically allied with the Town party at the time; and Edward Jordon, praised by Henry Taylor for being "as little like a man of colour as the Emperor of the French is like a Frenchman." During the following year, George Price, co-owner of Worthy Park, replaced Phillips, and William Hosack replaced Jordon, who was appointed governor's secretary. Jamaican workers and peasants could not expect to receive much assistance from this crew, and they didn't.[28]

As the depression intensified, the government took no positive steps to assist them, and many of its policies made their very survival more difficult. The burden of taxation had begun shifting from planters to smallholders in the early 1840s, when duties on imports became the revenue of choice. By the 1860s the disparity between the tax burden on property and that on people yawned wide. Between 1840 and 1865 the import tax on herrings rose 166 percent; on salt fish, 366 percent; on mackerel, 433 percent. All of these were main staples of the working classes. The tax on imported clothing rose 1,150 percent. Meanwhile, small farmers saw the taxes on their donkeys and horses jump 1,580 percent and 1,220 percent, respectively. Carts not used for plantation purposes now paid 18 shillings in annual taxes; they had paid none in 1840.[29]

On the other hand, plantation supplies that had paid 20s. per £100 value in 1840 were coming in duty-free by 1865. The tax rate on imported lumber had been reduced by 52 percent. Duties on plantation stock, horses, and mules were reduced by 40 percent. There were differential duties on imported manufactures versus the raw materials from which they were made: for example, a copper pan for an estate paid a duty of 4 percent of its value, while the copper metal, which might be used by local craftsmen to make a pan, paid 12.5 percent. Little wonder, then, that early in the fall of 1865, stump orators in Falmouth were urging people to resist paying their taxes—by force if necessary.[30]

All serious discussion of government assistance for growth and development focused on measures to assist the estates. This fact was graphically illustrated by the expenditures for road construction. Under the new Main Roads Law, ostensibly a reform to rebuild the island's infrastructure, money went to repair roads serving the great houses and estates but not the parochial roads serving the peasantry. A Baptist minister asserted that "when there is no sugar estate near the roads are almost given up, so that carts can scarcely pass, and are often broken. The bridges are in such a bad state that horses and saddles have been lost by falling through."[31]

Often, those main roads that did serve the peasant farmers were toll roads. These were not only very expensive and inconvenient but a constant irritant, driving home the second-class status of the settlers. The tollgates were especially objectionable to the people of Westmoreland, where they controlled peasants' access to markets and in some cases even estate workers' routes to their jobs. On three successive nights in February 1859, five hundred to six hundred small settlers, frustrated by the official indifference to their complaints, tore down the tollgates and tollhouses.[32]

When the interests of the smallholders and those of the estates came into direct conflict, the government, predictably, sided with the latter. For example, both Eyre and Darling expressed great sympathy for the small settlers' complaints about praedial larceny, perhaps because such charges accorded so well with their own views about the degraded morals and laziness of the black population. But smallholders were also victimized by the estates and pens, whose cattle often trampled their provision crops. This was, as Richard Hill pointed out, "an unceasing subject of complaint," and it exacerbated the tensions between planters and settlers. Here, the government not only failed to protect them, it reneged on the protection formerly accorded by law. In 1844 a law was passed that allowed the aggrieved party, usually a small provision grower, the option of impounding the offending animal or determining damages immediately through the mediation of three freeholders. The defendant, usually a penkeeper or sugar planter, could either pay the claim, dispute the claim and place the money in escrow with a magistrate pending a trial, or not pay and allow the animal to be impounded. In 1858 that legislation was repealed and superseded by a new law that placed the burden on the complainant to sue in Petty Debt Court for damages amounting to less than forty shillings and in Superior Court for larger amounts. This reversion to the older system of litigation meant delay and expense that often could not be recouped by the suit. In practice, therefore, it all but eliminated effective legal remedies for small freeholders and renters.[33]

Both British and Jamaican authorities were blind to the economic potential of peasant agriculture. This was not just a failure of imagination: there was a willful refusal to consider alternatives to the failing sugar industry. One of the petitions produced out of the mid-sixties crisis was arguably a model for more enlightened and forward-looking policies that the government might have pursued. In April 1865 the smallholders of St. Ann sent a memorial to the queen detailing grievances that would become all too familiar from the "Underhill meetings" later that spring and summer and asking that the government secure for them "a quantity of land." They would "put our hands and heart to work, and cultivate coffee, corn, canes, cotton and tobacco, and other produce. We will form a company for that purpose, if our Gracious Lady Victoria our Queen will also appoint an agent to receive such produce as we may cultivate, and give us means of subsistence while at work." They were *not* asking for free land; they proposed to pay for it in installments. They were, they assured her, "willing to work so that we may be comfortable." All they required was "land room."

Although government policies in the late nineteenth century would embrace proposals very similar to those in the St. Ann petition, the queen's ministers were not prepared to accept so seemingly radical a program in 1865. Henry Taylor, the most veteran of the colonial officers, drafted the queen's response, which took the form of a lecture in classical political economy.[34]

The petitioners were advised

> that the prosperity of the Labouring Classes, as well as of all other Classes, depends, in Jamaica, and in other Countries, upon their working for Wages, not uncertainly, or capriciously, but steadily and continuously, at the times when their labour is wanted, and for so long as it is wanted; and if they would use this industry, and thereby render the Plantations productive, they would enable the Planters to

pay them higher Wages for the same hours of work than are received by the best Field Labourers in this country; and as the cost of the necessaries of life is much less in Jamaica than it is here, they would be enabled, by adding prudence to industry, to lay by an ample provision for seasons of drought and dearth; and they may be assured, that it is from their own industry and prudence, in availing themselves of the means of prospering that are before them, and not from any such schemes as have been suggested to them, that they must look for an improvement in their condition; and that her Majesty will regard with interest and satisfaction their advancement through their own merits and efforts.

Delighted, Eyre ordered fifty thousand copies of the dispatch, referred to as "the Queen's Advice," distributed and posted in public places and read aloud in churches and other public meetings. The dispatch represented a victory for Eyre's policies and was consistent with his interpretation of the causes of Jamaican distress: the blacks were lazy.

"The Queen's Advice" also represented the culmination and conjuncture of several strains of British thought and policy; in particular, it marked the completion of a radical change in the basic racial assumptions underpinning that policy over the past two decades. In truth, Henry Taylor could have drafted this dispatch with scarcely a reference to the arguments of the petitioners. Which, in fact, he seems to have done. He assumed that they did not want to work, when in fact their whole object was to secure the means of production, land. He assumed that they wanted something for nothing, when their clearly stated intent was to earn their own way. But even more distressing, the dispatch displayed inexcusable ignorance of Jamaican conditions. It held out wage labor as a solution, when the main wage employers, the sugar estates, could not possibly absorb the labor force. It argued that the cost of living was low, a direct contradiction of readily available evidence in Colonial Office files. Obviously, Taylor and his colleagues now accepted fully the planters' view of the island's problems. But why? Why now? Why would they accept in 1865 arguments that they had rejected thirty years earlier?

The Road to Morant Bay: British Racial Ideology and Jamaican Policy

By 1865, Whitehall was deaf to any suggestion that peasant proprietorship might offer a road to economic recovery in Jamaica. That deafness reflected not only its commitment to capitalist agriculture in Jamaica but also its inability to even conceive of an alternative economy based on black initiative and enterprise. Indeed, *black* was no longer a credible adjective to modify *initiative* or *enterprise*. A powerful tradition had taken hold in which the ex-slaves were characterized as endowed with relatively simple material aspirations easily satisfied in a tropical environment.

Of course, this idea had long been an ingrained feature of white Jamaican folklore and conventional wisdom. Like their brethren elsewhere, West Indian slave keepers had insisted from the start that blacks would not work except by compulsion. They had ridiculed the liberal notions of incentives, "expanding wants," and such. And even though a few enlightened planters accepted aspects of the liberal dogma, most repeated the standard racist litany. The following excerpt from a letter written in the early 1840s by a Jamaican bookkeeper to his brother in England illustrates the genre and its pervasiveness among those connected with planter interests.

> I regret to say that this Country is no better and I fear there is no Immediate prospects of its being so, for the Negroes are Naturally a lazy Set of Individuals & there wants are but few. For instance they require no Hose or Stockings & in this warm Climate very little other Clothing and they have no Idea of luxuries for as they can satisfy there appetits with herbs & excellent Roots (Mixed with a little Herring Salt) which grow spontaneously with little or no Culture in this Country. So that they are Satisfied & will lay down under there Plantain trees & Sleep Soonder than work for fair wages.[35]

At the time of emancipation, ideas such as this had been rejected by informed British opinion. A critical assumption of the economic liberals of the 1830s—the men who had fashioned emancipation policy—was that blacks were endowed with the same material appetites as whites and with appropriate coaxing would respond to that innate desire for material gain that all men shared. Evidence during the first years following emancipation that some blacks might not choose to work on the estates could be accommodated to this guiding assumption about human character. British policymakers and many of the Jamaican officials responsible for implementing those policies seemed willing to concede that the peasants' provision trade was a vibrant and a sensible economic response to Jamaican conditions. For example, Henry Taylor and Lord Stanley had conceded the logic of this response and saw it as compatible, under certain conditions, with the survival of the estates. James Stephen had gone so far as to predict that peasants would replace the planters.[36] Officials could readily see that blacks refused to work on the estates because there were often more appealing, less oppressive alternatives. They were, however, still committed to estate agriculture as the mainstay of the Jamaican economy and avenue to civilization and culture for blacks.

Throughout the 1840s—in parliamentary hearings and debates, in memorials to the queen, in the popular press—planters had succeeded in drumming their particular construction of West Indian reality into British consciousness with little effective rebuttal. Meanwhile, the survival of Jamaica's sugar economy became more problematic and more expensive for the home government. More and more, black workers, or rather nonworkers, became the villains of the piece. By mid-century, the logic ran as follows: Blacks refuse to work on the sugar estates as needed and at the wages the planters feel they can afford to pay. Ergo, blacks will not work on the sugar estates. Ergo, blacks will not work. By this logical legerdemain, what freed people valued as the attainment of some measure of autonomy—that is, market gardening—came to be labeled simply "laziness." Working when, where, and as they chose became "They will not work." The defect was racial. Blacks somehow were missing that drive for material self-improvement innate in Europeans. Incapable of self-direction and inner restraint, they must be subjected to external controllers. Having failed to master themselves, they must have masters.

These notions were popularized most effectively by Thomas Carlyle's "Discourses on the Nigger Question," first published in *Fraser's Magazine* in December 1849 and reissued as a pamphlet four years later. As in the standard planter's complaint, Carlyle portrayed West Indian blacks as "sitting yonder with their beautiful muzzles up to the ears in pumpkins, imbibing sweet pulps and juices; grinders and incisor teeth ready for ever new work, and the pumpkins cheap as grass in those rich climates; while the sugar-crops rot round them uncut, because labour cannot be hired, or so cheap are the pumpkins." Meanwhile at home British taxpayers struggled to pay off the slave compensation grants and West Indian loans. Carlyle went on to repeat and even improve upon the planter myth that blacks could satisfy their scant wants by working less than a full day, adding to this a dig at liberal political economy. "Supply and demand, which, science says, should be brought to bear on him, have an uphill task of it with such a man. Strong sun supplies itself gratis, rich soil in those unpeopled or half-peopled regions almost gratis; there are *his* 'supply'; and half-an-hour a-day, directed upon these, will produce pumpkin, which is his 'demand.'"[37]

Carlyle's solution to the problem warmed the hearts of West Indian planters. The way to deal with this situation was to declare that no one refusing to work on the estates had any right "to eat pumpkin, or to any fraction of land that will grow pumpkin, however plentiful such land may be"; they had only the "indisputable and perpetual *right* to be compelled, by the real proprietors of said land, to do competent work for his living. This is the everlasting duty of all men, black or white, who are born into this world."[38] Blacks should be induced to work the estates as the coachman "induces" his horses. The alternative was the encroaching jungle: the idle "Black gentlemen" with "rum-bottle in his hand, no breeches on his body, pumpkin at discretion, and the fruitfulest region of the earth going back to jungle round him."

But the real objects of Carlyle's venom were "Exeter Hall Philanthropists" and proponents of "the Dismal Science." His attack on black liberty was part of a satiric attack on liberalism generally and a rejection of capitalist social relations, "the cash nexus."[39] He wrote "Discourses" after his second trip to Ireland, where he viewed firsthand the devastation wrought, he asserted, by British policy and Irish "laziness." The application of "Dismal Science" policies to the West Indies would produce "a Black Ireland."

His Irish tour merely reinforced and made more urgent Carlyle's earlier conclusions about the need for corporate societies under strongmen rulers. Liberty in modern times meant "to work sore and yet gain nothing; to be heart-worn, weary, yet isolated, unrelated, girt in with a cold universal Laissez-faire." Such sentiments won him the favorable attention of assorted contemporary radicals, including Friedrich Engels and the Young Ireland rebels, but Carlyle's answer for modern alienation and malaise was thoroughly reactionary.[40] The only "true Liberty" would come through compulsion, to be "forced to find out the right path, and to walk thereon. To learn, or to be taught, what work he actually was able for; and then, by permission, persuasion, and even compulsion, to set about doing the same! . . . Liberty requires new definitions."[41]

For England, the new liberty meant the destruction of feudalism, yet saving its essence, its mystery, its divinely ordained authority and social order. For the Irish, the new definition of liberty meant that "they will have to learn that man does need government, and that an able-bodied starving beggar is and remains (whatever Exeter Hall may say to it) a SLAVE destitute of a MASTER." For blacks, Carlyle pondered how one might "abolish the abuses of slavery, and save the precious thing in it." "You are not 'slaves' now; nor do I wish, if it can be avoided, to see you slaves again; but decidedly you have to be servants to those that are born *wiser* than you, that are born lords of you; servants to the Whites, if they *are* (as what mortal can doubt they are?) born wiser than you."[42]

"Blackness" was not simply a matter of biological endowment, however, but both consequence and manifestation of culture and labor. Indeed, the whiteness of the Irish was incidental and even something of an inconvenience, because "having a white skin and European features, [they] cannot be prevented from circulating among us at discretion, and to all manner of lengths and breadths." What they had in common with Quashee was the sin of savagery, "noisy, turbulent, irreclaimable savagery." It was "not the colour of the skin that determines the savagery of a man." It was willful ignorance and rebellion against "the laws of Nature," the chief of which was that men must work and be governed. Work rescued civilization from savagery; government rescued "the Cosmos" from "Chaos." Of course, none of this should be taken to mean that Carlyle's views were racially neutral. His public and private correspondence show consistent denigration of blacks, whereas some of his best friends were Irish.[43] Blacks were his emblem of degradation, of the level to which whites could sink.

Carlyle's racist diatribe should not be taken as necessarily representative of informed British opinion. Indeed, his essay drew immediate rebuttals, one of them from his former friend John Stuart Mill in the very next issue of *Fraser's*.[44] Mill, parodying Carlyle, condemned his essay as "a true work of the devil," because it bestowed a measure of legitimacy on racist ideas and gave aid and comfort to American slaveholders. Here was the slaveholders' propaganda in the mouth of one of Britain's most prominent men of letters. Other of Carlyle's peers had more affection for him as an intellectual gadfly and social satirist than as a serious thinker. In an anonymous estimate of Carlyle's work, James Fitzjames Stephen called it "unjust and injurious" and full of "the most wonderful errors." Though a "man of genius," he was the "most untrustworthy moralist and politician, of our age and nation. . . . The only way in which it is possible to criticise Mr. Carlyle's political writings favorably is by looking on them as addressed to an imaginary audience." Henry Taylor judged him to be a genuine man with unreal, extravagant opinions. He was an "iconoclast," delighting in "knocking over any pageantry of another man's setting up."[45]

But Taylor's description of Carlyle as a kind of intellectual court jester is suggestive. By articulating such extreme racist views, Carlyle opened the way for ostensibly more "moderate and judicious" opinion. It is conceivable that publication of Carlyle's extreme rhetoric shifted the terms for *public* discourse on race and public policy. Even so humane and able a critic as John Stuart Mill did not directly contest much of Carlyle's vicious caricature of blacks, although he disputed the causes and solutions. Mill devoted most of his long rejoinder to defending the humanitarian impulses of the abolitionists and the idealism of modern Britain. Although he disputed the accuracy of Carlyle's "half an hour a day," Mill conceded the key point: that blacks "can exist in comfort on the wages of a comparatively small quantity of work." The solution to the problem, in his view, was not physical coercion but immigration to bring the labor supply into balance with demand. On grounds of practical politics, Jamaican planters would hardly have objected to that.[46]

Respondents less committed to liberal political economy than Mill were more apt to rely on humanitarian arguments entirely. The deficiencies Carlyle lays to Quashee were not his own fault, wrote an anonymous critic to the *Inquirer*, but the errors of "his instructors." Britain's mission was to bring to him "the Divine gift" of civilization.[47] Though the sentiments were admirable, the author evaded the question of what the true character of the West Indian peasantry was, while basking in the afterglow of British benevolence. Indeed, by the late nineteenth century, a similar pride in Britain's civilizing mission would rationalize imperialism.[48]

Stripped of its rhetorical violence, then, Carlyle's essay simply restated an evolving and "respectable" set of ideas about race and underscored some of the key tenets regarding the universal applicability of liberal economy. In many ways his diatribe cleared space for fine-tuning classical liberalism, allowing it to accommodate increasingly recognized "racial realities." In essence, he held that free labor was not working in the West Indies because blacks abused it and refused to work. All that liberals like Mill could suggest in response was more of the same: the application of liberal economic principles and humanitarian values. But those charged with making and carrying out government policy were increasingly skeptical about the applicability of political economy to blacks at all and much less inclined to be humane. Whereas Carlyle coupled his slander of blacks with an equally sharp critique of liberal economics, colonial officials simply separated black deficiencies from liberal virtues. The Colonial and Emigration Commissioners' report to Herman Merivale in 1858 was not exceptional: blacks were "destitute of the very capacity for continuous industry."[49] In the end, what is most striking about Carlyle's polemic is its basic complementarity with official discourse, though not the official rhetoric and reasoning. In fact, he could easily have drawn the raw material for his essay from Henry Taylor, a close friend and associate he apparently had met through John Stuart Mill in the mid-1830s.

The Carlyle-Taylor friendship illuminates the social and intellectual milieu of policy formation at mid-century. Taylor, who had introduced Carlyle to major literary figures and organized a series of lectures on world literature for him in 1837–38, possibly thought of himself as benefactor and literary peer. But by the 1840s, Carlyle's "genius" was generally acknowledged, while Taylor remained a part-time, second-rate man of letters. Carlyle found Taylor personally attractive but thought he had a rather prosaic mind; he described him as "a solid, sound-headed, faithful, but not a well-read or wide-minded man, though of marked veracity, in all sense of that deep-reaching word, and with a fine readiness to apprehend new truth, and stand by it." His opinion of Taylor's work soon slipped out, however, and although they continued to see each other socially, there was a perceptible coolness in the relationship by late 1848. It was clear to Carlyle that Taylor did not understand him or his work, and Taylor's correspondence confirms that perception. "I fear he will grow to look on me as the very genius of Chaos," Carlyle wrote his wife, "for I see his understanding does not in the least discover my bearings and distances, unless his good honest heart may intimate to him some good tendency on my part in spite of all." Henry Taylor wrote to his wife in a similar vein: Carlyle "talks away lustily, and there is always something to take one's attention in his talk, and often a sort of charm in it; but less instructive talk I never listened to from any man who had read and attempted to think. His opinions are the most groundless and senseless opinions that it is possible to utter; or rather they are not opinions, for he will utter the most dogmatic and violent language in the course of half an hour. The real truth is that they are not opinions, but 'shams.'"[50]

But it is not clear just *which* of Carlyle's opinions Taylor considered sham. From 1846 on, he prepared a series of confidential memoranda—or what today might be termed "intelligence estimates"—for his superiors and colleagues at Whitehall that bear striking similarities to much that Carlyle would write for public consumption two years later. In the first of these he supported the Jamaican planters' effort to toughen the masters and servants ordinances and vagrancy laws with an explicitly racist argument. "An unsteady & capricious lightness is the prevailing infirmity of the Negro character, & I believe that it be for their advantage as well as that of their masters that they shd. be compelled to a moderate amount of perseverance in any work in which they are engaged." Their penchant to disappear at just the moment their labor was most needed justified more controls. "The Negroes, like children, require a discipline which shall enforce upon them steadiness in their own conduct & consideration for the interests of others."[51]

Thus Taylor, like Carlyle, saw wage labor as a source not so much of profit as of social discipline. And despite his criticism of Carlyle, he, too, profoundly distrusted democratic governance and urged a political order of "beneficent despotism." In his 1862 assessment of West Indian conditions (repeated in his *Autobiography* later), he bemoaned—in words Carlyle might well have claimed as his own—the fact that the home government had not had the power to carry out a thorough reconstruction of colonial societies. "I conceive that had the times admitted of a wise and strong Government at home taking this race into its own hands, levying an adequate revenue upon it, and insisting upon having it efficiently educated and trained, the present adult generation of negroes would have prospered accordingly."[52] Part of that education and training would come from disciplined wage labor on the estates.

By this time there was no one at the Colonial Office to raise an effective dissent to such views, and those who implemented policies in the colonies were even more blatantly racist. Jamaican governors had never been racial egalitarians, of course, but compared with their predecessors Darling and Eyre filled their dispatches with a harsher, less tentative judgment of black capacities and tendencies. Eyre has been heard from already, in his responses to the Underhill letters. His predecessor, Charles Darling, was scarcely any better. He thought blacks prone to public disorder because they were "incapable of forethought" and thus prudence. He implied that this was a biological rather than a cultural defect. Their "insensibility to consequences, whether immediate or more remote, . . . must be sought for I apprehend in their ethnological characteristics; prominent amongst which, are an incapacity to exercise forethought and reflection, amounting practically to an utter disregard of results: and a temperament so excitable as to render it an easy task to arouse their passions to a perfectly uncontrollable pitch." He asserted that these "peculiarities [were] highly developed . . . in the African, whether indigenous or imported from his original country," so presumably they were biological rather than cultural defects. This was the root cause of "nine-tenths of the serious crime and outrage" in Jamaica.[53]

The immediate, practical consequence of such views was callousness in policy discussions and brutality in the administration of the laws. Darling and Eyre drew their proofs for black incapacity from the social disorganization around them, which they took to be an effect of moral degradation rather than its cause. Consequently, the incidence of criminal behavior in particular became a test of Afro-Jamaicans' moral character. It was a test they failed. The increase in crime showed that there was "almost total absence of anything like moral feeling," declared Eyre. This declaration summed up the governor's interpretation of prison statistics that showed a startling 82 percent more incarcerations for 1863–64 than for 1861–62, mostly of young people. That 43 percent of these were convicted of larceny worried both the governor and his superiors, since it confirmed a growing "insecurity of property" and "barbarousness" that must be dealt with.[54]

Eyre's solution to the problem was greater prison discipline and less food and clothing for the inmates. During his tenure the prison population increased by 44 percent, while prison expenditures rose only 18 percent. But his determination not to "coddle" prisoners failed to stem the growth of the prison population. The jails filled, and there was no money to build more.[55] In fact, there was not even enough penal labor to occupy the prisoners. Kingston inmates had been put to work constructing and repairing the city's streets and building a new slip dock and a lunatic asylum, but these were temporary solutions at best. Legislation was passed during the late 1850s permitting leasing of convicts to private employers under certain conditions, but this was no longer adequate to absorb the prison population. Early in 1865, Eyre turned to an old method for combining labor, discipline, and punishment: he sent to England for a treadmill.[56]

But reversion to the penal methods of the apprenticeship era was still not enough to satisfy some Jamaicans. In their view, nothing less than the tried-and-true disciplinary methods of slavery could stem the tide of disorder and ruin and "check the progress of infamy among the hardened wretches." Since the early 1850s the demand for a return to corporal punishment had grown more and more insistent. One proponent, while making clear his repugnance toward slavery, noted that its abolition had permitted "a greater indulgence in the corrupt passions of a portion of our population." It was time for the government to ignore the protests of "mock philanthropists and characterless agitators," because "nothing less than the most degrading punishment to which a human being can be subjugated is likely to effect that wholesome reformation among the deprived." But, he insisted, the lash should fall irrespective of class or color, and it should not be wielded by local magistrates.[57]

In 1850, Governor Charles Grey had opposed legislation imposing corporal punishment but found the proponents "too strong for me." Grey's superiors were no more effective in opposing the law than he had been. The secretary urged amendment to rectify its "vagueness" but left it to its operation. Apparently, under this law whipping was reserved to the chief justice's discretion and was applied mostly in cases of arson. But early in 1865 the law was extended to cases of larceny and administered with increased severity, with up to fifty lashes inflicted on all male convicts except first offenders. The Colonial Office objected only to the number of lashes, not to the principle of the legislation. Henry Taylor, citing Governor Barkly as his authority, thought it a salutary remedy for praedial larceny and merely asked Jamaican authorities to limit the number of lashes to thirty-nine.[58]

Once one accepted that black Jamaican adults were demoralized wretches, it was easier to justify removing children from their authority to that of the planters. Thus a law passed in 1865 empowered magistrates to apprentice boys under sixteen years convicted of petty larceny, which was defined as the theft of anything worth less than one shilling. These youths could be indentured for five years or until they were twenty-one years old. Again, the Colonial Office objected to the execution rather than the principle of the law, urging amendments but letting it take effect without them. When it came up for renewal in 1866, Taylor's colleagues could not blink its palpable injustice. "As the Act stands at present," one wrote, "any two planters or agents who happen to be magistrates may take a boy of 16 who has plucked a sugar cane[,] from his parents & apprentice him to one of themselves for 5 years." This time the act was disallowed. Before that reversal, however, many Jamaican blacks had come to interpret the law, not unreasonably, as a plot to restore slavery; it figured prominently in the agitation and violence of 1865.[59]

Although the increase in antisocial behavior was real enough, there was also evidence that as in other societies in times of crisis, criminal behavior was being redefined. According to Richard Hill, the dramatic increase in larcenies and the growth of the prison population during the 1860s was as much a result of changes in the law as of criminal behavior. For example, all trespasses involving theft of produce were now defined as felonies, thus taking away the magistrates' discretion to levy fines rather than impose jail terms. Acts such as picking wild fruit or taking a small piece of cane, a Scottish missionary complained, were "acts that no man ever accounted a crime, and to which all classes thought they had a prescribed right"; they were now felonies.[60]

As creole employment on estates declined and planters and peasants came increasingly to occupy two different worlds, their main points of contact were in the courts of petty sessions. And there, more often than not, planters were the complainants and judges, while blacks were the defendants and losers. Between 1863 and 1865, for example, a third of the cases brought before the court of petty sessions in St. Thomas-in-the-East involved complaints for larceny, trespass, or stealing canes and fruit. Most of the persons complaining were planters or their attorneys; most of the persons complained of were black workers and peasants. Most of the judges—twenty-four of twenty-eight—were planters themselves. Most defendants were convicted.[61]

Repeated efforts had been made to tighten the planters' grip on the dispensing of justice by broadening the jurisdiction of the local magistrates. With Speaker Charles M. Morales's help, Hosack and the Planter party forced a measure through the Assembly in 1858 that increased the local magistrates' jurisdiction over cases up to twenty shillings (see chapter 7). Not until February 1865 was the law amended to restrict the local magistrates' jurisdiction to larcenies of ten shillings or less.[62]

During the early years of freedom, black workers could look to the special magistrates to blunt somewhat a judicial system that seemed stacked against them. But while there had been sixty-one special magistrates in Jamaica in 1838, there were only eleven in 1860; in 1865 there were six.[63] Those who remained found little of the support at King's House that they had received from Sligo, Smith, or even Metcalfe. Thomas Witter Jackson was one of the most effective of the surviving special magistrates protecting the rights of the black working class, but neither Darling nor Eyre supported him in his struggles with local magistrates, and eventually he was shunted off to Portland

Parish, where sugar cultivation was practically defunct and therefore labor discipline was less of a problem.[64]

Afro-Jamaicans could not expect equal justice in Jamaica's local courts, so they attempted to set up alternative court systems. William Miller, himself a magistrate, related how blacks held courts of their own in the interior districts of Manchioneal and in the Blue Mountain Valley district. Other courts were uncovered in St. Andrew, St. David, and St. Thomas-in-the-East. The so-called mock court in St. Thomas had been established in 1863 in the area of Serge Island and Plantain Garden River, where it issued summonses, tried cases, and levied fines. It involved a completely parallel judicial and police system, including a judge, clerk of peace, inspector, sergeant, and private, as well as a schedule of fees and fines. The prescribed fees and fines—one pound and four pounds—are suspiciously high, however, considering the poverty of the community. On the other hand, that those subject to the court's jurisdiction paid a "membership" fee of one shilling and that the sanction for defiance of its orders was to be declared "Unsivilise" suggests something similar to the mutual aid societies found in other African American communities. That is, it is likely that the courts' authority and sanctions were analogous to and probably linked with the larger church community, in which the power of expulsion was a formidable force for order. It is significant that the court in St. Thomas was organized and directed by a Native Baptist preacher and peasant farmer in the village of Stony Gut, Paul Bogle.[65]

"The Spirit of Rebellion"

Stony Gut was a black settlement about five miles into the hills northwest of Morant Bay (see map, p. 52). Like similar villages elsewhere in Jamaica, the settlement was not isolated in the backlands but was geographically contiguous to and economically interactive with several prosperous estates, many of which were owned or managed by members of the island's political elite. Like most others that survived and were prosperous, these estates relied on a core workforce of indentured Indian or African labor; indeed, more than a thousand of the latter had just arrived in Jamaica between 1861 and 1863. Native Jamaicans, a few resident on the estates but most living in settlements like Stony Gut, were recruited to fill out the workforce at certain seasons and for certain tasks. Even when resident on the estates, creole workers were housed separately from indentured laborers, which must have promoted a degree of social separation as well. Intermarriage and common economic needs eventually facilitated integration of Africans into creole communities, but this appears to have been more likely after they had finished their indentures and left the estates.[66] Thus estates and settlements constituted socially separate worlds, loosely tethered within a common economic and political space.

Paul Bogle and his neighbors relished their relative economic independence, and those same values were reflected in their religion and politics. At the center of their village stood a Baptist chapel, where Bogle preached. But this was not a church of which Jamaica's Baptist missionaries would have approved. It was Native Baptist, an independent sect organized in Jamaica at the end of the eighteenth century by black refugees from the American Revolution. Though its roots on the island predated those of the white Baptist missionaries, its potential political and spiritual force had developed quite recently.

The popular appeal and threat of the Native Baptists in 1865 must be understood in the context of postemancipation changes in Afro-Jamaican religious life generally. The influence of English Dissenter missionaries had peaked during the 1840s, with their sponsorship of the free village movement and political activism. The Baptist missionaries, strong abolitionists and energetic proselytizers, had made their denomination the largest in Jamaica, concentrated largely in the western parishes. The Methodists, with the second largest following, predominated in the central and eastern parishes but tended to concentrate in the cities and towns, where urban blacks and mulattoes made up the bulk of their membership.[67] With the 1850s and 1860s came economic distress, declining membership, internecine conflict, and challenges to European doctrines, faiths, and controls. In the five years between 1854 and 1859, for example, Methodist membership fell by 9 percent.[68]

Revivals in 1861 and 1862 stimulated renewed religious enthusiasm, but of a kind the regular denominations disdained and feared. People had visions, went into trances, threw themselves on the ground, jumped from windows apparently unhurt, went for three to four days without food, and, of course, did no work. But according to ministers and missionaries of the regular denominations, after the enthusiasm had passed, the new converts relapsed into a life of sin. The reversal of the secular decline in membership and faith was only temporary.[69]

Given their constituency among the agricultural working class, the

Baptists were particularly hard hit by both economic and religious retrenchment, since their missions depended heavily—even during slavery—on contributions from their members. Their congregations contributed much of the money and labor that built and maintained their chapels. Consequently, when disputes arose between competing factions within a church—a frequent occurrence after emancipation—they often led to counter claims to the church property itself. In 1850 Rev. James Phillippo, who had secured a court decree sustaining English Baptist claims to church property in Spanish Town, had to rely on a military guard to protect him from angry parishioners who surrounded and practically destroyed his house.[70] In Kingston three years later, Rev. Samuel Oughton, principal agent of the Baptist Missionary Society, confronted a similar crisis. In this incident, too, local members contested ownership claims of the Baptist Society in England, resulting in a court decree favoring the latter. Scorning that decree, church members took over the premises at night and erected barricades before being driven out by bayonet-wielding soldiers. On the following Sunday, Oughton preached to one hundred of the faithful in the recaptured chapel, but twelve hundred unrepentant dissidents gathered at another service nearby.[71]

These incidents suggest much about the content of religious conviction among Jamaican freed people. Their churches were venues for fostering community, legitimizing alternative world-views, and articulating political solidarity. Churches were political not in the narrow sense of partisan politics but in the broad sense of being arenas of contestation for the power, authority, and control of one's destiny that are fundamental to all political processes. The "political" schisms within the regular Baptist congregations, then, were merely suggestive of the latent political energies of those who had separated from the European churches completely—the Native Baptists.

The Native Baptist church nourished the island's most explicit expressions of the syncretic blending of Christian forms and rituals with African beliefs and values. Among Native Baptist congregations, for example, myalism flourished, and African beliefs and practices did not bring expulsion from among the faithful. At the heart of their value scheme was the subordination and control of individual desire and greed to the needs of the community. Here religion provided a vehicle for cultural resistance, giving moral authority to an alternative world-view.[72]

In Bogle's church at Stony Gut a religious world-view melded with an emerging political consciousness. Central to its functioning was

George William Gordon

the remarkable relationship between Bogle and George William Gordon. The chapel at Stony Gut had been opened during the Christmas season in 1864, and the following March Bogle was ordained deacon by Gordon. Gordon and Bogle were described as "like brothers." Part political and religious alliance, part friendship, their relationship was founded in resistance.

Gordon had been born a slave but was freed by his father, Joseph Gordon, then a wealthy planting attorney and proprietor. George ran a produce store in Kingston, a very successful venture from which he obtained capital to invest in several properties. Among these were three estates in St. Thomas-in-the-East that he leased out to tenants: Rhine Estate (near Bath), Bogg, and Spring, the latter about three miles from Stony Gut. Before 1860 Gordon's political views probably differed little from those of other Jamaican mulattoes. He had married an Irishwoman, joined the Anglican Church, and maintained an amicable though strained relationship with his father and former owner. When his father fell on economic hard times, the son rescued him from bankruptcy. In 1844 he took a seat in the Assembly, representing St. Andrew, and though a nominal member of the Town party, his voting record was centrist at best.[73]

By the 1860s all this had begun to change. Gordon was one of the leaders of the religious revival of 1860–61, and on Christmas Day, 1861, he converted to the Native Baptist faith. In fact, the revival in Kingston was launched from the Native Baptist tabernacle he had constructed on the Kingston Parade. He reentered the Assembly in 1863, this time representing St. Thomas-in-the-East; his ties to the Town party were as loose as before, but now he was clearly to its left. His passionate defense of the Jamaican poor earned him the condemnation of Darling and Eyre as a "fanatic." Meanwhile, his substantial landholdings were mortgaged, and he accumulated thirty-five thousand pounds in debts. In 1865 he was finding it difficult to pay his taxes.[74]

Gordon's political and religious activities were increasingly focused on St. Thomas. In February 1862 he lost to George Solomon in his first bid to represent the parish in the Assembly, and he was dismissed from the magistracy of that parish the following June. His fortunes were reversed somewhat the following year, when he was reelected to the Assembly and also won election to the parish vestry as churchwarden. But Rev. Stephen Cooke, the parish rector, and Maximillian August, Baron von Ketelhodt, who was the custos, both political foes of Gordon's, voided his election as churchwarden, claiming that his adult baptism into the Native Baptist church disqualified him.

This political infighting reflected a larger struggle in St. Thomas, where Gordon had founded his political base among its small settlements. His relationship to his constituents, in fact, had a superficial similarity to the relationship of the classic English patron and his retainers; the core of his political support appeared to come from tenants on his own estates, whose taxes and voter registration fees he paid on at least one occasion, and from the residents of neighboring settlements. On 25 July 1862, for example, Bogle wrote Gordon on behalf of "the people connected with small holdings" at Stony Gut, asking for £150 in order to register them as voters in the parish.[75]

The ties linking Gordon with his constituents were stronger than the ties of mere patronage, however. He was spiritual leader as well as political spokesman. Thus, shortly after Gordon's removal as churchwarden, Bogle wrote: "We want to see you at our village . . . for we have plans [to] arrange with you. Come up we beseach you as quick as posible, so that we may arange how the baptism is to go on at Spring." And then in a second letter that same day: "At a meeting held at the Liberal School Society meetings house at the above named

Baron von Ketelhodt

place [Stony Gut] to take into *consideration* what plans we might adopt for to recover your place that is lost in the *political* world, but in the *religious* one we are asurd your progress is great; may God grant it so. Among other plans we resolve to have an hundred tax payers put on, *independent of freehoders* and those who will or can pay without borrowing from us."[76]

The energy of the Bogle-Gordon alliance was rooted in the extraordinary religious enthusiasm of black Jamaica, particularly its Native Baptists. For both men, religion shaped their world-view and gave a strong millennial undercurrent to their vision of political entitlement and social justice. "The fact is, St. Thomas-in-the-East is about the *very worst* parish in the Island," Gordon wrote his friend and estate manager at Rhine, "and now the Governor has given *another* cheer to magisterial oppression, as if it were forcing matters to a point. Verily, this Governor is an evil doer. The Lord will plenteously reward him. Again and again the Baron and the Cookes are *gratified*." Having marked the political sinners in one letter, in his next he invoked their sure reward. "The enemies now exult, and justice is silenced for the time, but it will raise its head. . . . The Lord will soon pluck his hand out of his bosom, and so confound the whole band of oppressors. I believe this to be about one of their last *flickers*. Let us wait and see." And finally, on the eve of the incident at Morant Bay, he invoked the millennial faith one finds in Bogle's letters later. "The oppression still continues rife in St. Thomas-in-the-East, and there appears to be every effort put forth to exasperate the poor people! Their plan is to pray to God for deliverance. You may laugh at this and call it cant, but I assure you it is the most effectual plan. If you knew the number of ways in which God can, and often does destroy the evil-doer, you would agree."[77]

"The iron bar is broken"

It was Saturday, 7 October 1865. The large crowd gathered at the Morant Bay courthouse was not unusual, because the first Saturday of the month was both a market day and the time for convening the court of petty sessions. But on this particular day there was tension in the air. Francis Bowen, the proprietor of Coley Estate, and John Walton, the owner of Retreat, were the magistrates presiding over the court. Their calendar included the usual assortment of black-on-black crimes that had come to dominate proceedings at this level—assault, abusive language, and so on. A boy was found guilty of an assault and fined four shillings, but as so often happened in St. Thomas, the court costs—which paid the clerks' salaries—amounted to twelve shillings, six pence. James Geoghegan, a black spectator, urged the defendant to pay the fine but not the costs. Magistrate Walton ordered the police to seize him for disrupting the trial. Several members of the crowd rushed to his rescue. During the ensuing scuffle, Geoghegan escaped into the crowd, and the two black policemen pursuing him, John McPherson and John Burnett, were dragged down the steps and beaten "with sticks and stones." Later, Geoghegan's wife, Isabella, taunted Burnett to "step outside," and others in the crowd allegedly paraded through the streets boasting of their successful defiance. The incident was minor, but it reflected the people's growing impatience with and disdain for the system of law and justice in the parish.[78]

Most of the crowd that day actually had come to witness another case. Lewis Miller was charged with trespass onto Middleton, a pen adjoining Stony Gut owned by Wellwood Maxwell Anderson, a colored assemblyman and agent-general of immigration, but occupied largely by small provision-growing tenants. Since the late 1850s, Anderson had been unable to collect rents from his tenants, who had declared that "the land was free, and the estate belonged to the

Queen." Although a case of trespass had been brought and decided against some of the occupiers in 1858, they still resisted the judgment. In 1865 Anderson leased the property along with its subtenancies to another brown man, James Williams.

Williams specifically charged Miller with entering an enclosed pasture without permission to retrieve a horse. Technically, then, this was not a case of squatting, even though the issue of rightful possession underlay the entire dispute: Williams wanted to force Miller to pay for grazing his stock on the disputed land. The case ended as the previous suit had: Miller was found guilty of trespass and fined. When the verdict was announced, ten or twelve people yelled out urging Miller to appeal, which he did. Paul Bogle stood his bail.[79]

The following Monday, 9 October, parish authorities issued warrants for the arrest of Paul Bogle, his brother Moses, and several others for disrupting the court the previous Saturday during the Geoghegan incident. On Tuesday, six policemen and two rural constables made their way to Stony Gut. They found Bogle in his yard, beside the chapel in which he preached. He insisted that the warrant be read to him, after which he declared that he would not comply. When an attempt was made to apprehend him, he called out for help. William Grant, a tenant at Middleton and one of Bogle's "captains," yelled, "Turn out, men." With that command an estimated three hundred to five hundred men armed with cutlasses, sticks, and pikes poured out of the chapel and the adjoining cane field, while drums rolled and shells blew. The police were quickly overpowered and beaten. Three were detained for several hours and forced to swear an oath that they would "join their colour" and "cleave to the black," sealing the pact with a drink of rum laced with gunpowder. Bogle told the police that it was too late to go down to the bay that day but that he would come down on the following day for the scheduled vestry meeting. It is not clear whether his initial intent was to submit to arrest or to file a protest. But others among the crowd were said to have declared that they would come down "to kill all the white men and all the black men that would not join them."[80]

This information was relayed to the police inspector and to the custos, Baron von Ketelhodt, who summoned the volunteer militia and wrote Governor Eyre for troops. Although he had ordered the police and militia to muster at the courthouse the next day, the baron admitted that they had no powder and could not resist any determined assault.[81] His official tone could barely conceal his rising fear:

it was already 6:00 P.M., he wrote in a postscript, and he could hear shells blowing in the distance, collecting Bogle's forces.[82]

Meanwhile, Bogle and his confederates sat down to write the governor, too. Theirs was a formal complaint, but it contained the clear warning that their patience was at an end. They complained of "the mean advantages that has been taken of us from time to time, and more especially" Saturday, when "an outrageous assault was committed upon us by the policemen of this parish, by order of the Justices, which occasion an outbreaking, for which warrants have been issued against innocent parties of which we were compelled to resist." As "Her Majesty's loyal subjects," they asked for protection. If it were refused, they would "be compelled to put our shoulders to the wheels, as we have been imposed upon for a period of 'twenty-seven' years, with due obeisance to the laws of our Queen and country, and we can no longer endure the same."[83]

Coupled with subsequent events, this note renders Bogle's intentions enigmatic. Its procedural formality and tone, its appeal for redress of grievance, do not suggest violent intent. At least one witness quotes Bogle as saying he went to the bay merely to post bail.[84] On the other hand, it is doubtful that Bogle expected any sympathy from Eyre, and it is clear from his military organization and drilling that he was preparing for a violent showdown. The note was given to a messenger sometime after noon on the tenth for delivery in Spanish Town, some fifty miles away, between 10:00 and 11:00 the next morning. Meanwhile, Bogle and his men began preparations for the expected confrontation with the baron at Morant Bay.

Shortly after dawn the Stony Gut men, with womenfolk on their flanks, formed themselves into a column of twos and began marching down to the bay, pausing to collect additional recruits at neighboring settlements. Meanwhile, from early morning, roads east of the town were filled with country people, armed with sticks, cutlasses, and pikes, making their way down to the bay. By early afternoon they converged on the outskirts of town. They sacked the police station, taking its store of weapons, which were mostly old muskets without flints, powder, or shot. They were forced to load the few guns they had with gravel and stones. Between 3:00 and 4:00 P.M. the crowd, now numbering between five hundred and six hundred people, reformed and began marching toward the courthouse, where the vestry had been meeting since noon. Moving out, with shells blowing and drums beating, they rounded a bend onto the parade ground before the courthouse. Several conflicting reports suggest that they appeared to march, more or less, "in regular military order." Upon their approach, someone at the vestry meeting yelled: "There are the niggers coming."

Until that moment, the thirty-two militiamen commanded by Captain Edward Hitchins had been concealed in the schoolhouse. They now moved out to confront the crowd. Baron von Ketelhodt came out onto the courthouse steps and called to them, asking what they wanted. Receiving no reply, he pleaded for "Peace, peace." From the crowd came cries of "Hell peace!" "War!" With that the crowd surged forward. The militia retreated to the steps of the courthouse. The baron tried to read the Riot Act, but his words were muffled under a hail of stones, apparently unleashed by the women's phalanx. Hitchins ordered his men to fire. Several people, perhaps as many as a dozen, were cut down by this first volley. The crowd recoiled in horror, shuddering for an instant. Then came the fury.

They rushed the militiamen, ripping weapons from their hands, beating them with sticks and stones, slashing them with cutlasses. One of the militiamen, Edward Norman Harrison, charged into the crowd; his weapon was smashed into pieces, "split up the barrel, the stock splintered, and the ramrod." He and the other militiamen escaped the crowd's wrath by running into or under the courthouse, close on the heels of the baron and his vestry men. A few ran through the courthouse and escaped out of a back window. In vain the baron sent a black servant out with a white flag to sue for peace. Militiamen began firing from within the courthouse. A cry went up from the crowd: "Go and fetch fire." "Burn the brutes out." Bogle was heard to say: "Let us put fire upon the Court House. If we don't we will not manage the Volunteers and the Buckra."[85]

Fire was set to the adjoining schoolhouse, and leaping from the roof of one building to the other, it eventually spread to the courthouse. Sniping continued between the militia inside and those few rebels outside who had guns and powder. Most of their shots were ineffective, however, because they fired pebbles rather than lead shot. After two hours' burning, the roof of the stone courthouse began falling in and forced those barricaded inside to flee the building. Since it was now dark, many were able to hide among shrubbery or escape to other buildings, among them a privy. Several took refuge in a house close by, occupied by Charles Price, a black assemblyman and building contractor, who had come to the bay to rebuild the parish church. But very shortly after the magistrates had taken refuge there, Price's house was set afire, too.

This time, as the occupants tried to escape, they were set upon by the rebels. Dr. John Gerard and Dr. Edward Major were captured and released, because it was anticipated that their services might be needed later. Others were dragged out and beaten to death, one by one. The rebels hesitated before killing Charles Price but eventually decided that given his close association with the baron, his political complexion outweighed his skin color: "He has a black skin but a white heart." He was beaten to death. Before the night was over, seven militiamen and twenty-two civilians lay dead, and thirty-four others were seriously wounded. Although their battle cry had been "Kill all the buckras," it appears that men clothed with political or religious authority were their main targets. Ordinary white townspeople were not attacked; magistrates, parish priests, and plantation personnel were sought out. Magistrates Walton, Cooke, Smith, and police inspector Alberga met the fate of "black Price." Rev. Victor Herschell, a clergyman who had been among those opposing Gordon's election to the vestry as churchwarden, was found later with his throat cut. Baron von Ketelhodt was discovered with the fingers of his right hand gone, his skull crushed. The Lord had plenteously rewarded the "evil doers."[86]

The town was in the possession of the rebels. The jails were opened, and fifty-one prisoners were released. Over the following three days, the terrible retribution spread north and east of the bay, moving through Port Morant to Manchioneal, Mulatto River, and Elmwood. Armed with guns and bayonets on sticks, and blowing shells, two hundred people marched on Coley. Fifty others attacked Monklands. Amity Hall was attacked by a mixed group of creoles and Africans. Hordley, Wheelersfield, Holland, Winchester, Blue Mountain Valley, and other estates in the Plantain Garden River district were also sacked. Plantain Garden River, Duckenfield, and Golden Grove estates were plundered by their own people and those living nearby. Ironically, all of the white families in that area took refuge at Rhine Estate, George William Gordon's property near Bath.[87]

At its peak, the rebellion involved an estimated fifteen hundred to two thousand people, men and women, African and creole, estate workers and settlers. But at its core this was a peasant war. The most prominent participants in the agitation leading up to the violence and the key cadres of organized insurgents appear to have come from settlements surrounding Morant Bay: Stony Gut, Middleton, and Thornton to the west, John's Town, Cardiff, and Torrington to the east.[88] When troops marched on their villages, they found, to their amazement, a "class of people who are . . . not the poor, but a class of small freeholders who are, in every sense of the word, freeholders." The villagers owned "horses, pigs, poultry, and comfortable clothing" and "left behind large quantities of coffee and provisions of all kinds." All this indicated "the utmost comfort on the part of the people composing the rebellion."[89]

But its rapid spread among resident sugar workers suggests a broad base of support for the rebellion. The rebels' grievances included proletarian issues such as higher wages and better working conditions on the estates along with peasant issues such as lower taxes and more land.[90] The mixed character of their grievances reflected the hybrid character of the Jamaican peasantry. Most settlers worked on the estates at some time in their life cycle, if not their working year; and if they did not, they probably had kinfolk who did. This appears to have been true of many of the insurgents. Settlers at Middleton and Danby Village, for example, might own their house and yard but rented grounds on which to grow their provision crops. Work on nearby estates was necessary to earn money for the things they could not grow: for taxes, licenses, and school fees.

Grievances of peasants linked up with those of estate workers, and both with the overarching issue of equal justice before the local courts. In the person of the planter they found a single focus for their multiple complaints. As employer, the planter paid them low wages and sometimes no wages at all. As landowner, he charged them high rents or kept them out of possession of land for themselves. As magistrate, he weighted the law in favor of his own class and denied them justice. James McLaren, one of Bogle's key lieutenants, worked at Coley Estate, the property of magistrate Bowen. In a remarkable speech in Bogle's chapel at Stony Gut a month before the outbreak, he linked the key themes of the rebellion. Though born free of ex-slave parents, "I am still a slave by working from days to days. I cannot get money to feed my family, and I working at Coley estate for 35 chains for 1s., and after five days' working I get 2s. 6d. for my family. Is that able to sustain a house full of family?" To which his audience replied: "No." He went on to urge that they send a petition to the government for land. "And if they will give up the outside land to *we*, we shall work with cane, and cotton, and coffee like the white. But the white people say we are lazy and won't work." When he said that, the people said, "We have no land to work." McLaren went on to complain of the high rents he paid for his provision grounds and high taxes on his stock. If they had land, they could pay taxes and they would "not want anything from the white people, they would try to make their own living themselves." They must go down to Morant Bay, he concluded, "in lump, to let white people see there was plenty black in the island."[91]

If organization, preparation, and political consciousness distinguish a rebellion from a riot, then this was a rebellion.[92] Whether Bogle intended to ignite a rebellion on 11 October is irrelevant; once shots were fired, a preconceived, though ultimately abortive, plan of action ensued. Upon his return to Stony Gut immediately after the outbreak at the bay Bogle held a chapel service. Then he prepared his remarkable call to arms which is quoted in the epigraph to this chapter. "It is now time for us to help ourselves—skin for skin. The iron bar is now broken in this parish." He had his men construct a "rude field-work, by felling large trees," which were used to erect barricades across the roads. Bogle reportedly told his men—after drilling them on the twelfth—that the country belonged to them and they would take possession of it. They were ordered, as their ancestors in 1831 had been, not to destroy the sugar works, because they wanted "sugar to make for ourselves."[93]

Bogle felt that the only force standing in the way of success was the Maroons, the descendants of escaped ex-slaves who had established colonies in the rugged interior after the British took the island from the Spanish. The Maroons, the stuff of legend and myth, had waged a fierce and determined struggle in 1795 to maintain the independence of their mountain strongholds from the British. Eventually they won their own freedom by a treaty compelling them to assist their former enemies in putting down any future slave revolts, a role they had taken on with unseemly enthusiasm in 1831–32. Afro-Jamaicans had come to respect and fear them. The success of any uprising might well depend on whether they would be a welcome ally or a dreaded foe.

Bogle's letter suggests that he thought he had made allies of the Maroons, and there is circumstantial evidence to substantiate that belief. Three or four weeks before the rebellion, apparently, he and two of his lieutenants had visited the Maroon settlement at Hayfield, expecting to draw on their knowledge of warfare. Clearly, the rebels were anxious not to offend the Maroons. Several persons were released unharmed by the crowds upon identifying themselves or being recognized as Maroons. Bogle himself had released one of the policemen sent to apprehend him on the tenth once he discovered that he was a Maroon, declaring, "The Maroon is our back." Bogle went to Hayfield again on the Monday following the outbreak at the bay.[94]

But not only did the Maroons fail to rally to his side, they soon took the field against him. The Maroons at Hayfield were ordered to lift the rebel hold on Torrington and to guard Bath, and a detachment marched on Stony Gut from their western barracks at Moore Town in the Blue Mountains, thereby blocking any possible spread of the rebellion into the mountainous interior of the island. Heavy rains during this period washed away roads and bridges that British regular troops depended upon, making conditions ripe for the rebels to mount a guerrilla campaign, but the government's Maroon allies provided an effective antiguerrilla weapon. On the twenty-third, Bogle himself was captured by Maroons. A day later, he was court-martialed and hanged.[95]

Meanwhile, Eyre formed a council of war, carefully constituted of "nearly equal numbers from all the three leading classes, white, coloured, and Jews, and representing fairly all shades of politics," which unanimously approved a declaration of martial law covering the whole of Surrey County, except Kingston. Regular British ground and naval forces (some of them veterans of the Indian Mutiny suppression), island militia, and Maroons were mobilized to put down the rebellion. Holding his political enemy, Gordon, ultimately responsible for instigating the rebellion, Eyre had him arrested and taken to Morant Bay, where, on extraordinarily flimsy evidence, he was found guilty and hanged.[96]

When the final tallies of the government's repression were made, they revealed that a terrible vengeance had been unleashed: 439 dead, hundreds flogged, and 1,000 houses burned. On the eighteenth, 90 British marines and sailors had marched from Morant Bay to Stony Gut. Finding it deserted, they burned Bogle's chapel and 8 cottages. Despite orders for restraint, people were flogged with whips made of twisted, knotted wires, and scores were shot or hung after drumhead court-martials. Commanders were quite explicit about the objective of official violence: they intended to instill terror. They were aware, for example, of the people's awe of obeah. So when Arthur Wellington, an alleged obeahman, was captured, he was ordered shot and decapitated. Whether the intended message took is difficult to determine, since a heavy flood washed Wellington's head out of the grave and carried it downstream. White power could not contain obeah.[97]

Such excesses cost Eyre critical political support in Britain. Much as in 1832, the sympathy aroused by the first vague, exaggerated reports of rebel atrocities soon turned to revulsion against the military terror that followed. English abolitionists mobilized and demanded an investigation. Henry Taylor, a strong defender of Eyre's brutal repression, patiently explained to his friend that politically the government could not withstand the calls for an enquiry into his conduct. A royal commission of three members was constituted, chaired by Maj. Gen. Sir Henry Knight Storks, who was ordered to replace Eyre as governor immediately. Arriving in late January, the commissioners promptly began hearings, which they did not complete until 21 March.

Before he left office, however, Eyre engineered a major change in the Jamaican constitution. For weeks following the violence in St. Thomas, fears and rumors of fresh outbreaks swept across the island. Every seeming act of insolence became a harbinger of revolt. Such fears gained further support from Eyre's insistence that the Morant Bay incident had been merely a premature launching of a more general uprising planned for Christmas. Having thus incited these apprehensions, the governor then exploited the hysteria by pushing through the Assembly a resolution abrogating the Jamaican constitution and abolishing self-government. This, of course, was an objective long sought by Henry Taylor and some others at the Colonial Office. Over the past decade the idea had attracted support from a diverse array of Jamaicans as well, though for radically different reasons. Some of the planters feared eventual domination by black workers, while some of the black settlers were disgusted with the Assembly's failure to assist them.[98]

Although a small group of ten Afro-Jamaican and Jewish representatives resisted the imposition of crown colony government, an overwhelming majority of the frightened assemblymen were prepared to consent to their own political destruction.[99] On 22 December, after a mere two weeks of debate, the Assembly approved legislation abolishing itself and asking Parliament to reorganize it as a crown colony. On Christmas Eve, Eyre triumphantly sent the Colonial Office the new constitution, which provided for a partially elective, partially appointive governing body, with high-property qualifications for both members and the electorate. Eyre thought it provided a basis for a new order. "What we want mainly are a strong government, an organized detective Police Force, and an extensive white colonization of our interior lands." The Crown's legal officers concluded, however, that the Jamaica Assembly could not annihilate itself but must surrender its powers to the queen, who in turn would legislate for the island. By a subsequent vote of the Assembly this was done.[100]

Most of the Colonial Office's permanent staff, anxious to be rid of the Assembly, found ready arguments to urge the queen's assent to extinguishing Jamaica's democratic experiment. They were generally agreed, as Rogers put it, "that the planters—being the best educated class & most interested in the permanent prosperity of the c[oun-try]—should have great power controlling the Govt. & great share in the Govt. of the Island." To this Henry Taylor added the fanciful notion that the interests of the planters and those of the blacks were "in the main coincident"; consequently, there was little to fear from an oligarchic government. Indeed, such despotism might be the only way to ensure civilizing influences on the black population. With Car-lylean phrases, Taylor repeated the hoary myths that had now become official truths. The lessons of the past three decades had demonstrated that "in all but very exceptional seasons, the Negroes are able, thro' the fertility of the soil & the nature of their own bodily constitution & of the climate, to live in comfort without anything like what we in this country shd. call steady industry." Their moral development would be promoted "if they were to be placed in [circumstances] in which a moderate amount of such industry wd. become necessary for the sup-ply of their wants." Thus themes of liberal dogma and racism merged to justify white political hegemony.

Only one voice was raised in the Colonial Office to challenge these conclusions. W. E. Forster, the undersecretary for the colonies and of Quaker roots, argued that an oligarchic government might well be worse than the old, because as everyone agreed, it would represent just one class—the planters. Thus he found little justification for re-placing the present Assembly, "turbulent & unreasonable & corrupt though it be, by a class oligarchy especially now when 'class' feuds have culminated in terrible bloodshed."[101] Forster's arguments fell on deaf ears. On 9 April 1866 the queen approved the act abolishing the Jamaica Assembly.

On that same day the royal commission completed its report, con-cluding that the chief causes of the rebellion were the desire for land and the lack of confidence in the system of justice. They agreed with Eyre that though the outbreak was localized, it could have spread throughout the island, and so they praised him for his "skill, prompti-tude, and vigour" in the early stages of the crisis. But they condemned him for prolonging martial law until well after the pretext for sup-pressing violence had passed, for the illegality and injustice of Gor-don's trial, and for the excessive, even "barbarous," "wanton and cruel" punishments meted out to alleged rebels.[102]

Though its criticisms were modulated, the report gave Eyre little comfort. Prominent intellectuals and political figures in England had already organized a campaign to bring him to justice for his crimes against humanity, and especially his crime against George William Gordon. Enlisting in this cause were members of Parliament, scions of abolitionists, and prominent scientists, among whom were abolitionist leader Thomas Fowell Buxton's son Charles, who chaired the committee initially, and his successor, John Stuart Mill.[103]

Eyre had not awaited events before marshaling arguments in his defense but began his counterattack as soon as he sensed the shift in official opinion at home. His was essentially a racist defense: the defective moral character of black people required strong measures because the rebels intended "to exterminate the white and coloured classes, and obtain possession of the country for themselves." He recognized that this might seem "wild and visionary" to Englishmen, but the foreboding example of Haiti and the fact that Haitians were in Kingston "living in wealth and idleness" made it credible to Jamaicans. The brutality of the suppression was necessitated by the fact that "the negroes from a low state of civilization and being under the influence of superstitious feelings could not properly be dealt with in the same manner as might the peasantry of a European country." Punishment needed to be "prompt, certain, and severe." Effective suppression was necessary because "as a race the negroes are most excitable and impulsive, and any seditious or rebellious action was sure to be taken up and extended amongst the large majority of those with whom it came in contact." He was certain of the necessity for the actions he took but realized the difficulty involved in convincing "persons living at a distance, unacquainted with the country and with the negro character, and unable to appreciate the value of all the little incidents or circumstances which to my mind indicated a great and imminent danger."[104]

To his great relief, Eyre soon discovered that racist fears found a receptive public in Britain, too. British sympathy for colored peoples had been dulled by the Indian Mutiny of 1857 and the ongoing Maori War in New Zealand. Conservatives formed a defense committee to welcome him home, raised money to pay his legal fees, and lobbied the government in his behalf. For a short while Thomas Carlyle chaired this committee, and through him a number of prominent literary and cultural figures were enlisted in Eyre's cause. They, too, made explicitly racist appeals in Eyre's defense. Explaining his support of the Eyre Defence Committee, Joseph Hooker—a friend of Charles Darwin and T. H. Huxley and one of the few scientists to stand with

Eyre—declared: "We do not hold an Englishman and a Jamaican negro to be convertible terms, nor do we think that the cause of human liberty will be promoted by any attempt to make them so." Black insurrection could not be treated in the same way as a white one, because "the negro in Jamaica . . . is pestilential, . . . a dangerous savage at best."[105]

Liberal voices were raised to challenge such blatantly racist defenses of Eyre's actions. "We pardon Eyre because his error of judgment involves only negro blood," declared the *Spectator*, a Liberal weekly, "what would have otherwise been in our nation's eyes simply unpardonable." During the parliamentary debate on the Eyre case, W. E. Forster voiced similar sentiments, condemning the racist feelings "to which we were all tempted in dealing with weaker races," which allowed British officers to perpetrate "atrocities from which they would have shrunk had the victims been white people."[106] No doubt the leaders of the Jamaica Committee also deplored the racist appeals of Eyre's defenders, but they chose to ground their counterargument less in advocacy of racial equality than in the necessity for the rule of law, perhaps because they knew the British public would be more responsive to the latter. It was, they thought, "at bottom one of the most important constitutional battles in which Englishmen have for many years been engaged." Their most effective attack against Eyre was for his illegal treatment of the mulatto, George William Gordon, not his brutality to the black masses.[107]

The Eyre controversy was fought out against the backdrop of bread riots in the eastern end of London and Fenian uprisings in Ireland and England. As in the early 1830s, colonial events resonated with domestic strife, and the oppression of blacks provided metaphors for the treatment of whites. A renewed, militant agitation for universal suffrage had commenced in England following the resignation of Russell's Liberal ministry in June of 1866. The principals in the reform struggle overlapped with those in the Eyre controversy: Mill and the Jamaica Committee for political reform, Carlyle and the Eyre Defence Committee against. Working-class demonstrators gave Eyre a rude and violent welcome when he arrived in Southampton. Their orators linked Eyre's brutal repression of Jamaican blacks with the newly inaugurated Tory government's repression of the Hyde Park demonstration in July 1866. The following September at Clerkenwell Green in London a similar group of demonstrators burned Eyre in effigy. In all these situations much of the British middle class—whose members were fairly united in support of Eyre—connected the need to repel class challenges from below with support for racism and empire.[108]

The Jamaica Committee never succeeded in convicting Eyre for his crimes, neither in British courts nor in British public opinion. In the aftermath of Morant Bay and on the eve of its greatest imperialist adventures, British public opinion accorded more closely with Eyre and Carlyle than with Mill. In 1867, English workers won reform of Parliament and a new franchise. Black Jamaica would have to wait three-quarters of a century before receiving a similar boon.

Coda

The Morant Bay Rebellion, then, was taken afterwards as an explicit demonstration of the failure of British emancipation policy and as evidence of the ex-slaves' incapacity for responsible citizenship. The suppression of self-government in Jamaica set a precedent soon followed in other parts of the colonial empire. "Beneficent guardianship" over colored peoples, first implemented in Britain's former slave colonies, was an idea that gained ready assent from other British policymakers in the late nineteenth century. For example, Edward Stanley, son of the colonial secretary who had shepherded the British Abolition Act through Parliament in 1833 and while doing so had expounded at length on the innate fitness of blacks for freedom, declared in 1865 that the British had done enough for and spent enough resources on African peoples who seemed content with "a mere animal existence."[109]

The perceived failure of West Indian emancipation resonated with and helped sustain the rise of a virulent official racism, which in turn helped give shape and focus to the racial thought of the larger public. First, there was an unmistakable conjuncture between the racial ideology of the late nineteenth century and the general image of colonial peoples. Whether linked to a sense of religious mission, a need to rationalize economic exploitation, or, more often, a subtle blend of the two, ideas about colored peoples shared certain premises. The savage, the primitive, the yet to be civilized, were invariably stigmatized as underworked and oversexed, their material interests or drives unaroused, while their libidos were out of control. A common theme running through racist thought was that "the natives" had no inner controls; thus the need for external controllers.[110]

Second, this revolution in racial thinking was not simply an aberration, not some intemperate Carlylean backlash. Rather it was an extension of more general preexisting premises and assumptions about human nature, an outcropping from the still dominant classical liberal ideology. Advocates of slave emancipation had founded their policies on the liberal democratic presumption that all men—including blacks—shared certain innate traits and values. Although they did not recognize that the "human nature" they described was itself the product of a specific history, they did understand that the behavior and values of the slave were shaped by his or her experience. Since experience was the product of culture and condition, slavish conditions had to be altered and cultural deficiencies removed in order to free those innate material drives all humans shared. Human differences, then, were recognized as real but ephemeral; they could and would be dissolved in conformity with a larger, self-evident scheme of social progress.

This world-view implied social mobility and equality—anyone could be acculturated if they willed. But it also had its pessimistic side, which harbored the seeds of a later, harsher interpretation of resistance to these "self-evident" scripts of human progress. Arguing for his abolition plan in 1833, for example, Henry Taylor could easily and casually suggest that those slaves who *failed* to respond to market incentives were "a idle and spendthrift residue, whose liberation from arbitrary control could be duly retarded." In other words, the boon of freedom—the right to govern oneself—should be granted only to those who had assimilated certain internal controls. For liberals and conservatives alike, work-discipline was both the source and test of internal control, and those who failed to demonstrate that discipline were fit only to be ruled by others. By 1865, few voices disputed that ex-slaves had failed that test. Thus Charles Kingsley, a conservative and friend of Carlyle, explained to a friend a year after Morant Bay that the denial of "congenital differences" between races that Mill and his friends insisted upon was something he had been "cured of . . . by the harsh school of facts. . . . I have seen also, that the differences of race are so great, that certain races, e.g. the Irish Celts, seem quite unfit for self-government, and almost for the self-administration of justice involved in trial by jury."[111]

The fact that Kingsley singled out the Irish rather than the Jamaicans as an example of an unfit race suggests how much this world-view was consistent with the class relations of a maturing capitalism. This booming "age of capital" had, on the one hand, enlarged the social distance between the bourgeoisie and workers and, on the other, accelerated the segmentation of the working class into the deserving "respectables" and a "dangerous" residuum.[112] It may be that this "language of class" provided a vocabulary for thinking about race, or vice versa. It hardly matters; what is important is the symmetry of the discourse, which perhaps intensified the conviction that this vision of the world was just.

Given these terms, then, the large-scale economic failures following emancipation—failures attributed to the blacks' refusal to work—fueled racist thinking and imperialist ambitions. When ex-slaves chose to define the content of their freedom in apparent opposition to market forces, they became *themselves* vulnerable to redefinition; they were a different kind of human being, at least insofar as their suitability for normal political participation and economic self-determination were concerned. These wayward children of the human family were fit subjects for a "beneficent despotism." Projected to the world stage, beneficent despotism became "the white man's burden," the bittersweet fruit of his imperial adventure into the heart of darkness.

Part Four

The Road from Morant Bay

The English of those islands are melting away. That is a fact to which it is idle to try to shut our eyes. Families who have been for generations on the soil are selling their estates everywhere and are going off. Lands once under high cultivation are lapsing into jungle. . . . The white is relatively disappearing, the black is growing; this is the fact with which we have to deal.

JAMES ANTHONY FROUDE, *THE ENGLISH IN THE WEST INDIES* (1888)

The settlement of the labourer on the land has not, as a rule, been viewed with favour in the past by the persons interested in sugar estates. What suited them best was a large supply of labourers, entirely dependent on being able to find work on the estates, and, consequently, subject to their control and willing to work at low rates of wages. But it seems to us that no reform affords so good a prospect for the permanent welfare in the future of the West Indies as the settlement of the labouring population on the land as small peasant proprietors; and in many places this is the only means by which the population can in future be supported.

REPORT OF THE WEST INDIA ROYAL COMMISSION (1897)

The tendency of the time is against peasant proprietorships; it is in everything to concentration, not to separation. . . . It is that peasant proprietors would strengthen the existing system that makes schemes for creating them so popular among certain sections of the propertied classes of Great Britain. This is the ground on which these schemes are largely urged. These small landowners are desired that they may be used as a buffer and bulwark against any questioning of the claims of the larger owners.

HENRY GEORGE, *THE IRISH LAND QUESTION* (1881)

9

Political Economy and Race: Peasants in the Age of Empire

During the last week of December 1885, James Anthony Froude, protégé and biographer of Thomas Carlyle, boarded the West Indian mail steamer at Southampton to begin a trip to the West Indies. Embarking with Alfred Tennyson's "Locksley Hall"—a poem interpreted as bemoaning the moral degeneracy of the British nation—ringing in his ears, Froude framed the coming voyage with the ongoing debate over Britain's empire and racial destiny. Following his recent experiences in South Africa, where he had served as a special emissary for the colonial secretary, Froude expected this journey to provide even more material for challenging prevailing liberal ideas of laissez faire and statecraft.[1] His vision of Britain's leadership role in world affairs bore a strong resemblance to Carlyle's sermons on heroism, projected now onto the national character. His commentaries on the West Indies were punctuated with his political and cultural anxieties over the fate of the British Empire in a world of Gladstonian idealism. The loss of authority at home and of a sense of mission abroad were, he thought, reflected in the Liberal government's misguided policies in South Africa and Ireland as well as in the Caribbean. It is hardly surprising, then, that he saw in the West Indies in general, and in Jamaica in particular, societies in economic and social decay, poised to relapse into a primitive, jungle state, under Haitian-style black-dominated regimes.[2]

Given these preconceptions, Froude began writing his journal on shipboard, his first passages reiterating all the racist dogma that had become ingrained in public discourse following Morant Bay. Like Carlyle, he viewed blacks as primordial, amoral, in a state of nature. Having "escaped the consequences of the Fall . . . [they] must come of another stock after all." They were happy, having no aspirations or ambition and no guilty consciences. "They have food for the picking up. Clothes they need not, and lodging in such a climate need not be elaborate. They have perfect liberty." Carlyle's "Quashee" yet lived.[3]

Once he arrived in the West Indies, however, Froude confronted realities that challenged the Carlylean stereotype of lazy blacks. At first, he repeated pro forma the complaints he heard, current since emancipation, that "the blacks would not work for wages more than three days a week and not regularly even then." But noticing that these same "pale complaining beings" also conceded that the blacks worked their yams and sweet potatoes instead, Froude was soon forced to admit that he "could not see that there was much to complain of. The blacks were only doing as we do. We, too, only work as much as we like or as we must, and we prefer working for ourselves to working for others." Later, becoming clearly impatient with the incessant complaints of his white hosts, Froude declared that the blacks "do not deserve the ill that is spoken of them." When told that his host could hire a black woman to carry a load the twelve miles between his house and Kingston and return again for a mere shilling, it occurred to him that "with such material of labour wisely directed, whites and blacks might live and prosper together; but even the poor negro will not work when he is regarded only as a machine to bring grist to his master's mill."[4]

But Froude could not travel very far down that path without being forced to rethink his entire conservative philosophy. Thus, like Carlyle, he made a sharp right turn, his inchoate critique of capitalist labor relations deflected by racist mystifications. He met blacks in Jamaica in positions of authority, many of them self-made men. Must not it follow, he pondered, that individuals of any race were capable of bettering themselves, that theirs was not an innate or biological inferiority? Despite having conceded so much, he insisted that *as a group* blacks could not be expected to compete with whites: "The gulf which divides the colours is no arbitrary prejudice, but has been opened by the centuries of training and discipline which have given us the start in the race." In another mind such historical explanations for racial inequities might hold out promise for change, but as so often happened with Froude, his a priori racist convictions got the better of the facts before him. It was, he asserted, freedom, not slavery, that ruined blacks; after all, Africans had been free for thousands of years yet still were not civilized. "Generation has followed generation, and the children are as like their fathers as the successive generations of apes."[5]

Having evaded the implications of his direct observation of black economic enterprise and dispossession, Froude went on to declare that the ultimate issue was neither cultural nor economic, but political. "But it is as certain as any future event can be that if we give the negroes as a body the political powers which we claim for ourselves, they will use them only to their own injury. They will slide back into their old condition, and the chance will be gone of lifting them to the level to which we have no right to say that they are incapable of rising." Having come close to conceding the prospect of the race's eventual progress, Froude hastened to make crystal clear exactly what he meant, rendering yet again his gross caricature of Haiti as a land of cannibalism and snake worship. This was a condition to which Jamaican blacks could easily fall prey because their culture and civilization were only skin-deep. "Nature has made us unequal, and Acts of Parliament cannot make us equal. Some must lead and some must follow, and the question is only of degree and kind." The West Indians were a child race, incapable of self-government. Should political freedom be forced upon them, they would be driven back into "the condition of their ancestors, from which the slave trade was the beginning of their emancipation." Blacks had not demonstrated any capacity for civilization except "under European laws, European education, and European authority. . . . and the old African superstitions lie undisturbed at the bottom of their souls. Give them independence, and in a few generations they will peel off such civilisation as they have learnt as easily and as willingly as their coats and trousers."[6] From this it would appear that the day that Britain's tutelage could safely end was far off indeed.

Froude's intense concern about political liberalization in Jamaica was aroused by the current agitation there for reform of the crown colony system inaugurated after Morant Bay, a system justified as saving Jamaica from the perils of a black-dominated democracy by vesting extraordinary powers in the hands of the governor. Froude found support for his views in conversations with a Moravian missionary and an American capitalist, both of whom praised the work ethic of blacks but warned against prematurely giving them political privileges. Indeed Froude made much of the American capitalist's insistence that he would not invest in Jamaica if a black majority were allowed political equality.[7] Froude's elaborate historical argument, therefore, was designed to sever prospective economic reforms from any demands for changes in the island's political arrangements. Some leeway for black independent economic activity could be tolerated—was even necessary perhaps—but power must remain firmly in British hands.

Froude's travel journal was almost like a prologue to the reports of the official travelers who came later. Despite its tortured reasoning, his travelogue articulated connections left unstated, or stated more circumspectly, in many of the official analyses and state papers of that era. He was followed a decade later by a royal commission chaired by Sir Henry Norman, which, by contrast, emphasized the islands' future prospects rather than their imminent decay. Indeed, Norman and his colleagues saw great potential for economic prosperity and social development to be founded on the new peasant-based fruit industry and other heretofore minor cultivations. In their report, therefore, the commissioners broadly endorsed the longstanding demand of Jamaican workers: state support for peasant proprietorships and reforms in land tenure to achieve it. But for all their bold pronouncements on economic reform, the Norman commissioners fell silent on issues of political change.[8] Their confidential memoranda, however, suggested that the latter might have to be sacrificed to the former. If pressed, then, they probably would have responded—much as Henry Taylor had done three decades earlier—that in what modern analysts call plural societies economic progress required "a beneficent despotism." In keeping with the idea of imperial trusteeship, the government might be for the people, but by no means was it of the people. Black economic and moral progress depended on white guidance and control.

Indeed, in many ways the Norman Commission's recommendations merely echoed the rhetoric of a succession of reform-minded Jamaican governors, who, exploiting their unprecedented powers under the crown colony system, launched an impressive public works program and voiced support for peasant agriculture. Much more important to the island's agricultural development, however, were the private initiatives of Jamaican blacks to secure land and establish an economic alternative to the sugar estates. Between Froude's visit in 1886 and that of Norman and his colleagues in 1897, Jamaica had become a peasant society; the number of landowners had increased perhaps as much as 77 percent among a population that had grown only 12 percent. It was a trend that would continue; by the final years of the nineteenth century there were more than 72,000 owners of plots of ten acres or less, suggesting that over half the population lived on peasant-sized freeholds.[9] This infrastructure eventually provided the basis for the takeoff of the fruit industry in the mid-1880s, which in turn made peasant agriculture even more profitable and attracted the Norman Commission's favorable attention in 1897.

Yet, ironically, the commissioners' endorsement came just as the character of that fruit industry was changing. During the 1890s the growth of the peasant-sized freeholds stalled, and the industry that had provided a material basis for increased peasant proprietorship was rapidly falling under the domination of multinational capital.[10] By 1897, peasant proprietors were slipping into a de facto, and in many instances literal, proletarian status. Crucial to the consummation of that transformation, however, was the fact that Jamaican labor had been systematically dispossessed of political defenses. The government had changed its attitude toward Afro-Jamaican peasants, but not its abhorrence of Afro-Jamaican political power. Yet, ultimately, the fate of the peasantry depended on state power.

The racial dogma of Froude and the economic new deal signaled by the Norman Commission delineate an anomalous conjuncture of ideology and policy. Political, economic, and racial ideologies appear to have moved like separate strata of rock, slipping along fault lines of perception and misperceptions of reality. Jamaican peasants, defamed as indolent savages by the racial ideologists at mid-century, were apparently reclaimed as self-interested economic actors by the new imperialists of the late nineteenth century. During an era in which racist ideology was becoming more virulent and practically unchallenged, official policy was grounded paradoxically on the entrepreneurship of black Jamaicans. For example, Joseph Chamberlain and Lord Sydney Olivier, both advocates of Britain's imperial mission, were also among the chief proponents of government intervention on behalf of small landholders. Their simultaneous commitments to empire, racial superiority, and a reconstituted peasantry involved complex revisions of classical liberal belief and practice.[11]

How, then, does one explain, in ideological and/or political terms, this shift to advocacy of peasant proprietorship? The racist ideology articulated at mid-century was based on the presumed incapacity of blacks to be independent economic agents and on their supposed deficit of those innate desires for material improvement that whites possessed, qualities that fueled the progress of civilization. The "Queen's Advice" to Afro-Jamaicans was premised on their need of the social discipline provided by wage labor, even if they had to be coerced into the labor market. Yet, peasant production for export markets was by definition independent economic agency and presumably reflected a desire for material self-improvement. If much of the mid-century racist intellectual apparatus remained in place, then what had changed during the intervening thirty-odd years to make resolution of this apparent ideological and policy paradox possible?

Henry George deduced during his tour of Britain and Ireland in 1879 that conservatives found attractions in government sponsorship of peasant proprietors because it "strengthened the existing system" by deflecting "any questioning of the claims of the larger owners."[12] It does appear that for both Liberal and Conservative politicians the Irish experience played a large role in the transformation of ideology and policy and that the separation of economic from political self-determination was crucial to the resolution of the Irish crisis. In that crisis, too, racism mediated the contradictions between labor and politics. Perhaps, then, the answer to the seeming paradox in Jamaican policy must be sought outside the West Indian context. That policy, like the emancipation scheme earlier, may have been shaped in part by struggles in other, seemingly more distant domains.

The Irish Analogy: New Political Economy, Old Political Order

By the time the Norman Commission filed its report on the West Indies, state-aided creation of peasant proprietorship was accepted by leading elements in both the Conservative and Liberal parties. Although in their correspondence Jamaican governors do not appear to have taken much notice of events in Ireland, it is clear that the crisis there confronted British convictions about economics and social order with their greatest challenge in the late nineteenth century and that the resultant changes in classical liberal ideology and colonial policy was profound. So profound that even those who paid no explicit attention to Ireland were operating within a political world and discourse significantly altered by events there. Notwithstanding the silence of the record, then, those who made policy for the West Indies had to have been influenced by those changes.

In the fall of 1845 a fungus consumed half of Ireland's potato crop, its major food supply. The blight reappeared in each of the succeeding four years, destroying the harvest, triggering a general economic failure and a cataclysmic famine unequaled in modern European history. Between 1849 and 1853, thousands of Irish farmers, unable to pay their rent, were evicted. To escape starvation, hundreds of thousands left their native land for America, while still thousands more stayed to die of hunger and disease, despite private and public relief efforts. Over the decade, between the censuses of 1841 and 1851, the absolute decline in Ireland's population was about 20 percent, but when one considers the famine's impact on natural population growth, the depopulation was even more staggering.[13] Natural disaster alone did not account for this high mortality and emigration, however, as comparisons with the Netherlands and Belgium demonstrate.[14] In accounting for this unprecedented calamity, therefore, contemporary observers generally blamed the Irish agricultural system, even though they managed no consensus in assessing specific faults or recommending solutions.

England's prevailing racist views of the Irish certainly must have complicated their assessments of the cause of the emergency. At mid-century, Irishmen appeared on the pages of leading British newspapers and magazines—the *Times, Punch, Fraser's,* and *Blackwood's*—as indolent, improvident, alcoholic, ignorant, and superstitious. In words and illustrations they took on the features of "insensitive animals." Typical descriptions portrayed them as "brassy, cunning, brutalised," all images confirming their racial degeneration. They were, argued *Punch,* "the missing link between the gorilla and the Negro." Irish violence was an expression not of legitimate grievances but of innate character, insisted the *Times.* Brutish Irish character justified unconstitutional repression of Irish "outrages."[15] These contrasted sharply with images of Englishmen, who, according to *Fraser's,* were a "naturally industrious . . . energetic race, who for the most part comprehend their own interests perfectly, and sedulously pursue them." By contrast, members of the Celtic race were infamous for their "indolence and fickleness." "They will not work if they can exist without it."[16]

Liberals argued that Irish backwardness required an infusion of British capital and a rapid transition to capitalist-commercial agriculture. In their scenario, progressive commercial farmers would preempt the leadership of parasitic landlords, consolidate unproductive smallholdings, and transform backward tenants into wage laborers. For them the famine was a kind of validation of Malthus's theory of overpopulation. Consequently, John Russell's government, which came to power in the midst of the crisis, declined to intervene.

By mid-century, liberal political economy was dominant among British policymakers in both parties, however. Thus even Russell's Tory predecessor, Robert Peel, a recent convert to free trade, had addressed the crisis by sending £100,000 worth of Indian corn for sale in Cork, hoping to depress grain prices. But cheaper corn could not help those on the bottom rung of the agricultural ladder, the cottiers, because they normally functioned outside the market economy, growing their subsistence and paying their rent with labor. Peel's scheme only forced them to raise cash to purchase food by selling off their capital assets, such as pigs and other livestock, thus worsening their plight.[17] After the complete failure of the 1846 potato harvest, a Whitehall minister managing the relief effort was chastised by a local government agent: "You cannot answer the cry of want by a quotation from political economy."[18]

The liberal solution of consolidation and concentration was erroneous as well as callous: it overlooked the fact that land ownership was already more concentrated in Ireland than in England itself. A survey in 1870 found that about a thousand men—mostly British, Anglo-Irish, Protestant, and absentee—owned half of Ireland, with some estates engrossing tens of thousands of acres. Ireland's great landlords, who have been compared with Prussian Junkers, let their estates to middlemen, who sublet in turn to lesser middlemen or tenant farmers, the amount of rent per acre rising as one moved down the tenure ladder.[19] The large commercial farmers hired wage laborers, but the small tenant farmers, who generally worked ten to fifteen acres, relied mostly on family labor. In northern Ireland (Ulster) smallholders of five to ten acres commonly supplemented their farm income with earnings from weaving. In many cases they sublet to cottiers, providing them a loom, in exchange for shares of the cloth, thus giving rise to a semiproletarianized class of part-time weavers. As population pressed on the available land, a growing number of landless householders rented an acre or two to raise a single crop of potatoes or oats, a system called conacre. As in Jamaica, these smallholders and laborers were not isolated from the market but produced market goods as well as their family's subsistence needs.[20]

Given these facts, Irish reformers and political rebels argued a course just opposite that propounded by many liberals. In their view the problem was that the land was already concentrated in the hands of predatory landlords who gouged their tenants with excessive rents and abused them with unfair evictions. Their solution was to confirm and strengthen peasant-based agriculture by granting fixed tenure to the actual cultivators, thereby giving them an incentive to improve their property and increase production. They expressed this goal as the "3 F's"—fair rent, free sale, and fixed tenure—and offered the customs of Ulster as a model.[21]

In Ulster, the tenant, by custom rather than by law, had quasi-proprietary rights to the land. An incoming tenant made a lump-sum payment for "goodwill," often as high as eight to ten pounds per acre, to an outgoing tenant. Though ambiguous and elusive, the custom was said to be "deeply rooted in the Ulster popular consciousness." Irish nationalists justified the practice as an artifact of Ireland's social order before its subjugation to Britain, during which the peasantry had a claim to land held in common with Celtic chiefs. Thus James Fintan Lalor, an early Irish nationalist, argued that the land "belonged to the people, not to individuals." Ulster custom seemed a step toward that ideal because it established a de facto dual proprietorship.[22]

In practice the value of this "tenant right," as it was called, was often determined by open bidding at a public auction, with landlords sometimes setting an upper limit on the price.[23] Nonetheless, the custom was credited for the relatively stable tenures in Ulster, and it correlated with "fair" rents, that is, rates set by agreement rather than competition. Actually, evictions *were* much less frequent in Ulster than in the rest of Ireland, and though rents do not appear to have been any lower there, this probably reflected the prosperity of the diversified Ulster economy. There is some evidence, for example, that proximity to textile areas, where farm tenants could supplement their earnings from weaving, enhanced the value of tenant right. In any event, Ulster was relatively free of agrarian conflict.[24]

By contrast, in most of the rest of Ireland small tenants secured their land on short leases, most of them renewed annually, and they could be evicted upon six months' notice. There were no legal restrictions on rent increases, and the amount was determined by competitive bidding. At mid-century, 83 percent of the population lived in rural areas, and half of them were tenants; depending on agricultural conditions, therefore, the pressure of population could push rents to very high levels. Recent econometric work argues that rent increases were not excessive and that evictions were infrequent and declining during the postfamine decades. But it is clear that rents were *perceived* to be high relative to the tenants' economic circumstances and that the *threat* of eviction was a very real instrument of labor coercion.[25]

British authorities had difficulty assimilating the idea of tenant right or dual proprietorship to their classical liberal notions of absolute property right. Many writers reinterpreted it as merely a right to compensation for the improvements that a retiring tenant had made on his plot. In this way, "goodwill" was made consistent with capitalist property rights; that is, a tenant had a claim on the property only to the extent that he had added to its value. Those sympathetic to Irish reform were more inclined to concede this principle of compensation than the more radical notion of dual proprietorship that was embodied in Ulster custom. But many hardliners, fearing that the landlord's claims would be yielded by indirection, argued that even the right to compensation conceded too much. For much of the 1850s, therefore, the British government's policy was adamantly opposed to any concessions. Prime Minister Palmerston, for example, declaring that he favored "landlord-right," judged tenant right to be landlord wrong and "totally subversive of . . . all social order." Between 1845 and 1867, seven bills designed to allow some form of compensation to Irish tenants were defeated.[26]

The British government moved instead to establish conditions conducive to capitalist agriculture by encouraging greater concentration of holdings, a policy consistent with classical liberalism. During the famine, relief regulations forced owners of small plots to sell their land in order to qualify for assistance. Meanwhile, the Encumbered Estates Acts of 1848 and 1849 (on which similar laws in Jamaica were modeled) were designed to force the sale of an indebted estate upon petition by its creditors. The government's intent was to create a market in land that would attract new British investors, who were expected to reorganize and develop agriculture. Thus all problems would be solved once "a better class" of landlords was in place. But as in Jamaica, actually little British capital was invested; in fact, most purchases were made by local speculators.[27]

After mid-century the notion of peasant proprietorship began to attract more favorable attention, even from respected British political economists. Familiarity with European examples of efficient smallholdings operating under secure tenures—especially in Belgium,

Switzerland, and Prussia—encouraged the belief that smallholdings might actually lead to greater productivity. The most significant conversion was that of John Stuart Mill, whose name was synonymous with liberal political economy. Following his election to Parliament in 1865, Mill became a major political advocate of Irish land reform. In 1868 he published a pamphlet, *England and Ireland*, endorsing much of the program of the Irish radicals, including security of tenure and fair rents, and he argued the Irish case before Parliament in March of that year. Mill's conversion on this issue foreshadowed not only a broader transformation of classical liberalism during the last half of the nineteenth century but the increasing difficulties involved in accommodating that philosophy to the requirements of imperialism.

During the winter of 1846–47, Mill had put aside his work on the *Principles of Political Economy* to write articles on the Irish crisis for the *Morning Chronicle*. Later, Ireland figured prominently in each of the seven editions of *Political Economy*, wherever he discussed property, tenancy, and labor. Mill criticized the government's response to the 1840s crisis severely, arguing that only the massive immigration to America prevented a complete disaster. British authorities had misperceived the real causes of Ireland's agricultural collapse and were too prejudiced and parochial to adopt the correct remedies. The source of Irish distress, according to Mill, was that land was let by competition in a country where the overwhelming majority of people were dependent on agriculture for their subsistence. Consequently, rents rose with population rather than with farm values. The solution to the problem was security of tenure at fair rents, and that could be achieved by establishing the actual cultivators of the soil as the owners of the land—that is, by peasant proprietorship. All Irish land not cultivated by the owner should be let under "a permanent tenure, at an unchangeable rent, fixed by public authority." Mill repudiated those political economists who argued that peasant proprietorship would lead to overpopulation and backward agriculture as "discreditably behind the state of knowledge on the subject."[28]

Mill's embrace of peasant proprietorship involved two radical challenges to classical liberal doctrine. First, he repudiated liberalism's most sacred tenet: the inviolability of property rights. Second, he suggested that principles deduced from the British experience were not universally applicable to peoples of a different cultural and historical experience. Both propositions were heretical to many of Mill's peers. Robert Lowe, Gladstone's Chancellor of the Exchequer and one of Mill's opponents in the 1868 parliamentary debate on this issue, chided him for deserting orthodox political economy, declaring that "there is an oasis in the desert of politics upon which we may safely rest, and that is afforded us by the principles of political economy. . . . I entertain a prejudice, derived from Scotland and adopted by Adam Smith, that a man is at liberty to do what he likes with his own, and that having land, it is not unreasonable that he should be free to let his land to a person of full age upon the terms upon which they shall mutually agree. That I believe to be reason and good political economy." In reply, Mill ridiculed the notion "that a maxim of political economy if good in England must be good in Ireland," adding that "political economy has a great many enemies; but its worst enemies are some of its friends, and I do not know that it has a more dangerous enemy than my right hon. Friend."[29] Notwithstanding his rejoinder, Mill's views did represent a significant reversal of conventional liberal views and they marked out the path of future changes in liberal doctrine and provided the intellectual basis, even if unacknowledged, of future government policy.

The notion of absolute property right in land was merely English "superstition," Mill wrote in an 1848 article. Later he expanded on this theme in *Political Economy*, asserting that "the land of every country, belongs to the people of that country. The individuals called landowners have no right, in morality and justice, to anything but the rent, or compensation for its saleable value." Society, and thus government, has the right to determine the best, mutually beneficial use of the land itself. Land was different from other forms of property: because personal property is solely the product of labor, possessing it does not deprive others from acquiring it; but "whoever owns land, keeps others out of the enjoyment of it. Such privilege, or monopoly, is only defensible as a necessary evil; it becomes an injustice when carried to any point to which the compensating good does not follow it."[30]

In these bold pronouncements Mill appears at times practically to have appropriated James Fintan Lalor's thesis, "property is theft." Yet, in other parts of his text he drew distinctions and offered caveats that set up an interesting tension with his bolder rhetoric. "No man made the land," he wrote in *Political Economy*. "It is the original inheritance of the whole species. Its appropriation is wholly a question of general expediency. When private property in land is not expedient, it is unjust." But what constitutes socially justifiable "expediency"? It is expedient, he replied, to treat real property as indefeasible when the landlord improves that property. Although land is not absolute property, improvements, being the product of labor, are. But since in practice it is difficult to separate the value attributable to nature and that resulting from the investment of labor, and since the time period for realizing that investment can be very long, perhaps even indefinite, it is expedient to recognize the improving landlord's absolute right to the property. Of course, nineteenth-century Irish landlords, by and large, were not "improving" landlords.[31]

Structured this way, the implications of a radical argument were muted by allowing Ireland to be treated as an exception. In *Political Economy*, Mill tends to make the Irish merely the extreme example of the general pattern of landlord behavior. But in his 1868 pamphlet, which was written for British political consumption, he carefully distinguished the Irish from the English. He began his pamphlet with the declaration that land was "a thing which no man made, which exists in limited quantity, which was the original inheritance of all mankind, and which whoever appropriates, keeps others out of its possession." It is just, he went on, that one be able to reap what one sows; it is quite another thing to reap but not sow. This firm principle was followed by the expedient caveat. The usurpation of other people's rights *can* be justified if somehow culturally sanctioned: "It requires to be rooted in the traditions and oldest recollections of the people; the landed families must be identified with the religion of the country, with its nationality, with its ancient rulers, leaders, defenders, teachers, and other objects of gratitude and veneration, or at least of ungrudging obedience." This was the case, or nearly so, in England; it was the opposite in Ireland. Furthermore, the extreme inequality of land distribution made Ireland very different from England. Free contract in land was not applicable in a place where practically the whole population was dependent on the soil.[32]

Even in Ireland, Mill made it quite clear, he did not want to extirpate all the big landlords, nor did he want all the present cottiers to become proprietors. Rather his strategy—not unlike Henry George's suspicions—was aimed at encouraging long-term investment by progressive capitalist farmers, while placating unrest by giving a measure of justice to small tenants and cottiers. In the 1865 edition of *Political Economy*, Mill cited statistical evidence that cottier tenancy had declined and applauded the increased numbers of small capitalist farmers and landlords who cultivated their own estates. For this change he credited the Encumbered Estates Acts, which had brought in new investors, and the repeal of the Corn Laws, which had encouraged the shift from farming to grazing.[33]

In many ways, then, Mill was merely fine-tuning classical principles rather than abandoning them. Individual self-interest, cultivated through private property, was still the mainspring of his political economy. By guaranteeing individuals the fruits of their "labor and abstinence," society encouraged their best efforts and ensured innovation and progress. By putting land in the hands of the actual producers rather than a parasitical class of owners, agricultural progress was encouraged. Thus peasant proprietorship was made consistent with liberalism's first principle.

Drawing out the contrast between peasant owners and Irish cottiers made this consistency clearer. As long as rents were determined by competition, Mill argued, the cottier's livelihood would be determined not by his own efforts but by the extrinsic force of population increase; that is, competition made him bid for land at rents he could not possibly pay. Given excessive rents, the produce of extra exertion would be taken by the landlord. "Almost alone amongst mankind the cottier is in this condition, that he can scarcely be either better or worse off by any act of his own." His industry redounded entirely to the landlord's benefit; his indolence was solely at the landlord's expense. All he received was subsistence either way. "A situation more devoid of motives to either labour or self-command, imagination itself cannot conceive. The inducements of free human beings are taken away, and those of a slave not substituted. He has nothing to hope, and nothing to fear, except being dispossessed of his holding, and against this he protects himself by the *ultima ratio* of a defensive civil war."[34]

Other aspects of Mill's radical revision of liberal theory involved another kind of Irish "exceptionalism." In Mill's view, British cultural presumptuousness was a large part of the problem. His countrymen arrogantly applied their own institutions and solutions—such as absolute property in land—to Irish problems, but Ireland was quite different "in the whole constitution of its social economy." Indeed, Mill had been motivated to write *Political Economy,* he explained to Auguste Comte, because he recognized the cultural biases of existing English political economy. Economists had a simplistic view of human nature and hence of human motivation. Treating human behavior as if governed solely by market forces had ceased to be merely a convenient analytical abstraction, Mill recognized; it was now a misleading fiction.[35]

Contrary to the uninformed opinion of many British observers, argued Mill, by tradition Irish land was held in common rather than as private property. The appropriate model for Ireland, therefore, was India, not England. The Indian ryot, or peasant, was not regarded as a tenant at will, or even by lease, and his rent was set by custom rather than by competition. The British East India Company, by wisely choosing to reinforce the traditional system when it established its hegemony over the country, offered an example of Englishmen "shaking off insular prejudices" and adapting their administration to the culture they found. Moreover, India offered a useful model for developing a new Irish policy because the Hindu and Irish characters, as well as their traditional agricultural systems, were similar. "What has been done for India has now to be done for Ireland."[36]

The notion that Ireland and India were comparable did not go unchallenged by Mill's contemporaries. Historians as well as contemporaries have argued with good cause that an Irish tradition of communal ownership of land was a myth.[37] Similarly the proprietary rights of Indian ryots might also be questioned. In any event, the accuracy of this comparison is of less interest for this discussion than the use to which it was put in the argument for reform. Mill's main point was that Indian rent was set by custom rather than by competition and that the ryot had security of tenure.[38] In these two respects, he thought it offered an instructive solution for the Irish case.[39] The ancient Irish tradition invoked here may have been a myth, but it was a convenient myth. Convenient to Irish rebels seeking to establish a distinctly Irish nationality, and now convenient to reformers seeking a way out of the Irish imbroglio without establishing dangerous precedents for England itself. It is in this sense that the notion of Indian exceptionalism helped legitimize an exception for Ireland.

The way exceptionalism crept into Mill's argument may suggest something about how it functioned. Although many of the basic theoretical tenets for Mill's argument had been introduced as early as 1848, his unqualified acceptance of peasant proprietorship and his most radical case for Irish exceptionalism does not appear until his 1868 pamphlet. Despite the radical tenor of his theory, the policy recommendations in Mill's earlier works had been fairly tame: until 1852 the main recommendation was to settle peasant cultivators on reclaimed wastelands in western Ireland, thereby relieving competition for rents. In fact, Mill initially had rejected both fixity of tenure and compensation for improvements.[40] In 1868, however, he abandoned his earlier reforms, such as wasteland reclamation, because the situation now required revolutionary measures. This appears less an ideological conversion than a political one; Mill's basic ideas had not changed, but the political situation had.

Mill's arguments did not win over British public opinion, and apparently he never expected them to. His intent, he explained to his protégé J. E. Cairnes, was to shift the debate left of center by staking out a radical position, thereby making other progressive solutions appear more moderate.[41] Whatever the merits or truth of that stratagem, Mill's arguments did develop the major points that eventually made peasant proprietorship more palatable. His qualification of the notion of absolute property right and advocacy of state intervention cleared the way for even broader reinterpretations of liberal principles in the late nineteenth century.[42] Like Mill, the "advanced liberals" never pressed to its limit their modification of liberal doctrine. If culture and history shaped other peoples' economic behavior, then did it not follow that English capitalism was also just a phase of history and capitalist behavior the cultural artifact of a historical moment?

Mill was no racist, but variants of his argument for Irish exceptionalism might provide racist thinkers a way of evading the inherent contradictions in liberal democratic thought. A philosophy that pictured society as an aggregation of innately self-seeking individuals had difficulty accounting for the influence of communal values and the impact of culture and history on human thought and behavior. To the extent that racial differences could be invoked to explain deviations from expected behavior, no adjustments in basic propositions were required.[43] For racist ideologues the blacks' cultural differences were cause to cast them into outer darkness, as exceptions to humankind. For liberals like Mill, those same differences could be invoked to make them objects of special treatment. In both cases, their "otherness" meant that basic premises about human nature and behavior, as applied to Europeans, need not be reexamined.

Of course, many practicing politicians underwent no ideological conversion at all. For some of them, perhaps, the notion of granting economic concessions in order to forestall political demands was the most germane element in the proposed reforms for Ireland and the colonies. But this was the other string in Mill's bow, too. By 1868, ancient Irish economic grievances, long ignored, had given birth to Fenian uprisings in Ireland, England, and America, as well as to the demand for Irish independence. Mill not only strongly opposed Irish independence but felt that even limited home rule posed grave security dangers for Britain. On the other hand, Britain could not continue to rule Ireland against the will of the majority of the Irish people. That course being closed by both principle and expediency, the only one open was to decouple Irish economic grievances from Irish nationalism.[44] With the government's political and economic policies at an impasse, coercion proving ineffective, unrest rising, and increasingly militant Irish-American support, many other leaders had come by 1868 to share Mill's fear of a linkage between land reform and Irish nationalism.[45] The Irish problem seemed to require a bold new policy initiative, and the new Liberal party leader and prime minister, William Gladstone, was prepared to take it.

Although Gladstone entered office intent on shoring up his right flank—the landed element of the Liberal party, who distrusted him—he also felt the need for some radical initiative to solve the Irish question, which he was convinced threatened repercussions throughout the empire if left untended. Once he awakened to the depth of the malady in Ireland, Gladstone used his considerable national charisma to push through Parliament the Landlord and Tenant (Ireland) Act of 1870, which overturned, theoretically at least, prevailing ideas about property rights and government intervention and set a crucial precedent for its five successors passed between 1881 and 1903.[46]

Gladstone's conversion to Irish land reform was guided by George Campbell, a Scottish liberal of the Mill school and formerly a senior member of the Bengal civil service, who had toured Ireland in 1869 and published several pamphlets on the subject of land tenure. Campbell saw Ireland through the eyes of his Indian experience, and much like Mill, he developed in his pamphlets the idea of a conflict between two systems of property law, one based on contract and the other on custom. He described Irish "fixity of tenure" favorably, as the "crystallization by government of practices which were integral to the fabric of native society."[47] Reading Campbell's argument, Gladstone was impressed by the notion that property rights could be grounded in custom rather than law and soon became convinced that such customs should be given the sanction of law. This view he shared with his Cabinet as they considered his proposed land legislation in December 1869. The Irishman, he argued, might have history on his side in claiming that "without at all questioning the landlord's title, he too had by the old customs of the country his share in a tribal property which however rude in adjustment gave a right to him and his race to remain upon the soil." Although it was not now possible to reestablish those ancient rights, "the moral of it was a just, beneficial and humane idea to the substantial aim of which, if in altered form, it seems . . . time to give some measure of effect."[48]

The importance of the Indian example, then, was not that it served as a direct precedent for Ireland but that it helped prepare sympathetic British policymakers to recognize the significance of culture and nationality in economic behavior and thus the limits to the application of British liberal principles. Although Gladstone was moved most by the idea of "restitution" for historic wrongs suffered by the Irish at British hands and sought to rectify this with Ulster tenant rights, he, like Mill, did not want to destroy the Irish landlords. On the contrary, he hoped that reform would preserve their social leadership. Consequently, his own fears of too radical a departure from the status quo combined with the conservatism of his Whiggish Cabinet to produce a bill that merely legalized Ulster custom *where it existed*, mainly Ulster, and provided "compensation for improvements" in the rest of Ireland.[49]

In Parliament, many Liberal backbenchers were said to have come to the bill's support only after convincing themselves that it protected and reaffirmed property rights in general by punishing specific abuses of those rights by overbearing Irish landlords.[50] Others advocated the Irish exceptionalism argument in a different form. Whig-Liberal magnates in and out of the Cabinet feared that Irish legislation could be a precedent for Britain. There was already evidence that Irish laws could arouse demands for similar legislation in England; thus, failing to act quickly to stem the rising tide of agrarian radicalism in Ireland risked having it spill over at home.[51] In other words, landlord rights in one part of the United Kingdom must be sacrificed to preserve them in another. Indeed, the appeal of the government's proposals to many, such as landed magnate Lord de Grey, was that they were based on "the special state of things in Ireland, and . . . are not applicable to England."[52]

Even Robert Lowe, a conservative leader in the Cabinet, conceded at one point much of Mill's argument by declaring, according to one historian, that "the unsuitability of free contract to Irish conditions" was a reason "for interfering drastically with property," a concession Gladstone gleefully reminded him of in later debates. But in the floor debate Lowe defended the bill as a purely pragmatic measure "to save society from rushing down toward destruction; to give to property the security it is fast losing."[53] It was, then, legislation in the best Whig tradition, radical departures toward conservative ends.

The 1870 law is significant, therefore, more because it marks the initial breach in the liberal commitment to absolute property right than as an effective measure for land reform. One of its historians has summed it up as "in principle . . . a measure of great moment" but in practice "a monumental irrelevance."[54] The law's land purchase mechanism proved ineffective because the installments toward the sale price exceeded prevailing rents. Although it did not significantly increase the number of peasant proprietors through state-sponsored transfers, it might be argued that the law did legalize a form of dual proprietorship and made evictions more difficult because it imposed a de facto rent control. Consequently, when agricultural prices fell during the ensuing world depression, landlords became more favorably disposed to selling off their land, a process not unlike that operative during the same period among Jamaican sugar estates overrun by squatters. With the principle of peasant proprietorship established, however, this initial act was followed by five others in the 1880s and 1890s that devised increasingly efficient and simplified systems for land purchases by smallholders.

England, meanwhile, did not escape the pressure for land reform as conservatives had hoped. The issue, originally raised by the Chartists in the 1840s, was revived in Joseph Chamberlain's "Radical Programme," published in 1885. Chamberlain insisted that property ought to pay "ransom" to the community, his assumption being that "the land had originally belonged to the community and passed into private hands by force or fraud." The state was entitled to redistribute property for the commonweal, and so-called laws of political economy, when used to prevent the state from redressing these wrongs, were merely "the selfish cant of power and wealth." Chamberlain's friend Jesse Collings advocated expropriation or compulsory purchase for the purpose of creating smallholdings, a program that came to be labeled "three acres and a cow."[55]

Chamberlain never convinced his colleagues within the Liberal party to embrace his radical program. Apparently, what was good for Ireland was not necessarily suited for Britain. Instead, it was the Conservatives who embraced his radical agenda, their acquiescence to both Irish and English reforms being born of political need. By 1885, in a dramatic departure from the strategy of using economic reform to keep political reform at bay, Gladstone was prepared to grant Ireland home rule, as well as more extensive land reform. On this issue his Liberal party rival, Joseph Chamberlain, led a revolt, collecting into his splinter Liberal Unionist party many others who were committed to preserving the integrity of the empire. And by 1895, through Chamberlain, the Liberal Unionists brought their progressive social programs into the Conservative party. Adamantly opposed to Irish home rule, Chamberlain and the Conservatives pressed land reform as a way to lance the boil of Irish grievances.[56]

Consequently, during the 1880s and 1890s, four of the five laws

promoting Irish peasant proprietorships and state-aided land purchase schemes were initiated by Tory governments. Similarly, between 1887 and 1892, Conservatives were responsible for three of
the allotment schemes designed to increase English smallholdings.[57]
Their motive in the latter instance was to cement small landowners to
conservative principles, and to the Conservative party. After the British franchise was extended to county householders in the 1880s, Conservatives had adopted the idea of expanded property ownership as
a way of attaching the new working-class voters to themselves.[58]

Under Chamberlain's leadership the government's colonial policy
folded this newfound commitment to peasant proprietorship into the
older doctrine of imperial consolidation and expansion. Chamberlain
wanted "closer union," through trade and economic ties, with the
self-governing colonies and direct economic intervention in the crown
colonies. The latter colonies were like "undeveloped estates," he told
a cheering Parliament shortly after assuming office in 1895, and the
home government must lend them imperial assistance. "It appears to
me to be absurd," he added, "to apply to savage countries the same
rules which we apply to civilised portions of the United Kingdom."
Here Chamberlain consciously laid the basis for a departure from strict
free trade and laissez faire, but his language also echoed a more ancient tradition, when the colonies had been called "plantations" and
the Crown had ruled over them like a landlord. What this language
suggested was that for the colonies, the corollary of satisfying economic grievances at the expense of political demands was the renunciation of political self-rule in return for economic assistance.[59]

It is against this background that the spectacle of a Conservative
administration sending to the West Indies in 1896 a royal commission
that was prepared to endorse peasant proprietorship makes sense.
Moreover, it was the newly minted Conservative—erstwhile radical—Colonial Secretary, Joseph Chamberlain, who endorsed their report and made it the basis of official policy in 1897. The specific precipi-
tant of Chamberlain's action was the marketing crisis cane producers
confronted because of competition with state-subsidized beet sugar
growers. Not only were West Indian planters hurt by the plunge in
sugar prices—to less than ten shillings per hundredweight by
1897—but so was the social fabric of many colonial societies that were
dependent on sugar exports for the bulk or a substantial portion of
their public revenues.[60]

The commissioners, Sir Henry Norman, Sir David Barbour, and
Lord Edward Grey, each had Indian experience and/or familiarity with

the evolution of Irish policy. They probably found little in the Jamaican scene that would not have been evident twenty years earlier, but they looked upon that scene with new eyes, and with the benefit of the Irish-Indian analogy. Norman had been governor of Jamaica from 1883 to 1887, but he had spent most of his professional life in India. He had gone there at age sixteen to join his father, a businessman in Calcutta, and served for several years as a soldier in the Bengal army. Barbour, an economist, also had Indian experience, having gone there in 1862, fresh from his studies at Queens University, Ireland. He had held several posts in Punjab, Madras, and Bengal before serving as the chief financial advisor to the governor. Grey, the scion of a Whig magnate, overcame his preference for bird watching on his country estate to serve in several Liberal administrations, including Gladstone's last. Unlike Gladstone, however, he was a firm proponent of defending the empire. In 1899 he would be numbered among the Liberal imperialists who supported the Boer War.[61] Clearly these were not young radicals. Nonetheless, their previous experience—which very probably included the government's policy debates about peasant proprietorship in India and Ireland—together with their observations on the scene, prepared them to rethink colonial policy.

Sydney Olivier, the influential secretary to the Norman Commission, also underwent a change as a result of this mission. Olivier had entered the Colonial Office in the spring of 1882, bringing to his new job high academic honors and strong socialist views. Coming from a well-to-do family and exhibiting what George Bernard Shaw described as the "air of being a Spanish grandee," Olivier came to his socialism via Auguste Comte. But along with Shaw and his Colonial Office colleague Sidney Webb, he became active as a youth in London's radical politics, discovering Henry George, promoting land reform, and joining the Fabian Society in the early 1880s.[62]

It was very likely English socialist politics that prepared the ground for the relatively radical economic views on West Indian conditions that Olivier became identified with in later years, but he insisted that it was what he saw of West Indian realities that caused the transformation. "When I was a young man peasant proprietorship was thought the greatest fallacy in the world," he declared some years later, "but when I went out to the West Indies I saw that the people wanted land, and that it would be put to much better use."[63]

Olivier had opportunity to observe the weaknesses of sugar-based economies even before he witnessed the peasant-based alternative in Jamaica. "This place seems wealthy and prosperous," he wrote his

Lord Sydney Olivier

wife Margaret from Trinidad during one of the earliest stops on the commission's itinerary, "but the prosperity may collapse any day, as many of the big sugar works cannot keep on under present conditions. I think we shall have to clear away the plantation system. It hinders development, and though sugar is the most valuable crop these places can produce and its failure means a great scarcity of employment and wages, it is rather too dangerous a crop under present circumstances for one to wish to see it remain in perpetuity to provide these recurrent crises; especially since for the negro and coolie to develop at all they must come out of the plantation system and become small owners and cultivators for themselves."[64]

In Jamaica, Olivier and the commissioners were even more powerfully impressed with King Sugar's fall, finding that it made up only 18 percent of that island's total exports compared with 75 percent in the rest of the British West Indies and up to 95 percent in British Guiana, Barbados, Antigua, St. Kitts, and Nevis. Clearly Jamaica's future did not lie with the sugar industry. Jamaica was only the most obvious example of a general conclusion, however. Reporting for the commission in a confidential memorandum, Olivier wrote that "so far as the negro and negroid population of these Colonies is concerned the estate system of sugar production is either unworkable or oppressive and conduces to retrogression rather than to progress." The government's policy, therefore, should be only to assist in affecting a transition, "to break its fall."[65]

Although their published report expressed optimism for the sugar industry's prospects and recommended state support, these appear to have been merely a sop to the planter class to assuage their anticipated opposition to proposals to help the peasantry. "If we go to them bringing nothing in our hand," Olivier warned his colleagues in his confidential memorandum, "and simply say: you are going to be ruined, in part for the benefit of Great Britain, and we want you to give up your political constitutions and your land in order that the process of extinguishing you may be hastened, and your present command of your labor supply destroyed, we cannot expect to be met with cordiality."[66]

At the Colonial Office Joseph Chamberlain welcomed the commission's recommendations and sent a circular letter to governors of the West Indian islands urging them to encourage small landholdings through the purchase of private lands. He emphasized the need for these plots to be near roads and ports, and in continuous rather than scattered settlements. Perhaps to assuage planter opposition, he urged the governors to discourage squatting and insisted that his policy could be "pursued with due regard to the maintenance of the sugar industry, and in such a manner as not to withdraw from estates those who are under contract to work upon them." As this latter cautionary caveat suggests, unlike Olivier, Chamberlain and his staff did not interpret support for peasant proprietorship as meaning abandonment of the big sugar estates.[67]

Colonial land policies, then, were affected by Irish developments in at least two major ways. First, the mid-century liberal dogmas about absolute property rights and against state intervention were weakened, so that official rhetoric shifted toward support for small proprietorships long before land programs were initiated in Jamaica. Second, the specific legal and programmatic mechanisms for facilitating land sales in small allotments were tested, refined, and thereby made available for use elsewhere; consequently, it is not surprising that the basic features of the first land purchase schemes, implemented by Jamaican Governor Henry Blake in 1895, closely paralleled those devised for Ireland. Olivier complimented Blake years later as "the most valuable and progressive Governor that Jamaica has had during my acquaintance with her affairs, and the most truly appreciative, for his time, of the essential requirements of a public 'development' policy"; and, significantly, he credited Blake's insights to the fact that he was "an Irishman, born and bred in a country of small farmers and peasant cultivators."[68]

"A Beneficent Despotism": Race, Labor, and Jamaican Politics

Irish land reform not only cleared an ideological space and provided programmatic precedents for Jamaica, it also prefigured the motivations for and limitations of Jamaican developments. Although there was no nationalist insurgency in Jamaica approaching in extent or intensity that in Ireland in the late nineteenth century, and thus no need for economic concessions to deflect demands for greater political self-determination, Jamaican demands for and Colonial Office resistance to an expanded franchise and greater home rule persisted and even escalated between the 1880s and the 1920s. No linkage was articulated between a more progressive economic policy and a reactionary politics as clearly as with Ireland, but the strong analogy between these British possessions suggests the likelihood of similar motivations at work. Also, as in Ireland, the changes in Jamaican official rhetoric were seldom matched by the actual performance of its initial programs of land reform. Paradoxically, the most dramatic growth of peasant proprietors preceded the government's land programs, and their increase actually slowed after those programs were in place.

Under the crown colony system, the governor and state bureaucracy had gained what an American official on the scene called "despotic" powers. Ostensibly, the 1866 constitution was intended to preserve the political and economic power of the sugar planters, but in practice it had become something more complex than a mere instrument for class rule. Although Afro-Jamaicans were virtually eliminated as a political force, a succession of liberal, activist governors, most of them with prior service in India, initiated basic policy changes with respect to the peasantry. Olivier was fond of attributing their progressive policies to their exposure to Indian land tenure systems, but one might add as well that they also had been schooled in the Raj tradition of "enlightened autocracy."

The first of these governors, Sir John Peter Grant, came to Jamaica after thirty-four years in the Indian civil service, where he had earned commendations for his handling of land and labor problems. Arriving in 1867 convinced that the land issue had been at the bottom of the recent Morant Bay Rebellion, Grant quickly pushed through laws designed to ensure security of property ownership and to facilitate land transfers.[69] A Survey of Lands Department was set up to determine titles, maintain adequate records of abandoned grants, and settle unclaimed or illegally claimed property. One of the law's main effects, however, was to evict squatters. Grant is credited with making efforts to compensate such squatters for improvements that they had made on the land, and in some cases he allowed them to retain land at a rent charge calculated on its value. He also urged that squatters who had been long-term and unquestioned residents of a plot be given opportunities to buy it.[70] Grant's effort to establish legal machinery for the recovery of forfeited lands, however, appears to have become a dead letter until resuscitated by later governments to make grants to railways.[71]

For all these reforms, however, Grant was an autocratic ruler, who still "accepted the Estate and Planting system as necessarily the paramount interest of the community."[72] In the interests of that constituency he revived public-supported indentured Indian immigration, to pay for which he increased taxes dramatically. His fiscal policies intensified the regressive character of the island's tax system, a feature that became entrenched for the better part of the next century. From 1867 into the 1930s, the Jamaican government would draw three-fourths of its revenue from customs duties, primarily on food and fees. Meanwhile, the taxes on exports declined by more than 14 percent between 1867 and 1881, while the public debt rose 61 percent to pay for immigration expenses and railway bonds incurred almost entirely for the benefit of the planters.[73]

Sir Anthony Musgrave, governor of Jamaica from 1877 to 1882, further illustrates how great was the gap between official rhetoric and performance respecting the settler class. Reading a paper before the

Colonial Institute in London in 1880, Musgrave publicly disputed the importance of sugar to the island's prosperity, arguing that "the great mass of consumers who furnish the revenue, raised almost entirely by duties on imports and excise, are not labourers on sugar estates" but small settlers and peasants. Afro-Jamaicans were entitled to equal justice, insisted Musgrave, and the Jamaican elite must get over "the notion that any one class of men is bound to work for another class, unless it be to their interest that they should so work."[74] For all these brave words in support of black enterprise, however, nowhere in his official correspondence did Musgrave urge any specific imperial support for developing the Jamaican infrastructure or assisting small settlers, through land acquisitions, development of the roads, or technical assistance.[75] Peasant proprietors were now acknowledged as the backbone of the economy and mainstay of the public revenues, but the state was not prepared to expend public funds for their direct economic benefit.[76]

In fact, a program for land resettlement was not inaugurated until 1895, two years before the Norman Commission arrived. Governor Henry Blake secured legislation providing for the sale of Crown lands to applicants in lots of five to fifty acres at two pounds per acre, upon deposit of one-fifth of the purchase price plus two pounds for the survey. Once the purchaser had planted one-fifth of this acreage in a permanent crop, he would be forgiven one-fifth of the purchase money.[77] Following the Norman Commission's endorsement of the concept of peasant proprietorship, other schemes were enacted to provide advice and technical support to small producers.

Government purchase schemes had little direct impact on the growth of peasant cultivation and landownership, however. Despite its rhetoric, the government's policy favored concentration of land into large holdings; most of that sold under government auspices before 1900 went to planters and other elite purchasers. The Crown land available after 1895 under Blake's program tended to be of limited quantity, of poor quality, and inaccessible.[78] Meanwhile, peasant landholding grew phenomenally after Morant Bay and did not slow appreciably before the 1890s. Peasant marketing networks expanded, but their success owed little to the sputtering government road building efforts. Overall, the tax money collected from peasant freeholders and workers exceeded by far any expenditure for their benefit.[79] As we shall see below, the predominant factor in both the growth and the subsequent decline in peasant freeholds was not public efforts on their behalf but the parallel development of the fruit industry.

Veront Satchell's impressively detailed examination of *private* land transactions between 1866 and 1900 reveals a vital and vibrant land market in which 2.5 million acres of Jamaican soil changed hands. Although the bulk of this acreage was bought and sold in large lots by planters and other elites, the overwhelming majority of the acquisitions were by small settlers, and most of the purchases were under ten acres. The main theme of Satchell's story is that Jamaican peasants never controlled the majority of the arable land sold on the island during this period, but it is equally clear that an impressively large number of Jamaicans did manage for a generation to prosper outside the domain of the estates or dependency on wage labor.[80]

As in earlier years, peasant proprietors made the bulk of their purchases from planters, who were often forced by economic difficulties to sell portions and sometimes all of their estates. Such sales reached their peak during the 1870s, slowed in the 1880s, and practically stopped altogether in the 1890s. The decline involved marked shifts in the character of transfers, all of which suggest that most of the land sold was going to agrarian capitalists investing in the booming fruit trade. Whole estates or pens were sold rather than parcels, and mainly to buyers who were planters, merchants, professionals, or institutions, rather than small settlers. The pattern of transaction among the settler class, on the other hand, suggests increased fragmentation of holdings and a growing shortage of land relative to population. During the final decade of the century, small landholders were purchasing *from* each other and selling *to* merchants and institutions, often under pressure of defaulted mortgages and public seizures.[81]

Satchell convincingly demonstrates that these shifts in land concentration are important factors for any discussion of land inequality and the eventual proletarianization of rural Jamaica, but his data also demonstrate the continued vitality and expansion of the peasant sector through the 1880s.[82] Although other actors—planters, merchants, and other elites—were coming increasingly to dominate the land market and to engross larger and larger shares of Jamaica's arable land, peasants held their own until the 1890s, which ironically was precisely the moment that the British and Jamaican governments rhetorically embraced the promotion of small proprietorships as official policy. By the late 1890s, however, the government's minuscule, even lackluster effort was much like a finger in a dike holding back a capitalist flood. In the end, the apparent transformation reflected in the Norman Commission's report would prove fragile when buffeted by multinational capital and undermined by a now unquestioned racist ideology.

Racist ideology and the politics it produced explain much of the anomalous contradiction between the rhetoric and performance of the peasantry's "new deal." Although the government purported to act on behalf of the small settlers, ordinary peasants and workers had little or no voice in determining the state's policies. As a consequence, a racist discourse reminiscent of Carlyle's or Froude's and a social policy (as opposed to an economic one) familiar to Darling or Eyre was manifest even under ostensibly progressive governors. The American consul was shocked, for example, by the conditions of the penal system. "The prisons and penitentiaries of this island are conducted on the ideas prevailing fifty years ago—the treadmill, the stocks, and the whipping triangle being in full swing."[83] Much as the colonial officers had done in the early 1860s, staffers now devoted most of their time trying to regulate, but not abolish, corporal punishment. In grappling with such issues, both Jamaican officials and colonial officers divulged racial views that were little different from those expressed by Carlyle in the 1840s or Froude in the 1880s. In a confidential assessment presented in May 1897, Sir H. Hocking, a fifteen-year resident of Jamaica, explained the problem of praedial larceny wholly by the "fact" that blacks were a degraded race: "It must be remembered that the negro stands very low in the scale of humanity. The present black population are only a very few generations removed from wild cannibal savages." For its part, the Colonial Office merely praised Hocking's memo as "a valuable minute."[84]

The conviction that democratic government could not function in a racially mixed society continued to dominate official thinking for at least three decades more. The restrictive franchise established after Morant Bay was not modified until 1884, at which time Governor Norman made some concessions to increased local representation on the Legislative Council and an expanded franchise but adamantly opposed further democratic reforms.[85] As might be expected, the reforms that Norman did allow had little impact on increasing black political participation.[86] Electors had to be men of substantial property, qualifying by virtue of literacy, homeownership, and payment of at least one pound in property taxes. If not a homeowner, a prospective voter had to have paid thirty shillings in direct taxes on personal property.[87] The subsequent registration enrolled 98 Indians, 1,001 Europeans, 2,578 mulattoes, and 3,766 "African" voters, but this was less than half the 15,000 people (out of a total population of 580,804) the new law had been expected to enfranchise. Of course, even this limited enfranchisement suggests the potential for black political dominance even under crown colony rule. Indeed, Froude reports a widespread popular belief that the reforms conceded during Norman's tenure were merely a prelude to a future democratic, completely representative government in Jamaica.[88]

In the elections immediately following these reforms, however, not only were no Afro-Jamaicans elected to the new Legislative Council but all the councilmen were either planters or merchants, and only five were even natives of Jamaica. As in the pre-1866 era, high financial requirements for officeholders limited election contests to a small elite. Occasionally, during periods of crisis, a few politicians might appeal to the masses of black voters for support, mobilizing them around issues such as low wages, the harsh penal system, and the unequal allocation of public revenues. But as in the 1884 elections, as well as most that followed over the next several decades, not only were spokesmen for the people scarce but a majority of the legislative seats were not even contested.[89]

Consequently, the politics of the small settler class were likely to be directed into nonpartisan, nonelectoral channels. There were numerous public protests over the disproportionate tax burden that small landholders shouldered, although they were usually focused on the more visible, direct taxes on land and houses rather than on the less visible but more substantial levies on imported food, domestically consumed rum, and various licenses and fees.[90] In contrast with the early 1840s, however, the Colonial Office was much less sympathetic to such protests. In 1888, for example, Governor Norman attempted to reduce taxes on food imports by instituting an increased though regressive scale of taxes on land; it was disapproved at the Colonial Office.[91]

Their political emasculation and the indifference, even hostility, of the Colonial Office eventually proved the fatal flaw in the settlers' efforts to protect their hard-won economic gains. Stimulated by the fruit trade in the 1890s, agrarian capitalists reasserted themselves, snapping up the best and most arable land or bidding up land prices beyond the reach of small-scale purchasers. Heavily taxed small proprietors lost their land to mortgagees and to official seizures. The minuscule allotments of public land, usually undeveloped and often of poor quality, could not stem the receding tide of peasant freeholds. Thousands of Jamaicans, landless or reduced to landlessness, migrated to Panama and Central America, searching, as the Irish had a half-century earlier, for wages and a haven from callous treatment.

The success of peasant proprietorship, then, was as vulnerable as it was spectacular. It had been achieved, after all, in a society where the sugar industry was scarcely a shadow of its former self. There was, as Musgrave recognized in 1880, scarcely any viable alternative at the time; or, as the Norman Commissioners conceded in 1897, a peasant-based economy was "the only means by which the population can in future be supported." But the concessions made under a benign despotism could as easily be reversed under other circumstances, when there was an alternative, when initiatives from below could be more easily blunted, and when the appropriate congruence between the political, economic, and social orders could be more easily maintained.

Orange Grove . . . [is an] integrated societ[y] in which kinship plays an important role, whereas Sugartown is not so much a social entity as a conglomerate of disparate sections, held together only by a common involvement with the sugar estate. . . . Yet if I have been successful in the picture I have tried to draw of Sugartown it should be clear that in its diversity there was potential strength.

EDITH CLARKE, *MY MOTHER WHO FATHERED ME* **(1957)**

10

The Making of the Jamaican Working Class

Orange Grove and Sugartown were the names given to two of three Jamaican villages studied by anthropologist Edith Clarke shortly after World War II. Cradled in a fertile valley in the island's interior, Orange Grove was a community of small farmers enjoying a comfortable and stable living growing oranges for American and British markets. Clarke's description of one of its households, the Wrights', is reminiscent of the imagery conjured by special magistrate Richard Chamberlain in his advice to the freed people of St. Thomas-in-the-East on Emancipation Day, 1838. The Wright family, a legally married mother and father and their six children, lived together in a two-story house. They rose early each morning to share a family breakfast of coffee, eggs, and bread and butter or sometimes salt fish, ackee, and avocado. After breakfast the younger children went to school, the older boys assisted their father with the farm work, and the mother and older daughter tended house and prepared the substantial midday meal, which again the whole family gathered to share. There was always meat for this meal—beef, mutton, or chicken—along with yams, cocos, rice, and other vegetables. Once the father arrived home in the evening, the family gathered again for supper, which consisted of "home-made cake or biscuits, bread and butter and hot mint tea." Mr. Wright spent a generous portion of his leisure time playing with, admonishing, and teaching his children.[1]

The home life of a typical, but unnamed, Sugartown family presented a depressing contrast to that of the comfortable Wrights. Formerly a settlement of subsistence farmers from the postemancipation era, then a fruit-growing district, and now once again the site of a sugar factory, Sugartown was a fragmented community of migrant and resident workers, the former housed in estate barracks, the latter in one- or two-room huts, each of which was "little more than a dormitory." The town's population rose and fell with the sugar-growing seasons as migrant workers flooded in seeking work and out again once jobs grew scarce. The rhythm and ambience of a typical resident household contrasted sharply with the Wrights'. If lucky enough to be employed, the father went off early to the mill, having washed down bread, or an occasional cornmeal dumpling, with bush tea. He took his noon meal from vendors at work and returned late in the evening to a supper of bread and bush tea or cocoa. Meat was a rare item in this family's diet. Equally rare was time for the father to have a meaningful presence in his children's lives, for meals, conversation, or instruction.[2]

With these vignettes Clarke attempted to situate the polar extremes of Afro-Jamaican lives in the mid-twentieth century, but for most Jamaicans the realities were more varied and complex. For every family of Wrights, there were hundreds more in the hills struggling as their ancestors had to sustain an independent livelihood from small plots of family or rented land, growing, raising, and marketing root crops, fruits, and small animals. At sugar harvesting season they might send a father or son to the estates to cut and haul cane. For many such households, however, men were a transitory presence. Families were held together by women like Mother Brown, who, first with her mother and then with her daughter, cultivated a small plot of yams, potatoes, and cassava and raised goats, fowls, and pigs. Born on the eve of the Morant Bay Rebellion, in the 1970s Mother Brown was still working the family land inherited from her maternal grandfather.[3] For every permanent resident of a sugar town, moreover, there were thousands more crowding into the shantytowns of Kingston and other urban centers, working the docks, serving the middle and upper classes, or just "scuffling" to survive.

However overdrawn or unrepresentative the contrast Clarke depicts, it does reflect nonetheless a fundamental transformation in Jamaican economic and social life between the mid-nineteenth and twentieth centuries. The Wright family and Mother Brown's were, in their different ways, heirs to the victors in the struggles of freed people after emancipation to build an alternative economy to the sugar and coffee estates. Their ancestors had found in peasant crops such as bananas, coconuts, and oranges profitable export staples that reshaped the Jamaican economy in the late nineteenth century. But the resident workers in sugar towns and in the new bauxite plants and the casual laborers on Kingston's docks or in its yards and homes were casualties of those same struggles. By the mid-twentieth century they found the avenues to an independent livelihood increasingly closed. Bananas and coconuts were no longer export crops open to small producers, and sugar was once again king, drawing into its realm an increasingly proletarianized labor force of unionized resident employees and urban pools of casual workers.

And yet, as Clarke intuited, there was a paradoxical rebirth even in this defeat, as new social forces were unleashed by the transformation of labor relations. She observed anomie and deprivation at Sugartown, but she also gained appreciation for "the richness of personality and the reservoir of energy," the "intense vitality and opportunity," "a quickening of ideas, . . . and a crystallization of views on national as well as local problems—land, housing, labour, education, politics, religion, race, colour, class." She observed workers energetically debating these vital issues of the day "on streetcorners, in shops and taverns, in yards and in the canefields as men nested in the shade to eat their lunch."[4] By the time Clarke undertook her field studies a vast economic transformation, within the island and beyond its borders, had produced a Jamaican proletariat. Before exploring the political implications of that change, however, we must first examine its structural features and historical roots.

The Banana Trade and the Rise and Fall of the Peasantry

Between the year of the Morant Bay Rebellion in 1865 and the turn of the century, Jamaica's export trade shifted dramatically in direction and content as the growth of the fruit trade transformed the island economically by giving unprecedented prominence to peasant cultivation. Implicated in this revolution, too, was the eventual completion of a process that the sugar industry had been unable as yet to accomplish—the proletarianization of Jamaican labor. Ironically, then, while the fruit trade provided the basis for a dramatic expansion of the peasant population in the 1870s and 1880s, it eventually undercut the economic independence that that population cherished.

In 1865, Jamaica sold 79 percent of its exports to the United Kingdom and bought 61 percent of its imports there; by contrast, the United States received only 8 percent of Jamaica's exports and sold 26 percent of her imports there in 1865. Most of these goods arrived in British vessels, however, suggesting continued British dominance of shipping and tonnage.[5] By the early 1880s the beginnings of a dramatic shift in the trade balance between Jamaica, Britain, and the United States was discernible. The British share of Jamaican trade imports declined from 54 percent to 46 percent between 1876 and 1881, while U.S. imports grew from 29 percent to 39 percent.[6]

The bulk of this shift was accounted for by the dramatic growth of the fruit trade, both in absolute value and relative to other crops. The value of the fruit trade increased more than 700-fold between the Morant Bay Rebellion and the turn of the century, from a little over $300,000 per year to well over $2 million. In 1865, traditional crops—sugar, rum, coffee—accounted altogether for more than two-thirds of the island's export earnings, mostly from Britain, while non-plantation crops—fruit, pimento, ginger—accounted for only one-eighth. By the end of the century, however, fruit had become the single most important export (41.4 percent of the total value in 1898–99), and the United States, the most important trading partner in both exports and imports (59.1 percent and 45.1 percent, respectively).[7] By 1903, fruit made up 56 percent of the island's exports; bananas alone accounted for half the total, their value having increased 2.5 times since 1898. Sugar and rum, meanwhile, accounted for less than one-seventh of the island's production and were worth just one-quarter the value of bananas.

Bananas became the dominant export crop only after problems involved with their cultivation and shipping were resolved. In fact, during the early stages of the development of the fruit trade, other products were equally if not much more important. Between 1877 and 1882 the combined export of oranges, coconuts, limes, and pineapples exceeded the banana export crop; in fact, the value of oranges shipped from Kingston alone was almost twice that of bananas and probably equaled the export of bananas islandwide.[8] Originally introduced to the Caribbean by the Spanish in 1516 and brought to Jamaica from Santo Domingo, the banana plant is of the lily family and requires fertile soil with vegetable mold and good rainfall and drainage.[9] It does not do well on the red earths of limestone mountains or in dry areas such as in Vere, St. Elizabeth, Westmoreland, or the northern base of the mountains of St. James and lower Trelawny. Although it does do well in St. Catherine, in the interior of St. James, and in the Great River Valley, the plant was cultivated most successfully in the eastern parishes, St. Mary, St. Thomas-in-the-East, and especially in the rich black soils of Portland.[10] Superior port facilities in these three parishes also facilitated the rapid communications, loading, and embarkation that were important to the trade. In fact, by the twentieth century, Portland's Port Antonio had gained an overwhelming preeminence in the banana trade, clearing ninety-two ships for every twenty from other ports.[11]

Bananas and plantains had long been a staple in the peasant diet, and during the early days of the trade, production still remained in the hands of thousands of peasant growers, who supplied 80 percent of bananas exported to the United States; most of that production came from holdings of fewer than ten acres. In 1883–84 there were 2,880 such smallholdings in Portland alone, constituting 91 percent of the freeholds in that parish. During the last thirty years of the nineteenth century, Port Antonio's banana trade reached one-quarter of the island's total, increasing almost 26-fold during the first decade, 1870–80, 198 percent during the second, and another 260 percent between 1890 and 1900. A little sleepy town of 1,305 in 1880, the port was transformed with new wharfs, new roads and bridges, and a 37 percent increase in population.[12] The surge of depositors and savings in its government savings bank suggests both the impact of the fruit trade on the town and the role of the peasant class in the trade. The number of bank depositors and their total savings increased from 238 with £5,000 in 1880 to 778 with £10,155 in 1889, representing a 100 percent increase in the value of the deposits and better than 200 percent in depositors. Much of that growth came from small depositors, which suggests a more prosperous peasant class.[13]

The shift from exclusively domestic production to an export crop is credited by tradition to a number of enterprising Jamaican and American traders who began to speculate on shipping bananas to the United States during the late 1860s and early 1870s. They procured fruit from peasant producers, who brought it down from the hills, one stem at a time on their heads, to the seaports or to light boats plying the coast. Bananas, which sold for six pence per bunch on the local market, fetched about a shilling per bunch in 1871; by 1875 the price had doubled again.[14]

However, the key to the story of how bananas became Jamaica's dominant export crop for almost half a century and how the peasants who originated this crop soon lost their economic independence as a result lies in the development of a virtual monopoly by the United Fruit Company. The story of United Fruit begins with Captain Lorenzo D. Baker, whose original company, Boston Fruit, laid the basis for the formation of that multinational. Baker, owner of a Cape Cod fishing fleet, first visited Jamaica in 1872; by 1886, he was shipping 42 percent of Jamaica's bananas. A driven, moralistic man who did not drink, smoke, or swear, Baker formed his shipping company primarily of family and close friends from the Cape Cod area of Massachusetts. He saw his work in Jamaica as a divine, evangelical mission, his "wealth . . . only an indication from God that he was succeeding in the work to which he had been called." He moved to Jamaica permanently in 1881 and, except for occasional business trips back to the United States, remained there until his death in 1908. Baker also settled his family on the island, and many of his sons were involved, directly or indirectly, in the fruit trade. For example, the appointment of Lorenzo D. Baker, Jr., as U.S. consular agent at Port Morant in 1885 apparently gave the family important advantages over their competitors in arranging shipments.[15]

During the 1880s and 1890s Baker's company passed through a succession of organizational stages that eventually produced the multinational holding company United Fruit. In 1884 he formed the Boston Fruit Company in partnership with Jesse Freeman, who handled the marketing end of the business in the United States, while Baker oversaw production and purchasing in Jamaica. In 1888, on Baker's initiative, the Boston Fruit Company was reorganized as a limited partnership; and after Freeman died in January 1890, it was incorporated, with Baker as president. Andrew W. Preston, the company's marketing agent for New Orleans and the midwestern United States, became managing director of the Boston division, while Baker managed the tropical division. Over time Baker lost much of his control in the company to Preston; thus it was under Preston's guidance that the Boston Fruit Company affiliated with Minor Cooper Keith's banana-producing interests in Central America and eventually merged in 1899 to form the conglomerate United Fruit.[16]

Nonetheless, the groundwork for the eventual corporate control of banana production and monopoly control of the trade lay in Baker's

Lorenzo D. Baker

activities in the two decades preceding United Fruit's creation. Some of the reasons for Baker's success have to do with technical problems involved in raising and marketing bananas. The banana is not a tree but a herbaceous plant that can grow to over twenty feet and matures in thirteen to sixteen months, producing a single bunch of fruit on each plant. When the stem reaches maturity, the supporting stalk dies and a new one grows from underground runners, repeating the whole process. Once cut, the fruit immediately begins to ripen, a process that, depending on the temperature, takes no more than three weeks before the fruit is overripe and cannot be sold. Canning and preserving are not feasible, although there was a small market for a dried fruit called banana figs. Careful handling is necessary to avoid bruises, which show up as black marks on the fruit.[17] The keys to successful banana trading, therefore, were careful control of selection and handling and rapid shipment to market. In the era before refrigerated ships, the technology and organization of purchasing and shipping were crucial to the entire process, and here Baker outdid his competitors.

By the end of the 1880s Baker was shipping his bananas exclusively in steamships, an advantage he secured initially by cultivating a close relationship with the Atlas Steamship Company, a British-owned company headquartered at Liverpool that had obtained a contract in 1872 to carry mails twice each month from Jamaica to New York. By 1880 the company was also receiving an annual Jamaican government subsidy to reserve four hundred tons of its cargo space for fruit.[18] Shortly after his move to Jamaica, Baker became the agent for Atlas in Port Antonio and Morant Bay. He attended to the company's administrative duties and supervised the loading and unloading operations of its steamers. But more important than his 5 percent commission on all freight shipped via Atlas steamers, Baker had an option to ship bananas to New York on a "space available" basis at reduced rates. In practice he obtained the best space for his own fruit, leading his Kingston competitors to complain that he was monopolizing Atlas space and squeezing them out. By the end of the 1880s, however, when the relationship with Atlas had become much less advantageous, Baker turned to other shippers and eventually leased or bought his own British-made steamers.[19]

A mail steamer was not the most appropriate vessel for the booming fruit trade. As the American consul in Kingston pointed out, "While the company [Atlas] performs its obligations in regard to time, it cannot be said that it pays very much attention to the interests of the shippers of perishable commodities which form the greater part of their cargo each voyage." There were complaints of poor ventilation on the steamers, the arbitrariness of their agents and employees in general, and the damage done to fruit by other cargo. It was not unusual, for example, for a steamer to arrive with a large cargo of sugar and molasses, the steam from the latter having destroyed the fruit carried in the "between decks."[20] By the late 1890s, therefore, successful participation in the fruit trade required a fleet of specially designed and ventilated vessels. Superior shipping arrangements gave Baker's company a competitive advantage and eventually a virtual monopoly over the carrying trade, which, in turn, helped him establish control over production as well. The gradual extension of corporate control over the production of bananas led eventually to control of the entire trade by multinational capital.

The process of securing monopoly began at the point of sale; it was achieved once the buyer, rather than the sellers, dictated the price. But in order to dictate price, the buyer needed to control alternative sources of supply, either by securing other vendors or by producing fruit himself. The bananas' vulnerability to the Caribbean's frequent hurricanes led Baker in the late 1880s to seek other sources of supply in case there was a shortfall in Jamaica. The most important alternative sources were in Central America, especially Costa Rica.[21]

Between 1882 and 1888, however, Baker took steps to establish direct control over the production process by acquiring several major sugar properties in northeastern Jamaica and converting them to banana plantations. His objective was to supply five hundred bunches from his own properties in order to complete a cargo, thus securing further insurance against shortfalls in supply but at the same time improving his bargaining position with peasant producers. In the early 1890s, Baker spent about three hundred thousand dollars to purchase more plantations.[22] As a result of these activities, a significant portion of the shipments of Boston Fruit and its successor, United, always consisted of bananas produced from their own estates. By 1936 United Fruit's own estates produced one-seventh to one-sixth of the Jamaican fruit that the company handled.[23]

On properties he owned or leased Baker also maintained tenants, to whom in some cases he apparently made advanced commitments at the beginning of a growing season to purchase their produce. On one such estate, Bound Brook, he actually received more in rents than from the bananas grown. Indeed, one result of the increased demand by estates for property suitable for bananas was that buying or renting their own plots became more difficult for peasant growers. By the 1890s land rental rates in Portland soared to twenty to twenty-four shillings per acre per year, driving many peasant producers to become tenants to Baker or some other estate owner.[24]

Baker also tried to encourage the Jamaican sugar planters to shed their prejudice against growing bananas—the "backwoods nigger business," they called it. Although traditional planters were generally slow to shift to fruit production, fourteen of St. Thomas's eighteen sugar estates had converted by 1899.[25] At about the same time, many defunct sugar estates in the Rio Cobre delta around Spanish Town began growing bananas on irrigated lands. The American consul reported that between 1895 and 1897, two thousand acres had been planted in fruit in that area, quadrupling the value of land.[26] The transition to estate production of bananas is perhaps nowhere better illustrated than by the fact that the 2,745 East Indian laborers brought into Jamaica between 1899 and 1906 were intended to raise fruit rather than sugar.[27]

Of course, it was crucial to Baker's efforts at dictating prices to the producers that he control or eliminate competition among buyers. In the early 1880s there were so many fruit traders that it was impossible for any one to dominate the industry, and thus local producers had the advantage of a seller's market.[28] By the end of the decade, however, Baker had forced most of his competitors out of business by a calculated manipulation of the prices paid for fruit. In 1889, for example, he gave the following instructions to his son Loren regarding the purchase of fruit: "The price of fruit is varying in nearly every port. You must find out as near as possible what Atlas or James is paying and put on about ten shillings more to the small people and about 10 percent more to the plantations than what you pay the small people."[29] Most small traders were driven to the wall by such tactics, and by August 1889 even Baker's biggest rivals, the Atlas Company and Arthur James, were selling their fruit to Boston Fruit Company.[30]

By the 1890s, therefore, Baker controlled all Jamaican fruit going to the U.S. market, leaving the undeveloped European market as the only vulnerable flank of his monopolistic scheme. In 1896 some Jamaicans had experimented with shipping bananas to England in refrigerated storage, earning endorsement from the Norman Commission, which urged government assistance. Acting upon the commission's report, Colonial Secretary Joseph Chamberlain encouraged the managing director of Elders, Dempster, and Company, Sir Alfred Jones, who had established a successful fruit trade between England and the Canary Islands, to organize a similar trade between Jamaica and England. With a ten-year guaranteed annual subsidy, Jones set up the Imperial Direct Line of banana steamers in 1901 and formed a fruit and shipping company, Elders & Fyffes.[31]

Jones sent out Englishmen to buy fruit, but unfortunately they were not knowledgeable about either fruit or Jamaican trading conditions. His contract called for the delivery of twenty thousand bunches of bananas each fortnight, but this proved insufficient to support the line. Meanwhile, United Fruit diverted bananas that were contracted to the Jones Company by the tried-and-true method of selectively offering higher prices, drawing protests from Jamaican officials. The Colonial Office hesitated to intervene, however, thinking that United Fruit's investment would be good for the colony and noting that negotiations with Elders, Dempster that might resolve the matter amicably were under way. But the terms of the "amicable" resolution compelled Elders & Fyffes to buy its fruit from United in order to fill its ships. In 1900 the U.S. consul reported from Jamaica that the new direct steamer to England was in service but that "strange as it may seem," they had appointed United Fruit as their agent in buying fruit.[32]

Within fourteen years United Fruit had gained complete control of

Elders & Fyffes. In 1902 the American company purchased 45 percent of Elders & Fyffes's shares. When the 1903 hurricane exacerbated the problem of supplies in Jamaica, United Fruit diverted ships to its plantations in Costa Rica, thereby gaining even greater control over supplies and, with it, greater advantage over its junior partner in the Jamaican trade. In February 1904, Elders & Fyffes's capital was increased to £350,000, and United Fruit was given 50 percent. In August 1913 the capital was increased again to £1 million, but now United Fruit held 100 percent of that stock. In 1929, by special resolution, Elders & Fyffes was converted to a private company.[33]

After gaining control of Elders & Fyffes, United Fruit was then able to put pressure on the parent company, Elders, Dempster, and Company, and its subsidiary, the Imperial Direct Line, by cutting freight rates for the shipment of fruit. Finally, Jones and his associates in the Direct Line cut their losses and abandoned the company. The Elders, Dempster, Direct Line ceased to serve Jamaica; its ship *Port Kingston* was renamed *Tahiti*, and it eventually sank unobtrusively in the Pacific, carrying a load of mutton from New Zealand. Elders & Fyffes developed a fine fleet of fruit steamers, but they now carried *United's* fruit to England, principally from Costa Rica and Colombia rather than Jamaica. By 1914, with United now controlling supplies, the total value of Jamaican fruit sent to England was still only one-tenth that sent to U.S. markets.[34]

The effective monopoly control that United Fruit enjoyed not only depressed the prices that producers received but affected other aspects of their operations as well. Although growers had contracts with the company, the actual price that they received for their fruit depended upon its quality as judged by the buyers. Thus it could be "downgraded" in price or rejected outright upon delivery, leaving the grower with no redress. The small growers had to take whatever price the current supply-demand situation dictated, which, in absence of buyer competition, was always the bare minimum. Growers became even more dependent as fruit became the only viable cash crop available to them. As Sydney Olivier described it, "Only those actually acquainted with the manner in which bananas are purchased can appreciate how easily the buyer can convert a contract promising attractive prices into an unprofitable arrangement for the growers by means of heavy rejections and down-grading." Under these conditions, deprived of autonomy in the production process and of the ability to bargain over prices, peasant producers were more like wage workers paid at a piece rate than independent contractors.[35]

The earlier practices of Captain Baker, before the company's monopoly was secured, illustrate how the relation between peasant vendors and corporate procurers evolved. Baker insisted that his agents bargain hard with the peasant producers and, by requiring them to transport the fruit to the shipping points, contrived to have them share the risks as well. "You need not make any extra exertion for bananas," he instructed his son Loren. "Tell the people if they wish to sell their fruit they must bring it down."[36] He insisted that his agents buy only top-quality fruit, especially for the winter market, refusing unacceptable products even when rejection incurred ill-feeling among suppliers. "Never mind what people say," he wrote his son, "throw it back on their barrels, let them suffer for it if they will not mind you."[37] As United's monopoly control grew, therefore, peasant growers came to resemble even more the household production workers of England's prefactory textile industry. By the early twentieth century, then, the Jamaican banana trade was controlled from production to marketing by one multinational corporation, rendering the formerly independent peasant cultivators a virtual proletariat.

During the interwar years, one final effort was made to wrest control from United Fruit, motivated more by nationalistic sentiments and Jamaican local politics than by any principled objection to monopoly power per se. In 1925 a Jamaican government-appointed delegation convinced the Imperial Economic Committee meeting in London to strongly support the establishment of a cooperative of small fruit growers. The Jamaican government made an annual grant of twelve hundred pounds for a two-year period to assist in the organization of the cooperative.[38] In order to assist the cooperative in securing fruit, the Jamaican government passed a stringent new law to protect contracts for banana deliveries by imposing fines for violations. To finance the purchase of steamers, the secretary of state for the colonies arranged to guarantee debentures of the Jamaica Banana Producers' Association (JBPA), clearing the way for a loan of fifty thousand pounds from the recently established Colonial Development Fund.

All the while, however, United Fruit launched strong propaganda campaigns against the new organization in both England and Jamaica, threatening at one point, through *their* English company Elders & Fyffes, to withdraw from development plans on Africa's Gold Coast if the producers' cooperative was supported by the British government.[39] But despite their opposition, the JBPA began operations on 1 April 1929 and delivered over 4 million stems, or 2.6 million count bunches, of bananas from its 7,694 members the very first year. In

1932 its 11,628 contractors produced about 32 percent of the bananas shipped from the island. In sharp contrast with United Fruit, most of the JBPA's contractors farmed peasant-sized holdings (see fig. 10.1 and table 10.1).[40]

Although the new association had a salutary effect on the price of bananas, which rose as a result of its competition with United, there were problems with its organizational structure and operations. At its annual meetings, votes were allotted to members according to the number of bananas they had delivered the previous year, one vote for the first hundred counts and one for every additional two hundred counts. Furthermore, a cooperative normally pays its members after marketing the produce, but this was impractical in the case of bananas produced by small growers and shipped to a foreign market. Thus a system was adopted to pay two shillings upon receipt of deliveries and the balance at the end of the year, depending on the actual prices received in the British market. As a result, the JBPA remained vulnerable to the tactics, pioneered by Baker and continued by United Fruit, of manipulating prices in order to drive out competition. The legislation that had been passed to ensure the sanctity of contracts for deliveries failed to keep association contractors from selling their fruit to

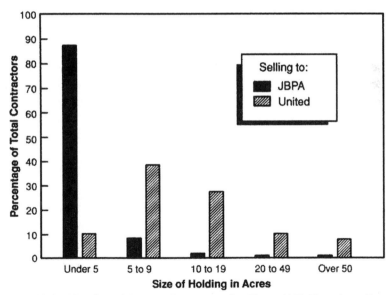

Figure 10.1. Number of Banana Contractors by Class, 1935. Data from *Report of the Jamaica Banana Commission*, 8.

Table 10.1. Acreage of Banana Contractors by Class, 1935

	JBPA		United	
Contractors	Acres	% of Total	Acres	% of Total
Under 5	21,657	43.6	700	1.3
5–9	6,924	13.9	7,336	13.9
10–19	3,522	7.1	8,263	15.7
20–49	4,776	9.6	10,021	19.0
Over 50	12,819	25.8	26,311	50.0
Total	49,698	100.0	52,631	100.0

Source: Report of the Jamaica Banana Commission, 8.

United. Many small growers had friends or relatives who were contracted to other companies and thus were easily able to sell "over the fence."[41]

The most intense competition for the JBPA came in 1933, when its production fell to 10 million stems (from 24 million the previous year), although it managed to hold its own on prices paid during this period. The situation became critical, however, after devastating hurricanes in 1934 and 1935 caused further shortages of fruit. Many small growers at that time succumbed to the higher prices being offered by United Fruit in its effort to divert bananas scheduled for delivery to the JBPA. Since the JBPA did not have adequate capital liquidity to take on the increased overhead resulting from the smaller consignments, its final dividends were reduced and its loyal members suffered as a result. There were other problems that undercut the loyalty of the JBPA members as well. In 1935 the American market for fruit collapsed, and as a result the final dividends were again much lower than had been anticipated. Consequently, the association's growers had been overpaid and had to return the difference. As one might expect, this was "disruptive of loyal support" that the JBPA had been receiving from its contractors previously.[42]

Unlike the United Fruit Company, the JBPA was not simply a buyer of fruit but also represented its members in many other areas of their business, including assisting them in getting loans for their operations after the hurricanes of the mid-1930s. Unfortunately, the JBPA also had to be involved in collecting these loans, during a period when the contractors found it difficult to repay them. Moreover, because the unregistered titles to land made small producers poor risks for commercial lenders, wholesale produce dealers had extensive involvements in loans to their producers.[43] After 1935, arrangements were made for a Banana Board to make loans to fruit growers of fifty or more acres, while local banks were supposed to service smaller producers. Although a sum of twenty-five thousand pounds was allotted by the government for both groups, banks in many districts did not want to handle loans to small growers. The Banana Board lent money on crops, on which it took a lien, and arranged to collect the loan payments from the pay of those under contract to the fruit companies. The amounts collected ranged upwards from 20 percent of the total value of their fruit. As a result, many contractors avoided the deductions of their debt payments by selling their fruit to companies with whom they did not have contracts. The chief beneficiary of such defections was United Fruit.[44]

All these problems shook the loyalty of many of the JBPA members and fueled predictions that many more of them would desert to United Fruit in 1936, when their contracts were due to expire. Surprising everyone, however, 87 percent of the association's contractors renewed their contracts.[45] This vote of confidence from its members came too late, however, to extricate the JBPA from its financial difficulties, because by the final months of 1935 the brunt of the crisis was upon it. In that year the combined forces of United Fruit's corporate power and an increasingly unsympathetic government forced the small producers' virtual capitulation.

With the collapse of the American fruit market in 1935, financial pressures on the JBPA increased, exacerbated by United Fruit tactics. The fact was that the JBPA could no longer match the prices offered by United Fruit. A. C. Barnes, the Jamaican secretary of agriculture, described the difficulties that the association confronted in trying to compete with the multinational. Lacking working capital, the JBPA deducted two pence per count bunch from the prices it paid its members in order to accumulate reserves, a practice members did not understand and resented, according to Barnes. The association was also handicapped by the fact that it dealt with sixteen thousand different contractors, while the United Fruit Company only had one-tenth as many, since it declined to make contracts with small growers, preferring to buy from them at the pier. United had a larger volume of business, especially given its properties in Central America, from which it could get fruit for as low as one shilling, three pence, per count bunch (about thirty cents) compared with one shilling, six pence, for Jamaican fruit. By combining bananas from both sources, it could sustain larger supplies and lower prices than its competitors. Furthermore, the cost of United Fruit's own estate produce was only ten and one-half pence per count bunch, and these made up one-sixth to one-seventh of the total Jamaican fruit it handled. All of these factors brought down the total cost of the fruit that United purchased. Owning no estates, the JBPA had no counters to these advantages. The multinational's extensive operations permitted it to divert cargoes, and its many sources allowed it to maintain a continuous supply despite adverse local conditions in Jamaica.[46]

Its strong hold on the English market prompted charges that United Fruit manipulated that market to hold prices down. "I understand that their regular customers are not permitted to sell bananas supplied from any other source," declared Barnes, "and that inspectors frequently visit retail shops to see that requirements are being complied with." Barnes went on to point out that for both United Fruit and the JBPA, the incomes of their agents were based on the amounts of fruit collected. Consequently, United Fruit's claim that it did not want JBPA fruit was not credible because the agent's interests would clearly be to maximize the number of his suppliers from any source. More money could go to growers if this system were changed, Barnes argued, because at present, producers were often left with considerable amounts of rejected fruit.[47]

In December 1935 the JBPA applied to the Jamaican government for direct intervention and financial assistance to save the cooperative. Reporting that its purchases had fallen off 11 percent, the association sought direct financial support and temporary relief from the interest payments on debts it had incurred to buy ships. These measures, the association argued, would allow it to offer competitive prices to its contractors. For the long term, it sought to renegotiate the terms of the competition through a legislatively mandated quota for each of the three major fruit buyers based on their existing shares of the market.[48]

United Fruit's counterproposal was that it would permit the JBPA to survive if it abandoned its marketing activities in the United Kingdom and sold its ships at their current valuation to United's subsidiary, Elders & Fyffes. Henceforth, the JBPA would merely collect the fruit of its members and sell it to United for marketing in the United Kingdom, the same kind of "amicable resolution" United had made earlier with its competitors for the American market. United Fruit continued to deny any interest in achieving a complete monopoly of Jamaican fruit, while simultaneously insinuating to government officials that it could easily achieve such monopoly any time it wished. It had looked upon the JBPA as a governmental concern, according to United's Jamaican representative, and "consequently had never taken steps such as they might have taken with an ordinary competitor, to drive them out of the market."[49] In conversation with Jamaican officials, United's officials betrayed the real crux of their objection to the JBPA: a successful cooperative movement represented an alien and potentially threatening principle of business organization that might undermine their vast interests in Central America.[50]

The ideological biases of the bureaucracy in Jamaica and Britain favored the arguments of United Fruit, and the predominantly peasant membership of the JBPA had little political leverage with which to command a fair hearing for its position. Periodic protests during the late nineteenth and early twentieth centuries had brought modifications but not fundamental changes in the crown colony system; the Colonial Office, acting through the governor, still retained fiscal control and a veto over any legislation considered of "paramount" importance to the Crown.[51] A suggestion for an expanded franchise and a more representative legislature was met with the disingenuous claim that the interests of the Afro-Jamaican masses were already represented by the colonial government itself.[52] Another suggestion for a minor modification in the procedures for selecting members of Jamaica's Executive Committee elicited a response reminiscent of Darling or Eyre during the previous century. "Responsible government is out of the question in Jamaica as elsewhere," declared a Colonial Office official. "The essence of Representative Government is that the Crown freely selects its officers, and the people control them by the legislative power. There is no halfway house. All over the world we are faced with attempts to get irresponsible ministers thrust on the Crown, and if we establish a precedent in Jamaica, it may do immense harm elsewhere."[53] Responding to increasing political agitation throughout the West Indies during the 1920s, therefore, the Colonial Office sought to tighten rather than relax its grip. By 1926 the case for crown colony rule had been raised to the level of fundamental philosophical doctrine, defended as the source of efficiency, public faith, and good government on the island.[54]

Although there were increasing numbers of nonwhites on the legislative councils of various West Indian governments, few were spokesmen for the popular majority, and given the structure of government, none could effectively represent the working class.[55] Indeed, one reason the Colonial Office opposed political reform so obstinately was the racial division in the colonies, or more accurately, the perceived need to protect whites from blacks.[56] For example, efforts to promote cooperation and closer union among West Indian colonies through political federation were rebuffed by the Colonial Office staff on the ground that federation might "encourage agitation everywhere in favour of more popular—i.e., coloured—control over finances & everything else."[57]

Consequently, the small settler class faced the fruit marketing crisis of the late Depression years without political representation or ideological support in either Whitehall or King's House. Only the potential for popular unrest should it openly abandon the JBPA caused the government to moderate its favoritism toward United. Therefore, though neither the governor nor the Legislative Council was favorably disposed toward the JBPA, they were reluctant to act against it because of its broad popular support in the Jamaican countryside. In August 1935, Governor Edward Denham, who had been in office little more than a year before the crisis broke, praised United Fruit's contribution to the Jamaican economy and discounted charges that it wanted to establish a monopoly there. At that time he defined the government's interest in the survival of the producers' cooperative primarily in terms of its unpaid government loans.[58]

Denham did express some interest in seeing the cooperative principle succeed but declared that the JBPA was not a true cooperative because its members were bound by contract and their roles in the organization depended upon the level of produce delivered.[59] In October, Denham seemed disposed to let events take their natural course, writing the Colonial Office: "I am not at all sure that masterly inactivity is not the only possible solution. But of course I want to do something definite." In his message to the Legislative Council a few days later, the governor confirmed his support of cooperative movements in general, while indirectly criticizing the operations of the JBPA.[60]

According to Secretary of Agriculture Barnes, the elected members of the Legislative Council were all supporters of United Fruit and would vote according to its dictates. Nevertheless, in December the council did give a positive response to the JBPA petition, granting a moratorium on its debt payments until 1 January and approving a guarantee of ten thousand pounds to the association. According to the governor, however, this was done despite the council's opposition to the JBPA, because it was not politic "to oppose financial aid if it goes to growers."[61]

At the Colonial Office, sentiment favored keeping the JBPA afloat until a special investigating commission could report its recommendations. But the records of its private deliberations make clear its bias favoring the position of United Fruit. Here, too, the alleged monopolistic designs of United Fruit were discounted. For example, G. L. M. Ransom reported favorably on a conversation with Keiffer, the company's Jamaican representative, who "told me, and I do not doubt that it is true," that his company actually preferred "a modicum of local competition" in order to determine prices. "A monopolist is always in danger, especially under modern conditions, when governments take so large an interest in economic matters, of being shot at when prices dissatisfy the growers (and what grower is ever satisfied?)." United's "real" objective was to limit the association's intrusion into the marketing phase of the business, he observed. The JBPA's inefficiencies and bad management could bring discredit on the whole trade, either by selling bad fruit or selling "it at any price so as to avoid it going bad on [its] hands" and thereby undermining "the whole price structure." Ransom agreed that the JBPA had been badly managed "and I expect they have upset the business."[62]

Others at the Colonial Office argued that monopolies could play a positive role in some situations, and the Jamaican fruit trade appeared to be one such situation. "Unscrupulous selfishness" tends to succeed where it is more efficient or best adapted to the character of the industry concerned, argued Sidney Caine in a confidential minute in November 1935. "There does, undoubtedly, seem to be something about the banana industry which favors monopoly." United Fruit could not have established nor sustained a monopoly "without the assistance of the natural conditions of the trade. It is, therefore, arguable that the proper ultimate solution is not conflict with the United Fruit Company but alliance with it on terms which will adequately secure [the] interests of Jamaican producers."[63]

In contrast, Jamaican authorities and colonial officers accepted the argument that the JBPA was not a *true* cooperative, implying that its failure to maintain the contractual commitments of its members was somehow proof of this. The association's problems were seen to be caused primarily by its own poor business practices; most important, they suspected, was the fact that something about Jamaican social conditions militated against successful economic cooperation. The main sources of these suspicions were racist evaluations of the capacities of the Jamaican peasants. "The Jamaican small-holder is unfitted both by his temperament and by his degree of education to be a cooperator," asserted Ransom. "He has only the shadowiest ideas even of the nature of a contract, let alone the nature of cooperation." This assertion was followed in the record by a note penned by the colonial secretary approving it as a "useful critique."[64]

Established to recommend solutions to the JBPA crisis, the Banana Commission merely confirmed basic conclusions already reached at the Colonial Office. However, the imprimatur of its distinguished members—W. Gavin of Imperial Chemical Industries, E. Furnival Jones, a chartered accountant and partner in Allen Charlesworth and Company, and J. H. Garwin, minister of agriculture and fisheries—may have been sought to deflect the potential political repercussions of decisions already taken.[65] Defining a true cooperative as "a union of persons and not capital," the commission confirmed the widely held view that the JBPA was not a *real* cooperative anyway. It also absolved United Fruit of charges that it had sought to monopolize the British market. The secular trend in fruit prices in the United Kingdom showed otherwise, and in principle it was not possible to manipulate the prices of perishable goods. The JBPA's problems were caused by its insufficient working capital and the consequent need to deduct money from sales in order to accumulate capital and to pay the interest on its loans, the commissioners argued. This, in turn, reduced the returns to its contractors (by as much as 3 and one-half pence per count bunch) and thus its ability to compete with United Fruit.[66] Suffice it to say, they concluded, that the JBPA's cooperative principle of business organization was an inherent disadvantage in its competition with United.

The commissioners were very pessimistic about the ability of cooperatives of any kind to compete against the vast resources of a multinational corporation, declaring in their conclusion that "the history of the Jamaican Association has indeed thrown into relief the difficulties with which a small cooperative organization has to contend when in competition with a company operating on a world-wide basis."[67] The only way for the JBPA to survive, then, was to cooperate with United Fruit. And since United insisted that the association abandon its cooperative structure, it had no choice but to reorganize as a limited-liability company. "The only reason for abandoning the cooperative structure is to enable the Association to coordinate its operations with others possessing the advantages which it cannot obtain."[68]

Consequently, in 1936 the Jamaica banana trade was reorganized along the lines recommended by the commission and on terms demanded by United Fruit: as a corporation rather than a cooperative. The government guaranteed the debentures issued by the new corporation, and United Fruit and the new association concluded a purchasing and marketing agreement. In the reorganized Jamaica Banana Producers Association, *Ltd.*, former members became shareholders, growing bananas and handing them over to the company, which paid them the market price. Former cooperators who had contributed toward the capital of the company received shares of a limited liability stock, up to a total of eight thousand in the reorganized company. The original shareholders, largely smallholding, illiterate men, paid a total of £226,000 for shares priced at 2s. 6d. per share. The reorganized company filled its ships to a stipulated capacity and sold any surplus to United Fruit at cost. If there were profits at the end of the year, they were treated like dividends and distributed to the "erstwhile cooperators, now shareholders, as in any other limited liability company."[69]

The legislation endorsing this arrangement was approved by the Jamaica Legislative Council on 26 November 1936 by a vote of 19 to 5, with two abstentions.[70] With this vote, the smallholders' last hope for genuine economic independence was dashed, the political system having failed them in their hour of greatest need. British and Jamaican authorities rationalized their decision on grounds Governor Eyre would have well understood: an efficient economy of peasant producers was not viable; black peasants were incapable of economic self-determination.

The Sugar Industry: Revival and Reorganization

When the Norman Commission visited Jamaica in 1897, its sugar industry was moribund. Between 1850 and 1910 the island's sugar production declined by 29 percent, dropping from 24,000 tons a year in the 1850s to 17,000 per year during the first decade of the twentieth century.[71] Just forty years later, however, sugar exports had increased 129 percent, a dramatic contrast with the 39 percent increase for all other agricultural exports. Much of that increase had come in the 1930s, when the sugar crop doubled, jumping from 59,000 tons in 1927–28 to 118,000 in 1937–38.[72] By 1948, output reached 180,318 tons per year (1946–48), a fifteenfold growth over the average pre–World War I annual output (11,401 tons in 1911–13).[73]

Clearly, World War I—like the Napoleonic Wars a century before—summoned the primary forces fueling this revival. The Napoleonic War blockades had encouraged European experimentation with beet sugar, which eventually undermined the profitability of cane production in the late nineteenth century. Ironically, World War I temporarily destroyed the European beet sugar industry, thus reducing supplies and pushing sugar prices up 500 percent. Although these prices could not be sustained in peacetime, world consumption continued to increase, nevertheless; the estimated 30,815,000 tons produced in 1938 represented an 18.5 percent increase over total world output just ten years before. Cane sugar was the source of 65 percent of that output. The British Empire accounted for 3.6 percent of the total sugar product (1,108,000 tons) and 5.5 percent of cane production. By 1938, total production from Britain's colonies was up 37 percent over 1933, two-thirds of it coming from Mauritius, British Guiana, Fiji, and Trinidad.[74]

Although the Jamaican sugar industry revived in response to these trends in the world market, its transformation involved more than simply expanded production and markets. By the late 1930s the very character of the industry was in the process of rapid change, the beginnings of which can be observed even in the half-century between Morant Bay and World War I. Most estates that survived the secular decline of the late nineteenth century had been able to undertake some measures to modernize production. Meanwhile, the strongest estates absorbed many of the weaker ones in a process of consolidation of territory and concentration of ownership that continued well into the twentieth century. These processes of modernization and concentration were parallel and interdependent; moreover, both were determined ultimately by transformations in the relationship of capital to labor that culminated in the creation of a new working class.

Since at least the mid-nineteenth century, most analysts of the problems of the island's declining sugar industry had agreed that adjustments in labor relations and new capital investment were necessary to its renewal. Greater command of workers would reduce production costs; greater capital investment in machinery would reduce the number of workers needed. In the 1840s, Governor Elgin had encouraged modernization of production, experimentation with new methods, and the stabilization of a technically skilled labor force. Later in the century, analysts took note of the Cuban example and urged the formation of central mills. All these changes, however, depended upon renewed capital investment. But capital's relation to labor was circular: it was not forthcoming to Jamaica, because of its unfavorable labor situation.

Consequently, the estates that remained in production survived largely by squeezing a greater surplus from their labor force and by curbing their labor needs, mostly by traditional means. The importation of indentured East Indians, beginning in 1858 and greatly accelerating after 1870, was critical to planters' gaining an advantage in the struggle to control labor costs and conditions. By 1917, when the importation ended, 36,000 East Indians had been brought to the island, of whom 18,000 remained as permanent residents. Estates also economized on labor by increasing the length of ratooning, that is, they left ratoons to bear for ten or more years, replacing them piecemeal when they were exhausted. This practice saved on the wage bill for planting, but at the cost of greatly reduced yields per acre.[75]

Planters faced a paradoxical situation in that the bulk of their labor expenditures went to field workers but the most important technical advances were applicable to manufacturing procedures rather than cultivation. The hilly terrain of most sugar parishes made adoption of the plow and mechanized transport impractical. One suspects that the planters' well-known prejudices concerning their "unreliable" labor force was also a factor here, making them reluctant to invest in the most labor-intensive phase of the production process. But even some factory innovations commonly found in competing sugar colonies made slow progress in Jamaica. The vacuum pan, for example, which boosted yields by controlling the final, crucial stage of the evaporation process, was introduced to Jamaica in 1846, but for years the only one in operation was at Albion Estate in St. Thomas. So unique were the fine yellow crystals produced there that they became known as "Albion sugar." As late as 1910, only seventeen factories used vacuum pans, which was only ten more than in 1881.[76]

The most effective innovations were made in the factory phase of production. Steam power replaced cattle, so that by 1900 only three out of one hundred twenty factories still used cattle, and even the thirty-six remaining water mills used steam as an auxiliary power source. Although the multiple-effect evaporation technique, which applied steam heat to evaporate cane juice before crystallization, was considered too expensive for most Jamaican estates, twenty estates did adopt other innovations using steam, such as the Wetzel and helical pans. The most widely adopted innovation was the centrifugal filter, which separated molasses from sugar more efficiently and more thoroughly. There were fifty-three of these in use in 1881, and sixty-one by 1900. The ease of its adoption was aided, no doubt, by the fact that it did not require new skills, could be simply integrated into the existing works, and reduced the loss in weight that took place in transit to market.[77]

Changes in the world market and in the marketing process were also important to the survivors of Jamaica's sugar debacle. Between 1850 and 1904 the United States imposed a countervailing duty on so-called bounty-fed European beet sugar and gave preferences to West Indian sugar in exchange for concessions to U.S. importers. Consequently, during the late nineteenth century, America became the main customer for British West Indian sugar as well as its fruit. America's imposition of new tariff barriers during the 1890s and 1900s was a setback to West Indian producers, but during the same period the adoption of the 1903 Brussels Sugar Convention prohibiting bounties made cane competitive with beet sugar again.

During this period there were important changes in the management and marketing of sugar as well. The estates' attorneys, who had always controlled the largest sugar estates, practically disappeared. Attorneys ran two-thirds of the estates in 1881 but only one-third in 1911. Only five of Westmoreland's seventeen estates in 1911 were managed through attorneys. Gone too were the even more ubiquitous English agents who had financed and supplied the estates from Britain and marketed their produce. By the 1880s Jamaican firms of produce dealers purchased and marketed sugar along with a diverse line of crops, including coffee, pimento, and dyewoods. Ironically, the rise of peasant-produced exports, by stimulating the development of local traders, may have indirectly furthered this transformation of marketing arrangements for the estates as well. In addition to these marketing services, and equally important, the larger corporations among the Jamaican merchant firms became sources for capital investment, which the industry so badly needed.[78]

Traditionally, the declining number of sugar estates had been taken as evidence of the morbidity of the industry as a whole, but by the late nineteenth century such decline was more likely to represent consolidation of ownership and more efficient organization of production. In 1896, 137 factories produced an average of 127 tons of sugar each. In 1926, only 38 factories remained in operation in Jamaica, but their average output was 1,620 tons, or more than twelve times that at the turn of the century. Indeed, for a quarter-century after 1926, production per unit grew geometrically: 3,160 tons per factory in 1937, which was almost double that just a decade before; it doubled again to 6,070 tons by 1944 and reached 11,650 tons by 1951. The increased scale of production showed clear advantages in costs and thus in the profitability of the estates. An examination of 1897 data from fifty-one estates showed that those producing over 500 tons achieved twice the yield per acre with two-thirds the labor and half the production cost, compared with smaller estates producing less than 100 tons.[79]

To operate efficiently, large modern factories required greatly increased supplies of cane, which could be secured best by reorganizing the smaller estates into farms producing cane for a central factory. There were several attempts to establish central mills in Jamaica in the late nineteenth century, but progress was slow, despite legislative changes intended to facilitate this form of organization. Success had to await the World War I boom, when higher prices made such reorganization profitable. Westmoreland Parish illustrates the pace of change: in 1911, estates cultivated 80 percent of the cane acreage in that parish, but by 1921 they farmed only 45 percent. Throughout the 1920s and 1930s, small cane farmers accounted for 25–35 percent of Jamaica's total sugar cane acreage.[80]

Simultaneous with this reorganization of the production process was the change from private to corporate ownership, at least of the largest estates. Traditionally, Jamaican law had not been favorable to the formation of limited-liability companies, and for years United Fruit had been the only corporate owner of estates, but by 1929 there were three such corporations.[81] Two of these—United Fruit and the West Indies Sugar Company (WISCO)—were multinational firms that would, in succession, control one-third of Jamaica's sugar output in the twentieth century. Their stories reveal the details not only of the roots of the process of the sugar industry's transformation but of its social consequences as well.

The central factories Frome and Moneymusk were located in the two major remaining sugar regions of the island, in the northwestern areas and in the south-central plains, respectively.[82] The contrasting histories of these two regions suggest some of the internal factors contributing to their survival and eventual dominance of the industry. A major factor in both places, although for different reasons, was the weakened bargaining position of laborers deprived of viable smallholdings.

The dry-weather parish of Vere, home of Moneymusk, enjoyed a reputation for a less conflictual apprenticeship period. Its sugar estates held on to their labor forces and survived the immediate postemancipation period largely intact. Its estates were unique in the slavery period in that they grew corn on the estates for their slaves' consumption. The usual "Negro grounds" were set aside as a unit and worked in common under the supervision of an overseer. It was the planter, not the slave family, who marketed the surplus produce of his workers. Consequently, a protopeasantry never developed in Vere.[83]

The ownership of estates in Vere was also very stable compared with the rest of Jamaica. In 1838 the parish contained 29 sugar estates,

5 cattle pens, and 8,275 apprentices. Vere planters resisted dissolution of their estates by exploiting their relatively close family ties to prevent borrowing from or sales to outsiders; family members were the first source of credit and had the first bids on estates up for sale. Over time, intermarriage among its small planter class had created a complex web of interlocking business and personal relationships. Major planter families such as the Morants, Gales, and Dawkins were all related, as were the Puseys, Edwardses, Crewses, and Mannings, as well as the Alpresses and Osbornes.[84]

Over time, of course, some families took advantage of the opportunities offered by hard times to absorb other properties and consolidate them with their own, a process accelerated by the 1884 depression. By 1900 only seven large sugar estates still functioned in Vere, and they belonged to "new" families with enterprises elsewhere. For example, in 1900, Messrs. Lascelles de Mercado and Company, a firm associated with de Pass and Company of London, acquired an interest in Vere Estates, whose produce they previously had marketed.[85] Between 1897 and 1929, the family estate system in Vere gave way completely to corporate ownership, leaving at the end of World War I only three large corporations: Lindo Brothers, Amity Hall Central, and Vere Estates.[86]

Moneymusk, the central factory for Lindo Brothers, and eventually for the entire parish, illustrates the pattern of consolidation. It was originally a small estate founded in the eighteenth century by the Grant family. Subsequently owned by the Rippon family, it was sold in the early nineteenth century to a cousin, one of the Sympsons. Before 1840 it was sold again to a Morant, who was a nephew of a Sympson. In 1884 the Morants sold it to Colonel Charles Ward, a member of a prominent landholding family but an outsider to the Vere district. Ward bought up other estates and added them to Moneymusk, making it the central mill for several different estates (Vizzard's Run, Knights', Carlisle, and Greenwich). The Lindo Brothers purchased the Moneymusk complex on the eve of World War I. By 1927 meanwhile, Vere Estates and Amity Hall had merged into Amity-Morelands Central. The following year, Clarendon Plantation Company, an obscure firm with offices in Canada, bought both Amity-Morelands and Lindo Brothers (including Moneymusk). Clarendon Plantation turned out to be a holding company for the United Fruit Company.[87]

United Fruit diversified production on these estates, bringing in bananas, coconuts, sheep pens, and pineapple fields. In fact, it actually reduced the acreage planted in canes. During the same year that it purchased Moneymusk, however, United also acquired the Bernard Lodge factory in St. Catherine, a large central sugar mill built during the postwar sugar boom. Consequently, during the early 1930s, United had not only a controlling share of Jamaica's fruit crop but one-third of its sugar as well. In 1937, United sold all its Vere estates to WISCO, the subsidiary of another multinational firm, Tate & Lyle. After World War II, when WISCO began full production at its two centrals, Moneymusk and Frome, their combined capacity reached seventy-five thousand tons.[88]

Frome, the other part of the factory tandem WISCO eventually came to control, had a history similar to Moneymusk's. Unlike in Vere, conditions in Westmoreland were not unfavorable to the development of peasant farming, but the exodus from the sugar estates after emancipation was comparatively slow. There was a spurt in the growth of smallholdings between 1867 and 1896, but this appears to have been among medium-sized cattle and logwood properties, not peasant-sized holdings. Most of the small freeholds in Westmoreland date from the sale of hilly lands previously attached to estates around the turn of the century.[89]

Westmoreland did suffer a precipitous decline in sugar production, notwithstanding the stability of estate control there. In the final years of slavery the parish produced 6,000 tons of sugar, but in 1847 it could manage barely half that. Although production recovered to 4,000 tons in 1881, it was not until 1911 that the parish's output, 6,500 tons, exceeded the slavery mark. By 1954, however, 60,000 tons was produced in the parish. Consolidation was marked but not as extensive as that found in Vere. There were thirty estates in Westmoreland during slavery; by 1867 there were twenty-five. There were fifteen by 1900 and only seven in 1937. In that year WISCO purchased practically all of the estates in the parish and centralized their operations at Frome.[90]

Frome sprawled across thirty thousand acres in the fertile central plain of Westmoreland. In 1931 it and the estates attached to it had produced a total of 12,000 tons of sugar. After their consolidation in 1937–38, production at the Frome complex and Moneymusk combined exceeded 37,900 tons, or 30 percent of Jamaica's total. By 1954, Frome alone would process 70,000 tons of sugar.[91] This complex would continue to be the island's dominant sugar producer until purchased by the government in 1972.

In a strategy similar to that of United Fruit ten years before, Tate

& Lyle used intermediaries to purchase Frome together with six other properties—Prospect and Blue Castle in Hanover; Friendship, Shrewsbury, Masemure, and Mint in Westmoreland. At about the same time, it acquired the Moneymusk complex in the Vere district of Clarendon. WISCO, incorporated in May 1937 and capitalized at six hundred thousand pounds, was owned by United Molasses, several insurance companies, and Tate & Lyle, the latter having a controlling interest.[92]

The board of directors of WISCO reflects something of the character of the new venture—with its interlocking directorate, its vertical integration of production enterprises, and its sprawling multinational interests. In 1936, Tate & Lyle had undertaken a project in Trinidad similar to the formation of the Frome Central, when it created Caroni, capitalized at £1 million. Four of the seven directors of WISCO were also directors of Tate & Lyle, and its chairman, Sir C. E. Leonard Lyle, a baronet, was not only president of Tate & Lyle but also a director of a South African sugar refinery. Two other WISCO directors were on the West India Committee in London, including Lt. Col. Ivan Davson, O.B.E., the chair of that committee. R. L. M. Kirkwood, the managing director of WISCO, was connected with Trinidadian sugar and mineral interests.[93]

Obviously, Tate & Lyle's investments in Jamaica and Trinidad were speculations designed to profit from the expected boom in the sugar market, especially after the conclusion of the International Sugar Agreement in 1937, which established national quotas. Crucial to its uninhibited operation was the company's ideology of public benefit produced through private gain. The prospectus for WISCO envisioned dramatic improvements in both the extraction process (sugar per ton of cane) and the cultivation process (canes per acre) to achieve a total output two to three times that of its original constituent properties.[94] A reorganization of this magnitude required thoroughgoing changes, not only in the operations of the small estates but also in the infrastructure of the entire community. Eventually, Frome would operate, as one observer described it, on a scale similar to that of a local governmental authority, providing water, electricity, roads, housing, and recreation to a community encompassing thousands of employees.[95]

In April 1938, Kirkwood informed the governor that his company planned to invest ten thousand pounds per year in Jamaica over a period of years. Workers would be rehoused at a cost of twenty thousand pounds in 1938 alone. The old-style barracks, many left over from the "coolie" labor era, would be razed. Two- and three-room cottages would be provided free to permanent laborers, and single-room, multiunit dwellings would house the migrant cane cutters who worked only at crop time. The company would try to provide separate family dwellings for all its workers, complete with kitchens and laundry facilities.[96]

Testifying before a government commission in the fall of 1938, Kirkwood, a relatively young man who prided himself for his "liberal" views, portrayed the WISCO venture as if its objectives were almost entirely philanthropic and paternalistic. He attributed the idea of building the central to recommendations of Sydney Olivier's commission in 1931, which credited centrals with providing better working conditions and a higher standard of living. In his written statement to the government commission, Kirkwood insisted: "So far as Jamaica is concerned, a few medium sized modern Central Factories, intelligently and sympathetically administered would lead to settled and properly housed and cared for communities in certain areas—each man with his own plot of land for vegetable cultivation and a regular week's work." It was "the considered opinion of the directors of WISCO that there is no surer method of bringing into being healthy and self-respecting settled communities . . . than the encouragement of the right type of investment in the sugar industry." It followed naturally, he added, that an increased sugar quota or colonial preference, or both, would better enable the company to achieve its objective of providing "a decent standard of life for all employees." The social welfare of workers, therefore, was best achieved through public subsidization of capital.[97]

WISCO was particularly proud of the work to improve the health of its workers. It established a free medical clinic, which emphasized preventive health measures as well as treatment, cleared swamps, and provided clean water and sewage disposal, all of which contributed to the value of the workers by reducing the incidence of such debilitating chronic illnesses as malaria, hookworm, and venereal diseases. The company's medical officer was particularly eloquent on the importance of what others would later refer to as "human capital." Strongly influenced by the successes of American capitalists in the Philippines, where economic progress came only after tropical diseases had been brought under control, Dr. Finlayson McKenzie concluded that health must be regarded from an economic as well as a humanitarian point of view. Human life has "a direct money value," even though difficult to estimate and variable with age and race. "To transform the Company's Employees from the weak and feeble Race they are into the strong, healthy, and enduring people that they might become is to lay the foundations for the future on a sound basis," he declared. "Healthy, happy, and contented labor is the best asset in any industry, and in the tropics, health takes first place."[98]

When questioned by the commissioners about the philosophy behind these "abnormal" capital expenditures for "welfare" or "social" work, general manager Kirkwood responded that such expenditures were essential to the company's reputation in Britain and to the contentment of the workers. But under close questioning, Kirkwood also made it clear that these expenditures on general welfare were in lieu of any significant wage increases. The company envisioned some rise in wages eventually but thought it desirable to obtain more accurate data on the subject "before taking any drastic action which might seriously embarrass the smaller planters." The island's "disorganized" labor force—referring apparently to the availability of subsistence plots to part-time workers and to the workers' migratory habits in general—made it impossible to determine a fair wage level. Asked directly whether the company would pay higher wages if its profits increased by virtue of higher quotas, Kirkwood demurred. Urging caution, he suggested that it might be better that "those companies which could afford to pay their labour more than the standard rates should devote their attention to housing, medical facilities, recreation grounds and clubs, rather than to embark upon a process of competitive wage increase." Improving conditions would "make the wage go a greater distance." Kirkwood and the commissioners agreed that this might in fact be considered an indirect payment to the worker. A Jamaican worker receiving regular wages of two to two and one-half shillings per day, a free house, free medical care, clean water, and "recreational facilities in the way of cricket, and so on," was as well off as the British farm laborer, they concluded.[99]

Kirkwood, like every other planter since 1838, complained that the workers did not work regularly. After earning ten to twelve shillings a week for three or four days' work, they quit; or they knocked off at lunch time after earning two or three shillings for the day. But somewhat contradictorily, he also asserted the company's policy of spreading the work "over a greater number of people than one would wish" because of the serious unemployment problem. Like so many other employers in Jamaica, therefore, WISCO deliberately created a situation of chronic *under*employment at low wages, ostensibly for a larger social good.[100]

Given the working and living conditions of sugar employees in the late Depression years, the benefits promised by monopoly capitalists such as Kirkwood had some appeal. Despite the vast transformations in the production processes arising from consolidation and corporate control of sugar estates, the basic structural characteristics of the labor force had changed very little since the mid-nineteenth century. Since the 1850s the labor force had been divided into at least two distinct categories: a small cadre of regular employees, usually resident on or near the estate, and a large group of seasonal employees, who lived and worked most of the year on properties rented or owned elsewhere. In 1937–38 an estimated forty thousand laborers were employed by the sugar industry at crop time. Half these laborers were migrants who came down from the hills after planting their yams, then left for two or three weeks to cultivate their own crops before returning to the estates again.[101] The resident workers, employed mostly in skilled jobs around the factory, received their houses and gardens free or for a nominal rent. For example, one observer reported that the four hundred such workers in his employ occupied 250 acres rent-free.[102]

This pattern, of course, was similar to that existing during the period of indentured labor, when the small East Indian group had constituted a core workforce supplemented by the more numerous black migrants employed at crop time. The conditions under which all of these people lived and worked had not changed much either, except perhaps to get worse. There were 381 estates of all crop types on the island in 1938, including 117 sugar and 94 banana properties. A survey of all properties recorded a total of 2,513 barracks accommodating a maximum of 22,620 persons in 8,596 rooms, fewer than half of which were judged to be in acceptable condition. Of the 2,513 barracks, 258 had no latrines and 567 others were unsanitary. Only about 1 of every 8 barracks was supplied with water, either piped or drawn from wells; 38 percent made no provision at all, and about half received water from open rivers and ponds. Worst of all were the sugar properties, whose facilities, reported the surveyors, "almost beggar description." And in practically all respects, Westmoreland Parish, the site of the Frome factory complex, was the worst offender.[103]

Banana properties had a much better record than the sugar estates, perhaps because fruit growing was a more recent enterprise that had enjoyed greater prosperity. Furthermore, the dominant firm in the fruit industry, United, enjoyed a favorable reputation for the physical facilities provided its workers. Perhaps it is understandable, then, that some observers entertained the hope that large corporations would bring greater prosperity and better living conditions.

But the replacement of individual proprietors by corporate managers portended other less favorable changes in the social relations of production. For the most part, the large central factories did not alter the overall structure of the labor force, that is, year-round, skilled resident employees and seasonal, unskilled nonresident workers. Furthermore, the provision of social and welfare services, such as housing, health care, and recreation, implied a kind of corporate paternalism. Nevertheless, it was a very different—and perhaps more insidious—relationship than that which had obtained before. In the 1970s an anthropologist interviewed workers who had been employed by Moneymusk during its takeover by United Fruit in the 1920s. The interviewees reported that "the coming of United Fruit and of [its] diversification [of production] tended to reduce somewhat the more personal, casual, slower pace of life and work. Relations became more impersonal, new and 'strange' managers and others were in charge; and the older social groupings and relationships which had arisen and developed among workers and their families in various work situations when sugar was dominant were now beginning to break up or to be lessened as workers engaged in new kinds of work with new or other workers whom, in some cases, they did not know so well." Evidently, these traditional personal relations and social groupings had survived the earlier consolidation of estates, but privileges and concessions, such as grazing goats and cutting estate wood, were curtailed with the advent of United Fruit.[104]

The interviewees suggested that their feelings of personal alienation were related to changes in the makeup of the labor force as well as in their relations with management. The creation of large central factories at Moneymusk and later at Frome stimulated a large in-migration to those areas. In Vere a centuries-old trend of out-migration was reversed in the 1930s and especially after World War II. Indeed, the new settlers were often descendants of the freed people who had moved into the upper Clarendon mountains in the 1840s and 1850s.[105] Meanwhile, in Westmoreland the Frome complex attracted a flood of new settlers out of the limestone hills into the fertile cane lands. One observer likened this demographic shift to the concurrent migration to Kingston. A 1951 survey of Frome village found that 57 percent of its heads of household had been born outside the parish. In the surrounding cane lands, this recency of settlement was true of only 35 percent of the heads of household, and in the hills, of only 17 percent.[106]

The demographic and ecological patterns associated with the new centrals involved both continuity and change. Though the basic ecological distinction between sugar and nonsugar zones persisted, the contrasts between those employees living contiguous to the factory and those in the hills grew sharper. Associated with the increase in the scale of operations and the number of employees, therefore, were changes in the social ecology of the sugar zone. By the early 1950s Frome consisted of about thirty properties that had been separate productive units formerly. The compound was its administrative center, including within its boundaries the factory, offices, and housing for the supervisory and managerial staffs. Across the road were the company houses that constituted Frome village, 80 percent of which included someone employed on the estate, mostly as skilled workers and foremen. Outside Frome village were more company-owned houses with gardens, rented at a nominal charge to the households, 64 percent of which included a WISCO employee.[107]

According to a 1951 survey, most workers resident at Frome neither owned nor worked land but were solely dependent on their wages. The further one moved from the village, however, the more marked the pattern of small-scale subsistence or truck gardening became. Almost all the employees from the more distant areas worked the land, and a much higher percentage owned the land they worked. In areas peripheral to the sugar zones, patterns of life and work continued much as they had been for a century. "The typical household lived in its own house and owned a piece of land adjacent to the house, on which were planted a score or so of the traditional food trees—ackee, breadfruit, plantain and others. Another piece of land was rented for cultivation at distances up to two miles."[108] This property was cultivated almost entirely with family labor, but one or more of the male members of the household traveled down to the cane lands for two or three months a year at crop time to cut cane. However, their earnings, though important, were only supplemental to the family's income.

The central mill's larger scale of operations involved significant changes for management as well. There was a sharper separation between the field and the factory. The cane farms—now operated by the company directly rather than under contract—were supervised by section managers, who reported in turn to a manager of cultivation. There were also separate managers for the factory and business operations. Overall responsibility for the Jamaican facility was in the hands of the general manager, but ultimate authority over the Frome complex lay with the corporate managers in Britain. Given this vast administrative hierarchy, the status and authority of those most immediately in charge of the workers tended to decline at the same time as the extent of their responsibilities—in terms of numbers of employees supervised—increased.[109]

Given these developments, it is easy to see why despite its special brand of corporate paternalism, the social relations of production in these centralized estates would tend to become more impersonal and rationalized, much like the corporation itself. In contrast with the old-style entrepreneurs, these new-style organization men claimed that they actually preferred a unionized labor force. "The general opinion," declared a representative of the Sugar Manufacturers' Association in 1938, "is that it certainly would be desirable to deal with organized and well-run trade unions." It would be helpful to the planters, explained another, to have a labor force "willing to obey its leaders."[110] Undoubtedly, this newfound appreciation of the virtues of trade unions was stimulated by the numerous unauthorized strikes during the 1930s, many of which eventually degenerated into uncontrolled violence. But it is also probable that bureaucratic channeling of the laborers' aspirations held some appeal for corporate bureaucrats. In any event, unionization of the sugar workers was one result of the reforms arising from or encouraged in the aftermath of labor rebellion at Frome in 1938. In the opinion of some observers, unionization completed the modernization process that the revival and transformation of the sugar industry had begun.[111]

Certainly organized labor could prove a valuable ally of monopoly capitalists. In 1938, WISCO officials were anxious to defend their company's labor relations policies in the aftermath of the labor violence that year, but they were also keenly interested in securing greater government assistance in the form of a higher sugar quota or higher colonial preferences, or both. The International Sugar Agreement, signed the year WISCO was incorporated, had established a quota too low for the Frome complex to operate efficiently, they complained. Technical reports prescribed a minimum factory output of 30,000 tons per crop, but the agreement set their salable quotas at only 17,000 tons for 1938–39, which was just 57 percent of the factory's capacity. Moreover, sugar prices did not rise as expected following the signing of the agreement; indeed, they fell by thirty shillings per ton and had recovered only ten shillings since.[112] The company could weather this adversity through necessary economies, but it would have "serious consequences from the social standpoint." Therefore, WISCO had chosen instead to honor its commitments to provide new housing and better living and working conditions. Implied by this was a concurrent obligation of the government to assist the company in turn. WISCO's strongest supporter in this request was none other than Alexander Bustamante, leader of the infant but growing union movement in Jamaica.[113]

Suggested in this vignette is the emergence of a more thoroughly proletarianized labor force and the potential conflict between its interests and those of Jamaica's traditional peasants, who had resisted the power of the sugar lobby since emancipation. Over the following two decades, Jamaica's increasingly unionized agricultural workers would experience impressive growth and, until the 1960s, important and frequent wage and benefits concessions from the planters. The benefits accrued, however, mainly to the minority of regular, full-time hourly and salaried employees, while excluding other groups, such as seasonal and part-time workers, women, and those paid by the task.[114] Like capitalist employers elsewhere, Jamaican planters were coming to appreciate more sophisticated means of controlling partly unionized, segmented labor forces.

Much like their nineteenth-century ancestors, many in this new Jamaican working class, whether resident employees or migrants from the hills, continued to depend on small plots of owned, rented, or company-allocated land for part of their subsistence. However, under twentieth-century conditions—chronic unemployment and underemployment, sharply curtailed emigration abroad, and growing demographic pressure on increasingly fragmented rural provision plots—this independent subsistence was no longer sufficient to ensure an autonomous bargaining position vis-à-vis the estates. In fact, the estates themselves now allocated plots to their workers with the express intent of countering wage demands and blunting labor militancy. Under modern conditions, access to small plots of lands no longer meant freedom—not for the peasant fruit growers who supplied United Fruit nor for the migrant workers cutting cane for WISCO. Under modern conditions, the freed people's century-old struggle for autonomy through peasant proprietorship appeared defeated, and their dream of an independent livelihood seemed a quaint anachronism. That defeat, however, simply gave rise to struggle on new terrain. In the twentieth century the struggle to be a free people would take new objectives, draw from newfound strengths, and confront new contradictions.

In 1833 there was reason to apprehend a universal Negro rebellion for freedom, and emancipation was granted from above to prevent the cataclysm [sic] of emancipation from below, as had occurred in San Domingo. Similarly today, when the rape of Ethiopia has given a great stimulus to growing Negro consciousness, it is not a question of rebellions if, but rebellions unless, democratic government is granted.

GEORGE PADMORE, FOR THE INTERNATIONAL AFRICAN SERVICE BUREAU (1938)

In 1865 the new class which was pressing for recognition and partnership in the society was the peasantry. In 1938 a similar role was played by the "proletarian" wage workers.

G. E. CUMPER, "LABOUR DEMAND AND SUPPLY IN THE JAMAICAN SUGAR INDUSTRY" (1954)

One of the most important problems in the West Indies with which Governments and employers alike are concerned arises from the extremely rapid development of self-consciousness among the labouring classes. This is a development which cannot be stayed, and lays upon those in responsible positions the duty of doing all in their power to help it into channels where it may work for the common good.

C. Y. CARSTAIRS, "MEMORANDUM [CONFIDENTIAL]" (1940)

Epilogue

"Better Must Come": The Problem of Freedom in the Twentieth Century

Nineteen thirty-eight marked the centennial year of slavery emancipation in the British West Indies. One hundred years earlier, the semi-slavery of apprenticeship had ended and Jamaican freed people had entered a brave new world of complete freedom. In striking contrast with the 1933 centennial of the Slavery Abolition Act, however, this anniversary would receive no official recognition; there would be no celebrations, no royal message to the people of the West Indies, no prideful speeches about the century's moral and social progress. Nineteen thirty-eight was a violent and troublesome year in Jamaica, the culmination of a difficult and troublesome decade in the West Indies generally. Angry confrontations in countryside and city exposed perplexing new developments and social relations that had taken shape over the past several decades. In its aftermath new forces emerged—some beneficial, some sinister—that would reshape the political, economic, and social futures not only of Jamaica but of the entire colonial empire. It was, then, a year as violent and as consequential as 1831–32 and 1865. And given the liberation movements that it spawned, it was a fitting centennial for 1838. Whitehall declined to notice this anniversary, however, apprehensive that doing so would call attention to the failed promise of freedom to a people grown more cynical about British intentions and more self-aware of their power to force change. There would be no celebrations.[1]

British anxieties were stimulated by a decade of escalating unrest during which strikes and riots had buffeted African and West Indian colonies like tropical storms. There were strikes by miners in Ghana and Rhodesia and by oil field workers in Trinidad. There had been rioting in St. Vincent, St. Lucia, St. Kitts, and British Guiana in 1935 and 1936. In Jamaica there had been serious riots at the docks in Falmouth and Kingston in May and October 1935 and strikes at Oracabessa and Port Antonio; 1938 opened with a canecutters' strike on Serge Island Estate in St. Thomas in January. In response, Governor Edward Denham fired off anxious telegrams to the Colonial Office. To head off trouble he appointed commissions to investigate wage rates and unemployment, followed by emergency public works initiatives and plans to increase the allocations for land settlement.[2] Despite these initiatives, however, it was clear that neither Denham nor his superiors at the Colonial Office were yet prepared to deal with the core issues implicated in this social unrest.

Emblematic of this unreadiness is the elaborate, glittering dinner party that the governor hosted at his residence on the very eve of the most serious violence of 1938. Among his guests was William Makim, the new editor of the *Jamaican Standard*, who had arrived in Kingston in the spring of 1938. Makim would stay only a year, returning to London from his tropical sojourn, like so many Europeans before him, a victim of ill-health and ruined fortune. But he left a vivid account of the events of that fateful year, informed by the insights that perhaps only an outsider could attain. The gathering at King's House, the governor's residence, was "British imperialism at its best," he observed. "I realized why these spacious grounds beyond had suggested an eighteenth century pleasance. Nothing changed here. It had been and would be."[3]

Dinner conversation was "pleasant and civilized," according to Makim, and after the ladies retired, leaving the gentlemen to their cigars, the conversation turned to joking about the island's high illegitimacy rate and the queer morality of Jamaican blacks. Implicit in their hilarity was the assertion that the poor Jamaicans' lack of progress could be traced to their fondness for leisure and careless sexual mores. Indeed, one might imagine a similar analysis being offered at a similar

Governor Edward Denham

dinner party presided over by Metcalfe, or Barkly, or Eyre. "With the excellent wines and foods," Makim felt "a growing conviction that not even an earthquake in Jamaica could upset the dignity and equanimity of that assembly." Yet hours earlier a minor payroll dispute at a sugar estate on the other side of the island had set in motion events that would soon engulf those gathered at the governor's house that evening. Although they were blissfully ignorant of it, the patience of Quashee had snapped; "the earthquake was already rumbling."[4]

Later that evening Makim talked privately with the governor as they smoked on the veranda. Denham was "a small, stout figure whose ruddy face carried a smile enticing and yet a shade cynical." This was the result, perhaps, of his many years in the colonial service, for his three years in Jamaica had been preceded by stints in British Guiana and Kenya. Makim judged him "a better diplomatist than an administrator." The governor found the island's problems as complex as Euclid's geometry and more difficult to solve. Wearily, he talked that night of returning to the cool air and green landscapes of England.[5]

Denham thought the real problems of Jamaica were less economic than political. The recent emergence of radical black politicians with "half-digested democratic ideas" posed the main threat to the delicately balanced equilibrium of British colonial rule. Denham's inner struggle was vividly clear to Makim that night. "Imperialism and democracy were as difficult to merge as black and white. But the British genius for compromise and putting blind eyes to telescopes that revealed all too clearly unpleasant facts, had indeed brought forth a workable system. It was that system of democratic ruling of native peoples—inexplicable to anyone outside the Empire—which Sir Edward Denham profoundly believed [in] and practised. It was a bitter realization for him, it was indeed his death-blow when he realized that the system had failed."[6] Denham would be dead before summer, and the colonial system as he had known it would be dying.

Earlier that afternoon the first shots had been fired that would ignite the summer's firestorms of protest. Ironically, the precipitating incident occurred at Frome Estate, the new central sugar mill on the main road from Savannah-la-Mar to Grange Hill in Westmoreland. Ironic because the construction of the central at Frome by WISCO, a subsidiary of the British multinational conglomerate Tate & Lyle, was part of a vast reorganization of the sugar industry in Jamaica that many assumed would help alleviate its worsening economic conditions. Beginning in November 1937, construction at Frome had employed a steadily increasing labor force that peaked at 911 workers by mid-April 1938. Newspaper reports of high wages—as much as a dollar a day was reported in the *Daily Gleaner*—brought hundreds of unemployed workers into the parish. But there were neither jobs enough nor housing enough to accommodate this influx. The disappointed aspirants simply camped out, their sullen despair barely softened by hope.[7]

Even so, WISCO's management system failed to keep pace with the dramatically expanded workforce. On Friday, 29 April, workers became restless because of the long delays in receiving their pay.

Rather than receiving their money in the traditional manner, "on the spot where they worked," they were required to queue up at the pay office. The progress of the line was painfully slow; disbursements that began at 3:00 P.M. were still not completed at 10:30 that evening. As Governor Denham's dinner guests drove home, many Frome workers still had not received either their pay or their supper. The situation grew uglier with each passing hour. Stones were thrown at the pay office. The pay clerk retaliated with a pistol shot over the heads of the crowd. The crowd's disposition did not improve.

Apparently the inefficiency of the pay office was not the only issue disturbing WISCO's employees. A delegation representing the construction workers complained to Frome's manager about unjustified deductions from their paychecks and the low rate of pay. They also demanded that the trigger-happy pay clerk be removed. The manager did make some adjustments in the pay scales, but the workers dismissed these as largely meaningless. On the following day they struck. Expecting even more trouble when the estate opened its gates on Monday, Westmoreland police inspector O'Donoghue called Kingston for reinforcements. Late Sunday afternoon, officers began pouring into the area from the capital city and surrounding parishes. On Monday morning a force of one hundred heavily armed policemen greeted protesters gathering at Frome.

Undaunted, the strikers stood their ground, armed with the traditional weapons of the dispossessed—sticks, stones, and iron pipes. They forced nonstriking workers to join them. They marched on the overseer's residence. They blocked all access roads into the estate, prevented the chief construction engineer from entering the property, damaged a company motor truck, and emptied bags of sugar into the road. By midmorning they were reported to be "in virtual control of the Company." Soon they turned their attention toward its general offices. The frightened manager fired into the air to attract the police, who moved in with fixed bayonets (a tactic severely criticized in the postmortem report). At first the crowd retreated, but then they unleashed a hail of stones. The police fired. After the barrage, four people lay dead and thirteen others writhing in pain, including innocent onlookers. One, an old woman, had her right side shot away. "The intestines of one man burst out into his shirt. Down the road another woman was painfully dragging herself along the ground and whimpering for help. Blood was spilled in the white dust."[8] Soon thereafter—as had occurred so often in past altercations when the people's rage was thwarted by the overwhelming firepower of authorities—smoke billowed over the estate, and the air was filled with the acrid, dense odor of burning sugar cane. When the fires were finally extinguished by heavy rains on Tuesday, 156 acres of cane had been destroyed.

The incident at Frome began as a strike but ended in riot; the particular grievances of the workers were sparks igniting a more general conflagration involving nonworkers as well. Police arrested 105 people for rioting, but only 22 of these were employed at Frome, and only 9 of those 22 were eventually found guilty. Thus at least the arrest pattern suggests that the most active rioters were found among the crowd of disappointed job-seekers rather than those employed on the estate.[9]

This particular pattern, wherein the grievances and job actions of the employed spilled over and agitated the more numerous unemployed, was typical of Jamaica's labor unrest during the late Depression years. Three weeks after the Frome riot, the scenario was repeated in Kingston. As with most earlier incidents, this one began among dock workers who were called out on strike on Saturday, 21 May. Shortly, the strike was made a general one, and by the following Monday, Kingston had been brought to a standstill as mobs surged through its streets halting streetcars, overturning cars and garbage cans, and firing shops. All this to the tune of "Onward Christian Soldiers."[10] In succeeding days and weeks the strike and its attendant violence spread across the island. Caymanas Estate in St. Catherine was blockaded. There was a hunger march through the normally sedate streets of Mandeville. At Islington, in St. Mary, police fired on a crowd of demonstrators. By the time the unrest subsided, 8 people had been killed, 32 had been wounded by gunshot, and another 139 had been injured by other means. Although no police were killed, 109 were wounded. In the riot's aftermath more than 800 people were prosecuted, of whom more than half were convicted.[11]

Sporadic outbreaks continued throughout the summer. Many believed that the rioting was centrally planned and coordinated. There were reports of arms shipments arriving in isolated ports and plans for a general rebellion scheduled for 1 August, to coincide with the emancipation centennial.[12] Although the local commission investigating the disorders catered to these fears by recommending increased police forces, better intelligence services, and the suppression of ganja, it also recognized the roots of the unrest in larger social developments. Rejecting the police conspiracy theory, the commission concluded that the idea of a general strike might be better explained as resulting from the precedents at Serge Island and Frome. What is more important, international developments as well as developments within Jamaica had created an unprecedented unemployment problem. Nations that had absorbed Jamaica's excess labor force now closed their doors to her migrants. Industries at home that had provided export crops for whole-time and part-time peasants, such as bananas, were now prostrated by plant diseases. Production in the reorganized sugar industry, the focus of much of the recent discontent, was constrained by international trade agreements. Furthermore, the systems governing labor relations had not been modernized and rationalized at the same pace as the technical systems of production. Since there was no systematic representation of the workers' grievances to management, strikes could be "used by extreme elements . . . and by those who were not concerned in the dispute to create disorder."[13] Thus one of the most immediate reforms called for by the commission was an official labor department to mediate disputes.

The local commissioners' findings suggested the need for a more thorough examination of colonial labor problems. Thus the Colonial Office sent out a special labor investigator, Major G. St. J. Orde Browne, to examine labor relations in the islands. Browne concluded that the real causes of labor unrest had less to do with unemployment than with deliberate underemployment. With the ending of indentured labor importation in 1917, there had been a shift to a more stabilized native workforce, which made customary claims on the estates for housing as well as employment. These workers considered the estates their homes and resisted eviction. As a result, the estates were stuck with an inelastic labor supply, were unable to lay off workers to adjust to market changes, and were unable to modernize their facilities. Employers were trying to carry a population appreciably larger than their economic conditions warranted. Browne recommended land reform to enlarge the peasantry, siphon off "superfluous labor," and restore elasticity to labor demand and supply. He also urged what economists would later call "import substitution" to reduce dependency on export markets.[14]

Browne's report described Jamaica's problems almost entirely in the passive voice; they were problems created by a situation of overpopulation. In an internal memorandum two years later, he also acknowledged that urban employers benefited directly from this labor surplus in reduced wage costs. "This suits the employers as it gives them a large and elastic supply of labor, and also tends to keep down wages. So the evil system of rotational engagement flourishes, especially on the waterfront." This observation notwithstanding, neither he nor any other colonial officer appears to have seen any contradiction in attempting to convince employers to support policies designed to reduce the labor surplus from which they benefited.[15]

In the months to come the enquiry commission's findings and Orde Browne's report would be replicated and expanded upon by other analysts, including the prestigious royal commission chaired by Lord Moyne. Despite their differences, common themes ran through all these analyses and recommendations: at root, Jamaica's labor unrest reflected its economic underdevelopment, its lack of social as well as economic modernization, and its marginal position in the world economy. The conclusion, inescapable for many in and outside Whitehall, was that Jamaica—indeed the entire colonial empire—must undergo a thorough reconstruction, a reconstruction that would demand of the home government commitment of resources and political will very similar to that made a century before. Yet that very same analysis and commitment raised the questions, By whom would that empire be governed? and For whom? Variations on this complex interplay of issues of development and issues of democracy would define the problem of freedom for much of the twentieth century.

Development versus Democracy

"The people of the West Indies had asked for bread; they received a Royal Commission." The commissioners were, Makim went on, "a group of well-meaning individuals burdened with a problem that the British Parliament finds convenient to put on other shoulders. Only a British democracy could conceive it."[16] Headed by Walter Edward, Baron Moyne, and comprising representatives of business and labor and various other experts, the royal commission of 1938 was part of a century-old tradition. It was a technique for mobilizing the British Parliament and public for major departures in social policy or major expenditures of public funds, and usually both. The commission had been appointed on 5 August and had begun hearing evidence in London in late September. The commissioners arrived in Jamaica in October; a few days later Baron Moyne arrived on his luxury yacht, *Rosaura*. At the Constant Spring Hotel, "in a jazz-painted dance-hall, at an improvised half-moon table and flanked by secretaries, short hand writers, and the inevitable blue books," the commissioners examined the causes of and possible solutions to the social ills that had brought the island to the brink of revolution.[17]

Significantly, their official report began with the one-hundred-year history that presaged the present unrest: emancipation, the free trade crisis, the adjustment to these twin crises through technological innovation and reorganization of the estates, the devastating effects of beet sugar competition and falling world sugar prices. They reviewed also the recommendations of the 1897 royal commission and the subsequent rise and fall of the fruit industry. Finally, they discussed the recent sugar boom of the postwar years, which was, they concluded, "reminiscent of the spacious days of the 18th century."[18] High sugar prices not only revitalized cane production but brought new producers into the market. These producers, together with revived world beet sugar production, created a surplus, however, which sent prices plummeting again by the late 1920s. Only increased subsidies and the quota system established under the International Sugar Agreement—measures that were a virtual renunciation of free trade policy—stabilized the industry.

Meanwhile, alternative crops were experiencing difficulties as well. Plant diseases, hurricanes, and other natural disasters severely limited crops such as bananas, limes, and cocoa. The fundamental problem of West Indian societies, therefore, was their inability to earn enough income to support their populations. Improved health led to more rapid population growth, while declining world demand and lower prices for tropical products produced inadequate income to support that population. Perhaps most important and troubling of all, simultaneous with this growing distress, the colonies had developed "an articulate public opinion," conscious of its grievances and insistent on improvement.[19]

The solutions that the commissioners sketched to these problems were as pessimistic as their analysis was gloomy. Although like every commission before them they recommended increased subsidies to the sugar industry in the form of trade preferences, this was clearly only a stopgap measure to prevent total social collapse. Like their predecessors forty years before, they also recommended public expenditures to develop alternatives to the sugar industry. Given the bleak outlook of other agricultural exports, however, they recommended food production primarily for the internal market to relieve the island's need for foreign exchange to buy exports. Even here, however, they held out little hope that this self-sufficiency strategy would much relieve the British Exchequer of its growing colonial burden.

Not only was this report more pessimistic than any previous West Indian commission's, it was also the most hortatory and moralistic. The economic fate of West Indians was in their own hands; it turned on nothing less than their moral regeneration. "This leads us to one final point of vital importance," the commissioners concluded their section on economic conditions. "One of the strongest and most discouraging impressions carried away by the investigator in the West Indies is that of a prevailing absence of a spirit of independence and self help, the lack of a tradition of craftsmanship and pride and good work, and a tendency on all matters to appeal to government for assistance with little or no attempt to explore what can be done by individual self help." But government assistance was useless under such circumstances, the commissioners argued. What was needed was a "sound and self-perpetuating social tradition." They identified improvidence, theft, sexual promiscuity, and inefficiency as the social evils that blocked West Indian progress. Although they recognized that the peculiar history of the West Indies helped explain this "pauperisation," they concluded, nevertheless, that "the material betterment of the West Indies must be accompanied, and is to a large extent conditional, on a moral resurgence among the peoples themselves."[20]

Interestingly, this moralistic posture was almost the only feature of the commissioners' report that found a receptive ear at the Colonial Office. Their more specific, practical remedies—import substitution through increased local food production and land settlement schemes to expand peasant proprietorship—were severely criticized. Colonial officer Sidney Caine rejected as "the most deceptive of mirages" the notion of achieving self-sufficiency, whether in food production or other consumer goods. Caine's analysis is particularly interesting because its perspective included the colonies as part of a broader world economic system, indeed a Third World, long before that term became fashionable. The problems found in the West Indies were a prognosis of what could happen not only to other British colonies, he argued, but to "tropical countries, or perhaps even more widely, [to] 'non-western' countries."[21]

These problems arose first of all from what West Indian economist W. Arthur Lewis had earlier referred to as "the gloomy prospects of agriculture the world over" and the increasing control by British and American monopolies of other tropical produce.[22] As a generalization, Caine thought that "the rapid rise in the standard of life in the advanced Western countries in recent generations has been at least assisted by the much lower standards of living prevailing in the countries where cheap raw materials and foodstuffs are produced —standards of living which are kept down by over-population and the obstacles imposed by natural inertia, by custom and increasingly by legislative restrictions on the movement of those populations to regions of higher standards."[23] Thus even as he blamed the victims of world poverty, Caine acknowledged that underdevelopment was an active rather than a passive process; *underdeveloped,* a verb as well as a noun.

Yet, despite having gone so far in their analysis, neither Caine nor his superiors could push further without raising fundamental questions about colonial power relationships. They settled therefore for a policy conundrum: West Indian economies were trapped in a cycle of dependency. Encouraging self-sufficiency, import substitution, and local industrialization would entail an even lower standard of living, Caine lamented. The only cereal that could be produced in the West Indies was rice, which was a "notorious low standard," and West Indian blacks, grown accustomed to semi-European standards, were not likely to accept it. Even if they did consume rice rather than wheat, Caine argued, they would likely import it from a lower wage area such as Burma rather than raise it themselves. Thus, they must still produce primary-good exports to pay for their finished-good imports, or accept an even lower standard of life. The latter option was implausible because West Indian consumption aspirations showed every evidence of expanding, not contracting, and for the sake of social order, these could not be safely denied.[24] A century earlier, policymakers had looked to such cultural-behavioral changes—"expanding wants"—as the salvation of the sugar industry; now, ironically, they seemed to pose a grave threat to social order. Here Caine anticipated the postwar development economists' orthodox injunction to developing nations: they should willingly accept austerity rather than indulge their aspirations for a better life.

Caine was similarly pessimistic about the prospects for developing infant industries; if these industries required tariff protection or subsidies, they would merely constitute transfer payments from the general population to a few producers whose industries generally added little to total employment. The small populations of the islands, moreover, provided inadequate internal markets; consequently, raising tariff barriers to the rest of the world would be suicidal. Thus Caine concluded that the main initiatives should be directed at research to develop new nonfood by-products from existing agricultural resources, at restoring the safety valve of out-migration by reducing legal barriers in other countries, and, most important of all, at a program of population control. In the latter recommendation Caine reiterated the commissioners' observations on the "fecklessness of the negro" and urged that "a moral revolution might have most welcome economic consequences."[25] A large part of the solution to Third World people's problems, it seemed, was to make fewer of them.

Colonial Office personnel were not the only ones voicing reservations and criticisms of the Moyne Commission's analysis of the West Indian situation. In contrast to its earlier history, by the 1930s Whitehall had to contend with lobbyists for the black residents of the colonies as well as those for the whites. During the interwar years increasing numbers of West Indian and African political activists, students, and other intellectuals came to colonial capitals. The synergy of an urban environment and the heady mix of radical ideologies, cultural innovations, and social-professional interactions that characterized New York City, London, and Paris created a new international black literature and sharpened political consciousness and commitment throughout the black world. The movements of Jamaican Pan-Africanist Marcus Garvey from Kingston to London to New York to Kingston and back to London again is an emblem of the interconnections within this flow of people, ideas, and issues. Conditions and events in the British colonies, therefore, focused the attention of black emigrants in all these capitals. George Padmore, C. L. R. James, and Jomo Kenyatta formed the International African Service Bureau specifically to enlighten the British public about conditions in the colonies. The League of Coloured Peoples was established in London in 1931 with the general aim of promoting and protecting "the social, educational, economic and political interests of its members."[26]

During the crisis years of the late 1930s representatives of these groups, especially the League of Coloured Peoples, were constant visitors at and correspondents with the Colonial Office. Although some officers of the West India Department grew impatient and disdainful of these "self-appointed" representatives, their political sophistication and growing influence with factions of Parliament made them difficult to ignore. General interest in West Indian affairs was stimulated in Parliament after the Trinidad riot in 1934. Shortly thereafter, in 1936, the Labour party's Imperial Advisory Committee became increasingly familiar with and invited experts on West Indian conditions to address them. A member of Parliament offered the League of Coloured Peoples their services in putting the group's questions to the ministers in Parliament (presumably during "question time").[27] In June 1937 several Labour members of Parliament (Creech-Jones, Major Millner, and Wilfred Paling) subjected Secretary of State Ormsby-Gore to severe criticism over labor conditions in the West Indies. Labour M.P.'s recommended extensions of the franchise and increases in the number of elected representatives on legislative councils. On 8 November 1938 a Committee for West Indies Affairs was formed by Labour M.P.'s with Creech-Jones as its chairman. Significantly, Peter Blackman, then chair of the League of Coloured Peoples, was this committee's secretary.[28]

Critics outside government were handicapped by the fact that the Moyne Commission's hearings were not published in 1940, only the summary of its findings and recommendations. The reason publicly offered for nonpublication was a necessity for economies during wartime, but the real reason was fear of supplying Germany propaganda materials at a crucial stage of the war. The British were especially sensitive to potential reactions in the United States, which had not yet entered the war and where sentiment against British imperialism was very strong.[29]

Of course, like most other critics of the Moyne Commission, the League of Coloured Peoples had already worked out positions on most of the critical issues addressed in the report. Apparently, W. Arthur Lewis, later Sir Arthur but at the time a Fabian socialist, was a strong influence within the League. A lecturer at the London School of Economics in the 1930s, Lewis was a native of St. Lucia, where he had worked as a clerk in the Department of Agriculture before coming to London to take a degree in economics. Most of the League's statements on economic issues appear to have been formulated by him.[30]

Lewis and the League took a position—not dissimilar in parts to Caine's—that continued dependence on agricultural exports would ensure poverty in the West Indies and that therefore alternative, nonagricultural industries must be developed. But they also endorsed the commission's recommendations to encourage mixed farming and increased production of foodstuffs, especially livestock, technical assistance to farms, more research on production and marketing, and dissemination of propaganda in favor of local produce. They anticipated some aspects of development policy that the Colonial Office would initiate in later years by linking welfare services to economic development. Thus the black West Indian lobbyists urged improvements in medical services especially. But they differed significantly from the Colonial Office in their insistence that improvements in wages and living conditions were prerequisites to better health care. They also endorsed expansion of land settlement as a partial solution to the unemployment problem but cautioned against schemes that would "encourage the conservative instincts of the peasantry. Peasant proprietorship must be linked with a definite scheme of co-operative education, production and distribution."[31]

League members had no illusions that such measures would solve the basic problems of the islands, however. Rather, all concerned must face the fact that the plantation system was "an economic anachronism" and that ultimate economic salvation lay outside of agriculture. Because there already were "too many agriculturalists in the world," that route could only lead to overproduction and further depression. Some of the League's strongest criticisms of the Moyne Commission's report were directed, therefore, at its "disparaging tone" regarding colonial industrial development. The West Indies had the raw materials for development ("on a modest scale"), they insisted. All that was required were skills and capital. The skills could be obtained through technical training schools and by selective recruitment of wartime refugees. Meanwhile, subsidies (but not protective duties) should be used to encourage prospective industrialists, "local or foreign," and a mechanism for national economic planning should be established. Furthermore, although they recognized the pressing need for expanded and better social services, in contrast with the Moyne Commission, the League gave priority to economic development over welfare because the former was ultimately necessary to fund the latter. "The real problem is to make the West Indies economically self-supporting, so that when the [proposed] grant comes to an end, they may be able to continue the new social services out of their own funds, and also to maintain a decent standard of living."[32]

The League's position on the primacy of development over welfare found some support at Whitehall. Indeed, determination of the right mix and relationship between these twin objectives continued to preoccupy Colonial Office planners well into the postwar period. But the other major objection raised by the League was more troublesome for British authorities. According to League spokesmen, the most glaring defect of the Moyne Commission report was its failure to recognize that far-reaching political reforms were a prerequisite to any meaningful economic change for social peace in the West Indies. The nature of the required reforms involved nothing less than the self-determination and democratic governance of West Indian societies: "We submit with deference [that] the progress of the West Indies depends only to a limited extent on the Colonial Office. If these colonies are to progress, it is their own people, led by their own leaders, who will play the major part."[33] Other West Indian and African activists also made clear their rejection of "being under the tutelage of England" and demanded self-government.[34]

The West Indians' specific demands for reform included an expanded franchise and lower qualifications for membership in the legislatures, but these potential changes in the power relations among local classes were clearly precursors to more extensive transformations of political relationships with Britain itself. A West Indian federation, with political and administrative powers, was recommended as a step toward dominion status for the islands. It was clear, too, that this rejection of dependence on Great Britain had racial as well as political overtones. "We would, however, like to utter here a word of warning to the conservative, self-confident and paternal Englishmen whose only conception is that if the coloured man is to advance, he can only advance safely and securely when tied to his apron strings. This idea is not absent even from such a generous report as that of the Royal Commission's, . . . and we meet it again and again in our efforts to procure the breakdown of the Colour Bar."[35]

In the League's analyses political self-determination, racial discrimination, and economic development were all linked. On the one hand, they observed that economic inequality was complicated by race and was therefore especially dangerous in the West Indian social context. On the other hand, they made it clear that they held the ruling, predominantly white local political leadership responsible for existing conditions and had little confidence in their capacity for reform. They chided the members of the Moyne Commission for recommending democracy as the ultimate goal yet declining to urge specific steps toward that goal. Disdainfully, they noted that the commission's recommendations regarding welfare and development were not new; they had been urged by popular leaders in the colonies for years but had been blocked by the local ruling classes, who held power through undemocratic franchises and the crown colony system of governance. The only solution was democratic reform, "so that those who have been advocating these policies for so many years may now get a chance to carry them out."[36]

With the recent rebellion as their mandate, they demanded such reforms immediately. "The issues at stake appear to be so clearly defined that we cannot see what further purpose would be served by appointing local committees to report on the franchise and membership qualifications (their reports, anyway will depend upon the political complexion of the members appointed)." They chided the Colonial Office for temporizing and reminded it of the manifest consequences of further delay. "Either the Colonial Office wishes to extend democratic institutions to these colonies now—in which case the drafting of the necessary Orders-in-Council is a[n] easy morning's work—or it does not. In the latter case, we fear that the result will be a continuance of that political tension between government and people which has ruled in the West Indies for the last twenty years and which came to a head in recent disturbances." Speaking for the now mobilized masses, they boldly asserted the urgency of their demand. "Rightly or wrongly, West Indians are 'fed up' with protestations that Britain holds democracy for them as their ultimate achievement; they will judge the Colonial Office by what it offers now, and not by what it promises for the future."[37] Until the political and constitutional changes that they recommended were effected, Arthur Lewis added in a separate communication, it was "useless to expect any substantial improvement in the standard of living, and useless to dismiss the inevitable disturbances as 'political agitation.'"[38]

Repeatedly, therefore, League lobbyists insisted that economics was "only half the problem." Reversing the order preferred by the Colonial Office, they insisted that the transfer of political power was the first requisite to social development and social improvement for the masses. Reforms in landholding, labor relations, health care, and trade unionism were important but essentially subordinate to the political question. Such reforms depended in turn on providing constitutionally sanctioned modes of popular expression. "Too long have the West Indies been dominated by bankrupt planters and absentee capitalist financeers [sic], interested only in the problems of labour supply, dividends and a remunerative price for sugar and oil. Crown Colony government has been found out." Although designed ostensibly as a system to protect the interests of the lower classes, it had degenerated into "a most effective means of tyrannising over them." The present system was a hybrid one of "partly representative institutions divorced from responsibility" and must be abolished. "Without drastic changes in the constitutions of these islands there seems little prospect of such [reform] measures, however strongly recommended, being carried out," they proclaimed in phrases reminiscent of Henry Taylor's trenchant memorandum of 1839, "since those who would carry them out cannot, those who can will not."[39]

In ringing phrases and urgent tones, therefore, West Indian and African colonial spokesmen insisted that political and economic freedom did not function in separable domains. To neglect one was to damn the other. This was not an unprecedented message. In somewhat different language, perhaps, it had been articulated in 1838 by peasant freeholders who staked their claims to land *and* votes and in 1865 by rebels at Morant Bay demanding land *and* justice in the magistrates' courts. And much like Morant Bay in 1865, or even the Baptist War of 1831–32, the Jamaica riots of 1938 underscored these demands and brought political and economic developments into sharper focus. As in these earlier instances, it was not so much the violence itself as what it portended for the future that moved a reluctant British government toward colonial reforms.

Shaping this commitment in 1938 was the fear that the economic grievances exposed by the Frome and Kingston unrest would soon be coupled with the equally profound political grievances propounded by the League and other West Indian activists. As Europe inched closer to a world war the stakes grew higher. Events during the war years and anticipation of postwar conditions gave greater impetus to a determination that had emerged late in 1938 to make a decisive break with past colonial policies. Britain became more sensitive to the political impact of unfavorable propaganda about the colonies on its war effort and on its prospective postwar role as a world leader. There was also concern that events in the West Indies prefigured the future of the entire colonial empire, especially the vast, important colonies of Africa. Indeed, for key British policymakers, the violence and protest in the West Indies brought into question the future of the entire colonial empire.[40] It was no longer simply workers rebelling against their poor living conditions but the growing class consciousness evident in their actions and the frightening political consequences should that class consciousness acquire worldwide content and direction.

Thus a new colonial philosophy emerged, already implicit in prewar discussions but now enshrined in landmark legislation: the Colonial Development and Welfare Acts of 1940 and 1945.[41] Development and modernization of social services, the British government concluded, would be the only way to delay the inevitable, irresistible demands for decolonization and, afterwards, to retain a predominant political influence in the newly independent nations.[42] In proposing increased colonial development and welfare funding in 1945, for example, Colonial Secretary George Hall made the connection between economic development and the postponement of colonial independence explicit. He argued that Britain did not intend to dominate other people, but then "neither was it their intention to abandon peoples who had come to depend upon us for their security and wellbeing." He went on to argue that "towards self-government the colonies would proceed as fast as they showed themselves capable of going. If these things were better understood, there would be less criticism of what was stigmatized as British imperialism."[43] In 1948, Creech-Jones would restate this policy for the Overseas League: "A higher standard of living is, in its turn, a necessary condition of the rapid and successful constitutional advance of these territories towards parliamentary institutions and ultimate self-government."[44]

In these formulations, therefore, economic development was an organic, politically neutral phenomenon; it required informed, technical decisions, not political and moral choices. Thus colonial populations could undergo the necessary economic transformation while delaying the more dangerous political changes. The postponement of political maturity until the completion of an economic and social adolescence also appealed to British policymakers determined to retain the essence of their classic compromise between democratic ideology and imperial ambition. But the assumption of colonial acquiescence to such postponement was a flaw even contemporaries could see. Perusing the government's colonial policy, a London *Times* editorialist noted Oliver Stanley's declaration that the greatest emphasis of colonial development must be on social and economic aspects and not political. "Ideally he may be right. It is no doubt more desirable that the peoples of the Colonial Empire should be paid adequate prices for their produce, should enjoy economic prosperity, and receive the foundations of an education than that they should engage prematurely in political agitation and demand rights which they are not yet fit to exercise. But this is not how things are likely to work out in practice."[45] The next two decades of British colonial history would prove this last observation correct.

"Freedom is a constant struggle"

On 6 August 1962, amid fireworks, street dancing, and solemn ceremonies, Jamaica became an independent nation and member of the British Commonwealth. As the *Times* editorialist had predicted, social changes set in motion by the 1938 labor rebellion and its wartime and postwar aftermath could not be contained within boundaries set by British authorities.[46] The Colonial Office resisted West Indian demands for political change, but they could not indefinitely deny them. By November 1944 Jamaicans had won the right to universal adult suffrage and governmental reform. In the elections the following month, ordinary Jamaicans were able, for the first time since 1865, to elect representatives to a national legislature. With this advent of the long-dreaded "party" or "responsible government," Jamaicans found vehicles for mobilizing and focusing their drive toward national independence. Two major leaders of that mobilization, Norman W. Manley and his cousin Alexander Bustamante, had themselves emerged out of the 1938 struggles, Manley as a moderate spokesman for the socialist left and Bustamante as leader of the largest labor union. As the leaders of the People's National Party (PNP) and the Jamaica Labour Party (JLP), respectively, they would dominate the politics of decolonization during the 1950s and early 1960s. Eventually, Bustamante became the first prime minister of the first new nation to emerge in the Western Hemisphere in more than half a century.[47]

With independence coming on the heels of a period of impressive economic growth, many Jamaicans entered this brave new world confident that the new nation was "better equipped than most of the new and even old nations of the world" to fashion a prosperous future. On independence eve newspaper editorials and features consciously linked its present state and future prospects with its historic struggles: from the Maroon rebels of the eighteenth century to the Baptist War of 1831–32, from the Morant Bay Rebellion in 1865 to the labor rebellion in 1938. Those same papers, however, carried other articles warning of troubles ahead, raising directly or obliquely the issue whether political independence could survive in a society so thoroughly dependent economically on the world's markets for agricultural and mineral commodities.[48]

Indeed, resolving the question of political independence did not determine how national sovereignty would be defined in a world of uncertain commodity markets and exigent international financial institutions. As Jamaicans sought to chart a path toward economic prosperity, they found themselves constrained within the boundaries set by powerful outsiders—outsiders whose precepts, now constructed as the "science of development economics," bore an uncanny similarity to the convictions of nineteenth-century laissez-faire radicals.

The precise parallels between the economic theories of classical liberalism and those of twentieth-century development economists need not be overdrawn, but there are strong family resemblances between the two exercises in shaping policy in the aftermath of a moment of symbolic liberation. In each case the meaning of freedom was in dispute. In each case a powerful group whose allegiances lay

Alexander Bustamante

Norman Manley

elsewhere sought to persuade Jamaicans that freedom was not self-determination and that submission to market forces was the essence of liberation. Like their predecessors', the development economists' putatively scientific analyses were grounded in moralistic judgments, hortatory pronouncements, and ideological assumptions.[49] In the decolonized world of the late twentieth century, it seemed, the problem of freedom would be both old *and* new.

The issue would not be resolved in that first decade of independence, nor in the two decades immediately following. Bustamante's Jamaica Labour Party led the new nation through that first decade, a period when the favorable economic expansion of the 1950s began to turn sour as foreign investment declined, the sugar industry stagnated, and the United Kingdom began to close its doors to immigrants from its former colonies. Norman Manley's son, Michael, would be elected prime minister in 1972 on a platform promising a socialist new deal for the Jamaican poor, appropriating from the patois of constituents his campaign slogan, "Better must come." He found instead that his field of action was severely limited by the constraints imposed by external powers, political and economic.[50]

Of course, Jamaicans were not alone in discovering that the issues of freedom and coercion required new definitions and must be fought on new terrain. Although the West Indies in general and Jamaica in particular had played major roles in bringing attention to the issue of colonial rule, they did not hold center stage in postwar independence campaigns. India and British Africa, two areas whose fates had been bound with the West Indies historically through slavery and indentured labor, were the foci of the main anticolonial struggles and shaped the major issues of nation building in a decolonized world. Colonies in Africa, not the West Indies, had attracted the lion's share of development funding under the Colonial Development and Welfare Acts.[51] Nonetheless, the histories of the former American colonies anticipated many of the ideological and policy issues of this new era of freedom in the sociopolitical and geographical zone called "the Third World," a phrase that resonates hauntingly with an earlier notion that some places were "beyond the line."

At the turn of the twentieth century, the great African American intellectual and activist W. E. B. Du Bois wrote: "The problem of the twentieth century is the problem of the color-line,—the relations of the darker to the lighter races of men in Asia and Africa and the islands of the sea."[52] With these words Du Bois introduced "Of the Dawn of Freedom," the second essay of a collection in which he challenged the conventional wisdom of his day about the role and fate of peoples of African descent in world history. His invocation of the color line can be read as merely an insistence on the salience of race and racial ideology in the establishment and maintenance of structures of inequality. But coming at the beginning of an essay on Reconstruction and the aftermath of the American Civil War, Du Bois's statement also links the central issues of the emancipation era with those of the twentieth century. Taken as a whole his essays argued that the fates of freed peoples and their descendants would be determined in a matrix formed by labor, politics, and an evolving racial ideology rather than in any one of these alone; that "work, culture, liberty" were merging pathways to self-fulfillment; and that the most important lessons taught by the experiences and struggles of freed peoples and their descendants had too soon been forgotten by the leaders of his generation. Thus from the perspective of that age of empire the problem of the color-line and the problem of freedom were inescapably linked.

On the eve of the twenty-first century these twin problems of negotiating human difference and of achieving human self-fulfillment confront us still, and the relevance of Du Bois's message about what could be learned from the travail and triumph of nineteenth-century freed people endures. Freedom, ex-slaves quickly learned, is not guaranteed by legal codes and proclamations; rather it must be realized in the contested process of fashioning social relations. Certainly, nothing in the ex-slave's experience authorizes the fanciful notion that Europeans, their self-congratulatory propaganda to the contrary, had any special talent for free institutions, any special legacy to bestow or to teach. Indeed the blindnesses and brutalities of the postemancipation era suggest that theirs was not an example worthy of uncritical emulation. Freedom's realization, for any people, is always specific and therefore historical, always contingent and therefore open to contestation. Freedom's meaning, for any era, has to be fashioned out of elements that are both ideological and material. We make the world as we know it; we know it by how we make it. The knowing and the making are, in the words of one of the protest songs of the American Civil Rights Movement, "a constant struggle."

Appendix 1

Sources for and Analysis of Data on Landholding and Migration

Estimating the Number of Peasant Freeholders

Multiple holdings and urban freeholders. The principal sources of data on the numbers, growth, and distribution of Jamaican freeholds are Douglas Hall's *Free Jamaica, 1838–1865: An Economic History* (New Haven: Yale UP, 1959), 160–62 (table 19), and Gisela Eisner's *Jamaica, 1830–1930: A Study in Economic Growth* (Manchester: Manchester UP, 1961), 220 (table 35). Hall's figures are collated from the published *Jamaica Almanacs* for the period 1840–45; Eisner's figure for 1860 is taken from contemporary testimony, and those for 1880–1930 are based on tax returns as reported in the *Handbook of Jamaica*. The major difficulty with using any of these figures to estimate the number of small freeholders is that there is no precise method of systematically adjusting for cases of multiple holdings and for urban plots not devoted to agriculture. (For a detailed discussion of these methodological difficulties and the limitations of the figures based on tax returns see Veront M. Satchell, *From Plots to Plantations: Land Transactions in Jamaica, 1866–1900* [Mona, Jamaica: Institute of Social and Economic Research, U of the West Indies, 1990], 7–8.) For this reason my tables and figures in chapter 5 refer to "freeholds" rather than "freeholders." I would argue, however, that the growth in the number of freeholds of ten acres or fewer is nonetheless an effective proxy for the growth in the number of peasant freeholders, especially during the 1840s, when urban populations were small and multiple holdings were unlikely to be numerous. For later years the shape of the graph (i.e., a dramatic upward slope) would remain much the same, and the magnitude of the growth in freeholds impressive, even if one were to apply a generous adjustment to the figures. Satchell's analysis (125–27 [table 6.7]), based on a count of actual real estate transactions, suggests that a deflation by 20 percent would be a generous correction factor in 1860. I have used that figure to establish the lower range of my estimates of the numbers of people and families involved in peasant agriculture in the mid-nineteenth century. It is unclear what correction figure would be appropriate for the late nineteenth and early twentieth centuries; Satchell states that over 70 percent of the smallholders reported in the tax returns possessed multiple holdings during that period. Of course, tax figures also *understate* the actual number of property holders because of tax avoidance. Given this indeterminacy, the numbers of freeholds recorded in the later years can only be taken as suggestive of the general trend in small-scale landowning. Significantly, the expansionist trend these figures delineate is consistent with that reflected in Satchell's own figures, which show that until 1890 there was a steady increase in the acreage in the hands of small settlers (131 [table 6.12]).

Squatting. Another source of indeterminacy in estimating the peasant population is the practice of squatting on abandoned estates, which was endemic during most of the postemancipation era. Of course, as long as the estimates are for total growth of peasant freeholds, the existence of squatting merely suggests the necessity for an indeterminate upward revision of the estimates. When one's objective is to estimate the geographical distribution of peasants, however, any significant number of squatters will complicate the calculations. Eisner, for example, estimates a total of "10,000 or more" squatters by 1846, basing her calculations on the estimated unemployment and underemployment caused by the abandoning of sugar estates. But the qualitative evidence she relies on to establish that squatting was prevalent very early appears to come from planter testimony at the 1847 hearings of the Select Committee on Sugar and Coffee Planting, which reflects the dramatic economic downturn and crisis following passage of the 1846 Sugar Duties Act (see Eisner, *Jamaica, 1830–1930*, 213–15). There is little in the special magistrates' reports for the early 1840s to suggest that 1847 testimony accurately characterizes the period 1840–45. As noted in chapter 4, the latter was a period during which there were actually efforts to expand sugar production. The areas hardest hit economically, the coffee parishes, were among those with large and rapidly increasing numbers of legally registered freeholds. Thus, whatever squatting did occur might be expected to augment rather than subtract from the numbers and distribution reported in chapter 5.

Estimating Internal Migration of the Working Population

The calculation of the interparish migration of black Jamaicans is based on the revised census figures reported in B. W. Higman's edition of the Jamaica censuses for 1844 and 1861 ("The Jamaican Censuses of 1844 and 1861: A New Edition, Derived from the Manuscript and Printed Schedules in the Jamaica Archives," [Mona, Jamaica: Social History Project, Department of History, U of the West Indies, 1980]) and on the 1834 distribution of the apprentice population (B. W. Higman, *Slave Population and Economy in Jamaica, 1807–1834* [Cambridge: Cambridge UP, 1976]). In-migration is defined as the percentage increase in the population of a given parish above the estimated rate of natural increase on the island, which is estimated in turn from islandwide population growth between the relevant census years. For example, the island population grew by 18 percent between 1844 and 1861; therefore, the parishes with smaller increases were assumed to have lost population through migration, while the seven parishes with larger increases were assumed to have gained. The calculation procedures vary slightly for the different periods:

1838–1844. Black migration for the period 1838–44 was determined by calculating the difference between estimates of a parish's black population growth and the islandwide growth figure. The growth of the black population is a good indicator of the migration of the ex-slave population, because "black" and "slave" described practically synonymous categories among rural populations. Both the colored slave population and the colored free population were heavily concentrated in urban areas (especially Kingston and Spanish Town), and colored slaves on the plantations were primarily in nonpraedial occupations. It is likely that after emancipation they too were attracted to the cities and towns, or remained in the skilled manufacturing sector of estate employment. Some probably became smallholders raising coffee or other crops. Given these tendencies, together with the overwhelming (90 percent) predominance of blacks in the total population, it seems fairly safe to assume that the relevant population from which 95 percent or more of the peasants would have been drawn comprised black ex-slaves. The figures for the 1838 black population are estimated, therefore, by taking the total 1838 apprentice population for a given parish and, using the inverse of Barry Higman's estimates of the percentage colored in each parish among the slave population in 1832, calculating an estimate of the number of black apprentices (see *Slave Population and Economy,* 58, 140, 256 [tables 7, 26, A3.7]).

1844–1861. The calculations for 1844–61 are restricted to the working-age black population, that is, those between ten and sixty years of age. Although changes in any parish's working population were highly correlated with changes in that parish's total population, most parishes that gained population also experienced a proportionate growth of the working population that was considerably greater than the growth of the total population. What this phenomenon suggests is the migration of young adults.

The direction of the postemancipation population flow was exactly opposite that of the slavery era. For example, Barry Higman's figures show that
eleven parishes were net exporters of slaves, while eight others were importers. Seven of the parishes that slaves left later became magnets for freed
people seeking to establish freeholds. Among the parishes losing slaves were
Manchester, Port Royal, St. Ann, Clarendon, and St. Thomas-in-the-Vale,
all of which had large increases in peasant freeholds in the 1838–44 period.
Westmoreland and St. Andrew also attracted black migrants (an indicator of
the growth of peasant holdings) in the 1844–61 period. Only one of the parishes showing a net in-migration in the 1844–61 period, St. Elizabeth, was
also an importer of slaves before emancipation. The exporters were Westmoreland, Hanover, Manchester, St. Ann, Clarendon, St. Thomas-in-the-
Vale, St. Andrew, Port Royal, St. George, St. David, Portland, and Kingston.
The importers were St. James, Trelawny, St. Elizabeth, Vere, St. Dorothy, St.
John, St. Catherine, St. Mary, and St. Thomas-in-the-East. Many of the slaves
moved to new parishes were probably nonpraedials (see Higman, *Slave Population and Economy*, 63–68 and table 8).

Appendix 2

Sources for and Analysis of Data on the Jamaica Assembly

Members of the Jamaica Assembly, 1837–1865

I have endeavored to identify the race, principal occupation, and party affiliation of members of the Jamaica Assembly for the period 1837–65. A number of the more prominent residents, especially in the earlier period, appear in the wills and inventories filed at the Island Record Office, most often as decedents but also as executors, administrators, or legatees. By far the most common source of information was the governors' correspondence with the Colonial Office. Where no specific information was available indicating that a member was Afro-Jamaican or Jewish, I have assumed that he was white and non-Jewish. For party affiliation I have used contemporary testimony, where it exists, together with the member's voting record; in cases of discrepancy I have given priority to the voting pattern. Gad J. Heuman's excellent study of the Afro-Jamaican assemblymen provided an indispensable starting point for the work of sorting out who was who in Jamaican politics during this period (*Between Black and White: Race, Politics, and the Free Coloreds in Jamaica, 1792–1865* [Westport, Conn.: Greenwood, 1981], 58–180 passim). His work was the source for or confirmed many of the identifications I have made. My other sources are listed below.

ISLAND RECORD OFFICE, SPANISH TOWN

Wills, Probate, and Inventories [Name, location (liber/folio), date entered]: Wellwood Maxwell Anderson, 135/33 (1888); Alexander Barclay, 130/20 (1864); Richard Barrett, 119/126 (1839); 154/133 (1840); Hiam Barrow, 132/65 (1872); Fitzherbert Batty, 124/216 (1848); Henry John Blagrove, 127/25 (1854); Wellesley Bourke, 133/359 (1877); Moses Bravo, 112/74 (1831); Hamilton Brown, 124/94 (1846); Samuel Constantine Burke, 137/76, 253 (1908); Colin Chisolm, 160/179 (1867); John Shea Clachar, 160/214 (1868); William Collman, 12/183 (1847); Henry Forbes Colthirst, 135/186 (1891); Henry Cox, 127/129 (1856); Charles Henry Darling, 137/381 (1919); James Davidson, 130/199 (1868); Foster Davis, 161/46 (1870); Robert Fairweather, 122/156 (1843); Alexander Forbes, 123/217 (1845); Henry Franklin, 128/28 (1857); William Frater, 119/222 (1839); Henry George Groves, 161/119 (1871); Edward Trueman Guy, 127/27 (1854); George William Hamilton, 155/184 (1852); Daniel Hart, 126/116 (1852); Lawrence Hyslop, 127/121 (1856); Wellwood Hyslop, 123/135 (1845); Maximillian August, Baron Ketelhodt, 160/165 (1866); Philip Lawrence, 129/226 (1864); Charles Levy, 136/196 (1896); Isaac Levy, 134/368 (1885); Moses Lyon, 130/76 (1866); Francis MacCook, 126/79 (1852); John Mais, 126/216 (1854); Arnold Lewis Malabre, 134/71, 230 (1878, 1881); Peter Moncrieffe, 162/77, 84 (1876); Michael Muirhead, 134/389 (1885); John Nunes, 160/198 (1868); Robert Nunes, 130/30 (1865); John Edward Wilson Panton, 159/1 (1854); Robert Pearson, 131/6 (1868); John Andrew Pillon, 132/91 (1873); John Vincent Purrier, 125/39 (1848); Findlater Roper, 135/469 (1898); Jacob J. Sanguinetti, 131/123 (1870); Henry Bridgewater Shaw, 136/147 (1900); Henry Houlton Shirley, 127/221 (1856); Raynes Waite Smith, 132/207 (1874); John Jacob Stamp, 150/151 (1834); George Radcliffe Stennett, 126/192 (1853); William Titley, 158/124 (1852); George Harrison Townshend, 124/71 (1846); Edward Vickars, 130/182 (1867) and 161/113 (1871); Robert Watt, 120/180 (1841); Hugh Anthony Whitelocke, 161/67 (1870); Benjamin Whittaker, 119/211 (1839); Joseph Stone Williams, 116/131 (1836); George Wright, 124/110 (1847).

JAMAICA ARCHIVES, SPANISH TOWN

Blagrove, Henry John. Journal, 1841–42. Private Gifts.
The Methodist Church in Jamaica, District Minutes, 1830–66. Ecclesiastical.
Sangster Family Collection, Private Gifts. Plummer, Oscar. "Biographical Sketch of Abraham Lindo, One of the Most Prominent Jamaica Characters of the 18th Century." In Scrapbook and Newspaper Clippings.

NATIONAL LIBRARY OF JAMAICA, KINGSTON

Cave, S. Memorandum Book: Sugar Estates, 1846–51, 70. MS18.

Hill, Richard of Jamaica. A Passport or *Laisser Passer*. 3 Dec. 1829. MS756A.

Hill, Richard. Biographical Information. R. E. Merren to Frank Cundall, 31 Dec. 1918. MS942.

Jordon, Edward. Obituary. *Morning Journal*, 9 Feb. 1869. MST901. Also in Frank L. Casserly Collection, Box 2, MS317.

Sligo Estate Papers. MS275D. Alexander Bravo to Marquis Sligo, 10 May 1839.

Whitelock(e) Collection, 1845–55. Letterbook of H. A. Whitelocke, 30 Sept. 1845–16 Sept. 1846. MS1633.

Young Collection. "Who's Who and What's What in Jamaica, 1879–80." MST318. No. 74.

PUBLIC RECORD OFFICE, KEW, ENGLAND

Colonial Office Records

Earl of Elgin to Edward G. Stanley, 3 Oct. 1843 (confidential), and 21 Nov. 1843 (confidential), CO 137/275.

Charles Grey to Earl Grey, 7 June 1847, no. 58, CO 137/292; 6 Mar. 1848, no. 26, CO 137/296; 6 Oct. 1848, no. 81, and 6 Nov. 1848, no. 81, CO 137/297; 20 Nov. 1848, no. 105, CO 137/298; 27 Feb. 1851, no. 17, and 15 Mar. 1851, no. 27, CO 137/309; 11 June 1851, no. 46, CO 137/309; 28 July 1852, no. 68, CO 137/310.

Henry Barkly to William Molesworth, 24 Oct. 1855 (confidential), CO 137/327; 28 Sept. 1855, no. 96, CO 137/331; Henry Barkly to Henry Labouchere, 14 Mar. 1856 (confidential) and 21 Apr. 1856, no. 57, CO 137/331.

Charles Darling to Duke of Newcastle, 24 Nov. 1860 (confidential), CO 137/346; 23 Nov. 1861 (confidential), CO 137/357.

Edward John Eyre to Duke of Newcastle, 7 Apr. 1863, no. 78, CO 137/371; 29 Sept. 1863 (confidential), CO 137/374; 9 Mar. 1864 (confidential) and 23 Mar. 1864, no. 109, CO 137/380.

NEWSPAPERS

Colonial Standard, 4 Jan. 1850.

Falmouth Post, 7, 10 Aug., 4 Sept. 1849.

New York Herald, 13 June 1853.

PUBLIC DOCUMENTS

Parliamentary Papers

"Papers in Explanation of Measures adopted for Giving Effect to the Abolition of Slavery Act." *PP* 1835 (177), 50:57, 60–61, 63–64, 94–96, 98–100, 107.

"Third Report from the Select Committee on Sugar and Coffee Planting." *PP* 1847–48 (167), 23:396–98.

"Report of the Jamaica Royal Commission (1866). Part II. Minutes of Evidence and Appendix." *PP* [3683-I], 31:95–96, 367, 502–3, 509, 511, 566–67, 641, 742–44, 795, 808, 856, 889.

Votes of the Honourable House of Assembly of Jamaica

1st sess., 1849–54, 253; 5th and 6th sess., 1849–54, 9, 391; 3d sess., 1854–59, 71, 186; 7th sess., 1854–59, 93; 1st sess., 1860–63, 1, 2.

Methods of Analyzing Roll Call Data

DATA SOURCES AND PREPARATION

Much of the discussion in chapter 7 is based on my analysis of roll call votes in the Jamaica Assembly between 24 October 1837 and 4 April 1865. (I did not find a complete copy of the proceedings of the final, post–Morant Bay Rebellion session, so it was not coded.) I used two computer-generated routines that I have authored to calculate agreement scores and success scores for each legislator (for elaboration of the algorithms on which these computer routines are based see Charles M. Dollar and Richard J. Jensen, *Historian's Guide to Statistics: Quantitative Analysis and Historical Research* [New York: Holt, Rinehart, & Winston, 1971], 111–16). The primary data sources for my analysis were the published roll calls available at the British Library, which I have coded in machine-readable form. I have edited the roll call files, however, by excluding some repeat votes (i.e., successive votes on the same issue with exactly the same outcome) and a few votes in which absenteeism was excessively high (two-thirds or more).

As in a parliamentary system, a legislature was elected for an undetermined time period pending the governor's call for new elections. Between 1837 and 1865 seven different assemblies were elected: 1837–38, 1838–44, 1844–49, 1849–54, 1854–60, 1860–63, 1863–65. These legislative terms were subdivided into varying numbers of sessions, usually annual but sometimes more frequent. For political purposes, however, the governor might choose not to disband a particularly fractious legislature but to "prorogue" it, that is, to proclaim a short recess lasting several hours, days, or weeks. Since the reconvened legislature would constitute an entirely new "session," the result might be a plethora of sessions in any given year and a confusing and cumbersome data set. To facilitate references to a more manageable set of legislative sittings, therefore, I have regrouped the roll calls into twenty-six consecutively numbered sets. A key for cross-referencing my consecutively numbered sets to the officially recorded sessions of the seven legislatures follows:

Set No.	Legislature and Actual Sessions
	1837–1838
1	Sessions 1–5, 24 Oct. 1837–3 Nov. 1838. 41 roll calls.
	1838–1844
2	Sessions 1–3, 18 Dec. 1838–22 Dec. 1840. 27 roll calls.
3	Sessions 4–5, 26 Oct. 1841–18 Jan. 1842. 22 roll calls.
4	Sessions 6–7, 25 Oct.–31 Dec. 1842. 18 roll calls.
5	Session 8, 24 Oct. 1843–Feb. 1844. 26 roll calls.
	1844–1849
6	Session 1, 15 Oct.–23 Dec. 1844. 38 roll calls.
7	Session 2, 21 Oct.–31 Dec. 1845. 43 roll calls.
8	Sessions 3–4, 19 Oct.–28 Dec. 1847. 33 roll calls [3d sess. missing].
9	Sessions 5–9, 3 Aug. 1848–6 July 1849. 37 roll calls.
	1849–1854
10	Sessions 1–2, 5 Sept. 1849–1 Feb. 1850. 108 roll calls.
11	Sessions 3–5, 25 June 1850–23 May 1851. 88 roll calls.
12	Session 6, 28 Oct. 1851–26 Feb. 1852. 64 roll calls.
13	Sessions 7–9, 9 Nov. 1852–20 May 1853. 67 roll calls.
14	Session 10, 18 Oct. 1853–13 Apr. 1854. 81 roll calls.
	1854–1860
15	Session 1, 28 Nov. 1854–10 Apr. 1855. 48 roll calls.
16	Session 2, 16 Oct. 1855–27 Feb. 1856. 48 roll calls.
17	Session 3, 11 Nov.–24 Dec. 1856. 22 roll calls.
18	Session 4, 10 Nov.–31 Dec. 1857. 40 roll calls.
19	Session 5, 9 Nov. 1858–11 Jan. 1859. 79 roll calls.
20	Sessions 6–8, 3 Nov. 1859–12 Apr. 1860. 32 roll calls [incomplete].
	1860–1863
21	Session 1, 8 Nov. 1860–22 Mar. 1861. 64 roll calls.
22	Session 2, 12 Nov. 1861–5 Feb. 1862. 35 roll calls.
23	Session 3, 4 Nov. 1862–29 Jan. 1863. 26 roll calls.
	1863–1865
24	Session 1, 24 Mar.–May 1863. 28 roll calls.
25	Session 2, 27 Oct. 1863–17 Feb. 1864. 60 roll calls.
26	Sessions 3–5, 1 Mar. 1864–4 Apr. 1865. 75 roll calls.

AGREEMENT SCORES

The agreement scores for pairs of legislators are my principal means of discerning and quantifying patterns in the voting behavior of the assemblymen. The scores for pairs of legislators can be averaged to give a collective score for any group or subgroup, such as partisan or ethnic groups. By identifying which members actually voted with whom, such aggregate scores provide a method for testing nominal party affiliations and for measuring the relative strength of that political alliance. Generally a group of members who vote with one another more frequently (over 50 percent) than with other legislators are considered a "party." By this method one can also identify factions or blocs or core groups within a party (those with average scores of 70–80 percent) or a loosely aligned group of "swing" voters operating independently of the major parties.

Although the calculation and meaning of an agreement score are simple and readily understood, the measure is extremely sensitive to absenteeism, which was endemic in the Jamaica Assembly during certain periods. The agreement score should be understood, therefore, to be an indicator of agreement in a procedural rather than a substantive sense; that is, a legislator may in fact share the same views as another, but his absence at roll call renders that substantive agreement moot in the practical legislative context. It is a situation, therefore, not unlike that of the 40–50 percent of the eligible American electorate that does not vote; in practical political terms their nonvoting is a concession that counts as a "vote" for the winning side in any given election. Similarly, those Jamaican assemblymen who were chronically absent can be treated for our purposes as politically absent as well.

SUCCESS SCORES

In a parliamentary system a majority party whose members attend and vote together consistently will be the consistent winner in legislative business. Although the Planter party enjoyed a working majority for most of the period examined here, its members neither attended regularly nor voted together consistently. All this produced a situation that contemporaries called "anarchy" and that historians find confusing. By giving measures for the relative legislative effectiveness of the main parties, factions, or other subgroups, success scores provide some help in sorting out the voting patterns and power relations in the Assembly. A success score is calculated by counting the number of times that a member votes with the winning side on a given set of roll calls. The scores of individual members can then be aggregated by party, ethnicity, or any other relevant category.

Because its denominator is the total number of roll calls, this measure is also affected by absenteeism. But it is appropriate that absenteeism reduce a member's success score, since an absent member is normally unable to exercise his legislative will. A party with a high absentee rate will lose more than it wins and will be less successful than an adversary whose members attend and vote.

Notes

Preface

1. For a useful exposition of both the connection between contemporary conservatism and traditional liberalism and the relation between the conservatives' economic and political theory see Conrad P. Waligorski, *The Political Theory of Conservative Economists* (Lawrence: UP of Kansas, 1990), 3–6, 22–31.

2. "The End of History?" *National Interest*, Summer 1989, 3–35, quote on 9.

Prologue: The Problem of Freedom in an Age of Revolution

1. Eric J. Hobsbawm's trilogy on the nineteenth century reminds us of both our debts to the nineteenth century, in language and thought, and our difficulty, especially with regard to its final forty years, seeing clearly through that "twilight zone between history and memory" (see esp. *The Age of Empire, 1875–1914* [New York: Pantheon, 1987], 1–12).

2. The idea of a "dual revolution" is developed by Eric J. Hobsbawm in *The Age of Revolution, 1789–1848* (Cleveland, Ohio: World Publishing, 1962).

3. C. B. Macpherson, *The Political Theory of Possessive Individualism: Hobbes to Locke* (Oxford: Clarendon, 1962), 1–4; idem, *Democratic Theory: Essays in Retrieval* (Oxford: Clarendon, 1973), 3–23, 185–94.

4. Conrad P. Waligorski elaborates the centrality of "methodological individu-

alism" in contemporary conservative theory as well (see *The Political Theory of Conservative Economists* [Lawrence: UP of Kansas, 1990], 25–28).

5. For a suggestive, though brief, discussion of the contrast between modern and traditional consciousness of freedom see Orlando Patterson, *Slavery and Social Death: A Comparative Study* (Cambridge: Harvard UP, 1982). On African notions about individualism see John S. Mbiti, *African Religions and Philosophy*, 2d ed. (Portsmouth, N.H.: Heinemann, 1990); Suzanne Meirs and Igor Kopytoff, eds., *Slavery in Africa: Historical and Anthropological Perspectives* (Madison: U of Wisconsin P, 1977); and Christopher Davis-Roberts, "Mango Na Mitishambe: Illness and Medicine among the Batabwa of Zaire" (Ph.D. diss., U of Chicago, 1980).

6. *Capital*, trans. Ben Fowkes, 3 vols. (New York: Vintage, 1977), 1:874.

7. "On Liberty," in *The Philosophy of John Stuart Mill: Ethical, Political, and Religious*, ed. Marshall Cohen (New York: Modern Library, 1961), 197–98. See also Graeme Duncan, *Marx and Mill: Two Views of Social Conflict and Social Harmony* (Cambridge: Cambridge UP, 1973), 217, 222–25, 229, 255–56.

8. Macpherson, *Political Theory of Possessive Individualism*, 60.

9. Their role in conservative doctrine suggests that the balkanization of the academic disciplines and embrace of positivism are neither ideologically nor politically neutral developments (cf. Waligorski, *Conservative Economists*, 15–16, 19–22).

10. In the United States, the Emancipation Proclamation and the Thirteenth Amendment emancipated almost 4 million slaves between 1863 and 1865. Although Brazil had more slaves than the British West Indies at mid-century (about 1.5 million), only about half that number (723,419) were affected by its final emancipation legislation in 1888 (see David W. Cohen and Jack P. Greene, eds., *Neither Slave Nor Free: The Freedman of African Descent in the Slave Societies of the New World* [Baltimore: Johns Hopkins P, 1972], 314, 335–39; and Robert Conrad, *The Destruction of Brazilian Slavery, 1850–1888* [Berkeley: U of California P, 1972], 285 [table 3]).

11. *Hegel's Phenomenology of the Spirit*, trans. A. V. Miller (New York: Oxford UP, 1977), 114. Hegel's *Philosophy of Right* (1821) is also relevant to the issues discussed here. My reading of Hegel has been aided greatly by the following critiques: J. M. Bernstein, "From Self-consciousness to Community: Act and Recognition in the Master-Slave Relationship," and Seyla Benhabib, "Obligation, Contract, and Exchange: On the Significance of Hegel's Abstract Right," in *The State and Civil Society: Studies in Hegel's Political Philosophy*, ed. Z. A. Pelcyzynski (Cambridge: Cambridge UP, 1984), 14–39 and 159–77, respectively.

Chapter 1. The Meaning of Freedom

1. Testimony of John Henry Morris, in "Report from the House of Assembly on the injury sustained during the recent Rebellion," *PP* 1831–32 (561), 47: 19–20; and "Despatches between the Government and the Colonies relating to the Recent Rebellion among the Slaves," *PP* 1831–32 (285), 47:21–23, both [IUP reprint, Slave Trade, vol. 80]. The citation refers, in the first case, to document no. 561 in volume 47 of the published House of Commons *Parliamentary Papers* for the year 1831–32. All subsequent citations to these papers will follow this convention: *PP* [year], ([doc. #]), [vol.]. Those volumes consulted in the Irish University Press reprint edition will be noted by "[IUP reprint, (series title and volume)]." All page references are to the original source.

2. Earl of Belmore to Viscount Goderich, 6 Jan. 1832, in *PP* 1831–32 (285), 47:13–18; Mary S. Turner, *Slaves and Missionaries: The Disintegration of Jamaican Slave Society, 1787–1834* (Urbana: U of Illinois P, 1982), 157; Michael Craton, *Testing the Chains: Resistance to Slavery in the British West Indies* (Ithaca: Cornell UP, 1982), 299; Edward Kamau Brathwaite, "The Slave Rebellion in the Great River Valley of St. James—1831/32," *Jamaican Historical Review* 13 (1982): 11–30.

3. Ibid. Among the factors contributing to the unrest that precipitated the rebellion may have been the growing demographic imbalances in the slave work-force, which forced women and mulattoes into field labor and curtailed opportunities for skilled slaves to escape the debilitating field work on sugar estates (Turner, *Slaves and Missionaries,* chap. 6).

4. *PP* 1831–32 (561), 47:3–4, 39–45; Craton, *Testing the Chains,* 312–15.

5. "This terrible event, . . . though failing of its object as a direct means, was indirectly a death blow to slavery" (Henry Taylor, *Autobiography of Henry Taylor, 1800–1875,* 2 vols. [London: Longmans, Green, 1885], 1:123).

6. *PP* 1831–32 (285): 47:17, 21–24, 30–33. For accounts of earlier revolts see Orlando Patterson, *The Sociology of Slavery: An Analysis of the Origins, Development, and Structure of Negro Slave Society in Jamaica* (Rutherford, N.J.: Fairleigh Dickinson UP, 1967), 266–73; and Craton, *Testing the Chains,* 125–39.

7. Extract, Belmore to Goderich, 10 Feb. 1832, in "Communications relating to Slave Insurrections and Trials of Missionaries," *PP* 1831–32 (482), 47:5–6 [IUP reprint, Slave Trade, vol. 80]; confessions of John Davis, Edward Morrice, William Binham, Thomas Dove, and Robert Gardner, in *PP* 1831–32 (561), 47:30–32, 34–38, quote on 38. See also Turner, *Slaves and Missionaries,* 152; and Craton, *Testing the Chains,* 299.

8. Turner, *Slaves and Missionaries,* 150.

9. Mary Turner argues that it should have been called a *Native* Baptist war. The rebel leaders were active with the Native Baptists, an independent sect founded by slave refugees from the American Revolutionary War, as well as regular converts of the missionary Baptists. This identification is not unproblematic, however, and it leaves the difficult problem of accounting for the extraordinary acculturation of the leaders. This acculturation was not generally a characteristic of Native Baptists, who tended to be strongly influenced by African religious practices. It may be that like slaves in the United States, these particular Jamaican slaves sustained their own "invisible" church, which whites took to be Native Baptist (Turner, *Slaves and Missionaries,* 153–54; cf. Brathwaite, "Slave Rebellion," 13–15. For the United States see Albert J. Raboteau, *Slave Religion: The "Invisible Institution" in the Antebellum South* [New York: Oxford UP, 1978]. See chapter 8, below, for more discussion of the relationship between religion and resistance).

10. *PP* 1831–32 (561), 47:3–4; *PP* 1831–32 (285), 47:8–13, last three quotes on 8. See also *PP* 1831–32 (482), 47:2–26, 28–31.

11. For a description of the popular mobilization see Roger Anstey, "Religion and British Slave Emancipation," in *The Abolition of the Atlantic Slave Trade: Origins and Effects in Europe, Africa, and the Americas,* ed. David Eltis and James Walvin (Madison: U of Wisconsin P, 1981), 37–62; and Howard Temperley, *British Antislavery, 1833–1870* (London: Longmans, 1972).

12. Goderich to Belmore, 1 Mar. 1832, in *PP* 1831–32 (285), 47:39–48.

13. Ibid., 44.

14. "A Meeting of the Freeholders . . . of St. Mary," in ibid., 10.

15. Linton's confession, in *PP* 1831–32 (561), 47:29.

16. [Henry Taylor], "Colonial Office, January 1833. Memo: for the Cabinet," 24–28, CO 884/1 (hereafter "Taylor Memorandum").

17. *Hansard*, 17:1211; 18:1171, 1194–95.

18. Ibid., 17:1194, 1229–30.

19. "The attack falls into three phases: The attack on the slave trade, the attack on slavery, the attack on the preferential sugar duties. The slave trade was abolished in 1807, slavery in 1833, the sugar preference in 1846. The three events are inseparable. The very vested interests which had been built up by the slave system now turned and destroyed that system" (*Capitalism and Slavery* [Chapel Hill: U of North Carolina P, 1944], 136).

20. Roger Anstey, *The Atlantic Slave Trade and British Abolition, 1760–1810* (London: Macmillan, 1975); Seymour Drescher, *Econocide: British Slavery in the Era of Abolition* (Pittsburgh: U of Pittsburgh P, 1977).

21. For example, both Seymour Drescher and Thomas L. Haskell admit that capitalism had something to do with abolition, but they insist that its effects were indirect and unrelated to the development of a capitalist class (Drescher, *Capitalism and Antislavery: British Mobilization in Comparative Perspective* [New York: Oxford UP, 1987], 2, 12; Haskell, "Capitalism and the Origins of Humanitarian Sensibility," pt. 1, *AHR* 90 [Apr. 1985]: 340–42).

22. Williams, *Capitalism and Slavery*, 136.

23. For more discussion of these issues and their general historiography see Thomas C. Holt, "Of Human Progress and Intellectual Apostasy," *Reviews in American History* 15 (Mar. 1987): 50–58; idem, "'An Empire over the Mind': Emancipation, Race, and Ideology in the British West Indies and the American South," in *Region, Race, and Reconstruction: Essays in Honor of C. Vann Woodward*, ed. J. Morgan Kousser and James M. McPherson (New York: Oxford UP, 1982), 286; and idem, "Explaining Abolition," *Journal of Social History* 24 (Winter 1990): 371–78.

24. David Brion Davis, *The Problem of Slavery in Western Culture* (Ithaca: Cornell UP, 1966); idem, *The Problem of Slavery in the Age of Revolution, 1770–1823* (Ithaca: Cornell UP, 1975); idem, *Slavery and Human Progress* (New York: Oxford UP, 1984). I have argued elsewhere that in some ways Davis's most recent book undercuts some of the bold themes spelled out in the second, but I believe that this is still a fair statement of Davis's core thesis (Holt, "Of Human Progress and Intellectual Apostasy"; see also Davis, "Reflections on Abolitionism and Ideological Hegemony," *AHR* 92 [Oct. 1987]: 797–812).

25. Davis, *The Problem of Slavery in the Age of Revolution*, 254.

26. Clifford Geertz's influential essay on ideology is a starting point for a definition. Rejecting the views of ideologies as merely forms of "higher cunning" or rationalizations of our interests, Geertz approaches them as "systems of interacting symbols," as "patterns of interworking meanings," as vocabulary, as "maps," as "metaphor." With them we unravel the complex relationship between objective reality and perceptions on the one hand and the ambiguities resulting when changes in perception and reality are not synchronized on the other. Similarly, Antonio Gramsci, in his *Prison Notebooks*, refers to ideology as "spontaneous philosophy," "language," "ways of seeing things and of acting" (Geertz, "Ideology as a Cultural System," in *Ideology and Discontent*, ed. David Apter [New York:

Free Press, 1964], 47–76; Gramsci, *Selections from the Prison Notebooks*, ed. and trans. Quintin Hoare and Geoffrey Nowell Smith [New York: International Publishers, 1971], 323, 375–77. Cf. Davis, "Reflections on Abolitionism and Ideological Hegemony," 799; and Göran Therborn, *The Ideology of Power and the Power of Ideology* [London: Verso & New Left Books, 1980], 2, 18).

27. Davis, *The Problem of Slavery in the Age of Revolution*, 41.

28. Here it is also useful to recall Geertz's observation that the "power of a metaphor derives precisely from the interplay between the discordant meanings it symbolically coerces into a unitary conceptual framework and from the degree to which that coercion is successful in overcoming the psychic resistance such semantic tension inevitably generates in anyone in a position to perceive it. When it works, a metaphor transforms a false identification. . . into an apt analogy; when it misfires, it is a mere extravagance." This comment, appropriately enough for our purposes, was in reference to organized labor's decrying the Taft-Hartley Act as legalizing "slave labor" ("Ideology as a Cultural System," 59).

29. Drescher, *Capitalism and Antislavery*, 1–24, 72–73, 130–32. See also idem, "Cart Whip and Billy Roller: Antislavery and Reform Symbolism in Industrializing Britain," *Journal of Social History* 15 (Fall 1981): 3–24.

30. Drescher, *Capitalism and Antislavery*, 93–94, 162–66.

31. Indeed, one of Williams's key failings is that by ranging over the whole movement and applying evidence indiscriminately at times to different time periods and phases, he hopelessly confused his argument. For example, as Drescher has shown, the West Indies trade did not decline by 1807. But on this point Williams's evidence specifically addresses the period *after* 1821, and for that period he actually is confirmed by Drescher's own evidence (Williams, *Capitalism and Slavery*, 132; Drescher, *Capitalism and Antislavery*, 10).

32. In his more recent book, Drescher provides a graph showing this decline in trade but emphasizes a different point: that the British colonies were relatively more important to Britain in the period 1810–30 than were the French colonies to France in 1825–46. Elsewhere Drescher emphasizes that the absolute value of the trade remained high, but this does not appear to have been the perspective contemporary officials took. In *Econocide*, however, he does concede that the abolition of the slave trade weakened West Indian interests economically and made it easier to abolish slavery itself in 1833 (*Capitalism and Anti-Slavery*, 10, 139, fig. 7.1; *Econocide*, 183).

33. "I am not quite certain that to some extent a diminution of that production would be matter of regret—I am not quite certain, that it might not be for the benefit of the planters and of the colonies themselves, in the end, if that production were in some degree diminished" (*Hansard*, 17:1211–12). Explaining his own abolition proposal to a reluctant John Russell, Grey declared: "The plan I have suggested I am quite willing to admit is not one which will probably enable the planter to produce any thing like the quantity of sugar he now does but I think it will enable him to raise a smaller quantity at a less expense & if so of course he need not be any the loser, but supposing that I am wrong & that he is a sufferer by the change, the question is can any other measure by which there will be less injury inflicted on him be devised? I believe not" (Howick [Henry George Grey] to Lord John [Russell], 11 Jan. 1833, Papers of Lord John Russell, P.R.O. 30/22/1C, Public Records Office, Kew, fols. 111–14). By 1840, James Stephen would draw similar conclusions.

34. Roger T. Anstey estimates a decline of West India interest M.P.'s from about thirty-nine in 1820 to twenty-eight in 1831. Barry Higman counts thirty-one in 1831 but only nineteen by 1833 (Anstey, "Capitalism and Slavery: A Critique," *Economic History Review*, 2d ser., 21 [Aug. 1968]: 307–20; Higman, "The West India 'Interest' in Parliament, 1807–1833," *Historical Studies* [Melbourne] 13 [Oct. 1967]: 3 [table 1]).

35. *Hansard*, 17:1234; Taylor Memorandum, 59, 85.

36. Taylor Memorandum, 85. For other evidence on the ideology of the governing elite see David Eltis, *Economic Growth and the Ending of the Transatlantic Slave Trade* (New York: Oxford UP, 1987), chap. 2; and idem, "Abolitionist Perceptions of Society after Slavery," in *Slavery and British Society, 1776–1846*, ed. James Walvin (Baton Rouge: Louisiana State UP, 1982), 193–213.

37. Temperley, *British Antislavery*, 69–71; Davis, *The Problem of Slavery in the Age of Revolution*, chap. 5.

38. Temperley, *British Antislavery*, 70, 73; Michael Ignatieff, *A Just Measure of Pain: The Penitentiary in the Industrial Revolution, 1750–1850* (New York: Pantheon, 1978), 143–44, 146–47, 151.

39. Ignatieff, *Just Measure*, 132, 149; J. R. Poynter, *Society and Pauperism: English Ideas on Poor Relief, 1795–1834* (London: Routledge & Kegan Paul, 1969), 61, 91–92; Peter Bailey, *Leisure and Class in Victorian England: Rational Recreation and the Contest for Control, 1830–1885* (London: Routledge & Kegan Paul, 1978), 106, 108, 112; Temperley, *British Antislavery*, 72.

40. Ignatieff, *Just Measure*, 65, 147; Stephen, quoted in Paul Knaplund, *James Stephen and the British Colonial System, 1813–1847* (Madison: U of Wisconsin P, 1953), 16. For discussion of elite media and its circulation see T. W. Heyck, *The Transformation of Intellectual Life in Victorian England* (New York: St. Martin's, 1982), chap. 2.

41. For Villiers biographies see *DNB* 20:318, 347, 353; and Taylor, *Autobiography*, vol. 1, chap. 5. Edward Gibbon Wakefield's demographic ideas are also relevant to Taylor's scheme, but there is no evidence that he read Wakefield. Possibly Wakefield's theories were such commonplaces by 1832 that Taylor did not need to read him to feel his influence.

42. Jeremy Bentham, *An Introduction to the Principles of Morals and Legislation*, ed. J. H. Burns and H. L. A. Hart (London: Athlone, 1970), 11.

43. Davis, *The Problem of Slavery in the Age of Revolution*, 49.

44. Various aspects of the argument that there was no necessary incompatibility between slavery, capitalism, and free trade are developed by Howard Temperley, "Capitalism, Slavery, and Ideology," *Past and Present* 75 (May 1977): 94–118; and Rebecca J. Scott, *Slave Emancipation in Cuba: The Transition to Free Labor, 1860–1899* (Princeton: Princeton UP, 1985), chap. 4.

45. Barbon and North, quoted in Joyce Oldham Appleby, *Economic Thought and Ideology in Seventeenth-Century England* (Princeton: Princeton UP, 1978), 169, 170.

46. Joyce Oldham Appleby, "Ideology and Theory: The Tension between Political and Economic Liberalism in Seventeenth-Century England," *AHR* 81 (June 1976): 499–513, quote on 510.

47. Ibid., 511.

48. Ignatieff, *Just Measure*, xiii.

49. Appleby, "Ideology and Theory," 513.

50. Davis, *The Problem of Slavery in the Age of Revolution*, 242.

51. Bailey, *Leisure and Class in Victorian England*, 47–94, quote on 55.

52. Neil McKendrick, "Josiah Wedgwood and Factory Discipline," *Historical Journal* 4 (Mar. 1961): 30–55, quotes on 34, 38; see also E. P. Thompson, *The Making of the English Working Class* (New York: Vintage, 1963), esp. 194, 402–5.

53. Quoted in Richard Johnson, "Educational Policy and Social Control in Early Victorian England," *Past and Present* 49 (Nov. 1970): 102.

54. *Hansard*, 20:143.

55. Ignatieff, *Just Measure*, 75, 177, 189, 215.

56. Ibid., 75.

57. Bentham, quoted in Gertrude Himmelfarb, "Bentham's Utopia: The National Charity Company," *Journal of British Studies* 10 (Nov. 1970): 94.

58. Poynter, *Society and Pauperism*, xvii.

59. James Spedding, *Reviews and Discussions: Literary, Political, and Historical, Not Relating to Bacon* (London: C. Kegan Paul, 1879), 39; Henry Richard Vassall Fox Holland, *Holland House Diaries, 1831–1840*, ed. Abraham D. Kriegel (London: Routledge & Kegan Paul, 1977).

60. School inspector, quoted in Johnson, "Educational Policy and Social Control," 104; testimony of William Taylor in "Report of the Select Committee on the Extinction of Slavery Throughout the British Dominions with the Minutes of Evidence, Appendix and Index," *PP* 1831–32 (721), 20:29 (question 257) [IUP reprint, Slave Trade, vol. 2]; also quoted in Taylor Memorandum, 5.

61. The character and tactics of the Jamaican slave rebels of 1831 were strikingly similar to those of the Swing uprising that swept England just months earlier (Eric J. Hobsbawm and George Rudé, *Captain Swing: A Social History of the Great English Agricultural Uprising of 1830* [New York: Norton Library, 1975], chap. 2).

62. Ibid., 224.

63. Ibid., 257, 262–63.

64. For an example of Cobbett's racism and ridicule of the abolitionists' cause immediately before the Swing outbreaks see *Cobbett's Weekly Political Register*, 26 June 1830. For a discussion of the influence of Cobbett and Methodism in the rebellious counties see Hobsbawm and Rudé, *Captain Swing*, 87–88, 186–87.

65. For a discussion of working-class abolitionists and their use of the slavery controversy see Drescher, "Cart Whip and Billy Roller," 8–10.

66. Hobsbawm and Rudé, *Captain Swing*, 265.

67. Taylor's chief works are the poetic drama *Philip Van Artevelde* and a Machiavelli-style collection of essays, *The Statesman* (*DNB* 19:410–12; see also Taylor, *Autobiography*, vol. 1).

68. Taylor Memorandum, 45–47.

69. Ibid., 7, 54, 55. Cf. the comment by James Spedding in *Reviews and Discussions*, 45.

70. Taylor Memorandum, 54–55, 72.

71. Ibid., 55, 67; Taylor, *Autobiography*, 1:127–28.

72. Slave children would come under the plan once they reached six years; infants born during their mother's apprenticeship would inherit her "status," that is, her original day of freedom and any others she had earned; and slaves over seventy years would be given the option of "gratuitous" freedom immediately or continued care from their masters as slaves (Taylor Memorandum, 75–76).

73. Ibid., 76–77.

74. *DNB* 22:786–89.

75. Grey to Russell, 11 Jan. 1833, Russell Papers.

76. "Abolition of Slavery. Outline of Plan on, 1832–3," 12, CO 320/8, Public Records Office.

77. Grey to Russell, 11 Jan. 1833, Russell Papers.

78. Taylor, *Autobiography*, 1:128.

79. Grey to Russell, 11 Jan. 1833, Russell Papers; Taylor Memorandum, 72; Mulgrave to Goderich, 2 Mar. 1833, Ripon Papers, 1833–42, 2:22–35, Add.Ms. 40,863. See also William Law Mathieson, *British Slavery and Its Abolition, 1823–1838* (London: Longmans, Green, 1926), 228–29; and W. L. Burn, *Emancipation and Apprenticeship in the British West Indies* (London: Jonathan Cape, 1937), 109–12.

80. Stephen to Alfred Stephen, 1829, and Stephen to Taylor, 12 July 1833, in *The Right Honourable Sir James Stephen: Letters With Biographical Notes*, biographical notes by Caroline Emelia Stephen (N.p.: Printed for Private Circulation Only, 1906), 16, 29–30; "The Diary of James Stephen, 1846," ed. T. Barron and K. J. Cable, *Historical Studies* (Melbourne) 13 (Apr. 1969): 503–19; *DNB* 18:1049–51.

81. Stephen, *James Stephen*, 28–29.

82. *Hansard*, 17:1231–59, quotes on 1233, 1235, 1241, 1248.

83. Temperley, "Capitalism, Slavery, and Ideology," 107; report quoted in Poynter, *Society and Pauperism*, xvii n. 4.

84. John Earl Russell, *Recollections and Suggestions, 1813–1873* (London: Longmans, Green, 1875), 65–66; Kingsley, quoted in Douglas A. Lorimer, *Colour, Class, and the Victorians: English Attitudes to the Negro in the Mid-Nineteenth Century* (Leicester: Leicester UP, 1978), 195.

85. Taylor Memorandum, 66. On the Whigs' preference for controlled change, Kriegel observes: "The stratagem of concession for the sake of stability, so evident in the Whigs' implementation of Parliamentary reform, recurred so often as to assume the dimension of government policy" (*Holland House Diaries*, xxxiv).

Chapter 2. An Apprenticeship for Ex-Slaves

1. Madden, *A Twelvemonth's Residence in the West Indies during the Transition from Slavery to Apprenticeship*, 2 vols. (Philadelphia: Carey, Lea, & Blanchard, 1835), 2:6; Spedding, *Reviews and Discussions: Literary, Political, and Historical, Not Relating to Bacon* (London: C. Kegan Paul, 1879), 52–53, quote on 52.

2. Sligo to Spring Rice, 13 Aug. 1834, CO 137/192; Sligo to Sir George Cockburn, 31 Aug. 1834, Letterbooks of Peter Howe Browne, vol. 5, Private Letters, MS228, National Library of Jamaica, Kingston (hereafter "Sligo Letterbooks"); *Montego Bay Standard*, quoted in *Kingston Chronicle and City Advertiser*, 6 Nov. 1835; Walter Dendy to John Dyer, 12 Aug. 1834, Various Missionaries to Jamaica, Papers relating to the West Indies, 1813–1914, WI/5, Baptist Missionary Society, London.

3. W. L. Burn, *Emancipation and Apprenticeship in the British West Indies* (London: Jonathan Cape, 1937), 172.

4. Spedding, *Reviews and Discussions*, 38; Sligo to Edward Stanley, 5 June 1834, CO 137/192.

5. Burn, *Emancipation and Apprenticeship*, 18–30; Spedding, *Reviews and Discussions*, 77–78.

6. Burn, *Emancipation and Apprenticeship*, 183–230.

7. Ibid., 197–200, 203.

8. B. W. Higman, *Slave Population and Economy in Jamaica, 1807–1834* (Cambridge: Cambridge UP, 1976), 71–74, 208; Michael Craton, *Searching for the Invisible Man: Slaves and Plantation Life in Jamaica* (Cambridge: Harvard UP, 1978), 142–49.

9. Roderick Alexander McDonald, "'Goods and Chattels': The Economy of Slaves on Sugar Plantations in Jamaica and Louisiana" (Ph.D. diss., U of Kansas, 1981), 7–14.

10. Thomas McNeil to Lord Holland, 4 June 1835, 17 Nov. 1836, Holland House Papers, Add.Ms. 51,816; McDonald, "Goods and Chattels," 15.

11. Sligo to Spring Rice, 12 Oct. 1834, CO 137/193; Sligo to Richard Barrett, 23 Aug. 1834, and Sligo to Colonel Doyle, 1 Nov. 1834, Sligo Letterbooks; McNeil to Holland, 16 Feb. 1838, Holland House Papers.

12. Sligo to Spring Rice, 4 Oct. 1834, CO 137/193; Sligo to Secretary for the Colonies, 29 Jan. 1835, CO 137/197. Herbert N. Jarrett experienced difficulties similar to Cuthbert's. When he tried to cut back allowances, his trash house was burned down (Hearings before the Jamaica Assembly, 6 Nov. 1834, encl. with Sligo to Spring Rice, 29 Dec. 1834, in "Papers in Explanation of Measures adopted for Giving Effect to the Abolition of Slavery Act," PP 1835 [177], 50:77–108). For a description of other conflicts between planters and apprentices see Swithin Wilmot, "Not 'Full Free': The Ex-Slaves and the Apprenticeship System in Jamaica, 1834–1838," *Jamaica Journal* 17 (Aug.–Oct. 1984): 2–10.

13. Sligo to Charles Grant, 26 June 1835, no. 30, and Grant to Sligo, 26 Aug. 1835, no. 81, CO 137/199; *Falmouth Post*, 20 Jan. 1836.

14. Burn, *Emancipation and Apprenticeship*, 170–71; Sligo to Barrett, 23 Aug. 1834, and Sligo to Thomas McCornock, 18 July 1834, Sligo Letterbooks.

15. Hearings before the Jamaica Assembly, 6 Nov. 1834, 77–108.

16. For very similar descriptions of militant initiatives by freedwomen see Thomas Holt, *Black over White: Negro Political Leadership in South Carolina during Reconstruction* (Urbana: U of Illinois P, 1977), 34–35; Rebecca J. Scott, "Exploring the Meaning of Freedom: Postemancipation Societies in Comparative Perspective," *Hispanic American Historical Review* 68 (Aug. 1988): 427–28; and Lawrence N. Powell, *New Masters: Northern Planters during the Civil War and Reconstruction* (New Haven: Yale UP, 1980), 108–9.

17. Testimony of Melmoth, in *Votes*, 4th sess., 1832–34, app. 48, pp. 768–69.

18. Baines to Sligo, 9 Feb. 1836, encl. with Sligo to Glenelg, 9 Apr. 1836, in "Papers relative to the Abolition of Slavery in the British Colonies," PP 1837 (521-I), 53:34–36. The apprentices at Gibraltar Estate, in Port Royal, went on strike when the overseer attempted to arrange extra long work shifts. The special magistrates and the planters were unanimous in singling out women as the frequent leaders of protests and strikes among the workers (Sligo to Secretary for the Colonies, 7 Feb. 1835, CO 137/197).

19. Hearings before the Jamaica Assembly, 6 Nov. 1834, 108–9; R. S. Cooper to Sligo, 11 Aug. 1835, in "Papers relating to the Abolition of Slavery," PP 1836 (166), 48:118.

20. Sligo to Sir George Cockburn, 31 Aug. 1834, Sligo Letterbooks. S. H. Cooke to Sligo, 2 Mar. 1836; John Daughtrey to Sligo, 29 Dec. 1835; and Cooper to Sligo, 11 Aug. 1835, in PP 1836 (166), 48:118, 202, 291. Edward D. Baynes to Sligo, 30

June 1836; R. Chamberlaine to Sligo, 6 July 1836; and W. H. Bell to Sligo, 5 July 1836, in *PP* 1837 (521-I), 53:62–65. Sligo to Aberdeen, 20 May 1835; testimony of Samuel Anderson and Rudolph Lewis before Jamaica Assembly, 6 Nov. 1834, in *PP* 1835 (177), 50:84, 90, 164.

21. McDonald, "Goods and Chattels," 51, 55–57. On historical development of system and variations among parishes see Mary S. Turner, "Ground Provision Production and the Transition to Freedom in Jamaica" (Paper presented at the Conference on Cultivation and Culture, University of Maryland at College Park, 12–14 Apr. 1989). For similar descriptions of slaves selling goods to plantation personnel see Rebecca J. Scott, *Slave Emancipation in Cuba: The Transition to Free Labor, 1860-1899* (Princeton: Princeton UP, 1985).

22. McDonald, "Goods and Chattels," 53, 57, 59, 261–62.

23. Golden Grove workers were said to have shipped seventeen wagonloads of provisions in 1834 (Baines to Sligo, 4 Aug. 1835, in *PP* 1836 [166], 48:92–93; Henry Blake to Sligo, 17 Mar. 1835, and Hearings before the Jamaica Assembly, 6 Nov. 1834, 94–96, 142, 151).

24. McDonald, "Goods and Chattels," 63–64, 104–5.

25. *PP* 1835 (177), 50:361. The practice of selling to higglers was found during slavery, too (see McDonald, "Goods and Chattels," 89).

26. For wage comparisons, one might consider that an overseer received £200 to £300 sterling per year, and an attorney received several thousand pounds, sometimes as much as £10,000 (Hearings before the Jamaica Assembly, 31 Oct., 6 Nov. 1834, 53, 77–108, 361).

27. Spedding, *Reviews and Discussions,* 67–68; Hearings before the Jamaica Assembly, 31 Oct. 1834, 63–64. Henry Shirley was proprietor of Hyde Hall and Elingdon in Trelawny Parish, which had a total of thirteen hundred apprentices.

28. Spedding, *Reviews and Discussions,* 66–67; Hearings before the Jamaica Assembly, 31 Oct. 1834, and S. B. M. Barrett to Sligo, 16 Dec. 1834, encl. with Sligo to Spring Rice, 13 Dec. 1834, in *PP* 1835 (177), 50:60–62, 71; Report of H. H. Ives for Good Hope Estate, Tharp Family Papers, Letters and Accounts, Cambridge Records Office, Cambridge, England; Burn, *Emancipation and Apprenticeship,* 271.

29. *Falmouth Post,* 23 Dec. 1835. See chapter 4, below, for discussion of regional differences in production and adjustment to emancipation.

30. Alston to [Charles] Scott, 29 Oct. 1832, in Georgia Estate, St. Thomas-in-the-East, Jamaica, Letterbooks and Accounts, Mar. 1822–May 1835, vol. 3, MST132, National Library of Jamaica. Cf. Kathleen Mary Butler, "Slave Compensation and Property, Jamaica and Barbados, 1823–1843" (Ph.D. diss., Johns Hopkins U, 1986), 32.

31. Hearings before the Jamaica Assembly, 13 Nov. 1834, Sessional Papers, CO 137/193; and 31 Oct. 1834, in *PP* 1835 (177), 50:63–64. E. B. Lyon to Sligo, 12 Aug. 1835, and E. Fishbourne to Sligo, 31 Aug. 1835, in *PP* 1836 (166), 48:116, 120.

32. Sligo to Glenelg, 9 July 1836, in *PP* 1837 (521-I), 53:60–61.

33. Baynes to Sligo, 30 June 1836, ibid., 62–63. Daughtrey to Sligo, 25 Aug., 29 Dec. 1835; Cooper to Sligo, 11 Aug. 1835; and A. J. Fyfe to Sligo, 29 Dec. 1835, all in *PP* 1836 (166), 48:117–18, 202, 243–44. Daughtrey to Sligo, 24 Mar. 1835, in *PP* 1835 (177), 50:143.

34. Glenelg to Governors of the West India Colonies, 6 Nov. 1837, in "Papers in Explanation of the Measures Adopted For Giving Effect to the Act For the Abolition of Slavery," *PP* 1837–38 (154-I), 49:9–11.

35. Glenelg to Governors of the West India Colonies, 16 Nov. 1835, in *PP* 1836 (166), 48:49–57.

36. Glenelg to Sligo, 15 Oct. 1835; Dunne to Sligo, 30 Dec. 1835; Baynes to Sligo, 1 Jan. 1836; and Daughtrey to Sligo, 29 Dec. 1835, in ibid., 177, 207, 198–99, 204.

37. Glenelg to Governors of the West India Colonies, 30 Jan. 1836, in ibid., 58–60.

38. Ibid.

39. Ibid.

40. Ibid.

41. Ibid.

42. Trelawny Memorial, enclosed with Sligo to Aberdeen, 20 May 1835, in *PP* 1835 (177), 50:164; see also *Royal Gazette*, 15 June 1835, reprinted in *Falmouth Post*, 30 Sept. 1835: "We must not be deluded—our present apprentices will answer our necessities only in proportion to the facilities of their becoming petty settlers being withheld from them."

43. Mulgrave to Stanley, 14 Mar. 1834, CO 137/192. Sligo to Spring Rice, 26, 22 Dec. 1834, nos. 112, 107, CO 137/194; 17 Nov. 1834, no. 71, CO 137/193.

44. Richard Hill, "Continuation of Diary," 17 Mar.–3 May 1832, MS756C, National Library of Jamaica.

45. *Morning Journal*, 17 Aug. 1838.

46. Ibid.

47. Ibid.

48. Hill to Lionel Smith, 8 Jan. 1837, in *PP* 1837 (521-I), 53:268–69.

Chapter 3. An Apprenticeship for Former Masters

1. Mulgrave to Goderich, 2 Mar. 1833, Ripon Papers, 1833–42, 2:22–35, Add.Ms. 40,863.

2. Taylor, "Colonial Office, January 1833. Memo: for the Cabinet," 74, CO 884/1 (hereafter "Taylor Memorandum").

3. *DNB* 27:562–64, 566–68; Henry Richard Vassall Fox Holland, *Holland House Diaries, 1831–1840*, ed. Abraham D. Kriegel (London: Routledge & Kegan Paul, 1977), xvi–xviii, xxi.

4. Henry Taylor was a frequent visitor at Holland House at one time but stopped attending parties there because he did not like Lady Holland. Evidently he took offense at a cutting remark she once made about the poetry of Wordsworth, one of Taylor's literary heroes (*DNB* 20:115–17; Henry Taylor, *Autobiography of Henry Taylor, 1800–1875*, 2 vols. [London: Longmans, Green, 1885], 1:201).

5. Lord Glenelg to Holland, 27 May 1836; Thomas McNeil to Holland, 17 Aug. 1832; Lord Seaford to Holland, 29 Jan. 1834; and McNeil to Holland, 17 Nov. 1836, in Holland House Papers, Add.Ms. 51,819.

6. *DNB* 6:691–92.

7. B. W. Higman, *Slave Population and the Economy of Jamaica, 1807–1834* (Cambridge: Cambridge UP, 1976), 158.

8. Seaford to Holland, 10 Dec. 1831, Holland House Papers; Holland, *Holland House Diaries*, 137, 140.

9. Seaford to Holland, 2 Aug. 1833, Holland House Papers.

10. Seaford to Holland, 2 Aug. 1833, 14 Oct. 1834, 24 Dec. 1839, n.d., 29 Jan. 1834, ibid.

11. W. L. Burn, *Emancipation and Apprenticeship in the British West Indies* (London: Jonathan Cape, 1937), 152, 153.

12. McNeil to Holland, 25 Oct. 1836, and Seaford to Holland, 27 May 1834, Holland House Papers.

13. McNeil to Holland, 25 Oct. 1836, 28 July 1837, 26 Apr. 1836, 24 Oct. 1837, 4 June 1835, ibid.

14. McNeil to Holland, 4 June 1835, 28 July 1837, ibid.

15. Edward Kamau Brathwaite, *The Development of Creole Society in Jamaica, 1770–1820* (Oxford: Clarendon, 1971), 105; Gisela Eisner, *Jamaica, 1830–1930: A Study in Economic Growth* (Manchester: Manchester UP, 1961), 127; John Stewart, *A View of the Past and Present State of the Island of Jamaica* (1823; reprint, New York: Negro UP, 1969), 179; idem, *An Account of Jamaica and Its Inhabitants* (London: Longman, Hurst, Rees, & Orme, 1808), 253; Burn, *Emancipation and Apprenticeship*, 29; "Jamaica through French Eyes," *Kingston Daily Chronicle*, 25 Mar. 1916.

16. Richard B. Sheridan, *Sugar and Slavery: An Economic History of the British Indies, 1623–1775* (Baltimore: Johns Hopkins UP, 1974), 216–17, 229–33.

17. Ibid., 216–17, 231; Higman, *Slave Population and Economy*, 69.

18. Sheridan, *Sugar and Slavery*, 229; Stewart, *Past and Present State of Jamaica*, 184.

19. Sheridan, *Sugar and Slavery*, 385.

20. The careers of three prominent families—the Tharps, the Dawkins, and the Prices—illustrate the major patterns of absenteeism (see Tharp Family Papers, Letters and Accounts, Cambridge Records Office, Cambridge, England; Sheridan, *Sugar and Slavery*, 224–27; and Michael Craton, *Searching for the Invisible Man: Slaves and Plantation Life in Jamaica* [Cambridge: Harvard UP, 1978], 268. See also Michael Craton and James Walvin, *A Jamaica Plantation: The History of Worthy Park, 1670–1970* [London: W. H. Allen, 1970]).

21. Stewart also noted that the great attorneys refused to take salaries, which would have amounted to considerably less than one-half of what they would have received on a commission basis. Their numbers declined in the 1820s (Stewart, *Past and Present State of Jamaica*, 183–87, quotes on 183, 187; Brathwaite, *Creole Society*, 139).

22. Douglas Hall, "Absentee-Proprietorship in the British West Indies to About 1850," *Jamaican Historical Review* 4 (1964): 17; Craton, *Searching for the Invisible Man*, 266–69.

23. Sheridan, *Sugar and Slavery*, 368–70; Orlando Patterson, *The Sociology of Slavery: An Analysis of the Origins, Development, and Structure of Negro Slave Society in Jamaica* (Rutherford, N.J.: Fairleigh Dickinson UP, 1967), 45; Higman, *Slave Population and Economy*, 41; Stewart, *Past and Present State of Jamaica*, 183–87.

24. Brathwaite, *Creole Society*, 124–28, 267.

25. Brathwaite, *Creole Society*, 100. By contrast, Jack Greene's assessment of this same dichotomy suggests that the differences were ones of degree and not kind: "To one degree or another each colonial society is a new society that exists within a symbiotic relationship with one or more metropolitan societies" (Jack P. Greene, "Society and Economy in the British Caribbean during the Seventeenth and Eighteenth Centuries," *AHR* 79 [Dec. 1974]: 1499–1517, quote on 1516).

26. James Spedding, *Reviews and Discussions; Literary, Political, and Historical, Not Relating to Bacon* (London: C. Kegan Paul, 1879), 38; Sligo to Spring Rice, 25 Dec. 1834, in "Papers in Explanation of Measures adopted for Giving Effect to the Abolition of Slavery Act," *PP* 1835 (177) 50:72–74. See the epigraph at the beginning of this chapter.

27. Dunne to Sligo, 30 June 1835, in *PP* 1835 (177), 50:374. Other magistrates also blamed the attorneys for the failure of the apprenticeship system; as one put it, "the attorneys and overseers refused to forget their former power" (Henry Walsh to Sligo, 30 June 1835, ibid.).

28. Stewart, *Past and Present State of Jamaica*, 181; *Falmouth Post*, 14 Oct. 1835.

29. Richard S. Dunn, *Sugar and Slaves: The Rise of the Planter Class in the English West Indies, 1624–1713* (Chapel Hill: U of North Carolina P, 1972), 149; Stewart, *Past and Present State of Jamaica*, 218–19, 204, 168.

30. Ibid., 173. Richard S. Dunn finds the male-female ratio in 1673 to be 2.02 (*Sugar and Slaves*, 149). Wills and probate papers of Jamaican legislators were examined at the Jamaica Archives and the Island Record Office in Spanish Town. See appendix 2 for discussion of data collection.

31. Bryan Edwards, *The History, Civil and Commercial, of the British Colonies in the West Indies*, 2 vols. (London: J. Stockdale, 1793), 2:9.

32. "Reply of the House of Assembly of Jamaica to the Governor's Opening Speech," 8 Oct. 1833, in *PP* 1835 (177), 50:28; Spedding, *Reviews and Discussions*, 48.

33. Spedding, *Reviews and Discussions*, 48–49, 50.

34. Aberdeen to Sligo, 15 Jan. 1835, in "Papers in Explanation of the Proceedings of the Legislature of Jamaica, in reference to the Amendment of Their Original Act For Giving Effect to the Act of Parliament for the Abolition of Slavery," *PP* 1836 (0.44), 48:9–10.

35. "Governor's Speech to the Jamaican Assembly, August 1835," in ibid., 13–16; see also Thomas F. Buxton's objections to the Jamaican vagrancy laws in Buxton to Glenelg, 23 Dec. 1835, CO 137/207.

36. Taylor, *Autobiography*, 1:206.

37. Seaford to Holland, 29 Jan. 1834, Holland House Papers; Burn, *Emancipation and Apprenticeship*, 148–49, 150. Sligo's ship, the *Pylades*, was a sixteen-gun brig that carried letters of marque permitting him to seize enemy cargo.

38. Aberdeen to Sligo, 14 Apr. 1835, Aberdeen Papers, Add.Ms. 43,333; Holland, *Holland House Diaries*, 335; Spedding, *Reviews and Discussions*, 51.

39. Sligo to Holland, n.d., and Sligo to Countess of Desart, 29 Aug. 1834, Letterbooks of Peter Howe Browne, vol. 5, Private Letters, MS228, National Library of Jamaica, Kingston (hereafter "Sligo Letterbooks"); editorial encl. with Sligo to Stanley, 5 June 1834 (confidential), CO 137/192.

40. Spedding, *Reviews and Discussions*, 89–90; Burn, *Emancipation and Apprenticeship*, 159–60.

41. Sligo to Suffield, 10 Jan. 1834, and Sligo to George Gordon, 22 Sept. 1834, Sligo Letterbooks; Sligo to Stanley, 15 Apr. 1834 (private), CO 137/192; Sligo to Spring Rice, 14 Oct. 1834 (confidential), and 1 Nov. 1834 (confidential), both in CO 137/193; Sligo to Glenelg, 5 Sept. 1835, no. 100, CO 137/201, and 9 Aug. 1835 (confidential), CO 137/202.

42. Sligo to Stanley, 15 Apr. 1834 (private), CO 137/192.

43. Sligo to Stanley, 8 May 1834 (private), CO 137/192; Sligo to Glenelg, 8 July 1835, no. 52, CO 137/200, and 26 Sept. 1835, no. 135, CO 137/202.

44. *Montego Bay Standard,* quoted in *Kingston Chronicle and City Advertiser,* 6 Nov. 1835; *Falmouth Post,* 7 Oct. 1835.

45. Burn, *Emancipation and Apprenticeship,* 152–53; *Jamaica Standard,* quoted in *Kingston Chronicle and City Advertiser,* 6 Oct. 1837; *Kingston Chronicle and City Advertiser,* 4, 5 Oct., 12 Sept. 1837.

46. "Jamaica Acts, 1834," nos. 3145–80, CO 139/73.

47. Sligo to Spring Rice, 31 Dec. 1834, no. 126, CO 137/194; Glenelg to Sligo, 13 June 1835, no. 37, CO 137/198; Jordon's observations encl. with L. C. Lecesne to Earl of Aberdeen, 27 Mar. 1835, CO 137/206.

48. "Jamaica Acts, 1834," nos. 3145–80; see also Burn, *Emancipation and Apprenticeship,* 323–24.

49. Burn, *Emancipation and Apprenticeship,* 295–99, 193.

50. Ibid., 296–98; Holland, *Holland House Diaries,* 335; Sligo to Glenelg, 9 Aug. 1835, no. 82, CO 137/201.

51. Burn, *Emancipation and Apprenticeship,* 300–305; Sligo to Glenelg, 15 Nov. 1835, no. 193, and 22 Nov. (confidential), both CO 137/204, and 14 Dec. 1835, no. 217, CO 137/205; Holland, *Holland House Diaries,* 335.

52. Given the failure of the Jamaica Assembly to act, Parliament renewed the old act-in-aid on 24 March 1836, extending it until 1840, with a provision that local legislative action could supersede it. Subsequently, the Assembly passed a local act-in-aid on 15 June 1836 (Glenelg to Sligo, 15 May 1836, and Sligo to Clanricarde, 18 July 1836, Sligo Papers, 1836, MS275C, National Library of Jamaica; William Burge to Glenelg, 19, 21 Mar. 1836, in "Correspondence relative to the Abolition of Slavery in Jamaica," *PP* 1836 [174], 48:37–47; extract from Glenelg to Sligo, 23 Oct. 1835, in *PP* 1836 [0.44], 48:27; Burn, *Emancipation and Apprenticeship,* 242–48, 312–13).

53. Burn, *Emancipation and Apprenticeship,* 319–23; Taylor, *Autobiography,* 1:243–44.

54. Spedding, *Reviews and Discussions,* 91.

55. Burn, *Emancipation and Apprenticeship,* 324, 326, 328–29; Taylor, *Autobiography,* 1:244.

56. Burn, *Emancipation and Apprenticeship,* 330; William Law Mathieson, *British Slavery and Its Abolition, 1823–1838* (London: Longmans, Green, 1926), 291–93.

57. Sligo to Glenelg, 6 July 1835 (confidential), CO 137/200.

58. Burn, *Emancipation and Apprenticeship,* 282–83; Michael Ignatieff, *A Just Measure of Pain: The Penitentiary in the Industrial Revolution, 1750–1850* (New York: Pantheon, 1978), 176–77; Jeremy Bentham, "Principles of Penal Law," in *The Works of Jeremy Bentham,* ed. John Bowring, 11 vols. (Edinburgh: William Tait, 1843), 1:415. See also Michel Foucault, *Discipline and Punish: The Birth of the Prison,* trans. Alan Sheridan (New York: Vintage, 1979), esp. 200–209, 215–22.

59. Sligo to Glenelg, 5 Mar. 1836, in "Papers relating to the Abolition of Slavery," *PP* 1836 (166), 48:328–32; "Report of Captain J. W. Pringle on Prisons in the West Indies," *PP* 1837–38 [596-I&II], 40:255–363, 364–416. There were several deaths in the workhouses and on the treadmills in particular, which, together with the celebrated narrative of ex-apprentice James Williams, exposed many of the abuses of the Jamaican prison system (Burn, *Emancipation and Apprenticeship,* 287–88).

60. Taylor, *Autobiography*, 1:248, 243.

61. Burn, *Emancipation and Apprenticeship*, 361; William Law Mathieson, *British Slavery and Emancipation, 1838–1849* (London: Longmans, Green, 1932), 20–21, 23.

62. Taylor, *Autobiography*, 1:246–49.

63. [Taylor], "Memorandum on the Course to be Taken with the West Indian Assemblies," 19 Jan. 1839, CO 884/II.

64. Taylor's argument received some support from Governor Smith, who declared: "If the Assembly is let alone as it hopes, the bulk of the people will be again placed in slavery." He urged that Jamaica be governed by order in council. After Smith dissolved the Assembly, new elections were held in which, by and large, the old members were returned, except for Richard Hill of Trelawny, who received only 4 votes out of 176 cast (Burn, *Emancipation and Apprenticeship*, 361).

65. Taylor, *Autobiography*, 1:249–61, quote on 261.

66. In his autobiography Taylor described Glenelg as "an amiable man and exceedingly averse from strong measures." Holland described Glenelg as "a good, and in some respects, very able man, without gall and without guile and of a gentle spirit" (Taylor, *Autobiography*, 1:232; Holland, *Holland House Diaries*, 389–90).

67. John Earl Russell, *Recollections and Suggestions, 1813–1873* (London: Longmans, Green, 1875), 140–41; Burn, *Emancipation and Apprenticeship*, 303.

Chapter 4. The Planters: Managing a Free Labor Economy

1. Henry Barkly to Duke of Newcastle, 14 Jan. 1854, no. 8, CO 137/322, also in "Papers relative to the Affairs of the Island of Jamaica," *PP* 1854 [1848], 43:123–25.

2. *PP* 1854 [1848], 43:91, 96.

3. Edward John Eyre to Edward Cardwell, 10 Sept. 1864, no. 256, CO 137/384.

4. *PP* 1854 [1848], 43:101–5.

5. Noel Deerr, *The History of Sugar*, 2 vols. (London: Chapman & Hall, 1950), 2:531.

6. Ibid., 2:377. B. W. Higman, *Slave Population and Economy in Jamaica, 1807–1834* (Cambridge: Cambridge UP, 1976), 55–57.

7. Population and production declines calculated from figures in Higman, *Slave Population and Economy*, 256 (table A3.7), and Deerr, *History of Sugar*, 1:198–99, respectively. Quote from G. D. Gregg, "diary" for June 1835, in "Papers in Explanation of Measures adopted for Giving Effect to the Abolition of Slavery Act," *PP* 1835 (177), 50:365.

8. See Deerr, *History of Sugar*, 2:377.

9. E. B. Lyon to Marquis of Sligo, 12 Aug. 1835, and E. Fishbourne to Sligo, 31 Aug. 1835, in "Papers relating to the Abolition of Slavery," *PP* 1836 (166) 48:120; Lyon to Sligo, Apr. 1835, in *PP* 1835 (177) 50:341; Sligo to Lord Aberdeen, 27 Mar. 1835, no. 60, CO 137/198. Similar apprehensions may have affected plantings in the late 1830s.

10. Higman, *Slave Population and Economy*, 16 (table 2), 62–64.

11. B. W. Higman, "Jamaican Coffee Plantations, 1780–1860: A Cartographic Analysis," *Caribbean Geography* 2 (Oct. 1986): 74.

12. Exports from regional ports were collated from information reported in *Votes*, 4th sess., 1832–34, 49; 2d sess., 1838–44, 138; 2d sess., 1844–49, 207; 4th sess., 1849–54, 39, for the years 1834, 1840, 1845, and 1850, respectively.

13. Ibid.

14. The count of properties for 1836 was collated from a running tabulation collected by special magistrates ("Return of the Number of Properties and Their Descriptions in each Special Magistrate's District on Feb. 1, 1836," encl. with Sligo to Lord Glenelg, 13 Feb. 1836, in *PP* 1836 [166], 48:276ff. Cf. Douglas Hall, *Free Jamaica, 1838–1865: An Economic History* [New Haven: Yale UP, 1959], 82 [table 10]).

15. Barkly's report on his tour in *PP* 1854 [1848], 48:122; Michael Craton, *Searching for the Invisible Man: Slaves and Plantation Life in Jamaica* (Cambridge: Harvard UP, 1978), 292.

16. See Henry Taylor's analysis for the Colonial Office in "Memorandum on the Progress of the Free System in the West India Colonies, 1840," no. 6, CO 884/1.

17. Encl. with Charles Grey to Earl Grey, 22 Dec. 1847, no. 125, CO 137/293.

18. "Sugar Duties (confidential)," no. 8, CO 884/1.

19. Of course, the figures for a single year should be used only as a general indication, because in 1842 Aboukir expended £281 for wages against receipts of £1,585, or 18 percent. Another example of the differences in slave versus free labor cost is Vauxhall Estate in 1829, which expended £797 19s. for maintenance and received £2,069 14s. for its exports; thus maintenance costs were 38 percent of the receipts (Accounts Current, liber 27, fols. 73–75, Government Documents, Jamaica Archives, Spanish Town. For discussion of applying rum proceeds to cover slave maintenance see "Papers in Explanation of the Measures Adopted For Giving Effect to the Act For the Abolition of Slavery," *PP* 1837–38 [154-I], 49:92–126; for planter expenditures during slavery generally see Roderick Alexander McDonald, "'Goods and Chattels': The Economy of Slaves on Sugar Plantations in Jamaica and Louisiana" [Ph.D. diss., U of Kansas, 1981], 95–96, 249, 260).

20. Craton, *Searching for the Invisible Man*, 279, 281, 291.

21. Pringle's calculation involves adding the £528 in compensation and interest that the planter received for his four hundred slaves during their four years of apprenticeship, computed at 5 percent interest, to the slavery side of the ledger and adding £150 sterling, which represents the charge on £10,000 annual value (i.e., forgone interest), to the freedom expenses (Earl of Elgin to Edward Stanley, 6 June 1842, no. 6, CO 137/263).

22. "Papers relative to the Abolition of Slavery in the British Colonies," *PP* 1837 (521-I), 53:176.

23. Taylor, "Memorandum on the Progress of the Free System in the West India Colonies, 1840."

24. S. Cave, Memorandum Book: Sugar Estates, 1846–51, 62, MS18, National Library of Jamaica, Kingston.

25. Elgin to Stanley, 6 June 1842, no. 6.

26. For an excellent discussion of the problems of supervision and labor autonomy see Gerald David Jaynes, *Branches Without Roots: Genesis of the Black Working Class in the American South, 1862–1882* (New York: Oxford UP, 1986), chap. 11, esp. 199–208.

27. The official wage rate in 1844 was reported to be one shilling for a day's work in many parts of the island, but actually a nine-hour day was paid at 1s. 6d. sterling because labor could not be obtained at the lower price. Children under sixteen years of age received one shilling or nine pence, depending on their age.

Tradesmen received two, three, and four shillings per diem. Masons' and carpenters' wages fell steadily (Elgin to Stanley, 27 Feb. 1845, no. 23, CO 137/283, and 21 Nov. 1844, no. 130, CO 137/280. Views of Colonial Office staff are reflected in "Sugar Duties [confidential]").

28. "Report of Captain J. W. Pringle on Prisons in the West Indies," *PP* 1837–38 (596-I&II), 40:265ff.

29. "Statistical Report of the Sickness, Mortality and Invaliding among the Troops in the West Indies," *PP* 1837–38 [138], 40:462–91.

30. Walter Dendy to Rev. J. Angus, 15 Aug. 1848, Baptist Missionary Society, 1844–54, MS378, National Library of Jamaica; *PP* 1854 [1848], 43:93; Barkly to George Grey, 18 Sept. 1854, no. 101, CO 137/324; *Wignall v. John Woodrow* in Morant Bay, 1 Aug. 1863, in Diary of Thomas Witter Jackson, Private Gifts, Jamaica Archives; *Falmouth Post*, Dec. 1844. See esp. the case in Hanover court session, 1840–43, of *Robert Kerr v. Isaac Jackson*, 20 Aug. 1840, on Tryall Estate, where seven weeks' pay was owed to Kerr's daughter (*New York Daily Tribune*, 9 June 1854).

31. See James L. Roark, *Masters without Slaves: Southern Planters in the Civil War and Reconstruction* (New York; W. W. Norton, 1977), 132–34, 152–70, 199–200; and Lawrence N. Powell, *New Masters: Northern Planters during the Civil War and Reconstruction* (New Haven: Yale UP, 1980), 41–42, 61.

32. Barkly to Grey, 15 Nov. 1854, no. 114, CO 137/324; Lord [Sydney Haldane] Olivier, *Jamaica: The Blessed Island* (London: Faber & Faber, 1936), 256n, 273–74.

33. See, e.g., a report from St. Elizabeth in 1842 stating that pens were better able to attract labor at a lower price than either sugar or coffee estates (Elgin to Stanley, 28 Dec. 1842, no. 64, CO 137/264). See also Verena A. Shepherd, "The Effects of the Abolition of Slavery on Jamaican Livestock Farms (Pens)," *Slavery & Abolition* 10 (Sept. 1989): 187–211.

34. Journal of Henry John Blagrove, 1841–42, July 1841, 21, 23 Mar. 1842, Private Gifts, Jamaica Archives.

35. Whitelocke to Arthur Playford, 31 July 1846, Letterbook of H. A. Whitelocke, 30 Sept. 1845–16 Sept. 1846, Whitelock(e) Collection, 1845–55, MS1633, National Library of Jamaica.

36. Fort George Penn: Jamaica Account Book, 1852–57, vol. 1, MS274, National Library of Jamaica.

37. Elgin to Stanley, 28 Dec. 1842, no. 64.

38. See, e.g., Barkly, in *PP* 1854 [1848], 43; and Hall, *Free Jamaica*, 60–80.

39. Elgin to Stanley, 20 Apr. 1843, no. 112, CO 137/273; *PP* 1854 [1848], 43.

40. Journal of Henry John Blagrove, 14–15 Apr. 1842.

41. Lord Howard de Walden, "H. de W., General Instructions for Montpelier and Ellis Caymanas Estates in Jamaica," June 1852, 5–6, Private, British Library, London.

42. Kathleen Mary Butler, "Slave Compensation and Property, Jamaica and Barbados, 1823–1843" (Ph.D. diss., Johns Hopkins U, 1986), 4, 22, 158.

43. Ibid., 98 (table 1), 173–74, 215, 220; T. W. Jackson and Peter Brown in Elgin to Stanley, 6 June 1842, no. 6; "Sugar Duties (confidential)."

44. Butler, "Slave Compensation," 153.

45. Charles Grey to Earl Grey, 4 Nov. 1848, no. 96, CO 137/298 (emphasis added).

46. *Falmouth Post*, 19 Nov., Dec. 1844; see also "Letter from Civis," ibid., 18 Sept. 1835, 28 July and 7 Apr. 1846.

47. Barkly, in *PP* 1854 [1848], 43:130; Rev. J. T. Dillon, "One Hundred Years, 1838–1938," in Canon Jolly, F.G., *Private Gifts, Jamaica Archives*; S. Cave, Memorandum Book; Butler, "Slave Compensation," chap. 4.

48. "Search for the Marquis of Sligo. Respecting Cocoa Walk and Kelly's Plantations in the Island of Jamaica," Sligo Estate Papers, with [Maurice Morris] to Sligo, 22 July 1852, MS275D, National Library of Jamaica; Berkeley to W. E. Gladstone, 7 Aug. 1846, no. 24, CO 137/289. See also Butler, "Slave Compensation," 249–50.

49. Whitelocke to Sir [Charles Armstrong], 30 May 1846, 30 Sept. 1845; to Benjamin Vickers, 15 Oct. 1845; to Wallace, 19 Dec. 1845; to Storer, 30 Dec. 1845; to Plummer Dewar, 1 Feb. 1846; to Robert Wallace, 20 Apr., 20 May 1846; to Charles Armstrong, 20 May 1846; to Armstrong and Lockwood, 21 July, 5 Sept. 1846; to Moyne, 29 June 1846, Whitelock(e) Collection.

50. Whitelocke to Charles Armstrong, 20 May 1846, ibid.

51. *PP* 1837 (521-I), 53:263–64.

52. McDonald, "Goods and Chattels," 233–63.

53. Elgin to Stanley, 6 June 1842, no. 6; 27 Feb. 1845, in "Copies or Extracts of Correspondence relative to the Labouring Population in the West Indies," *PP* 1845 (642), 31:379ff.; 28 Dec. 1842, no. 64. The special magistrate's report from Port Royal in 1842 found some families paying 3s. to 5s. per week in rent (Elgin to Stanley, 28 Dec. 1842, no. 64).

54. Seaford to Holland, [1838–40], Holland House Papers, Add.Ms. 51,818; McNeil to Holland, 17 Nov. 1836, ibid., Add.Ms. 51,816. Holland had also urged the establishment of schools on the estates in order to strengthen the laborers' attachment (see chapter 5, below, for discussion of this strategy).

55. Three separate samples—for 1832, 1842, and 1852—were drawn from the accounts produce ledgers located in the Jamaica Archives. They were analyzed separately for a cross-sectional picture of production for the year and then through three separate longitudinal, or "trace," files, which were produced by tracing a given property through successive five-year intervals. The estimates of sugar receipts are based on a gross price of £37 per ton, excluding duties.

56. Craton, *Searching for the Invisible Man*, 288.

57. Fort George Penn: Estate Book, 1840–49, vol. 1, MS274B, National Library of Jamaica. See also entries for 1865 and 1872 in Mount Pleasant Plantation Book, 1838–44, MS88, National Library of Jamaica.

58. Taylor, "Memorandum on the Progress of the Free System in the West India Colonies, 1840."

59. Metcalfe to Lord John Russell, 30 Mar. 1840, no. 50, CO 137/248.

60. Fort George Penn: Estate Book, vol. 2, 1843.

61. de Walden, "General Instructions for Montpelier and Ellis Caymanas Estates in Jamaica," 53.

62. Metcalfe to Russell, 30 Mar. 1840, no. 50.

63. Metcalfe to Russell, 26 Mar. 1840, no. 49, CO 137/248.

64. Journal of Henry John Blagrove, 25 Jan. 1842.

65. Fort George Penn: Jamaica Account Book, 1852–57, vol. 1.

66. *Baptist Herald and Friend of Africa*, 14 Sept. 1839.

67. "Jamaica Acts, 1834," CO 139/76.

68. Metcalfe to Russell, 12 Jan. 1840, no. 41, CO 137/248.

69. Metcalfe to Stanley, 19 Jan. 1842, no. 58, CO 137/261.

70. Metcalfe to Russell, 26 Mar. 1840, no. 49.

71. Taylor, "Memorandum on the Progress of the Free System in the West India Colonies, 1840."

72. Elgin to Stanley, 21 Nov. 1844, no. 130.

73. Elgin to Stanley, 20 Apr. 1843, no. 112.

74. *Votes*, 1844–49, appendix to 1845, 671, in Sessional Papers, CO 140/138.

75. "Account Book of Richard Hind & Jack Jackson for Content Estate, St. James, 1850–1891," MS133, National Library of Jamaica.

76. Fort George Penn: Jamaica Account Book; Fort George Penn: Estate Book.

77. Metcalfe to Russell, 30 Mar. 1840, no. 50.

78. They were attempting to reduce wages from 1s. 3d. and 1s. 6d. to 1s. sterling in exchange for giving up their demands for rent on houses and gardens (Elgin to Stanley, 6 June 1842, no. 6).

Chapter 5. Peasants and Workers: Building a Free Society

1. Reprinted in *Falmouth Post*, 30 Sept. 1835.

2. "Papers in Explanation of Measures adopted for Giving Effect to the Abolition of Slavery Act," PP 1835 (177), 50:373.

3. "Papers relative to the Abolition of Slavery in the British Colonies," PP 1837 (521-I), 53:254.

4. Marquis de Sligo to Lord Glenelg, 9 July 1836, in PP 1837 (521-I), 53:123.

5. PP 1837 (521-I), 53:263–64.

6. From three dollars to five dollars per acre (*New York Observer*, [1838]). Kathleen Mary Butler argues that land prices also increased in response to disbursement of slave compensation funds ("Slave Compensation and Property, Jamaica and Barbados, 1823–1843" [Ph.D. diss., Johns Hopkins U, 1986], 246, 268–69).

7. *Baptist Herald and Friend of Africa*, 14 Sept. 1839. Applicants for freeholds were encouraged to apply at the *Herald* offices.

8. Charles Metcalfe to Lord John Russell, 9 June 1840, no. 84, CO 137/249.

9. The estimate of 3.2 persons per family is taken from Barry Higman's calculations of slave family size (*Slave Population and Economy in Jamaica, 1807–1834* [Cambridge: Cambridge UP, 1976], 159 [table 31]). The statistics on freeholds are taken from Douglas Hall, *Free Jamaica, 1838–1865: An Economic History* (New Haven: Yale UP, 1959), 160–62 (table 19). Of course, there may have been some double counting because of multiple holdings, but this may not have been as extensive in the earlier years as later. For discussion of other limitations on the use of these data on peasant holdings see appendix 1.

10. "Memorandum on the Progress of the Free System in the West India Colonies, 1840," no. 6, CO 884/1; Lord Elgin to Edward Stanley, 6 June 1842, no. 6, CO 137/263. For more general discussion of the growth of interior towns, trading, consumption of imports, and currency problems see Hall, *Free Jamaica*, 12, 210–12, 234–35.

11. "Diagram of Retirement Estate, St Ann," Tweedie Estate Records, Private Gifts, Jamaica Archives, Spanish Town.

12. Henry Barkly to Sir William Molesworth, 2 Oct. 1855, no. 97, CO 137/327.

13. Lt. Gov. E. Wells Bell to Henry Labouchere, 24 Mar. 1857, no. 24, CO 137/334.

14. *Leisure Hour*, [1864]. Hall estimates that there were about four thousand small farmers by 1865. He describes them as owners of more than ten acres, for which they hired day laborers to assist them. They raised coffee, "cheap sugar," and minor crops for export, such as ginger (Hall, *Free Jamaica*, 182–84).

15. See appendix 1 for discussion of methods and problems in estimating the growth of peasant freeholders.

16. William A. Green, *British Slavery Emancipation: The Sugar Colonies and the Great Experiment, 1830–1865* (Oxford: Clarendon, 1976), 188, 194, quote on 188; Philip D. Curtin, *Two Jamaicas: The Role of Ideas in a Tropical Colony, 1830–1865* (Cambridge: Harvard UP, 1975), 113, 121, 143, 156–57, quotes on 121, 143. Of course, to say that economic success "meant less" is not to say that it meant nothing, but Curtin never specifies precisely what he means by this and other references to an alternative culture and ideology. As I will argue, recognizing the "otherness" of a freed people's experience does not require seeing them as economically irrational or reactionary.

17. John Daughtrey to Sligo, 29 Dec. 1835, in "Papers relating to the Abolition of Slavery," *PP* 1836 (166), 48:204.

18. William G. Sewell, *The Ordeal of Free Labor in the British West Indies* (New York: Harper & Brothers, 1861), 176, 186.

19. *Jamaica, 1830–1930: A Study in Economic Growth* (Manchester: Manchester UP, 1961), 192–95. Cf. Hall, *Free Jamaica*, 164.

20. *Jamaica: The Blessed Island* (London: Faber & Faber, 1936), 194.

21. Ibid., 197.

22. Sidney W. Mintz, *Caribbean Transformations* (Chicago: Aldine, 1974), 135, 144, 155; see also idem, "A Note on the Definition of Peasantries," *Journal of Peasant Studies* 1 (Oct. 1973): 91–106. For a comparative perspective see Dale W. Tomich, *Slavery and the Circuit of Sugar: Martinique and the World Economy, 1830–1848* (Baltimore: Johns Hopkins UP, 1990), 259–80.

23. Higman, *Slave Population and Economy*, 38 (table 4).

24. Testimony of Samuel Anderson before Jamaica House of Assembly, 6 Nov. 1834, and J. W. Baynes to Sligo, 1 July 1835, in *PP* 1835 (177), 50:84, 371.

25. S. H. Cooke to Sligo, 2 Mar. 1836, in *PP* 1836 (166), 48:291.

26. E. B. Lyon to Sligo, 9 Sept. 1835, ibid.

27. "Copy of a Report from C. J. Latrobe, Esq., on Negro Education in Jamaica, with Correspondence relating thereto," *PP* 1837–38 (113), 48:141, 144.

28. Patrick Dunne to Sligo, 30 Dec. 1835, and William Marlton to Sligo, 28 Dec. 1835, in *PP* 1836 (166), 48:207, 220.

29. "Report from C. J. Latrobe, Esq., on Negro Education in Jamaica," 71, 132–33. The estimate of school-age apprentices was calculated from Barry Higman's figures in *Slave Population and Economy*, 38 (table 4).

30. Michael Craton, *Searching for the Invisible Man: Slaves and Plantation Life in Jamaica* (Cambridge: Harvard UP, 1978), 74–75, 286.

31. Holland House Papers, Add.Ms. 51,819, 54–57. A second list showed that females made up 45 percent of the workforce, or about 19 out of 42, but were 54 percent of the field labor force. All of the women were assigned to the fields, in contrast with 70 percent of the men.

32. Higman's figures also show variation by nativity (the African population was more male than the creole) and crop (the sugar estates had more females

than did pens or coffee plantations) (Higman, *Slave Population and Economy,* 71–81; Craton, *Searching for the Invisible Man,* 135–87).

33. Charles Darling to Duke of Newcastle, 8 Sept. 1859, no. 114, CO 137/346.

34. *Massachusetts Abolitionist,* 6 June 1839. In this survey, 2,031 people were at work, of whom one-third were female, whereas formerly there had been 4,341, three-fifths of them female. Hence, of the 1,736 men originally on the estates, 383, or 22 percent, had left; of 1,929 women, 74 percent had left. On sixty-nine sugar estates in St. James, 4,494 laborers were at work from Baptist congregations alone.

35. Craton, *Searching for the Invisible Man,* 286.

36. Green Park Estate, Trelawny, Account Book, 1848–52, Private Gifts, Jamaica Archives.

37. "Third Report from the Select Committee on Sugar and Coffee Planting," *PP* 1847–48 (167), 23:2, 6, 56 (quoted reply in response to question 5165).

38. Craton, *Searching for the Invisible Man,* 289.

39. Metcalfe to Russell, 30 Mar. 1840, no. 50, CO 137/248.

40. In June 1853 a two-year-old heifer was "cruelly maimed by the tenants" while they were delivering cattle to Montpelier. The manager responded by ejecting all in the district. In July a three-year-old steer was killed in the area of Old Coffee Piece. It would appear that in some of these cases the tenants were exercising their rights against trespassing cattle (Fort George Penn: Jamaica Account Book, 1852–57, vol. 1, MS274, National Library of Jamaica, Kingston). Roderick Alexander McDonald describes similar fencing practices and territorial claims from the slavery period ("'Goods and Chattels': The Economy of Slaves on Sugar Plantations in Jamaica and Louisiana" [Ph.D. diss., U of Kansas, 1981], 255, 261–63).

41. Taylor, "Memorandum on the Progress of the Free System in the West India Colonies, 1840."

42. For sugar workers the standard expectation for productivity was one hogshead per worker per year.

43. Parish size correlates strongly with the number of new peasant holdings. Regressing the latter on the former gives an R^2 of 0.50, which means that parish size "explains" 50 percent of the variation in the absolute growth of peasant holdings. No other interpretatively significant variables revealed strong correlations. (The above correlation was statistically significant as well, but since the data are for a total population, measures of significance are not relevant.)

44. The value of fixed capital assets, taken here as an index of economic activity, are represented by the hereditament tax that was imposed in 1840 and discontinued after 1858. In the 1840s this tax was not collected from peasant landholders (see Hall, *Free Jamaica,* 177).

45. Several of the main peasant parishes had been net exporters of slaves during the three years preceding abolition, which suggests a corresponding diminution of production and perhaps even dissolution of estates (data on estates collated from special magistrates' reports in *PP* 1836 [166], 48:276ff.).

46. On the rapid decline of coffee and the willingness of the proprietors to sell out see Hall, *Free Jamaica,* 185; and B. W. Higman, "Jamaican Coffee Plantations, 1780–1860: A Cartographic Analysis," *Caribbean Geography* 2 (Oct. 1986): 73–75.

47. Barkly to Molesworth, 2 Oct. 1855, no. 97; Bell to Labouchere, 24 Mar. 1857, no. 24; Darling to Newcastle, 8 Sept. 1859, no. 114; Edward John Eyre to Edward Cardwell, 10 Sept. 1864, no. 256, CO 137/384. Cf. Woodville K. Marshall,

"Notes on Peasant Development in the West Indies since 1838," *SES* 17 (Sept. 1968): 260–63.

48. Reports by Hill and Crew, encl. with Barkly to Molesworth, 2 Oct. 1855, no. 97.

49. Hall, *Free Jamaica*, 18.

50. Black interparish migration is estimated here as the difference between the growth of a parish's black population and the islandwide growth of the black population, which is taken to approximate the natural increase of the population (see appendix 1 for further detail).

51. The population movement after emancipation was almost exactly opposite to the pattern found in the movement of the slave population earlier (see appendix 1).

52. Of course, it is possible that the masculinization of the field labor force after emancipation might have compensated somewhat for this loss of labor time, since in many key field tasks the labor required of women appears to have been much less—10 percent to 33 percent, in fact—than that required of men. For example, in Hanover's stiff clay soils, men were required to dig 90 holes per task, as compared with 30 for women. In lighter soils, 100–110 were required of men, while 80–90 were required of women (Elgin to Stanley, 27 Feb. 1845, in "Copies or Extracts of Correspondence relative to the Labouring Population in the West Indies," *PP* 1845 [642], 31:379ff.; "Papers in Explanation of the Measures Adopted For Giving Effect to the Act For the Abolition of Slavery," *PP* 1837–38 [154-I], 49:48–88. For the U.S. South see Gerald David Jaynes, *Branches Without Roots: Genesis of the Black Working Class in the American South, 1862–1882* [New York: Oxford UP, 1986], 228–32).

53. Such a family division of labor is very similar to that described by a twentieth-century Alabama sharecropper: see Nate Shaw, *All God's Dangers: The Autobiography of Nate Shaw*, ed. Theodore Rosengarten (New York: Knopf, 1974). For a different kind of family strategy see Rebecca J. Scott, *Slave Emancipation in Cuba: The Transition to Free Labor, 1860–1899* (Princeton: Princeton UP, 1985), 242–54.

54. "Papers relative to the Affairs of the Island of Jamaica," *PP* 1854 [1848], 43:106; see also Sidney W. Mintz and Richard Price, *An Anthropological Approach to the Afroamerican Past: A Caribbean Perspective* (Philadelphia: Institute for the Study of Human Issues, 1976), 40.

55. For example, Craton finds that women were 70 percent of the cane cutters on Worthy Park. Examination of the wage list of Sheldon coffee plantation in 1847 shows women constituting approximately one-half of the pickers during harvest (*PP* 1847–48 [167], 23:168).

56. Metcalfe to Russell, 30 Mar. 1840, no. 50, CO 137/248.

57. Journal of Henry John Blagrove, 1841–42, 21 Jan. 1842, Private Gifts, Jamaica Archives.

58. Peter Brown to Richard Hill, 1 May 1842, encl. with Elgin to Edward Stanley, 6 June 1842, no. 6.

59. Elgin to Stanley, 26 June 1844, no. 80, CO 137/279; 6 June 1842, no. 6; 28 Dec. 1842, no. 64, CO 137/264.

60. Elgin to Stanley, 28 Dec. 1842, no. 64.

61. Ibid.

62. Sligo to Glenelg, 9 July 1836, in *PP* 1837 (521-I), 53:60–61.

63. Journal of Henry John Blagrove, 1 and 3 Aug. 1841.

64. Thomas Scattergood, "Jamaica-Haitian Diary," 7 Mar.–24 Apr. 1888, 6, MST107, National Library of Jamaica.

65. Metcalfe to Lord Holland, 18 June 1840, Holland House Papers, Add.Ms. 51,819, 141–46.

66. Elgin to Stanley, 27 Feb. 1845, in *PP* 1845 (642), 31:379ff.

67. Jackson to Austin, 31 Jan. 1854, in *PP* 1854 [1848], 43:108.

68. *Colonial Standard*, 12 Jan. 1850.

69. Barkly to Labouchere, 21 Apr. 1856, no. 57, CO 137/331.

70. *PP* 1854 [1848], 43:39–40, 96.

71. Ibid., 25–26.

72. Cf. Lawrence W. Levine, *Black Culture and Black Consciousness: Afro-American Folk Thought from Slavery to Freedom* (New York: Oxford UP, 1977).

73. W. A. Bell to Austin, 1 Jan. 1854, in *PP* 1854 [1848], 43:106–7; Journal of Henry John Blagrove, 3 July 1841. For observations about slaves refusing to inform on each other see McDonald, "Goods and Chattels," 77, 84–85.

74. Only between 1815 and 1825 was Jamaica a net importer of slaves from other American colonies. The internal trade became more important after abolition of the slave trade, but there was no geographical area of natural increase that could supply newly settled regions as in the United States and Brazil. Between 1829 and 1832 almost 5,000 slaves moved to new parishes, but most only a short distance to a contiguous parish. Fewer than half of 1 percent of slaves were manumitted between 1829 and 1832; hardly any ran away (446); and fewer than 2 percent were moved to another parish, mostly to another unit connected to the property of origin. A law in 1735 regulated the internal trade and required that families be maintained; an 1831 law made it illegal to transport great gangs for display and sale (Higman, *Slave Population and Economy*, 62–63; idem, "Household Structure and Fertility on Jamaican Slave Plantations: A Nineteenth-Century Example," *Population Studies* 27 [1973]: 527–50; idem, "The Slave Family and Household in the British West Indies, 1800–1834," *Journal of Interdisciplinary History* 6 [Fall 1975]: 261–87. For the "social chaos" interpretation see Orlando Patterson, "From Endo-deme to Matri-deme: An Interpretation of the Development of Kinship and Social Organization among the Slaves of Jamaica, 1655–1830," *Eighteenth-Century Florida and the Caribbean*, ed. Samuel Proctor [Gainesville: U Presses of Florida, 1976], 50–59).

75. McDonald, "Goods and Chattels," 236, 239–40.

76. Raymond T. Smith, *Kinship and Class in the West Indies: A Genealogical Study of Jamaica and Guyana* (Cambridge: Cambridge UP, 1988), 149–50; Erna Brodber, "Afro-Jamaican Women at the Turn of the Century," *SES* 35 (Sept. 1986): 34.

77. Most of the material in this paragraph is based on Brodber, "Afro-Jamaican Women at the Turn of the Century," 23–50. See also Helen Safa, "Economic Autonomy and Sexual Equality in Caribbean Society," *SES* 35 (Sept. 1986): 1–22.

78. Smith, *Kinship and Class*, 31n, 45, 47, 49. Twelve years after emancipation, in the midst of a cholera epidemic, a Baptist missionary reported that almost no Afro-Jamaican orphans had become public charges, which is strong corroboration of the strength of their kin networks (Walter Dendy to Edward B. Underhill, 3 May 1851, Baptist Missionary Society, 1844–54, MS378, National Library of Jamaica).

79. Brodber, "Afro-Jamaican Women at the Turn of the Century," 34.

80. Mintz, *Caribbean Transformations*, 225–50; Jean Besson, "A Paradox in Caribbean Attitudes to Land," in *Land and Development in the Caribbean*, ed. Jean Besson and Janet Momsen (London: Macmillan Caribbean, 1987), 13–45; Edith Clarke, *My Mother Who Fathered Me: A Study of the Family in Three Selected Communities in Jamaica* (London: George Allen & Unwin, 1957), 65–78. Though published in the 1950s, the data on which Clarke's conclusions are based were apparently collected in the 1930s. See her testimony before the Moyne Commission: Testimony of Edith Clarke, 10 Nov. 1938, 8th sess., Oral Evidence, West India Royal Commission, 1938–39, vol. 2, CO 950/925.

81. Clarke, *My Mother Who Fathered Me*, 65; Cf. Mintz, *Caribbean Transformations*, 242.

82. Clarke, *My Mother Who Fathered Me*, 78; Mintz, *Caribbean Transformations*, 239, 247. For further discussion of the symbolic, noneconomic aspects of landownership see Jean Besson, "Symbolic Aspects of Land in the Caribbean: The Tenure and Transmission of Land Rights among Caribbean Peasantries," in *Peasants, Plantations, and Rural Communities in the Caribbean*, ed. Malcolm Cross and Arnaud Marks (Guildford: Department of Sociology, U of Surrey, 1979), 86–116.

83. "Family Land as a Model for Martha Brae's New History: Culture Building in an Afro-Caribbean Village," in *Afro-Caribbean Villages in Historical Perspective*, ed. Charles V. Carnegie (Kingston: African-Caribbean Institute of Jamaica, 1987), 100–132, quote on 104. In this same volume, Charles Carnegie argues for a more nuanced understanding of the dialectical relation of family land to the market but confirms its multiple symbolic significance as well ("Is Family Land an Institution?" ibid., 83–99).

84. Elgin to Stanley, 6 June 1842, no. 6.

85. Unless, of course, one includes autonomy within the definition of utility. But then the concept would become so all-inclusive that it ceases to be of much use in explaining anything.

86. Metcalfe to Lord Holland, 18 June 1840, Holland House Papers, Add.Ms. 51,819, 141–46; Metcalfe to Russell, 30 Mar. 1840, no. 50, CO 137/248. The persistence of this problem is suggested by a report from St. Dorothy in 1854 that showed that it was still a matter of supply at critical moments, especially during the planting, or rainy, season, when workers took off to tend their own grounds (Bell to Austin, 1 Jan. 1854, in *PP* 1854 [1848], 43:105–6; see the epigraph at the beginning of this chapter).

87. Elgin to Stanley, 28 Dec. 1842, no. 64.

88. *PP* 1847–48 (167), 23:70 (question 5165). In 1865 Peter Alexander Espeut, a colored planter and assemblyman, expressed much the same sentiment during a hearing on the Morant Bay Rebellion ("Report of the Jamaica Royal Commission [1866]. Part II. Minutes of Evidence and Appendix," *PP* 1866 [3683-I], 31:96 [IUP reprint, Colonies: West Indies, vol. 5]). See chapter 8, below.

89. John Salmon to T. F. Pilgrim, 25 June 1848, encl. with Charles Grey to Earl Grey, 7 July 1848, no. 64, CO 137/299.

90. *Massachusetts Abolitionist*, 6 June 1839; Elgin to Stanley, 28 Dec. 1842, no. 64; *PP* 1835 (177), 50:365.

91. For a stimulating discussion of this problem in another context see Frederick Cooper's review of the literature on African peasants, "Peasants, Capitalists, and Historians: A Review Article," *Journal of Southern African Studies* 7 (Apr. 1981):

284–314. "The attachment of a label," he writes, "can delude us into thinking that we understand the nature and causes of a process when we are only beginning to see what is going on" (312).

92. In the twentieth-century American South, both black and white tenant farm families supplemented their income with nonfarm labor whenever possible (see Shaw, *All God's Dangers;* and Margaret Jarman Hagood, *Mothers of the South: Portraiture of the White Tenant Farm Woman* [Chapel Hill: U of North Carolina P, 1939]).

93. For other Caribbean examples of the complex interaction between peasants and proletarians in the context of kinship and community bonds see Sidney W. Mintz, "The Rural Proletariat and the Problem of Rural Proletarian Consciousness," *Journal of Peasant Studies* 1 (Apr. 1974): 291–324; and idem, "Note on the Definition of Peasantries."

94. In 1882 Governor Musgrave reported that roving gangs of laborers traveled from estate to estate, not as one body under a single leader, but as an "accidental collection of individuals coming from different places and acting quite independently of each other as to their personal proceedings, and merely directed as to the work on the Estate by an overlooker" (A. W. Musgrave to Earl of Kimberley, 23 Jan. 1882, no. 34, CO 137/504). Edith Clarke describes the labor migration in the twentieth century in "Land Tenure and the Family in Four Selected Communities in Jamaica," in *Peoples and Cultures of the Caribbean,* ed. Michael Horowitz (New York: Natural History P, 1971), 211–42.

Chapter 6. Liberal Democratic Society in Theory and Practice

1. Glenelg to Governors of the West India Colonies, 6 Nov. 1837, "Papers in Explanation of the Measures Adopted For Giving Effect to the Act For the Abolition of Slavery," *PP* 1837–38 (154-I), 49:9–11.

2. Cf. Eric J. Hobsbawm, *The Age of Capital, 1848–1875* (New York: Charles Scribner's Sons, 1975), 3.

3. "M. de Tocqueville on Democracy in America," in *The Philosophy of John Stuart Mill: Ethical, Political, and Religious,* ed. Marshall Cohen (New York: Modern Library, 1961), 131.

4. Hobsbawm, *Age of Capital,* 29–47, quote on 47.

5. "On Liberty," in *The Philosophy of John Stuart Mill,* 197–98.

6. Grey's statement quoted in second epigraph, above (Charles Grey to Earl Grey [confidential], CO 137/302). The literature on this notion of plural society is extensive and need not detain us here. For further discussion see Charles W. Mills, "Race and Class: Conflicting or Reconcilable Paradigms?" *SES* 36 (June 1987): 69–108; and M. G. Smith, *The Plural Society in the British West Indies* (Berkeley: U of California P, 1965), together with his critical exchange with Don Robotham: Robotham, "Pluralism as an Ideology," *SES* 29 (Mar. 1980): 69–89; Smith, "Robotham's Ideology and Pluralism: A Reply," *SES* 32 (June 1983): 103–39; and Robotham, "The Why of the Cockatoo," *SES* 34 (June 1985): 111–51.

7. The interpretation is my own but is based on the following: Donald G. Southgate, *The Passing of the Whigs, 1832–1886* (London: Macmillan, 1962); Derek Beales, *From Castlereagh to Gladstone, 1815–1885* (New York: W. W. Norton, 1969); Asa Briggs, *The Age of Improvement, 1783–1867* (London: Longmans, 1959); and

Norman Gash, *Reaction and Reconstruction in English Politics, 1832–1852* (Oxford: Clarendon, 1965).

8. Earl of Elgin to Edward Stanley, 28 Dec. 1842, no. 64, CO 137/264; Stanley to Elgin, 14 Dec. 1843, no. 178, CO 137/275.

9. This includes the Baptist and Methodist missionaries. See, e.g., James M. Phillippo to Sligo, 24 Oct. 1835, encl. with Sligo to Glenelg, 25 Oct. 1835, no. 174, CO 137/203.

10. Hill to Colonel Bruce, 22 June 1846, in L. H. Berkeley to W. E. Gladstone, 23 July 1846, no. 17, CO 137/289.

11. John Scoble to Joseph Beldam, 8 Aug. 1838, Joseph Beldam Papers, MS321, no. 23, National Library of Jamaica, Kingston.

12. Mavis Christine Campbell, *The Dynamics of Change in a Slave Society: A Sociopolitical History of the Free Coloreds of Jamaica, 1800–1865* (Rutherford, N.J.: Associated Universities P, 1976), 220–23; Gad J. Heuman, *Between Black and White: Race, Politics, and the Free Coloreds in Jamaica, 1792–1865* (Westport, Conn.: Greenwood, 1981), 112.

13. Marginal note, Stephen to Russell, 14 Aug. 1840, in marginal notes and memoranda "re. Jamaica Acts passed in the Session of 1839/40," encl. with Metcalfe to Russell, 12 Jan. 1840, no. 41, CO 137/248 (microfilm copy).

14. Summary prepared by Mr. Barrow, 14 Aug. 1840, in marginal notes, memoranda, and draft dispatches, ibid.; Russell to Metcalfe, 25 May 1840, no. 76, CO 137/248.

15. Metcalfe to Russell, 29 July 1840, no. 99, CO 137/249.

16. Besides the 5 that were disallowed, 21 (32 percent) were allowed, 10 were amended, in 10 decisions were suspended, and 19 were under consideration. Fewer than 8 percent of the 65 laws passed during the session were vetoed. Almost half were either confirmed or left to their operation, 15 percent were returned to Jamaica for amendments, and 29 percent were still awaiting a decision (Minute by Russell, 10 Nov. 1840, encl. with Metcalfe to Russell, 12 Jan. 1840, no. 41).

17. Elgin to Stanley, 8 Mar. 1844, no. 39, CO 137/278.

18. Stanley had approved this policy rather than accede to the governor's wish to abolish the specials outright (Metcalfe to Stanley, 7 Jan. 1842, no. 42 [with CO notations appended to back]; Stanley to Metcalfe, 1 Mar. 1842, no. 55, CO 137/261).

19. Elgin to Stanley, 21 Jan. 1845, no. 8, CO 137/283; 5 Jan. 1846, no. 2, CO 137/287.

20. Metcalfe to Russell, 10 Apr. 1841, no. 210, CO 137/255; Elgin to Stanley, 28 Dec. 1842, no. 64, and Stanley to Elgin, 21 Feb. 1843, no. 86, CO 137/264; Elgin to Stanley, 30 Jan. 1843, no. 81, CO 137/273.

21. Myalism was a syncretic belief system; its practitioners found Baptist doctrines and practices—the Holy Spirit and total immersion—reminiscent of spirit possession and river spirits in African religious traditions (Monica Schuler, *"Alas, Alas, Kongo": A Social History of Indentured African Immigration into Jamaica, 1841–1865* [Baltimore: Johns Hopkins UP, 1980], 32–44, quote on 44).

22. Elgin to Stanley, 28 Dec. 1842, no. 64; Rev. J. T. Dillon, "One Hundred Years, 1838–1938," in Canon Jolly, F.G., Private Gifts, Jamaica Archives, Spanish Town.

23. Elgin to Stanley, 30 Jan. 1843, no. 81, and 28 Dec. 1842, no. 64.

24. Elgin to Stanley, 30 Aug. 1844, no. 104, CO 137/280; Summary of "Half-Yearly Magistrates Reports for Jamaica," by Henry Taylor, 14 Feb. 1843, encl. with Elgin to Stanley, 28 Dec. 1842, no. 64.

25. Early in 1850, Governor Charles Grey reported several sentences of thirty-nine lashes, though all of these were for arsonists (Charles Grey to Earl Grey, 23 Mar. 1850, no. 30, CO 137/303).

26. Elgin to Stanley, 5 Aug. 1845 (confidential), CO 137/284.

27. [Sligo], *Jamaica under the Apprenticeship System* (London: J. Andrews, 1838), in Joseph Beldam Papers, MST321R, no. 28, National Library of Jamaica.

28. Elgin to Stanley, 5 Aug. 1845 (confidential).

29. Elgin to Stanley, 20 Apr. 1843, no. 112, CO 137/273.

30. Elgin to Stanley, 5 Aug. 1845 (confidential).

31. Ibid.

32. Elgin to Stanley, 20 Apr. 1843, no. 112.

33. Elgin to Stanley, 5 Aug. 1845 (confidential).

34. Elgin to Stanley, 23 Oct. 1844, no. 119, CO 137/280. Stanley expressed his hearty concurrence with Elgin's views (Stanley to Elgin, 24 Nov. 1844, no. 303, CO 137/280).

35. Elgin to Stanley, 5 Aug. 1845 (confidential).

36. Elgin to Stanley, 7 Nov. 1843, no. 176, CO 137/275.

37. Elgin to Stanley, 23 Oct. 1844, no. 119, CO 137/280; J. Woolfreys, 1 May 1844 (St. Ann), encl. with Elgin to Stanley, 26 June 1844, no. 80, CO 137/279.

38. Elgin to Stanley, 5 Aug. 1845 (confidential).

39. Journal of Henry John Blagrove, 1841–42, 3 July 1841, Private Gifts, Jamaica Archives.

40. Richard Lewis to Messrs. N. & H. Mayo, 27 Oct. 1841, Ballard's Valley Plantation Papers, 1766–1873, Unbound Docs., 1840–48, Duke University Library, Manuscript Collection, Durham, North Carolina. I am grateful to Rebecca Scott for bringing this letter to my attention.

41. Elgin to Stanley, 23 Oct. 1845 (private), CO 137/285.

42. "Reply of Assembly to the Governor," 23 Oct. 1845, encl. with Elgin to Stanley, 23 Oct. 1845, no. 90, CO 137/285.

43. Sligo to Secretary for the Colonies, 19 Jan. 1835, no. 4, CO 137/197. See also commentary of missionaries in Walter Dendy et al. to Rev. J. Angus, 9 Feb. 1849, Baptist Missionary Society, 1844–54, MS378, National Library of Jamaica; J. E. Henderson to Baptist Missionary Society, 21 Dec. 1858, John Edward Henderson Letters, 1841–63, MS817, National Library of Jamaica; and K. V. B. Donaldson, "The Contribution of Baptist Missionaries to Education in Jamaica during the First Half of the Nineteenth Century, 1814–67" (Master's thesis, U of London Institute of Education, 1967), 80.

44. Sir George Grey to C[harles] Latrobe, 23 Feb. 1837, in "Copy of the Instructions addressed to the Inspector appointed to visit the Schools in the West Indies," *PP* 1837 (393), 43:311–17; Metcalfe to Russell, 10 Sept. 1841, no. 243, CO 137/256. See also Carl Campbell, "Towards an Imperial Policy for the Education of Negroes In the West Indies after Emancipation," *Jamaican Historical Review* 7 (1967): 68–102.

45. Stanley did approve the reduction of the number of special magistrates by attrition, however (Metcalfe to Stanley, 7 Jan. 1842, no. 42 [with CO notations appended to back], and Stanley to Metcalfe, 1 Mar. 1842, no. 55).

46. Elgin to Stanley, 15 Jan. 1845, no. 5, CO 137/283. Although more schools were located in the central part of the island, where the bulk of peasant settlers were, the western and eastern sections showed higher proportions of their school-age populations enrolled, with daily attendance averaging two-thirds of those enrolled (Charles Grey to Earl Grey, 20 Sept. 1847, no. 91, CO 137/293).

47. Charles Grey to Earl Grey, 20 Sept. 1847, no. 91; see also Donaldson, "Contribution of Baptist Missionaries to Education in Jamaica," 75–82.

48. By contrast, the Methodists were early supporters of industrial education (see James M. Phillippo to Sligo, 24 Oct. 1835, encl. with Sligo to Glenelg, 25 Oct. 1835, no. 174).

49. Charles Grey to Earl Grey, 20 Sept. 1847, no. 91.

50. Apparently there had been some expansion after 1844, followed by an equally precipitous decline. Barkly reported that one-third of Jamaica's sixty-five thousand school-age children (ages five to fifteen) were in school. Although this was higher than the one-fifth reported in the mid-1840s, the governor still claimed a 50 percent reduction in enrollment (Barkly to Henry Labouchere, 18 Mar. 1856, no. 47, CO 137/331).

51. *Colonial Standard*, 21 Jan. 1850.

52. Heuman, *Between Black and White*, 140, 148.

53. Barkly to Labouchere, 18 Mar. 1856, no. 47.

54. Mary Elizabeth Thomas, *Jamaica and Voluntary Laborers from Africa, 1840–1865* (Gainesville: U Presses of Florida, 1974), 16.

55. Metcalfe to Russell, 27 Aug. 1840, no. 108, CO 137/249.

56. Elgin to W. E. Gladstone, 21 Feb. 1846, no. 33, CO 137/288; Eyre to Newcastle, 20 Sept. 1862, no. 81, CO 137/367.

57. Elgin to Stanley, 14 Aug. 1845, no. 75, CO 137/284.

58. Metcalfe to Stanley, 9 Feb. 1842, no. 72, CO 137/261; Thomas, *Jamaica and Voluntary Laborers*, 28, 38, 42.

59. Elgin to Stanley, 5 Aug. 1845 (confidential).

60. Marginal note, Merivale to Hawes, 1 Feb. 1848, encl. with Charles Grey to Earl Grey, 21 Dec. 1847, no. 123, CO 137/303; Marginal note, Berkeley to Earl Grey, 23 Oct. 1846, no. 37, CO 137/289; William A. Green, *British Slave Emancipation: The Sugar Colonies and the Great Experiment, 1830–1865* (Oxford: Clarendon, 1976), 284 (table 17).

61. Whitelocke to Charles Armstrong, 20 May 1846; Whitelocke to Robert Wallace, 20 May, 20 Apr. 1846, all in Letterbook of H. A. Whitelocke, 30 Sept. 1845–16 Sept. 1846, Whitelock(e) Collection, 1845–55, MS1633, National Library of Jamaica.

62. Entries 30 Apr. 1853 and 30 June 1854 in Fort George Penn: Jamaica Account Book, 1852–57, vol. 1, MS274, National Library of Jamaica. See also Richard Hill's report in 1848 showing estates to which indentured laborers had been assigned (Charles Grey to Earl Grey, 6 Mar. 1848, no. 26, CO 137/296).

63. Charles Grey to Earl Grey, 22 Jan. 1847, no. 8, CO 137/291. For discussion of patterns in the U.S. South see Gerald David Jaynes, *Branches Without Roots: Genesis of the Black Working Class in the American South, 1862–1882* (New York: Oxford UP, 1986), 207–8.

64. Charles Grey to Earl Grey, 9 Mar. 1849, no. 30, CO 137/302. See also Schuler, *"Alas, Alas, Kongo,"* 58–60.

65. Charles Grey to Earl Grey, 7 June 1847, no. 59, CO 137/292.

66. This second petition, along with six others, was tabled. In addition to the immigration issue, these petitions from Trelawny and Westmoreland protested granting tax money to Anglican churches and excessive import duties ("Memorial to Lord John Russell from Jamaica Baptist Western Union," encl. with Charles Grey to Earl Grey, 21 Mar. 1848, no. 32, CO 137/296; "Petition of certain labourers and others of the parish of Westmoreland," 1 Nov. 1844, in *Votes*, 1844–49, 112, in Sessional Papers, CO 140/136).

67. Heuman, *Between Black and White*, 101, 140.

68. Berkeley to Earl Grey, 23 Oct. 1846, no. 37, and 21 Nov. 1846, no. 44, CO 137/289.

69. Charles Grey to Earl Grey, 6 Feb. 1850, no. 13, CO 137/303. Cf. Green, *British Slave Emancipation*, 245, 363.

70. Darling to Stanley, 25 May 1858, no. 77, CO 137/337; Darling to E. B. Lytton, 21 July 1859, no. 90, CO 137/345.

71. Charles Grey to Earl Grey, 10 Mar. 1849, no. 32, CO 137/304.

72. Responding to charges by Baptist missionaries, Lord Russell queried Metcalfe concerning whether the duty imposed on sugar and coffee sold and consumed within the island was aimed at the peasantry and would be oppressive. Metcalfe responded that the law had been allowed to expire because it was ineffective, since the peasants had avoided paying it. Thus no action was taken by the Colonial Office (Metcalfe to Stanley, 17 Jan. 1842, no. 53 [with reference to Russell to Metcalfe, 28 Aug. 1841, no. 251], CO 137/261).

73. Draft of Stanley to Elgin, 12 Apr. 1843, no. 99, CO 137/274.

74. Marginal note, J. S. [James Stephen] to Mr. Hope, 6 July 1843; Stanley to Elgin, 31 Aug. 1843, no. 145; Elgin to Stanley, 20 May 1843, no. 124, CO 137/274. Elgin to Stanley, 24 Jan. 1843, no. 77, CO 137/273.

75. Draft of Glenelg to Thomas Lack [of Board of Trade], 19 Nov. 1835, CO 137/206.

76. Draft of Stanley to Elgin, 1 May 1843, no. 107, CO 137/274.

77. Elgin to Stanley, 15 May 1843, no. 121, CO 137/274.

78. Reply of Assembly to Elgin's opening speech, encl. with Elgin to Stanley, 1 Nov. 1843, no. 169, CO 137/275.

79. Enclosures with Elgin's dispatch included testimony before a committee of the House of Assembly by local merchants, who generally agreed that consumer preferences and lower shipping costs gave American pork an advantage over Irish competitors. The price of pork in 1843 at retail was 6d. per pound (Elgin to Stanley, 1 Jan. 1844, no. 2, CO 137/278).

80. Meanwhile, £25,944 was spent on the ecclesiastical establishment, not including £3,657 in other special grants, and only £8,110 on roads and bridges (*Votes*, 2d sess., 1844–49, in Sessional Papers, CO 140/137, 314–19 [2 Dec. 1845]).

81. Metcalfe to Stanley, 27 Dec. 1841, no. 32, CO 137/257.

82. Charles Grey to Earl Grey, 22 Dec. 1849, no. 113, CO 137/303, and 21 Dec. 1847, no. 123.

83. Grey's response was to recommended substitution of a uniform acreage tax rather than the system of assessments and valuation then used, which had led to the discontent. But in a later report Grey appears to have confused the issue, claiming that there was discontent because the planters defaulted on wages and colluded to lower the wage rates. Also, certain overseers had taunted blacks with

the idea of Jamaica's being annexed to the United States (Charles Grey to Earl Grey, 19 Sept. 1848, no. 78, CO 137/297; Charles Grey to Earl Grey, 20 Oct. 1848, no. 91, and Henry Walsh to T. F. Pilgrim, 21 Aug. 1848, CO 137/297).

84. Sir Charles Edward Grey, the younger son of R. W. Grey, who was at one time Sheriff Northumberland, was educated at Oxford. Called to the bar in 1811, he served as a supreme court judge in India and chief justice for Bengal. Charles had had to leave England to escape his chronic debts. He was a commissioner investigating Canadian discontent in 1835 and sat in Commons for Tynemouth in 1838. Prior to Jamaica he was governor of Barbados (*DNB* 8:623, 22:786–89; Heuman, *Between Black and White*, 141).

85. Earl Grey to Charles Grey, 1 Dec. 1849 (private), Richard Hart Collection, nos. 1–10, MST1813, National Library of Jamaica.

86. Ibid., 31 Mar. 1848 (private).

87. Ibid., 16 Feb. 1850.

88. Ibid., 10 Aug. 1847.

89. Ibid.

90. Ibid., 1 Dec. 1847 (private). Grey also urged Charles to talk with Thomas Jelly, of "Wilbro' Hall," Westmoreland, who had expressed similar views in a recent pamphlet.

91. Annual exports from the West Indies had declined by 30 percent below preemancipation levels, while per capita consumption in the United Kingdom fell from twenty pounds in 1830 to fifteen pounds in 1840. In 1846 British West Indian sugar cost 34s. 5d., as compared with 19s. 11d. for Brazilian sugar and 24s. 6d. for Cuban (Green, *British Slave Emancipation*, 229–31).

92. Actually Peel had reduced the duty on foreign sugar in 1844 and again in 1845, but this had proved inadequate to relieve the burden on consumers (ibid., 229–30).

93. Earl of Musgrave to E. G. Stanley, 2 Jan. 1834; Minutes by J. L. [Lefevre] and H. T. [Taylor], CO 137/192.

94. The dissenting voters were W. W. Anderson, Charles Darling, James Taylor, and Robert Osborn (*Votes*, 1st sess., 1844–49, 422–29, in Sessional Papers, CO 140/136 [18 Dec. 1844]; see also Green, *British Slave Emancipation*, 245–48).

95. Heuman, *Between Black and White*, 141–42.

96. Green, *British Slave Emancipation*, 234–35, 237–38.

97. Ibid., 239–40, 244n.

98. Heuman, *Between Black and White*, 142.

99. Charles Grey to Earl Grey, 19 Sept. 1848, no. 78.

100. Green, *British Slave Emancipation*, 240–42.

101. Charles Grey to Earl Grey, 6 Nov. 1848 (confidential), CO 137/298; Green, *British Slave Emancipation*, 242–43.

102. In the winter of 1847, Alexander Barclay, of St. Thomas-in-the-East, proposed to abolish differential duties between foreign and British imports. Aside from creating a loss of about £25,000 in revenue, this bill would have made the government even more dependent upon annual revenue acts. Since the differential duties were established by an imperial act, they provided some consistent revenue for the government. The following month, Grey reported that Barclay's bill removing the differential duties had passed, presenting the prospect of having no permanent revenue. Colonial officials were a bit perplexed as to how they

might counter this new ploy, finding no legitimate grounds to refuse assent to it. Since a mere £25,000 out of a civil establishment costing £130,000 annually was affected by Barclay's measure, they allowed it to stand (Charles Grey to Earl Grey, 9 Mar. 1847, no. 20, and 6 Apr. 1847, no. 30, CO 137/291).

103. Earl Grey to Charles Grey, 7 May 1849 (confidential), CO 137/302.

104. Charles Grey to Earl Grey, 6 Apr. 1847, no. 30, CO 137/291.

105. Minute by Earl Grey, encl. with Charles Grey to Earl Grey, 19 Feb. 1849, no. 21, CO 137/301. A draft confidential dispatch from Earl Grey to Charles Grey, with no number or date [approximately Apr. 1849], disclaimed any responsibility or power to intercede on the supplies issue but simply warned of the consequences and approved the governor's course.

106. Earl Grey to Charles Grey, 16 Apr. 1849, Hart Collection.

107. After a year on the island, the governor wrote that racial differences were the real cause of political conflicts in Jamaica, but because "political power has been for some years past so evenly balanced in Jamaica, and the outward manifestation of prejudices in such respects has grown so repugnant to the spirit of the age,—that the effects of these distinctions have to a superficial observer been veiled, and their mention concealed under the ordinary terms of party nomenclature" (Barkly to George Grey, 19 Oct. 1854, no. 107, CO 137/324).

Chapter 7. Politics and Power in a "Plural Society"

1. Barry W. Higman, ed., "The Jamaican Censuses of 1844 and 1861: A New Edition, Derived from the Manuscript and Printed Schedules in the Jamaica Archives" (Mona, Jamaica: Social History Project, Department of History, U of the West Indies, 1980), 3, 16 (tables 2, 7). Although they were not counted separately from other whites in the censuses, William A. Green estimates that there were about 5,000 Jews in Jamaica in the 1830s (*British Slave Emancipation: The Sugar Colonies and the Great Experiment, 1830–1865* [Oxford: Clarendon, 1976], 9n). Until they began to assimilate in the late nineteenth century, however, Jews were a distinct group socially and politically. In fact, they did not gain full political rights until 1830, *after* the mixed-race, or colored, Jamaicans (see Thomas August, "Jewish Assimilation and the Plural Society in Jamaica," *SES* 36 [June 1987]: 109–22).

2. Illustrative, perhaps, of the political implications of such a semantic shift is the modern debate over whether to classify Jamaica as a "plural society" (see Charles W. Mills, "Race and Class: Conflicting or Reconcilable Paradigms?" *SES* 36 [June 1987]: 69–108). For an incisive unmasking of a somewhat similar process in twentieth-century America see Barbara Jeanne Fields, "Slavery, Race, and Ideology in the United States of America," *New Left Review* 181 (May–June 1990): 95–118.

3. See esp. Governor Barkly's characterization of "parliamentary anarchy" in Barkly to George Grey, 19 Oct. 1854, no. 107, CO 137/334; see also Barclay [Barkly] to Newcastle, 23 Nov. 1853, no. 18, in "Papers relative to the Affairs of the Island of Jamaica," *PP* 1854 [1848], 43:15. Among historians this view is best represented by Mavis Christine Campbell, *The Dynamics of Change in a Slave Society: A Sociopolitical History of the Free Coloreds of Jamaica, 1800–1865* (Rutherford, N.J.: Associated Universities P, 1976).

4. In the first year after emancipation (1838–39), 2,074 freeholders registered their properties under twenty acres, and 934 of them also registered to vote. By

1845 there were at least 20,000 such freeholders. Of course, the low registration figures also suggest that it was not just black peasants who failed to exercise the franchise. In St. John, where no more than 23 votes in each election were cast in the 1840s, there were 125 planters listed in the 1844 census; certainly more than 20 of these were eligible to vote. For registered freeholders see Metcalfe to Russell, 9 June 1840, no. 84, CO 137/249; and Douglas Hall, *Free Jamaica, 1838–1865: An Economic History* (New Haven: Yale UP, 1959), 160–64 (table 19). See also Gad Heuman, *Between Black and White: Race, Politics, and the Free Coloreds in Jamaica, 1792–1865* (Westport, Conn.: Greenwood, 1981), 119.

5. Heuman, *Between Black and White*, 117–19, 122–23, esp. table 6.

6. "General Report on the State of the Island of Jamaica," encl. with Charles Grey to Earl Grey, 10 Mar. 1849, no. 32, CO 137/304.

7. Metcalfe to Stanley, 9 Feb. 1842, no. 72, CO 137/261; Earl Grey to Charles Grey, 16 Mar. 1849 (private), Richard Hart Collection, nos. 1–10, MST1813, National Library of Jamaica, Kingston. Of course, it was not a problem confined to the colonies; Eric J. Hobsbawm has called it "the basic dilemma of nineteenth-century liberalism" (*The Age of Empire, 1875–1914* [New York: Pantheon, 1987], 85).

8. There were six brown men in the Assembly in 1835, but Price Watkis died in 1836, John Manderson resigned, and Aaron Deleon became ill and missed most sessions, reducing their effective strength to three votes by 1836–37. Seven brown men served in 1837–38, but one of them, Richard Hill, was defeated in the 1838 election (Heuman, *Between Black and White*, 92–93, 96n, 99, 100, 104–5).

9. The white members of the government faction included Christopher Good and William Wemyss Anderson, who were later associated with the Town party. Occasionally, Planter party members Alexander Barclay, Daniel Hart, E. C. Smith, Jacob Sanguinetti, and Edward Thompson defected to the government side (see appendix 2 for discussion of identification of Assembly members; see also Heuman, *Between Black and White*, 103–7, quote on 104).

10. Heuman, *Between Black and White*, 100–101. For general discussion of British politics after the Reform Act of 1832 see Norman Gash, *Reaction and Reconstruction in English Politics, 1832–1852* (Oxford: Clarendon, 1965), 122–30, quote on 125.

11. See appendix 2 for discussion of methods of roll call voting analysis.

12. Of course, by the late 1850s and early 1860s a few of the colored politicians also had acquired estates—Peter A. Espeut and Alexander Heslop were prominent examples—but in most cases their primary occupations remained in law or other urban professions. Cf. Heuman, *Between Black and White*, 63.

13. This language is from a petition by George William Gordon and others protesting the 1859 election laws (C. H. Darling to Sir E. Bulwer-Lytton, 12 Mar. 1859, no. 45, CO 137/344). Richard Hill disagreed, however, arguing that the estates and small freeholders could be mutually supportive (Heuman, *Between Black and White*, 64, 68).

14. See *Falmouth Post*, 19 Nov., Dec. 1844; and *Morning Journal*, Oct. 1856. Cf. Heuman, *Between Black and White*, 64, 67.

15. There is little doubt that such statements accurately reflected the deep resentments of the assemblymen's constituents. In March 1833, for example, William Griffiths, a brown militiaman, complained at a court of enquiry that colored men were not being promoted to officer ranks in the militia. He put the matter bluntly: "This is our native country—we have nowhere to go; and consider it a

hardship to be superseded by foreigners who have been in the country for 10 or 12 months and who brought nothing with them" (quotes in Heuman, *Between Black and White*, 67, 72).

16. Heuman, *Between Black and White*, 97, 101–2, 108; *Votes*, 2d sess., 1838–44, 17.

17. Heuman, *Between Black and White*, 138.

18. Absenteeism of the colored minority in this legislature reached 31 percent during the first seven sessions. Curiously, among the issues on which they divided were various proposals to reappoint and to vote a gift of silver plate to William Burge, Jamaica's British lobbyist who had earned the contempt of abolitionists during the preceding decade with his strong defense of slavery and of the Assembly's prerogatives (*Votes*, 1st through 4th sess., 1838–44).

19. The shopkeepers were David Judah Alberga (who kept a canteen at the Newcastle barracks), Hiam Barrow (a provisions merchant in Spanish Town and St. Thomas-in-the-Vale), Hugh M. Henry, Isaac Levy, George Lyons, Aaron Salom, Simon Magnus, and Moses Lyon (the latter two were tavernkeepers). Charles Levy of Kingston, Robert Nunes of Montego Bay (who was also an agent of the Colonial Bank), and Daniel Hart (who was briefly identified with the Town party for the 1837–38 period) were merchants also but probably had larger establishments. Andrew Henry Lewis was a small penkeeper. The occupations of Edward Lucas and Robert J. Macpherson have not been identified.

20. Cf. Heuman, *Between Black and White*, 128–29.

21. The lawyers were Samuel B. Hylton, Francis R. Lynch, and Joseph Stone Williams. I have included Charles Farquharson and Samuel Jackson Dallas, even though both were identified with the Planter party, because each supported the government in later years. Henry G. Groves, Andrew Gregory Johnston, Thomas Wheatle, Charles Royles, Charles Farquharson, and William Wemyss Anderson were planters. Because of their voting records, I have classified two other men sometimes identified with the Town party as Planter party members, James Davidson and George Solomon; the latter was also a merchant (Barkly to Molesworth, 24 Oct. 1855 [confidential], CO 137/327; *Votes*, 2d sess., 1854–60, 271).

22. Heuman, *Between Black and White*, 140.

23. As with the Town party, I have used primarily voting records to identify 114 members of the Planter party. Eleven were Jews and 6 were Afro-Jamaicans. Planters (42) and merchants (11) account for most of the occupations that can be identified (51 percent); there were 4 lawyers (2 of them barristers) and 2 surgeons.

24. Heuman, *Between Black and White*, 122; *Falmouth Post*, 7 Aug. 1849.

25. Since it took the island secretary one year to register new electors, scheduling elections early did blunt the Baptist voter registration drive. Baptist candidates won only in St. Thomas-in-the-Vale and St. Mary, but the latter win was voided for alleged electoral corruption (Heuman, *Between Black and White*, 120–21).

26. See appendix 2 for fuller discussion of success scores.

27. This reasoning was apparently attributed to Jordon and Osborn by the *Falmouth Post* when it vehemently attacked them for "inconsistent" and "self-interested" opposition to retrenchment in their newspaper, the *Morning Journal* (*Falmouth Post*, 10 Aug. 1849. Cf. Heuman, *Between Black and White*, 143).

28. Through roll call analysis I have identified "core" voting blocs within and across the parties, defined as members present at least half the time who agreed

with each other at least 70 percent of the time. The Planters formed a core group of 21 members with an average agreement score of 83 and a success index of +56. Peter Moncrieffe was the only colored member in this core. By contrast, 13 of the 20 Town party members—all but 4 of them colored—formed a core group with an average agreement score of 85. Their success ratio was -26. This is consistent with the findings of Heuman, who uses Guttman scaling for 1848–49 and 1849–51 to show the unity and cohesion of what he calls "the Liberals" (Heuman, *Between Black and White*, 145–47).

29. Charles Grey to Earl Grey, 8 Oct. 1849, no. 94, CO 137/303.

30. Heuman, *Between Black and White*, 124.

31. Some sense of the obvious political revolution this election seemed to portend can be gleaned from the unusually large number of Planter challenges to Afro-Jamaican victors that followed. James Taylor was challenged by James Porteous in Port Royal; John Samuel Brown of St. James by Henry George Groves; Alexander Heslop of Kingston by James Davidson. Planter party electees William Girod and John Fowles from St. George were also challenged (*Votes*, 1st sess., 1849–54, 23–24, 26, and 2d sess., 1849–54, 10).

32. Two of the new colored members were formally allied with the Planter party. The expansion of numbers also drew in different class and racial strata. Samuel Q. Bell, John Nunes, and Robert L. Constantine either worked with their hands or were small businessmen. Edward Vickars, Charles Price, Robert Clementson, and probably Christopher Walters were black; Clementson's election was voided, however (Heuman, *Between Black and White*, 62–63).

33. The Planters' absentee rate varied between 25 percent in the first session of 1860–63 and 55 percent in the third session of 1854–60; the Town party's between 20 percent in 1837–38 and 49 percent in session 5 of 1863–65. These rates are understated because they are based on "edited" roll call files; that is, roll calls with high absentee rates were deleted before the analysis was done. See appendix 2 for discussion of data analysis.

34. James Taylor, for example, served for more than a decade (cf. Heuman, *Between Black and White*, 143–46).

35. Charles Grey to Earl Grey, 7 Sept. 1849, no. 79, CO 137/303.

36. In this session, a Planter party "core" had an average agreement score of 83 and a success ratio of 47. The Town party "core" scored 91 and -13, respectively. Several Jews voted with the Planters in 1849–51, but they joined the Afro-Jamaicans in opposing Planter attempts to impose an income tax instead of taxing the estates. The two Town party defectors were Aaron Salom and Moses Lyon, both Jewish merchants. The Planter party defectors were Charles Miller Farquharson and Samuel Jackson Dallas, both Jamaican creoles, descended from two of the oldest families on the island.

37. *Votes*, 2d sess., 1849–54, 38. Cf. Heuman, *Between Black and White*, 145–46.

38. The political controversy subsided and absenteeism rose (39 percent for the Town party and 43 percent for the Planters) during the frightening cholera epidemic, to which 30,590 deaths were attributed by 1852 (*Votes*, 6th sess., 1849–54, 377; Heuman, *Between Black and White*, 148–49). William Green suggests that the collapse of Guianese efforts at retrenchment in August 1849 weakened the Jamaicans' will to resist the free trade policy (Green, *British Slave Emancipation*, 242).

39. *New York Herald*, 13 June 1853; Heuman, *Between Black and White*, 149.

40. Charles Grey to Duke of Newcastle, 10 May 1853, no. 40, CO 137/316.

41. Enclosed letter, Alexander Bravo, custos of Vere, to R. Bruce, 3 Sept. 1845, CO 137/284.

42. *Falmouth Post,* 4 Sept. 1849.

43. Among those indicted was the half-brother of Edward Jordon, Robert, who was later acquitted (Charles Grey to Earl Grey, 27 Feb. 1851, no. 17, and 15 Mar. 1851, no. 27, CO 137/309; Campbell, *Dynamics of Change,* 243).

44. Heuman, *Between Black and White,* 65–66, 121, 148.

45. Ibid., 148; Charles Grey to Duke of Newcastle, 26 May 1853, no. 50, CO 137/316; Grey to Newcastle, 25 June 1853, no. 68, in *PP* 1854 [1848], 43:2.

46. Of the island's six hundred prisoners, one hundred were released unconditionally and one hundred more were granted pardons on condition that they work for an employer at nine pence a day plus board (T. F. Pilgrim, Governor's Secretary, 8 June 1853, encl. with Grey to Newcastle, 10 June 1853, no. 56, and Grey to Newcastle, 5 Oct. 1853, no. 98, in *PP* 1854 [1848], 43:1–2, 7–8).

47. Grey to Newcastle, 9 July 1853, no. 73, and 25 July 1853, no. 76, and Newcastle to Grey, 1 July 1853, no. 57, all in *PP* 1854 [1848], 43:4, 114.

48. My survey of the literature on British politics during this period confirms that the 1840s and 1850s marked a period of weak governments and that every government between 1852 and 1867 was vulnerable in the House of Commons. Most analysts agree that the party system itself was fragile, and governments were brought down by Commons votes rather than by general elections. Norman Gash argues that despite constantly shifting coalitions, the roots of the party system are to be found in this period, nevertheless (Asa Briggs, *The Age of Improvement, 1783–1867* [London: Longmans, 1959], 417; Derek Beales, *From Castlereagh to Gladstone, 1815–1885* [New York: W. W. Norton, 1969], 198–99; Gash, *Reaction and Reconstruction,* 122–30).

49. Donald Southgate, *The Passing of the Whigs, 1832–1886* (London: Macmillan, 1962), 193, 229; *DNB* 15:666. For a slightly different perspective see Gash, who argues that Russell was weakened by the 1849 agricultural depression and political vacillation (*Reaction and Reconstruction,* 196).

50. Southgate, *Passing of the Whigs,* 240; *DNB* 8:200–203.

51. *DNB* 4:554–55.

52. *Hansard,* 128:947–77, quote on 948.

53. Ibid., quotes on 948, 951.

54. Ibid.; see esp. 952, 961, 963–64, quote on 964.

55. Stephen to Mr. Cunningham, 20 Mar. 1850, quoted in *The Right Honourable Sir James Stephen: Letters With Biographical Notes,* biographical notes by Caroline Emelia Stephen (N.p.: Printed for Private Circulation Only, 1906), 143–44.

56. "Colonial Policy," 7 Jan. 1850, Miscellaneous, no. 7, CO 885/1.

57. Ibid.

58. During a parliamentary debate in 1849, Stanley claimed to see in the Montreal riots "the most formidable of all wars, a war of races" (Phillip A. Buckner, *The Transition to Responsible Government: British Policy in British North America, 1815–1850* [Westport, Conn.: Greenwood, 1985], 73–75, 192–234, quote on 314; *The Collected Works of Edward Gibbon Wakefield,* ed. M. F. Lloyd Prichard [Glasgow: Collins, 1968], 43).

59. Wakefield, *Collected Works,* 43; Buckner, *Transition to Responsible Government,* 191–92.

60. Jacques Monet, *The Last Cannon Shot: A Study of French-Canadian National-ism, 1837–1850* ([Toronto]: U of Toronto P, 1969), 90.

61. Wakefield, *Collected Works*, 44, 45, quote on 45.

62. The following discussion is generally based on information culled from Buckner, *Transition to Responsible Government*; Monet, *The Last Cannon Shot*; and John W. Cell, *British Colonial Administration in the Mid-Nineteenth Century: The Policy-Making Process* (New Haven: Yale UP, 1970).

63. Buckner, *Transition to Responsible Government*, 251.

64. As late as 1849, for example, Earl Grey "denounced it as a 'somewhat incorrect' way to describe the 'system of administration' in Canada" (Buckner, *Transition to Responsible Government*, 257ff., quote on 258; see also "Colonial Policy," 8 Feb. 1849).

65. Monet, *The Last Cannon Shot*, 25; Buckner, *Transition to Responsible Government*, 261, 312, 323.

66. Buckner, *Transition to Responsible Government*, 280, 306.

67. Hincks to LaFontaine, 17 June 1840, quoted in Monet, *The Last Cannon Shot*, 66 (emphasis in the original); see also 44–45, 47.

68. Nova Scotia set the precedent in August 1839 when Colonial Secretary Normanby instructed its governor that the Executive Council must command "co-operation" on *most* matters in order to function (Normanby to Campbell, 31 Aug. 1839, no. 34, CO 218/32, fols. 197–218, cited in Buckner, *Transition to Responsible Government*, 261).

69. The first government organized under the Act of Union went only halfway toward majority rule. Given the Tories' election victories, it was not necessary to bring *Canadiens* into the government, the reformers could be ignored for a time, and the policy of Anglicization mandated by the Act of Union implemented; but Peel thought even then that responsible government was, nonetheless, "on the eve of exposure" (Buckner, *Transition to Responsible Government*, 262–64, quote on 264).

70. Buckner, *Transition to Responsible Government*, 259. For Elgin's views see Elgin to Sir George Grey, 9 Sept. 1854, quoted in J. L. Morison, *The Eighth Earl of Elgin: A Chapter in Nineteenth-Century Imperial History* (London: Hodder & Stoughton, 1928), 138–39.

71. Bagot to Stanley, 28 Oct. 1842, cited in Buckner, *Transition to Responsible Government*, 267.

72. Wakefield, *Collected Works*, 50; Buckner, *Transition to Responsible Government*, 266–67.

73. The recognition became explicit in Nova Scotia as early as December 1846, when the governor found it impossible to maintain a coalition ministry. Actually, in that instance it was Russell, now prime minister, who first recognized the inevitability of party government in Nova Scotia and advised Grey to revise his dispatch to reflect that fact. After an exchange of correspondence with Elgin, Grey conceded responsible government de facto in Canada. Although it is usually seen as a commitment to party government, Buckner argues that it was motivated really by the need to control the damage over the patronage issue (Buckner, *Transition to Responsible Government*, 297, 300; Elgin to Grey, 26 Apr. 1847, in *The Elgin-Grey Papers, 1846–1852*, ed. A. Doughty, 4 vols. [Ottawa, 1937], 1:29, quoted in Cell, *British Colonial Administration*, 113).

74. Elgin rather enjoyed his reputation as "an ultra-liberal" (Elgin to Sir George Grey, 15 Sept. 1854, quoted in Morison, *Eighth Earl of Elgin*, 140–41).

75. Russell to Metcalfe, 25 June 1840, and Metcalfe to Russell, 12 Jan. 1840, no. 41, CO 137/248; Metcalfe to Russell, 12 Feb. 1841, no. 189, CO 137/255. See also J. S. [James Stephen] to Vernon Smith, 24 Mar. 1841; and [Taylor?] to Russell, 24 Mar. 1841, encl. with Metcalfe to Russell, 12 Feb. 1841.

76. In response to this chastisement, Charles Grey explained that he had proposed the idea of responsible government merely to deflect the Assembly's attention from the retrenchment issue and that he did not mean to equate it with a ministry in the English style but merely to secure permanent funding of the executive and judicial bureaucracy. Once that had been secured, he saw no problem with "humoring" the Assembly majority by appointing and removing executive officers. But during a debate in May 1853, Robert Osborn urged responsible government as the way to safeguard colored interests: "Do away with the Assembly, and the coloured people would sink into the insignificance from which they had risen" (Earl Grey to Charles Grey, 13 Sept. 1848 [confidential], and Charles Grey to Earl Grey, 5 Aug. 1848, no. 70, CO 137/297; Earl Grey to Charles Grey, 15 Sept. 1848, Hart Collection; Charles Grey to Earl Grey, 6 Nov. 1848 [confidential], CO 137/298; Heuman, *Between Black and White*, 143, 150 [Osborn cited on 150]. See also *Morning Journal*, 11 July 1849).

77. *Hansard*, 128:963–64.

78. Aeneas Barkly, Henry's father, bought estates in Berbice, British Guiana, in 1822 and had interests in fourteen estates via his merchant firm Davidson & Barkly, for all of which he received £18,555 in slave compensation money in 1833. Barkly inherited all this upon his father's death in 1836 (Mona Macmillan, *Sir Henry Barkly, Mediator and Moderator, 1815–1898* [Cape Town: A. A. Balkema, 1970], 6–11).

79. *Hansard*, 82:1295–1310; Macmillan, *Sir Henry Barkly*, 9–15, 17.

80. Macmillan, *Sir Henry Barkly*, 57–58.

81. Barkly to Newcastle, 21 Feb. 1854, no. 24, CO 137/322. See also Newcastle to Barkly, 28 July 1854, no. 19, and Barkly to Newcastle, 22 Mar. 1854, no. 37, both in *PP* 1854 [1848], 43:58.

82. Barkly to George Grey, 19 Oct. 1854, no. 107; Barclay [Barkly] to Newcastle, 23 Nov. 1853, no. 18; "Jamaica," *New York Daily Tribune*, 12 Oct. 1853; Heuman, *Between Black and White*, 150, 156.

83. More than half the Planter party members missed more than half the roll calls, while only 21 percent of the Town party members were that delinquent. But even when those who were present often enough to be paired with another member on 50 percent of the votes are selected out, one finds that only 19 percent of Planter party members that could be scored (15 percent of the total) agreed on 80 percent or more of the roll calls, and less than 4 percent on 70 to 79 percent of the roll calls. Meanwhile, 20 percent of Town party members scored (43 percent of the total) achieved agreement above 80 percent, and 36 percent agreed 70 to 79 percent of the time.

84. During the early 1850s, death claimed Alexander Finlay and James Dunstone, Raynes Smith vacated his seat in April 1853, George Price was promoted to the Legislative Council in December 1853, and James Davidson lost to John Castello, the fiery, colored editor of the *Falmouth Post*.

85. Regarding the constitutional crisis, Heuman argues that Jackson wanted

an executive committee of limited power and sought to abolish or weaken the Legislative Council and strengthen the Assembly but feared that full responsible government would further divide the colony from the Crown (Heuman, *Between Black and White*, 153–55).

86. The opposing factions had comparable cohesion, but the Jackson group controlled voting. The opposition coalition had an average agreement score of 86 and an average success ratio of +56. The government coalition had an agreement score of 82 and a success ratio of -6.7.

87. The defectors were Edward Vickars, Peter A. Espeut, John Nunes, and John Castello. David Mason, a white Town party member, and Thomas Mason, a Planter, also supported the government. The agreement score for this core group was 81, and its success ratio was +18, compared with 73 and +9.5, respectively, for Jackson's group (cf. Heuman, *Between Black and White*, 155–56).

88. Newcastle to Barkly, encl. with Barkly to Newcastle, 9 Dec. 1853, no. 28, in *PP* 1854 [1848], 43:37–41, quote on 37.

89. Barkly to Newcastle, 10 Feb. 1854, no. 23, in *PP* 1854 [1848], 43:49–58.

90. Barkly to Newcastle, 26 Dec. 1853, no. 36, in *PP* 1854 [1848], 43:45–48.

91. Just over a year later Barkly would call for amendments to the Better Government Act in order that he might bring the attorney general into his Cabinet (Barkly to Molesworth, 26 Sept. 1855, no. 96, CO 137/327; Barkly to Newcastle, 7 Apr. 1854, no. 43, and 10 Apr. 1854, no. 46, in *PP* 1854 [1848], 43:86–98 [copy of act on 98–109]; Newcastle to Barkly, 12 June 1854, no. 94, in *PP* 1854 [1848], 43:124–25).

92. Barkly to Newcastle, 19 Jan. 1854, no. 9, CO 137/322.

93. Barkly to George Grey, 17 Aug. 1854 (confidential), CO 137/324.

94. Barkly to Herbert, 10 Apr. 1855, CO 137/326. Significantly, the governor's arguments for an appointment were always couched in terms of the political as well as the personal qualities of the candidate. For example, Barkly urged the appointment of Bryan Edwards and Richard Hill to the Privy Council or the Advisory Council because of "the degree of confidence reposed in them by large and influential sections of the community" (Barkly to George Grey, 17 Aug. 1854 [confidential]).

95. Taylor's marginal note, encl. with Eyre to Cardwell, 24 Oct. 1864, no. 275, CO 137/385.

96. The motion to censure Jordon was supported by Bourke and Constantine, both colored members allied with the Planter faction, and Charles Jackson. Opposing censure were William T. March, Osborn, Russell, and Taylor (*Votes*, 2d sess., 1854–60, 27).

97. At the core of the ministerial cluster were Jordon, Westmorland, William Hosack, and Charles Royles, who voted together over 96 percent of the time, joined by Baron von Ketelhodt, Peter Espeut, Paterson, George Geddes, William Rose, and Colin Chisholm. Their average agreement score was 82; their success ratio was +46. The five opposition members had an average agreement score of 58 with each other and 38 with Jordon and Westmorland; their success ratio was +4.8. The six colored members constituting the swing group had a collective average agreement score of 65; they also voted with the ministerial coalition 64 percent of the time and had a success rate of +46, matching that of the government's core group. Since absenteeism on most roll calls exceeded 45 percent, the

government was able to marshal enough votes to control the House. In the second session of the new Assembly most of the swing group was reintegrated with the government coalition, which now attracted fifteen members, of whom eight were identified with the Town party, seven were colored, and two were Jewish (a large merchant and a planter). But this larger group was not nearly as cohesive or as successful as during the previous session. By contrast, six Town party members (three of them colored) joined three Planter party members to form a tight opposition coalition. The average agreement score for the government coalition was 74, and its success ratio was $+23$, compared with the opposition's 87 and $+9.4$, respectively.

98. Of fifteen Afro-Jamaicans, six opposed and nine supported the government on the import duties bill. Although Jewish merchants joined the government's opponents, they were unable to defeat the bill (Heuman, *Between Black and White,* 157–59).

99. *Votes,* 2d sess., 1854–60, 281.

100. The tax produced a yield of £12,000, from a levy of 8 shillings on the first £10 value of a house, graduated by 10 shillings for every additional £10 in value. Houses on estates for the temporary accommodation of laborers, that is, huts rented by the planters, were exempt. Among colored members, only William T. March opposed the measure; Bourke and Jackson were absent (*Votes,* 2d sess., 1854–60, 211; Barkly to Henry Labouchere, 18 Mar. 1856, no. 47, CO 137/331. See also Barkly to Newcastle, 7 Dec. 1853, no. 23, in *PP* 1854 [1848], 43:34–35. Cf. Heuman, *Between Black and White,* 159, 160–61).

101. Barkly to Henry Labouchere, 9 Apr. 1856 (confidential), CO 137/331.

102. The new governor arrived in Jamaica in time for the fifth session of the 1854–59 Assembly, which began in November 1858. Opposition to him brought the Town party and the Afro-Jamaican members their greatest unity of the 1850s decade (see figs. 7.2 and 7.3). A cohesive nine-member opposition (including seven colored members and three Town party whites) had a success ratio of $+34$, compared with the government's $+26$.

103. *Votes,* 5th sess., 1854–60, 50; Heuman, *Between Black and White,* 161–62.

104. Tenants were required to obtain a rental receipt from their landlord, who for political reasons might refuse to give one; and assessors could undervalue the land of peasant freeholders. In 1847, for example, freeholders in St. Ann discovered that their property had been undervalued and thus they were ineligible to vote (Metcalfe to Russell, 4 Jan. 1841, no. 158, and 19 Sept. 1841, and Stanley to Metcalfe, 29 Nov. 1841, no. 18, in CO 137/254, 256; Heuman, *Between Black and White,* 129). The amended law was 5 Victoria, chaps. 39 and 57 (Metcalfe to Stanley, 9 Feb. 1842, no. 72, CO 137/261).

105. Earl Grey to Charles Grey, 10 Aug. 1847, Hart Collection.

106. The decisive votes were cast by two Planter representatives, Dr. Hinton Spalding and John Fowles, while two colored members, Wellesley Bourke, a planter, and Robert Russell, a lawyer, supported the amendment (*Votes,* 6th sess., 1849–54, 286).

107. Barkly to Newcastle, 22 Mar. 1854, no. 37.

108. Barkly to Henry Labouchere, 9 Apr. 1856 (confidential); Heuman, *Between Black and White,* 159–60. Among the colored Town party members, only Jordon's business partner, Robert Osborn, supported him on this vote. For Castello's call for a broader suffrage see *Falmouth Post,* 29 Sept. 1854.

109. Darling later recanted his concession that the new law would discourage voters, saying that he simply meant that they would fail to register because of their reluctance "to part with money for any purpose that does not directly minister to their wants or gratifications" (Darling to Lytton, 10 Feb. 1859, no. 31, CO 137/343; Heuman, *Between Black and White*, 130–31; Darling to Lytton, 24 Feb. 1859, no. 34, CO 137/343).

110. Heuman, *Between Black and White*, 131.

111. On the first vote, the Afro-Jamaican opponents were James Taylor, Christopher Walters, Charles Price, John Nunes, Foster March, and Robert Constantine, the latter ostensibly a member of the Planter party. On the second vote, William T. March joined them. The government's supporters consisted of thirteen Planter and eight Town party members. Two of the four Afro-Jamaicans who favored retaining the duty were identified with the Planter party (*Votes*, 5th sess., 1854–60, 112–13; memorial to Queen from Joseph Brown, chairman of meeting in St. David, 15 Jan. 1859, encl. with Darling to Lytton, 24 Feb. 1859, no. 34; Heuman, *Between Black and White*, 163).

112. Darling was promised the Knighthood Commander of the Bath by Labouchere upon taking the governorship, and he grew increasingly anxious about it as his troubles in Jamaica worsened (H. Merivale Minute, 30 July, in Darling to Lord Stanley, 10 June 1858 [private and confidential], CO 137/337).

113. Minute by Fortesque to Duke of Newcastle, 27 Dec., and H. Taylor, 22 Dec. 1860, encl. with Darling to Newcastle, 23 Nov. 1860, no. 156, CO 137/351.

114. Minute by Duke of Newcastle, 14 Jan., encl. with Darling to Newcastle, 23 Nov. 1860, no. 156; see also Henry Taylor's minute in Darling to Newcastle, 7 Dec. 1860, no. 157, all in CO 137/351.

115. Darling to Newcastle, 24 Dec. 1860 (confidential), CO 137/351; Heuman, *Between Black and White*, 165.

116. Benj. Vickers to Messr. Thomson Hankey & Co., 24 Nov. 1860, encl. with Darling to Newcastle, 24 Nov. 1860 (confidential), CO 137/351.

Chapter 8. "A War of the Races"

1. Darling to Newcastle, 10 Oct. 1859, no. 123, CO 137/346. For examples of Baptist complaints see "Letter from Dr. Underhill . . . and Correspondence relative to Disturbances in Jamaica," *PP* 1866 (380), 51:45ff.; and Don Robotham, "'The Notorious Riot': The Socio-Economic and Political Bases of Paul Bogle's Revolt," *Anales del Caribe* (Havana) 3 (1983): 91–100.

2. Darling to Newcastle, 8 Sept. 1859, no. 114, CO 137/346.

3. Robotham, "Notorious Riot," 83–87.

4. Among numerous other examples, Alexander Chisolm, the overseer at Golden Grove, insisted that a worker could earn 16s. a week, but his records showed that 5s. to 6s. was the average pay. Chisolm claimed that this was because the blacks refused to work more than five days a week, and four to five hours a day. Similarly, on Hordley Estate field workers averaged just 4s. to 5s. a week. On Coley the maximum ranged from 4s. 6d. in May to 7s. in April, the average from 2s. in April to about 4s. 6d. in May. Moreover, even among skilled Coley workers the maximum wages per week fell well below what was theoretically possible: a journeyman tradesman could get 10s. for five days, a mill hand, 10s. 6d. for five

and one-half days, and a boiler man, 12s. for five and one-half days; but the average wages for a five-day week in these categories were 7s. 6d., 8s., and 8s. 9d., respectively ("Report of the Jamaica Royal Commission [1866]. Part II. Minutes of Evidence and Appendix," PP 1866 [3683-I], 31:1047 [questions 47874–96], 1108–11 [appendix] [IUP reprint, Colonies: West Indies, vol. 5] [hereafter "Report of the Jamaica Royal Commission, Pt. 2"]).

5. Testimony of Alexander Chisolm, ibid., 1047 (questions 47896–907); quote from Robotham, "Notorious Riot," 83.

6. "Report of the Jamaica Royal Commission, Pt. 2," 96 (questions 4340–41).

7. Robotham, "Notorious Riot," 80.

8. Edward Bean Underhill, The West Indies: Their Social and Religious Condition (London: Jackson, Walford, & Hodder, 1862), 285.

9. The minister was Henry Clarke, an Anglican in Westmoreland (quoted in Lord [Sydney Haldane] Olivier, The Myth of Governor Eyre [London: Hogarth, 1933], 129).

10. Regina v. Sutherland et al., 16 Apr. 1859, in Darling to Newcastle, 10 Nov. 1859, no. 135, CO 137/346.

11. I. R. Kitchen and Fred. L. Castle to Hugh W. Austin, 2 Aug. 1859, in Darling to Newcastle, 9 Aug. 1859, no. 103, CO 137/345.

12. A coroner's inquest found justifiable homicide in killings of two women on 1 August by police, but the verdict was not unanimous. A second inquest was abortive, as only seven of thirteen jurors concurred in the verdict and the coroner dismissed the charges (Darling to Newcastle, 11 Oct. 1859, no. 125, and Regina v. Sutherland et al., 16 Apr. 1859).

13. George D. Ramsay to W. R. Myers, 17 July 1865, "Report of the Jamaica Royal Commission, Pt. 2," 987–88 (question 46571).

14. Augustus Hire to W. R. Myers, July 1865, ibid., 988 (question 46571); see also 330–31 (questions 16435–46).

15. The net number of acres of patented land in 1838 was 3,403,359; quitrents had been paid on 2,588,056, giving a difference of 815,303 acres. The term "backlands" is problematic, since it appears to have been commonly used to designate uncultivated portions of estates, but Richard Hill defines backlands as all "unpatented lands," that is, land never granted out and yielding no quitrents and thus "actually at the disposition of the Government." Since there had never been a survey, the actual acreage was undetermined ("Report of the Jamaica Royal Commission, Pt. 2," 815–17 [esp. questions 39591, 39595, 39601]; cf. Robotham, "Notorious Riot," 71–72).

16. Bruce A. Knox, for example, argues that such expectations were "naïve." But there was no question that abandoned properties could be seized by the Crown where the owners had failed to pay quitrents. Indeed, this is the premise of Hill's discussion, cited above (see Knox, "The Queen's Letter of 1865 and British Policy towards Emancipation and Indentured Labour in the West Indies, 1830–1865," Historical Journal 29 [June 1986]: 345–67; and "Report of the Jamaica Royal Commission, Pt. 2," 817 [question 39601]. On the practice of repossessing land for which quitrents were in arrears see Veront M. Satchell, From Plots to Plantations: Land Transactions in Jamaica, 1866–1900 [Mona, Jamaica: Institute of Social and Economic Research, U of the West Indies, 1990], 67).

17. Edward Bean Underhill, The Tragedy of Morant Bay: A Narrative of the Disturbances in the Island of Jamaica in 1865 (London: Alexander & Shepeard, 1895), xi–xii.

18. Underhill especially deplored the discouragement of capital investment (Underhill to Edward Cardwell, 5 Jan. 1865, in "Papers Laid before the Royal Commission of Inquiry by Governor Eyre," *PP* 1866 [3682], 30:511ff. [IUP reprint, Colonies: West Indies, vol. 4] [hereafter "Eyre Papers"]; Underhill, *Tragedy of Morant Bay*, xvi).

19. Geoffrey Dutton, *The Hero as Murderer: The Life of Edward John Eyre, Australian Explorer and Governor of Jamaica, 1815–1901* (London: Collins, 1967), 218ff.; Olivier, *Myth of Governor Eyre*, 53–91; Gad J. Heuman, *Between Black and White: Race, Politics, and the Free Coloreds in Jamaica, 1792–1865* (Westport, Conn.: Greenwood, 1981), 175–76, 178–81.

20. Eyre to Cardwell, 6 Aug. 1864, no. 234, CO 137/384.

21. The governor also enclosed a copy of a letter from the *Jamaica Guardian* of 25 Feb. 1865 by Samuel Oughton, a Baptist minister, who asserted that the causes of distress were "the inveterate habits of idleness and the low state of moral and religious principles which prevail to so fearful a degree in our community" (Eyre to Cardwell, 2 Mar. 1865, enclosing Hosack to Eyre, 28 Feb. 1865, in "Papers relating to Disturbances in Jamaica," *PP* 1866 [3595], 51:517).

22. Eyre to Cardwell, 19 Apr. 1865, in *PP* 1866 (3595), 51:539–44.

23. Eyre to Cardwell, 10 Sept. 1864, no. 256, CO 137/384.

24. Eyre to Cardwell, 19 Apr. 1865, in *PP* 1866 (3595), 51:541.

25. Gordon to Lawrence, 14 Sept. 1865, in "Report of the Jamaica Royal Commission, Pt. 2," 1154–55 (appendix); Heuman, *Between Black and White*, 173–75.

26. Eyre to Cardwell, 19 Dec. 1864, no. 303, CO 137/385. The "poll tax" took the form of requiring a stamp on every application for registration. The voting-age population, defined as all males over twenty-one years old, was estimated by taking the total age cohort of persons aged twenty years and over (220,783), deducting the twenty-year-olds, estimated at 7,436, and multiplying by the male percentage of the population (48 percent), which yields 102,406, 1.9 percent of whom were registered (all figures taken from Barry W. Higman, ed., "The Jamaican Censuses of 1844 and 1861: A New Edition, Derived from the Manuscript and Printed Schedules in the Jamaica Archives" [Mona, Jamaica: Social History Project, Department of History, U of the West Indies, 1980], 16, 22).

27. Eyre to Newcastle, 7 Apr. 1863, no. 78, and 8 Apr. 1863 (confidential), CO 137/371; Heuman, *Between Black and White*, 177–78. Eyre despaired of being able to keep party government indefinitely at bay, however (Eyre to Cardwell, 20 July 1865 [confidential], CO 137/392).

28. Later, Jordon was recommended for Receiver General, a position normally reserved for an Englishman, but it was decided to appoint him to a combined position of island secretary and governor's secretary instead. It was in that context that Taylor praised him for being "unlike every other man of the Coloured Race that has cast up in the Colonial Service" and, given his influence, important "to have a permanent hold upon." Eyre to Edward Cardwell, 24 Oct. 1864, no. 275, CO 137/385; Heuman, *Between Black and White*, 182–83.

29. Robotham, "Notorious Riot," 77.

30. Ibid., 78; testimony of assemblyman Andrew Henry Lewis, "Report of the Jamaica Royal Commission, Pt. 2," 839 (question 40444); Heuman, *Between Black and White*, 190.

31. Darling to Newcastle, 8 Sept. 1859, no. 114, CO 137/346; Robotham, "Notorious Riot," 78.

32. An interesting feature of this riot was the prominence of African indentured workers in the leadership, against whom the government deliberately used African troops, believing they would have the best effect on the rioters (Darling to E. B. Lytton, 25 Mar. 1859, no. 48, and 26 Apr. 1859, no. 57, CO 137/344; Darling to Secretary of State, 22 July 1859, no. 96, CO 137/345; Monica Schuler, *"Alas, Alas, Kongo": A Social History of Indentured African Immigration into Jamaica, 1841–1865* [Baltimore: Johns Hopkins UP, 1980], 99–102).

33. Testimony of Richard Hill and Bryan Edwards, "Report of the Jamaica Royal Commission, Pt. 2," 816–17 (questions 39568–82), 835 (question 40283).

34. A minute by Henry Taylor to Sir F. Rogers, dated 30 June, became the draft for the dispatch later referred to as "the Queen's Advice." The minute and the dispatch are identical, except that "some" was substituted for "fewer" hours work. There is no evidence of any disagreement within the Colonial Office over this soon-to-be controversial dispatch (J. R. note, dated 6 June: "I agree"; Eyre to Cardwell, 25 Apr. 1865, no. 117, CO 137/390).

35. Stephen Harmer to Saal [Harmer], 21 June 1842, Stephen Harmer Letters, MS765, National Library of Jamaica, Kingston.

36. In 1840 James Stephen had almost casually accepted the inevitable supersession of the planters by the peasants. "I am convinced," he wrote, "that the inevitable tendency of things is toward the substitution of small holdings and a Peasantry living on detached Plots of Land, for the old system of large Plantations." He also anticipated their eventual political supremacy (quoted in William A. Green, *British Slave Emancipation: The Sugar Colonies and the Great Experiment, 1830–1865* [Oxford: Clarendon, 1976], 85).

37. There are two versions of the essay. The first appeared with the less offensive title, "Occasional Discourse on the Negro Question," in *Fraser's Magazine* 40 (Dec. 1849): 670–79. Four years later the essay was expanded and reprinted as a separate pamphlet with the new title "Occasional Discourse on the Nigger Question" (London, 1853), which was much harsher and more vitriolic than the first, as the change in title suggests. In between these versions, in 1850 Carlyle published *Latter-day Pamphlets*, the writing of which Carlyle's protégé and biographer, James Anthony Froude, described as a "discharge of spiritual bile"—a characterization that might well have been applied to "Discourse" as well. All references here are to the reprinted 1853 version of the essay in *Thomas Carlyle, "The Nigger Question," John Stuart Mill, "The Negro Question,"* ed. Eugene R. August (New York: Crofts Classics, 1971), 4; Froude, *Life of Carlyle,* abr. and ed. John Clubbe (Columbus: Ohio State UP, 1979), 491–94.

38. Cf. Carlyle's use of the St. Simonian phrase "A chacun selon sa capacité, à chaque capacité selon ses oeuvres," in his review of Boswell's "The Life of Samuel Johnson" in Thomas Carlyle, *Critical and Miscellaneous Essays: Collected and Republished,* 7 vols. (London: Chapman & Hall, 1872), 4:93.

39. For example, writing in 1843, he declared that man could not live his life by "'enlightened Egoism' . . . 'Laissez-faire,' 'Supply-and-demand,' 'Cashpayment for the sole nexus,' and so forth. . . . Alas, he thinks that man has a soul in him, *different* from the stomach in any sense of this word; that if said soul be asphyxied, and lie quietly forgotten, the man and his affairs are in a bad way" ("Hero-Worship," in *Past and Present* [London: Chapman & Hall, 1843], 38).

40. Engels's favorable opinion was short-lived. In a review of *Latter-day Pam-*

phlets, Marx and Engels criticized Carlyle's view of history and, indirectly, all racist ideologies. For Carlyle, they charged, "historically created class differences are made into natural differences which people must recognize and revere as part of the eternal law of nature by bowing before wise and noble ones in nature: the cult of genius" (*On Literature and Art* [New York: International Publishers, 1947], 110–11).

41. He goes on to condemn modern liberty "which has to purchase itself by social isolation, and which each man standing separate from the other, having 'no business with him' but a cash-account; this is such a liberty as the Earth seldom saw" ("Democracy," in *Past and Present,* 210–12, 218).

42. The comment on the Irish is found in Carlyle to Ralph Waldo Emerson, 19 Apr. 1849, in *Correspondence of Thomas Carlyle and Ralph Waldo Emerson, 1834–1872,* ed. C. E. Norton, 2 vols. (London: Chatto & Windus, 1883), 2:179. The statement about blacks is found in "Discourse."

43. In *Past and Present,* he asserted that Lancashire weavers were worth the whole lot of West Indian Quashees, who were small in number and worth. Carlyle had close friends among the Young Ireland group (see chapter 9, below, for more comparisons with popular English attitudes toward Irish).

44. Carlyle and Mill had been friends earlier. Carlyle had read the anonymous series entitled "The Spirit of the Age" in the *Examiner* (Jan.–June 1831) and declared the author a "new mystic," a veritable soul mate. The author was Mill, who had been equally impressed with Carlyle's early essays. There was a kind of convergence of the respective personal and intellectual odysseys of Mill and Carlyle at that time, in their "crisis of faith," in their criticism of their era, and in their enthusiasm about its possibilities for reformation. At one point, Mill suggested a new periodical for "radical" opinion, which Carlyle aspired to edit. He became one of Carlyle's personal benefactors. Mill was a reader of Carlyle's first draft of *The French Revolution,* and the indirect cause of its destruction: Mill's maid accidentally burned the manuscript. Later, Mill suggested the Cromwell biography but did not like it when it came out. Indeed, by the time *Cromwell* was published in 1845, their friendship had cooled.

45. Stephen, "Mr Carlyle," in *Essays by a Barrister* (London: Smith, Elder & Co., 1862), 242–53 (originally published anonymously in *Saturday Review,* 19 June 1858); Taylor, *Autobiography of Henry Taylor, 1800–1875,* 2 vols. (London: Longmans, Green, 1885), 1:269–74.

46. Mill, "The Negro Question," in Carlyle and Mill, *"The Nigger Question,"* 41, 47–48.

47. *Inquirer* 8, no. 388 (8 Dec. 1849), quoted in Carlyle and Mill, *"The Nigger Question,"* 55.

48. Cf. David Brion Davis, *Slavery and Human Progress* (New York: Oxford UP, 1984), 298–309.

49. Merivale, quoted in Knox, "The Queen's Letter," 360.

50. Carlyle, *Reminiscences,* ed. Charles E. Norton, 2 vols. in 1 (London: Macmillan, 1887), 2:278; Carlyle to [Jane Carlyle], 17 Jan. 1848, in *Thomas Carlyle: Letters to His Wife,* ed. Trudy Bliss (London: V. Gollancz, 1953), 244–45; Henry Taylor to [Theodosia Alice Taylor], 19 Sept. 1848, *Correspondence of Henry Taylor,* ed. Edward Dowden (London: Longmans, Green, 1888), 184–85.

51. Henry Taylor, "Legislation Affecting the Labouring Classes in the West Indies," 15 Feb. 1846, "West Indies: Miscellaneous, 1846," CO 318/169.

52. Henry Taylor, "State of the West Indies in 1862," July 1862, no. 12, CO 884/1; this is a revision of the 1855 memorandum.

53. Darling to Newcastle, 9 Aug. 1859, no. 103.

54. Eyre to Cardwell, 30 Mar. 1865, no. 69, and Taylor's minute attached to Eyre to Cardwell, 22 Mar. 1865, no. 59, both in CO 137/388. The words quoted are Henry Taylor's.

55. The prison population had increased from 400 inmates costing £10,883 in 1860 to 575 costing £12,828 in 1864 (Eyre to Cardwell, 16 Mar. 1865, no. 48, CO 137/388).

56. Ibid. The laws governing the use of convict labor were passed between 1854 and 1864: 18 Victoria, chap. 22 (1854); 21 Victoria, chap. 14 (1857); and 28 Victoria, chap. 22 (1864).

57. "The Suppression of Crime by Corporal Punishment," *Falmouth Post*, Mar. 1850, clipping in J. E. Pieterez, "Scrapbook, compiled by J. E. Pieterez. Miscellaneous Newspaper Clippings dated from 1826–1944," MS227, National Library of Jamaica. Cries for severer punishment came from all quarters; for example, stipendiary magistrate Henry Laidlaw of Mandeville urged convict lease as an appropriate remedy for thefts from provision grounds (Darling to Newcastle, 8 Sept. 1859, no. 114).

58. Charles Grey to Earl Grey, 23 Mar. 1850, no. 30, CO 137/303. Henry Roberts to Charles Grey, 20 Apr. 1850; Earl Grey to Charles Grey, 8 June 1850, no. 342; Charles Grey to Earl Grey, 7 May 1850, no. 41, CO 137/303. Eyre to Cardwell, 22 Mar. 1865, no. 59.

59. The quotation is from a minute dated February 1866 and signed by "WET." The amendments that the Colonial Office sought initially were that for first offenders the permission of the parent be required and that the indenture should be limited to one year and not go beyond the eighteenth birthday (Eyre to Cardwell, 22 Mar. 1865, no. 60, enclosing Cardwell to Storks, 29 Jan. 1866, CO 137/388).

60. Testimony of Richard Hill, "Report of the Jamaica Royal Commission, Pt. 2," 815–16 (questions 39446–551); quote in Robotham, "Notorious Riot," 72–73. Cf. E. P. Thompson, *Whigs and Hunters: The Origins of the Black Act* (London: Allen Lane, 1975).

61. In 1864 more than 50 percent of the cases were brought by planters against workers, while less than 0.5 percent of the cases were brought by workers against planters. In 1863 there were 219 cases, of which 210 involved laborers as defendants but only 4 involved planters; 71 of the complainants were laborers, 96 were planters. In 1864 there were 256 cases, in 250 of which laborers were defendants, while 139 involved planters as plaintiffs. There were no appeals and 2 dismissals ("Report of the Jamaica Royal Commission [1866]. Part I. Report," *PP* 1866 [3683], 30:1103, 1083–1101 [appendix] [IUP reprint, Colonies: West Indies, vol. 4] [hereafter "Report of the Jamaica Royal Commission, Pt. 1"]. See also Robotham, "Notorious Riot," 88–90, 96–99 [tables 2 and 3]).

62. According to Eyre, the new act substantially returned to the old law (16 Victoria, chap. 42, secs. 2–4; 23 Victoria, chap. 14). It gave summary jurisdiction to two justices as before 27 Victoria, and larceny of plants or other property valued at more than ten shillings value was now triable by indictment only (Eyre to Cardwell, 8 Feb. 1865, no. 22, CO 137/388; Heuman, *Between Black and White*, 162).

63. Darling to Newcastle, 18 Oct. 1860, no. 140, CO 137/346; testimony of Richard Hill, in "Report of the Jamaica Royal Commission, Pt. 2," 817 (question 39583).

64. The Jackson controversy was extended and complex. The flavor of it is revealed in the voluminous correspondence over his removal from St. Thomas-in-the-East, upon the insistence of Eyre's political ally, Baron von Ketelhodt (Eyre to Cardwell, 4 Sept. 1865, no. 220, CO 137/393).

65. "Report of the Jamaica Royal Commission, Pt. 2," 1160–61; William C. Miller statement encl. with Eyre to Cardwell, Jan. 1866, "Eyre Papers," 10, 51–52; Robotham, "Notorious Riot," 85.

66. Schuler, "Alas, Alas, Kongo," chap. 5.

67. In 1830 the Methodists enrolled 3,110 free Negro, 83 white, and 8,937 slave members, heavily concentrated (64 percent) in the southeastern part of the island. For some indication of denominational strength and location after emancipation see "Return of marriages registered in Island Secretary's office . . . by Dissenting Ministers, 1 April 1844 to 1 July 1845," in Votes, 2d sess., 1844–49, CO 140/137, 304.

68. There were 17,792 Methodists in 1854 and 16,222 in 1859. Enos Nuttall blamed the Methodist losses on their itinerant system of ministry and their failure to recruit natives into the ministry, an analysis that might well apply to the Baptists as well (Enos Nuttall to Rev. J. Mearns [chairman of the Jamaica District], 31 Jan. 1866, and minutes for 1866, in The Methodist Church in Jamaica, District Minutes, 1830–66, Ecclesiastical, Jamaica Archives; Philip Chapman to General Secretary, 7 Apr. 1840, MMS196, and S. Burrell to General Secretary, 9 Oct. 1858, MMS199, Methodist Missionary Society, Jamaica Correspondence, 1840–42, School of Oriental and Asian Studies, University of London. See also Robotham, "Notorious Riot," 80–81).

69. See testimony of Rev. George Truman, Native Baptist, describing revival practices, in "Report of the Jamaica Royal Commission, Pt. 2," 415–16 (questions 20475–514); John Mearns to General Secretary, 22 Nov. 1860, and W. Clark Murray to Rev. Elijah Hoole, 8 Oct. 1862, in MMS199, Methodist Missionary Society.

70. Actually there were two riots: the first, on New Year's Eve, was led mainly by women (16 of the 20 people arrested were women); the second involved 500 people, who practically destroyed Phillippo's house (Thomas Witter Jackson to T. F. Pilgrim, 25 July 1851, which encloses a report dated 19 July 1851 enclosed in turn in Charles Grey to Earl Grey, 27 Feb. 1851, no. 17, CO 137/309; Charles Grey to Earl Grey, 26 July 1851, no. 65, and 28 July 1851, no. 67, CO 137/310).

71. Barkly to Newcastle, 19 Jan. 1854, no. 9, CO 137/322; Barkly to Henry Labouchere, 12 Mar. 1855, no. 24, CO 137/326.

72. As noted in chapter 6, above, myalists found African resonances in Baptist doctrines and practices. For more discussion see Schuler, "Alas, Alas, Kongo," 32–44.

73. Apparently, Gordon was also briefly a member of the Presbyterian denomination (see letters from Gordon to a business associate indicating an active and successful business: George W. Gordon to James Bell, 24 Apr. 1855, 1 May 1862, and 6 Oct. 1863, in George William Gordon Letters, MST892, no. 1, National Library of Jamaica; "Report of the Jamaica Royal Commission, Pt. 1," 29–30; W. Adolphe Roberts, Six Great Jamaicans: Biographical Sketches [Kingston: Pioneer, 1951], 25–31; and Heuman, Between Black and White, 61).

74. For scattered evidence on Gordon's finances see "Eyre Papers," 248–49; and testimony of Maria Jane Gordon, "Report of the Jamaica Royal Commission, Pt. 2," 722–27 (questions 35374–614). For Gordon's own account of and statement regarding his finances see his will dated 14 Oct. 1865, the probate entered 13 June 1871, and the inventory of property dated 25 Oct. 1873 in the wills and probate records, liber 131, fol. 180, and in the inventories, liber 161, fol. 210, Island Record Office, Spanish Town.

75. "Report of the Jamaica Royal Commission, Pt. 1," 19; Robotham, "Notorious Riot," 76–77. See also the tax records submitted by W. P. Kirkland, collector of dues in St. Thomas-in-the-East. Gordon paid a total of £16 8s. 8d. for various tenants ("Eyre Papers," 29).

76. "Report of the Jamaica Royal Commission, Pt. 2," 1150 (appendix).

77. Gordon to Henry James Lawrence, 11, 18 and 21 Sept. 1865, "Eyre Papers," 209, 213–14. Lawrence was executed for alleged complicity in the Morant Bay Rebellion.

78. The testimony on this incident is contradictory on many details but generally consistent on the overall scenario. Sgt. John Burnett claimed that he saw Bogle involved in the rescue, but no one else corroborated this ("Report of the Jamaica Royal Commission, Pt. 2," 1–2, 155–56, 229–30 [questions 1–7, 7581–7652, 11564–631]).

79. Ibid., "Pt. 1," 10–11, and "Pt. 2," 34–37, 124–31, 184–85, 566–67 (questions 1614–1712, 5886–6211, 9336–81, 9400–9412, 28630–81).

80. Ibid., "Pt. 1," 11, and "Pt. 2," 31–32, 79–82 (questions 1463–1511, 3643–3837); "Eyre Papers," 23.

81. The Jamaica militia had suffered as a fighting force after abolition largely as a result of government policies, most of them motivated by its uneasiness about relying largely on black enlistment. Under 7 Victoria, chap. 64, arms and accouterments were removed from the custody of foot militia and put in the hands of the governor, "thereby precluding the possibility of the employment of that portion of the force without the Governor's express sanction." Early in 1865, Eyre announced plans to reduce the West India Regiment, dispensing with black troops and keeping the whites for internal policing. Fearing that black militiamen would be unwilling to act against friends and relatives, he wanted a force of three hundred white troops (Elgin to Stanley, 30 June 1845, no. 59, CO 137/284; Eyre to Cardwell, 13 Mar. 1865 [confidential], CO 137/388).

82. "Shell" refers to a horn made by knocking off the end of a conch shell. Such horns had been used during slavery to send people back to work after breakfast; the sound carried up to two or three miles ("Report of the Jamaica Royal Commission, Pt. 2," 4–5, 6, 83–84 [questions 89, 96–97, 221, 3858–60).

83. Ibid., 1081 (appendix).

84. Matthew Cresser quoted Bogle's claim following the violence that he had gone to Morant Bay merely to post bail and that the militia had started the fight when they fired on the crowd (ibid., 144 [question 6960]).

85. This account is a composite one, drawn from testimony of eyewitnesses to the Royal Commission. The discrepancies are fairly minor, often reflecting different vantage points of observation. For example, the Royal Commission noted conflicting evidence concerning whether stones were thrown before the order to fire was given, but apparently the stones were thrown by people—mostly

women—on the side of the main body of the crowd (ibid., "Pt. 1," 11–13, and "Pt. 2," 1–9, 26–33 [questions 8–147, 210–336, 1210–1352, 1381–1462, 1524–71]).

86. Ibid., "Pt. 1," 11–14, and "Pt. 2," 1081 (appendix) and see also 10 (questions 420–23).

87. "Eyre Papers," 412, 428; "Report of the Jamaica Royal Commission, Pt. 1," 15–16, and "Part 2," 11, 22–23 (questions 457–60, 1023–28, 1107).

88. Peter A. Espeut, a brown St. Thomas planter and assemblyman, asserted that the rebels were mostly small settlers who "never worked on the estates," but this is contradicted by the numerous specific identifications others made of accused rebels (see the testimony of William Lake, a policeman at Morant Bay, and Robert William Kirkwood, a planter at Bath, "Report of the Jamaica Royal Commission, Pt. 1," 16, and "Pt. 2," 79, 96, 114 [questions 3657, 4344, 5406–8]; "Eyre Papers," 433). Richard Ogilvie described one of the accused rebels, Austin Stewart, as "a well conducted man" who owned land at Mount Lebanus that was "doing well with coffee on it" (deposition taken 18 Nov. 1865 in Kingston by Henry J. Bicknell, P.M., enclosures in Eyre to Cardwell, Jan. 1866, "Eyre Papers," 52, 423). Monica Schuler concludes that most African indentured laborers were not involved in the rebellion, except in trying to escape it. Since the militia applied a rather suspect definition of rebellion—that is, refusing to halt when commanded—it is impossible to know with certainty its extent (Schuler, "Alas, Alas, Kongo," 107–8).

89. Col. H. J. Francis Hobbs to Major General O'Connor, 15 Oct. 1865, "Report of the Jamaica Royal Commission, Pt. 2," 1,120 (appendix).

90. Several others coupled a rise in wages with land reform. See testimony by James Paterson, Matthew Cresser, Wallace Wood McGowen, and William Anderson, "Report of the Jamaica Royal Commission, Pt. 2," 97, 117, 144, 165 (questions 4390, 5549, 6960, 8243).

91. See testimony by William Anderson, ibid., 165 (question 8243).

92. Douglas Hall dismisses the Morant Bay incident as merely one of the many "local riots" that occasionally erupted in Jamaica, insisting that it was not the "inevitable outcome of any long previous chain of events." I agree with Don Robotham, however, who argues that it was definitely a premeditated act of rebellion, even though spontaneous and poorly organized once in motion because it relied on a peasant "army" that was not easily disciplined (Douglas Hall, *Free Jamaica, 1838–1865: An Economic History* [New Haven: Yale UP, 1959], 250; Robotham, "Notorious Riot," 62–66).

93. "Eyre Papers," 404, 427; "Report of the Jamaica Royal Commission, Pt. 1," 16, 25.

94. Paul Bogle et al., 17 Oct. 1865, in "Eyre Papers," 427; testimony of John Orgill McKenzie and George Fuller Osborne, "Report of the Jamaica Royal Commission, Pt. 1," 17, and "Pt. 2," 19, 32 (questions 883–86, 1489–92, 1511).

95. "Report of the Jamaica Royal Commission, Pt. 1," 17, 22, 25–26, and "Pt. 2," 1136 (appendix).

96. Gordon was arrested on Monday, 16 October, by Eyre himself and the custos of Kingston at the commanding general's house, where he had gone to surrender himself. Since the martial law decree did not cover Kingston, he was sent to Morant Bay on Friday, 20 October, tried on the twenty-first, and executed on Monday, the twenty-third. Gordon's letters do not suggest complicity in or advanced knowledge of the rebellion, and the Royal Commission found the evi-

dence against him "wholly insufficient" ("Report of the Jamaica Royal Commission, Pt. 1," 28–38, quote on 37, and "Pt. 2," 1034–35 [question 46260], 1150–57 [appendix]).

97. Enclosures in Eyre to Cardwell, Jan. 1866, "Eyre Papers," 17; Eyre to Cardwell, 24 Dec. 1865 (confidential), CO 137/396; "Report of the Jamaica Royal Commission, Pt. 1," 18–28.

98. Eyre could produce letters from both white planters and Afro-Jamaicans favoring abolition of the Assembly (Forbes Jackson to Eyre, 27 Feb. 1864, and John Castello to Austin, 1 Mar. 1864, encl. with Eyre to Newcastle, 9 Mar. 1864, no. 92, CO 137/380). The British government had already succeeded in exploiting internal divisions to get crown colony government in Dominica in 1863 (C. V. Gocking, "Early Constitutional History of Jamaica [with Special Reference to the Period 1838–1866]," *Caribbean Quarterly* 6 [May 1960]: 114–33).

99. Heuman argues that lack of cohesion among the colored members led to abolition of the representative government, but actually Afro-Jamaicans were as cohesive as ever and indeed fairly united in their willingness to see the Assembly abolished. Mavis Campbell also lays abolition of representative government at the door of Jordon and the free coloreds, charging them with moral cowardice and greed. Given the material interests of men such as Peter Espeut, however, they were more likely than not to make common cause with white property holders (Heuman, *Between Black and White*, 193–94; Campbell, *The Dynamics of Change in a Slave Society: A Sociopolitical History of the Free Coloreds of Jamaica, 1800–1865* [Rutherford, N.J.: Associated Universities P, 1976], 367–68).

100. Eyre to Cardwell, 7, 24 Dec. 1865 (confidential), CO 137/396; Opinion of the Law Officers of the Crown, 19 Jan. 1866 (confidential), CO 884/2.

101. Although these discussion were held with reference to the constitution Eyre had given notice of in his 7 December dispatch, they are equally applicable to the decision to impose crown colony government (marginal notes and minutes in Eyre to Cardwell, 7 Dec. 1865, no. 313, CO 137/396).

102. "Report of the Jamaica Royal Commission, Pt. 1," 5, 36–37, 40–41.

103. Charles Darwin and Herbert Spencer were among the prominent new men of science; James Fitzjames Stephen, grandson of the elder James Stephen, drew up the legal opinion to indict Eyre for murder. Bernard Semmel describes the membership as "radical in politics, non-conformist in religion, men whose ties were to middle-class business enterprise, rather than to the land; professors, journalists, political economists, non-conformists ministers" (*Democracy versus Empire: The Jamaica Riots of 1865 and the Governor Eyre Controversy* [1963; reprint, Garden City, N.Y.: Anchor, 1962], 67–68, 151).

104. "Eyre Papers," 1–3.

105. Prominent among Eyre's early defenders was Rev. Charles Kingsley, the poet, novelist, and Regius Professor of Modern History at Cambridge. Kingsley held antidemocratic views very similar to Carlyle's (Semmel, *Democracy versus Empire*, 105, 132).

106. *Spectator*, June 1868, quoted in Semmel, *Democracy versus Empire*, 105, 132; *Hansard*, 31 July 1866, 184:1812.

107. Semmel, *Democracy versus Empire*, 128–29, 133.

108. Semmel, *Democracy versus Empire*, 101–2, 139–41; Cheryl Marguerit Cassidy, "Islands and Empires: A Rhetorical Analysis of the Governor Eyre Contro-

versy, 1865–1867" (Ph.D. diss., U of Michigan, 1988), chap. 1. Relying solely on his sympathetic reading of Colonial Office views, Bruce A. Knox rejects the connection of the Eyre controversy and the Reform debate ("The British Government and the Governor Eyre Controversy, 1865–1875," *Historical Journal* 19 [Dec. 1976]: 899–900).

109. Douglas A. Lorimer, *Colour, Class, and the Victorians: English Attitudes to the Negro in the Mid-Nineteenth Century* (Leicester: Leicester UP, 1978), 124.

110. Comparable to this discourse on the colonial "other" are Henry Mayhew's contemporaneous observations on the London underclass, in which he links *in the same sentence* "repugnance to regular labour," "extraordinary powers of enduring privation," "love of libidous dances," "delight in warfare," and "absence of chastity among his women" (quoted in Cassidy, "Islands and Empire," 19).

111. Quoted in Cassidy, "Islands and Empire," 27.

112. Henry Mayhew's mid-century commentaries on the London underclass provide excellent illustrations of the rhetorical linkages between racial and class ideology (Cassidy, "Islands and Empire," 18–22. See also, *inter alia*, Gareth Stedman Jones, *Outcast London: A Study in the Relationship between Classes in Victorian Society* [New York: Pantheon, 1984]; idem, "Working-Class Culture and Working-Class Politics in London, 1870–1900: Notes on the Remaking of a Working Class," in *Language of Class: Studies in English Working-Class History, 1832–1982* [Cambridge: Cambridge UP, 1983], 179–238; and Eric Hobsbawm, *The Age of Capital, 1848–1875* [New York: Charles Scribner's Sons, 1975]).

Chapter 9. Political Economy and Race: Peasants in the Age of Empire

1. In 1874, Lord Carnarvon, the Tory Colonial Secretary, had prevailed upon Froude to undertake a mission as a special emissary to South Africa, where his strong advocacy of the empire undercut Governor Henry Barkly's efforts to maintain amicable relations between the English and the Boers, leading eventually to Barkly's dismissal (Mona Macmillan, *Sir Henry Barkly, Mediator and Moderator, 1815–1898* [Cape Town: A. A. Balkema, 1970], 228–67; Waldo Hilary Dunn, *James Anthony Froude: A Biography*, vol. 2 [Oxford: Clarendon, 1963]).

2. See James Anthony Froude, "England and Her Colonies," *Fraser's Magazine*, n.s. 1 (Jan. 1870): 1–16; idem, *The English in the West Indies, or, The Bow of Ulysses* (1888; reprint, New York: Charles Scribner's Sons, 1900), 372–73. See also idem, *Two Lectures on South Africa* (London: Longmans, Green, 1880).

3. Froude, *The English in the West Indies*, 49–50.

4. Ibid., 211–12, 221.

5. Ibid., 124–25.

6. Ibid., 125–26, 235–36, 247, 286–87.

7. Ibid., 250–54.

8. Olivier addressed the matter indirectly while writing about how to assuage planter reaction by offering countervailing sugar duties ("Memorandum of Mr. Olivier," in "Minutes Relating to the Report of the West India Royal Commission of 1896–7," 28 Sept. 1897, no. 79, CO 884/5).

9. Sydney Olivier revises these figures in his 1936 book, arguing that the 1882

figures were underestimated. The growth was purported to be from 52,608 to 92,979, of which 81,924 were under ten acres (Lord [Sydney Haldane] Olivier, *Jamaica: The Blessed Island* [London: Faber & Faber, 1936], 256n, 273–74; H. Jardine Hallowes to Joseph Chamberlain, 15 Nov. 1898, CO 137/594). Of course, the number of freeholders does not necessarily equal the number of freeholds (see appendix 1).

10. For discussion of the slowdown and then reversal of growth in peasant freeholds see Veront M. Satchell, *From Plots to Plantations: Land Transactions in Jamaica, 1866–1900* (Mona, Jamaica: Institute of Social and Economic Research, U of the West Indies, 1990), 149. For the role of multinationals in the fruit industry see chapter 10, below.

11. Chamberlain's commitment to imperialism is well-known, but Olivier's advocacy of more enlightened colonial economic policies did not imply political self-determination either. He wrote in a 1918 pamphlet endorsing the international protectorate system that mankind (meaning Europeans) had a right to free access to the natural resources in lands occupied by primitive people, and "under proper control" the development of those resources would be advantageous to the natives. Abuses by some imperial powers did not invalidate the generally beneficial effects of European penetration; it only argued for a controlling authority guided by human conscience (Olivier, *The League of Nations and Primitive Peoples* [London: Oxford UP, 1918], 6. See also idem, *Imperial Trusteeship*, Fabian Tract No. 230 [London: Fabian Society, 1929]).

12. *The Irish Land Question, What It Involves, and How Alone It Can Be Settled: An Appeal to the Land Leagues* (New York: D. Appleton & Co., 1881), 23.

13. Until recently the number of deaths above the normal death rate was estimated at less than a million, but this has been revised upward to as many as 1.5 million by Joel Mokyr. The census commissioners reported a gap of 2.5 million persons between the actual 1851 census figure and one projected on the basis of expected growth, which could mean a population loss of 28 percent (Joel Mokyr, *Why Ireland Starved: A Quantitative and Analytical History of the Irish Economy, 1800–1850* [London: George Allen & Unwin, 1983], 263–71, 276. Cf. Barbara Lewis Solow, *The Land Question and the Irish Economy, 1870–1903* [Cambridge: Harvard UP, 1971], 54–57).

14. Both the Netherlands and Belgium were hard hit by the same potato blight, but their mortality rates amounted to 2 percent and 1.1 percent of the population, respectively, compared with estimates six to twelve times higher for Ireland. Ireland's depopulation continued for the balance of the century, declining to 5,799,000 in 1861, 5,175,000 in 1881, and 4,459,000 by 1901.

15. *Punch* 14 (1849): 54, 17 (1851): 26, 231, cited in Richard Ned Lebow, *White Britain and Black Ireland: The Influence of Stereotypes on Colonial Policy* (Philadelphia: Institute for the Study of Human Issues, 1976), 38–43, 45–50, 67. According to Lebow, the *Morning Chronicle*, the *Westminster Review*, and the radical *Northern Star* were the only journals that rejected these stereotypes. For iconography of the Irish in British publications see L. Perry Curtis, Jr., *Apes and Angels: The Irishman in Victorian Caricature* (Newton Abbot, England: David & Charles, 1971).

16. *Fraser's Magazine* 36 (Mar. 1847): 373, cited in Lebow, *White Britain and Black Ireland*, 40. The striking similarities between Irish and Afro-Jamaican caricatures hardly require comment.

17. Mokyr, *Why Ireland Starved*, 265–68, 276.

18. James C. Beckett, *The Making of Modern Ireland, 1603–1923* (London: Faber & Faber, 1966), 338–39.

19. By contrast, in England and Wales four thousand people owned 60 percent of the land, averaging 4,500 acres each (E. D. Steele, *Irish Land and British Politics: Tenant-Right and Nationality, 1865–1870* [Cambridge: Cambridge UP, 1974], 3; Liam Kennedy, "The Rural Economy, 1820–1914," in *Economic History of Ulster, 1820–1940*, ed. Liam Kennedy and Philip Ollerenshaw [Manchester: Manchester UP, 1985], 31–33; W. E. Vaughan, *Landlords and Tenants in Ireland, 1840–1904*, Studies in Irish Economic and Social History, 2 [Dublin: Dundalgan, 1984], 4–6).

20. Kennedy, "Rural Economy," 31–33.

21. Ibid., 38; R. D. Collison Black, *Economic Thought and the Irish Question, 1817–1870* (Cambridge: Cambridge UP, 1960), 28–29; Steele, *Irish Land and British Politics*, 27–28.

22. Quote in text from Kennedy, "Rural Economy," 39. Sharman Crawford, a longtime advocate of Ulster custom, understood it to be tantamount to peasant proprietorship, "a letting in perpetuity subject to a revaluation of the rent from time to time." It is not clear how this theory worked for Ulster, which was culturally and demographically the most English part of the island (quoted in John E. Pomfret, *The Struggle for Land in Ireland, 1800–1923* [Princeton: Princeton UP, 1930], 57; see also Steele, *Irish Land and British Politics*, 7–9, 19, 21–22, 29).

23. Although W. E. Vaughan tries to reconcile tenant right with classical economic principles by defining the payments as "capitalized rent," his argument still confirms that tenant right was a practice established by custom; that is, the landlord conceded a property right to his tenant, which he was not legally obligated to do, and the calculation of the value of that right also had to be "customary," since no reasonably accessible and specifiable set of economic calculations would have determined it (Vaughan, *Landlords and Tenants*, 20; see also Kennedy, "Rural Economy," 38–41).

24. Vaughan, *Landlords and Tenants*, 17–20.

25. Recent revisionist studies by O. Robinson, James S. Donnelly, Jr., and Barbara Solow dispute the tradition that excessive rent charges, evictions, or even agrarian unrest were widespread. Though in general agreement with these arguments, Vaughan still concedes that the threat of eviction was "an important part of estate management." All these findings are summarized in ibid., 3, 10–20.

26. Steele, *Irish Land and British Politics*, 34, 68, 70, quote on 69. Since the total paid might be ten times the annual rent of a farm, the notion of compensating the tenant for improvements must have played a small role in determining the amount. In any event, such payments conceded to tenant farmers an effective property right in the land which they could sell (Kennedy, "Rural Economy," 38–41, quote on 39).

27. Black, *The Irish Question*, 10, 18–19, 23; Steele, *Irish Land and British Politics*, 14, 50–51.

28. Interestingly, Mill referred specifically to Edward H. Stanley as being among the ignorant, citing Stanley's speech at Brighton as reported in the *Times* on 23 Jan. 1868. Mill used the French experience as evidence that overpopulation and backwardness need not result from smallholdings (Mill, *Principles of Political Economy, with Some of Their Applications to Social Philosophy*, ed. Sir W. J. Ashley

[New York: Augustus M. Kelly, 1965], xvii–xviii, 318–24, 329–42; idem, "England and Ireland," in *Essays on England, Ireland, and the Empire: The Collected Works of John Stuart Mill*, ed. John M. Robson [Toronto: U of Toronto P, 1982], 527–29, quote on 529).

29. Quoted in Black, *The Irish Question*, 60–61, 64.

30. Mill, "What Is To Be Done with Ireland," in *Essays on England, Ireland, and the Empire*, 501–3; *Political Economy*, 235, 331.

31. Apparently, their eighteenth-century predecessors' reputation as "improvers" was much better (*Political Economy*, 230–31, 233).

32. "England and Ireland," 512.

33. *Political Economy*, 329–42. Mill's favorable analysis of the effects of the Encumbered Estates Acts has been disputed by recent historians (see Joseph Lee, *The Modernisation of Irish Society, 1848–1918* [Dublin: Gill & Macmillan, 1973]).

34. *Political Economy*, 318–24, quote on 323. In bk. 2, chaps. 6 and 7, "Of Peasant Proprietors" and "Continuation of the Same Subject," Mill deplores the ignorance of English political economists about peasant proprietorship. He discusses the literature on systems in France, Switzerland, Norway, Belgium, and Germany, showing not only that such proprietorship led to prosperous and "improving" agriculture but that it best developed the capacities of the laborer, because he was applying his skills and knowledge in his own self-interest. Smallholding need not lead to unrestrained population growth, because the peasant knew exactly how many mouths the land he farmed would feed and could be expected to act accordingly. To the wage laborer, however, the notion that increased population would reduce his wages was an abstraction. Thus peasant owners possessed "prudence, temperance, and self-control," while day laborers were "improvident," tended to spend "carelessly," and "let the future shift for itself" (256–301, quote on 286).

35. "England and Ireland," 511. In his *Autobiography*, Mill credits Harriet Taylor, his intellectual companion and later his wife, for influencing his thinking in making the distinction between production and distribution. The first was materially determined and could be studied as a matter of physical laws; the second was socially determined and required a science of human nature not yet available. In his *System of Logic*, he had aspired to develop a new field of study he called "ethology," the study of human character, thinking that the absence of such a study weakened the practical application of political economy because it induced economists to neglect the impact of custom or folkways on market behavior. Mill cited Indian ryots, métayers, and serfs as examples of such influences (Mill, *Autobiography*, ed. Jack Stillinger [Boston: Houghton Mifflin, 1969], 148; ibid., *Political Economy*, xvi–xvii, xix–xx, 199–200, 224–28, 242–48).

36. Mill acknowledged that in some areas of India, peasant tenures were on a precarious footing, but in most villages the "descendants or representatives of the original inhabitants, and even many mere tenants of ancient date, are thought entitled to retain their land, as long as they pay the customary rents" ("England and Ireland," 513, 519; *Political Economy*, 243–44, 324–28).

37. Cf. Lee, *Modernisation of Irish Society*, 94–97.

38. Modern scholars generally describe five types of Indian land tenure in different geographical areas during the era of British rule, all resulting from a combination of traditional Hindu and Mogul legacies and British interventions (for

details see Sachchidananda Bhattacharya, "Land Tenure Systems," in *A Dictionary of Indian History* [New York: George Braziller, 1967], 541–43). On the more general point that the East India Company tried to work with rather than replace the traditional system, there is general agreement (see David Ludden, *Peasant History in South India* [Princeton: Princeton UP, 1985]).

39. "The case of Ireland is similar in its requirements to that of India," Mill wrote (*Political Economy*, 332).

40. In the first two editions of *Political Economy* Mill opposed compensation for improvements because it would be impossible to measure the peasant's improvements, since they would be in the form of labor rather than money. He also opposed the legalization of Ulster custom, because it would deprive the landlord of compensation. Meanwhile, he devoted five pages to explaining the land reclamation solution (*Political Economy*, 329–42).

41. E. D. Steele, "J. S. Mill and the Irish Question: Reform, and the Integrity of the Empire, 1865–1870," *Historical Journal* 13 (Sept. 1970): 439–40, 442–43.

42. For discussion of Mill's influence on "advanced liberal" thought see Michael Freeden, *The New Liberalism: An Ideology of Social Reform* (Oxford: Clarendon, 1978).

43. Mill explicitly rejected racist ideas. "Of all vulgar modes of escaping from the consideration of the effect of social and moral influences on the human mind, the most vulgar is that of attributing the diversities of conduct and character to inherent natural differences." For the Irish, as for everyone else, social environment determined behavior (*Political Economy*, 324).

44. "England and Ireland," 509, 518, 521–22.

45. James Fintan Lalor, an early martyr for the cause, had argued in 1848 for linkage of the land issue with Irish nationalism, but this was not done effectively until 1879, when Michael Davitt and Charles Stewart Parnell formed the Land League. Gladstone's chief fear was that Irish agitation would embolden Irish-Americans to make trouble in Canada (Black, *The Irish Question*, 71; Steele, *Irish Land and British Politics*, 28, 31–32; Solow, *The Land Question*, 128–30).

46. Steele, *Irish Land and British Politics*, 40–42, 46, 75. Cf. Black, *The Irish Question*, 64–71.

47. One of Campbell's pamphlets on Indian land tenure was brought out by the Cobden Club in 1870, along with others on Ireland, Europe, and America (see "Tenure of Land in India," in *Systems of Land Tenure in Various Countries: A Series of Essays Published under the Sanction of the Cobden Club*, 2d ed. [London: Macmillan, 1870], 149–231; see also Steele, *Irish Land and British Politics*, 104–8).

48. Quoted in Steele, *Irish Land and British Politics*, 253. The 1881 Land Act would be based on this principle. On the other hand, it was but a short step from this realization to racist premises about group differences, that is, that different peoples required different rules of governance.

49. At one point Gladstone considered giving the law a temporary character to limit its damage to free contract principles. He also considered giving the occupiers long leases (thirty-one years and renewable) in exchange for a 10 percent rent increase and a prohibition of eviction without compensation for improvements (ibid., 126, 143, 184, 200, 277, 298, 314).

50. Ibid., 302–3; Pomfret, *Struggle for Land in Ireland*, 84–85.

51. Some advocates of franchise reform—which had carried in 1867—had

linked that issue to a demand to nationalize Irish land, and the issue was being featured more and more among radical demands in various international meetings. In its 18 November 1869 issue, the *Saturday Review* declared: "English landowners who venture to criticize any of the numerous projects for dealing with Irish tenures are constantly reminded . . . if they make themselves troublesome, they will find that in England also there is a land question" (quoted in Steele, *Irish Land and British Politics,* 56, 267, quote on 270).

52. de Grey to Fortescue, 13 Dec. 1869, quoted in Steele, *Irish Land and British Politics,* 214; see also 101, 111, 114, 116, 132.

53. Steele, *Irish Land and British Politics,* 288, 306, quote on 306.

54. Ibid., 313.

55. Donald G. Southgate, *The Passing of the Whigs, 1832–1886* (London: Macmillan, 1962), 364, 388–89, quote on 389. Sidney Webb, Chamberlain's compatriot in the Colonial Office, declared all such plans for free land, peasant proprietorship, or leasehold enfranchisement to be "survivals of the Individualistic Radicalism which is passing away" (Webb, "The Basis of Socialism: Historic," quoted in Freeden, *New Liberalism,* 146).

56. Catherine B. Shannon, "The Ulster Liberal Unionists and Local Government Reform, 1885–98," *Irish Historical Studies* 18 (Mar. 1973): 407–23; Michael Balfour, *Britain and Joseph Chamberlain* (London: George Allen & Unwin, 1985), 154–225.

57. The laws were the Allotments Acts of 1887 and 1890, which empowered local authorities to purchase land for renting at economic rates, and the Smallholdings Act in 1892. Conservative attitudes were probably also influenced by the fact, according to Pomfret, that English farm rents declined by up to 50 percent between 1870 and 1900. There was additional legislation in 1902 and 1908; by 1918, 183,877 acres had been purchased at a cost of £395,955, providing 12,702 holdings ("Agriculture: Land Settlement," CO 950/50; Pomfret, *Struggle for Land in Ireland,* 215; Martin Pugh, *The Making of Modern British Politics, 1867–1939* [New York: St. Martin's, 1982], 60–61).

58. See Pomfret's discussion of W. H. Smith and the memorandum written by Chief Justice Longfield in 1882 (Pomfret, *Struggle for Land in Ireland,* 222–23, 271).

59. For Chamberlain's speech see *Hansard,* 36:639–45; see also Denis Judd, *Radical Joe: A Life of Joseph Chamberlain* (London: Hamish Hamilton, 1977).

60. Richard A. Lobdell, "Patterns of Investment and Sources of Credit in the British West Indian Sugar Industry, 1836–97," *Journal of Caribbean History* 4 (May 1972): 46–47.

61. *DNB,* 2d suppl., 3:21–24.

62. Sydney Haldane Olivier, *Letters and Selected Writings,* ed. Margaret Olivier (London: George Allen & Unwin, 1948), 9, 20, 30, 36.

63. "Verbatim Report of the First Session of the [Royal West India] Commission, held at the Colonial Office," 20 Sept. 1938, 22–23, encl. with "Lord Olivier: Memorandum of Evidence," CO 950/28.

64. Olivier, *Letters,* 99.

65. "Memorandum of Mr. Olivier," 28 Sept. 1897, no. 79.

66. Ibid.

67. See also the minute by C. P. Lucas, who suggested, interestingly enough,

that the slave compensation provided a precedent for such direct economic aid (Chamberlain circular letter to governors, 26 July 1898, West India No. 86, and "Memorandum by C. P. Lucas," Oct. 1897, both in CO 884/5). It should be noted, however, that there is also evidence of reservations and some half-hearted efforts in the Colonial Office toward this new policy. For example, when toward the end of 1898 Governor Hemming urged Chamberlain to seek an imperial government grant to build roads to open new lands to small settlers in Jamaica, he was rebuffed (A. W. Hemming to Chamberlain, 30 Nov. 1898; Chamberlain to Hemming, 24 Jan. 1898, no. 30; and minute by W.A.K., 1 Dec. [1898], all in CO 137/595. See also H. A. Will, "Colonial Policy and Economic Development in the British West Indies, 1895–1903," *Economic History Review*, 2d ser., 23 [Apr. 1970]: 129–47).

68. Olivier, *Jamaica*, 251.

69. Grant to Buckingham, 23 Aug. 1867, CO 137/425; see also Vincent John Marsala, *Sir John Peter Grant, Governor of Jamaica, 1866–1874: An Administrative History* ([Kingston]: Institute of Jamaica, 1972).

70. The impact on squatters was devastating nonetheless; very few of the repossessed tracts were relet to small settlers (Satchell, *From Plots to Plantations*, 71).

71. Olivier, *Jamaica*, 288.

72. Ibid., 191.

73. Memorandum by G.W.K., 7 Dec. 1882, CO 884/4; D. N. East to William Grey, 6 Oct. 1876, encl. with W. Grey to Carnarvon, 10 Oct. 1876, CO 137/482.

74. Olivier, *Jamaica*, 215–17, 219.

75. Musgrave to Derby, 2 Feb. 1883, CO 137/508.

76. Olivier, *Jamaica*, 220.

77. Ibid., 259, 263, 317; Hallowes to Chamberlain, 15 Nov. 1898, CO 137/594.

78. Satchell, *From Plots to Plantations*, 79–80, 97–98, 102.

79. The bulk of public expenditures and the resultant debt was for roads and public works (see Will, "Colonial Policy and Economic Development," 146 [table 2]).

80. Given his keen interest in refuting the traditional view that there was remarkable peasant progress through state assistance, Satchell is inclined to understate the equally extraordinary story of independent peasant success that his evidence reveals (Satchell, *From Plots to Plantations*, 153–55).

81. Ibid., 140–53.

82. Ibid., 56–131 passim, esp. tables 3.7, 6.2, 6.11, 6.12.

83. Hoskinson to Seward, 3 June 1879, in Despatches from U.S. Consuls in Kingston, Jamaica, British West Indies, 1796–1906, Microfilm ed., T31, vol. 28, General Records of the Department of State, Record Group 59 (hereafter "U.S. Consular Papers").

84. "Correspondence relevant to the Question of Punishment by Flogging," May 1900, misc. no. 112, CO 885/7.

85. Arthur E. Burt argues that Norman had been committed to expanding the black electorate when he came out to Jamaica but that after a tour of the island in January 1884 be began to have "grave doubts as to the wisdom of making any constitutional changes." Thereafter he insisted that social and economic reforms were more important than political change ("The First Instalment of Representative Government in Jamaica, 1884," *SES* 11 [Sept. 1962]: 246; see also Norman to Derby, 19 Feb., 8 Oct. 1884, CO 137/513 and 518).

86. There was only one contested seat in the general election of 1889, and in the 1892 special election only one-third of registered voters participated. In 1906,

six candidates were unopposed and just 1,628 votes were cast in eight other districts. In 1911, five were unopposed and 7,449 of 17,958 registered voters (41 percent) voted in the nine remaining districts. There were 38,376 registered voters in 1896; 16,256 in 1901; 18,607 in 1905–6; and 27,257 in 1910–11. In 1920 there were nine uncontested seats, and in the five remaining districts only 3,858 of 17,958 bothered to vote. Attendance at Legislative Council meetings was very poor (Ronald V. Sires, "The Experience of Jamaica with Modified Crown Colony Government," *SES* 4 [June 1955]: 152, 155n, 156).

87. The literacy qualification was waived for the first elections under the new law. George Stiebel, a planter representative on the Franchise Commission, had favored eliminating the literacy provision altogether. He argued that given the high officeholding qualifications, voters would have to select their representatives from among the two or three planters who offered themselves for election anyway. This, he reasoned, was protection enough for the interests of property. At that time, the main taxes in the country districts were house taxes (6 shillings), horse taxes (11 shillings), sanitary taxes (9 pence); and a tax on cultivated land. Arthur Burt calculates that a man who paid all of the above and had nine acres or more under cultivation would have been eligible to vote. According to an 1883 royal commission report, only one in twelve blacks could read (Burt, "Representative Government in Jamaica," 249; Hemming to Chamberlain, 12 June 1901, CO 137/620).

88. Norman to Granville, 19 Apr. 1886, CO 137/525; Froude, *The English in the West Indies*, 202–3.

89. For example, during a political crisis in 1900, not unlike that of 1883, opposition speakers clearly pitched their appeals to the concerns of the peasantry—opposing the flogging bill as a "relic of slavery," and the subsidy to steamer service to England as money that should have been spent to help people buy land, blaming low wages for praedial larceny, and disputing the value of technical assistance to small settlers if they did not own land (see Ethebert Watts to David J. Hill, 6 Mar. 1900, no. 9, U.S. Consular Papers, vol. 37). Qualifications for Legislative Council membership included £150 clear annual income from land, or clear annual income of £200 partly from land, or £300 clear annual income from any freehold or business, or payment of £10 annually in direct taxes or export duty. Members were not paid (Burt, "Representative Government in Jamaica," 243–44).

90. Hallowes to Chamberlain, 31 Oct. 1898, CO 137/594. Olivier reported that small settlers approved Governor Blake's special taxes on lands because they were specifically linked to parochial road construction intended to benefit them (Olivier, *Jamaica*, 241).

91. Norman's proposal called for a 1s. levy per acre on landholdings of 0.5–100 acres, 16d. on 100–500 acres, and 1.5d. on 500 acres and above. At the same time he called for a reduction of duties on food, especially flour, bread, and fish, which would be cut by 50 percent or more, and the abolition of export duties (Norman to H. T. Holland, 12 Mar. 1888, CO 137/534).

Chapter 10. The Making of the Jamaican Working Class

1. Edith Clarke, *My Mother Who Fathered Me: A Study of the Family in Three Selected Communities in Jamaica* (London: George Allen & Unwin, 1957), 26–27, 143–44, quote on 144.

2. Ibid., 22–24, 147–48, quote on 147.

3. Erna Brodber, "Afro-Jamaican Women at the Turn of the Century," *SES* 35 (Sept. 1986): 30–35.

4. Clarke, *My Mother Who Fathered Me,* 189.

5. Using mostly heavy steamers, British shippers controlled 96 percent of the combined U.S. and British steamer tonnage in and out of Jamaica ("Annual Report on the Trade and Commerce of the Island of Jamaica, Year Ending September 1879," in Hoskinson to John Hay, 8 Mar. 1880, no. 230, Despatches from U.S. Consuls in Kingston, Jamaica, British West Indies, 1796–1906, Microfilm ed., T31, vol. 28, General Records of the Department of State, Record Group 59 [hereafter "U.S. Consular Papers"]).

6. Canada accounted for 10 percent of Jamaica's imports but only 0.3 percent of her exports (Hoskinson to Robert Hitt, 19 July 1881, U.S. Consular Papers, vol. 28; "Total Value of Imports and Exports into Colony of Jamaica Year Ending 31 December 1865," *Blue Book for the Island of Jamaica for the Year 1865* [Kingston: Colonial Standard Office, 1865]).

7. A. W. Hemming to Alfred Lytteton, 23 Dec. 1904, CO 137/637.

8. Hoskinson to Secretary of State, 24 July 1882, U.S. Consular Papers, vol. 28.

9. The Gros Michel species of banana was introduced into Jamaica from Martinique in the nineteenth century. The plantain, another peasant staple, is of the same botanical family as the banana (which bears more heavily) but was brought from Africa and grown by slaves in their gardens. Unlike bananas, plantains are always eaten cooked, and they are used more like a vegetable than like a fruit.

10. Wilson Randolph Bartlett, Jr., "Lorenzo D. Baker and the Development of the Banana Trade between Jamaica and the United States, 1881–1890" (Ph.D. diss., American U, 1977), 51–54; Lord [Sydney Haldane] Olivier, *Jamaica: The Blessed Island* (London: Faber & Faber, 1936), 377–78.

11. Hemming to Lytteton, 23 Dec. 1904.

12. Bartlett, "Lorenzo D. Baker," 51–54; Olivier, *Jamaica,* 377–79; Hoskinson to Seward, 3 Jan. 1879, U.S. Consular Papers, vol. 28.

13. Hoskinson to Seward, 3 Jan. 1879.

14. Olivier, *Jamaica,* 378; Hoskinson to Assistant Secretary of State, 24 July 1882; Bartlett, "Lorenzo D. Baker," 48–51, 60, 119.

15. W. R. Estes to L. D. Baker, Jr., 12 Jan. 1891, in Bartlett, "Lorenzo D. Baker," 171–72, 224, 231, 233, quote on 171. See also Official Letters Received, Port Morant, 6 Mar. 1884–8 Mar. 1898, Port Morant, Jamaica; and Despatches from U.S. Consuls in Port Antonio, British West Indies, 1895–1906, Microfilm ed., T650, General Records of the Department of State, Record Group 59.

16. Bartlett, "Lorenzo D. Baker," 152–55, 180, 198–216, 227.

17. Ibid., 51–54.

18. Indeed, by 1881 the American consular agent reported that the Atlas line was growing and driving American sailing vessels out of Jamaican ports (Olivier, *Jamaica,* 263, 380–81; Robert Nunes [agent at Falmouth] to W. M. Evarts, 22 Oct. 1880, U.S. Consular Papers, vol. 28).

19. Bartlett, "Lorenzo D. Baker," 131–35, 183–96.

20. The consul also noted that the governor paid $22,500 to subsidize this service annually (Hoskinson to Assistant Secretary of State, 24 Jan. 1882, U.S. Consular Papers, vol. 28).

21. The banana industry developed in Central America simultaneously with its development in Jamaica, and Jamaicans had a significant role there as well. The banana industry in Costa Rica was begun by Minor Keith with Jamaican workers whom he had employed to build an ill-fated railway. At the same time the Lindo Brothers, a Jamaican family with coffee and sugar estates in Costa Rica, promoted the cultivation of bananas there. And by 1911 United Fruit itself had over fifty thousand acres of land in Costa Rica, after having absorbed Keith's and Lindo's operations, together with those of other competitors in Cuba and Santo Domingo. By the late nineteenth century there were at least forty thousand Jamaicans working in Costa Rica (Olivier, *Jamaica*, 380–81; Bartlett, "Lorenzo D. Baker," 176).

22. Baker's biographer argues that competition was mainly responsible for his initial decision to purchase large properties for banana cultivation. In 1882, apparently with capital supplied by Freeman, he purchased Bound Brook Estate in Port Antonio (formerly Bog Estate) and Bowden Estate in Port Morant; Golden Vale, with thirty-five hundred acres, in 1884; and Williamsfield, a twelve-hundred-acre estate near Port Antonio, in 1885. All of these properties were located near the sea and had good harbors (Bartlett, "Lorenzo D. Baker," 76–77, 80–81; Olivier, *Jamaica*, 378).

23. A. C. Barnes to Harold Beckett, 7 Aug. 1935, Jamaica Banana Producers' Association, Marketing Bananas, CO 137/805/68552 (hereafter "JBPA file").

24. Bartlett, "Lorenzo D. Baker," 72–75, 80, 83–84. On inflation in land prices see Veront M. Satchell, *From Plots to Plantations: Land Transactions in Jamaica, 1866–1900* (Mona, Jamaica: Institute of Social and Economic Research, U of the West Indies, 1990), 113.

25. A geographer's study of St. Thomas shows most peasant holdings located on the fringes of the estates, which were still intact, although some had been broken up and sold in small lots. Of the 2,288 acres devoted to bananas in 1899, only 83 acres were cultivated on farms under 20 acres. By contrast, all of St. Andrew's 586 acres in fruit were cultivated on peasant-sized holdings (Joseph B. Thornton, "The Agricultural Transformation of 19th Century Jamaica" [Ph.D. diss., Clark U, 1980], 160; Olivier, *Jamaica*, 378–79, quote on 379).

26. Some of this activity involved not only bananas but also oranges, which had attracted a number of Florida investors during the late 1890s (Lewis A. Dent to William R. Day, 20 Dec. 1897, no. 31, U.S. Consular Papers, vol. 35; enclosure in Message of Governor to Legislative Council, 23 Feb. 1897, in Eckford to W. W. Rockhill, 24 Feb. 1897, ibid., vol. 34; Olivier, *Jamaica*, 377–78).

27. "West Indies and Imperial Aid," Dec. 1905, West India no. 92, CO 884/6.

28. Bartlett, "Lorenzo D. Baker," 72–75, 164.

29. L. D. Baker to Loren Baker, 25 Apr. 1889, quoted in ibid., 190.

30. Ibid., 83–84, 191.

31. Elders & Fyffes was registered in Britain in May 1901 with an original capital of £150,000, to grow, buy, and import fruit and vegetables ("Brief Particulars of Operations of Elders & Fyffes, Limited, from formation to date," no. 37, encl. with JBPA file).

32. Watts to Hill, 13 Mar. 1900, no. 10, U.S. Consular Papers, vol. 37. In 1899 Jamaica's Governor Hemming sent a telegram to the Colonial Office: "Boston Fruit Company seeks monopoly; direct steam line needed. Boston Fruit seeking to drive competitors out of market and afterwards lower the price" (telegram, Hemming to [Joseph Chamberlain], 12 Apr. 1899, CO 137/600; see also Olivier, *Jamaica*, 382–84).

33. "Brief Particulars of Operation of Elders & Fyffes"; Olivier, *Jamaica*, 382–84.

34. In its twelve years of operation, the Direct Line only earned an average of £83,500 a year, or about twice the government subsidy. The company also had been intended to develop markets for other fruits, that is, oranges and grapefruits, but that movement collapsed completely (Olivier, *Jamaica*, 383–84).

35. Olivier, *Jamaica*, 386–98, quote on 398. For parallel processes of proletarianization in Colombia and in the U.S. South, respectively, see Catherine LeGrand, "Colombian Transformations: Peasants and Wage-Labourers in the Santa Marta Banana Zone," *Journal of Peasant Studies* 11 (July 1984): 178–200; and Harold D. Woodman, "Post–Civil War Southern Agriculture and the Law," *Agricultural History* 53 (Jan. 1979): 319–37.

36. Bartlett, "Lorenzo D. Baker," 62.

37. Ibid., 60–61.

38. Meanwhile, through negotiations with Canada at the Canada–West Indies Trade Convention of 1925 in Ottawa, Jamaica's independent banana producers concluded an agreement to ship their fruit to Canada under conditions that would put the control of shipping space in the hands of the Jamaican and Canadian governments rather than United Fruit (Olivier, *Jamaica*, 392–93).

39. *Liverpool Post*, cited in Olivier, *Jamaica*, 392. Earlier attempts to form a cooperative had been thwarted in the immediate postwar years by United Fruit's influence on the American government, which ruled that non-American shippers would need a license in order to deliver fruit to the United States. During the war such shippers had been required to obtain their licenses from "the Caribbean Committee," which was controlled by United Fruit and Atlantic Fruit Company representatives. This procedure was relaxed after the war but revived again briefly after the Jamaican Imperial Association announced its intention to form a producers' cooperative. Although the licensing requirement was soon withdrawn after protest from the Jamaican government, it had the effect of validating United Fruit's threats that growers would be shut out of the U.S. market if they went along with this new producers' cooperative (Olivier, *Jamaica*, 390–98).

40. *The Report of the Jamaica Banana Commission, 1936* ([Kingston], Jamaica: Government Printing Office, 1936), 8, 15–37, encl. with "Economic: Commodities. Bananas–Jamaica. Banana Commission Report," CO 852/31/10. A count bunch was a whole stem of nine hands or more, while a bunch of fruit consisted of four to twelve hands, each hand comprising eight to ten bananas. A bunch of seven hands was the standard size for shipping fruit (Bartlett, "Lorenzo D. Baker," 120).

41. *Report of the Jamaica Banana Commission*, 20, 37–38; testimony of C. E. Johnston and R. F. Williams, 5 Dec. 1938, West India Royal Commission, Oral Evidence, vol. 4, CO 950/927 (hereafter "Moyne Commission"). See also Barnes to Beckett, 7 Aug. 1935.

42. "Memorandum: Position of Association in Accounting to Growers for the net sale of proceeds of Bananas and Surplus Assets," encl. with "Jamaica Banana Producers Association Petition," CO 137/806/68552/2 (hereafter "JBPA petition"); *Report of the Jamaica Banana Commission*, 6; Olivier, *Jamaica*, 397–98. In their testimony in 1938, the leaders of the JBPA testified that the causes of their problems were (1) insufficient operating capital and (2) a series of hurricanes that depleted supplies "and undermined to a very great extent the loyalty of our members." Members were enticed to sell their fruit to United Fruit by offers of three shillings per bunch on the spot, while JBPA could offer two shillings with the prospect of an additional shilling much later (testimony of C. E. Johnston and R. F. Williams).

43. G. C. Wainwright also testified that many small settlers had only a receipt of payment for their lands and not a certificate of title (testimony of G. C. Wainwright, 3 Nov. 1938, 64–104, Moyne Commission, Oral Evidence, vol. 1, CO 950/924; Wainwright, "Memorandum re. Agricultural Credit in General and the Operations of the Banana Industry Aid Board in Particular," Oct. 1938, 6, Moyne Commission, Written Evidence, vol. 1, CO 950/943).

44. Wainwright, "Memorandum re. Agricultural Credit," 6.

45. *Report of the Jamaica Banana Commission*, 43.

46. Barnes to Beckett, 7 Aug. 1935.

47. Ibid.

48. Minute of J. E., 2 Dec. 1935, and telegram from JBPA, 11 Dec. 1935, both in JBPA petition.

49. Copy of cable to deputation, 6 Dec. 1935, encl. with JBPA petition; Barnes to Frank A. Stockdale, 27 Sept. 1935; note by H. Beckett on meeting with Keiffer, 13 Aug. 1935; and testimony of Downer, of Standard Fruit, in "Proceedings At a Meeting to Discuss Proposed Quota Systems for Bananas" (confidential), all in JBPA file.

50. Barnes to Beckett, 7 Aug. 1935; Denham to W. G. A. Ormsby Gore, 9 June 1936, both in JBPA file.

51. E. R. Darnley minute, 28 Nov. 1920, in Neal R. Malmsten, "Colonial Office Policy to Major Constitutional and Administrative Problems in the West Indies, 1919–1939" (Ph.D. diss., U of London, 1976), 8.

52. See E. P. L. Wood, "Report by Parliamentary Undersecretary of State for the Colonies: A Visit to the West Indies and British Guiana, 1921–22," *PP* 1922 [Cmd. 1679], 16.

53. Minute by Gilbert Grindle, 2 July 1923, quoted in Malmsten, "Colonial Office Policy," 48.

54. Amery to [Self?], 31 Mar. 1926, in ibid., 50–51.

55. Ibid., 158a.

56. In an internal minute, E. R. Darnley specifically identified this as the purpose for retaining the governor's appointive powers over the Legislative Council of Grenada (18 Jan. 1921, in ibid., 37–38).

57. Minute by Gilbert Grindle, 30 Dec. 1930, quoted in ibid., 120.

58. Denham to M. MacDonald, 20 Aug. 1935 (confidential), JBPA file.

59. Denham to MacDonald, 11 Nov. 1935 (confidential), encl. with JBPA petition.

60. Extract, Denham to Beckett, 3 Oct. 1935, and extract, Minutes of the Honourable Legislative Council of Jamaica, 15 Oct. 1935, both in JBPA file.

61. Barnes to Beckett, 16 Aug. 1935, JBPA file; confidential telegram, Denham to Secretary of State, 19 Dec. 1935, JBPA petition.

62. Minute by G. L. Ransom, 27 Nov. 1935; note by H. Beckett, 13 Aug. 1935, both in JBPA file.

63. Minute by S. Caine, 22 Nov. 1935, ibid.

64. Minute by Ransom, 27 Nov. 1935, ibid. (note penciled by J. McDonald, 28 Nov.). This notion was also prominent in the United Fruit arguments (see report of conversation, Keiffer with Beckett, note by H. Beckett, 13 Aug. 1935, ibid.).

65. Minute by S. Caine, 22 June 1936, ibid.; "Jamaica Banana Producers Association Investigative Commission," CO 137/806/68552/1.

66. *Report of the Jamaica Banana Commission*, 20–21.

67. Ibid., 49.

68. Ibid.

69. Testimony of C. E. Johnston and R. F. Williams, 5 Dec. 1938.

70. Interestingly enough, the nays came from members representing Hanover, Trelawny, St. Elizabeth, St. Ann, and Clarendon; the last four were traditionally peasant but not fruit parishes. Five other members were challenged because they were connected to the association or Standard Fruit as officers or agents ("Minutes of the Hon. Legislative Council of Jamaica," 26 Nov. 1936, encl. with JBPA file).

71. G. E. Cumper, "Labour Demand and Supply in the Jamaican Sugar Industry, 1830–1950," *SES* 2 (Mar. 1954): 58, 70.

72. "The Sugar Manufacturers' Association Testimony," Moyne Commission, Oral Evidence, 3:5, CO 950/926.

73. Cumper, "Labour Demand and Supply," 71 (table 9).

74. "Economic Survey. Commodities. Sugar and Sugar Products," CO 852/96/20.

75. Cumper, "Labour Demand and Supply," 58–59, 69–70.

76. Ibid., 62–65.

77. Ibid.

78. Ibid., 62–63. Cf. Richard A. Lobdell, "Patterns of Investment and Sources of Credit in the British West Indian Sugar Industry, 1836–97," *Journal of Caribbean History* 4 (May 1972): 46–47.

79. Cumper, "Labour Demand and Supply," 67–68, 74 (table 10).

80. Ibid., 77.

81. "Economic Survey. Commodities. Sugar and Sugar Products," CO 852/96/20; Cumper, "Labour Demand and Supply," 62.

82. One-half of all sugar estates were located in the northwestern and north-central coastal parishes, but the largest ones were in the south-central area and St. Thomas-in-the-East. In contrast, just under half the banana estates were in three eastern parishes—Portland, St. Thomas, and St. Andrew ("Memorandum on Estate Barracks, Medical Dept.," serial no. 156, CO 852/96/20).

83. James J. Phillips, "Fe Wi Land a Cane: Choice and Change on a Jamaican Sugar Plantation" (Ph.D. diss., Brown U, 1976), 169.

84. Ibid., 182, 189–93.

85. Cumper, "Labour Demand and Supply," 63; H. G. De Lisser, *Twentieth Century Jamaica* (Kingston: Jamaica Times, 1913), 172.

86. Phillips, "Fe Wi Land a Cane," 189, 193, 206.

87. Ibid., 189ff., 218–19.

88. Cumper, "Labour Demand and Supply," 78.

89. G. E. Cumper, "A Modern Jamaican Sugar Estate," *SES* 3 (Sept. 1954): 122–25.

90. Ibid., 122, 125.

91. Ibid., 199, 125–35; "A Memorandum Respectfully Submitted to the West India Royal Commission by the West Indies Sugar Company, Limited (Jamaica), by R. L. M. K[irkwood], 13 Sept. 1938," Memorandum of Evidence, Moyne Commission, CO 950/46 (hereafter "WISCO Memo").

92. WISCO Memo; "Notes Regarding Messers. Tate & Lyle Ltd.' Interest in the West Indies," 8 Feb. 1938, CO 318/432/5.

93. "The West Indies Sugar Company, Limited: List of Directors and Details of Their Interests in Other Companies," encl. with WISCO Memo.

94. WISCO Memo.

95. Cumper, "A Modern Jamaican Sugar Estate," 141, 143.

96. R. L. M. Kirkwood to Commander Rushbrooke, private secretary to the governor, 6 Apr. 1938, "West Indies Labour Conditions," CO 318/432/5.

97. WISCO Memo, 6–7. Kirkwood subsidized the *Jamaica Standard* and brought its editor William Makim to Jamaica in 1938. For a description of Kirkwood and his sometimes difficult relations with his home office see Ken Post, *Strike the Iron: A Colony at War: Jamaica, 1939–1945*, 2 vols. (Atlantic Highlands, N.J.: Humanities P, 1981), 2:329–36.

98. "The West India Sugar Co. Ltd., Extracts from the Report of the Medical Officer of the Company, Dr. Finlayson McKenzie, M.B., B.S., London," 30 July 1938, encl. with WISCO Memo.

99. WISCO Memo, 22, 25.

100. Ibid.

101. "Sugar Manufacturers' Association," 20, CO 854/96/20.

102. Testimony of Mr. Cuthill, CO 852/06/20.

103. "Memorandum on Estate Barracks, Medical Dept.," serial no. 156, CO 852/96/20.

104. Phillips, "Fe Wi Land a Cane," 220–21.

105. Ibid., 85.

106. Cumper, "A Modern Jamaican Sugar Estate," 144, 155–56.

107. Ibid., 140–43; cf. Michael Craton, *Searching for the Invisible Man: Slaves and Plantation Life in Jamaica* (Cambridge: Harvard UP, 1978), 316–25.

108. Cumper, "A Modern Jamaican Sugar Estate," 143–49, quote on 148.

109. Ibid., 140–41.

110. Testimony of Verity and Muschett (Sugar Manufacturers' Association), Moyne Commission, Oral Evidence, 3:5, CO 852/96/20.

111. Cumper, "Labour Demand and Supply," 79–85; Carl Henry Feuer, "Better Must Come: Sugar and Jamaica in the 20th Century," *SES* 33 (Dec. 1984): 20–23.

112. WISCO Memo.

113. Bustamante testimony, 16 Nov. 1938, Moyne Commission, Oral Evidence, 2:21–25; Bustamante claimed twenty-five thousand dues-paying members, a phenomenal growth for the five-month-old union (Trevor Munroe, *The Politics of Constitutional Decolonization: Jamaica, 1944–62* [Kingston: Institute of Social and Economic Research, U of the West Indies, 1972], 21–23).

114. Feuer, "Better Must Come," 20–23.

Epilogue. "Better Must Come": The Problem of Freedom in the Twentieth Century

1. W. M. Macmillan, author of a political treatise on the West Indies in 1936, reported rumors that workers would seize the sugar estates on 1 August and suggested that a commemoration of the end of apprenticeship might help ease tensions by showing the working classes that the government had not forgotten them (telegram, "Seizure of Land in Jamaica," 16 July 1938, and "Emancipation Day. Proposed Message," [1938], CO 318/435/1).

2. Denham to Malcolm MacDonald, 18 July 1935, and Denham to P. Cunliffe-Lister, 30 May 1935, both in "Disturbances at Falmouth," CO 137/806/68557. Ken Post argues that the offer of land settlement schemes during the 1938 rebellion was a cynical move to divide peasant from wage laborers. It is less clear, however,

that this tactic succeeded, given the Jamaican workers' complex relations to the land (see *Arise Ye Starvelings: The Jamaican Labour Rebellion of 1938 and Its Aftermath,* 2 vols. [The Hague: Martinus Nijhoff, 1978], 1:269, 283, 294–96).

3. William J. Makim, *Caribbean Nights* (London: Robert Hale, 1939), 51.

4. Ibid., 52.

5. Ibid., 50.

6. Ibid., 52.

7. "Report (with Appendices) of Commission appointed to enquiry into the Disturbances which occurred on the Frome Estate in Westmoreland on 2nd May 1938" (Kingston: Government Printing Office, 1938), CO 950/132 (hereafter "Frome Riot Report"); *Daily Gleaner,* 26 Mar. 1938.

8. Makim, *Caribbean Nights,* 57.

9. "Frome Riot Report."

10. Makim, *Caribbean Nights,* 61.

11. "Report (with Appendices) of the Commission appointed to Enquiry into the Disturbances which occurred in Jamaica between the 23 May and the 8th June 1938." CO 950/132.

12. Makim, *Caribbean Nights,* 73–74, 79–88; telegram, "Seizure of Land in Jamaica," 16 July 1938, and "Emancipation Day. Proposed Message," [1938], CO 318/435/1.

13. "Frome Riot Report," 3.

14. G. St. J. Orde Browne, *Labor Conditions in the West Indies* (London: HMSO, 1939), 736–37.

15. Browne, *Labor Conditions;* "Visit of Major Orde Brown," CO 137/830/68989; G. St. J. Orde Browne, "Some Comments on Mr. Carstairs's Memorandum," 8 Aug. 1940, CO 318/445/48. For more on casualization of the workforce see Post, *Arise Ye Starvelings,* 120–21. Cf. Frederick Cooper, *On the African Waterfront: Urban Disorder and the Transformation of Work in Colonial Mombasa* (New Haven: Yale UP, 1987), chap. 2.

16. Makim, *Caribbean Nights,* 88–89.

17. Ibid., 89.

18. Ibid., 5.

19. *West India Royal Commission Report* (London: HMSO, June 1945), 8.

20. Ibid., 35.

21. Sidney Caine, "Economic Position of the West Indian Colonies," May 1940, CO 318/445/47/60563.

22. "Mr. W. Arthur Lewis, B. Com., Memorandum of Evidence," 6, Moyne Commission, CO 950/56 (hereafter "Lewis Memorandum").

23. Caine, "Economic Position of the West Indian Colonies," May 1940.

24. Ibid.

25. Ibid.

26. Neal R. Malmsten, "Colonial Office Policy to Major Constitutional and Administrative Problems in the West Indies, 1919–1939" (Ph.D. diss., U of London, 1976), 258.

27. Ibid., 258–59.

28. Ibid., 242–43, 259, 270.

29. Draft from Secretary of State to Anthony Eden (Foreign Office), Dec. 1943, CO 448/2.

30. The League's formulations are almost identical in language to oral and written presentations made by Lewis at various times (see, e.g., notes on interviews at the Colonial Office with League representatives [Moody, Lewis, and C. B. Clarke] on Aug. 16 and 29, 1940, minute by Carstairs, 3 Sept. 1940, CO 318/445/47). For a discussion of how Lewis's Fabian sympathies colored his critique and agreement with the Moyne Commission see John Gaffar LaGuerre, "Arthur Lewis and the Moyne Commission" (Paper presented at the fourteenth annual conference of the Caribbean Studies Association, Bridgetown, Barbados, May 1989).

31. "Memorandum on the Economic, Political and Social Conditions in the West Indies and British Guiana presented by the International African Service Bureau, the League of Coloured Peoples, and the Negro Welfare Association," 9 Sept. 1938, quote on 13, CO 950/30 (hereafter "African Service Bureau Memorandum").

32. Ibid., 16; "Memorandum on the Recommendations of the West India Royal Commission (Cmd. 6174). Prepared for H. M. Secretary of State for the Colonies," by the League of Coloured Peoples, May 1939, in "Royal Commission Correspondence with the League of Coloured Peoples," quotes on 3, 6–7, CO 318/445/47 (hereafter "League Memo").

33. League Memo.

34. "Testimony of Mr. Brown of Jamaica Progressive League," 17 Nov. 1938, 28, Moyne Commission, Oral Evidence, vol. 3, CO 950/926.

35. Harold A. Moody, preface to League of Coloured Peoples "News Letter," Apr. 1940, encl. with League Memo.

36. League Memo.

37. Ibid.

38. Lewis Memorandum, 16.

39. African Service Bureau Memorandum, 26–27; first and final quotes in Lewis Memorandum, 12–14.

40. "One of the most important problems in the West Indies with which Governments and employers alike are concerned arises from the extremely rapid development of self-consciousness among the labouring classes. This is a development which cannot be stayed, and lays upon those in responsible positions the duty of doing all in their power to help it into channels where it may work for the common good." Significantly, it was realized that these developments in the colonies resembled those in Britain, except that "a century or so is being telescoped into roughly one-tenth of the time in the West Indies" (Memorandum by C. Y. Carstairs, 1940, CO 318/445/48/60458 [confidential]; see also G. St. J. Orde Browne, "Some Comments on Mr. Carstairs's Memorandum," 8 Aug. 1940).

41. Under the first law, £20 million (the same amount voted to compensate slaveholders in 1833) was appropriated to underwrite development initiatives and improve welfare services in the colonial empire. Because of critical wartime shortages of technical staff, materials, and manpower, as well as delays in planning and start-up, only £3.79 million was actually expended by late 1944. On 25 April 1945, new legislation was passed that increased the appropriation to £120 million over a ten-year period, with an added £1 million per year for research ("Future Provision for Colonial Development and Welfare," Memorandum by the Secretary of State for the Colonies to the War Cabinet, Secret, W.P. [44] 643, 15 Nov. 1944, CO 852/588/11/60303).

42. In a secret memorandum urging Cabinet adoption of the 1945 Colonial Development and Welfare Act, Oliver Stanley declared that it presented "an opportunity which may never recur, at a cost which is not extravagant, of setting the Colonial Empire on lines of development which will keep it in close and loyal contact with us" (ibid. Cf. Howard Johnson, "The West Indies and the Conversion of the British Official Classes to the Development Idea," *Journal of Commonwealth and Comparative Politics* 15 [Mar. 1977]: 55–83; and J. M. Lee, *Colonial Development and Good Government: A Study of the Ideas Expressed by the British Official Classes in Planning Decolonization, 1939–1964* [Oxford: Clarendon, 1967], 45–53).

43. Quoted in *Scotsman*, 10 July 1946, encl. with "Colonial Welfare and Development Act, Preparation and Enactment, [1946]," CO 852/588/13.

44. "Some Aspects of Colonial Economic Policy, an Address by the Right Honourable the Earl of Listowel, Minister of State for Colonial Affairs, to the Overseas League in London," 30 Sept. 1948, encl. with "Planning of Economic and Social Development," CO 852/854/1.

45. Editorial, "Colonial Policy," London *Times*, n.d. [c. 1945], encl. with "Colonial Welfare and Development Act, Preparation and Enactment, [1946]," CO 852/588/13.

46. It should be noted that this linkage was also made by some of the key participants in these events (see, e.g., speeches during debates on the West India Bill in 1962 by Arthur Creech-Jones and G. M. Thompson, respectively, in *Hansard*, 5th ser., 656:874–76, 925–26).

47. For detailed discussions of the postwar developments see Trevor Munroe, *The Politics of Constitutional Decolonization: Jamaica, 1944–62* (Kingston: Institute of Social and Economic Research, U of the West Indies, 1972); and Ken Post, *Strike the Iron, A Colony at War: Jamaica, 1939–1945*, 2 vols. (Atlantic Highlands, N.J.: Humanities P, 1981).

48. Vic Reed, "The lure of gold brought them, . . . ," quote on 5, and "Midnight Tonight—a date with destiny. . . ," 1, both in *Sunday Gleaner*, 5 Aug. 1962; "Hard Times seen for Jamaica 'unless. . . ," *Daily Gleaner*, 10 Aug. 1962, 1; "Price-Crisis in Bananas," *Farmer's Weekly*, 11 Aug. 1962, 1.

49. Munroe argues that Jamaica's was a "false decolonization": "Decolonization did not involve the 'transfer of power' but at most the transfer of authority" (*Politics of Constitutional Decolonization*, 179–92, quotes on 179, 189). For discussion of the favorable and problematic postwar trends in Jamaica's economic development and the problems external authorities posed for political expression within Jamaican society see Evelyne Huber Stephens and John D. Stephens, *Democratic Socialism in Jamaica: The Political Movement and Social Transformation in Dependent Capitalism* (Princeton: Princeton UP, 1986), 10–60, 199–250. For the curious twists and turns of development and free labor ideologies see Frederick Cooper, "Free Labor Ideology and Colonial Rule: Universal Values and Ambiguities of Labor Capital" (Typescript, [c. 1987]).

50. Stephens and Stephens, *Democratic Socialism in Jamaica*, 199–250.

51. "Colonial Development and Welfare Act. Preparation and Enactment, 1945," CO 852/588/12; and "Colonial Development and Welfare Act. Allocation of Funds, Jamaica," CO 852/590/1.

52. W. E. Burghardt Du Bois, "Of the Dawn of Freedom," in *The Souls of Black Folk: Essays and Sketches* (Chicago: A. C. McClurg, 1903), 13.

Works Cited

Primary Sources

MANUSCRIPT SOURCES

Jamaica

Island Record Office, Spanish Town.
    Wills, Probate, and Inventories, libers 12–150.
Jamaica Archives, Spanish Town.
    Ecclesiastical
      The Methodist Church in Jamaica, District Minutes, 1830–66.
    Government
      Accounts Current.
      Accounts Produce.
    Local Government
      Hanover Parish. Lucea Court of Petty Sessions, 1816–1936.
    Private Gifts
      Blagrove, Henry John. Journal, 1841–42.
      Green Park Estate, Trelawny. Account Book, 1848–52.
      Jackson, Thomas Witter. Diary.

Jolly, Canon, F.G., Manuscript.

Sangster Family Collection.

Tweedie Estate Records.

National Library of Jamaica, Kingston.

"Account Book of Richard Hind & Jack Jackson for Content Estate, St. James, 1850–1891." MS133.

Baptist Missionary Society, 1844–54. MS378.

Beldam, Joseph. Papers. MS321 and MST321R.

Buxton, Thomas Fowell, and Beldam, Joseph. Letters [1824–38]. MST321B.

Casserly, Frank. Collection. "Papers of Casserly on Kingston in the Nineteenth Century and Correspondence, 1938–50." MS317.

Cave, S. Memorandum Book: Sugar Estates, 1846–51. MS18.

Fort George Penn: Estate Book, 1840–49. 2 vols. MS274B.

Fort George Penn: Jamaica Account Book, 1852–57. 3 vols. MS274.

Fort George Penn: Journal, 1850–64. MS274A.

Georgia Estate, St. Thomas-in-the-East, Jamaica. Letterbooks and Accounts, Mar. 1822–May 1835. Vol. 3. MST132.

Gordon, George William. Letters. MST892. No. 1.

Harmer, Stephen. Letters. MS765.

Hart, Richard. Collection. MST1813.

Harvey, C. Letters. MS854.

Henderson, John Edward. Letters, 1841–63. MS817.

Henderson, John Edward. Letters, 1851–57. MS817A.

Hill, Richard. Biographical Information. R. E. Merren to Frank Cundall, 31 Dec. 1918. MS942.

Hill, Richard. "Continuation of Diary," 17 Mar.–3 May 1832. MS756B.

Hill, Richard of Jamaica. A Passport or *Laisser Passer*. 3 Dec. 1829. MS756A.

Jordon, Edward. Obituary. *Morning Journal*, 9 Feb. 1869. MST901.

Mahagony Hall Estate Collection, 1857–1907. 12 vols. MS1634.

Mount Pleasant Plantation Book, 1838–44. MS88.

Pieterez, J. E. "Scrapbook, compiled by J. E. Pieterez. Miscellaneous Newspaper Clippings dated from 1826–1944." MS227.

"Proposal for establishing a Company of Proprietors." MS803.

Scattergood, Thomas. "Jamaican-Haitian Diary." 7 Mar.–24 Apr. 1888. MST107.

Sligo, Marquis of. Letterbooks of Peter Howe Browne. 8 vols. MS228.

Sligo Estate Papers. MS275D.

Sligo Papers, 1836. MS275C.

Sligo Papers, 1837–38. Letters. MS275.

Whitelock(e) Collection, 1845–55. Letterbook of H. A. Whitelocke, 30 Sept. 1845–16 Sept. 1846. MS1633.

Williams, James. "Narrative of Events since 1 August 1834, by James Williams, an Apprenticed Labourer in Jamaica." London, 20 June 1837. MS321R.

Young Collection. "Who's Who and What's What in Jamaica, 1879–80." MST318. No. 74.

Great Britain

Baptist Missionary Society, London.
  Papers relating to the West Indies, 1813–1914.
    Phillippo, James M. WI/2.
    Various Missionaries to Jamaica. WI/5.
British Library, London. Manuscript Division.
  Additional Manuscripts
    Aberdeen Papers.
    Holland House Papers.
    Ripon Papers. Vol. 2, 1833–42.
  Documents.
    Colonial Office. Confidential Print. Reels 2–10.
  Private
    de Walden, Lord Howard. "H. de W., General Instructions for Montpelier and Ellis Caymanas Estates in Jamaica." June 1852.
Cambridge Records Office, Cambridge.
  Tharp Family Papers. Letters and Accounts.
Public Records Office, Kew.
    P.R.O. 30/48. Papers of Edward Cardwell.
    P.R.O. 30/22. Papers of Lord John Russell.
  Colonial Office Records.
    137. Original Correspondence of Jamaican Governors.
    139. Acts. Jamaica.
    140. Sessional Papers.
    318. Original Correspondence. West Indies.
    320. Miscellanea. West Indies.
    323/50. Original Correspondence. Report of Law Officers.
    448. Royal Commission.
    852. Original Correspondence. Economic, 1935–43.
    859. Original Correspondence. Social Service, 1939–51.
    884. Confidential Print (microfilm).
    885. Miscellaneous. Confidential Print (microfilm).
    950. West India Royal Commission, 1938–39.
  School of Oriental and Asian Studies, University of London.
    Methodist Missionary Society. Jamaica Correspondence, 1840–42.

United States

Duke University Library, Durham, North Carolina. Manuscript Collection.
  Ballard's Valley Plantation Papers, 1766–1873. Unbound Docs., 1840–48.
National Archives, Washington, D.C.
  General Records of the Department of State. Record Group 59.

Despatches from U.S. Consuls in Kingston, Jamaica, British West Indies, 1796–1906. Microfilm ed. T31.

Despatches from U.S. Consuls in Port Antonio, British West Indies, 1895–1906. Microfilm ed. T650.

NEWSPAPER SOURCES

Baptist Herald and Friend of Africa. 14 Sept. 1839–16 Feb. 1840.

Cobbett's Weekly Political Register. 26 June 1830.

Colonial Standard. Jan.–June 1850.

Falmouth Post. 18 Sept. 1835–29 Sept. 1854.

Kingston Chronicle and City Advertiser. 6 Nov. 1835–6 Oct. 1837.

Kingston Daily Chronicle. 25 Mar. 1916.

Leisure Hour. [1864].

Massachusetts Abolitionist. 6 June 1839.

Missionary Herald. Feb. 1841–Dec. 1865.

Morning Journal. 17 Aug. 1838–Oct. 1856.

New York Daily Tribune. 12 Oct. 1853, 9 June 1854.

New York Herald. 13 June 1853.

New York Observer. [1838].

Times (London). [c. 1945].

PUBLIC DOCUMENTS

Browne, G. St. J. Orde. *Labour Conditions in the West Indies.* London: HMSO, 1939.

Great Britain. Parliament. House of Commons. *Parliamentary Papers.*

   1831–32 (721), 20. "Report of the Select Committee on the Extinction of Slavery Throughout the British Dominions with the Minutes of Evidence, Appendix and Index." [IUP reprint, Slave Trade, vol. 2]

   1831–32 (285), 47. "Despatches between the Government and the Colonies relating to the Recent Rebellion among the Slaves." [IUP reprint, Slave Trade, vol. 80]

   1831–32 (482), 47. "Communications relating to Slave Insurrections and Trials of Missionaries." [IUP reprint, Slave Trade, vol. 80]

   1831–32 (561), 47. "Report from the House of Assembly on the injury sustained during the recent Rebellion." [IUP reprint, Slave Trade, vol. 80]

   1835 (177), 50. "Papers in Explanation of Measures adopted for Giving Effect to the Abolition of Slavery Act."

   1836 (0.44), 48. "Papers in Explanation of the Proceedings of the Legislature of Jamaica, in reference to the Amendment of Their Original Act For Giving Effect to the Act of Parliament for the Abolition of Slavery."

   1836 (166), 48. "Papers relating to the Abolition of Slavery."

   1836 (174), 48. "Correspondence relative to the Abolition of Slavery in Jamaica."

1837 (393), 43. "Copy of the Instructions addressed to the Inspector appointed to visit the Schools in the West Indies."

1837 (521-I), 53. "Papers relative to the Abolition of Slavery in the British Colonies."

1837–38 [138], 40. "Statistical Report of the Sickness, Mortality and Invaliding among the Troops in the West Indies."

1837–38 (596-I&II), 40. "Report of Captain J. W. Pringle on Prisons in the West Indies."

1837–38 (113), 48. "Copy of a Report from C. J. Latrobe, Esq., on Negro Education in Jamaica, with Correspondence relating thereto."

1837–38 (154-I), 49. "Papers in Explanation of the Measures Adopted For Giving Effect to the Act For the Abolition of Slavery."

1842 (479), 13. "Report from the Select Committee on West India Colonies; together with the Minutes of Evidence, Appendix and Index."

1845 (642), 31. "Copies or Extracts of Correspondence relative to the Labouring Population in the West Indies."

1847–48 (167), 23. "Third Report from the Select Committee on Sugar and Coffee Planting."

1854 [1848], 43. "Papers relative to the Affairs of the Island of Jamaica."

1866 [3682], 30. "Papers Laid before the Royal Commission of Inquiry by Governor Eyre." [IUP reprint, Colonies: West Indies, vol. 4]

1866 [3683], 30. "Report of the Jamaica Royal Commission (1866). Part I. Report." [IUP reprint, Colonies: West Indies, vol. 4]

1866 [3683-I], 31. "Report of the Jamaica Royal Commission (1866). Part II. Minutes of Evidence and Appendix." [IUP reprint, Colonies: West Indies, vol. 5]

1866 (380), 51. "Letter from Dr. Underhill . . . and Correspondence relative to Disturbances in Jamaica."

1866 (3595), 51. "Paper relating to Disturbances in Jamaica."

1898 [c. 8655], 50. "Report of the West India Royal Commission, with Subsidiary Report and Statistical Tables." [IUP reprint, Colonies: West Indies, vol. 7]

1898 [c. 8656], 50. "Appendix C, Vol. I, Proceedings, Evidence, and Documents received in London." [IUP reprint, Colonies: West Indies, vol. 7]

1898 [c. 8657], 50. "Appendix C, Vol. II, Proceedings, Evidence, and Documents relating to British Guiana, Barbados, Trinidad, and Tobago." [IUP reprint, Colonies: West Indies, vol. 7]

1922 [Cmd. 1679], 16. "Report by Parliamentary Undersecretary of State for the Colonies [E. P. L. Wood]: A Visit to the West Indies and British Guiana, 1921–22."

Hansard's Parliamentary Debates. 3d and 5th series.

Royal Commission Report on the West Indies, 1938–39. London: HMSO, 1945.

"Total Value of Imports and Exports into Colony of Jamaica Year Ending 31

December 1865." *Blue Book for the Island of Jamaica for the Year 1865*. Kingston: Colonial Standard Office, 1865.

Votes of the Honourable House of Assembly of Jamaica. 1832–65.

PRINTED PRIMARY SOURCES

Bentham, Jeremy. *An Introduction to the Principles of Morals and Legislation*. Edited by J. H. Burns and H. L. A. Hart. London: Athlone, 1970.

———. *The Works of Jeremy Bentham*. Edited by John Bowring. 11 vols. Edinburgh: William Tait, 1843.

Bruce, James [Earl of Elgin] and Henry George Grey. *The Elgin-Grey Papers, 1846–1852*. Edited by Arthur George Doughty. 4 vols. Ottawa: J. O. Patenaude, 1937.

Campbell, George. "Tenure of Land in India." In *Systems of Land Tenure in Various Countries: A Series of Essays Published under the Sanction of the Cobden Club*, 149–231. 2d ed. London: Macmillan, 1870.

Carlyle, Thomas. *Critical and Miscellaneous Essays: Collected and Republished*. 7 vols. London: Chapman & Hall, 1872.

———. *Latter-day Pamphlets*. Boston: Philips, Sampson, 1850.

———. "Occasional Discourse on the Negro Question." *Fraser's Magazine* 40 (Dec. 1849): 670–79.

———. *Past and Present*. London: Chapman & Hall, 1843.

———. *Reminiscences*. Edited by Charles E. Norton. 2 vols. in 1. London: Macmillan, 1887.

———. *Thomas Carlyle: Letters to His Wife*. Edited by Trudy Bliss. London: V. Gollancz, 1953.

Carlyle, Thomas, and Ralph Waldo Emerson. *Correspondence of Thomas Carlyle and Ralph Waldo Emerson, 1834–1872*. Edited by C. E. Norton. 2 vols. London: Chatto & Windus, 1883.

Carlyle, Thomas, and John Stuart Mill. *Thomas Carlyle, "The Nigger Question," John Stuart Mill, "The Negro Question."* Edited by Eugene R. August. New York: Crofts Classics, 1971.

Edwards, Bryan. *The History, Civil and Commercial, of the British Colonies in the West Indies*. 2 vols. London: J. Stockdale, 1793.

Froude, James Anthony. "England and Her Colonies." *Fraser's Magazine*, n.s. 1 (Jan. 1870): 1–16.

———. *The English in the West Indies, or, The Bow of Ulysses*. 1888. Reprint. New York: Charles Scribner's Sons, 1897.

———. *Life of Carlyle*. Abridged and edited by John Clubbe. Columbus: Ohio State UP, 1979.

———. *Two Lectures on South Africa*. London: Longmans, Green, 1880.

George, Henry. *The Irish Land Question, What It Involves, and How Alone It Can Be Settled: An Appeal to the Land Leagues*. New York: D. Appleton & Co., 1881.

Gramsci, Antonio. *Selections from the Prison Notebooks.* Edited and translated by Quintin Hoare and Geoffrey Nowell Smith. New York: International Publishers, 1971.

Hegel, Georg Wilhelm Friedrich. *Hegel's Phenomenology of the Spirit.* Translated by A. V. Miller. New York: Oxford UP, 1977.

———. *Hegel's Philosophy of Right.* Translated by T. M. Knox. London: Oxford UP, 1952.

Holland, Henry Richard Vassall Fox. *Holland House Diaries, 1831–1840.* Edited by Abraham D. Kriegel. London: Routledge & Kegan Paul, 1977.

Madden, Richard Robert. *A Twelvemonth's Residence in the West Indies during the Transition from Slavery to Apprenticeship.* 2 vols. Philadelphia: Carey, Lea, & Blanchard, 1835.

Makim, William J. *Caribbean Nights.* London: Robert Hale, 1939.

Marx, Karl. *Capital.* Translated by Ben Fowkes. 3 vols. New York: Vintage, 1977.

Marx, Karl, and Friedrich Engels. *On Literature and Art.* New York: International Publishers, 1947.

Mill, John Stuart. *Autobiography.* Edited by Jack Stillinger. Boston: Houghton Mifflin, 1969.

———. "England and Ireland." In *Essays on England, Ireland, and the Empire: The Collected Works of John Stuart Mill,* edited by John M. Robson. Toronto: U of Toronto P, 1982.

———. "M. de Tocqueville on Democracy in America." In *The Philosophy of John Stuart Mill: Ethical, Political, and Religious,* edited by Marshall Cohen. New York: Modern Library, 1961.

———. "On Liberty." In *The Philosophy of John Stuart Mill: Ethical, Political, and Religious,* edited by Marshall Cohen. New York: Modern Library, 1961.

———. *Principles of Political Economy, with Some of Their Applications to Social Philosophy.* Edited by Sir W. J. Ashley. New York: Augustus M. Kelly, 1965.

———. "What Is To Be Done with Ireland." In *Essays on England, Ireland, and the Empire: The Collected Works of John Stuart Mill,* edited by John M. Robson. Toronto: U of Toronto P, 1982.

Olivier, Lord [Sydney Haldane]. *Imperial Trusteeship.* Fabian Tract No. 230. London: Fabian Society, 1929.

———. *The League of Nations and Primitive Peoples.* London: Oxford UP, 1918.

———. *Sydney Olivier: Letters and Selected Writings.* Edited by Margaret Olivier. London: George Allen & Unwin, 1948.

Russell, John Earl. *Recollections and Suggestions, 1813–1873.* London: Longmans, Green, 1875.

Sewell, William G. *The Ordeal of Free Labor in the British West Indies.* New York: Harper & Brothers, 1861.

Shaw, Nate. *All God's Dangers: The Autobiography of Nate Shaw.* Edited by Theodore Rosengarten. New York: Knopf, 1974.

Spedding, James. *Reviews and Discussions: Literary, Political, and Historical, Not Relating to Bacon*. London: C. Kegan Paul, 1879.

Stephen, James. "The Diary of James Stephen, 1846." Edited by T. Barron and K. J. Cable. *Historical Studies* (Melbourne) 13 (Apr. 1969): 503–19.

———. *The Right Honourable Sir James Stephen: Letters with Biographical Notes*. Biographical Notes by Caroline Emelia Stephen. N.p.: Printed for Private Circulation Only, 1906.

Stephen, James F. "Mr Carlyle." *Essays by a Barrister*. London: Smith, Elder & Co., 1862.

Stewart, John. *An Account of Jamaica and Its Inhabitants*. London: Longman, Hurst, Rees, & Orme, 1808.

———. *A View of the Past and Present State of the Island of Jamaica*. 1823. Reprint. New York: Negro UP, 1969.

Taylor, Henry. *Autobiography of Henry Taylor, 1800–1875*. 2 vols. London: Longmans, Green, 1885.

———. *Correspondence of Henry Taylor*. Edited by Edward Dowden. London: Longmans, Green, 1888.

Underhill, Edward Bean. *The Tragedy of Morant Bay: A Narrative of the Disturbances in the Island of Jamaica in 1865*. London: Alexander & Shepeard, 1895.

———. *The West Indies: Their Social and Religious Condition*. London: Jackson, Walford, & Hodder, 1862.

Wakefield, Edward Gibbon. *The Collected Works of Edward Gibbon Wakefield*. Edited by M. F. Lloyd Prichard. Glasgow: Collins, 1968.

Secondary Sources

Anstey, Roger. *The Atlantic Slave Trade and British Abolition, 1760–1810*. London: Macmillan, 1975.

———. "Capitalism and Slavery: A Critique." *Economic History Review*, 2d ser., 21 (Aug. 1968): 307–20.

———. "Religion and British Slave Emancipation." In *The Abolition of the Atlantic Slave Trade: Origins and Effects in Europe, Africa, and the Americas*, edited by David Eltis and James Walvin. Madison: U of Wisconsin P, 1981.

Appleby, Joyce Oldham. *Economic Thought and Ideology in Seventeenth-Century England*. Princeton, N.J.: Princeton UP, 1978.

———. "Ideology and Theory: The Tension between Political and Economic Liberalism in Seventeenth-Century England." *American Historical Review* 81 (June 1976): 499–513.

August, Thomas. "Jewish Assimilation and the Plural Society in Jamaica." *Social and Economic Studies* 36 (June 1987): 109–22.

Bailey, Peter. *Leisure and Class in Victorian England: Rational Recreation and the Contest for Control, 1830–1885*. London: Routledge & Kegan Paul, 1978.

Balfour, Michael. *Britain and Joseph Chamberlain*. London: George Allen & Unwin, 1985.

Bartlett, Wilson Randolph, Jr. "Lorenzo D. Baker and the Development of the Banana Trade between Jamaica and the United States, 1881–1890." Ph.D. diss., American U, 1977.

Beales, Derek. *From Castlereagh to Gladstone, 1815–1885*. New York: W. W. Norton, 1969.

Beckett, James C. *The Making of Modern Ireland, 1603–1923*. London: Faber & Faber, 1966.

Benhabib, Seyla. "Obligation, Contract, and Exchange: On the Significance of Hegel's Abstract Right." In *The State and Civil Society: Studies in Hegel's Political Philosophy*, edited by Z. A. Pelcyzynski, 159–77. Cambridge: Cambridge UP, 1984.

Bernstein, J. M. "From Self-consciousness to Community: Act and Recognition in the Master-Slave Relationship." In *The State and Civil Society: Studies in Hegel's Political Philosophy*, edited by Z. A. Pelcyzynski, 14–39. Cambridge: Cambridge UP, 1984.

Besson, Jean. "Agrarian Relations and Perceptions of Land in a Jamaican Peasant Village." In *Small Farming and Peasant Resources in the Caribbean*, edited by John S. Brierley and Hymie Rubenstein, 39–61. Manitoba Geographical Studies, 10. Winnipeg: U of Manitoba Department of Geography, 1988.

———. "Family Land as a Model for Martha Brae's New History: Culture Building in an Afro-Caribbean Village." In *Afro-Caribbean Villages in Historical Perspective*, edited by Charles V. Carnegie, 100–132. Kingston: African-Caribbean Institute of Jamaica, 1987.

———. "Land Tenure in the Free Villages of Trelawny, Jamaica: A Case Study in the Caribbean Peasant Response to Emancipation." *Slavery & Abolition* 5 (May 1984): 3–23.

———. "A Paradox in Caribbean Attitudes to Land." In *Land and Development in the Caribbean*, edited by Jean Besson and Janet Momsen, 13–45. London: Macmillan Caribbean, 1987.

———. "Symbolic Aspects of Land in the Caribbean: The Tenure and Transmission of Land Rights among Caribbean Peasantries." In *Peasants, Plantations, and Rural Communities in the Caribbean*, edited by Malcolm Cross and Arnaud Marks. Guildford: Department of Sociology, U of Surrey, 1979.

Bhattacharya, Sachchidananda. "Land Tenure Systems." In *A Dictionary of Indian History*. New York: George Braziller, 1967.

Black, R. D. Collison. *Economic Thought and the Irish Question, 1817–1870*. Cambridge: Cambridge UP, 1960.

Blassingame, John W. *The Slave Community: Plantation Life in the Antebellum South*. New York: Oxford UP, 1972.

Brathwaite, Edward Kamau. *The Development of Creole Society in Jamaica, 1770–1820*. Oxford: Clarendon, 1971.

————. "The Slave Rebellion in the Great River Valley of St. James—1831/32." *Jamaican Historical Review* 13 (1982): 11–30.

Briggs, Asa. *The Age of Improvement, 1783–1867*. London: Longmans, 1959.

Brodber, Erna. "Afro-Jamaican Women at the Turn of the Century." *Social and Economic Studies* 35 (Sept. 1986): 23–50.

Buckner, Phillip A. *The Transition to Responsible Government: British Policy in British North America, 1815–1850*. Westport, Conn.: Greenwood, 1985.

Burn, W. L. *Emancipation and Apprenticeship in the British West Indies*. London: Jonathan Cape, 1937.

Burt, Arthur E. "The First Instalment of Representative Government in Jamaica, 1884." *Social and Economic Studies* 11 (Sept. 1962): 241–59.

Butler, Kathleen Mary. "Slave Compensation and Property, Jamaica and Barbados, 1823–1843." Ph.D. diss., Johns Hopkins U, 1986.

Campbell, Carl. "Towards an Imperial Policy for the Education of Negroes in the West Indies after Emancipation." *Jamaican Historical Review* 7 (1967): 68–102.

Campbell, Mavis Christine. *The Dynamics of Change in a Slave Society: A Sociopolitical History of the Free Coloreds of Jamaica, 1800–1865*. Rutherford, N.J.: Associated Universities P, 1976.

Carnegie, Charles V. "Is Family Land an Institution?" In *Afro-Caribbean Villages in Historical Perspective*, edited by Charles V. Carnegie, 83–99. Kingston: African-Caribbean Institute of Jamaica, 1987.

Cassidy, Cheryl Marguerit. "Islands and Empires: A Rhetorical Analysis of the Governor Eyre Controversy, 1865–1867." Ph.D. diss., U of Michigan, 1988.

Cell, John W. *British Colonial Administration in the Mid-Nineteenth Century: The Policy-Making Process*. New Haven: Yale UP, 1970.

Clarke, Edith. "Land Tenure and the Family in Four Selected Communities in Jamaica." In *Peoples and Cultures of the Caribbean*, edited by Michael Horowitz, 211–42. New York: Natural History P, 1971.

————. *My Mother Who Fathered Me: A Study of the Family in Three Selected Communities in Jamaica*. London: George Allen & Unwin, 1957.

Cohen, David W., and Jack P. Greene, eds. *Neither Slave Nor Free: The Freedman of African Descent in the Slave Societies of the New World*. Baltimore: Johns Hopkins P, 1972.

Conrad, Robert. *The Destruction of Brazilian Slavery, 1850–1888*. Berkeley: U of California P, 1972.

Cooper, Frederick. "Free Labor Ideology and Colonial Rule: Universal Values and Ambiguities of Labor Capital." Typescript. [c. 1987].

————. *From Slaves to Squatters: Plantation Labor and Agriculture in Zanzibar and Coastal Kenya, 1890–1925*. New Haven: Yale UP, 1980.

————. *On the African Waterfront: Urban Disorder and the Transformation of Work in Colonial Mombasa*. New Haven: Yale UP, 1987.

————. "Peasants, Capitalists, and Historians: A Review Article." *Journal of Southern African Studies* 7 (Apr. 1981): 284–314.

Craton, Michael. *Searching for the Invisible Man: Slaves and Plantation Life in Jamaica.* Cambridge: Harvard UP, 1978.

———. *Testing the Chains: Resistance to Slavery in the British West Indies.* Ithaca: Cornell UP, 1982.

Craton, Michael, and James Walvin. *A Jamaica Plantation: The History of Worthy Park, 1670–1970.* London: W. H. Allen, 1970.

Cumper, G. E. "Labour Demand and Supply in the Jamaican Sugar Industry, 1830–1950." *Social and Economic Studies* 2 (Mar. 1954): 37–86.

———. "A Modern Jamaican Sugar Estate." *Social and Economic Studies* 3 (Sept. 1954): 119–60.

Curtin, Philip D. *Two Jamaicas: The Role of Ideas in a Tropical Colony, 1830–1865.* Cambridge: Harvard UP, 1975.

Curtis, L. Perry, Jr. *Apes and Angels: The Irishman in Victorian Caricature.* Newton Abbot, England: David & Charles, 1971.

Davis, David Brion. *The Problem of Slavery in the Age of Revolution, 1770–1823.* Ithaca: Cornell UP, 1975.

———. *The Problem of Slavery in Western Culture.* Ithaca: Cornell UP, 1966.

———. "Reflections on Abolitionism and Ideological Hegemony." *American Historical Review* 92 (Oct. 1987): 797–812.

———. *Slavery and Human Progress.* New York: Oxford UP, 1984.

Davis-Roberts, Christopher. "Mango Na Mitishambe: Illness and Medicine among the Batabwa of Zaire." Ph.D. diss., U of Chicago, 1980.

Deerr, Noel. *The History of Sugar.* 2 vols. London: Chapman & Hall, 1950.

De Lisser, H. G. *Twentieth Century Jamaica.* Kingston: Jamaica Times, 1913.

Dollar, Charles M., and Richard J. Jensen. *Historian's Guide to Statistics: Quantitative Analysis and Historical Research.* New York: Holt, Rinehart, & Winston, 1971.

Donaldson, K. V. B. "The Contribution of Baptist Missionaries to Education in Jamaica during the First Half of the Nineteenth Century, 1814–67." Master's thesis, U of London Institute of Education, 1967.

Drescher, Seymour. *Capitalism and Antislavery: British Mobilization in Comparative Perspective.* New York: Oxford UP, 1987.

———. "Cart Whip and Billy Roller: Antislavery and Reform Symbolism in Industrializing Britain." *Journal of Social History* 15 (Fall 1981): 3–24.

———. *Econocide: British Slavery in the Era of Abolition.* Pittsburgh: U of Pittsburgh P, 1977.

Du Bois, W. E. Burghardt. "Of the Dawn of Freedom." In *The Souls of Black Folk: Essays and Sketches,* 13–40. Chicago: A. C. McClurg, 1903.

Duncan, Graeme. *Marx and Mill: Two Views of Social Conflict and Social Harmony.* Cambridge: Cambridge UP, 1973.

Dunn, Richard S. *Sugar and Slaves: The Rise of the Planter Class in the English West Indies, 1624–1713.* Chapel Hill: U of North Carolina P, 1972.

Dunn, Waldo Hilary. *James Anthony Froude: A Biography.* 2 vols. Oxford: Clarendon, 1961–63.

Dutton, Geoffrey. *The Hero as Murderer: The Life of Edward John Eyre, Australian Explorer and Governor of Jamaica, 1815–1901*. London: Collins, 1967.

Eisner, Gisela. *Jamaica, 1830–1930: A Study in Economic Growth*. Manchester: Manchester UP, 1961.

Eltis, David. "Abolitionist Perceptions of Society after Slavery." In *Slavery and British Society, 1776–1846*, edited by James Walvin, 193–213. Baton Rouge: Louisiana State UP, 1982.

———. *Economic Growth and the Ending of the Transatlantic Slave Trade*. New York: Oxford UP, 1987.

Feuer, Carl Henry. "Better Must Come: Sugar and Jamaica in the 20th Century." *Social and Economic Studies* 33 (Dec. 1984): 1–50.

Fields, Barbara Jeanne. *Slavery and Freedom on the Middle Ground: Maryland during the Nineteenth Century*. New Haven: Yale UP, 1985.

———. "Slavery, Race, and Ideology in the United States of America." *New Left Review* 181 (May–June 1990): 95–118.

Foucault, Michel. *Discipline and Punish: The Birth of the Prison*. Translated by Alan Sheridan. New York: Vintage, 1979.

Freeden, Michael. *The New Liberalism: An Ideology of Social Reform*. Oxford: Clarendon, 1978.

Fukuyama, Francis. "The End of History?" *National Interest*, Summer 1989, 3–35.

Gash, Norman. *Reaction and Reconstruction in English Politics, 1832–1852*. Oxford: Clarendon, 1965.

Geertz, Clifford. "Ideology as a Cultural System." In *Ideology and Discontent*, edited by David Apter. New York: Free Press, 1964.

Glory, Robertson, comp. "Members of the Assembly of Jamaica from the General Election of 1830 to the Final Session, Jan. 1866." Kingston: West India Reference Library, Institute of Jamaica, 1965.

Gocking, C. V. "Early Constitutional History of Jamaica (with Special Reference to the Period 1836–1866)." *Caribbean Quarterly* 6 (May 1960): 114–33.

Green, William A. *British Slave Emancipation: The Sugar Colonies and the Great Experiment, 1830–1865*. Oxford: Clarendon, 1976.

Greene, Jack P. "Society and Economy in the British Caribbean during the Seventeenth and Eighteenth Centuries." *American Historical Review* 79 (Dec. 1974): 1499–1517.

Gutman, Herbert G. *The Black Family in Slavery and Freedom, 1750–1925*. New York: Pantheon, 1976.

Hagood, Margaret Jarman. *Mothers of the South: Portraiture of the White Tenant Farm Woman*. Chapel Hill: U of North Carolina P, 1939.

Hall, Douglas. "Absentee-Proprietorship in the British West Indies to About 1850." *Jamaican Historical Review* 4 (1964): 15–35.

———. "The Flight from the Estates Reconsidered: The British West Indies, 1838–42." *Journal of Caribbean History* 10–11 (1978): 7–24.

———. "Fort George Pen, Jamaica: Slaves, Tenants and Labourers,

1832–1843." Paper presented at the eleventh conference of Caribbean Historians, Curaçao, 5–10 Apr. 1979.

———. *Free Jamaica, 1838–1865: An Economic History*. New Haven: Yale UP, 1959.

Hart, Ansell. "The Banana in Jamaica: Export Trade." *Social and Economic Studies* 3 (Sept. 1954): 212–29.

Haskell, Thomas L. "Capitalism and the Origins of Humanitarian Sensibility." Pts. 1 and 2. *American Historical Review* 90 (Apr., June 1985): 339–62, 547–66.

Heuman, Gad J. *Between Black and White: Race, Politics, and the Free Coloreds in Jamaica, 1792–1865*. Westport, Conn.: Greenwood, 1981.

———. "White over Brown over Black: The Free Coloureds in Jamaican Society during Slavery and after Emancipation." *Journal of Caribbean History* 14 (1981): 46–69.

Heyck, T. W. *The Transformation of Intellectual Life in Victorian England*. New York: St. Martin's, 1982.

Higman, B. W. "Household Structure and Fertility on Jamaican Slave Plantations: A Nineteenth-Century Example." *Population Studies* 27 (1973): 527–50.

———. "Jamaican Coffee Plantations, 1780–1860: A Cartographic Analysis." *Caribbean Geography* 2 (Oct. 1986): 73–75.

———. "The Slave Family and Household in the British West Indies, 1800–1834." *Journal of Interdisciplinary History* 6 (Fall 1975): 261–87.

———. *Slave Population and Economy in Jamaica, 1807–1834*. Cambridge: Cambridge UP, 1976.

———. "The West India 'Interest' in Parliament, 1807–1833." *Historical Studies* (Melbourne) 13 (Oct. 1967): 1–19.

———, ed. "The Jamaican Censuses of 1844 and 1861: A New Edition, Derived from the Manuscript and Printed Schedules in the Jamaica Archives." Mona, Jamaica: Social History Project, Department of History, U of the West Indies, 1980.

Himmelfarb, Gertrude. "Bentham's Utopia: The National Charity Company." *Journal of British Studies* 10 (Nov. 1970): 80–125.

Hobsbawm, Eric J. *The Age of Capital, 1848–1875*. New York: Charles Scribner's Sons, 1975.

———. *The Age of Empire, 1875–1914*. New York: Pantheon, 1987.

———. *The Age of Revolution, 1789–1848*. Cleveland, Ohio: World Publishing, 1962.

Hobsbawm, Eric J., and George Rudé. *Captain Swing: A Social History of the Great English Agricultural Uprising of 1830*. New York: Norton Library, 1975.

Holt, Thomas C. *Black over White: Negro Political Leadership in South Carolina during Reconstruction*. Urbana: U of Illinois P, 1977.

———. "'An Empire over the Mind': Emancipation, Race, and Ideology in the British West Indies and the American South." In *Region, Race, and Reconstruction: Essays in Honor of C. Vann Woodward*, edited by J. Morgan Kousser and James M. McPherson. New York: Oxford UP, 1982.

———. "Explaining Abolition." *Journal of Social History* 24 (Winter 1990): 371–78.

———. "Of Human Progress and Intellectual Apostasy." *Reviews in American History* 15 (Mar. 1987): 50–58.

Ignatieff, Michael. *A Just Measure of Pain: The Penitentiary in the Industrial Revolution, 1750–1850*. New York: Pantheon, 1978.

Jaynes, Gerald David. *Branches Without Roots: Genesis of the Black Working Class in the American South, 1862–1882*. New York: Oxford UP, 1986.

Johnson, Howard. "The Political Uses of Commissions of Enquiry (1): The Imperial-Colonial West Indies Context, The Forster and Moyne Commissions." *Social and Economic Studies* 27 (Sept. 1978): 256–83.

———. "The West Indies and the Conversion of the British Official Classes to the Development Idea." *Journal of Commonwealth and Comparative Politics* 15 (Mar. 1977): 55–83.

Johnson, Richard. "Educational Policy and Social Control in Early Victorian England." *Past and Present* 49 (Nov. 1970): 96–119.

Jones, Gareth Stedman. *Outcast London: A Study in the Relationship between Classes in Victorian Society*. New York: Pantheon, 1984.

———. "Working-Class Culture and Working-Class Politics in London, 1870–1900: Notes on the Remaking of a Working Class." In *Languages of Class: Studies in English Working-Class History, 1832–1982*. Cambridge: Cambridge UP, 1983.

Judd, Denis. *Radical Joe: A Life of Joseph Chamberlain*. London: Hamish Hamilton, 1977.

Kennedy, Liam. "The Rural Economy, 1820–1914." In *Economic History of Ulster, 1820–1940*, edited by Liam Kennedy and Philip Ollerenshaw, 31–33. Manchester: Manchester UP, 1985.

Knaplund, Paul. *James Stephen and the British Colonial System, 1813–1847*. Madison: U of Wisconsin P, 1953.

Knox, Bruce A. "The British Government and the Governor Eyre Controversy, 1865–1875." *Historical Journal* 19 (Dec. 1976): 877–900.

———. "The Queen's Letter of 1865 and British Policy towards Emancipation and Indentured Labour in the West Indies, 1830–1865." *Historical Journal* 29 (June 1986): 345–67.

LaGuerre, John Gaffar. "Arthur Lewis and the Moyne Commission." Paper presented at the fourteenth annual conference of the Caribbean Studies Association, Bridgetown, Barbados, May 1989.

———. "The Moyne Commission and the Jamaican Left." *Social and Economic Studies* 31 (Sept. 1982): 59–94.

Lebow, Richard Ned. *White Britain and Black Ireland: The Influence of Stereotypes on Colonial Policy*. Philadelphia: Institute for the Study of Human Issues, 1976.

Lee, J. M. *Colonial Development and Good Government: A Study of the Ideas Expressed by the British Official Classes in Planning Decolonization, 1939–1964.* Oxford: Clarendon, 1967.

Lee, Joseph. *The Modernisation of Irish Society, 1848–1918.* Dublin: Gill & Macmillan, 1973.

Lee, Sidney, ed. *Dictionary of National Biography.* 2d suppl. New York: Macmillan, 1912.

LeGrand, Catherine. "Columbian Transformations: Peasants and Wage-Labourers in the Santa Marta Banana Zone." *Journal of Peasant Studies* 11 (July 1984): 178–200.

Levine, Lawrence W. *Black Culture and Black Consciousness: Afro-American Folk Thought from Slavery to Freedom.* New York: Oxford UP, 1977.

Litwak, Leon F. *Been in the Storm So Long: The Aftermath of Slavery.* New York: Knopf, 1979.

Lobdell, Richard A. "Patterns of Investment and Sources of Credit in the British West Indian Sugar Industry, 1836–97." *Journal of Caribbean History* 4 (May 1972): 31–53.

Lorimer, Douglas A. *Colour, Class, and the Victorians: English Attitudes to the Negro in the Mid-Nineteenth Century.* Leicester: Leicester UP, 1978.

Ludden, David. *Peasant History in South India.* Princeton: Princeton UP, 1985.

McDonald, Roderick Alexander. "'Goods and Chattels': The Economy of Slaves on Sugar Plantations in Jamaica and Louisiana." Ph.D. diss., U of Kansas, 1981.

McKendrick, Neil. "Josiah Wedgwood and Factory Discipline." *Historical Journal* 4 (Mar. 1961): 30–55.

Macmillan, Mona. *Sir Henry Barkly, Mediator and Moderator, 1815–1898.* Cape Town: A. A. Balkema, 1970.

Macpherson, C. B. *Democratic Theory: Essays in Retrieval.* Oxford: Clarendon, 1973.

———. *The Political Theory of Possessive Individualism: Hobbes to Locke.* Oxford: Clarendon, 1962.

Malmsten, Neal R. "Colonial Office Policy to Major Constitutional and Administrative Problems in the West Indies, 1919–1939." Ph.D. diss., U of London, 1976.

Marsala, Vincent John. *Sir John Peter Grant, Governor of Jamaica, 1866–1874: An Administrative History.* [Kingston]: Institute of Jamaica, 1972.

Marshall, Woodville K. "Notes on Peasant Development in the West Indies since 1838." *Social and Economic Studies* 17 (Sept. 1968): 252–63.

Mathieson, William Law. *British Slavery and Emancipation, 1838–1849.* London: Longmans, Green, 1932.

———. *British Slavery and Its Abolition, 1823–1838.* London: Longmans, Green, 1926.

Mbiti, John S. *African Religions and Philosophy.* 2d ed. Portsmouth, N.H.: Heinemann, 1990.

Meirs, Suzanne, and Igor Kopytoff, eds. *Slavery in Africa: Historical and Anthropological Perspectives.* Madison: U of Wisconsin P, 1977.

Mills, Charles W. "Race and Class: Conflicting or Reconcilable Paradigms?" *Social and Economic Studies* 36 (June 1987): 69–108.

Mintz, Sidney W. *Caribbean Transformations.* Chicago: Aldine, 1974.

———. "A Note on the Definition of Peasantries." *Journal of Peasant Studies* 1 (Oct. 1973): 91–106.

———. "The Rural Proletariat and the Problem of Rural Proletarian Consciousness." *Journal of Peasant Studies* 1 (Apr. 1974): 291–324.

———. *Sweetness and Power: The Place of Sugar in Modern History.* New York: Penguin, 1985.

Mintz, Sidney W., and Richard Price. *An Anthropological Approach to the Afroamerican Past: A Caribbean Perspective.* Philadelphia: Institute for the Study of Human Issues, 1976.

Mokyr, Joel. *Why Ireland Starved: A Quantitative and Analytical History of the Irish Economy, 1800–1850.* London: George Allen & Unwin, 1983.

Monet, Jacques. *The Last Cannon Shot: A Study of French-Canadian Nationalism, 1837–1850.* [Toronto]: U of Toronto P, 1969.

Moreno Fraginals, Manuel. *El ingenio: complejo económico social cubano del azúcar.* Havana: Editorial de Ciencias Sociales, 1978.

Morison, J. L. *The Eighth Earl of Elgin: A Chapter in Nineteenth-Century Imperial History.* London: Hodder & Stoughton, 1928.

Morrissey, Marretta. "Aspects of Jamaican Economic Development, 1830–1930." Ph.D. diss., Michigan State U, 1977.

Munroe, Trevor. *The Politics of Constitutional Decolonization: Jamaica, 1944–62.* Kingston: Institute of Social and Economic Research, U of the West Indies, 1972.

Olivier, Lord [Sydney Haldane]. *Jamaica: The Blessed Island.* London: Faber & Faber, 1936.

———. *The Myth of Governor Eyre.* London: Hogarth, 1933.

Patterson, Orlando. "From Endo-deme to Matri-deme: An Interpretation of the Development of Kinship and Social Organization among the Slaves of Jamaica, 1655–1830." In *Eighteenth-Century Florida and the Caribbean,* edited by Samuel Proctor, 50–59. Gainesville: U Presses of Florida, 1976.

———. *Slavery and Social Death: A Comparative Study.* Cambridge: Harvard UP, 1982.

———. *The Sociology of Slavery: An Analysis of the Origins, Development, and Structure of Negro Slave Society in Jamaica.* Rutherford, N.J.: Fairleigh Dickinson UP, 1967.

Phillips, James J. "Fe Wi Land a Cane: Choice and Change on a Jamaican Sugar Plantation." Ph.D. diss., Brown U, 1976.

Pomfret, John E. *The Struggle for Land in Ireland, 1800–1923.* Princeton: Princeton UP, 1930.

Post, Ken. *Arise Ye Starvelings: The Jamaican Labour Rebellion of 1938 and Its Aftermath.* The Hague: Martinus Nijhoff, 1978.

———. *Strike the Iron: A Colony at War: Jamaica, 1939–1945.* 2 vols. Atlantic Highlands, N.J.: Humanities P, 1981.

Powell, Lawrence N. *New Masters: Northern Planters during the Civil War and Reconstruction.* New Haven: Yale UP, 1980.

Poynter, J. R. *Society and Pauperism: English Ideas on Poor Relief, 1795–1834.* London: Routledge & Kegan Paul, 1969.

Pugh, Martin. *The Making of Modern British Politics, 1867–1939.* New York: St. Martin's, 1982.

Raboteau, Albert J. *Slave Religion: The "Invisible Institution" in the Antebellum South.* New York: Oxford UP, 1978.

Roark, James L. *Masters without Slaves: Southern Planters in the Civil War and Reconstruction.* New York: W. W. Norton, 1977.

Roberts, W. Adolphe. *Six Great Jamaicans: Biographical Sketches.* Kingston: Pioneer, 1951.

Robotham, Don. "'The Notorious Riot': The Socio-Economic and Political Bases of Paul Bogle's Revolt." *Anales del Caribe* (Havana) 3 (1983): 51–111.

———. "Pluralism as an Ideology." *Social and Economic Studies* 29 (Mar. 1980): 69–89.

———. "The Why of the Cockatoo." *Social and Economic Studies* 34 (June 1985): 111–51.

Rodney, Walter. *A History of the Guyanese Working People, 1881–1905.* Baltimore: Johns Hopkins UP, 1981.

Safa, Helen I. "Economic Autonomy and Sexual Equality in Caribbean Society." *Social and Economic Studies* 35 (Sept. 1986): 1–22.

Satchell, Veront M. *From Plots to Plantations: Land Transactions in Jamaica, 1866–1900.* Mona, Jamaica: Institute of Social and Economic Research, U of the West Indies, 1990.

Schuler, Monica. *"Alas, Alas, Kongo": A Social History of Indentured African Immigration into Jamaica, 1841–1865.* Baltimore: Johns Hopkins UP, 1980.

Scott, Rebecca J. "Exploring the Meaning of Freedom: Postemancipation Societies in Comparative Perspective." *Hispanic American Historical Review* 68 (Aug. 1988): 407–28.

———. *Slave Emancipation in Cuba: The Transition to Free Labor, 1860–1899.* Princeton: Princeton UP, 1985.

Semmel, Bernard. *Democracy versus Empire: The Jamaica Riots of 1865 and the Governor Eyre Controversy.* 1963. Reprint. Garden City, N.Y.: Anchor, 1969.

Shannon, Catherine B. "The Ulster Liberal Unionists and Local Government Reform, 1885–98." *Irish Historical Studies* 18 (Mar. 1973): 407–23.

Shepherd, Verena A. "The Effects of the Abolition of Slavery on Jamaican Livestock Farms (Pens)." *Slavery & Abolition* 10 (Sept. 1989): 187–211.

Sheridan, Richard B. *Sugar and Slavery: An Economic History of the British Indies, 1623–1775.* Baltimore: Johns Hopkins UP, 1974.

Sires, Ronald V. "The Experience of Jamaica with Modified Crown Colony Government." *Social and Economic Studies* 4 (June 1955): 150–67.

———. "The Jamaica Constitution of 1884." *Social and Economic Studies* 3 (June 1954): 64–81.

Smith, M. G. *The Plural Society in the British West Indies.* Berkeley: U of California P, 1965.

———. "Robotham's Ideology and Pluralism: A Reply." *Social and Economic Studies* 32 (June 1983): 103–39.

Smith, Raymond T. *Kinship and Class in the West Indies: A Genealogical Study of Jamaica and Guyana.* Cambridge: Cambridge UP, 1988.

Solow, Barbara Lewis. *The Land Question and the Irish Economy, 1870–1903.* Cambridge: Harvard UP, 1971.

Southgate, Donald G. *The Passing of the Whigs, 1832–1886.* London: Macmillan, 1962.

Steele, E. D. *Irish Land and British Politics: Tenant-Right and Nationality, 1865–1870.* Cambridge: Cambridge UP, 1974.

———. "J. S. Mill and the Irish Question: Reform, and the Integrity of the Empire, 1865–1870." *Historical Journal* 13 (Sept. 1970): 419–50.

Stephen, Leslie, and Sidney Lee, eds. *Dictionary of National Biography.* 22 vols. London: Oxford UP, 1885–1901.

Stephens, Evelyne Huber, and John D. Stephens. *Democratic Socialism in Jamaica: The Political Movement and Social Transformation in Dependent Capitalism.* Princeton: Princeton UP, 1986.

St. Pierre, Maurice. "The 1938 Jamaica Disturbances: A Portrait of Mass Reaction against Colonialism." *Social and Economic Studies* 27 (June 1978): 171–96.

Temperly, Howard. *British Antislavery, 1833–1870.* London: Longmans, 1972.

———. "Capitalism, Slavery, and Ideology." *Past and Present* 75 (May 1977): 94–118.

Therborn, Göran. *The Ideology of Power and the Power of Ideology.* London: Verso & New Left Books, 1980.

Thomas, Mary Elizabeth. *Jamaica and Voluntary Laborers from Africa, 1840–1865.* Gainesville: U Presses of Florida, 1974.

Thompson, E. P. *The Making of the English Working Class.* New York: Vintage, 1963.

———. *Whigs and Hunters: The Origins of the Black Act.* London: Allen Lane, 1975.

Thornton, Joseph B. "The Agricultural Transformation of 19th Century Jamaica." Ph.D. diss., Clark U, 1980.

Tomich, Dale W. *Slavery and the Circuit of Sugar: Martinique and the World Economy, 1830–1848.* Baltimore: Johns Hopkins UP, 1990.

Trouillot, Michel-Rolph. "Discourses of Rule and the Acknowledgement of the Peasantry in Dominica, W.I., 1838–1928." *American Ethnologist* 16 (Nov. 1989): 704–18.

Turner, Mary S. "Ground Provision Production and the Transition to Freedom in Jamaica." Paper presented at the Conference on Cultivation and Culture, U of Maryland at College Park, Apr. 12–14, 1989.

————. *Slaves and Missionaries: The Disintegration of Jamaican Slave Society, 1787–1834*. Urbana: U of Illinois P, 1982.

Vaughan, W. E. *Landlords and Tenants in Ireland, 1840–1904*. Studies in Irish Economic and Social History, 2. Dublin: Dundalgan, 1984.

Waligorski, Conrad P. *The Political Theory of Conservative Economists*. Lawrence: UP of Kansas, 1990.

Wiener, Martin J. "Social Control in Nineteenth-Century Britain." *Journal of Social History* 12 (Winter 1978): 314–20.

Will, H. A. "Colonial Policy and Economic Development in the British West Indies, 1895–1903." *Economic History Review*, 2d ser., 23 (Apr. 1970): 129–47.

Williams, Eric. *Capitalism and Slavery*. Chapel Hill: U of North Carolina P, 1944.

Williams, Raymond Lambert. "The Growth, Structure, and Performance of the Coffee Industry in Jamaica." Ph.D. diss., Columbia U, 1973.

Wilmot, Swithin. "Not 'Full Free': The Ex-Slaves and the Apprenticeship System in Jamaica, 1834–1838." *Jamaica Journal* 17 (Aug.–Oct. 1984): 2–10.

————. "Race, Electoral Violence, and Constitutional Reform in Jamaica, 1830–54." *Journal of Caribbean History* 17 (1982): 1–13.

Woodman, Harold D. "Post–Civil War Southern Agriculture and the Law." *Agricultural History* 53 (Jan. 1979): 319–37.

Index

Related Titles in the Series

Dale W. Tomich, *Slavery in the Circuit of Sugar: Martinique and the World Economy, 1830–1848*

Richard Price, *Alabi's World*

Richard M. Morse, *New World Soundings: Culture and Ideology in the Americas*

Philippe I. Bourgois, *Ethnicity at Work: Divided Labor on a Central American Banana Plantation*

Michel-Rolph Trouillot, *Peasants and Capital: Dominica in the World Economy*

David Barry Gaspar, *Bondmen and Rebels: A Study of Master-Slave Relations in Antigua, with Implications for Colonial British America*

B. W. Higman, *Slave Populations of the British Caribbean, 1807–1834*

Walter Rodney, *A History of the Guyanese Working People, 1881–1905*